T0235120

Collective Management of Copyright and Related Rights

KLUWER LAW INTERNATIONAL

Collective Management of Copyright and Related Rights

Second Edition

Editor

Daniel Gervais

Wolters Kluwer

Law & Business

AUSTIN   BOSTON   CHICAGO   NEW YORK   THE NETHERLANDS

Published by:
Kluwer Law International
PO Box 316
2400 AH Alphen aan den Rijn
The Netherlands
Website: www.kluwerlaw.com

Sold and distributed in North, Central and South America by:
Aspen Publishers, Inc.
7201 McKinney Circle
Frederick, MD 21704
United States of America
Email: customer.service@aspenpublishers.com

Sold and distributed in all other countries by:
Turpin Distribution Services Ltd.
Stratton Business Park
Pegasus Drive, Biggleswade
Bedfordshire SG18 8TQ
United Kingdom
Email: kluwerlaw@turpin-distribution.com

Printed on acid-free paper.

ISBN 978-90-411-2724-2

Printed in Great Britain.

Summary of Contents

Table of Contents

Chapter 7
Collective Rights Management in Germany   215
Prof. Dr Jörg Reinbothe

Chapter 9
Collective Management in the Nordic Countries   **283**
Tarja Koskinen-Olsson

Chapter 11
Copyright Collectives and Collecting Societies: The United States Experience   **339**
Glynn Lunney

Chapter 14
Collective Management of Copyright in Latin America 465
Karina Correa Pereira

Introduction

Note Concerning This New Edition

This new edition of *Collective Management of Copyright and Related Rights* is different from the previous edition in several ways. Amongst the useful comments on the first edition was that it did not contain a general introduction to collective management. It was, in other words, a book for experts only. This has been remedied by the addition to the first chapter of a description of the operations of a collective management organization (CMO), in addition to a sharper focus on the history of collective management and its possible futures. A new chapter on multi-territorial licensing was added to address the topic – even though it was discussed in the European chapter of the first edition and in the same chapter in this edition. All individual chapters were updated to reflect not just changes that have occurred since 2005 but also constructive critiques received after the publication of the first edition.

The topic of this book is collective management, which refers to licensing (i.e., the grant of an authorization to use a protected work) performed by a CMO on behalf of a plurality of right holders. It implies that a group of right holders pooled some or all of their rights so that users can obtain a license to use such pooled rights from a single source, namely the CMO.

CMOs function in a variety of ways. Collective management, therefore, does not refer to a particular legal structure, regime or model. Some CMOs function as mere agents of a group of right holders who voluntarily entrusted the licensing of one or more uses of their works to a collective. Other collectives are assignees of copyright. In some cases, right holders transfer rights to all their present and future works or rights to a CMO; in other cases, they are allowed to choose which works or objects the CMO will administer on their behalf. Some CMOs license work-by-work, some offer users a whole 'repertory' of works; and others do both. This may be combined with an indemnity clause or equivalent.[1]

In most cases, the structure of a particular collective management model can be explained by looking at the history and 'vision' that governed at the time of its creation. Was the CMO viewed merely as a tool to improve economic efficiency of the licensing process (by reducing transaction costs and delays, etc.), or was it viewed more as a 'union' with a mission to defend the economic and, to a certain extent, moral interests of its members? The circumstances surrounding the birth of a particular collective management model may influence the drafting of accompanying legislation and shape the underlying policy of the state toward collective management. For instance, are CMOs considered a tolerated encroachment on competition law, an essential part of a well-functioning copyright system or rather viewed as a necessary policy instrument to defend the weaker party (authors) in transactions with large users?

CMOs generally belong to one of the two main 'families' of CMOs, namely the International Confederation of Societies of Authors and Composers (CISAC),[2] the largest and oldest association of CMOs, or to the International Federation of Reproduction Rights Organizations (IFRRO).[3] There are also several CMOs representing holders of related rights, and those may belong to other associations.[4] These organizations have played and continue to play an important role in debates concerning international copyright norms and their implementation in national and regional legislation. They have tended to emphasize both the need to defend authors and the efficiencies for both right holders and users of collective licensing when compared to individual licenses by right holders.

CMOs are facing the challenges of the digital age. Claims that 'copyright does not work' in the digital age are often the result of the inability of users to use protected material lawfully. On the Internet, users of copyright material can easily access millions of works and parts of works, including government documents; legal, scientific, medical and other professional journals; and newspapers, but also of course music and audiovisual content. Although digital access is fairly easy once a work has been located (though it may require identifying oneself and/or paying a subscription or other fee), obtaining the right to use the material beyond the initial contact (which is usually only listening, viewing or reading all of or a part of the work) is more difficult unless already allowed under the terms of the license or subscription agreement or as an exception to the exclusive rights contained in copyright laws around the world. Although in some cases, this is the result of

---

1. An 'indemnity clause' is an undertaking by the CMO in favour of the user to defend the user for using any work/right in the CMO's repertory of works/rights if the work/right was used according to the terms of the license. This indemnity often takes the form of an obligation to defend the user in court proceedings.
2. See online: <www.cisac.org>.
3. See online: <www.ifrro.org>.
4. Examples would include the International Federation of Musicians ('FIM'), online: <www.fim-musicians.com/eng/index.html> and the International Federation of the Phonographic Industry ('IFPI'), online: <www.ifpi.org>.

the right holders' unwillingness to authorize the use – a priori a legitimate application of their right to prohibit – there are several other cases in which it is the unavailability of adequate licensing options that makes authorized use impossible. Both right holders and users are losers in this scenario – right holders because they cannot provide authorized (controlled) access to their works and lose both income and the benefits of orderly distribution of their works, and users because there is no often easy authorized access to the right to use or reuse digital material. In other words, this inability to 'control' means that copyright works are simply unavailable (legally) on the Web. The *Napster, KaZaa* and *Grokster* cases[5] come to mind in that respect.

Whatever the optimal answer to those questions may be, one fact remains – a large amount of copyright material is (and more will be) available on the Internet and that 'market' will need to be organized in some way. By 'organized', it is suggested that users will want access and the ability to use and reuse material lawfully. These uses include putting the material on a commercial or educational website or an Intranet, emailing it to a group of people, reusing all or part of it to create new copyright material, storing it and distributing it. Authors and other right holders will want to ensure that they can put some reasonable limits on those uses and more importantly get paid for uses for which they decide that users should pay (again, absent a specific exemption or compulsory license in the law).

CMOs will be critical intermediaries in this process. Their expertise and knowledge of copyright law and management will be essential to make copyright work in the digital age. To play that role fully and efficiently, these organizations must acquire the rights they need to license digital uses of protected material and build (or improve current) information systems to deal with ever more complex rights management and licensing tasks.

The Approach Chosen for This Book

This book is divided into two main parts. Part I presents horizontal issues that affect collective management in almost every country. The part begins with an introductory chapter that describes collective management models and paints a brief historical overview of the evolving role of CMOs. It explains how copyright collectives are organized and the various models under which CMOs operate and discusses the current role of collectives and their likely evolution over the coming years. The chapter also considers whether extended repertoire systems (also known as extended collective licensing), which seem to be playing an increasingly important role in policy discussions, is compatible with the prohibition of certain formalities and conditions contained in Article 5(2) of the Berne Convention.

Chapter 2, by Dr Mihály Ficsor, former Assistant Director General of the World Intellectual Property Organization (WIPO) and Director General of the

---

5. *A&M Records, Inc. v. Napster, Inc.* 284 F.3d 1091 (9th Cir., 2002); *Universal Music Australia Pty Ltd v. Sharman License Holdings Ltd*, [2005] FCA 1242; and *Metro-Goldwyn-Mayer Studios Inc. v. Grokster, Ltd*, 125 S.Ct. 2764 (US Sup. Ct., 2005).

Hungarian CMO ARTISJUS, discusses the role of collectives in the digital age, using the Berne Convention (particularly the three-step test) and the 1996 WIPO Copyright Treaties (and the 'making available' right) as a backdrop. Dr Ficsor reminds us that 'with the advent of ever newer and better technologies, the areas in which individual exercise became equally difficult, and – in certain cases, even impossible – began widening. It was in those cases that right holders established collective management systems'. He then considers the impact of the US Digital Millennium Copyright Act[6] and the Napster[7] case, along with the EU Papers and the Copyright (Infosoc) Directive.[8] Dr Ficsor offers key insights into the changing nature of collective management and the relationship between collective management, rights to remuneration and the ways in which CMOs acquire the rights they need to function (i.e., the authority to license). Insisting on the freedom of right holders to choose between individual and collective management of rights, he concludes that the cases in which mandatory collective management is possible are limited, but notes that extended repertoire (extended collective licensing[9]) is allowed, provided certain important safeguards are in place.

In Chapter 3, Professor Laurence Helfer tackles the interface between collective management and human rights issues. That interface is seldom discussed, but collectives manage rights in human knowledge, the creation of and access to which are crucial in every country, notably as a basis for a well-functioning democratic system. The chapter is one of the deepest analyses of that crucial rights intersection available. The chapter begins with a reminder that the Universal Declaration of Human Rights (UDHR) and the 1966 International Covenant on Economic, Social and Cultural Rights (ICESCR or 'the Covenant') protect the moral and material interests of authors and inventors,[10] as well as the public's right 'to enjoy the arts and to share in scientific advancement and its benefits',[11] but that 'without elaboration, however, these provisions provide only a skeletal outline of how to develop human rights – compliant rules and policies for governments to promote creativity and innovation'. Suggesting that a 'human rights framework for intellectual property puts the public's interest front and centre and on an equal footing with property rights in intangibles', Professor Helfer then examines how Article 15(1)(c) of the Covenant could be expanded into a coherent framework. His analysis includes a detailed review of the work done by the Committee on Economic, Social and Cultural Rights (and its 'general comments') and difficulties stemming form the fact that both authors' rights and access to copyright works may

---

6. *Digital Millennium Copyright Act of 1998*, Pub. L. No. 105-304, 112 Stat. 2860 [DMCA].
7. See *supra* n. 6.
8. EC, *Directive 2001/29/EC of the European Parliament and the Council of 22 May 2001 on the harmonisation of certain aspects of copyright and related rights in the information society* (2001), OJ L 167/10, online: <http://europa.eu.int/eur-lex/en/consleg/pdf/2001/en_2001L0029_do_001.pdf> (last visited: 19 Oct. 2005).
9. See Ch. 1 and the study of the Nordic countries by Ms. Koskinen-Olsson in Ch. 11.
10. *Universal Declaration of Human Rights*, Art. 27(2); *International Covenant on Economic, Social and Cultural Rights*, Art. 15(1)(c) & 15(1)(b).
11. UDHR, *ibid.*, Art. 27(1).

be considered fundamental rights (thus limiting the ability of states to legislate). He notes that in the comments[12] concerning Article 15(1)(c) of the Covenant (a 'non-binding, albeit highly persuasive' interpretation of the Covenant), the Committee mentioned affirmative measures to facilitate 'the formation of professional associations', and 'to ensure the active and informed participation' of authors in those associations to protect their moral and material interests.[13] Professor Helfer concludes that 'a human rights framework for intellectual property offers a possible focal point around which all parties can structure a revised regulatory regime' instead of the increasingly 'corporate' approach to copyright regulation.

The last chapter in this part, by Tanya Woods, discusses the issue of transnational licensing and the possible role of multi-territorial licensing. In doing so, using historical and theoretical approaches, she notes that copyright was and is fundamentally territorial. She considers efforts by CMOs and dissects the well-known Santiago Agreement with great acuity. She then suggests the parameters of an optimal post-Santiago multi-territorial solution, concluding that 'CMOs must expand their traditionally restrictive approach to licensing by injecting more clarity into the process, cooperating with users, finding creative or unconventional solutions, relinquishing some control over the way content is used and, perhaps above all else, abandon their habit of not globally working together.'

Part II of the book is divided on a geographical basis. The purpose of Part II is not encyclopaedic in nature; it does not aim to present in exactly the same way how collective management operates in every country. Rather, various national systems were selected as representatives of the principal models that are applied in various countries and regions. The basic structure of all of the country-specific chapters is the same. Each begins with a historical overview and a presentation of existing CMOs and their activities. Where available, financial information is also provided. Then, the authors explain how CMOs are supervised or controlled by legislation, a governmental authority or both. Finally, the chapters offer thoughts about the challenges facing CMOs in the country or region concerned. Naturally, the length and exact structure of each part of the chapters varies, owing to the important differences among CMOs and how they operate in various parts of the world.

The exception in Part II is its first chapter, which examines efforts to regulate CMOs at the European level. Prepared by Dr Lucie Guibault and Stef van Gompel of the Institute for Information Law of the University of Amsterdam, the chapter begins with an analysis of the existing regulatory context, in particular, key decisions by the European Court of Justice and the European Commission,[14]

---

12. Committee on Economic, Social and Cultural Rights, 'The right of everyone to benefit from the protection of the moral and material interests resulting from any scientific, literary or artistic production of which he is the author (Art. 15(1)(c) of the Covenant), Draft General Comment No. 18' (15 Nov. 2004), (Reporter: Eibe Riedel).
13. *Ibid.*, at paras 36 and 50.
14. Notably *Gesellschaft fur Musikalische Auffuhrungs- und Mechanische Vervielfaltigungsrechte (GEMA) v. Commission of the European Communities*, (1971) OJ L 134/15; *Belgische Radio en Televisie (BRT) v. SABAM*, (1974) ECR 51 [*BRT v. SABAM*]; *Musik-Vertrieb Membran GmbH v. GEMA*, (1981) ECR 147; *GVL v. Commission*, (1983) ECR 483; *Ministère public v. Tournier*, (1989) ECR 2521; and the *Lucazeau v. SACEM*, (1989) ECR 2811.

which dealt with, on the one hand, the relationship among CMOs, between CMOs and users and, on the other hand, relations between CMOs and their members. The chapter contains an analysis the most recent normative efforts and work on a Community framework and relevant cases, including *MyVideo v. CELAS* (25 June 2009) and CISAC (16 July 2008). The authors also discuss the impact of recent measures on the market for cross-border licensing of rights, noting that among

> the biggest concerns is the fear that the implementation of the Recommendation will lead to the emergence of monopolies or regional oligopolies for the management of online music rights which, in the long term, could have a negative effect on the cultural diversity. By allowing right-holders to assign their online rights to the CMO of their choice, competition will arise at the level of the repertoires, which leads to a segmentation of the market, favouring the establishment of monopolies and the appearance of network effects.

Other chapters in Part II focus on one or more national systems. They were prepared by some of the most well established and recognized experts in each region. In *Europe*, the cradle of collective management, France, Germany, the United Kingdom and Ireland and the Nordic countries were selected and a specific chapter is devoted to each one. The contributors of those chapters are, respectively, Ms Nathalie Piaskowski, LL.M., former legal director of French CMO SCPP; Dr Jörg Reinbothe, former head of the Intellectual Property Unit at the European Commission, where he oversaw the development and application of several key directives; Professor Paul Torremans, who teaches intellectual property law at the University of Nottingham; and Ms Tarja Koskinen-Olsson, former director of the Finnish RRO KOPIOSTO and former Chair of IFRRO. Each country and region has a different approach to collective management In *France*, where copyright and copyright management are anchored in post-Revolution human rights doctrines, collectives have undergone very significant changes since 2000. *Germany*, whose model was considered by several CMOs in Central and Eastern Europe, has developed a unique system of government oversight, located in the Patent Office. The *United Kingdom*, whose copyright law served as a model for the laws of most Commonwealth members, uses a specialized tribunal to settle tariff disputes. Finally, the extended repertoire system (or extended collective licensing) is examined, discussed also in Chapters 1 and 2; it was developed in the highly socially cohesive system of the *Nordic countries*. It is now under consideration in a number of other countries.

Moving to the Americas, the *Canadian* chapter was contributed by Mr Mario Bouchard, General Counsel of the Copyright Board. Canada's collective management system is in transition, after the introduction in the late 1990s of both neighbouring rights and a private copying levy. Canada's Copyright Board has also adopted fairly unique measures to improve collective management over the past several years. The chapter compares the situation in Canada with developments in *Australia*. Like Canada, Australia inherited its copyright legislation from Britain. It is also a smaller market. The analysis of the parallels between the two systems thus offers unique insights into the role and function of collective licensing and the 'counterintuitive' impact of a higher degree of governmental scrutiny based on empirical observations in the two countries.

The situation in the *United States* is presented by Professor Glynn Lunney of Tulane University in New Orleans, Louisiana, one of the most prolific and original intellectual property scholars in that country. The US situation is somewhat different from that of other countries. Controlled and 'tolerated' under antitrust (competition) law judicial decrees (though there are tariff hearings administered by the Copyright Office), several collectives 'compete' in the same area of licensing, namely, the public performance of music. In recent years, however, copyright specific supervisory mechanisms were established.

Collective management is a very important activity in *Japan*, where CMOs collect more than United States Dollar (USD) 1 billion per year. It is also well organized. The situation may seem complex to observers outside the Land of the Rising Sun in part because of the way in which CMOs are supervised, which differs to a certain extent from methods now in use elsewhere. Yet, the Japanese collective management system seems to work quite well. In a detailed chapter, Associate Professor Koji Okumura from the Faculty of Business Administration at Kanagawa University offers one of the first complete presentations of collective management in Japan.

In the rest of the *Asia-Pacific region*, Mr Ang Kwee Tiang, the representative of CISAC in the region for more than a decade, authored a veritable tour de force. He manages to offer a detailed, up-to-date portrait of this huge region (minus Japan) in a single chapter. Again, this is the only complete presentation of CMO activity in that part of the world. Mr Ang is one of the best qualified persons to author this chapter. He personally assisted in the establishment of many of the CMOs now in operation.

In *Latin America*, the systems of Argentina, Brazil, Costa Rica, Chile, Mexico, Peru and Venezuela were selected to represent the region. That chapter was prepared by Ms Karina Correa Pereira, a Brazilian attorney specializing in copyright issues.

Daniel Gervais
Nashville, June 2010

Chapter 1

Collective Management of Copyright: Theory and Practice in the Digital Age

*Daniel Gervais**

1 INTRODUCTION

This initial chapter examines, first, the basic features of 'collective management' of copyright and related rights.[1] This is useful both to delineate the scope of this book and to explain to readers less familiar with collective management where it comes from and what it does. Second, the chapter aims to provide theoretical foundations for the collective management of copyright and to that end discusses both the paradox of copyright and the fragmentation of rights.

The apparent paradox of copyright is that in order to maximize the creation and dissemination of new works of art and the intellect while adequately rewarding authors and other owners of copyright and related rights, intellectual property law seemingly poses obstacles both to the creation of new works – because authors may not create derivative works without authorization, and to their

---

* Professor at Vanderbilt University Law School.
1. I use the term 'related rights', as does the World Trade Organization Agreement on Trade-Related Aspects of Intellectual Property Rights (TRIPS Agreement), to refer to rights owned not by authors (creators) and their successors in title but by performers, broadcasting organizations and sound recording producers. The term 'neighboring right' is also used in this context. Unless the context requires otherwise, the expression 'collective management of copyright' includes related rights.

Daniel Gervais (ed.), *Collective Management of Copyright and Related Rights*, pp. 1–28.

dissemination – because it provides copyright owners with a right to exclude others from copying, performing and communicating those new works.

The fragmentation of rights[2] may be defined as the fact that copyright and related rights are expressed as a bundle of rights applicable to various types of use and defined by their technical nature, such as making copies (reproduction), performing in public, communicating (by wire or wireless means), renting, displaying, etc. Making matters even more complex, each right in the bundle can be shared by co-authors or their successors in title and it can be divided contractually by territory, language, type of media, etc. This means that, for a single use of a copyright work, a user may need several authorizations.

Let us take a concrete example. A radio station (broadcaster) wishing to copy music on its computers and then use that copy to broadcast the music will need to clear two rights: the right to copy (reproduction) and the right to communicate the work to the public.[3] The radio station will need both rights in respect to three different objects: (1) the musical work, (2) the sound recording and (3) the musical performance of the musical work incorporated in the sound recording.[4] Our hypothetical broadcaster will need, at least occasionally but probably very frequently, to use works, sound recordings or performances, the rights in which are owned in whole or in part by foreign nationals and entities.[5] The broadcaster probably uses thousands of songs from around the world each week. However, a typical broadcaster does not know in advance which songs it will play enough to seek individual licenses. Or the broadcaster may have a change of mind. For example, after the death of Michael Jackson, several radio stations decided to play his music much more than usual. In sum, a broadcaster may need up to twenty licenses (or payments) if some of the rights have been transferred to are split among various right holders. That clearance process will be required for each song, performance and recording used by the station.

---

2. The chapter does not, however, analyse the economics of collective management. Some of the economic aspects are discussed in various chapters of this book (e.g., Professor Lunney's chapter on the United States). For a more complete look at the economics of collective management, the reader might consult Hansen, Gerd and Schmidt-Bischoffshausen, Albrecht, Economic Functions of Collecting Societies – Collective Rights Management in the Light of Transaction Cost – and Information Economics (19 Oct. 2007). Available at SSRN: <http://ssrn.com/abstract=998328>. That paper focuses on the transaction costs for the licensee. For a different view, see Ariel Katz, 'Is Collective Administration of Copyrights Justified by the Economic Literature?', in *Competition Policy and Intellectual Property*, ed. Marcel Boyer, Michael Trebilcock & David Vaver (Toronto: Irwin Law, 2009), 451–461.
3. Referred to in the United States as part of the right of public performance and in some jurisdictions as part of the right of representation.
4. Some countries grant only some of those rights. As of this writing (2010), the United States is one of the very few World Trade Organization (WTO) Members that does not grant performers a statutory right in public performances. Many other countries do grant such a right but only as a right to 'remuneration' (payment) – that is, not as a full exclusive right.
5. In fact, the broadcaster may not know whether the work, performance or recording is in fact from this or that country, and it may be from several. The composer might be American, the lyricist Canadian, the performer Nigerian and the producer German.

This leads us to another issue – who are these right holders, and where are they? Why would a broadcaster not go online and find out who owns every piece of the work the broadcaster wants to use and obtain rights that way? There are at least three sets of reasons. First, because under Article 5(2) of the Berne Convention – most substantive provisions of which were incorporated into the TRIPS Agreement – mandatory formalities – such as registration with a governmental entity – cannot be imposed by the State as a condition for the normal exercise or enjoyment of copyright. Put differently, a country party to the Berne Convention and/or member of the World Trade Organization (WTO) cannot impose a mandatory registration system for copyright, at least not if the sanction is a reduction in copyright rights below the minimum thresholds established under the Berne Convention and the TRIPS Agreement.[6] Second, where registration systems exist (e.g., the United States), not only are right holders, especially foreign ones, not required to use them, but once a work is registered, total or partial transfer of rights are often not registered, at least not in a timely fashion. This means that a radio station, even if it wanted to, could not find some or all of the right holders it needs. Third, it is also rather obvious that the transaction costs would likely be astronomical and make it probably impossible to run the business.

What is needed, therefore, to make the copyright system work for the broadcaster, is a license to use *all the right fragments* (reproduction, communication, etc.) for the copyright work(s) (music and lyrics) and the objects of related rights (performance and sound recording). The license must be for all or as close to all existing works, performances and recordings that the radio station might use, which in practice means a worldwide license. This is exactly what collective management organizations (CMOs) do. They perform those licensing functions not just for radio stations, but also for small and large music users (hotels, cinemas, television stations, discotheques, restaurants, public events, etc.) and in areas other than music as well (including the reproduction of printed and online material for business and education, reproduction of images and photographs and use of theatrical plays in theatres).

2   COLLECTIVE MANAGEMENT IN HISTORICAL PERSPECTIVE

Understanding collective management may be easier in historical context. The story of the rise of collective management has become a quaint and famous tale. It begins in France with the French playwright Pierre-Augustin Caron de Beaumarchais in the dark and dingy Parisian theatres in the 1700s.[7] Theatrical

---

6. This was confirmed by a WTO panel report issued in January 2009 examining a complaint filed by the United States against China, in which copyright was denied for works that failed censorship review. See D. Gervais, 'World Trade Organization Panel Report on China's Enforcement of Intellectual Property Rights', *American Journal of International Law* 103, no. 3 (2009): 549–554.
7. A more detailed history is contained in the chapter on France.

companies at the time were enthusiastic in their encouragement of promoting plays and artists, but were less generous when it came time to share in the revenues. The term 'starving artist' was more literal than figurative.[8] Beaumarchais was the first to express the idea of collective management of copyright. In 1777, he created the General Statutes of Drama in Paris. What began as a meeting of twenty-two famous writers of the *Comédie française* over some financial matters turned into a debate about collective protection of rights. 'They appointed agents, conducted the now famous pen strike and laid a foundation for the French Society of Drama Authors (*Société des auteurs dramatiques*).'[9] In 1838, Honoré de Balzac and Victor Hugo established the Society of Writers,[10] which was mandated with the collection of royalties from print publishers.

A net of authors' societies, shaped by the cultural environment of each country, slowly spread throughout the world. The collective management of copyright was seen as a practical and efficient way of allowing creators to be compensated. In Italy the *Società Italiana degli Autori ed Editori* (SIAE), under the direction of Barduzzi, was empowered them to collect theatre and cinema taxes.[11]

Developments were not limited to the domestic scene, however. As CMOs flourished in their own national States, the need for cooperation and harmonization on the international level became apparent. In 1925, Romain Coolus organized the Committee for the Organization of Congresses of Foreign Authors' Societies. This Committee was founded to tackle some of the insurmountable problems involving international issues.[12] Around the same time, Firmin Gémier succeeded in creating the Universal Theatrical Society.[13] Both of these initiatives led to the founding congress meeting in 1926 of the International Confederation of Societies of Authors (CISAC).[14] The founding members identified the need to establish both uniform principles and methods in each country for the collection of royalties and

---

8. Although this may be an exaggeration on the authors' part, this cliché remains, nonetheless, a somewhat accurate portrait of financially struggling artists both then and now.
9. See CPTech's Page on Collective Management of Copyright, online: <www.cptech.org/cm/copyrights.html> (last visited: 7 Jan. 2010).
10. Société des gens de lettres, see online: <www.sgdl.org/> (last visited: 17 Oct. 2009).
11. For a complete historical account of the formation of CMOs, see International Confederation of Societies of Authors and Composers (CISAC), *As Long as There Are Authors* (International Confederation of Societies of Authors and Composers, 1996), 64.
12. As one commentator noted:

    The Portuguese Society of Authors offered to represent French authors, and the theatre managers of Lisbon immediately threatened to boycott French plays. The Spanish society SGAE would not allow the SACD to deal with its members on an individual basis.

    Ibid., at 10.
13. The biography of Firmin Gémier may be found online: <www.answers.com/topic/firmin-g-mier> (last visited: 17 Jan. 2010).
14. See online: <www.cisac.org> (last visited: 8 Feb. 2010).

the protection of works and to ensure that literary and artistic property[15] were recognized and protected throughout the world.[16] Today, CISAC has 225 member societies in 118 countries,[17] a majority of which license either the public performance and communication of musical works or the reproduction of those works. Other CISAC members license reprography and reproduction of works of the fine arts and performance in theatres (the so-called 'grand rights'). Many countries have fostered the growth of CMOs through legislative initiatives in the belief that CMOs offer a viable solution to the problem of individually licensing, collecting and enforcing copyright.

Although the formation of CMOs may have once been considered revolutionary, the pivotal role that they continue to play as facilitators in the copyright system is more properly characterized as evolutionary. CMOs facilitate the establishment of unified methods for collecting and dispersing royalties and negotiate licensing arrangements for works. Yet, licensing and royalty payment, while still important, is not the only preoccupation of CMOs. Over time the role of CMOs has evolved to oversee copyright compliance, fight piracy and perform various social and cultural functions.[18] Collective management has also allowed authors to use the power of collective bargaining to obtain more for the use of their work and negotiate on a less unbalanced basis with large multinational user groups.[19] That being said, most collective schemes value all works in their repertory on the same economic footing, which may be unfair to those who create works that may have a higher value in the eyes of users.

Although CMOs were initially promoted as an efficient way to collect and disburse monies to compensate right holders for copyright works, increasingly the structure of CMOs, on both a national and an international level, has raised questions about their efficiency.[20] In addition to those significant structural issues, the market conditions and business trends of copyright owners are changing, and CMOs must adapt.[21] Just as the role of CMOs is evolutionary, so is their underlying

---

15. The French law on authors' rights (the civil law version of copyright) is actually known as the *Code of Literary and Artistic Property*, Law No. 92–597 of 1 Jul. 1992, as amended by Laws No. 94–361 of 10 May 1994, and 95–4 of 3 Jan. 1995.
16. By 'world', I am referring only to the Western World. This is inclusive of the Anglo-Saxon and *droit d'auteur* traditions of copyright.
17. See *supra* n. 14.
18. See M. Ficsor, *Collective Management of Copyright and Related Rights* (World Intellectual Property Organization, 2002), at 99–106.
19. For instance, imagine if corporations such as music video television (e.g., MTV) negotiated the use and fee for each song/video it broadcasted with individual artists. Although artists such as U2 or Madonna would be in a position to negotiate on a balanced power basis, the same would not be said for new groups struggling to find airtime.
20. For example, often rights are governed by multiple CMOs within a particular nation. Coordination is therefore required not only among national CMOs, but also on an international basis among CMOs. There is a significant lack of standards among many CMOs. Identification alone of an underlying right and right holder can be a convoluted process.
21. As one author notes, 'efficiency will be what, in the end, members and music users most want and will most easily recognize, however it is measured'. See J. Hutchinson, 'Collection and

stated efficiency.[22] Although the current milieu of CMOs may have served both creators and users reasonably well in the past, the system must adapt to remain both efficient and relevant.[23]

3   HOW COLLECTIVE MANAGEMENT OPERATES

As this book shows, CMOs in various countries, and even sometimes within the same country, operate and are regulated differently; however, their basic modus operandi is fairly linear.

Once established (sometimes an authorization is required to operate as a CMO), it must acquire the authority to license (or collect) and create the repertory of works, performances or recordings. Such authority to license may be granted by law or by contracts with right holders or other CMOs. Then it must license on the basis of agreed tariffs or, if agreement with the user is not possible, prices set by a third party (court, tribunal, board, etc.).[24] The CMO will then collect usage data, process them and apply those data to distribute the funds to right holders. CMOs may also engage in other activities, such as cultural promotion, awards, etc. Let us look at each of those areas of operation.

– Obtaining the authority to license

Once established – sometimes with the support of a governmental authority – CMOs, most of which are private entities, obtain from a group of right holders (e.g., music composers, music publishers, book publishers, music performers) the ability to license on behalf of those right holders. This can be done by a full transfer of copyright (assignment) or by an agency agreement (license) allowing the CMO to represent the right holder, whether on an exclusive or non-exclusive basis.

Most CMOs operate alone in their field in their territory, which means they are a de facto (and sometimes de jure) monopoly and as such subject to competition law scrutiny or to another, more specific form of governmental supervision. The one CMO per territory model is not uniform worldwide, however. As Professor Lunney's chapter on the United States shows, in that country there are three

---

Distribution of Performing and Mechanical Royalties: A View from the UK', *Copyright World* 84 (1998): 30, at 32.

22. As Peter Drucker notes, 'efficiency is doing better what is already being done'. See P. Drucker, *Innovation & Entrepreneurship: Practices and Principles* (New York: Harper & Row, 1985), 277. Drucker discusses the nexus between technology, innovation and efficiency.

23. Licensing, collecting and enforcing copyright may now be done on an individual basis through the aid of technologies such as digital rights management systems. While most authors' do not adopt the view that collectives will no longer have a role to play in the digital environment, the point is that new technologies alleviate some of the concerns relating to the inefficiency of individual licensing, collecting and enforcement of copyright.

24. Sometimes the price is set by a governmental authority without the need to seek a voluntary agreement first.

organizations licensing the same right to publicly perform music although there is usually one CMO per country (per field of activity). In Europe, as Dr Guibault and Stef van Gompel's chapter demonstrates, CMOs operating in the field of music may 'compete' within the territory of the European Union (EU).

There is no uniformity in the type of government supervision either. In some jurisdictions (e.g., the United States), the matter is dealt with under normal competition law – and enforced by the Department of Justice's antitrust division. In many European countries, a specific governmental body or commission was established for that purpose, sometimes operating in conjunction with the competition law enforcement agency.

Once a CMO has acquired the right to license on behalf of a plurality of right holders, it can enter into 'reciprocal representation agreements' with similar CMOs in other territories. Those agreements allow the parties to license each other's pool of rights, known as their repertoire (sometimes called repertory) in the other party's territory. For example, GEMA (the German music CMO) has such an agreement with the Society of Composers, Authors and Music Publishers of Canada (SOCAN), its counterpart in Canada. As a result, SOCAN can license GEMA's repertoire in Canada and GEMA can license SOCAN's repertoire in Germany.

– Setting licensing terms and tariffs

Having acquired right to as much of the world repertoire as possible, a CMO then turns to users. Often, the users and the CMO will disagree on the terms of the license. Each jurisdiction basically decides which type of state intervention is warranted in that context. To take just a few examples, in the United States, a federal judge is empowered (for music performing rights organizations the American Society of Composer, Authors and Publishers (ASCAP) and Broadcast Music, Inc. (BMI)) by the agreement entered into between those CMOs and the Department of Justice to decide the appropriate rate for the licenses. In Australia, Canada and the United Kingdom, a specialized copyright tribunal or board was established for that purpose. The power of the tribunal varies greatly from one jurisdiction to another, as the respective chapters explain. In other cases, the matter is left entirely to civil courts, and in yet other jurisdictions, the terms of the license, or some of them, are set by government regulation or decree.

There is also a layer of regulation decided by the CMOs themselves, particularly in their reciprocal representation agreements. Most CMOs belong to CISAC.[25] CISAC developed over the years a model for reciprocal representation agreements among its members. One of its features, for example, it to limit the percentage (10%) of a CMO's total collections that be used for social or cultural purposes. However, for private copying income, the percentages of funds collected used for such purposes may be much higher and that percentage is often prescribed by statute.

---

25. See *supra* n. 14.

This takes us to the next phase in our analysis of the work of CMOs. Once a license has been signed by a user – often after a price-setting intervention by a court, specialized body or other third party, the CMO will receive payments from that user. In some cases, the payment is received not as consideration for the license but as a form of regulatory compensation for a form of use that is otherwise considered not licensable (as a practical and/or normative matter). A major example of this is the 'private copying' levies on blank media and on recoding, copying, computer and other equipment. The monies are typically paid to a CMO according to applicable legislation or sometimes a decision by an administrative or quasi-judicial body (tribunal or board).

– Usage data collection and distribution

The CMO's task then is to distribute the funds. To do so, it will need data. From an operational standpoint, CMOs are essentially data collecting and processing entities.

CMOs need and process two types of information: identification and ownership. The former is used to identify works, performances and recordings in the CMO's repertoire. The latter is used to know whom to pay for the use of a particular work, recording or performance. The rights to a musical work composed by x may well have been sold to y and then to z. That work may have been performed by several artists and find itself on several recordings. Usage data reported by a user may use the name of the performer, song, recording, composer or any combination of the above. That identification data will not necessarily match current ownership data, and the CMO needs both. Worldwide databases of identification data have been created by CISAC and the International Federation of Reproduction Rights Organisations (IFRRO) for reprographic rights.[26] This allows their members to identify foreign works, performances and recordings licensed to them under reciprocal representation agreements. Each CMO tends to keep some or all of the ownership data (contact information, etc.) confidential.

Identification data will be used to match usage data reported by users or generated by the CMO to specific works, recordings or performances. License contracts with users typically will require usage reporting for all or part of the works, performances or recordings used. A radio station may use computer logs, for example, to report the music used. For other types of users (e.g., hotels, bars, restaurants), it is more difficult to require 100% reporting. Sometimes surveys are used. For example, some (hopefully a representative number) of users may be surveyed for a specific period, and the data thus gathered will then be extrapolated to the class of users concerned using statistical regressions and other similar models.

Despite some work by CISAC in this area, there is little uniformity and each CMO decides for itself the extent of the surveys and the type and accuracy of data capture tools it wants to use and/or request its users to use. Typically, a larger pool of data will produce more accurate results and present a more fine-grained picture

---

26. See <www.ifrro.org>.

of works, performances and recordings actually used and the frequency of such use by each user of class of users, but it will increase the data processing costs, thereby diminishing the amount available for distribution. A CMO will normally distribute all of its collections after deduction of its administrative expenses, a small reserve and possible deductions for other purposes (e.g., social and cultural purposes, including promotion of members, pension funds, award ceremonies, training programmes, etc.). A CMO's revenue includes not just the actual license fees or levies paid to it but interest earned on the 'float', that is, the period of time between the day a payment is received from a user and the day on which it will be paid (distributed) to a right holder or a foreign CMO.

Having matched usage data to identification data and knowing which works, performances or recordings have been used, the CMO then matches that dataset against ownership data to apportion the funds to each right holder and to foreign CMOs. Funds owed to right holders represented by CMO A through a reciprocal representation agreement with CMO B are typically not paid to the right holder directly. They are sent to CMO B together with appropriate usage data. CMO B will add this (foreign) income to its own income and distribute it to the right holders it represents. In some (fairly rare) cases, two CMOs will agree to let the other party to a reciprocal representation agreement license their respective repertoire but not exchange data or money. In other words, under this arrangement (known as a 'B' agreement in CISAC terminology), CMOs keep funds generated by the use of foreign works, performances or recordings in the other CMO's repertoire as part of their own revenue. This type of arrangement is less expensive to administer and may be helpful to fledgling CMOs or in situations in which strict currency exchange controls hamper cross-border financial flows. Yet, it is much less fair to right holders whose works, performances or recordings were used. For that reason, it is generally considered a temporary arrangement.

To increase fairness and accuracy, several CMOs keep discrete data pools. For example, a music performing right CMO may separate data from radio stations, television stations, cinemas, background music users (e.g., large stores), etc. It can then separate those revenue streams and use separate datasets for distribution. CMOs also sometimes use keys or factors that are applied to usage data before distribution. One model of distribution is known as 'follow the dollar' (or euro or yen, etc.). It means simply that each right holder will receive the exact share of the CMO's distribution pool that usage data has determined. Under other models, a further processing of the data occurs.[27] For example, some CMOs will give greater 'weight' to a work performed for the first time on their territory. Because first worldwide use typically occurs in the country where the composer or creator of the work resided, this tends to favour domestic right holders. Some CMOS actually evaluate the 'quality' of works and may give greater weight to a performance of contemporary music than to the latest pop single.

---

27. Even 'follow the dollar' distribution systems are sometimes tweaked to reflect other concerns.

– Transparency issues

As this brief *tour d'horizon* has shown, collective management of copyright is complex. In several areas (e.g., rights ownership, financial data), CMOs tend to maintain secrecy (even from other CMOs) as a matter of policy. In other areas, the data (survey methods, distribution keys, etc.) is not released for a variety of reasons and often leads to claims of opaqueness. There is undoubtedly room for greater transparency, although many CMOs do provide annual reports and try to provide some insight into their operations.[28] What is arguably lacking is a uniform standard or code of conduct in that respect.

4 THEORETICAL APPROACHES

4.1 FRAGMENTATION

Copyright is a bundle of rights (reproduction, public performance, communication to the public, translation, adaptation, etc.). Each sub-right (or copyright 'fragment') can be split among many right holders. For music, there are several distinct layers of rights: rights in the musical work – itself a combination of music and lyrics; the performance; and the recording. Right fragments[29] such as 'reproduction' or 'public performance' are complex and increasingly a source of frustration for users because they no longer map out discrete uses, especially on the Internet. Put differently, a single use of a copyright work or object of a related right (e.g., performance, recording) often requires multiple authorizations (right fragments) from several different right holders. The way in which right fragments are expressed no longer matches who does what, and for which purpose, with a work or object of a related right. Contracts present a partial solution to fragmentation. A contract can define a 'use' that is allowed rather than which fragments of rights are licensed, but that simplification is apparent only if right fragments are owned by, and a license negotiated with, multiple entities.

Fragmentation has its roots in the pre-Internet history of copyright (from the late seventeenth century until the 1990s – approximately 300 years), which was essentially that of the adaptation to new forms of creation (e.g., cinema, computer programs) and dissemination of copyright works (radio, then television broadcasting, cable and satellite). Copyright adapted and was able successfully to regulate new markets made possible by these new technologies because they were created by *professionals* who were willing to live with a certain degree of complexity as

---

28. CISAC also releases an annual survey of collections. The 2008 edition was available (as of February 2010) at <www.cisac.org/CisacPortal/consulterDocument.do?id=17829#>. It shows 2008 stable compared to the previous year, with total collections of over Euro (EUR) 7 billion.
29. Fragment or fragmentation is derived from the Latin adjective 'fractus'. See Kimberly Wertenberger, Fractals, Mandelbrot Sets & Julia Sets, available at <www.ms.uky.edu/~lee/ma502/fractals/FRACTALS.html>.

part of their compliance efforts. However, many new technologies added a layer of complexity because the right fragments in the copyright bundle grew, usually by analogy, to bring many new uses under the copyright umbrella. For example, playwrights and music composers were able to obtain rights in respect to the live performance of their works by arguing that this was their main economic use. When radio was invented, those same live performances (mostly of opera and music) were then broadcast directly to the homes of listeners. People did not attend the live performance, and the existing exclusive right of live public performance did not apply. Yet broadcasters were making a commercial use of the material similar to the use made by theatre or concert hall operators. It was quite logical then, to extend the right of public performance to the communication of the performance of a work by radio (or Hertzian waves). It was only a small step after that to add television and later communication by cable and satellite. The result of this historical process is the bundle composed of 'copyright rights' we find in most national copyright laws.

The fragmentation of copyright, therefore, occurs on many different levels – rights contained in national laws, which recognize several economic rights (reproduction, communication to the public, adaptation, rental, etc.); within market structures; within licensing practices; within a repertory of works; within different markets (language, territory); and through the interoperability (or lack thereof) of rights clearance systems. Fragmentation has an impact directly on all affected parties, whether they be right holders, users of copyright works or regulatory authorities that oversee the process; it also affects, of course, CMOs.

Although the division of labour among traditional rights 'fragments' (reproduction, performance, communication, etc.) is less relevant in mapping newer uses (as already mentioned, a broadcaster making a copy of the recording and then broadcasting it requires at least a license to copy the content on a server and another to communicate the work to the public[30]), collective management is (still) organized mainly around those traditional fragments. Quite often, one CMO licenses the right of communication to the public/public performance, while another license the right of reproduction (for musical or textual works). Although so-called 'one-stop shops' have been set up in some countries, they often operate as services that copy or transfer authorization requests to the various CMOs concerned. A 'one-stop-shop' set up in this fashion assumes that at least one member CMO actually has the authority to license each fragment that the user requires and is willing to license the user in question, which may not be the case. Perhaps no CMO in the group has the right, or perhaps they do not issue license to the type of user concerned. In short, even when reasonably efficient systems are available, rights clearance may prove a difficult task.

The inherent difficulty in rights clearance in today's world is perhaps best illustrated by way of examples. If the hypothetical broadcaster mentioned in the

---

30. Or its public performance. In some jurisdictions, the right fragment is not the right to communicate to the public but the right to authorize that communication, which is yet another fragment.

opening pages of this chapter wanted to put music on the Internet, at least four right fragments could be involved, namely:

- reproduction on the emission server[31];
- authorization of communication to the public in territory of emission;
- communication to the public in territory of reception; and
- reproduction in territory of reception.[32]

In fact, this rights matrix is more complex because there are three levels of rights involved in music:

- composers and lyricists;
- performing artists; and
- makers (producers) of the sound recording.

The rights matrix is demonstrated in Table 1.1.

Table 1.1   Rights Matrix to License a Point-to-Point Internet Communication of a Sound Recording Containing a Performance of a Protected Musical Work

Right →Rightholder ↓	*Composer/Lyricist*	*Performer*	*Producer*
Reproduction on emission server	C/PC?	C/PC?	PC?
Authorization of communication in territory of emission	C	C/R	C/R
Communication to the public in territory of reception	C	C/R	C/R
Reproduction in territory of reception	C/PC?	C/PC?	PC?

C, Right likely administered by a collective; PC, use possibly covered by private copying regime; R, right is only to remuneration (as opposed to exclusive).

In short, twelve different analyses are required. Actually, if the composer and lyricist's rights are administered separately or if multiple authors and performers are involved, the matrix would be even more complex. Naturally, there are ways in which the situation could be simplified, notably by agreements among CMOs that allow one participating CMO to grant a worldwide license on behalf of all other participating entities, especially with respect to the right of communication to the

---

31. Unless, at the time the copy is made, it is a 'private copy'. Even then theories based on the right of destination might apply.
32. Which is also potentially a 'private copy'.

public. Still, one must proceed with each of the rights analyses in Table 1.1 to avoid a potential finding of infringement. In other words, the rights clearance process involves multiple layers of rights. Clearing each of these rights can be a labyrinthine process even if each such process is in itself efficient. Because rights ownership and licensing arrangements change through time, the matrix becomes four-dimensional.

Rights analyses concerning audiovisual works add another layer of complexity to the analysis. A film might include rights to a screenplay, a book on which the screenplay was based, musical works incorporated in the film, any art or photographs used in the setting, as well as the end product of the film itself. Each of the works[33] in turn involve several different rights fragments and, consequently, multiple right holders and systems of rights clearance and possibly also guilds or unions. Some right holders may have moved or died. And of course any one of the right holders who has an exclusive right may prevent the use and stop or force a rearrangement of the entire project. Each holder of a right fragment has a potential veto. CMOs can help because, as de facto or de jure monopolies, they usually cannot refuse to grant a license. Still, several organizations may be involved. Additionally, one CMO may represent a creator for part of its repertoire and another CMO for the remainder.[34]

Fragmentation may not be an essential ingredient of an optimal national copyright system, but it is the reality for most if not all such systems. CMOs can do much to alleviate the burden of users by bundling fragments. For example, as Mario Bouchard explain in the chapter on Australia and Canada, the Copyright Board of has essentially forced CMOs to work together to offer a single fee license to users who need multiple right fragments. This allows them to pay a single fee and it allows the Board to determine the entire value of the copyright bundle (all of the fragments) needed by the user. The bundle must then be split for distribution purposes (as the Board did) between the various CMOs representing different groups of right holders. But that is of no concern to the user.

4.2   THE COPYRIGHT PARADOX

Another role of CMOs is to provide an 'answer' to the copyright paradox. It may indeed seem paradoxical that, in order to maximize the creation, dissemination and access to new human knowledge expressed as works of art and of the intellect, the law chooses to provide those who create, publish, produce or otherwise disseminate this knowledge with exclusive rights to prohibit many forms of use of the knowledge. That paradox is real, but only up to a point. The rights to prohibit contained in the bundle of copyright rights (and related rights) apply in specific

---

33. Or object of a related right.
34. Many composers change their US performing right affiliation from ASCAP to BMI or to the Society of European Stage Authors and Composers (SESAC) and back, etc. They thus have rights that at a certain point in time were administered by one society and later by another, adding a temporal element to the complexity equation.

cases and, in theory at least, with the principal aim of *organizing* access, not denying it, at least for published content.[35]

4.3 CMOs AND THE TWO WORLDVIEWS

The 1710 *Statute of Anne* emerged 300 years ago after the demise of a licensing monopoly that allowed only members of the Stationers' Company (publishers' guild) to publish books in England. That monopoly had expired, and stationers were unable to justify a renewal of their publishing monopoly, which many saw as a form of censorship. They joined authors in a petition to Parliament in demanding a 'copy-right' to be vested initially in authors but then normally assigned to publishers. This led to the adoption of the *Statute of Anne*, which contained a fourteen-year monopoly granted to authors (fully assignable). The Statute also renewed for a limited period of time the Stationers licensing monopoly. British authors' already had common law rights to prevent first publication and false attribution.[36] British 'copyright' was thus born by merging two quite different approaches – on the one hand, there was the economically motivated desire of publishers to prevent copying of their books, and, on the other, the demands of authors to 'own' their works, anchored in a natural rights perspective and based on the Lockean principle that all persons should own the fruits of their labour.

The last justification seemed perhaps more morally acceptable for public opinion. It was also a view very strongly held on the Continent after the 1789 French Revolution and before that date in Germany, and defended by philosophers such as Kant and later Hegel. Yet, even if the *droit d'auteur/Urheberrecht* tradition can be seen as a child of the European Enlightenment tradition of individual human rights, Josef Kohler made it clear that copyright's purpose was to be used by and between professionals.[37] Interestingly, similar debates took place also in the United States, with Thomas Jefferson advocating an 'economic' approach to copyright while James Madison apparently supporting the author's natural right.[38]

To this day, the difference between the economic/instrumentalist view of copyright prevalent in common law jurisdictions and inspired by British legal principles and history and the natural right (indeed human right) approach

---

35. A right to decide when the first publication will occur is a key component of the copyright bundle.
36. After long debated before British courts, it was determined in *Donaldson v. Becket* ((1774) 4 Burr. 2408, 98 Eng. Rep. 257) that there is no common law right in published works that could be used to prevent copying of books after the expiry of the statutory monopoly.
37. J. Kohler. *Das Autorrecht* (1880), 230. Whether CMOs can solve the copyright paradox for individual (non-professional) user is explored in s. 5 below.
38. See M. Rose, *Authors and Owners* (Cambridge: Harvard University Press, 1993), 176; and L. Ray Patterson, *Copyright in Historical Perspective* (Nashville: Vanderbilt University Press, 1968), 264.

defended in civil law jurisdictions inspired by, *inter alia*, French and German thinkers, is seen as profound.[39]

Yet the history of European and then American copyright since the eighteenth century shows that the picture is more complex, and that copyright is both an economically justifiable right required to organize markets for certain types of works of art or the intellect, *and* a 'moral' right that authors have to prevent the publication of their works without consent and to be recognized as the authors of such works.[40] Trying to squeeze copyright on one side of that philosophical fence is incorrect in historical perspective, both in common law and civil law jurisdictions.

Many if not most CMOs are a good reflection of this history. They see themselves as champions of the rights of their members (or represented right holders if not a membership organization) and recognize the value of administering rights that can be justified as human rights or natural rights.[41] But they also operate as 'businesses', handling large sums of money. They are part of the multibillion dollar business of copyright, and their work determines the economic livelihood of many an author worldwide. More importantly, CMOs can solve the copyright paradox, by proving that the role of copyright (for published works, performances and recordings) is not to deny access and use but rather to *organize it* by making it reasonably simple, if not always inexpensive, for users to secure the rights they needs. Naturally, much more can be done. If right holders want to license individual and small-scale users beyond what fair use and other exceptions allows them to do freely, then it behoves them to offer user-friendly systems to obtain such licenses; a collective approach would seem to present efficiency gains.

5 CMOS AND THE INTERNET

5.1 THE CHALLENGES

As mentioned in the previous section, from the seventeenth century until the 1990s copyright was aimed at, and used by, professional entities, either legitimate ones such as broadcasters, cable companies or distributors, or illegitimate ones, such as makers and distributors of pirated cassettes and later CDs and DVDs. In many cases, these professionals were intermediaries with no particular interest in the content itself.

In recent years, however, and especially since the advent of the Internet, copyright has also been used to try to prevent *mass individual uses* (e.g., music

---

39. See A. Strowel, *Droit D'auteur et Copyright: Divergences et Convergences* (Bruxelles: Bruylant, 1993), 722 and Laurence Helfer's chapter.
40. Philosophically, one may derive the right to prevent mutilation from the latter. It may be linked either to the right to protect one's reputation or in the link that united the author and his or her work.
41. See the chapter by Professor Helfer.

and video file-sharing), in many cases without providing an equivalent market (e.g., legal downloads; monetized file-sharing). In addition, to enforce copyright, many right holders have tried to obtain usage information concerning individual users, thus confronting the right of privacy, a duel between rights not seen before because copyright was used by (or against) and transacted between professionals of the copyright industries, such as authors, publishers, producers, distributors and professional pirates, not by or against individual end-users.

Even more strikingly, the invention of peer-to-peer (P2P) software, also known as 'file-sharing', has radically altered the copyright landscape. P2P started as a centralized system known as Napster,[42] the demise of which was made possible, in large part, by its easily locatable and controllable nature. Napster was, in reality, only a few Internet servers, which made their owner and operators an easy enforcement target; put differently, Napster was very easy to shut down. The recording industry then tried to stop file-sharing software. In addition to lawsuits, it is using technological locks to make it harder to 'rip' music from compact discs. It also uses spoofing (sending corrupted files into peer-to-peer networks). Yet, exchanges of music files have apparently continued to grow, and events since 2001 seem to beg the question whether the music industry underestimated the strength of the demand for, and the societal role of, file-sharing and 'free music'. Distributed file-sharing technologies such as torrents are extremely hard to pin down, and music users are now turning to anonymizing software and secure USENET access to continue to 'share' music undetected.[43] Even if the authors of the software and/or some operators of sites promoting the technology can be fined, as in the PirateBay case, trying to stop file-sharing is essentially impossible short of kicking users off the Internet, a solution that some countries (e.g., France) may put into practice. Yet, this may reduce Internet traffic and commerce, and it raises privacy concerns, two undesirable side effects. For example, if one file-sharer is identified among a group of users (e.g., a family), the entire group will be punished collectively and denied access to email, online governmental and commercial services, etc. This hardly seems an optimal solution. More importantly, although the focus of the approach is strictly a limited, property-based view of music designed to minimize unauthorized use, *no one can demonstrate conclusively that the industry will in fact make more revenue* because it is able to shut down Internet accounts of music users. As stores selling physical media disappear or morph into

---

42. Napster was shut down after injunctions were issued by various courts in the United States. See *A&M Records, Inc. v. Napster, Inc.*, 284 F. 3d 1091 (9th Cir., 2002).
43. See Lior Strahilevitz, 'Charismatic Code, Social Norms, and the Emergence of Cooperation on the File-Swapping Networks', *Virginia Law Review* 89 (2003): 505; and Bobbie Johnson, 'Internet Pirates find "Bulletproof" Havens for Illegal File Sharing', *The Guardian* 5 Jan. 2010 (noting that '[b]efore going completely dark in October 2009, Demonoid physically moved their servers to Ukraine, and remotely controlled them, said John Robinson, of Big-Champagne, a media tracking service based in Los Angeles. Ukrainian communications law, as they paraphrase it, says that providers are not responsible for what their customers do. Therefore, they feel no need to speak about or defend what they do'). Available at <www.guardian.co.uk/technology/2010/jan/05/internet-piracy-bulletproof> (last visited: 21 Jan. 2010).

retail outlets for other types of products (e.g., DVDs, games and consoles) and the resentment of users whose Internet accounts were suspended (even if they were prepared to pay for a download) grows, the likelihood of a steep upward curve in the revenue stream of the music industry as a result of the crackdown remains low. Historically, copyright industries have done well, one could argue, *when their primary focus was not to minimize unauthorized uses but rather to maximize authorized use.*

In reality, the Internet-based picture is far more complex than the 'piracy' label implies.[44] File-sharing software is used in ways that mirror social sites. People use the Internet to share music and music preferences. This is widely acknowledged as a form of free advertising, though one that does not necessarily compensate for lost sales. Yet, it seems clear that a significant, though admittedly hard to quantify, portion of music that is file-shared would never be purchased. It may remain on a user's computer because of today's computers huge storage capacity, but it will be seldom if ever listened to. If recipients of the file like the music, they might become new fans and buy some music (data analyses show that many people get some of their music for free and pay for some – perhaps a form of self-appraisal of what music is worth to them in aggregate).

If this analysis is correct, even in part, online mass and P2P uses should be a market that needs to be organized not quashed, absent a paradigmatic change in the technology itself. Part of that organization could be a broad license to use the music – and perhaps other types of content as well, and CMOs would be well placed to be partners in such an endeavour. In fact, it is difficult to see how such a system could operate without them.

Some observers argue that, with the aid of technology such as Digital Rights Management (DRM), the individual exercise of rights will become not only feasible but a more efficient solution, at least in certain cases.[45] A layer of individually or collectively managed transactional uses can coexist with a free or uncontrolled space that would be covered by a general license, perhaps one that would be paid as part of a monthly Internet or other subscription.

The role that CMOs will play in managing transactional uses and/or general online use licenses (which one could then compare to a compensation regime) is

---

44. For a discussion of the use of the term 'piracy', see William Patry, *Moral Panics and the Copyright Wars* (Oxford: Oxford University Press, 2009). Whereas the term is now used for its apparent rhetorical appeal, it has been in use for centuries as a fairly technical term of the art to refer, *inter alia*, to an unauthorized printing of a book etc.

45. M. Kretschmer, 'The Failure of Property Rules in Collective Administration: Rethinking Copyright Societies as Regulatory Instruments', *European Intellectual Property Review* 24 (2002): 126, at 133. Under this theory, right holders will use digital rights management systems to control and disseminate the use of their works. The author explains:

> In short, the transaction cost argument for collective administration from the cost of individual contracting may support not a universal rights administration system (to which all right holders have access on similar terms), but a system where the major rightholders selectively decide, supported by sophisticated information technology, whether collecting licence fees is worthwhile.

unclear, and it depends in large part to the degree that they can facilitate and develop new business models. It may be the case that the advancement of new technologies will minimize the role of CMOs, but it could also lead to a significant expansion of their role. Whatever view is taken, the rationalization of the collective management of copyright remains an important task. In fact, if CMOs are to play the role of intermediary fully and efficiently, these organizations must acquire the rights they need to license digital uses of protected material and build (or improve current) information systems to deal with ever more complex rights management and licensing tasks.

The ability of CMOs to meet the needs of both authors and users is contingent on the evolution of both their internal practices, and the framework in which CMOs work to alleviate the many concerns of fragmentation within the current system.[46] Countries and CMOs throughout the world must adapt their laws and infrastructure to meet the challenges of digital technology irrespective of the philosophical underpinnings of each nation's copyright system – that is, whether it is rooted in economic rights, natural/human rights, utilitarian rights or any combination of these.

CMOs also will face possible competition from new players. Commercial entities that offer music on the Internet, whether on a subscription basis or individual song downloads, could combine their service with rights management in order to circumvent CMOs altogether. This is unlikely to work for individual authors, given the sheer number of composers and lyricists concerned, but could apply to other right holders, especially publishers and producers, in light of the high concentration of the music market among major labels and the decreasing daylight between music publishers and producers.

In countries where collective management is not mandatory and non-exclusive (e.g., the United States), one could see these new entities offering their services to authors as well. New 'de facto CMOs' of that sort could operate on a trans-national basis, which raises the spectre of territoriality. The example of the Google Book Settlement and the proposed establishment of a new CMO whose purpose would be precisely the administration of that settlement is another example of possible new players intersecting with existing CMOs.

After this analysis of the problems that copyright faces, illuminated by the spotlight of history and public policy and of the chaotic nature of copyright and related rights, it is time to turn to the role that CMOs are playing or may be called upon to assume in finding a way out of this rights maze.

5.2   THE DEFRAGMENTATION OF DIGITAL USES

Rights clearance systems are often based on the rights fragments discussed earlier, and each tends to come with its 'practices' and other idiosyncrasies. This means

---

46. The proliferation of digital technology presents problems both to authors and copyright holders, as well as for users. See S. Handa, *Copyright Law in Canada* (Markham: Butterworths, 2002) at 354.

that even if each such 'sub-system' (for a clearance process requiring several clearance transactions performed through different intermediaries (including several CMOs)) is efficient, the efficiency of the process as a whole is in jeopardy.

Collective management is not a neutral service. Given the fragility of Internet-based business models for delivery of copyright content on the Internet, economically efficient clearance 'should ensure that copyright administration favours no one delivery method over another'.[47] In fact, regardless of whether digital technology is involved, the standardization of practices among CMOs would lead to greater efficiencies and would alleviate some of the fragmentation under the current system. To play that role fully and efficiently, however, these organizations must acquire the rights they need to license digital uses of protected material and build (or improve current) information systems to deal with ever more complex rights management and licensing tasks. Additionally, CMOs need to cooperate more fully on both a national and international scale to fully achieve their role as facilitators of rights clearance. The following suggestions are offered as potential means of achieving this goal.

Technology and, in particular, copyright management systems (CMS), are a useful tool in copyright clearance because they assist with proper identification of the works, performances, recordings and right holders involved and the rights that will need to be cleared. CMS are basically databases that contain information about content – works, discrete manifestations of works and related products and, in most cases, the author and other right holders.[48] They may be used by individual right holders or by third parties who manage rights on behalf of others. A rights holder might use the system to track a repertory of works or products embodying such works (or substantial parts thereof), or an organization representing a group of right holders might use a CMS to track each right holder's rights and works. Such an organization might be a literary agent representing multiple writers or, more commonly, a CMO.

Some CMS allow right holders or CMOs to automatically grant transactional licenses to users without human intervention, which has the benefit of keeping transaction costs low and making licensing an efficient, Internet-speed process: licenses to use a specific work can be granted online, twenty-four hours per day, to individual users. Ideally, such licenses will be tailored to a user's needs.[49] For example, a company may want to post a flattering newspaper article on its website

---

47. M. Einhorn & L. Kurlantzick, 'Traffic Jam on the Music Highway', *Journal of the Copyright Society of the USA* 8 (2002): 417, at 420.

48. See J. Cunard, 'Technological Protection of Copyrighted works and Copyrighted Management Systems: A Brief Survey of the Landscape', ALAI Congress 2001; and D. Gervais, 'Electronic Rights Management and Digital Identifier Systems', *Journal of Electronic Publishing* 4, no. 3 (March 1999), online: <http://quod.lib.umich.edu/cgi/t/text/text-idx?c=jep;view=text;rgn=main;idno=3336451.0004.303> (last visited: 8 Feb. 2010).

49. Many licenses to use a work are granted where the user obtains permission for several different uses of a work. It may be the case that the user requires the work for only a specific purpose. Why should the user pay to acquire rights to use a work in a manner for which the user has no intention of using it?

or send it via email to its customer base; an individual author may decide to purchase the right to use an image, video clip or song to use in her or his own creative process; a publishing house might purchase the right to reuse previously published material.[50] CMS may also be used to deliver content in cases in which the user does not have access to such content in the required format or to create licensing sites or offer licensing options at the point at which the content is made available.

To be optimally efficient and able to deal with digital usage information, online members and work registration, user requests and online transactional licensing (where such licensing on reasonably standard terms is possible), CMOs need CMS with both an efficient 'back-end' system and a user-friendly online interface ('front-end'). However, building an all-encompassing online multimedia licensing system operated jointly by all CMOs in a country is hard to justify under current licensing practices or indeed in light of prevailing market conditions.[51]

The sheer number of CMOs that may be involved in the licensing of a single economic use of a protected work (or works and possibly combined with one or several related rights) poses another problem. To implement an efficient system, CMOs should cooperate within appropriate groupings (i.e., CMOs having a sufficient degree of commonality) to limit the number of systems to be developed, and they should develop compatible systems and standards to ensure that the exchange of data will be possible.[52]

A repertoire license (i.e., one that allows the user to use any work or object contained in the repertory of works licensed by a CMO) presents an attractive alternative in the online environment. The two most relevant uses of such licenses are where there are inherent difficulties in advance clearance of rights and where consolidation is more practical from a user's (and sometimes creator's) perspective. From a functional point of view, CMOs are a practical substitute for a compulsory license because of the multitude of uses and the difficulty of advance clearance. This solution has the advantage of being fairer to users and

---

50. Copyright Clearance Center, Inc. (CCC) licenses reproduction of printed material for inclusion in 'digital coursepacks', reuse of material on websites, intranets, CD-ROMs and other digital media. CCC also offers a repertory-based license for internal digital reuse of material by corporate users. Interestingly, in the latter programme, users can only scan material not made available by the publisher in digital form. CCC's ability to license digital uses is entirely based on voluntary and non-exclusive rights transfers from right holders. See <www.copyright.com>.

51. These systems often perform several functions. The first, if so required, is to break down the rights in a work (more the case with multimedia works). The second function is to identify the right holder(s) of the work. The third function is then to clear these rights, followed by establishing license terms, and payment of fees for the use of a work. Such technologies facilitate the expediency and efficiency of licensing content online. See T. Koskinen-Olsson, 'Secure IPR-Content on the Internet', ALAI Congress 2001.

52. These would seem to follow the best practices emerging from ongoing efforts in countries other than the United States. This will be explored in greater detail when addressing centralized licensing regimes or one-stop-shop services.

potentially achieves administrative efficiencies for both creators and users. Such a system would be fairer to users in that there would no longer be a discrepancy in fees to be paid for similar uses of a work.[53] In essence, a single tariff could be established for different types or uses of works. Put differently, a user would pay an 'admission fee' at the entrance.

5.3   THE EXTENDED REPERTOIRE SYSTEM AND INTERNET USES

One system that may be worth a second look to make the licensing of mass online uses more efficient and workable is the extended repertoire system (ERS – also known as 'extended collective licensing'), used in all Nordic countries[54] and under consideration or being implemented in other parts of the world, including Central and Eastern Europe, Africa and possibly also Canada.[55] ERS is a voluntary assignment or transfer of rights from right holders to a CMO followed by a *legal extension of the CMO's repertoire* to encompass non-member right holders. It greatly simplifies the acquisition of rights. In fact, it has been called a 'backup legal license', but this expression is confusing because the right holder can opt out of the system. This, of course, is not possible under a compulsory or legal license.[56]

Usually the legal extension applies after a determination that a 'substantial' number of right holders in a given category have agreed to join a CMO.[57] Then the repertoire of the CMO is automatically extended (for the licensing scheme concerned) to other domestic right holders in the same category and to all foreign right holders. The license also extends to deceased right holders, particularly in cases in which estates have yet to be properly organized. Thus, ERS is a powerful solution to the orphan works issue.

The extended repertoire is an interesting model for countries where, on the one hand, right holders are reasonably well organized and informed, and, on the other hand, a great part of the material that is the object of licenses comes from foreign countries. It is often more difficult and time consuming to obtain an authorization for the use of foreign material. The extended repertoire provides a legal solution to this situation, because the agreements struck between users and right holders

---

53. As it stands, collectives sometimes negotiate different licensing terms and fees with users regardless of whether the actual 'use' of the work is similar in nature.
54. See the chapter by Tarja Koskinen-Olsson.
55. See D. Gervais, 'Application of an Extended Collective Licensing Regime in Canada: Principles and Issues Related to Implementation (2003)', study prepared for and published by the Government of Canada, online: <http://aix1.uottawa.ca/~dgervais/publications/extended_licensing.pdf> (last visited: 2 Feb. 2010).
56. Internationally, very few countries have adopted *compulsory* licensing of digital uses. Such a system exists in the Danish legislation but has yet to be applied in practice. It would be an extension of the license existing under ss 13 and 14 of the Danish *Copyright Act*, 14 Jun. 1995, No. 395.
57. Substantiality is contextual. A new collective organizing right holders in a given area for the first time should have a much lower substantiality threshold to pass than a well-established collective trying to obtain an extension of repertoire for a new licensing scheme.

will include all non-excluded domestic and foreign right holders. Finally, by accelerating the acquisition of rights, the extended repertoire also increases the efficiency and promptness of royalties' collection. The monies redistributed to right holders are thereby increased.

An argument raised against the ERS is its alleged incompatibility with Article 5(2) of Berne, which prohibits formalities concerning the existence and exercise of the rights granted by virtue of the Convention. This argument must fail.

Article 5(2) came into being in the very early days of the Berne Convention. It was then and remains part of the Convention's provisions dealing with the treatment of foreign authors (i.e., national treatment) and place of (first) publication. In the first draft of the Convention published in 1884[58] the relevant part of Article 2 read as follows:

> Authors who are nationals of one of the countries of the Contracting Countries shall enjoy in all the other countries of the Union, in respect of their works, whether in manuscript or unpublished form or published in one of those countries, such advantages as the laws concerned do now or will hereafter grant to nationals. The enjoyment of the above rights shall be subject to compliance with the conditions of form and substance prescribed by the legislation of the country of origin of the work or, in the case of a manuscript or unpublished work, by the legislation of the country to which the author belongs.[59]

It is clear from the above that the principal intent was to grant to foreign authors the same rights as nationals. This was confirmed by the Drafting Committee, which also clarified the meaning of the expression 'conditions of forms and substance', originally a German proposal, which was changed to 'formalities and conditions'. The Minutes of the First Conference held in Berne in 1884 are very useful to illuminate the meaning and purpose of the expression:

> Dr. Meyer said the following: 'It is merely a question of noting that the wording proposed by the German Delegation, '*conditions of form and substance*' has been replaced by the words '*formalities and conditions*', and that the word '*formalities*' being taken as a synonym of the term '*conditions of form*', included, for instance, registration, deposit, etc.; whereas the expression '*conditions*', being in our view synonymous with '*conditions of substance*', includes, for instance, the completion of a translation within the prescribed period. Thus the words '*formalities and conditions*' cover all that has to be observed for the author's rights in relation to his work to come into being, whereas the effects and consequences of protection, notably with respect to the extent of protection have to remain subject to the principle of treatment on the same footing as nationals.

---

58. See WIPO, *Berne Convention Centenary: 1886–1986* (Geneva: WIPO, 1986) at 94.
59. *Ibid.*

The President noted that the Conference agreed with Dr. Meyer on the scope of the words *'formalities and conditions'*.[60]

The Report of 1896 Paris Conference contains the following:

> Under the text of the Convention, the enjoyment of copyright shall be subject to the accomplishment of the *conditions and formalities prescribed by law in the country of origin of the work.* The meaning of this provision does not seem to be seriously debatable. As a result of it, the author needs only to have complied with the legislation of the country of origin, to have completed in that country the conditions and formalities which may be required there. He does not have to complete formalities in the other countries where he wished to claim protection. This interpretation, which is in keeping with the text, was certainly in the minds of the authors of the 1886 Convention. (Emphasis in original.)[61]

Clearly, the conditions and formalities are those mentioned in 1884, namely registration, deposit, mandatory translation or publication etc., not the need to sign contracts, file statements of claims in courts, join or otherwise deal with copyright agencies, etc. This was further reinforced at the 1908 Berlin Conference, a slightly different version of Article 2, which from 1908 until 1967 became 4(2) – now Article 5(2) – was adopted. There it was very clear that the provision is related to publication and similar requirements. The relevant part read as follows:

> Authors who are nationals of any of the countries of the Union shall enjoy in countries other than the country of origin of the work, for their works, whether unpublished or first published in a country of the Union, the rights which the respective laws do now or may hereafter grant to their nationals as well as the rights specially granted by this Convention. The enjoyment and the exercise of these rights shall not be subject to any formality; such enjoyment and exercise are independent of the existence of protection in the country of origin of the work. Consequently, apart from the provisions of this Convention, the extent of protection, as well as the means of redress afforded to the author to protect his rights, shall be governed exclusively by the laws of the country where protection is claimed.[62]

The Report of the 1908 Conference is also worth quoting *in extenso* on this point. It begins with a statement that the provision does not apply to domestic authors and then explains the shift from the single formality requirement (in the country of origin) to the no formality formulation we have in the Convention text today:

> *The enjoyment and exercise of these rights shall not be subject to any formality.* It should be noted that it is exclusively the rights claimed by virtue of the Convention that are involved here. The legislation of the country in which the

---

60. *Ibid.*, at 94–95.
61. *Ibid.*, at 137.
62. *Ibid.*, at 149.

work is published and in which it is nationalized by the very fact of publication continues to be absolutely free to subject the existence or the exercise of the right to protection in the country to whatever conditions and formalities it thinks fit; it is a pure question of domestic law. Outside the country of publication, protection may be requested in the other countries of the Union not only without having to complete any formalities in them, but even without being obliged to justify that the formalities in the country of origin have been accomplished. This is what results, on the one hand, from a general principle which is going to be stated and explained and, on the other, from the deletion of the third paragraph of Article 11 of the 1886 Convention. This paragraph provides that:

> It is, nevertheless, agreed that the courts may, if necessary, require the production of a certificate from the competent authority to the effect that the formalities prescribed by law in the country of origin have been accomplished, in accordance with Article 2.

That Article does indeed state, at the beginning of its paragraph 2, that 'the enjoyment of these rights shall be subject to the accomplishment of the conditions and formalities prescribed by law in the country of origin of the work' and, to remove difficulties which had arisen in certain countries, the Paris Interpretative Declaration had emphasized the idea – which was evidently that of the authors of the 1886 Convention – that the protection depends solely on the accomplishment, in the country of origin, of the conditions and formalities which may be required by the legislation of that country. This was already a great simplification which will be appreciated if it is recalled that there was a time not so long ago when, to guarantee a work protection in a foreign country, even by virtue of an international convention, it was necessary to register and often even to deposit that work in the foreign country within a certain time limit.

The new Convention simplifies matters still further since it requires no justification. Difficulties had arisen with regard to the production of a certificate from the authority of the country of origin – this production having been considered, occasionally, as the preliminary to infringement action, which caused delays. The new provision means that a person who acts by virtue of the Convention does not have to provide proof that the formalities in the country of origin have been accomplished, as the accomplishment or non-accomplishment of these formalities must not exert any influence. However, if it is in his interest to produce a certificate to establish a particular fact, he cannot be prevented from doing so (the Article in the draft only refers to *formalities*, but it is meant to cover the *conditions and formalities* to which the 1886 Convention refers.)[63] (Emphasis in original.)

Unquestionably, in light of the above, the formalities that are prohibited under Article 5(2) are essentially registration with a governmental authority, deposit of a

---

63. *Ibid.*, at 148.

copy of the work or similar formalities when they are linked to the existence of copyright or its exercise, especially in enforcement proceedings.

Interestingly, in its pre-1908 incarnation, the provision was arguably derogating from national treatment, though it was clearly not intended as such. Rather, Convention drafters saw it as a simplification of the multiple registration/deposit requirements.[64] If 'pure' national treatment had been applied, it would have been sufficient to grant protection to foreign authors on the condition of accomplishing the same formalities as nationals in every country. In 1908, the provision was realigned along the principle of national treatment by making it a provision against mandatory formalities while maintaining the meaning of the expression 'conditions and formalities' defined in 1884–1886. Formal requirement in existence at the time essentially involved registration, deposit (in national libraries) and, in rare cases, translation. For many reasons, although it was necessary to respect each country's ability to impose such requirements, they had to be decoupled from copyright. Deposit is still required for published works in many countries, but the sanction for failure to provide free copies to the national library cannot be the removal of copyright. The issue of mandatory translation is similarly separate from copyright, though its political importance led to the adoption of the Appendix to the Paris Act in 1971 allowing developing countries to impose compulsory translation licenses. The provision does not prevent requirements of other types.

This is further confirmed in World Intellectual Property Organizations (WIPO's) latest commentary on the Convention:

> Formalities are any conditions or measures – independent from those that relate to the creation of the work (such as the substantive condition that a production must be original in order to qualify as a protected work) or the fixation thereof (where it is a condition under national law) – without the fulfillment of which the work is not protected or loses protection. Registration, deposit of the original or a copy, and the indication of a notice are the most typical examples.[65]

'Enjoyment' is thus the very existence of the right, whereas exercise refers in particular to enforcement.[66] It would be patently incongruous to read Article 5(2) as preventing the mandatory doing of anything. Should authors just have to walk into a courtroom (itself a 'formality') without having to file a statement of claim? Not have to deal with foreign publishers and distributors because those are 'formalities'? Not have to deal with foreign tax authorities to avoid deductions at source in a foreign country? Not have to deal with foreign CMOs to ensure the protection of their rights in cases in which they cannot or do not want to join a

---

64. *Ibid.*
65. M. Ficsor, *Guide to the Copyright and Related Rights Treaties Administered by WIPO and Glossary of Copyright and Related Rights Terms* (Geneva: WIPO, 2004), at 41. See also WIPO, WIPO *Intellectual Property Handbook.* (Geneva: WIPO, 2004) at 262 ('protection is granted automatically and is not subject to the formality of registration, deposit or the like').
66. See Ficsor, *ibid.,* at 42.

worldwide system through their national CMO (if any)? That is clearly not the intent or meaning of Article 5(2). Those are all normal acts that authors and other copyright holders must perform routinely to exploit their copyright works and not – as was made abundantly clear during the adoption and revision of the Convention, 'formalities' prohibited under Article 5(2).

The application of Article 5(2) hinges on whether the formality is (a) copyright-specific and (b) government-related. On the first element, as examples above show, it is self-evident that authors are not somehow free of all civic or judicial formalities. The second element is a distillate of the drafting history of Article 5(2). It cannot simply be assumed that the prohibition on government (legislatively imposed) formalities such as registration or deposit necessarily extend to dealings with private entities, which most CMOs are.

To consider restriction on the freedom to exercise one's rights fully, see Table 1.2.

Table 1.2   Copyright Restriction Levels

LEVEL	TYPE OF RESTRICTION
0	Full Individual Exercise
1	Voluntary Collective Management (opt in)
2	Collective Management With Extended Repertoire (and opt out)
3A	Mandatory Collective Management/Presumption
3B	Limitation of Damages to Tariff
4	Compulsory Licensing
5	Exception[67]

Several countries routinely impose restrictions of levels 3A, 3B and 4.[68] Damages available to a right holder are limited to what would be available under a tariff, if that right holder was a member. In effect, although membership is not mandatory, the effect of membership is. In other cases, as in Germany, there is a 'presumption' that all right holders are members of the CMO. Those are simply ways in which the exploitation of the works concerned is organized and tasks that copyright holders must fulfil. Even at Level 0, authors must still negotiate and sign exploitation contracts, file statements of claim, testify in court or before an arbitration panel, for example, and, of course, deal with CMOs.

---

67. Admittedly, Level 5 is conceptually different from the other types of restriction, but for our purposes it can be argued that it is a compulsory license with a tariff of 0 for all users who benefit from the exemption. The link between the three-step test and Art. 5(2) is thus established.
68. See Gervais, 'Collective Management of Copyright and Neighbouring Rights in Canada: An International Perspective' (2001), online: <www.docstoc.com/search/Neighbouring-Rights-Collective-of-Canada> (last visited: 2 Feb. 2010).

Properly structured, ERS is not a prohibited formality under Berne. It guarantees an orderly exploitation of the repertoire that will be licensed but offers authors the option of going back to Level 0 by sending a simple notice, perhaps even as simple as an email. The ERS provides CMOs with the immediate ability to license all or almost all works that users may need to license. Although not affecting the scope of exceptions, it ensures that uses that go beyond such exceptions are paid for; that is, that the objective of providing a fair reward is fulfilled. At the same time, licensing removes the (theoretical) obstacle and frustrating attempts by certain right holders to stop Internet use. This would fulfil the other side of the equation, namely the promotion of the public interest in the encouragement and dissemination of works of the arts and intellect.

6   CONCLUSION

CMOs are easier to defend to the extent that the level of quality of services is perceived as efficient by both authors and users, taking into account available administrative technologies. Initially, CMOs developed out of necessity; it was not feasible for authors and publishers to maintain a direct relationship with users. With the advent of new technologies, however, authors and publishers are increasingly able to initiate and maintain a direct relationship with users. Although this does not necessarily diminish the role of CMOs, it highlights the need to reform the existing CMO structure to justify their continued existence on one level and to alleviate the problems stemming from the fragmentation of both copyright rights proper and rights clearance. This is not to say that the role and justification of CMOs is vanishing. It is that they are changing.

There is a similar motif that runs through each of the outlined solutions, namely that centralization and standardization are prerequisites to efficiency, particularly in the digital era. There may in fact be a greater role for CMOs in the area of mass online uses. If copyright's excludability does not easily reach individual end-users, neither does it reach without difficulty users who have no direct (one-on-one) transactional contact with the right holders concerned. To maximize efficiency, it seems that copyright's power to exclude should be limited to cases in which an exclusive distributorship (or other form of dissemination) is negotiated by the first owner of copyright or someone else who acquired rights from that first owner and in cases of commercial piracy. It was thus not an obvious step for copyright to try to reach Internet users who do not consider themselves pirates or act with intent of commercial gain.

What does it mean for the future of copyright? We should recognize that copyright is not intended to be used to stop uses by end-users completely. Historically, it has been used to organize markets for those uses. Additionally, copyright works best, as an exclusion tool, when its rules are internalized by users. If one abandons attempts to *stop* end-users, by essentially preventing use and reuse and even terminating their access to the network copyright remains as a market organization tool, an entitlement to remuneration for mass uses at least when such uses reach the level of interference with normal commercial exploitation under the Berne Convention and the TRIPS Agreement's three-step test.[69] Unfortunately, by treating file-sharers as pirates, they may push the majority of Internet users into the 'deviant' camp and damage respect for the rule of law. The solution – at this point, the only solution – is to *license* massive Internet uses in a way that respects all of those involved in the creation, performance, publication, production and use of copyright content. Naturally, this includes respect for existing exceptions. Soft enforcement measures may be used to help convince users to accept the scheme, but it cannot be overly emphasized that the best way to ensure adoption is to offer users practicable terms they will perceive as fair. The best way to achieve this, barring a major technological paradigm shift, is collective management.

---

69. See Martin Senftleben, *Copyright, Limitations and the Three-Step-Test* (The Hague: Kluwer Law International, 2004); and D. Gervais, 'Towards a New Core International Copyright Norm: The Reverse Three-Step Test', *Marquette Intellectual Property Law Review* 9 (2005): 1–37, available at <http://papers.ssrn.com/sol3/papers.cfm?abstract_id=499924> (last visited: 1 May 2010).

Chapter 2

Collective Management of Copyright and Related Rights from the Viewpoint of International Norms and the *Acquis Communautaire*

*Dr Mihály Ficsor**

1   INTRODUCTION

One may ask the question as to what kind of treaty obligations the title of this chapter might refer to, because there is no provision on collective management in the international treaties on copyright and related rights – the Berne Convention, the Universal Copyright Convention (UCC), the 'old' related rights conventions (i.e., the Rome Convention, the Geneva Phonograms Convention, the Brussels Satellite Convention), the TRIPS Agreement or the two WIPO 'Internet Treaties,' the WIPO Copyright Treaty (WCT) and the WIPO Performances and Phonograms Treaty (WPPT). There is no mention whatsoever in any of these treaties about this form of exercising rights.

　　　Nevertheless, WIPO, as the international organization in charge of the administration of the Berne Convention – and along with UNESCO and the International Labour Organization (ILO) also of the 'old' related rights conventions – in the late

———————
*　　Former Assistant Director General of the World Intellectual Property Organization in charge of copyright, President of the Hungarian Copyright Council.

Daniel Gervais (ed.), *Collective Management of Copyright and Related Rights*, pp. 29–74.
© 2010 Kluwer Law International BV, The Netherlands.

1970s and in the 1980s, began paying growing attention to collective management of copyright and related rights. This was due to the recognition that collective management was becoming the desirable – or, in certain cases, the only workable – way of exercising copyright and related rights in an ever broader field.

WIPO's activities in that period culminated in the publication of a study on 'Collective Administration of Copyright and Related Rights'[1] (hereinafter: the WIPO study) in 1990, which had been prepared in accordance with the decision adopted by the WIPO Governing Bodies at their 1989 annual sessions.[2] As Dr Arpad Bogsch, the then Director General described in the Introduction to the book in which the WIPO study was published, one of its main objectives was to analyze 'what conditions should be met so that such a system be compatible with the international obligations in respect of the protection of copyright and so-called neighboring rights, particularly, with the minimum provisions and the principle of national treatment of the Berne Convention . . . and . . . the Rome Convention'.[3]

In this chapter, first, it is discussed why and in which forms WIPO, as the administrator of international copyright and related rights treaties, has dealt with collective management with growing attention in the last decades (section 2). Then, cases in which it is justified to exercise copyright and related rights through collective management and what impact such management may have on the rights concerned are examined (section 3). This is followed by discussion of issues that seem to be the most relevant from the viewpoint of treaty obligations – the questions of in which cases and under what conditions collective management may be made mandatory (section 4) and the effect of voluntary collective management may be extended (section 5). The chapter is closed by a brief review of other issues that have also been found more or less relevant from the viewpoint of the international treaty obligations as reflected in the basic WIPO study on collective management (section 6).

2   WIPO'S ACTIVITIES IN RECOGNITION OF THE GROWING IMPORTANCE OF COLLECTIVE MANAGEMENT FROM THE VIEWPOINT OF THE INTERNATIONAL TREATIES ON COPYRIGHT AND RELATED RIGHTS

2.1   JOINT WIPO-UNESCO PROGRAMMES TO ADDRESS THE ISSUES RAISED BY NEW TECHNOLOGIES IN THE 1970s AND 1980s

The Berne Convention was revised in 1971 in Paris for the last time. This was followed by a the so-called guided development period[4] in the 1970s and 1980s

---

1. WIPO publication No. 688 (E).
2. See the Introduction to the book mentioned in the preceding footnote by Dr Arpad Bogsch, 3.
3. *Ibid.*
4. *Sam Ricketson* referred to this period of international copyright development in his book on the Berne Convention, published in 1986, as follows: 'In essence, "guided development" appears to

when the competent bodies of WIPO and UNESCO tried to give answers to certain emerging new technologies on the basis of the interpretation of the existing international treaties (the Berne Convention, the UCC and the Rome Convention) in joint meetings and projects.[5] Before that period, there were only two categories of rights – musical 'performing rights' (meaning the rights of public performance and broadcasting) and mechanical rights (concerning recording of music) – in the case of which truly widespread systems of collective management had been applied. On the basis of the studies prepared for, and the discussions held at, the joint WIPO-UNESCO meetings, it became clear that collective management was emerging as a desirable way of exercising copyright and related rights for a growing scope of rights.

The very first of such meetings in the 'guided development' period was the session of the Sub-Committees of the Executive Committee of the Berne Union and the Intergovernmental Committee of the UCC dealing with the copyright questions raised in regard to reprographic reproduction, which was held in Washington, DC, in June 1975. The Subcommittees studied the various options worked out by a previous working group (e.g., contractual schemes, non-voluntary licenses, levies on equipment) but in the short resolution – in addition to the general statement that it was up to each country to resolve the problems raised by this new form of reproduction by adopting appropriate measures in harmony with the international conventions – the Subcommittees identified concretely only one possible way of responding to those new challenges; they stated that, 'States where the use of processes of reprographic reproduction is widespread, such States could consider, among other measures, *encouraging the establishment of collective systems to administer the right to remuneration*'[6] [emphasis added].

The WIPO/UNESCO Group of Experts on Unauthorized Private Copying of Recordings, Broadcasts and Printed Matter, in Geneva in June 1984, also found that in cases in which it was not justified or possible to maintain the exclusive nature of the right of reproduction, only those solutions were desirable that could function only through a collective management system. The Group of Experts suggested that, in the case of 'home taping' (i.e., private copying of phonograms

---

be the present policy of WIPO, whose activities in promoting study and discussions on problem areas have been fundamental importance to international copyright protection in recent years.' (See: Sam Ricketson, *The Berne Convention for the Protection of Literary and Artistic Works: 1886–1986* (London: Kluwer Law International, 1986), 919 (hereinafter: Ricketson).

5.   The intensive joint activities were due to the fact that the UCC administered by UNESCO had a much more important role in international copyright relations than now; for example, the United States of America and the Soviet Union, as well as several Latin American countries, were only party to that convention. Since then, however, the overwhelming majority of the countries party to the UCC have acceded to the Berne Convention, and because between countries party to both conventions, the Berne Convention applies (see Art. XVII of the UCC and the Appendix Declaration related thereto), the importance of the UCC has decreased to a great extent.

6.   See point 2 of the Resolution adopted by the Sub-Committees; *Copyright*, WIPO's monthly review (hereinafter: Copyright), August 1975 issue, 175.

and audiovisual works), a right to remuneration should be recognized to be exercised by a collective management organization (CMO).[7]

WIPO's and UNESCO's copyright programmes also addressed the issues of computer-related uses of works quite early. The second session of the WIPO/ UNESCO Committee of Governmental Experts on Copyright Problems Arising from the Use of Computers for Access to or the Creation of Works, in Paris in June 1982, drew up recommendations on the protection and exercise of rights concerned by storage in, and retrieval from, computer systems of protected works. It was emphasized that such uses should be based on contractual agreements concluded either on an individual basis or through a collective management. The Committee stated that, because of the rapid technological developments, the exercise of copyright on an individual basis was becoming extremely difficult in the case of these new forms of exploitation and stressed that of the possible solutions to this problem, collective management was preferable to a non-voluntary license system.[8] (At that time, only these two major choices were considered; the potentials of a third possible answer to the challenges of electronic uses of works – the 'answer to the machine in the machine'[9] in the form of digital rights management (DRM) systems – were not yet recognized.)

Even greater attention was paid to collective management in the '*Annotated Principles of Protection of Authors, Performers, Producers of Phonograms and Broadcasting Organizations in Connection with Distribution of Programs by Cable*' adopted by the meeting of the Subcommittees of the Executive Committee of the Berne Union and the Intergovernmental Committees of the UCC and of the Rome Convention, respectively.[10] The Annotated Principles emphasized that, in case of cable retransmission of broadcast programmes, the clearance of rights on a programme-by-programme basis with every owner of rights was impracticable and, in such cases, collective management was the only workable solution.[11] The Annotated Principles also dealt with the necessary conditions of, and guarantees for, appropriate operation of this way of exercising rights.

The WIPO/UNESCO Group of Experts on Rental of Phonograms and Videograms, meeting in Paris in November 1984, was a kind of 'cuckoo's egg' in the process of the recognition of the importance of the application of collective

---

7. See para. 17 of the Report, *Copyright*, July–August 1984 issue, 281–282.
8. See paras 11 and 12 of the 'Recommendations for Settlement of Copyright Problems Arising from the Use of Computer Systems for Access to or the Creation of Works', *Copyright* (September 1982 issue): 246.
9. See Charles Clark, 'Publishers and Publishing in the Digital Age', in *WIPO Worldwide Symposium on Copyright in the Global Information Infrastructure – Mexico City* (22–24 May 1995), WIPO publication No. 746 (E/S), 346–348. The relevant part of the paper, under the title 'The Answer to the Machine is in the Machine', pointed out that digital technology – through the application of the technological protection measures and rights management information – may solve the problems created by the same technology.
10. See the April 1984 issue of *Copyright* devoted exclusively for the publication of the Annotated Principles and the Report of the Subcommittees.
11. *Ibid.*, 150–151.

management. It expressed the view for the first time that there were certain categories of rights of certain categories of owners of rights in the case of which collective management would not be desirable and appropriate. In the conclusions adopted by the Group of Experts, it was stated that

the soliciting and granting of licenses may, specially where the number of rightholders is big, require legislative measures which facilitate the negotiations of licenses and their implementation measures preferably resulting in the collective administration of the rights.

There was, however, a fairly strong opposition at the meeting against the idea of imposing (mandatory) collective management for the exercise of rental right (which was proposed as an alternative in the working document). The report of the meeting reflected this, *inter alia*, in the following way:

'Representatives of film producers and several other participants said that, with regard to the special conditions of producing and marketing cinematographic works, the film industry needs control over each form of using its productions, and the rental or lending of videograms should be exempted from collective administration of the rights therein. In their view, the film industry is in a position to control the rental or lending of each videogram individually . . . . Some experts felt that the authors cannot be obliged to entrust a society with the administration of their rights' and 'expressed their concern that the system of collective administration may easily become a kind of non-voluntary licensing, in particular with regard to authors and producers who did not entrust the society giving collective authorization to represent them'.[12]

2.2   ORGANIZATIONAL ASPECTS OF COLLECTIVE
           MANAGEMENT ORGANIZATIONS

WIPO and UNESCO also had a joint project that concentrated on the organizational aspects of collective management in parallel with the previously mentioned meetings addressing the issues raised by the emerging new technologies. A Committee of Governmental Experts on the Drafting of Model Statutes for Institutions Administering Authors' Rights in Developing Countries met twice, in Paris in June 1980 and in Geneva in October 1983, and, at its second session, adopted two Model Statutes for CMOs; one for public institutions and another one for private societies.[13] It followed from the terms of reference of the Committee that it dealt with only the organizational aspects and legal status of CMOs, and thus it undertook no analysis of the substantive issues of such management.

---

12. See paras 28, 29 and 31 of the Report of the Group of Experts, *Copyright*, January 1985 issue, 18.
13. See the Report of the Committee, *Copyright*, December 1983 issue, 351–357.

In regard to related rights, it was a Subcommittee of the Intergovernmental Committee of the Rome Convention that, in Geneva in January to February 1979, discussed in detail the questions concerning collective management of such rights. The Subcommittee adopted a Recommendation that contained a subchapter on 'Guidelines for the establishment and operation of collective societies for Article 12 rights.'[14] ('Article 12 rights', of course, meant the right to a single equitable remuneration under Article 12 of the Rome Convention for performers and/or producers of phonograms in respect to broadcasting or other communication to the public of phonograms published for commercial purposes.)[15]

2.3   ANALYSIS OF THE VARIOUS LEGAL ISSUES OF
               COLLECTIVE MANAGEMENT

From the middle of the 1980s, under WIPO's programme – as a result of the recognition of the growing importance of collective management – the analysis was extended to all the substantive legal issues that seemed to be relevant from the viewpoint of the obligations under the international treaties.

Between October 1985 and March 1986, seven comprehensive studies were published in WIPO's monthly review 'Copyright' (and its French version *'Le Droit d'auteur'*) under the overall title: 'Collective Administration of Authors' Rights'. The following subjects were covered (in the order of the publication of the articles): 'Collective Administration of Authors' Rights in the Developing Countries';[16] 'Development and Objectives of Collective Administration of Authors' Rights';[17] 'Music Performing Rights Organizations in the United States of America: Special Characteristics, Restraints and Public Attitudes';[18] 'Collective Administration: The Relationship Between Authors' Organizations and Users of Works';[19] 'Technical Problems in Collective Administration of Authors'

---

14. See 'Recommendation concerning the Protection of Performers, Producers of Phonograms and Broadcasting Organizations', *Copyright*, 108–109.
15. Article 12 of the Rome Convention which reads as follows: 'If a phonogram published for commercial purposes, or a reproduction of such phonogram, is used directly for broadcasting or for any communication to the public, a single equitable remuneration shall be paid by the user to the performers, or to the producers of the phonograms, or to both. Domestic law may, in the absence of agreement between these parties, lay down the conditions as to the sharing of this remuneration.' (Art. 16.1(a) of the Convention provides for the possibility of reservations to Art. 12, which may go even so far as to no application of the Article) It is to be noted that Art. 15 of the WPPT also provides for similar rights to remuneration for performers *and* producers of phonograms.
16. By Salah Abada, *Copyright*, September 1985 issue.
17. By Mihály Ficsor, *Copyright*, October 1985 issue.
18. By John M. Kernochan, *Copyright*, November 1985 issue.
19. By Michael Freegard, *Copyright*, December 1985 issue.

Rights';[20] 'The Relations between Authors and Organizations Administering Their Rights';[21] and 'Collective Administration and Competition Law'.[22]

The publication of the series of articles was part of the preparation of the WIPO International Forum on the Collective Administration of Copyrights and Neighbouring Rights that was held in Geneva in May 1986. The Forum was attended by some 160 participants (government representatives, observers from intergovernmental organizations and international non-governmental organizations, as well as members of the general public (in general, representatives and members of various national CMOs)). Dr Arpad Bogsch, the then Director General of WIPO, spoke about the objectives of the Forum as follows:

> With galloping technological developments, *collective administration of such rights is becoming an ever more important way of exercising copyright and neighboring rights.* Taking into account its increasing importance, much more attention should be paid to it, both at the national and at the international levels. *Guarantees should be worked out and applied for the correct functioning of collective administration systems to make sure that they will not lead to a disguised version of non-voluntary licensing or to the unjustified collectivization of rights.*[23]

At the three-day Forum, twenty-one invited speakers presented their papers. They were mainly the representatives of international non-governmental organizations interested in the field of CMOs and such national organizations from all parts of the world: Africa, the Americas, Asia, Australia and the Pacific and Europe; from both developed countries and developing countries and from both market-economy countries and centrally-planned-economy countries.

In conclusion of the Forum, the participants adopted a *Declaration* in which they, *inter alia*, expressed the view that:

> the establishment of collective administration systems should be encouraged wherever individual licensing is not practicable and as a preferable alternative to non-voluntary licenses, even where such licenses could be admitted under the Berne Convention . . . and the Rome Convention.[24]

The Declaration stated that the participants would welcome it 'if WIPO were to continue to make governments and the concerned interested circles increasingly aware of the importance of appropriate systems of collective administration of copyrights and neighboring rights and were to stimulate further international discussion in this field'. They considered it desirable that 'WIPO collect, study and make available to governments and the concerned interested circles information' on various aspects of joint management of copyright and neighbouring rights and

---

20. By Ulrich Uchtenhagen, *Copyright*, January 1986 issue.
21. By Gunnar Karnell, *Copyright*, February 1986 issue.
22. By Jean-Loup Tournier & Claude Joubert, *Copyright*, March 1986 issue.
23. Unnumbered WIPO publication, available in the archive of the author of this chapter.
24. *Ibid.*

that it 'continue to pay particular attention to rendering assistance in the setting up or strengthening of collective administration systems in developing countries'.[25]

The programme of studying the legal and practical aspects of collective management continued in the same programme period (1986–1987) when WIPO, together with UNESCO, concentrated its programme on the copyright and related rights questions concerning various categories of works. The results of the discussions on nine categories of works, by a series of meetings of committees of governmental experts, were then finalized by the Committee of Governmental Experts on the Evaluation and Synthesis of Principles on Various Categories of Works in Geneva in June – July 1988. A number of principles – accompanied by detailed comments – had been worked out that were not considered to be binding but were intended to offer guidance to governments and legislators.[26]

The categories of works in connection with which the questions of joint management were discussed were the following: audiovisual works, phonograms, dramatic and choreographic works, musical works, and works under the heading 'the printed word' (practically all kinds of literary works other than computer programs). The principles regarding joint management related more specifically to the following issues: 'home taping' of audiovisual works and phonograms, rental of such productions, cable distribution of such productions, performing rights relating to musical works ('small rights') and reprographic reproduction of writings and graphic works. At the end of the meeting of the Committee of Governmental Experts on the Evaluation and Synthesis of Principles on Various Categories of Works, it was recommended that the results of the discussions on the principles be taken into account by WIPO in the then foreseen future work on model provisions for national legislation in the field of copyright.

In accordance with the just mentioned recommendation, the *draft Model Provisions* prepared by the International Bureau of WIPO for the Committee of Experts on Model Provisions for Legislation in the Field of Copyright contained a chapter (Chapter VIII) on 'Collective Administration of Economic Rights'.[27] The Committee discussed the draft Model Provisions in three sessions. At the first and second sessions (in February–March 1989 and November 1989), discussions took place about all provisions; at the third session (July 1990),[28] those provisions of what, at that time, was already called the 'draft Model Law on Copyright' were only discussed again in respect of which further consideration seemed to be necessary. The Model Law – the last version of which contained quite detailed provisions on collective management – were not, however, adopted officially. The reason was that, by the time of its 'third reading', a new important WIPO project had been launched; namely, the preparation of a 'protocol to the Berne Convention' – which became six years later the WCT, one of the two WIPO

---

25. *Ibid.*
26. Published in three parts in *Copyright*, October, November and December 1988 issues.
27. WIPO document CE/MPC/III/2.
28. See the Report of the Committee in *Copyright*, September 1990 issue, 241–301, at 276 and 299.

'Internet treaties' (the other one being the WPPT, the result of an extension of the original project). Because the preparation of new binding norms was foreseen, there was agreement that it would not be timely to publish the Model Law.

2.4   THE ISSUES OF COLLECTIVE MANAGEMENT DISCUSSED IN THE FRAMEWORK OF THE PREPARATION OF THE WIPO 'INTERNET TREATIES'

The preparatory document prepared by the International Bureau of WIPO and submitted to the second session of the Committee of Experts working on the proposed 'protocol to the Berne Convention', held in February 1992, emphasized the increasing importance of collective management and suggested that the protocol cover provisions on five issues, in respect to which appropriate new norms on joint management might contribute to establishing more balanced and transparent conditions in international copyright relations.

In the working paper, the following proposals were submitted:

- *First*, it should be provided that government intervention in the determination of fees and conditions of authorizations given by a collective administration organization is only allowed if, and to the extent that, such intervention is indispensable for prevention or elimination of *actual* abuse (particularly abuse of a de jure or de facto monopoly position) by a collective administration organization.
- *Second*, it should be prescribed that the fees collected by a collective administration organization be distributed to the interested copyright owners as proportionally to the actual use of their works as possible (after deducting the actual costs of administration).
- *Third*, it should be prohibited to use the fees collected by collective administration organizations on behalf of copyright owners without the authorization of the copyright owners concerned, or by persons or bodies representing them, for purposes other than distribution of fees to them and covering the actual costs of collective administration of the rights concerned.
- *Fourth*, foreign copyright owners should enjoy the same treatment as copyright owners who are members of the collective administration organization and nationals of the country where the organization operates.
- *Fifth*, it should be provided that national legislation may only prescribe (in an obligatory way) collective administration of those rights for which the Berne Convention allows determining the conditions of their exercise; that is, in the cases where non-voluntary licenses or the application of a right to remuneration are allowed by the Convention (broadcasting, recording, certain reproductions, *droit de suite*), because the condition that a right can only be exercised through collective administration is clearly a condition of the exercise of that right.

These proposals seem to be overly ambitious retrospectively and too optimistic as to the chance for any possible agreement concerning such thorny issues (which have never been the topic of international treaties). It seemed that the Committee was somewhat relieved when it 'had to' state, at the end of the session, that there remained no time for the discussion of this topic (which was the last one in the working paper), and the discussion thereon would take place at the third session. Before the third session of the Committee, however, the competent assemblies of WIPO reduced the terms of reference to an exhaustive list of ten issues, and collective management of copyright was not among them.

Two of the remaining issues on the agenda of the 'Berne Protocol Committee' concerned the possible abolition and 'phasing out' of non-voluntary licenses for broadcasting (at least, as far as 'primary broadcasting' and satellite communication were concerned) and for sound recording of musical works under Articles 11*bis*(2) and 13(1), respectively, and this had a certain importance from the viewpoint of collective management. The relevant proposals 'survived' the preparatory work and were still included in the basic proposal (the draft of the treaty that became the WCT), but, at the Diplomatic Conference in December 1996, they were not adopted.[29]

However, this does not mean that the WCT and the WPPT have not brought about changes that may influence the future of collective management of copyright and related rights. The treaties and the agreed statements have clarified the application of existing rights, as well as the permissible exceptions to and limitations of them and also adapted certain rights to the digital online environment (recognizing some new aspects of the application thereof or even completing them with new ones). The new obligations on protection of technological measures and rights management information – of course, along with the actual application of such measures and such information – however, are even more important; they may transform the legal and technical conditions of protection, exercise and enforcement of copyright and related rights, including the collective forms thereof.

2.5   SEVILLE INTERNATIONAL FORUM

It was exactly in view of the new technical and legal possibilities of individual and collective exercise of rights that WIPO organized in Seville, Spain, in May 1997, in cooperation with the Ministry of Education and Culture of Spain and with the assistance of the General Authors' and Publishers' Society of Spain (SGAE), an International Forum on the Exercise and Management of Copyright and Neighboring Rights in the Face of the Challenges of Digital Technology. It was attended by some 400 participants from approximately 50 countries.

---

29. See 'Records of the Diplomatic Conference on Certain Copyright and Neighboring Rights Questions – Geneva 1996', WIPO publication No. 348 (E), 8, 187, 395–396, 398, 440, 465, 485, 487–488, 503, 600, 603, 606, 610, 618, 622–623, 647–650, 737, 739, 742–743, 755–756, 763 and 778–779.

At the Seville Forum, four keynote presentations were made by Thierry Desurmont, Ralph Oman, Charles Clark and Tarja Koskinen-Olsson jointly, and Santiago Schuster, and nine panel debates took place with the participation of representatives of authors, performers, publishers, producers of phonograms, producers of audiovisual works, software makers, broadcasting organizations, cable distributors and Internet service providers. The topics of the nine panels were the impact of digital technology on the protection and exercise of copyright and neighbouring rights, the role of the state concerning the exercise and management of copyright and neighbouring rights, exercise of rights in respect of 'multimedia' productions, technological means of protection and rights management information, new alternatives for centralized management, one-stop shops, 'traditional' collective management in the face of digital technology, overview of the present situation of collective and centralized management of rights, review of the principles outlined in the 1990 version of the WIPO study, and collective management in developing countries. The rich material of the Seville Forum was published by WIPO in a book in 1998.[30]

The Forum identified the challenges raised by the digital, networked environment to joint management systems and outlined those directions in which adequate responses should be sought. The findings of the Forum served as a basis for an updated version of the 1990 WIPO study published in 2002 under the title of 'Collective Management of Copyright and Related Rights'[31] (hereinafter: the WIPO Study (2002)).

2.6   COLLECTIVE MANAGEMENT IN WIPO'S DEVELOPMENT
           COOPERATION PROGRAMME

The development cooperation programmes of WIPO extended, also in the past, to advising governments concerning legislative and administrative aspects of collective management, to cooperation in the establishment of new CMOs and further developing the existing ones, as well as to training of the officials of state copyright administrations who supervise CMOs and the managers of such organizations themselves. However, from the beginning of the 1998–1999 biennium, these activities have become more intensive and extended to new areas of cooperation. Not only have the regional bureaus and the WIPO Academy dealt with the various aspects of the relevant programmes, but a separate collective management division has also been set up to take care of the coordination and carrying out of the specific projects in this field.

The objectives of institution building in the field of collective management are also highlighted in WIPO's programme and budget for the 2010–2011 biennium:

> Formulating, developing and deploying collective management as a competitive tool demands a complex web of technical and managerial skills

---

30. WIPO publication No. 756(E).
31. Mihály Ficsor, 'Collective Management of Copyright and Related Rights', WIPO publication No. 855 (E) (WIPO Study [2002]).

harnessed to the need to create a critical mass of collective management specialists and set up and improve institutional capacity. The system has been dramatically complicated by digital technology which poses challenges to its rationale as well as to its capacity to adapt to new business licensing models and forms of content delivery. The 1996 WIPO Internet Treaties have strengthened the effectiveness and accuracy of collective management in the digital environment by safeguarding the integrity of rights management information. Facilitating access to international databases and data distribution networks, as well as integration of digital technologies in collective management operations for emerging or existing copyright and related rights societies will be undertaken in the biennium in cooperation with relevant partner non governmental organizations. The development, design and deployment of WIPOCOS, as well as any related activities would undergo systematic professional streamlining process to support the creation, modernization and digital networking of all ranges of collective management organizations' (CMOs) activities. The legal and technical assistance provided by WIPO will address in a development oriented way the promotion and creation of collective management infrastructures, as well as the institutional and operational capacities of CMO's, both at national and regional levels.[32]

3	SCOPE OF RIGHTS IN WHICH COLLECTIVE MANAGEMENT MAY BE JUSTIFIED; ITS IMPACT ON THE NATURE OF THE RIGHTS CONCERNED

It is a legal commonplace that the exclusive rights of authors to exploit their works or authorize others to do so form a basic element of copyright, and, where recognized, such rights are also important for the beneficiaries of related rights. The exclusive nature of a right means that its owner – and its owner alone – is in a position to decide whether to authorize or prohibit the performance of any act covered by the right, and if the owner authorizes such an act, under what conditions and for what remuneration. It goes without saying that an exclusive right may be enjoyed to the fullest possible extent if it is exercised individually by the owners of the right. In such a case, the owners maintain control over the exploitation and dissemination of their works[33] and may closely monitor whether their rights are duly respected.

At the time of the establishment of the international copyright system, there were certain rights – first of all, the right of public performance of non-dramatic musical works – in which case individual exercise was extremely difficult. Later, with the advent of ever newer technologies, the areas in which individual exercise became difficult, and – in certain cases, even impossible – began widening.

---

32. WIPO document A47/3: Program and Budget for the 2010/11 Biennium, 35.
33. In the rest of this chapter, unless the contrary follows from the given context, 'copyright' means also related rights, and 'work' also means objects of related rights.

In those cases, owners of rights established collective management systems in many countries.

In the case of a traditional, fully fledged collective management system, owners of rights authorize CMOs to monitor the use of their works, negotiate with prospective users, grant licenses, collect remuneration, and distribute it among the owners of rights. In such a system, many elements of the management of rights are standardized or it may be said 'collectivized'. The same tariffs, the same licensing conditions and the same distribution rules apply to all works that fall into a given category.

In certain cases, owners of rights do not authorize an organization to carry out all the functions just mentioned, but rather only some of them. For example, in certain countries, authors of dramatic works leave collective bargaining and the establishment of framework agreements (with the representatives of theaters, etc.) to their societies, but as a rule they directly conclude contracts with theaters and only entrust their societies with monitoring performances, collecting remuneration and transferring it to them. This form of exercising rights is sometimes referred to as 'partial collective management'.[34] However, it may also be regarded as a kind of agency-type management of rights.

For producers, publishers and other corporate owners of rights, it is also inevitable or, at least, desirable in certain situations that, for exercising their rights, they form a CMO. Although some of them – for example, music publishers – are members of traditional CMOs and accept the rules thereof, others prefer to choose other forms of exercising rights with as few collectivized elements as possible. This also leads to a kind of agency-type system, in which the only or main task of the jointly established organization is the collection and transfer of royalties as quickly, precisely and economically as possible and as much in proportion to the value and actual use of the productions involved as possible. The most developed form of such agency-type systems – managed by so-called rights-clearance centers – is where the tariffs and licensing conditions are individualized, but a single licensing source is offered with significant reduction of transaction costs for both owners of rights and users. In this system there are no real 'collectivist' elements; thus, it is usually referred to as 'centralized management' to differentiate it from real, 'traditional' 'collective management'. In legal literature, the expression 'joint management' has been chosen to cover both 'collective management' and 'centralized management' in contrast with 'individual exercise' of rights.[35]

'Traditional,' fully fledged CMOs and such agency-type bodies function side by side. Sometimes they also establish alliances – coalitions – to pursue common interests or to exercise and/or enforce certain rights together.

A form of collective management needs special mention; namely, the management of mere rights to remuneration (where the reason for which the management system is not full is that the rights themselves are not exclusive rights). There may be quite significant differences between the various rights to remuneration from the viewpoint of their roots and their copyright status. In some cases, what is involved is

---

34. See for this, WIPO Study (2002), 57–60.
35. See WIPO Study (2002), 22–24.

a limitation of an exclusive right to a right to remuneration (e.g., in regard to 'private copying' and reprographic reproduction, where in several countries the exclusive right of reproduction – at least in certain cases – is limited to a mere right to remuneration). In other cases, the right itself is granted as a mere right to remuneration (such as the *'droit de suite'* (resale right) or the 'Article 12 rights'[36] of performers and producers of phonograms). In other cases, the right to remuneration is a 'residual right' (e.g., the Rental Directive[37] of the European Union (EU) has introduced such a right – an 'unwaivable right to equitable remuneration' – for authors and performers in respect to the rental of phonograms and audiovisual works (into which their works or performances, respectively, are incorporated)).

Digital technology, and in particular the online use of works and related rights through the Internet has had double impact on collective management: on the one hand, it has raised complex challenges to the owners of rights and, on the other hand, individual exercise of rights – through the application of technological protection measures (TPMs), electronic rights management information (RMI), and their combination as complex digital rights management systems (DRMs) – has become possible and practical in a broadening field.

As discussed earlier, collective management – in particular, when it results in fully fledged 'collectivization' of the various management elements – from the viewpoint of owners of rights, goes along with quite extensive restriction of exclusive rights. Therefore, it is justified to raise the question of in which cases, and under what conditions, such restriction may be justified and acceptable. In the following subchapters, this question is discussed in respect to three forms of non-voluntary collective management – mandatory collective management (subchapter 4), presumption-based collective management and extended collective management (subchapter 5) – from the viewpoint of the international copyright norms and the *'acquis communautaire'* of the EU.

4   MANDATORY COLLECTIVE MANAGEMENT

4.1   MANDATORY COLLECTIVE MANAGEMENT AND THE
            INTERNATIONAL TREATIES

4.1.1   Limited Scope of Exclusive Rights for Which the
            Prescription of Mandatory Collective Management
            Is Allowed

Before the analysis of the Berne Convention from the viewpoint of when and under what conditions mandatory collective management may be permitted (of course,

---

36. See *supra* n. 15.
37. Originally adopted as Council Directive (EEC) 92/100 of 19 Nov. 1992, on Rental Rights and Lending Right and on Certain Rights Related to Copyright in the Field of Intellectual Property; in codified form, published as Directive 2006/115/EC of 12 Dec. 2006.

this analysis is relevant also from the viewpoint of the TRIPS Agreement and the WCT, which incorporate the substantive provisions of the Berne Convention by reference),[38] it is worthwhile asking the following questions:

- is it *determining/imposing a condition* if someone is in the position to do something, but it is provided in the law that the person can only do so in a certain way?
- is it *determining/imposing a condition* if someone owns something, but it is provided in the law that the person can only use it in a certain manner?
- is it *determining/imposing a condition* if someone is granted a right, but it is provided in the law that he can only exercise it through a certain system?

It seems obvious that an affirmative answer should be given to each of these questions.

The Berne Convention contains provisions – namely Article 11*bis*(2) and Article 13(1) – under which it is a matter for legislation in the countries of the Berne Union to determine/impose *conditions* under which certain exclusive rights may be exercised.

Article 11*bis*(2) reads as follows:

It shall be a matter for legislation in the countries of the Union *to determine the conditions under which the rights mentioned in the preceding paragraph*[39] *may be exercised*, but these conditions shall apply only in the countries where they have been prescribed. They shall not in any circumstances be prejudicial to the moral rights of the author, nor to his right to obtain equitable remuneration which, in the absence of agreement, shall be fixed by competent authority. [Emphasis added.]

Article 13(1) reads as follows:

Each country of the Union may *impose* for itself reservations and *conditions on the exclusive right granted to the author* of a musical work and to the author of any words, the recording of which together with the musical work has already been authorized by the latter, to authorize the sound recording of that musical work, together with such words, if any; but all such reservations and conditions shall apply only in the countries which have imposed them and shall not, in any circumstances, be prejudicial to the rights of these authors to obtain equitable remuneration which, in the absence of agreement, shall be fixed by competent authority. [Emphasis added.]

---

38. See Art. 9.1 of the TRIPS Agreement and Art. 1(4) of the WCT.
39. Under the preceding paragraph – paragraph (1) of the same Article – '[a]thors of literary and artistic works shall enjoy the exclusive right of authorizing: (i) the broadcasting of their works or the communication thereof to the public by any other means of wireless diffusion of signs, sounds or images; (ii) any communication to the public by wire or by rebroadcasting of the broadcast of the work, when this communication is made by an organization other than the original one; (iii) the public communication by loudspeaker or any other analogous instrument transmitting, by signs, sounds or images, the broadcast of the work'.

In general, these provisions are regarded as a legal basis for the application of *compulsory licenses*. This is deduced from the way thèy define the minimum requirement to be respected when such conditions are applied; namely, that determining/imposing conditions must not, under any circumstances, be prejudicial to the right to obtain an equitable remuneration. This does not mean, however, that non-voluntary licenses may be regarded as the only possible 'conditions' mentioned in those provisions; also, other conditions of the exercise of the exclusive rights concerned may be applied.

Mandatory collective management of rights is such a condition, since, it means – referring to the questions above – that:

- although the owners of these rights are in the position to do something (namely, to enjoy the exclusive right of authorizing the acts in question), it is provided that *they can only do so in a certain way*;
- although they own such exclusive rights, it is provided that *they can only exploit those rights in a certain manner*; and
- although they are granted such rights, it is provided that *they can only exercise those rights through a certain system* (i.e., through collective management).

Since the possibilities of 'determining/imposing conditions' are provided for in the Convention in an exhaustive way, on the basis of the *a contrario* principle, it can be deduced that, in general, mandatory collective management of exclusive rights may only be prescribed practically in the same cases as non-voluntary licenses (which result in mere rights to remuneration).

4.1.2 Mandatory Collective Management of Rights to Remuneration

Under the previous subtitle, the issue of mandatory collective management of exclusive rights is analysed. It is necessary to emphasize this to point out that what was discussed earlier should not be interpreted as to mean that mandatory collective management may be prescribed only in cases in which the Berne Convention – or other international treaty on copyright and related rights – allows the determination or imposition of conditions for the exercise of exclusive rights. Mandatory collective management is permissible also in cases

- in which a right is not provided as an exclusive right of authorization but rather as a mere right to remuneration (as in the case of the resale right *(droit de suite)* under Article 14*ter* of the Convention or the so-called 'Article 12 rights'[40] of performers and producers of phonograms);

---

40. See *supra* n. 15.

– in which the restriction of an exclusive right to a mere right to remuneration is allowed (as under Article 9(2) concerning the right of reproduction);[41] and
– in which a 'residual right' is concerned; that is, a right to remuneration (usually of authors and performers) that survives the transfer of certain exclusive rights (such a residual right by definition allows the exercise of the exclusive right concerned, because it is only applicable after that the latter has been transferred).

4.2   MANDATORY COLLECTIVE MANAGEMENT UNDER THE *ACQUIS COMMUNAUTAIRE*

4.2.1   Rental Directive

For mandatory collective management of residual rights mentioned at the end of the preceding section, the best example is the unwaivable right to remuneration under Article 4 of the Rental Directive.[42] Following its mention in the previous section, it is justified to begin the review of the *acquis communautaire* from the viewpoint of the issue of mandatory collective management, with the provisions on this right.

Paragraph 1 of Article 4 of the Rental Directive provides as follows: 'Where an author or performer has transferred or assigned his rental right concerning a phonogram or an original or copy of a film to a phonogram or film producer, that author or performer shall retain the right to obtain an equitable remuneration for the rental.' Paragraph 2 of the same article adds that '[t]he right to obtain an equitable remuneration for rental cannot be waived by authors or performers'.

Paragraphs 3 and 4 of the Directive deal with the issues of collective management. First, paragraph 3 provides that '[t]he administration of this right to obtain an equitable remuneration *may* be entrusted to collecting societies representing authors or performers' [emphasis added]. Then, paragraph 4 provides for the *possibility* of imposition of collective management. Its relevant part reads as

---

41. Article 9(2) uses the expression 'to permit the reproduction of . . . works'. This may mean – subject to the said test – either free uses or, as it is clarified in the report of Main Committee I of the 1967 Stockholm revision conference (see para. 85 of the report), the reduction of the exclusive right to remuneration to a mere right to equitable remuneration. It is on this basis, that, in case of widespread and uncontrollable private copying, in certain countries, a right to remuneration is applied (usually in the form of a levy on recording equipment and material) to which is, of course, the obligation to grant national treatment extends without any reasonable doubt whatsoever.
42. Paragraph 1 of Art. 4 of the Rental Directive provides as follows: 'Where an author or performer has transferred or assigned his rental right concerning a phonogram or an original or copy of a film to a phonogram or film producer, that author or performer shall retain the right to obtain an equitable remuneration for the rental.' And para. 2 of the same article adds that '[t]he right to obtain an equitable remuneration for rental cannot be waived by authors or performers'.

follows: 'Member States *may* regulate whether and to what extent administration by collecting societies of the right to obtain an equitable remuneration *may* be imposed' [emphasis added].

In the text of the quoted provisions of the Rental Directive, the word 'may' is emphasized to point out the fact that what is involved is that the Directive grants permission to impose (mandatory) collective management for the exercise of this residual right. The drafters of the Directive found it necessary to state that, in this case, collective management *may* be imposed; by this they expressed the position implicitly that, under the *acquis communautaire* – unless this possibility does not follow directly from the provisions of an international treaty to which the Member States are party – there is a need for such a permission. This has an inevitable *a contario* implication because it seems to reflect the position that, in the EU, the prescription of mandatory collective management is allowed only if it is exceptionally permitted by the international norms on copyright and – in accordance with those norms – by the *acquis communautaire*. The provisions of other directives on mandatory collective management referred to in the following section confirm this *a contrario* effect.

4.2.2 Satellite and Cable Directive

The Satellite and Cable Directive[43] goes further than just allowing the determination or imposition of collective management of rights; in the case of cable retransmission, it makes such management mandatory. Article 9.1 of the Directive provides as follows: 'Member States *shall* ensure that the right of owners of copyright and related rights to grant or refuse authorization to a cable operator for a cable retransmission may be exercised only through a collecting society' [emphasis added]. The Directive also regulates the legal technique through which all such rights of owners of copyright and related rights may be concentrated in the repertoire of a CMO (or possibly more than one organizations among which owners of rights may choose).[44]

---

43. Council Directive 93/83/EEC of 27 September 'on the coordination of certain rules concerning copyright and rights related to copyright applicable to satellite broadcasting and cable retransmission'.
44. Article 9.2 and 3 of the Satellite and Cable Directive provide as follows:

    2. Where a rightholder has not transferred the management of his rights to a collecting society, the collecting society which manages rights of the same category shall be deemed to be mandated to manage his rights. Where more than one collecting society manages rights of that category, the rightholder shall be free to choose which of those collecting societies is deemed to be mandated to manage his rights. A rightholder referred to in this paragraph shall have the same rights and obligations resulting from the agreement between the cable operator an collecting society which is deemed to be mandated to manage his rights as the rightholders who have mandated that collecting society and he shall be able to claim those rights within a period to be fixed by the Member State concerned, which shall not be shorter than three years from the date of the cable retransmission which includes his work or other protected subject matter.

The provision of the Satellite and Cable Directive just quoted is in accordance with the principle just stated, namely, that in the case of an exclusive right, mandatory collective management may be prescribed only where the relevant international norms allow, through either permitting the prescription of conditions for the exercise of exclusive rights or limiting it to a right to remuneration in certain cases (in which cases, the exclusive nature of the rights concerned disappears not only in respect of the decisive 'upstream' stage – that is, in the relationship between the owners of rights and the CMOs – but also in respect to the downstream stage between the CMOs and the users). This is so because, as quoted earlier, in respect of authors' 'exclusive right of authorizing . . . any communication to the public by wire . . . of the broadcast of [their] works' granted by paragraph (1) of Article 11*bis*, paragraph (2) of the same Article provides that '[i]t shall be a matter for legislation in the countries of the [Berne] Union to *determine the conditions under which the rights mentioned in* [paragraph (1)] *may be exercised*'. (In the case of related rights, neither the Rome Convention nor the *acquis communautaire* provided for exclusive rights of authorization concerning cable retransmissions. This situation has not changed with the adoption of the Satellite and Cable Directive. The international norms adopted in the meantime – the relevant provisions of the TRIPS Agreement and the WPPT – also have not introduced such exclusive rights.)

Article 10 of the Satellite and Cable Directive provides for *an exception to mandatory collective management* of cable retransmission rights; namely in respect of the rights of broadcasting organizations.[45] This refers to and confirms one of the basic principles concerning collective management, according to which collective management is justified only where individual exercise of rights – because of the number of owners of rights, the number of users or other circumstances of uses – is impossible or, at least, highly impracticable.[46] Broadcasting organizations are relatively less numerous (in contrast with authors and the owners of related rights other than broadcasting organizations); they are able to manage their rights individually.

---

3. A Member State may provide that, when a rightholder authorizes the initial transmission within its territory of a work or other protected subject matter, he shall be deemed to have agreed not to exercise his cable retransmission rights on an individual basis but to exercise them in accordance with the provisions of this Directive.

45. Article 10 of the Satellite and Cable Directive provides as follows: 'Member States shall ensure that Article 9 [prescribing mandatory collective management] does not apply to the rights exercised by a broadcasting organization in respect to its own transmission, irrespective of whether the rights concerned are its own or have been transferred to it by other copyright owners and/or holders of related rights.'

46. This is the very first principle stated in the Conclusions chapter of both versions of the WIPO Study. In the 2002 version, this principle reads as follows: '(1) Collective management or other systems of joint management of copyright and related rights is justified where individual exercise of such rights – due to the number and other circumstances of uses – is impossible or, at least, highly impracticable. Such joint management of rights should be chosen, whenever possible, as an alternative to non-voluntary licenses.'

4.2.3 Resale Right Directive

The Resale Right Directive[47] – similarly to the case of the Rental Directive in respect to the residual right to remuneration provided in it – does not prescribe mandatory collective management for the collection and distribution of the royalties due for the resale right, but allows Member States to do so. Its Article 6.2 reads as follows: 'Member States *may* provide for compulsory or optional collective management of the royalty provided for under Article 1' [emphasis added].

As discussed earlier, in this case, the prescription of mandatory collective management is allowed under the international copyright norms, because it corresponds to the nature of the resale right *(droit de suite)* under Article 14*ter* of the Berne Convention, namely, that it is a mere right to remuneration (it is also only such a right under Article 1 of the Resale Right Directive).

In the text of Article 6.2 of the Directive emphasis added to the word 'may' to indicate that permission is involved. The drafters of the Directive found it necessary to state that, in the case of this right, prescribing mandatory collective management is allowed. This confirms the result of the earlier analysis, according to which such provisions have an *a contrario* implication.

4.3 THEORIES ON GENERAL APPLICABILITY OF MANDATORY COLLECTIVE MANAGEMENT OF EXCLUSIVE RIGHT

Silke von Lewinski has developed a theory according to which Articles 11*bis*(2) and 13(1) of the Berne Convention do not include limitations of the exclusive rights concerned. She has argued as follows:

> Such provisions have been introduced with a view to allow member countries to establish compulsory licenses in favour of broadcasting organizations and record companies. Historically, in both cases, the potential users, namely, broadcasting organizations and record companies, were afraid of being hindered by the right owners from obtaining the necessary broadcasting and recording licenses, particularly where they were represented by collecting societies. They claimed unimpeded access for the purposes of their use.[48] Consequently, these provisions allow, in particular, the replacement of the exclusive right by a right to equitable remuneration. Although the mandatory collective administration may be covered by the wording of Article 11*bis*(2) BC, a 'condition under which the right . . . may be exercised', it becomes clear from the purpose of the previously mentioned provisions that the Berne

---

47. Directive 2001/84/EC of the European Parliament and the Council of 27 Sep. 2001 on the resale right for the benefit of the author of an original work of art.
48. Footnote 14 in the text quoted: Ricketson, *The Berne Convention: 1886–1986*, note 9.48 and notes 9.41 et seq.

Convention thereby addresses only restrictions of the exclusive rights in favour of the users (broadcasting organizations, record producers). As the historical background of Article 11*bis*(2) BC reveals, the potential conflict was seen between collecting societies (as the representatives of authors) and broadcasting organizations, rather than between authors and collecting societies. Indeed, the relationship between the author on the one hand and the user on the other hand is not at stake in the cases of mandatory collective administration.

As the kinds of exceptions and limitations addressed in the Berne Convention relate only to certain interests of the public at large and specific interests of particular groups of users, it is well possible that the mandatory collective administration of the exclusive rights in question is beyond the concern of the Berne Convention and is not considered at all as a restriction to the minimum rights.[49]

I rarely disagree with the views of Silke von Lewinski, but, with due respect to her position, this is one of the rare cases. There are weighty reasons for this.

As for the interpretation of any treaty provisions, also for the interpretation of Article 11*bis*(2) (as well as for Article 13(1) of a similar nature) it is necessary to take into account the relevant provisions of the Vienna Convention on the Law of Treaties.[50]

Those provisions read as follows:

Article 31

General rule of interpretation

1. A treaty shall be interpreted in good faith in accordance with the ordinary meaning to be given to the terms of the treaty in their context and in the light of its object and purpose.
2. The context for the purpose of the interpretation of a treaty shall comprise, in addition to the text, including its preamble and annexes:
   (a) any agreement relating to the treaty which was made between all the parties in connexion with the conclusion of the treaty;
   (b) any instrument which was made by one or more parties in connexion with the conclusion of the treaty and accepted by the other parties as an instrument related to the treaty.
3. There shall be taken into account, together with the context:
   (a) any subsequent agreement between the parties regarding the interpretation of the treaty or the application of its provisions;

---

49. Silke von Lewinski, 'Mandatory Collective Administration of Economic Rights – A Case Study on its Compatibility with the International and EC Copyright Law', UNESCO e-Copyright Bulletin, January–March 200 issue, 5–6.
50. For the reasons for which it is justified to apply these provisions of the Vienna Convention for the interpretation of the Berne Convention, see Ricketson (1986), 134.

(b) any subsequent practice in the application of the treaty which establishes the agreement of the parties regarding its interpretation;

(c) any relevant rules of international law applicable in the relations between the parties.

4. A special meaning shall be given to a term if it is established that the parties so intended.

Article 32

Supplementary means of interpretation

Recourse may be had to supplementary means of interpretation, including the preparatory work of the treaty and the circumstances of its conclusion, in order to confirm the meaning resulting from the application of article 31, or to determine the meaning when the interpretation according to article 31:

(a) leaves the meaning ambiguous or obscure; or

(b) leads to a result which is manifestly absurd or unreasonable.

As provided in Article 31.1 of the Vienna Convention, the basic, decisive rule is that a treaty should be interpreted, in good faith, in accordance with the ordinary meaning of the terms used in the given context in the light of the object and purpose of the treaty.

As discussed above, it could hardly be denied that the ordinary meaning of the term 'determination or imposition of conditions' covers the case in which a given exclusive right may be exercised only through collective management (it covers it, at least, as much as the case of compulsory licenses). The context is the regulation itself of how the rights concerned may be exercised. Therefore, from the viewpoint of the interpretation of which conditions may be prescribed for the exercise of those rights, the context hardly changes the validity of what is found on the basis of the ordinary meaning of the term or the object and purpose of the Berne Convention, which, as stated in the Preamble, is 'to protect, in as effective and uniform manner as possible, the rights of authors in their literary and artistic works'.

This is, in a way, also recognized by von Lewinski, because – as quoted earlier – she states that 'mandatory collective administration may be covered by the wording of Article 11*bis*(2) BC, a "condition under which the right . . . may be exercised"'. Nevertheless, according to her view, the preparatory work of the provision reveals the contrary; namely, that such a condition does not mean any possible conditions but only conditions that favour certain users. It follows from this that she does not base her interpretation on the Article 31.1 of the Vienna Convention, but rather on its Article 32.

It is submitted, however, first, that it is quite doubtful whether it is justified at all to apply Article 32 of the Vienna Convention, and, second, that, if the preparatory work is still taken into account, it does confirm that conditions mentioned in Article 11*bis*(2) (and in Article 13(1)) should be interpreted in accordance with its original meaning; namely, that it means conditions in general rather than only specific conditions favouring certain users.

Under Article 32 of the Vienna Convention, recourse may be had to the preparatory work of a treaty only as a supplementary source of interpretation for two purposes: (i) to confirm the meaning of a term resulting from the application of Article 31, or (ii) to determine the meaning when the interpretation according to Article 31: (a) leaves the meaning ambiguous or obscure; or (b) leads to a result that is manifestly absurd or unreasonable. It also follows from von Lewinski's earlier quoted finding, namely, that mandatory collective management may be regarded by the term 'conditions under which the right...may be exercised' – that there is no reason for the application Article 32 under its item (ii): there is (a) no ambiguity or obscurity about the term and (b) no manifestly absurd or unreasonable result whatsoever.

Therefore, there is good reason to presume that, according to her position, it is rather due to what she sees as a failure to confirm, under item (i) of Article 32, the meaning of the term 'conditions' resulting from Article 31 that it should be interpreted, on the basis of the preparatory work, in a way different from what follows from its ordinary meaning, that is, that 'conditions' does not mean any conditions as the text of Article 11*bis*(2) suggests, also according to her, but only a certain limited scope of the conditions (i.e., those favouring certain users).

As pointed out earlier, this conclusion is not in accordance with the relevant provisions of the Vienna Convention and, therefore, it is not well founded.

First of all, there is nothing in the preparatory work to which reference is made that would indicate any kind of agreement emerging among the delegations that would correspond to what is described by von Lewinski. It is true that Sam Ricketson, in reviewing the preparatory work, refers in paragraph 9.48 of his book on the Berne Convention, as quoted by von Lewinski and as reproduced earlier, to the wish of broadcasters to have unimpeded access to protected works as a basis for the proposals to introduce compulsory licenses.[51] However, Sam Ricketson' analysis, after that paragraph, continues as follows[52]:

> 9.49 These issues were extensively debated at the Rome Conference where the recognition of the broadcasting right was first proposed.[53] Many delegations favoured restrictions on the exercise of this right, in particular Norway, Australia and NZ.[54] However, *the nature of the suggested restrictions varied considerably: from the imposition of a straightforward compulsory licence*[55] *to limited exceptions for particular uses*[56] *and more general controls over abuses of the new right, particularly by collecting societies.*[57] *By contrast, some delegations, led by the French, were opposed to any restrictions at*

---

51. Ricketson (1986), 522.
52. *Ibid.*, 522–523.
53. Footnote 241 in the text quoted: *Actes* 1928, 256–260 (résumé of discussions).
54. Footnote 242 in the text quoted: *Ibid.*
55. Footnote 243 in the text quoted: Norway: *ibid.*, 112 and 257. Czechoslovakia: *ibid.*, 257.
56. Footnote 244 in the text quoted: Denmark ('certain exceptions' to be allowed): *ibid.*, 256; Hungary (similar exceptions as for the press): *ibid.*, 259.
57. Footnote 245 in the text quoted: Australia, NZ, the Netherlands, Sweden and Norway: *ibid.*, 25–259.

all, arguing that in this new area the Convention should uphold the cause of authors' rights by protecting the new right in absolute terms.[58] *These conflicting proposals were sifted by a special sub-committee which sought to effect a compromise.[59] The latter was essentially based on a French amendment which avoided any reference to the recognition of a conventional compulsory licence, but proposed reserving to national legislation the power to regulate the conditions under which the broadcasting right could be exercised*, subject to three conditions:

1. the effect of such restrictions were to be confined to the country which imposed them;
2. they were not to affect the author's moral rights; and
3. they should not prejudice the author's right to an equitable remuneration, fixed by the competent authority.[60]

Although some states would have preferred the formulation of a more generous exception that explicitly recognized the overriding interest of the public,[61] *the sub-committee's text was finally adopted by the general commission and duly became article 11bis(2) of the Rome Act.[62]* In this regard, it is worth noting the view of the sub-committee that a 'country should only avail itself of the possibility of making limitations to copyright, in the case of broadcasting, where the necessity for them had been established by the experience of that country'.[63]

This full description of the preparatory work of Article 11*bis*(2) of the Berne Convention by Sam Ricketson does not raise doubts; just the contrary – it confirms that the term 'conditions' does not only mean those kinds of conditions that broadcasters wished to be allowed, but any kinds of conditions, including a condition according to which the right concerned may be exercised only through collective management. There is nothing in the text or the preparatory work of Article 11*bis*(2) to suggest that such a condition would not be covered.

Otherwise, von Lewinski's characterization of the determination or imposition of mandatory collective management for the exercise of a right in a way that it is a matter for the relationship between authors and their CMOs is hardly well founded and does not correspond to the context of Article 11*bis*(2) (and Article 11(3)) of the Berne Convention either. This is so because the issue covered by these provisions is not the relationship that exists between an author and a CMO, but rather a prior question before an author would become a member of a CMO at all, that is, the question of whether the author's exclusive right may be limited by

---

58. Footnote 246 in the text quoted: *Ibid.*, 256ff. France, however, later proposed that exceptions in respect to education and popular instruction might be allowed: *ibid.*, 259.
59. Footnote 247 in the text quoted: *Ibid.*, 259.
60. Footnote 248 in the text quoted: *Ibid.*, 183 (report of sub-committee).
61. Footnote 249 in the text quoted: For example, Sweden: *ibid.*, 259.
62. Footnote 250 in the text quoted: *Ibid.*, 260.
63. Footnote 2516 in the text quoted: *Ibid.*, 183 and 260.

subjecting it to the condition that the author cannot exercise as desired, but only through a CMO.

Silke von Lewinski deduces from her interpretation – according to which the term 'conditions' is restricted to conditions in favour of broadcasters and, therefore, this term does not cover the determination or imposition of collective management – that the latter kind of provision does not mean a limitation of the exclusive right. On that basis, she adopts the theory that, because the prescription of mandatory collective management is not a restriction of an exclusive right, it may be prescribed also in those cases in which the Berne Convention – or another copyright or related rights treaty – does not allow for the possibility of providing for conditions of an exclusive right.

This interpretation does not seem to be well founded not only because it involves a non-sequitur inference, but also because the premise serving for its basis, as discussed earlier, does not stand a closer scrutiny. In fact, (1) the 'conditions' mentioned in Article 11*bis*(2) – and equally in Article 13(1) – mean any conditions of exercising the exclusive right, including the condition that it may be exercised only by a CMO, (2) such a condition limits the exclusive right of authors because they are no longer in the position to decide when and under what conditions they authorize use of their works, and (3) consequently, because such a limitation is allowed only in an exhaustively determined scope of exclusive rights, it follows from the *a contrario* principle that, in the case of other exclusive rights, it is not allowed to provide for such a limitation.

Christoph Geiger, to a great extent, bases his position on arguments similar to those presented by von Lewinski's when he also expresses the view that mandatory collective management is not a limitation of exclusive rights and that there is nothing in the international treaties that would restrict the freedom of national legislation in this respect. What seems to be the essence of his opinion reads as follows[64]:

> It must be underlined at the outset that none of the aforementioned treaties expressly settle the question of mandatory collective management. As we have seen they only state that any restriction to the exclusive right must be compatible with the three-step test. Moreover international conventions set the conditions for the implementation of non-voluntary licenses. Certain provisions are designed to allow Member countries to set up non-voluntary licenses for the benefit of certain groups of users, notably broadcasting organizations. These conditions are stated in article 11*bis* of the Berne Convention, to which the TRIPS Agreement (article 9(1)) and the WIPO Copyright Treaty (article 1(4)) refer. The idea is therefore to replace the exclusive right by a right to fair remuneration. Once again we are faced with a restriction to the exclusive right since the use is allowed by law.[65]

---

64. Christoph Geiger, 'The Role of the Three-step Test in the Adaptation of Copyright Law to the Information Society', UNESCO Copyright e-Bulletin, January – March 2007 issue, 9–11.
65. Footnote 52 in the quoted text: See, however, M. Ficsor, *La gestion collective du droit d'auteur et des droits voisins à la croisée des chemins: doit-elle rester volontaire, peut-elle être 'étendue' ou rendue obligatoire?* e-Copyright Bulletin, October – December 2003, 4, according to whom

Hence the real question is to determine whether to subject the exclusive right to mandatory collective management is incompatible with international law, for it constitutes a restriction to the exclusive right, a limitation or an exception to the right of the author. It is not fitting to revisit terminology issues, as there are numerous scholarly interpretations of the terms 'limitation' or 'exception'.... One thing is certain however: a limitation or exception affects the existence of the exclusive right, because the author loses control of the use in question. The use is subject to his exclusive right, regardless of remuneration.

When remuneration is provided, one speaks of 'statutory license', even if this term may be misleading. Indeed, the term 'license' seems to imply that the use enters the perimeter of the right, but that authorization is not from the author, but from the law. However, it is not the case since the use is located outside the field of exclusiveness. In our opinion it would thus be more appropriate to speak of an 'exception with remuneration', or even a 'right to remuneration'. Yet mandatory collective management does not deal with the existence of an exclusive right, which remains intact and is not questioned. It only intends to solve the question of the exercise of rights, of modalities of implementation: the exclusive right can only be exercised through the collective management society. It is in fact clearly the substance of Community case law, which specifies that collective management deals only with the exercise of rights and not with their existence.[66]

---

mandatory collective management would also be included under these provisions since it constitutes a restriction to the exclusive right. See also in this sense P. Sirinelli, *Logiques de concurrence et droit d'auteur*, Contribution to the seminar Peer-to-Peer: *droit d'auteur et droit de la concurrence*, reproduced in: *RLDC* April/June 2007, no.11, 185, who believes, relying of a study led by M. Ficsor for WIPO (M. Ficsor, Collective Management of Copyright and Related Rights, Report prepared by WIPO, 1989, 327 et seq., spec. no. 261 of the Report), that collective management can only be imposed in cases where non-voluntary licenses can be implemented. An analysis of the history of article 11*bis* al. 2 of the Berne Convention seems to indicate however that this article only deals with the restrictions to exclusive rights *for the benefit of users* (non-voluntary license). Because mandatory collective management does not deal with the relationship between authors and users, it would thus not fall under this article (see in this sense S. v. Lewinski, *La gestion collective obligatoire des droits exclusifs et sa compatibilité avec le droit international et le droit communautaire du droit d'auteur: e-Copyright Bulletin*, January – March 2004, 5).

66. Footnote 55 in the text quoted: European Commission Decision of 8 Oct. 2002, relating to a proceeding under Art. 81 of the EC Treaty and Art. 53 of the EEA (European Economic Area) Agreement COMP/C2/38.014 – IFPI '*Simulcast*'), Official Journal of the European Communities (OJ) L 107/58, dated 30 Apr. 2003, 58, point no. 66. See also more recently in the framework of the mandatory collective management set up by Art. 9(2) of Council Directive 93/83/EEC of 27 Sep. 1993 on the coordination of certain rules concerning copyright and rights related to copyright applicable to satellite broadcasting and cable retransmission., CJCE, 1 Jun. 2006, *Uradex SCRL c/ Union Professionnelle de la Radio et de la Télé-distribution (RTD) et Sté Intercommunale pour la Diffusion de la Télévision (Brutele)*, case C-169/05, where the Court of Justice reaffirms that the Directive has, for legal certainty and simplification of procedures, implemented a mandatory collective management of the exclusive right of cable retransmission. For a commentary see F. Pollaud-Dulian, *RTDcom.* July/September 2006, 603.

Collecting societies carry out these exclusive rights on behalf of authors, according to, most of the time, their mandate. The author, by joining a collecting society, may (theoretically) have an influence on the modalities of exercise of his right, since by becoming a member he will be able to participate in the determination of the licensing fees. Sometimes he will even be able to designate the society of his choice. Besides, collecting societies do not always need to grant licenses. Indeed if it is true that, in some countries, they have a legal obligation to do so (like in Germany) it is not always the case (namely in Switzerland and France). Absent such an obligation to enter into a contract, the society could in principle refuse to grant authorization if the conditions are deemed unsatisfactory,[67] even if in practice this will rarely be the case (especially to avoid infringing competition law). There is a very important theoretical nuance to be made with the remuneration rights (or statutory licenses) which are most of the time also collected by collecting societies, since in that case the collecting society is only used to collect a remuneration right (i.e., a claim), the distribution conditions of which are often determined by law. In the case of mandatory collective management, it is the exclusive right that is enforced, which gives the collecting society greater bargaining power.

Comparison with French law offers an additional clue. Indeed in France there are two cases of mandatory collective management. The first one is the management of the reprographic reproduction right (Article L. 122-10 of the Intellectual Property Code (hereinafter CPI)) and the second is cable retransmission right management of a broadcast work (Article L. 132-20-1 CPI for copyright; Article L. 217-2 CPI for performers, phonogram and videogram producers). In the first case, Article L. 122-10, CPI states the principle that the publication of a work implies granting the right to a certified collecting society. Yet French doctrine is unanimous to argue that it is not at all a case of 'statutory license', since only the modalities of the exercise of the exclusive right are settled.[68] In addition, it must be underlined that some Community directives sometimes authorize, or even impose, mandatory collective management. It is the case of Directive of 27 September 1993 for cable retransmission,[69] but also of Directive of 19 November 1992, which allows

---

67. Footnote 56 in the text quoted: See in this sense F. Siiriainen, *Le caractère exclusif du droit d'auteur à l'épreuve de la gestion collective*, Thesis, Nice, 1999, 441. According to this author, this would link mandatory collective management closer to the exclusive right than to the nonvoluntary license.

68. Fotnoote 57 in the text quoted: P.-Y. Gautier, *Propriété littéraire et artistique*, 5e éd., Paris, PUF, 2004, n. 195; A. et H.-J. Lucas, *Traité de la propriété littéraire et artistique*, 3rd edn (Paris: Litec, 2006), 562, note 43; F. Pollaud-Dulian, *Le droit d'auteur* (Paris, Economica, 2005), n° 746 et seq. and n° 1644.

69. Fotnoote 58 in the text quoted: Council Directive 93/83/EEC of 27 Sep. 1993 on the coordination of certain rules concerning copyright and rights related to copyright applicable to satellite broadcasting and cable retransmission, *JOCE* L 248 of 6 Oct. 1993, 15; Art. 9.1, entitled '*Exercise of the cable retransmission right*', 'Member States shall ensure that the right of copyright owners and holders or related rights to grant or refuse authorization to a cable operator for a cable retransmission may be exercised only through a collecting society.'

mandatory collective management of the rental and lending right,[70] as well as Directive of 27 September 2001 for the *droit de suite*.[71] Compliance of these solutions with international law has never been questioned.

The following comments seem to be necessary in respect of the above-outline arguments:

(1) In the first paragraph quoted above, it is stated that 'none of the . . . treaties expressly settle the question of mandatory collective management'. Then it is added that '[c]ertain provisions are designed to allow Member countries to set up non-voluntary licenses.'

Both statements seem to be correct. However, as discussed earlier, it would also be correct to state that 'none of the treaties expressly settle the question of compulsory licenses' (because, in the text of the treaty provisions concerned, just as there is no express reference to mandatory collective management, there is no express reference to compulsory licenses). Then it would equally be correct to add that 'certain provisions are designed to allow countries party to the treaties to prescribe mandatory collective management'.

This is so because the provisions of the treaties concerned (more closely Article 11*bis*(2) and 13(1) of the Berne Convention, which are also applicable by reference under the TRIPS Agreement and the WCT) use only the expression 'determining/imposing conditions for the exercise' of the exclusive rights concerned (in a way that such conditions must not be prejudicial to moral rights of authors, nor to their right to an equitable remuneration). As discussed earlier, both the application of compulsory licenses and the prescription of mandatory collective management are limitations of the exclusive rights concerned in the form of conditions for the exercise of those rights, and – if duly applied – both of them are suitable to fulfil the criteria of not prejudicing moral rights and the right to equitable remuneration.

(2) At the end of the first paragraph quoted earlier, a footnote is added referring to differing views (including my views) on the interpretation of Article 11*bis*(2) of the Berne Convention. *Inter alia*, the text of the footnote includes the following statements: 'This article only deals with the restrictions to exclusive rights *for the benefit of users* (non-voluntary

---

70. Fotnoote 59 in the text quoted: Council Directive 93/83/EEC of 27 Sep. 1993 on the coordination of certain rules concerning copyright and rights related to copyright applicable to satellite broadcasting and cable retransmission, *JOCE* L 248 of 6 Oct. 1993, 15; Art. 9.1, entitled '*Exercise of the cable retransmission right*', 'Member States shall ensure that the right of copyright owners and holders or related rights to grant or refuse authorization to a cable operator for a cable retransmission may be exercised only through a collecting society.'

71. Footnote 60 in the text quoted: Directive 2001/84/EC of the European Parliament and of the Council of 27 Sep. 2001 on the resale right for the benefit of the author of an original work of art, *JOCE* L 272 of 13 Oct. 2001, 32; Art. 6. 2: 'Member States may provide for compulsory or optional collective management of the royalty provided for under Article 1.'

license). *Since mandatory collective management does not deal with the relationship between authors and users, it would thus not fall under this article'* [emphasis added].

This corresponds to von Lewinski's argument discussed earlier, and the same response may be given to it, that is, that the preparatory work of the provision contradicts this thesis: conditions mentioned in Article 11*bis*(2) – as also the text of the provision suggests where there is no restriction concerning the meaning of the term – means any conditions, and not only certain conditions (namely, only those that benefit certain users).

Mandatory collective management – as soon as it is imposed – truly does not concern the relationship between authors and users, because authors are not in the position anymore to exercise their rights in relation to users (only the CMO may do so). However, when an exclusive right is granted, it is granted exactly in respect to the relationship between authors and users. It is on the basis of such a right that authors are in the exclusive position to decide on authorizing or prohibiting use of their work and, if authorizing it, under what conditions. Where the law imposes the condition that an exclusive right cannot not be exercised by the author but only by a CMO according to its internal rules, *this relationship with users ceases to exist* as far as the author is concerned. The essence of the limitation of authors' exclusive right consists exactly in this transformation of relationship, losing the possibility to decide about the use of their works and accepting that only the CMO forms relationships with users and applies its uniform conditions and tariffs. That is, while the existence of mandatory collective management truly reduces the authors' relationship to the CMOs, the possibility of the imposition of mandatory collective management does concern the relationship between authors and users as the very essence of fully fledged exclusive rights; the question is exactly in which cases the international treaties allow the limitation of exclusive rights by imposing conditions of the exercise of such rights as a result of which this relationship is eliminated.

(3) In the third paragraph quoted above, the following is stated: '[M]andatory collective management does not deal with the existence of an exclusive right, which remains intact and is not questioned. It only intends to solve the question of the exercise of rights, of modalities of implementation: the exclusive right can only be exercised through the collective management society.'

I do agree that mandatory collective management concerns 'the question of the exercise of rights' and the modalities by which rights may be exercised. In the logic and linguistic context – which is relevant from the viewpoint of the interpretation of legal texts – 'modalities' means the classification of propositions on the basis of whether they assert or deny the possibility, impossibility, contingency or necessity of their content. This is in accordance with the finding in this chapter according to which the imposition of mandatory collective management is a condition (determining a single possibility) for the exercise of the exclusive rights concerned.

In regard to the first sentence of the text referred to above, according to which, in the case of mandatory collective management, the exclusive rights of authors remain 'intact', simply does not correspond to reality. An intact exclusive right means that those to whom it is granted are in the exclusive position to decide whether they authorize or prohibit certain uses. Where mandatory collective management is imposed the owners of rights to which such rights are granted are not anymore in such a position; their exclusive right is not 'intact' at all. The description of the relationship between authors and CMOs in the case of mandatory collective management in the fourth paragraph quoted earlier, contrary to the apparent intentions of the author thereof, also indicates this. Certain atypical aspects are mentioned in trying to prove that, in case of mandatory collective management, authors may still exercise their right to authorize or prohibit use and in the case of authorization to determine the conditions of use. It is crystal clear, however, that in reality this not the case.

(4) At the end of the third paragraph quoted earlier, the following statement may be found: 'It is in fact clearly the substance of Community case law, which specifies that collective management deals only with the exercise of rights and not with their existence.'

It is submitted that the community case law to which reference is made does not concern the interpretation of Articles 11*bis*(2) and 13(1) of the Berne Convention; it is irrelevant because it differentiates between the existence and exercise of rights from the competition, anti-trust viewpoint and it concerns the relationship between CMOs and users. The question of whether the exclusive rights of authors and other owners of rights may be limited by prescribing the condition that such rights may be exercised only through a CMO is a completely different matter.

(5) Finally, in the fifth paragraph quoted above, certain cases of mandatory collective management under the French law and the *acquis communautaire* are described and the description is closed by this sentence: 'Compliance of these solutions with international law has never been questioned.'

The author of this chapter does agree with this statement. Nobody questioned that, in the cases mentioned in that paragraph, mandatory collective management is in accordance with the international norms. Also the author of this chapter not only has never questioned this, rather the contrary, as also earlier in this chapter, he has always stressed that, in these cases, there is harmony with the international treaties. The prescription of mandatory collective management in these cases is in accordance with the treaties because they belong to those cases in which – either due to the nature of the rights (i.e., that they are mere rights to remuneration) or to the fact that the Berne Convention allows determination or imposition of conditions for the exercise of the exclusive rights concerned – mandatory collective management may be applied exceptionally.

This, however, also means that – *a contario* – in the case of those exclusive rights where such exceptional possibility is not allowed by the international treaties, it would be in conflict with the treaties to extend this limitation to such rights on the basis of which authors and other owners of copyright may decide whether they trust a CMO with the management thereof or they rather maintain the option for themselves to authorize or prohibit uses and grant authorization and to also decide under what conditions they do so.

4.4　　　　　EXCLUSIVE RIGHTS IN THE CASE OF WHICH THE INTERNATIONAL TREATIES DO NOT ALLOW PRESCRIPTION OF MANDATORY COLLECTIVE MANAGEMENT

As emphasized earlier, it may be deduced from the *a contrario* principle that, where the provisions of an international treaty or the *acquis communautaire* provide for an exclusive right and does not allow the determination or imposition of *conditions* for its exercise (nor permit its limitation to a mere right to remuneration), it would be in conflict with those norms to submit the exercise of such a right to the condition that it may be exercised *only* through collective management.[72] It follows from this finding that no prescription of mandatory collective management is allowed under the international copyright norms (and under the *acquis communautaire*) in the case of the rights of translation, public performance, public recitation and adaptation (Articles 8, 11, 11*ter* and 12, respectively) or the right of 'making available to the public' (Article 8 of the WCT and Articles 10 and 16 of the WPPT).[73]

---

72. The Conclusions chapter of the WIPO Study (2002) contains the following principle: '(4) As regards the choice of rights owners between individual exercise and joint management of rights, their freedom of association should be respected. Joint management should not be made obligatory in respect of exclusive rights which, under the international norms on the protection of copyright and related rights, must not be restricted to a mere right to remuneration.' (158) On the basis of the sub-chapter of the Study on the issue of mandatory collective management (the Study uses the synonym: 'obligatory collective management'), it is clear, however, that this principle is a 'short-hand' description of all the cases discussed above (concentrating on the common denominator of all of them); namely, (i) where determination/imposition of mandatory collective management is allowed in the same cases where the Berne Convention also allows the application of compulsory licenses resulting in de facto rights to remuneration; (ii) where the international treaties provide rights as mere rights to remuneration; (iii) where the treaties allows the limitation of an exclusive right to a mere right to remuneration; and (iv) where the exercise of an exclusive right is not subject to limitations/conditions, but after the exercise of it, a 'residual' right to remuneration is maintained. (137–139)
73. Articles 10 and 16 of the WPPT provides separately for 'rights of making available' of fixed performances and phonograms, while, under Art. 8 of the WCT, such a right is provided for as a 'sub-right' of the right of communication to the public in the following way: Without prejudice to the provisions of Articles 11(1)(ii), 11*bis*(1)(i) and (ii), *11ter*(1)(ii), 14(1)(ii) and 14*bis*(1) of

This does not mean that owners of rights may not, and do not, create collective management systems where it is not mandatory, since, for example, the oldest and most efficiently functioning collective management system, both at national level and – through the International Confederation of Societies of Authors and Composers (CISAC) – at international level, has been established exactly for the management of the public performance right. Also, in such cases, extended collective management systems may be applied (see later discussion). However, in the case of voluntary collective management, any owner of rights may decide not to authorize the CMO to represent and exercise the owner's rights, and, also in the case of extended collective management, as discussed later, there must be a possibility of any owner of right to opt out of the collective system.

5   PRESUMPTION-BASED AND EXTENDED COLLECTIVE MANAGEMENT

5.1   CONSIDERATIONS FROM THE VIEWPOINT OF THE INTERNATIONAL TREATIES

One of the most important advantages of fully developed collective management systems is the possibility that CMOs may grant blanket licenses to users for the use of quasi the entire world repertoire of works or objects of related rights in regard to a given right of a given category of owners of rights.

However, even where the system of bilateral agreements is fairly developed (e.g., as in the case of musical performing rights), the repertoire of works in respect to which a CMO has been *explicitly* given the power to manage exclusive rights, in

---

the Berne Convention, authors of literary and artistic works shall enjoy the exclusive right of authorizing any communication to the public of their works, by wire or wireless means, *including the making available to the public of their works in such a way that members of the public may access these works from a place and at a time individually chosen by them* (the text relating to the right of 'making available', as a sub-right of the right of communication to the public, is emphasized). It is to be noted that the 1996 Diplomatic Conference having adopted the WCT has also adopted an agreed statement concerning the above-quoted Article 8, which states as follows: 'It is . . . understood that nothing in Article 8 precludes a Contracting Party from applying Article 11*bis*(2)' [of the Berne Convention]. Article 11*bis*(2) provides for the possibility of countries of the Berne Union 'to determine the conditions under which the rights mentioned in the preceding paragraph may be exercised'. The rights mentioned in that 'preceding paragraph' – paragraph 11*bis*(1) – are the right of broadcasting and the rights of retransmissions and certain 'public communications' of broadcast works; that is, sub-rights of the right of communication to the public clearly other than the right of making available to the public Thus, Article 11*bis*(2) obviously is not applicable in respect of the right of 'making available'. It is another matter that recital (26) of the Information Society Directive contains the following statement: 'With regard to the making available in on-demand services by broadcasters of their radio or television productions incorporating music from commercial phonograms as an integral part thereof, collective licensing arrangements are to be encouraged in order to facilitate the clearance of the rights concerned.' This is another matter since encouraging collective management does not mean making it mandatory.

fact, is never truly an entire world repertoire (because, in certain countries, there are no appropriate partner organizations to conclude reciprocal representation agreements, or because certain authors do not trust and CMO with the exercise of their rights).

There are two basic legal techniques for ensuring the operation of blanket license systems. The first one is the 'guarantee-based' system, which involves the following elements: (1) the lawfulness of authorizing the use of works not being covered by the repertoire of a given organization is recognized by law (either by statutory law or by case law); (2) the organization guarantees that individual right owners will not claim anything from users to whom blanket licenses are granted, and that, if they still try to do so, such claims will be settled by the organization and that any user will be indemnified for any prejudice and expense caused to the user as a result of justified claims by individual owners of rights; and (3) the organization also guarantees that it treats owners of rights who have not delegated their rights to it in a reasonable way (certainly not discriminating them in favour of those authors who have delegated the excursion of their rights to the CMO), taking into account the nature of the right involved. In this system, there is an 'automatism' that may not be compatible with the exclusive nature of the rights involved. Because it does not extend to the possibility of opting out (see later discussion), its compatibility with the relevant international is, as a minimum, doubtful.

The other legal technique for ensuring the applicability of blanket licenses seems to be more appropriate in the case of exclusive rights, because it avoids the paradox situation of leaving the solution to the problem created for those owners of rights who do not wish to participate in the collective system to the very CMO in which they do not wish to participate (as in the case of the 'presumption-based' systems). This legal technique is the so-called extended collective management. The essence of such a system is that, if there is an organization authorized to manage a certain right by the overwhelming majority of – both domestic and foreign – owners of rights and thus it is sufficiently representative in the given field,[74] the effect of such collective management is extended by the law also to the rights of those owners of rights who have not entrusted the organization to manage their rights.

This condition, in fact, includes two criteria. First, it is a basic criterion of the compatibility with the international norms that such an extended effect is granted only where collective management is a justified normal way of exercising a right. The second criterion is that the extended effect should concern only a relatively marginal scope of rights not covered by the repertoire established on a voluntary basis, for the reasons mentioned earlier.

---

74. The condition of sufficiently representative repertoire is stated in respect to both 'presumption-based' and 'extended' collective management systems in the Conclusion chapter of the WIPO Study (2002): '(13) The operation of blanket licenses granted by duly established and *sufficiently representative* joint management organizations should be facilitated by a legal presumption that such organizations have the power to authorize the use of all works covered by such licenses and to represent all the rights owners concerned.' (Emphasis added.)

The second indispensable condition of an extended collective management system for its compatibility with the international norms is that there should be special provisions for the protection of the interests of those owners of rights who have not joined the organization and who do not wish to participate in the collective system. Those owners of rights should have the option of freely choosing between either claiming remuneration (as in the case of the application of the guarantee-based system) or opting out (i.e., declaring that they do not want to be represented by the organization). In the latter case, of course, they are supposed to take care of the exercise of their rights.

In regard to opting out from the collective system, a reasonable deadline should be given to the organization in order that it may exclude from its repertoire the works or objects of related rights concerned. At the same time, the procedure of 'opting out' should be simple and not burdensome (e.g., an owner of right should be able to opt out in a simple declaration with all of the owner's present and future works, without being obliged to offer an exhaustive list, because without this, the opting out system might be transformed into a de facto formality).[75]

5.2   EXTENDED COLLECTIVE MANAGEMENT UNDER THE *ACQUIS COMMUNAUTAIRE*

5.2.1   Satellite and Cable Directive

The fact that an extended collective management system better corresponds to the exclusive nature of rights – and to the related requirements of the international copyright norms and/or the *acquis communautaire* – than a simple 'guarantee-based' system is duly recognized also under the *acquis communautaire*.

This is reflected in the provisions of Articles 2–4 of the Satellite and Cable Directive. After that Article 2 provides that 'Member States shall provide an exclusive right for the author to authorize the communication to the public by satellite of copyright works'; and then Article 3.1 adds that 'Member States shall ensure that the authorization referred to in Article 2 may be acquired only by agreement' (i.e., it must not be subject to a non-voluntary licensing system) – Article 3.2 outlines what may be regarded as an extended collective management system. It reads as follows:

> A Member State may provide that a collective agreement between a collecting society and a broadcasting organization concerning a given category of works

---

75. The requirement of the possibility of 'opting out' is stated in the Conclusions chapter of the WIPO Study (2002) as follows: '(14) . . . In an extended joint management system, there should be provisions for the protection of the interests of those owners of rights who are not members of a joint management organization. They should have the possibility of "opting out" (that is, declaring – with a reasonable deadline – that they do not want to be represented by the organization) and/or claiming individual remuneration. Unless such possibilities exist and may be applied in practice without any unreasonable difficulties, an extended joint management system is to be regarded a form of obligatory joint management'.

may be extended to right holders of the same category who are not represented by the collecting society, provided that:

– the communication to the public by satellite simulcasts a terrestrial broadcast by the same broadcaster, and
– the unrepresented right holder shall, at any time, have the possibility of excluding the extension of the collective agreement to his works and of exercising his rights either individually or collectively [emphasis added].

This provision allows Member States to introduce an extended collective licensing system (the 'may' language clearly indicates this), which reflects the position that (1) such an authorization is needed and such a system cannot be applied in respect to any exclusive right, and (2) where such a system is applied, there are certain conditions to be taken into account.[76]

This is confirmed by Articles 3.3 and 4, which indicate that extended collective management is justified only where it is indispensable and where owners of rights usually do not intend to – or could hardly – exercise their exclusive rights on an individual basis. Article 3.3 identifies a category of works in which this is not the case. It provides that '[p]aragraph 2 shall not apply to cinematographic works, including works created by a process analogous to cinematography,' whereas Article 3.4 underlines the exceptional nature of extended collective management by introducing a specific notification procedure.[77]

5.2.2 Copyright Directive

There is one more directive in which mention is made of extended collective management. The so-called Copyright (or Information Society) Directive[78] in recital (18) states as follows: 'This Directive is without prejudice to the arrangements in the Member States concerning the management of rights such as extended collective licenses.'

It seems obvious that this may hardly be interpreted as an authorization for applying any kinds of arrangements – including extended collective management systems – in respect to any uses and any category of protected subject matter under

---

76. It goes without saying that, because the *acquis commuautaire* does not cover all aspects of copyright and related rights, it does not provide an exhaustive list of rights either where the application of extended collective management may be justified. For example, the right of public performance of authors is not covered by the *acquis communautaire*. In the case of that right, for example, extended collective management may be justified (but, since it is an exclusive right in the case of which it is not allowed to determine/impose conditions for its exercise, mandatory collective management obviously is not permitted).
77. Article 3.4 provides as follows: 'Where the law of a Member State provides for the extension of a collective agreement in accordance with the provisions of paragraph 2, that Member States shall inform the Commission which broadcasting organizations are entitled to avail themselves of that law. The Commission shall publish this information in the *Official Journal of the European Communities* (C series).'
78. Directive 2001/29/EC of the European Parliament and the Council of 22 May 2001 on the harmonization of certain aspects of copyright and related rights in the information society.

any conditions. The principles reflected in Article 3 of the Satellite and Cable Directive certainly must be duly taken into account.

6   OTHER ISSUES IDENTIFIED IN THE WIPO STUDY AS RELEVANT FROM THE VIEWPOINT OF COMPATIBILITY OF COLLECTIVE MANAGEMENT SYSTEMS WITH THE INTERNATIONAL TREATIES

6.1   INTRODUCTORY REMARKS

I was the author of both the 1990 and the 2002 versions of the WIPO Study mentioned earlier. However, the two versions differed in the viewpoint of the way they had been prepared.

As in the Introduction to the 1990 original version of the WIPO Study, Dr Arpad Bogsch the then Director General of WIPO clarified, it had been prepared under the instructions of the competent Governing Bodies of WIPO 'in order to offer advice to governments',[79] and for its finalization, the comments of an experts body – established in accordance with the decisions of the Governing Bodies – had also been taken into account.[80] That is, the 1990 version of the WIPO Study was also an official WIPO document and, in the relevant aspects, represented an interpretation of the relevant international copyright norms from the viewpoint of collective management (although not of a binding nature, but issued at the request of the competent WIPO Governing Bodies and vetted by both the International Bureau and a special WIPO experts body).

In contrast, the 2002 version of the Study was prepared just at the request of the International Bureau to update the original 1990 version in the light of new technological, legal, social and business-method developments. Nevertheless, in regard to those aspects that are relevant from the viewpoint of the compatibility of the regulation and operation of collective management systems with the international norms, the new version, in general (with the exception of the issue of 'extended collective management', in respect to which a more 'liberal' position was presented in view of certain new legal developments[81]), the new version either

---

79. Excerpt from the Introduction: 'The Governing Bodies of WIPO instructed the International Bureau of WIPO in 1989 to prepare a study which would be the has is of appropriate advice to governments in respect of the collective administration of certain rights in the field of copyright and neighboring rights . . . The present document contains the said study'. (WIPO Study [1990], 3.)
80. As the Introduction to the Study refers to it, the WIPO Group of Consultants on the Collective Administration of Copyright and Neighbouring Rights discussed the draft study in Geneva from 19–23 Mar. 1990, and made a few minor comments.
81. In the original 1990 version of the WIPO Study (see footnote, above, the Conclusions chapter still contained the following principle (h): 'No extended collective administration (i.e., statutory permission to use, without authorization but against payment of remuneration, works belonging to the same category in respect of which a collective administration

have reproduced the same principles as those included in the 1990 version or, at maximum, have made some insubstantial wording changes.

Under the following titles, those principles of the WIPO Study (common in both versions) are quoted that, in addition to the previously discussed key aspects of compatibility with the international treaties (regarding the scope and conditions of mandatory and 'extended' collective management), also have direct or indirect relevance from the viewpoint of the question of compliance with the treaties. Certain comments are added to them, on the understanding that, on the one hand, these principles relate to certain more complex issues, the detailed analysis of which would go beyond the framework of the present chapter, and, on the other hand, the book includes other chapters devoted to the issues concerned.

6.2   GOVERNMENTAL REGULATION AND SUPERVISION GUARANTEEING
        PROPER OPERATION OF COLLECTIVE MANAGEMENT SYSTEMS

Principle (15) of the Conclusions chapter of the WIPO Study (2002) reads as follows:

> (15) Government supervision of the establishment and operation of joint management organizations seems desirable. Such supervision may guarantee, *inter alia*, that only those organizations which can provide the legal, professional and material conditions necessary for an appropriate and efficient management of rights may operate; that the joint management system be made available to all rights owners who need it; that the terms of membership of the organizations be reasonable and, in general, that the basic principles of an adequate joint management (for example, the principle of equal treatment of rights owners) be fully respected.[82]

In this book, the chapters on the copyright systems of various countries also describe how the conditions of the establishment of CMOs are regulated and how their operation is supervised by governmental bodies. Here, as mentioned earlier, this issue emerges from the viewpoint of obligations governments may have in this respect in the light of the international norms.

The WIPO Study (2002) contains the following comments in this respect:

> If the given organization does not operate properly, such a situation may lead to negligence, or to practical denial or restriction, of the rights of owners of rights. Therefore, under the present circumstances, when ever more rights are

---

organization authorizes the use of its own repertoire, with some guarantees in favour of right owners who do not accept such administration) should be applied in the case of exclusive rights if, under the Berne Convention or the Rome Convention, those rights may not be restricted to a mere right to remuneration.' (88–89 of the Study). However, on the basis of the discussions of the issue in the 1990 version (see 72–74), it turns out that, at that time, the possibility of 'opting out', as an important guarantee – was not yet duly taken into account.

82. WIPO Study (2002), 162.

managed jointly, *it seems to be justified to introduce and apply appropriate legal provisions to ensure the proper operation of joint management systems. This seems*, in fact, *to be an obligation of countries party to the Berne Convention, the Rome Convention, the TRIPS Agreement and the WIPO 'Internet Treaties'* (in the same way as they are obliged to take appropriate measures against other possible violations of rights which they are supposed to protect under these instrument).[83] [Emphasis added.]

The validity of the comment according to which it seems an obligation of governments to guarantee that only those organizations may be established and operating the activities of which do not lead to negligence, or to practical denial or restriction, of the rights of right owners to be by the international treaties may be confirmed by the 'mother' of all principles concerning international treaties: *pacta sunt servanda*. The copyright and related rights treaties, where they provide in 'shall language' that certain rights *must be granted* to authors and owners of related rights, cannot be interpreted in good faith in a manner that it is sufficient to simply state the existence of those rights in the law. A country hardly fulfils its obligations to grant the rights concerned where it is obvious that, in practice, the owners of rights cannot enjoy their rights, although through adequate governmental measures the enjoyment thereof could be guaranteed. This is true not only in a country where certain rights do not prevail because of piracy, but also where they do not prevail for any other reasons – including the reason that as a result of an inappropriate collective management system, they are unduly curtailed or simply misappropriated – that could be eliminated with due and proportional governmental measures.

Article 36 of the Berne Convention provides as follows:

(1) Any country party to this Convention undertakes to adopt, in accordance with its constitution, the measures necessary to ensure the application of this Convention.
(2) It is understood that, at the time a country becomes bound by this Convention, it will be in a position under its domestic law to give effect to the provisions of this Convention.

Article 26 of the Rome Convention includes, with certain wording differences, in substance, the same provisions.

Article 14 of the WCT and Article 23 of the WPPT contain the following identical provisions:

(1) Contracting Parties undertake to adopt, in accordance with their legal systems, the measures necessary to ensure the application of this Treaty.
(2) Contracting Parties shall ensure that enforcement procedures are available under their law so as to permit effective action against any act of infringement of rights covered by this Treaty, including expeditious remedies to prevent infringements and remedies which constitute a deterrent to further infringements.

---

83. *Ibid.*, 141–142.

As can be seen, paragraph (1) of Article 14 of the WCT and Article 23 of the WPPT correspond to paragraph (1) of Article 36 of the Berne Convention with the difference that they refer to the legal systems in general, rather than just to the constitutions of the Contracting Parties in accordance with which they are obligated to ensure the application of these Treaties. In turn, paragraph (2) is an adapted version of the first sentence of Article 41(1) of the TRIPS Agreement, stating basic obligations regarding the enforcement of rights.[84] In the case of the TRIPS Agreement, of course, respect for the obligations of the WTO Members under the TRIPS Agreement is also guaranteed by the efficient dispute settlement mechanism.

It is submitted that these provisions also cover the obligations of countries party to the international treaties to guarantee adequate applicability of the rights – the granting of which is their obligation – in those cases in which they are exercised through collective management. This obligation is particularly clear where collective management is not voluntary but prescribed by law, either as mandatory or as 'extended' collective management.

The WIPO Study (2002) also includes certain principles that concern more concrete issues relevant from the viewpoint of governmental regulation and supervision and their compatibility with the international treaties. These relate partly to conditions necessary for the operation of collective management and partly to guarantees that collective management does not lead to curtailment or misappropriation of rights.

Principle (22) is part of the former category:

(22) Appropriate legislative and administrative measures should facilitate the monitoring of uses and collection of royalties by joint management organizations. The fullest possible cooperation by users – including application for licenses and supply of programs – should be prescribed as an obligation, and enforcement measures and sanctions should be applied against those users who create any unreasonable obstacles to such activities of joint administration organizations.[85]

On the other hand, the following principles fall into the latter category; that is, these are principles to guarantee that a collective management system is not in conflict with the international treaties and with the national laws duly implementing them:

(23) No remuneration collected by a joint management organization should be used for purposes other than covering the actual costs of management and the distribution of the remuneration to rights owners, except where the rights owners concerned, including foreign rights owners, or bodies representing

---

84. The first sentence of Art. 41 of the TRIPS Agreement reads as follows: 'Members [of the WTO] shall ensure that enforcement procedures as specified in this Part [Part III of the Agreement on Enforcement of Intellectual Property Rights] are available under their law so as to permit effective action against any act of infringement of rights covered by this Agreement, including expeditious remedies to prevent infringements and remedies which constitute a deterrent to further infringements.'
85. WIPO Study (2002), 164.

them under the statutes of their collective management organizations, authorize such a use of the remuneration (for example, for cultural or social purposes). It should, however, be taken into account that authorizing deductions for cultural and social purposes may establish a favorable basis for the operation of joint management organizations in an efficient way, as well as for sufficient political support and social respect for copyright and related rights (in particular in developing and other 'net importer' countries).

(24) The remuneration collected by a joint management organization – after the deduction of the actual costs of management and of other possible deductions that rights owners may have authorized according to the preceding point – should be distributed among individual rights owners in proportion to the actual use of their works and objects of related rights as much as possible. Individual distribution may only be disregarded where the amount of remuneration is so small that distribution could not be carried out at a reasonable cost.[86]

These principles relate partly to the internal regulations and partly to the practical operation of CMOs. It is submitted that the previously mentioned obligations of governments of the countries party to the international treaties to grant certain rights and to ensure their application extends to providing adequate rules and mechanisms concerning the establishment and monitoring the operation of CMOs guaranteeing respect for these basic principles. In the absence of this, no less would be involved than that the government would not provide adequate protection against the misappropriation of certain parts of the remuneration for the exploitation of rights to be granted under the international treaties in those cases in which CMOs are not adequately established and/or operated.

It is also important, however, to emphasize the need for due balance in respect to the previously mentioned principles. In the second part of principle (23) quoted earlier, reference is made to this. The WIPO Study (2002) elaborates on the considerations mentioned there as follows:

Recently, attempts have been made by some performing rights societies of CISAC to eliminate, from bilateral contracts between societies, the possibility of deduction for cultural and/or social purposes from the remuneration due to their members, or, at least, heavily reduce the level of deductions much below the 10% level allowed under the CISAC Model Contract. Although this is legally possible, and although it is a legitimate wish of such societies to get as high an amount of remuneration, and with as little deductions, as possible, this in itself may not justify a heavy reduction of deductions for cultural and social purposes. If the sums obtained through such deductions are used in due harmony with the objectives thereof, this may contribute to a significant strengthening of the 'public relations' position of copyright in the country concerned. Through grants for the promotion of creativity, prizes for the recognition of

---

86. *Ibid.*, 164.

outstanding creative achievements, and/or financial support for young talents or for authors in need, it may be made more easily perceivable that copyright operates for those noble objectives that it is supposed to serve.

It is, however, even more important than such a direct 'public relations' impact that, through all this, the creative community of the country will stand more firmly behind the collective management organization and the entire copyright system. With the readiness of this community to fight for its own interests and rights – and, through this, for efficient, high level copyright protection, in general – it is easier to obtain the support of the government and the legislators for creating the necessary legal and practical conditions for such protection. This is particularly indispensable in countries that are 'net importers' in the field of cultural and information productions, since it is obviously more difficult to get political and social support for a strong copyright system if the operation of national collective management organizations only, or nearly exclusively, benefits foreign owners of rights without any apparent results in the country which might correspond to the 'advertised' objective of copyright, namely the recognition and promotion of creative activities.[87]

These considerations are also relevant from the viewpoint of the issue discussed below; namely the question of what kind of governmental intervention may be justified from the viewpoint of competition, 'anti-trust' considerations into the operation of collective management systems. Principle (16) stresses that although government regulation and supervision of the operation of CMOs is justified and even necessary from the viewpoint of the obligations under the international treaties, it must not go beyond what is needed for guaranteeing that their activities are in accordance with the relevant legal norms. Governmental intervention beyond this limit may involve unjustified interference into the rights concerned and inappropriate limitation of the exclusive nature thereof:

(16) Decisions about the methods and rules of collection and distribution of remuneration, and about any other important general aspects of joint management, should be taken by the rights owners concerned or by bodies representing them under the statutes of their organization.[88]

6.3   GOVERNMENTAL INTERVENTION INTO THE OPERATION OF
       COLLECTIVE MANAGEMENT SYSTEMS FOR COMPETITION AND
       'ANTI-TRUST' REASONS

The WIPO Study (2002) contains two principles concerning this issue:

(18) Government supervision of, and interference in, the establishment and operation of tariffs and other licensing conditions applied by joint

---

87. *Ibid.*, 152–153.
88. *Ibid.*, 162.

management organizations which are in a *de facto* or *de jure* monopoly positions *vis-à-vis* users, is only justified if, and to the extent that, such supervision or interference is indispensable for preventing abuse of such a monopoly position.

(19) A certain level of tariffs (for example, a higher level than in other countries) should not be regarded in itself as a sufficient basis for presumption of abuse. In that respect, it should be taken into account that the tariffs should correspond to the exclusive nature of rights and should represent an appropriate remuneration to owners of rights which, in certain countries, may be ensured in a much fuller way than in others, and the actual value of the repertoire and service offered by a joint management organization, as well as the economic and social conditions of the country concerned should also be taken into account.[89]

There is a provision of the Berne Convention (more precisely a kind of 'agreed statement' adopted in connection with it) that is relevant from the viewpoint of the possible need, justification and desirable limits of governmental intervention for competition and 'anti-trust' reasons.

Article 17 of the Convention reads as follows:

The provisions of this Convention cannot in any way affect the right of the Government of each country of the Union to permit, to control, or to prohibit, by legislation or regulation, the circulation, presentation, or exhibition of any work or production in regard to which the competent authority may find it necessary to exercise that right.

This provision has been part of the Berne Convention from its original 1886 Act and has remained unaltered. It has always been interpreted as a provision authorizing censorship if, for example, the protection of basic human rights, public moral or public security justifies it.

It is interesting to note that none of the three acts mentioned in the provision – circulation, presentation and exhibition of works – are covered explicitly by any right to be granted under the Convention, although 'presentation' may be understood as broad enough to refer implicitly to all non-copy-related rights (e.g., public performance, broadcasting, communication to the public by wire), and, of course, 'circulation' (a term that seems to mean distribution after the first sale of copies) and 'exhibition', if covered by any right in a given country, are to be subject to the obligation to grant national treatment.

In spite of the understanding that the objective of the article is to make it clear that countries of the union are allowed to exercise censorship in respect to the public uses of works referred to by the previously mentioned three terms, its text – in particular, the use of the verb 'to permit' – could have been misinterpreted if it had been considered outside its appropriate context. To avoid this kind of wrong interpretation, at the 1967 Stockholm revision conference, Main Committee

---

89. *Ibid.*, 164.

I adopted a statement – included in the report – that clarified the meaning of this article. It reads as follows:

> This article referred mainly to censorship: the censor had the power to control a work which it was intended to make available to the public with the consent of the author and, on the basis of that control, either to 'permit' or to 'prohibit' dissemination of the work. According to the fundamental principle of the Berne Union, countries of the Union should not be permitted to introduce any kind of compulsory license on the basis of article 17. In no case where the consent of the author was necessary for the dissemination of the work, according to the rules of the convention, would it be possible for countries to permit dissemination without the consent of the author.[90]

If one reads the text of Article 17 and the previously quoted agreed statement, one may be surprised about any allegation that they have anything to do with the possibility of intervening in the operation of CMOs for competition and 'anti-trust' reasons. What kind of permission, control or prohibition of circulation, presentation or exhibition of works (in the framework of censorship) might be involved in a case in which the intervention concerns only the licensing conditions of certain rights? The obvious answer is that hardly anything.

Nevertheless, as one of the anachronisms of the history of the Berne Convention, another agreed statement was adopted on the previously mentioned unrelated at the 1967 Stockholm diplomatic conference, which reads as follows:.

> The Committee accepted, without opposition, the proposal of its Chairman that mention should be made in this Report of the fact that questions of public policy should always be a matter for domestic legislation and that *the countries of the Union would* therefore *be able to take all necessary measures to restrict possible abuse of monopolies.* Whereupon, the proposals of Australia and the United Kingdom relating to abuse of monopoly were withdrawn.[91] [Emphasis added.]

The adoption of this agreed statement put an end to a long debate that started at the 1928 Rome diplomatic conference and continued at the 1948 Brussels diplomatic conference. Several delegations raised the issue of what they saw as a possibility for CMOs to abuse their de facto or de jure monopoly position. At those conferences, general but somewhat vague references were made to the freedom of countries of the Berne Union to regulate this issue in their domestic legislation.[92]

At the 1967 Stockholm revision conference, however, the delegation of the United Kingdom and Australia wanted to settle this problem through an express provision in the Convention. The United Kingdom presented a concrete proposal; it suggested that a new paragraph be inserted into Article 17 to read as follows: 'Each country of the Union is free to enact such legislation as is necessary to prevent or

---

90. Records of the 1967 Stockholm conference, 1174–1175, para. 262.
91. *Ibid.*, 1175, para. 263.
92. See Ricketson (1986), 546–547.

deal with any abuse, by persons or organizations exercising one or more of the rights in a substantial number of different copyright works, of the monopoly position they enjoy.'[93] This proposal received certain support, but also opposition, that resulted in the adoption of the quoted agreed statement.

In the text of the agreed statement the way it is quoted, emphasis is added to the part that clarifies that any measures interfering in the exploitation of rights granted under the Convention because of competition and 'anti-trust' reasons may serve only the objective *'to restrict possible abuse of monopolies'*. This confirms the full validity of the previously quoted principles stated in the WIPO Study (2002), according to which governmental interference in the licensing conditions applied by CMOs that are in de facto or de jure monopoly positions vis-à-vis users, 'is only justified if, and to the extent that, such supervision or interference is indispensable for preventing abuse of such a monopoly position'.

It is submitted that any governmental intervention – by citing alleged competition, anti-trust, anti-monopoly or any other market-regulation reasons – that is not truly necessary for preventing abuse of a de facto or de jure monopoly position involves limitations of the exclusive rights concerned tends to be in conflict with the international norms prescribing the obligation of granting certain exclusive rights.

6.4   COLLECTIVE MANAGEMENT AND NATIONAL TREATMENT

In the Berne Convention, the basic provision on the obligation to grant national treatment to the nationals of other countries of the Berne Union is included in Article 5(1):

> Authors shall enjoy, in respect of works for which they are protected under this Convention, in countries of the Union other than the country of origin, the rights which their respective laws do now or may hereafter grant to their nationals, as well as the rights specially granted by this Convention.

The Convention allows certain limited, exhaustively determined exceptions to this principle,[94] but none of them applies to collective management.

There are conflicting interpretations about the nature of the national treatment principle under the Rome Convention; however, the text of the relevant provisions and the preparatory work of the Convention indicate that basically a Berne-type national treatment principle was originally adopted by the 1961 Rome diplomatic conference.[95]

---

93. Records of the 1967 Stockholm conference, 704, doc S/171.
94. For those exceptions, see Mihály Ficsor, 'Guide to the Copyright and Related Rights Treaties Administered by WIPO', WIPO publication No. 891 (E), 2003, 40–41, para. BC-5.3. (hereinafter: the WIPO Guide)
95. See *ibid.*, 136–138.

In respect to copyright, both the TRIPS Agreement[96] and the WCT[97] adopt the provisions of the Berne Convention. In contrast, in regard to related rights, both the TRIPS Agreement[98] and the WPPT[99] have given up the Berne-Rome-type national treatment model and adopted instead – anachronistically, under the title 'national treatment' – a principle that could rather be characterized as material reciprocity (just contrary to national treatment).

The issue of national treatment of rights exercised through collective management emerges at two levels. The first is at the level of whether a certain right normally exercised through collective management is also duly recognized for the nationals of other countries party to the same international treaties, and the second is at the level of rights granted to such nationals as influenced by the regulation and operation of collective management systems.

In this chapter, the latter aspect is the focus of attention. In regard to the issue of whether national treatment is duly recognized for rights normally exercised by CMOs, the framework of this chapter permits only a short statement, namely, that this is not always the case. Theories with highly dubious legal foundation have developed – mainly with protectionist purposes and for avoiding negative balance of payment in the given context – how national treatment may be denied. For example, the theory has been developed in certain countries that when, in the case of private copying, the exclusive right of reproduction is limited to a mere right to remuneration, that right is not covered by national treatment.[100] In other cases, the principle of public order is applied in an unjustified way as a basis for avoiding national treatment.[101]

---

96. By reference in Art. 9.1, as well as directly in Art. 3 of the Agreement.
97. By reference in Art. 1(4).
98. The second sentence of Art. 3 of the Agreement provides as follows: 'In respect of performers, producers of phonograms and broadcasting organizations, this obligation [granting national treatment] only applies in respect of the rights provided in this Agreement.'
99. Article 4 of WPPT reads as follows:

> (1) Each Contracting Party shall accord to nationals of other Contracting Parties, as defined in Article 3(2), the treatment it accords to its own nationals with regard to the exclusive rights specifically granted in this Treaty, and to the right to equitable remuneration provided for in Article 15 of this Treaty.
>
> (2) The obligation provided for in paragraph (1) does not apply to the extent that another Contracting Party makes use of the reservations permitted by Article 15(3) of this Treaty.

100. In fact, since such limitation to a mere right to remuneration – no matter that, for national-treatment-avoidance purposes, it may be referred to by the mystifying term 'fair compensation' – is still clearly provided under the Berne Convention by virtue of Art. 9(2) (and therefore, also under Art. 9.1 of the TRIPS Agreement and Art. 1(4) of the WCT) and under Arts 7, 11 and 16(2) of the WPPT, even the issue of national treatment hardly emerges in a justified way. What is involved rather is a matter of minimum obligations under the treaties. For the discussion about this issue, see the WIPO Guide, 240–241.
101. For an example, see Mihály Ficsor, 'Prospects for Improving the Protection of Audiovisual Performers at the International Level', published as WIPO document WIPO/CR/KYI/09/2, available at <www.wipo.int/edocs/mdocs/copyright/en/wipo_cr_kyi_09/wipo_cr_kyi_09_2.pdf> (last visited: 17 Nov. 2009).

However, as stressed earlier, in the context of this chapter, the focus of attention is the application of national treatment in those cases in which a right is recognized also for foreign nationals and is exercised through collective management.

Principle (25) of the Conclusions chapter of the WIPO Study (2002) reads as follows:

> (25) Foreign rights owners represented by a joint management organization should enjoy, in all respects (such as the monitoring of uses, the collection of remuneration, the deduction of costs and, especially, the distribution of remuneration), the same treatment as those rights owners who are members of the organization and nationals of the country concerned.[102]

It is hardly necessary to elaborate on the reasons for which there is a need in respect to this principle that a country may confirm its obligations to grant national treatment. It seems sufficient to stress that the application of this principle means two requirements. First, the statutory regulation of collective management must not contain any element that might be in conflict with it, and, second, governments – when they fulfil their previously discussed tasks regarding the establishment and supervision of the operation of CMOs – should ensure that both the internal rules and the actual activities of the CMOs are in accordance with it.

---

102. WIPO Study (2002), 165.

Chapter 3

Collective Management of Copyrights and Human Rights: An Uneasy Alliance Revisited

Prof. Laurence R. Helfer*

1   INTRODUCTION

Public and private organizations and associations that collectively administer copyright and neighbouring rights on behalf of creators and rights owners operate under a diverse array of contracts, laws and regulations. At the centre of this regulatory matrix are agreements that define the organizations' relationship with the individuals and corporations that are its members. These agreements address issues such as the criteria for membership and affiliation, the licensing, monitoring and enforcement authority that the organization possess, and the rules for allocating and distributing royalties. Moving outward from this contractual core are specialized laws that recognize collective management organizations (CMOs) and regulate their activities. Laws of general applicability form the outermost layer of regulation. These laws include copyright statutes, legislation regulating corporations and business associations and, most famously, competition laws that prevent abuses of the dominant market positions that often follow from the

*   Harry R. Chadwick, Sr. Professor of Law and Co-director, Center for International and Comparative Law, Duke University School of Law. Thanks to Graeme Austin, David Boyd, and Allison Danner for helpful suggestions on an earlier draft, and to Lauren Winter, Vanderbilt University Law School Class of 2010, for excellent research assistance.

Daniel Gervais (ed.), *Collective Management of Copyright and Related Rights*, pp. 75–103.
© 2010 Kluwer Law International BV, The Netherlands.

concentration of licensing authority within a single entity or a very small number of entities.[1]

Given this complex regulatory environment, it may be surprising and perhaps unwelcome news to CMOs and their members that another body of law is relevant to the collective administration of copyright. Yet for more than fifty years, treaties and customary international law have recognized certain moral and material interests of creators of intellectual property as human rights. Until recently, the conceptualization of these interests as internationally protected human rights was all but unexplored. Although both the 1948 Universal Declaration of Human Rights (UDHR) and the 1966 International Covenant on Economic, Social and Cultural Rights (ICESCR or 'the Covenant') protect the moral and material interests of authors and inventors,[2] as well as the public's right 'to enjoy the arts and to share in scientific advancement and its benefits',[3] these provisions provide only a skeletal outline of how to develop human rights-compliant rules and policies for governments to promote creativity and innovation. They also leave unanswered the critical question of how those rules and policies interface with existing intellectual property protection systems.

Recent events have highlighted the need to address these issues and to develop a distinctive 'human rights framework' for intellectual property.[4] Over the last decade, intellectual property protection standards have expanded dramatically, both in their subject matter and in the scope of the economic interests they protect. Nation states have also linked these rights to the world trading system, creating new opportunities for enforcement at the international and national levels. These twin developments have made intellectual property protection rules relevant to an expanding array of value-laden economic, social and political issues, including public health, education, agriculture, privacy and free expression.[5]

This chapter considers in depth one aspect of this emerging human rights framework – the relevance of the 'creators' rights'[6] provisions of the ICESCR

---

1. For a comprehensive discussion of these laws, regulations, and contacts, see D. Sinacore-Guinn, *Collective Administration of Copyrights and Neighboring Rights: International Practices, Procedures, and Organizations* (Boston: Little Brown & Co., 1993), 866 at 519–620.
2. Universal Declaration of Human Rights, Art. 27(2); International Covenant on Economic, Social and Cultural Rights, Art. 15(1)(c) & 15(1)(b).
3. UDHR, *ibid.*, Art. 27(1).
4. L. Helfer, 'Toward a Human Rights Framework for Intellectual Property', *U.C. Davis Law Review* 40 (2007): 971. For a more detailed analysis, see L. Helfer & G. Austin, *Human Rights and Intellectual Property: Mapping the Global Interface* (Cambridge: Cambridge University Press, 2011) (forthcoming).
5. For further discussion of these trends, see L. Helfer, 'Human Rights and Intellectual Property: Conflict or Coexistence?' *Netherlands Quarterly of Human Rights* 22 (2004): 167, at 171–175; L. Helfer, 'Regime Shifting: The TRIPS Agreement and New Dynamics of International Intellectual Property Lawmaking', *Yale International Law Journal* 29 (2004): 1, at 26–45.
6. To avoid confusion with terms such as *droit d'auteur*, this chapter uses the phrase 'creators' rights' to describe the legal entitlements for authors and inventors recognized in international human rights law. As explained in greater detail below, these legal protections are not coterminous with those of copyright or *droit d'auteur*. For a general discussion of the distinctions

to the collective administration of copyright in general and to the policies and practices of CMOs in particular. It also addresses other human rights treaty provisions and international court rulings that are relevant to collective rights management.

The chapter focuses primarily on two documents issued by the Committee on Economic, Social and Cultural Rights ('the ICESCR Committee' or 'the Committee'). The Committee is a supervisory body of eighteen human rights experts who monitor the implementation of the Covenant – a treaty that imposes legally binding obligations upon 156 member nations.[7] Because many of the Covenant's provisions are ambiguously worded, one of the Committee's principal functions is to provide guidance to member nations as to the treaty's meaning. This guidance takes the form of nonbinding but persuasive recommendations that can serve as focal points for legal change at the national level. Formally, these recommendations are directed to governments and other state actors. But their scope – like that of the ICESCR itself – is not limited to public laws or regulations. They extend as well to individuals, groups and business associations – including CMOs – whose actions implicate social, economic and cultural rights. Although these non-state actors have no direct human rights responsibilities under the Covenant, governments are required to regulate their activities to satisfy their own treaty obligations.[8]

The ICESCR Committee's initial foray into the intellectual property arena began in 2001, when it published an official Statement on Human Rights and Intellectual Property[9] that contained a preliminary analysis of creators' rights and their relationship to other economic and social rights. The Statement contemplated that the Committee would eventually publish more extensive 'general comments' on Article 15, the provision of the Covenant most relevant to intellectual property issues.[10] The first of these general comments, an exegesis on Article 15(1)(c) – 'the

---

between the latter two concepts, see A. Strowel, *Droit D'auteur et Copyright: Divergences et Convergences* (Paris: Librairie générale de droit et de jurisprudence, 1993) (comprehensively comparing *droit d'auteur* and copyright).

7. United Nations Treaty Collection, International Covenant on Economic, Social and Cultural Rights, Signatories and States Parties, online: <http://treaties.un.org/Pages/ViewDetails.aspx?src=TREATY&mtdsg_no=IV-3&chapter=4&lang=en> (last visited: 9 Sep. 2009).

8. For a thoughtful and influential analysis of these issues, see A. Clapham, *Human Rights in the Private Sphere* (Oxford: Clarendon Press, 1996), 422.

9. Committee on Economic, Social and Cultural Rights, 'Substantive Issues Arising in the Implementation of the International Covenant on Economic, Social and Cultural Rights, Follow-up to the day of general discussion on Article 15.1(c), Monday, 26 November 2001' (14 Dec. 2001), E/C.12/2001/15, [Statement on Human Rights and Intellectual Property], online: <www.unhchr.ch/tbs/doc.nsf/0/1e1f4514f8512432c1256ba6003b2cc6/$FILE/G0146641.pdf> (last visited: 9 Sep. 2009).

10. *Ibid.*, at para. 2. In addition to reviewing periodic reports by States on the measures they have taken to comply with the Covenant, the ICESCR Committee periodically issues 'general comments' that infuse the treaty with greater clarity and meaning. Although these interpretative statements do not bind states parties, they create widely shared expectations as to the meaning of the treaty's text. See M. Craven, *The International Covenant on Economic, Social and Cultural Rights: A Perspective on Its Development* (Oxford: Clarendon Press, 1995). General comments

right of everyone to benefit from the protection of the moral and material interests resulting from any scientific, literary or artistic production of which he is the author' – was published by the Committee in 2005.[11]

These two documents provide a partial outline of a human rights framework for intellectual property, one aspect of which I analyse in the remainder of this chapter. Most importantly, the documents demonstrate that such a framework is not restricted to protecting creators and innovators and the fruits of their intellectual endeavours. Rather, it gives equal importance to protecting the rights of the public to benefit from the scientific and cultural progress that intellectual property products can engender. However, one of the most challenging tasks for the ICESCR Committee is how to strike an appropriate balance between these two sets of rights – a balance that promotes compliance with treaty obligations and their underlying human rights values, and that provides a coherent interface with national and international intellectual property laws.

A few caveats are in order before turning to an analysis of how these issues play out in the specific context of CMOs. This chapter assumes that readers have at least a rudimentary understanding of copyright and neighbouring rights laws and how creative works protected by such laws are collectively administered,[12] but it does not presume familiarity with international human rights law or its recent application to intellectual property issues. In addition, the chapter does not provide an exhaustive treatment of the many intersections between human rights and copyright,[13]

---

specify States' commitments in far greater detail than the treaty itself, for example, by identifying certain core obligations for states to provide 'at the very least, minimum essential levels of each of the rights' in the treaty. See Committee on Economic, Social and Cultural Rights, 'General Comment No. 3, The nature of States parties obligations (Art. 2, para. 1 of the Covenant)' (1990), E/1991/23 at para. 10 [General Comment No. 3], online: <www.unhchr. ch/tbs/doc.nsf/(Symbol)/94bdbaf59b43a424c12563ed0052b664?Opendocument> (last visited: 9 Sep. 2009) (in which core obligations are distinguishable from 'obligations of result', which States may achieve by a variety of means over time).

11. Committee on Economic, Social and Cultural Rights, 'The right of everyone to benefit from the protection of the moral and material interests resulting from any scientific, literary or artistic production of which he is the author (Art. 15(1)(c) of the Covenant)', General Comment No. 17 (21 Nov. 2005) [hereinafter General Comment], online: <www.unhchr.ch/tbs/doc.nsf/ (Symbol)/E.C.12.GC.17.En?OpenDocument> (last visited: 9 Sep. 2009). In December 2009, the Committee issued General Comment No. 21 'Right of everyone to take part in cultural life (art. 15, para. 1 (a), of the International Covenant on Economic, Social and Cultural Rights)', online: <http://www2.ohchr.org/english/bodies/cescr/comments.htm> (last visited: 4 May 2010).
12. For a 'basic definition' of the functions that collective management organizations perform, see M. Ficsor, *Collective Management of Copyright and Related Rights* (Geneva: World Intellectual Property Organization, 2002), 165 at 17 (stating that the 'owners of rights authorize collective management organizations to monitor the use of their works, negotiate with prospective users, give them licenses against appropriate remuneration on the basis of a tariff system and . . . collect remuneration, and distribute it among the owners of rights').
13. Readers seeking additional analysis of these issues may wish to consult the following sources: P. Torremans (ed.), *Intellectual Property and Human Rights* (The Hague: Kluwer Law International, 2008); P. Torremans (ed.), *Copyright and Human Rights: Freedom of*

but instead analyses a selection of salient legal and policy issues relating to collective.

The remainder of the chapter proceeds as follows. Section 2 provides an overview of the ICESCR Committee's statement on human rights and intellectual property and of its General Comment. It highlights basic distinctions between the Committee's approach to protecting creators and the approach adopted in intellectual property treaties and national intellectual property laws, with the goal of making the Committee's analysis more accessible to intellectual property lawyers and legal scholars. Section 3 provides an overview of the key concepts in the Committee's analysis relevant to the collective administration of copyright and neighbouring rights. It argues that a human rights framework for intellectual property supports many of the functions that CMOs already perform. Part 3 notes, however, that certain practices and policies of CMOs may be in conflict with the analysis of the Covenant enunciated by the ICESCR Committee. Section 4 considers in greater depth two legal and policy issues with important human rights implications: whether membership in CMOs should be mandatory or voluntary and whether CMOs should promote national culture. Section 5 concludes with an analysis of the practical implications of adopting a human rights framework for analysing the collective administration of copyright and for the international intellectual property system more generally.

2 INTRODUCING A HUMAN RIGHTS FRAMEWORK FOR INTELLECTUAL PROPERTY

If intellectual property lawyers were asked to list the freedoms and liberties that international human rights law protects, they would likely name widely recognized civil and political rights, such as the prohibitions of slavery, torture and the crime of genocide or perhaps due process rights and freedom of expression, association or privacy. More internationally minded responses might mention economic and social guarantees, including the right to health care, food and education. These are also internationally protected human rights, although their precise scope – as well as their recognition by a few countries such as the United States – remains a subject of genuine debate.

But few observers, if any, would list the rights of authors, creators and inventors as human rights. Yet such rights were recognized at the birth of the international human rights movement. No less an august statement of foundational principles than the UDHR includes in its catalogue of rights and freedoms a statement that 'everyone has the right to the protection of the moral and material interests resulting from any scientific, literary or artistic production of which he

---

Expression – Intellectual Property – Privacy (The Hague: Kluwer Law International, 2004), 181; J. Griffiths & U. Suthersanen (eds), *Copyright and Free Speech: Comparative and International Analyses* (Oxford: Oxford University Press, 2005), 474; J. Sterling, *World Copyright Law* (London: Sweet & Maxwell, 2003), 1357.

[or she] is the author'.[14] The UDHR's drafting history makes clear that the protection of creators' rights was no accident, even if the drafters' precise intentions remain elusive.[15] Support for these rights also finds expression in nearly identical language in the ICESCR, which makes the UDHR's economic and social guarantees binding as a matter of treaty law.[16]

The endorsement of creators' rights in these documents establishes broad areas of overlap between human rights law and intellectual property law. But these texts also suggest many important differences between the two fields – differences in philosophy, regulatory objectives and the subject matter and scope of legal protection for the products of human creativity.

In part, these differences are textually engendered. The thrust of multilateral intellectual property treaties such as the Berne, Rome and Paris Conventions and the Trade-Related Aspects of Intellectual Property (TRIPS) Agreement is to establish minimum standards of protection for authors, inventors and other owners of intellectual property products.[17] These treaties also recognize the public's interest in the distribution of and access to those products. However, they do so principally in the form of carefully constrained exceptions and limitations to authors' and inventors' exclusive rights. Two provisions of the TRIPS Agreement, which set out the treaty's 'objectives' and 'principles', indicate that the protection and enforcement of intellectual property rights should contribute to the 'mutual advantage' of 'producers and users of technological knowledge'[18] and should 'promote the public interest in sectors of vital importance to [members'] socio-economic and technological development'.[19] But these provisions are, at least at present, under-enforced and have yet

---

14. UDHR, *supra* n. 2, Art. 27(2).
15. J. Morsink, *The Universal Declaration of Human Rights: Origins, Drafting and Intent* (Philadelphia: University of Pennsylvania Press, 1999), 378 at 220–221. As one scholar recently observed, although the motivations of governments who favoured inclusion of Art. 27 in the UDHR are somewhat obscure, the proponents appear to be divided into two camps:

> What we know is that the initial strong criticism that intellectual property was not properly speaking a Human Right or that it already attracted sufficient protection under the regime of protection afforded to property rights in general was eventually defeated by a coalition of those who primarily voted in favour because they felt that the moral rights deserved and needed protection and met the Human Rights standard and those who felt the ongoing internationalization of copyright needed a boost and that this could be a tool in this respect.

> P. Torremans, 'Copyright as a Human Right', in *Copyright and Human Rights: Freedom of Expression – Intellectual Property – Privacy, supra* n. 13 at 6.
16. See M. Green, 'Drafting History of the Article 15(1)(c) of the International Covenant on Economic, Social and Cultural Rights' (9 Oct. 2000), E/C.12/2000/15, online: <www.unhchr.ch/tbs/doc.nsf/0/872a8f7775c9823cc1256999005c3088/$FILE/G0044899> (last visited: 9 Sep. 2009).
17. Berne Convention for the Protection of Literary and Artistic Works [Berne Convention]; International Convention for the Protection of Performers, Producers of Phonograms and Broadcasting Organizations [Rome Convention]; Agreement on Trade-Related Aspects of Intellectual Property Rights [TRIPS Agreement].
18. TRIPS Agreement, Art. 7.
19. *Ibid.*, Art. 8.1.

to affect the interpretation of TRIPS' substantive intellectual property provisions by World Trade Organization (WTO) dispute settlement panels.[20]

In contrast to this approach, a human rights framework for intellectual property puts the public's interest front and centre and on an equal footing with property rights in intangibles. Indeed, the very same ICESCR article that protects the rights of creators also requires states to protect 'the right of everyone' to 'enjoy the benefits of scientific progress and its applications' and to take steps 'necessary for the conservation, the development and the diffusion of science and culture'.[21] The Committee will eventually elucidate these rights of the public when it issues general comments interpreting the relevant provisions of the Covenant. In the discussion that follows, however, the analysis focuses more heavily on the creators' rights provisions of the ICESCR.

2.1   THE ICESCR COMMITTEE'S GENERAL COMMENT NO. 17

The Committee's General Comment on creators' rights reveals the difficulties of translating the text of Article 15(1)(c) of the Covenant into a coherent framework for analyzing intellectual property from a human rights perspective. The General Comment is a lengthy, densely worded and somewhat repetitive document of 57 paragraphs divided into six parts: (1) an introductory section that explains the basic's premises of the Committee's analysis; (2) a close textual reading of Article 15(1)(c)'s 'normative content'; (3) a section outlining States parties' legal obligations, including general, specific, core and related obligations; (4) an analysis of actions or omissions that would violate the Article; (5) a section on how creators' rights are to be implemented at the national level; and (6) a short discussion of the obligations of non-state actors and intergovernmental organizations.

This organizational structure may seem unfamiliar or even mystifying to intellectual property lawyers, in particular the distinction between 'legal obligations' and 'violations'. But the methodology should be recognizable to foreign ministries, human rights scholars and others familiar with social and economic rights, who have followed the Committee's efforts, in past general comments, to provide detailed and concrete interpretations of the ICESCR's many ambiguous clauses. The Committee has struggled to clarify the meaning of a treaty whose open-ended provisions are to be realized over time, taking into account the limited resources available to Member States, particularly to developing countries.[22]

---

20. See R. Howse, 'The Canadian Generic Medicines Panel: A Dangerous Precedent in Dangerous Times', *Journal of World Intellectual Property* 3 (2000): 493 at 502; R. Okediji, 'Public Welfare and the Role of the WTO: Reconsidering the TRIPS Agreement', *Emory International Law Review* 17 (2003): 819 at 914.

21. ICESCR, *supra* n. 2, Art. 15(1)(b) & 15(2). For a comprehensive analysis, see A. Chapman, 'Towards an Understanding of the Right to Enjoy the Benefits of Scientific Progress and its Applications', *Journal of Human Rights* 8 (2009): 1.

22. The ICESCR requires States' parties to 'take steps, individually and through international assistance and cooperation, especially economic and technical, to the maximum of its available resources, with a view to achieving progressively the full realization of the rights recognized in

To prevent these limiting principles from emptying the Covenant's economic, social and cultural rights of all meaning, the Committee has developed a 'violations approach' that distinguishes 'core obligations' – to which all States must give immediate effect – from other obligations that may be achieved progressively as additional resources become available.[23]

These core commitments include obligations to respect, protect and fulfil the rights of authors. As the Committee explains:

> The obligation to respect requires States to refrain from interfering directly or indirectly with the enjoyment of the right to benefit from the protection of the moral and material interests of the author. The obligation to protect requires States to take measures that prevent third parties from interfering with the moral and material interests of authors. Finally, the obligation to fulfill requires States to adopt appropriate legislative, administrative, budgetary, judicial, promotional and other measures towards the full realization of article 15, paragraph 1 (c).[24]

These three core obligations, although framed in the distinctive language of human rights law, should, on further reflection, seem reasonably familiar to intellectual property lawyers and scholars. Taken seriatim, they bar States from violating creators' material and moral interests, most notably in the form of infringements by government agencies or officials;[25] they mandate 'effective protection' of those interests by means of legislation recognizing creators' rights and specifying the modes for their protection, including protection of 'works which are easily accessible or reproducible through modern communication and reproduction technologies',[26] and they require States to provide judicial and administrative remedies and other measures for creators to prevent unauthorized uses of their works (i.e., injunctions), to recover compensation for such uses (i.e., damages) and, more broadly, to facilitate creators' participation in decisions that affect their moral and material interests.[27]

These obligations also overlap with certain provisions in intellectual property treaties, most notably the Berne Convention's reproduction right, the 'making available' right in the World Intellectual Property Organization (WIPO) Copyright Treaty and the WIPO Performances and Phonograms Treaty and the enforcement provisions in the TRIPS Agreement.[28] This commonality suggests that States can

---

the present Covenant by all appropriate means'. ICESCR, *supra* n. 2, Art. 2(1). These provisions establish programmatic and flexible commitments that are to be achieved over time.

23. General Comment No. 3, *supra* n. 10 at para. 10. See also A. Chapman, 'Conceptualizing the Right to Health: A Violations Approach', *Tennessee Law Review* 65 (1998): 389.
24. General Comment, *supra* n. 11 at para. 28; see also *ibid.*, at paras 44–46 (discussing actions and omissions that violate these three obligations).
25. *Ibid.*, at paras 30 and 44.
26. *Ibid.*, at paras 31 and 45.
27. See *ibid.*, at paras 34 and 46.
28. Berne Convention, Art. 9; WIPO Copyright Treaty, Art. 8; WIPO Performances and Phonograms Treaty, Art.10; TRIPS Agreement, Arts 41–51 & 61.

meet the requirements of Article 15(1)(c), at least in part, by ratifying international intellectual property agreements and enacting national copyright and neighbouring rights laws. The ICESCR's reporting procedures strongly support this claim.[29] Since the early 1990s, States parties have regularly cited such treaties and laws to demonstrate their compliance with the creators' rights provisions in the Covenant.[30]

Notwithstanding the commonalities between these two legal regimes, the Committee's core obligations approach to creators' rights leaves many issues unresolved. Most notably, it does not itself define the content of 'moral and material interests' which states are required to 'respect, protect, and fulfil'. Nor does it specify whether – and if so, how – a human rights framework for creators' rights differs from the legal rules contained in intellectual property treaties and domestic legislation. The next section considers the Committee's treatment of these key definitional issues.

2.2   DEVELOPING A DISTINCTIVE HUMAN RIGHTS FRAMEWORK
         FOR CREATORS' RIGHTS

The General Comment gives detailed attention to the differences between creators' moral and material interests and the provisions of intellectual property treaties and statutes. The Committee begins with the basic and uncontroversial assertion that the 'scope of protection' of creators' rights in Article 15(1)(c) 'does not necessarily coincide with what is termed intellectual property rights under national legislation or international agreements'.[31] But what, precisely, are these differences in scope?

---

29. ICESCR, *supra* n. 2, Art. 16 (requiring states to submit periodic 'reports on the measures they have adopted and the progress made in achieving the observance of the rights recognized' in the Covenant).

30. See, for example, Committee on Economic, Social and Cultural Rights, 'Implementation of the International Covenant on Economic, Social and Cultural Rights, Third periodic report: Cyprus' (6 Jun. 1996), E/1994/104/Add.12 at para. 420, online: <www.unhchr.ch/tbs/doc.nsf/(Symbol)/ E.1994.104.Add.12.En?Opendocument> (last visited: 9 Sep. 2009) (citing ratification of Berne Convention and domestic copyright legislation to demonstrate compliance with Art. 15(1)(c)); Committee on Economic, Social and Cultural Rights, 'Implementation of the International Covenant on Economic, Social and Cultural Rights, Initial report: Israel' (20 Jan. 1998), E/ 1990/5/Add.39(3) at paras 782–788, online: <www.unhchr.ch/tbs/doc.nsf/23a89bf90e53e6ccc1 25656300593189/41e674c4a2affbd480256617004768f5?OpenDocument#PART%20III> (last visited: 9 Sep. 2009) (discussing evolution and expansion of copyright legislation and ratification of numerous international agreements to demonstrate compliance with Art. 15(1)(c)); Committee on Economic, Social and Cultural Rights, 'Implementation of the International Covenant on Economic, Social and Cultural Rights, Second periodic report: Jordan' (23 Jul. 1998), E/1990/6/ Add.17 at para. 151, online: <www.unhchr.ch/tbs/doc.nsf/(Symbol)/7eb0986e8af3f29c8025672 40056ca4c?Opendocument> (last visited: 9 Sep. 2009) (citing amendments to Copyright Protection Act that conform to international copyright treaties and government's intent to ratify such treaties to demonstrate compliance with Art. 15(1)(c)).

31. General Comment, *supra* n. 11 at para. 2; see also *ibid.*, at para. 3. ('It is ... important not to equate intellectual property rights with the human right recognized in Article 15, paragraph 1(c).')

The Committee first compares foundational principles. It notes that:

> human rights are fundamental as they are inherent in the human person as such, whereas intellectual property rights are first and foremost means by which States seek to provide incentives for inventiveness and creativity for the benefit of society as a whole.[32]

Intellectual property rights are granted by the State, and thus they may also be taken away by the State. They are temporary, not permanent; they may be 'revoked, licensed or assigned';[33] and they may be 'traded, amended or even forfeited',[34] commensurate with the regulation of a 'social product [that] has a social function'.[35] By contrast, human rights are enduring, 'fundamental, inalienable and universal entitlements'.[36] These statements reflect a vision of creators' rights that exist independently of the vagaries of state approval, recognition or regulation.

Turning from lofty principles to specifics, the Committee identifies several distinctive features of creators' rights. For example, Article 15(1)(c) applies only to 'individuals, and under certain circumstances groups of individuals and communities'.[37] Corporations and other legal entities are expressly excluded.[38] This represents a profound departure from Anglo-American copyright laws, which have long recognized that legal entities can enjoy the status of authors of intellectual property products, for example, of works made for hire.[39]

Moreover, the legal protections provided to natural persons have a distinctive human rights flavour. Consider the issue of equality. A cornerstone of intellectual property treaties is the 'national treatment' of foreign authors.[40] A human rights approach also encompasses the principle of equality between domestic and foreign creators. But it goes much further, including many additional prohibited grounds of discrimination and mandating equal access to legal remedies for infringement,

---

32. *Ibid.*, at para. 1.
33. *Ibid.*, at para. 2.
34. *Ibid.*
35. Statement on Human Rights and Intellectual Property, *supra* n. 9 at para. 4.
36. *Ibid.*, at para. 6.
37. General Comment, *supra* n. 11 at para. 1.
38. See *ibid.*, at para. 7 (stating that the drafters of ICESCR Art. 15 'considered authors of scientific, literary or artistic productions to be natural persons'); Statement on Human Rights and Intellectual Property, *supra* n. 9 at para. 6 (contrasting human rights approach authors' rights with that of intellectual property regimes which 'are increasingly focused on protecting business and corporate interests and investments').
39. 17 U.S.C. § 201(b). ('In the case of a work made for hire, the employer or other person for whom the work was prepared is considered the author . . . and . . . owns all of the rights comprised in the copyright.')
40. See, for example, S. Ricketson, *The Berne Convention for the Protection of Literary and Artistic Works: 1886–1986* (London: Centre for Commercial Law Studies, Queen Mary College, 1987), 981 at 17–38; D. Vaver, 'The National Treatment Requirements of the Berne and Universal Copyright Conventions' *International Review of Industrial Property and Copyright Law* 17 (1986): 577.

including access for 'vulnerable or marginalized groups'.[41] Equality also has a process dimension, which requires states to provide creators with information 'on the structure and functioning of . . . legal or policy regime[s]', and to facilitate their participation in 'any significant decision-making processes with an impact on their rights and legitimate interests', either directly or through 'professional associations'.[42]

These comparisons between human rights law and intellectual property law have some surprising consequences. If the moral and material interests of creators are fundamental, then the ability of governments to regulate them – either to protect other human rights or to achieve other social objectives – ought to be exceedingly narrow. Indeed, the Committee has developed a stringent test for assessing the legality of state limitations of social and economic rights,[43] a standard that it reaffirms in the General Comment on Article 15(1)(c).

According to this test, governmental restrictions on creators' rights must be '[1] determined by law, [2] in a manner compatible with the nature of these rights, [3] must pursue a legitimate aim, and [4] and must be strictly necessary for the promotion of the general welfare in a democratic society'.[44] In addition, such limitations must 'be [5] proportionate, meaning that [6] the least restrictive measures must be adopted when several types of limitations may be imposed'.[45] This highly restrictive, multi-part standard is far more constraining than the now ubiquitous 'three-step test' used to assess the treaty-compatibility of exceptions and limitations in national copyright laws.[46]

Yet if restrictions on creators' rights are to be so rigidly scrutinized (and, presumably, so rarely upheld), how, then, are governments to strike a balance between those rights on the one hand and the public's interest in access to knowledge on the other – a balance that the Committee views as a key feature of Article 15(1)(c) and that it emphasizes throughout the draft?[47] A close parsing

---

41. General Comment, *supra* n. 11 at para. 39; see also Statement on Human Rights and Intellectual Property, *supra* n. 9 at para. 7 (stating that 'human rights instruments place great emphasis on protection against discrimination', and that the rights guaranteed in the Covenant 'must be exercised without discrimination of any kind as to race, colour, sex, language, religion, political or other opinion, national or social origin, property, birth or other status').

42. General Comment, *supra* n. 11 at paras 18 and 14.

43. See Committee on Economic, Social and Cultural Rights, 'General Comment No. 14 – The Right to the Highest Attainable Standard of Health (Article 12 of the International Covenant on Economic, Social and Cultural Rights)' (8 2000), E/C.12/2000/4 at para. 28, online: <www.unhchr.ch/tbs/doc.Nsf/(symbol)/E.C.12.2000.4.En?OpenDocument> (last visited: 9 Sep. 2009) (discussing government's burden to demonstrate legality of limitations on the right to health).

44. General Comment, *supra* n. 11 at para. 22 [bracketed numbers added].

45. *Ibid.*, at para. 23 [bracketed numbers added].

46. See J. Ginsburg, 'Toward Supranational Copyright Law? The WTO Panel Decision and the "Three-Step Test" for Copyright Exceptions', *Revue Internationale du Droit d'Auteur* 187 (2001): 3; M. Ficsor, 'How Much of What?: The "Three-Step Test" and Its Application in Two Recent WTO Dispute Settlement Cases', *Revue Internationale du Droit d'Auteur* 192 (2002): 110.

47. See General Comment, *supra* n. 11 at paras 22, 35 and 39.

of the text suggests a blueprint from which the Committee may ultimately construct a distinctive human rights framework for intellectual property.

The key to understanding this framework is to identify the purposes of recognizing authors' moral and material interests as human rights. According to the Committee, such rights serve two essential functions. First, they 'safeguard the personal link between authors and their creations and between people or other groups and their collective cultural heritage'.[48] Second, they protect 'basic material interests which are necessary to enable authors to enjoy an adequate standard of living'.[49]

These two statements, which recur throughout the document,[50] suggest the existence of an irreducible core of rights – a zone of personal autonomy in which creators can achieve their creative potential, control their productive output and lead independent intellectual lives that are essential requisites of any free society.[51] Legal protections in excess of those needed to establish this core zone of autonomy may serve other salutary social purposes. But they are not required under Article 15 of the Covenant and, as a result, are not subject to the restrictive exceptions and limitations test quoted above. Stated differently, once a country guarantees creators these two core rights – one moral and the other material – any additional intellectual property protections the country provides 'must be balanced with the other rights recognized in the Covenant', and must give 'due consideration' to 'the public interest in enjoying broad access to authors' productions'.[52] The ICESCR thus gives each State discretion to eschew these additional legal protections altogether or, alternatively, to shape them to take account of the particular economic, social and cultural conditions within its borders.[53]

Seen from this perspective, creators' rights are both more and less expansive than copyright and neighbouring rights regimes. They are more expansive in that rights within the core zone of autonomy are subject to a far more stringent test for restrictions than the test applicable to exceptions and limitations in copyright and

---

48. *Ibid.*, at para. 2. This 'personal link' is protected by legislation that enables authors 'to claim authorship for their works and to object to any distortion, mutilation or other modification of, or other derogatory action in relation to, their works, which would be prejudicial to their honour or reputation'. *Ibid.*, at para. 41(b). The Committee's language closely tracks the moral rights provisions in Art. 6*bis* of the Berne Convention and in many national laws.
49. *Ibid.*, at para. 2.
50. The Committee repeats variants of the 'personal link' language a total of six times, and it reasserts the 'adequate standard of living' formulation no less than nine times – repetitions that suggest the importance of these concepts to its analysis.
51. Cf. Torremans, *supra* n. 15 at 5 (drafters of UDHR believed that the best way to avoid recurrence of abuses of science, technology and copyrighted propaganda that occurred during Second World War would be 'to recognize that everyone had a share in the benefits and that . . . those who made valuable contributions were entitled to protection').
52. General Comment, *supra* n. 11 at paras 22 and 35. See also *ibid.*, at para. 11 (stating that nothing in Art. 15(1)(c) prevents states parties from 'adopting higher protection standards' in intellectual property treaties or national laws, 'provided that these standards do not disproportionately impede the enjoyment by others of their Covenant rights').
53. See *ibid.*, at para. 18 (stating that 'the precise application' of authors' and inventors' moral and material interests 'will depend on the economic, social and cultural conditions prevailing in a particular State party').

neighbouring rights treaties and national laws. They are less expansive, however, in that a state need not recognize additional creators' rights lying outside of this zone or, if it does recognize such rights, must give appropriate weight to other human rights, to the public's interest and to other policy objectives – calibrations that may permissibly vary from one country to another.

3   HUMAN RIGHTS AND THE COLLECTIVE
         ADMINISTRATION OF COPYRIGHT:
         A PRELIMINARY ASSESSMENT

Where does the collective administration of copyright and neighbouring rights fit within this emerging legal paradigm? Although the General Comment references issues of collective administration only sparingly, the Committee's detailed analysis of Article 15(1)(c) suggests several ways in which CMOs can help to enhance creators' rights. However, that analysis also reveals certain collective management practices that are in tension with the Covenant's intellectual property provisions. The discussion below provides an overview of these competing perspectives.

The only express mention of CMOs in the General Comment appears in the discussion of how to protect creators against infringement by third parties. This is hardly surprising, inasmuch as the obligation 'to protect' is the legal 'hook' that the ICESCR Committee has used to require governments to regulate the activities of non-state and private actors (in contrast to other Covenant provisions that impose obligations on state actors alone).[54] One method for States to provide such protection is 'by establishing systems of collective administration of authors' rights'.[55] Collective administration is particularly appropriate, in the Committee's view, where works are 'easily accessible or reproducible through modern communication and reproduction technologies'.[56] A second, more oblique reference to CMOs appears in the discussion of the obligation 'to fulfil', which requires governments 'to promote the realization' of Article 15(1)(c).[57] These conditions include funding and other affirmative measures to facilitate 'the formation of professional associations', and 'to ensure the active and informed participation' of authors in those associations to protect their moral and material interests.[58]

3.1   CMO ACTIVITIES THAT ENHANCE THE HUMAN RIGHTS OF
         CREATORS AND USERS

Although the references to collective administration in the General Comment are sparse, the document's overall analysis supports many of the activities that

---

54. *Ibid.*, at para. 31.
55. *Ibid.*
56. *Ibid.*
57. *Ibid.*, at para. 46.
58. *Ibid.*, at paras 34 and 46.

CMOs perform. In fact, where prevailing modes of exploiting protected works make it difficult or impossible for authors to control their creations on an individualized basis, CMOs are likely to be essential features of human rights-compliant, twenty-first century copyright systems.

Distilled to their essence, CMOs enable copyright owners to enforce their rights where the transaction costs of negotiating individual licenses and pursuing individual enforcement preclude mutually beneficial transactions with users.[59] In particular, CMOs perform two functions that the Committee identifies as necessary for the 'effective protection' of creators' rights: (1) they prevent infringement by third parties, and (2) they collect and distribute compensation for authorized uses of protected works.[60] CMOs also make it possible for copyright owners to retain exclusive control over their creative output in situations in which user groups are likely to pressure legislators to convert such control into the lesser right to receive remuneration from compulsory licenses.[61]

In addition to these core functions, CMOs also carry out a variety of ancillary activities that provide human rights benefits. These include representing the interests of creators before legislatures and administrative agencies, providing social services such as health benefits and pensions for authors, and promoting creativity through awards, prizes and fellowships.[62] By engaging in these additional functions, CMOs not only assist States in complying with Article 15(1)(c) but also help them to satisfy the obligations of other United Nations (UN) treaties.[63] It is not

---

59. See L. Helfer, 'World Music on a U.S. Stage: A Berne/TRIPS and Economic Analysis of the Fairness in Music Licensing Act', *Boston University Law Review* 80 (2000): 93 at 110. ('These [transaction] costs include identifying numerous potential licensees in disparate locations, negotiating with them over payment terms, monitoring compliance with each licensing agreement and taking legal action to prevent infringements.')

60. See General Comment, *supra* n. 11 at paras 31 and 45; see also Helfer, *ibid.*, at 110 (stating that CMOs 'reduce transaction costs in several significant ways. They provide a clearinghouse for users seeking licenses, they collect and distribute revenues to the songwriters, composers and publishers who are their members, they monitor the activities of licensees and they take enforcement action where necessary to vindicate their members' rights'.).

61. See Ficsor, *supra* n. 12 at 17 (arguing against pressures to abolish exclusive rights and convert them to a 'mere right to remuneration' and proposing collective management of rights as an alternative).

62. See, for example, *ibid.*, at 149–50; Sinacore-Guinn, *supra* n. 1 at 211–212.

63. The UN Convention on the Protection and Promotion of the Diversity of Cultural Expressions, adopted 20 Oct. 2005 and entered into force 18 Mar. 2007, recommends that States parties adopt measures to encourage the 'creation, production, dissemination, distribution and enjoyment of . . . domestic cultural activities, goods and services' and those 'aimed at nurturing and supporting artists and others involved in the creation of cultural expressions'. Article 6(2)(b) and 6(2)(g). The Convention also encourages States parties 'to create in their territory an environment which encourages individuals and social groups to create, produce, disseminate and have access to their own cultural expressions [and] to have access to diverse cultural expressions from within their territory as well as from other countries of the world'. Article 7(1)(a) and 7(1)(b). CMOs could serve as vehicles for helping States to achieve these objectives.

CMOs could also assist States parties to the Convention on the Rights of Persons with Disabilities, adopted 13 Dec. 2006 and entered into force 3 May 2008, to meet their obligation to

surprising, therefore, that several States parties to the ICESCR have referred favourably to legislation establishing collective management systems in their reports to the Committee.[64]

'take all appropriate steps . . . to ensure that laws protecting intellectual property rights do not constitute an unreasonable or discriminatory barrier to access by persons with disabilities to cultural materials'. Art. 30(3). For example, CMOs may facilitate – either on their own or in response to government incentives – the conversion of copyrighted materials into media accessible to persons with disabilities, and the distribution of those materials to such persons by means of blanket licensing agreements.

64. See, for example, Committee on Economic, Social and Cultural Rights, 'Fourth Periodic Reports: Mexico, Implementation of the International Covenant on Economic, Social and Cultural Rights' (25 Feb. 2005), E/C.12/4/Add.16 at para. 883, <www.unhchr.ch/tbs/doc.nsf/898586b1dc7b4043c1256a450044f331/5e44a3f92c77e707c12570ab0059563c/$FILE/G0540525.pdf> (last visited: 9 Sep. 2009) (referring to 'the National Copyright institute authoriz[ing] the formation and operation of collectively managed societies'); Committee on Economic, Social and Cultural Rights, 'Initial Reports: Slovenia, Implementation of the International Covenant on Economic, Social and Cultural Rights' (26 May 2004), E/1990/5/Add.62 at para. 915, online: <www.unhchr.ch/tbs/doc.nsf/898586b1dc7b4043c1256a450044f331/ba2445d14057821cc1257067003238cd/$FILE/G0441926.pdf> (last visited: 9 Sep. 2009) (discussing the difficulty of establishing 'collective organizations for creative (copyright) workers'); Committee on Economic, Social and Cultural Rights, 'Initial Reports: China, Implementation of the International Covenant on Economic, Social and Cultural Rights' (4 Mar. 2004), E/1990/5/Add. 59 at paras 234, 258, <www.unhchr.ch/tbs/doc.nsf/898586b1dc7b4043c1256a450044f331/9fbfe806f28f1eb4c1256f4a004bc5d8/$FILE/G0440656.pdf> (last visited: 9 Sep. 2009) (referring to 'collectively administering copyright' as a means of 'protect the cultural rights of [China's] citizens' and discussing China's 'first institution for the collective management of intellectual property rights'); Committee on Economic, Social and Cultural Rights, 'Fourth Periodic Reports: Norway, Implementation of the International Covenant on Economic, Social and Cultural Rights' (26 Feb. 2004), E/C.12/4/Add.14 at para. 461, <www.unhchr.ch/tbs/doc.nsf/898586b1dc7b4043c1256a450044f331/4b7cddf05a594cbac1256f42004d4d3b/$FILE/G0442518.pdf> (last visited: 9 Sep. 2009) (referring to laws created 'to provide for collective arrangements whereby remuneration is paid through the state budget to funds administered by various copyright organizations'); Committee on Economic, Social and Cultural Rights, 'Third Periodic Reports: Chile, Implementation of the International Covenant on Economic, Social and Cultural Rights' (14 Jul. 2003), E/1994/104/Add. 26 at paras 877–881, <www.unhchr.ch/tbs/doc.nsf/898586b1dc7b4043c1256a450044f331/91ef5d1ff1e1525cc1256f16004aa896/$FILE/G0343617.pdf> (last visited: 9 Sep. 2009) (discussing the emergence of collective management societies protecting rights in the music sector, and protecting rights of image artists, playwrights and screenwriters, and actors); Committee on Economic, Social and Cultural Rights, 'Initial Reports: Lithuania, Implementation of the International Covenant on Economic, Social and Cultural Rights' (9 Dec. 2002), E/1990/5/Add. 55 at paras 657–658, 667, <www.unhchr.ch/tbs/doc.nsf/898586b1dc7b4043c1256a450044f331/1eaf91a2843227dfc1256e78004a2b55/$FILE/G0246237.pdf> (last visited: 9 Sep. 2009) (discussing the importance of collective administration of copyright and referring to the Lithuanian laws and agency that govern collective administration of copyright); Committee on Economic, Social and Cultural Rights, 'Initial Reports: Greece, Implementation of the International Covenant on Economic, Social and Cultural Rights' (23 Oct. 2002), E/1990/5/Add. 56 at paras 670, 678, online: <www.unhchr.ch/tbs/doc.nsf/898586b1dc7b4043c1256a450044f331/fc0f67050f79d862c1256d5f00565ee6/$FILE/G0245183.pdf> (last visited: 9 Sep. 2009) (discussing both self-managed and publicly managed collective management organizations); Committee on Economic, Social and Cultural Rights, 'Initial Reports: Bolivia, Implementation of the International Covenant on Economic, Social

Collective management of copyright also enhances the rights of consumers under Article 15 of the Covenant, although the benefits are more equivocal than those accruing to creators.[65] Blanket licenses, the mainstay of so many CMOs, authorize the unlimited use of all works within the organization's repertoire for a specific period of time. Such licenses avoid the time and expense of negotiating specific uses for specific works. For users who require immediate access to a broad array of creative consent, blanket licenses also promote spontaneity in exploiting protected works.[66] For those with more particularized needs, however, the benefits of blanket licenses are less clear, because the 'all or nothing' bargains they embody compel consumers to purchase more works at higher prices than they would otherwise be willing to pay.[67] Whether the aggregate benefits to the public outweigh the costs depends in part on the extent to which governments regulate CMO licensing practices, a subject addressed in greater detail below.

3.2   CMO ACTIVITIES THAT DETRACT FROM THE HUMAN RIGHTS OF CREATORS AND USERS

Some form of collective management of creators' rights is essential to ensure compliance with Article 15(1)(c) where the transaction costs of individual licenses are high. Not all of the functions that CMOs perform are human rights enhancing, however. On the contrary, the monopoly position that CMOs enjoy – both in relation

---

and Cultural Rights' (9 Dec. 1999), E/1990/5/Add.44 at para. 506, <www.unhchr.ch/tbs/doc.nsf/898586b1dc7b4043c1256a450044f331/5e41566ff361c211c12569220048364e/$FILE/G9946227.pdf> (last visited: 9 Sep. 2009) (discussing the Copyright Act's 'establishment of societies of authors and artists, with a view to assuming responsibility for the administration of their property rights'); Committee on Economic, Social and Cultural Rights, 'Second periodic reports: Belgium, Implementation of the International Covenant on Economic, Social and Cultural Rights' (5 Mar. 1998), E/1990/6/Add. 18, <www.unhchr.ch/tbs/doc.nsf/0/9b1e64652f3a69cc8025678a00318bfb?OpenDocument> (last visited: 9 Sep. 2009) (describing provisions of new copyright law that 'provides for the formation of royalty management companies (or collective management)' which 'makes it obligatory for these societies to intervene to ensure that certain types of remuneration are received').

65. See generally, G. Davies, 'The Public Interest in the Collective Administration of Rights' *Copyright* (March, 1989), 81 at 84–87.

66. See *Broadcast Music, Inc. v. Columbia Broadcasting System, Inc.* (1979), 441 U.S. 1 at 20 (United States Supreme Court), <caselaw.lp.findlaw.com/scripts/getcase.pl?court=us&vol=441&invol=1> (last visited: 9 Sep. 2009). ('Most users want unplanned, rapid, and indemnified access to any and all of the repertory of compositions, and the owners want a reliable method of collecting for the use of their copyrights.') This need for immediate access is one reason why blanket licenses are the norm for public performance rights for musical works. See Ficsor, *supra* n. 12 at 37–48 and Sinacore-Guinn, *supra* n. 1 at 747–768.

67. See A. Katz, 'The Potential Demise of Another Natural Monopoly: New Technologies and the Future of Collective Administration of Copyrights' (May 2004), *U Toronto Law and Economics Research Paper No. 04-02*, <http://ssrn.com/abstract=547802> or <law.bepress.com/cgi/viewcontent.cgi?article=1034&context=alea> (last visited: 9 Sep. 2009); Stanley M. Besen, S. Kirkby & S. Salop, 'An Economic Analysis of Copyright Collectives', *Virginia Law Review* 78 (1992): 383 at 393.

to users and, in some cases, in their dealings with the creators who are their members – generate incentives for the organizations to behave in ways that limit the human rights of both groups. These incentives highlight the need for governments to regulate (1) the licenses that CMOs offer to users, (2) the relationships between CMOs and their members and (3) the relationships among the members themselves.[68]

As to the first issue, governments in nearly all countries in which CMOs operate exercise some form of regulatory control over licensing practices to prevent abuse of their dominant positions. The source, extent and enforcement of these regulations vary widely, however. In some countries, copyright laws limit CMO activities. In others, administrative agencies, tribunals or other specialized regulatory bodies monitor CMO activities and adjudicate complaints by licensees. In yet other nations, users seek relief from the courts by filing competition or antitrust claims against CMOs, leading to judicial monitoring of licensing practices in the form of detailed consent decrees.[69]

How do human rights principles inform government regulation of CMOs? As explained above, a human rights framework for intellectual property requires a balance between the rights of creators and the rights of the public. In striking this balance, 'the private interests of authors and inventors should not be unduly advantaged and the public interest in enjoying broad access to new knowledge should be given due consideration'.[70] Regulation of licensing practices is one way to avoid such undue advantage. According to the ICESCR Committee, states must prevent private parties from imposing 'unreasonably high' license fees or royalties that interfere with other rights in the Covenant, including the right to education and to culture.[71]

The consequences of this statement for government regulation of CMOs are somewhat uncertain, however. The Committee provides no guidance for determining when royalties are unreasonably high. In addition, the examples that it identifies as potentially problematic – high costs of access to essential medicines, plant seeds, schoolbooks and other learning materials[72] – do not include the works of entertainment or popular culture that are often subject to collective management. Nevertheless, the Committee's reference to the price that consumers pay to access copyrighted works as part of the overall balance of creators' rights suggests that States must provide some form of meaningful regulation of CMO licensing practices to comply with their obligations under the Covenant.

---

68. Cf. Sinacore-Guinn, *supra* n. 1 at 237. ('The disadvantages of private [CMOs] fall into two general categories: problems in relationship to the organization's activities on the creator's behalf and problems related to the relationship between the organization and the creator.')
69. See Ficsor, *supra* n. 12 at 142–44; Helfer, *supra* n. 59 at 110–111 and n. 64; see also S. Helm, 'Intellectual Property in Transition Economies: Assessing the Latvian Experience', *Fordham Intellectual Property Media & Entertainment Law Journal* 14 (2003): 119 at 200–201 (discussing supervisory functions performed by Ministry of Culture in relation to Latvian copyright collectives).
70. General Comment, *supra* n. 11 at para. 35; see also Statement on Human Rights and Intellectual Property, *supra* n. 9 at para. 17 (similar quotation).
71. General Comment, *supra* n. 11 at para. 35.
72. *Ibid.*

The second and third areas of human rights scrutiny concern the relationship between CMOs and their members, and among their members *inter se*. Two provisions of the General Comment are relevant to these issues: the restriction of creators' rights to natural persons and the more capacious equality norms that the ICESCR endorses.

The exclusion of corporations and other business entities from the rights protected in Article 15(1)(c) suggests that States parties must give special solicitude to individual creators who are compelled, either by law or as a practical matter, to enforce their rights through collective management systems. This is particularly true for CMOs organized in a form other than an authors' association, in which creators may exercise somewhat greater control.[73] Government supervision to ensure equal treatment of individual creators encompasses a broad range of issues, including the terms of CMO membership, transfers of rights from individuals to the collective, the distribution of royalties and participation by copyright owners in CMO decisions that affect their interests.[74]

Corporate and equality issues also arise in another area of CMO governance – the relationship between individual creators and business owners who belong to the same CMO. Several scholars have noted the growing conflicts between these two classes of rights holders from the agglomeration of intellectual property-related businesses and the concomitant expansion of corporate influence over CMO decision making.[75] Although principles of 'equity' and 'solidarity' among rights holders are enshrined in many CMO charters, the recent erosion of these principles highlights the potential of the Covenant's broader non-discrimination rules to bolster equality for individual creators in their relations with corporate rights owners.[76]

4   TWO HUMAN RIGHTS CONCERNS OF COLLECTIVE
      ADMINISTRATION: MANDATORY MEMBERSHIP
      AND PROMOTING NATIONAL CULTURE

The preceding section provided a thumbnail sketch of a human rights framework for the collective administration of copyright and neighbouring rights, emphasizing both the benefits and the detriments of CMOs for achieving the balanced

---

73. See Sinacore-Guinn, *supra* n. 1 at 235–236 (discussing distinction between 'membership organizations' and 'corporate non-membership organizations').
74. See Ficsor, *supra* n. 12 at 21, 132 and 143. Where a CRO is a public entity – as is often true in developing countries – the government is required to address these issues as part of its obligation 'to respect' the rights of creators. See General Comment, *supra* n. 11 at paras 30 and 44.
75. See R. Wallis, C. Baden-Fuller, M. Kretschmer & G. Klimis, 'Contested Collective Administration of Intellectual Property Rights in Music: The Challenge to the Principles of Reciprocity and Solidarity', *European Journal of Communication* 14 (1999): 5 at 6–8 (analysing the consequences of increasing concentration of ownership and integration in the music industry); G. Jokhadze, 'The Big Ones of the Music Industry: Copyright and Human Rights Aspects of the Music Business', in *Expanding The Horizons of Human Rights Law*, ed. I. Ziemele (Boston: Martinus Nijhoff Publishers, 2005), 290 at 237–238 (same).
76. See Wallis et al., *supra* n. 75 at 14–15, 19 and 22–23.

protection of creators' rights indicated by the ICESCR Committee. This section contains a more detailed analysis of two legal and policy questions with important human rights implications: (1) whether participation in CMOs should be voluntary or mandatory and (2) whether such organizations should promote national culture in addition to the licensing, enforcement and royalty distribution activities that comprise the core of their work.

4.1   SHOULD MEMBERSHIP IN CMOS BE MANDATORY
             OR VOLUNTARY?

The question of whether creators should be required to join CMOs has long vexed intellectual property commentators. On the one hand, mandatory membership, and the exclusion of other modes of exploitation it implies, help to achieve the economic efficiencies and practical benefits that justify collective administration in the first instance, such as issuing blanket licenses and reducing the costs of negotiations, enforcement actions and royalty distributions. However, mandatory participation in a CMO also raises serious concerns for creators. In its most extreme incarnation, compulsory membership precludes creators from issuing individual licenses for their own works, compels participation in an organization whose policies they may disfavour (and that they may be legally or practically precluded from modifying) and requires affiliation with other creators with whom they may not wish to associate.[77]

Similar concerns led the European Court of Human Rights (ECHR) to find 'closed-shop agreements' – contracts that require employees to join a trade union as a condition of gaining or maintaining employment – to violate the right to freedom of association.[78] Article 11 of the European Convention on Human Rights guarantees freedom of association, 'including the right to form and to join trade unions'.[79] It does not, however, expressly mention a right *not* to associate. Nevertheless, in *Sørensen and Rasmussen v. Denmark*, the ECHR found that compelling an employee to join a union impermissibly interfered with the rights guaranteed by Article 11.[80]

In reaching this result, the court explained that States have a positive obligation to intervene in private employment relationships to secure the rights

---

77. For a discussion of these competing viewpoints, see Sinacore-Guinn, *supra* n. 1 at 289–303. For an analysis of when compulsory membership is compatible with international copyright and neighbouring rights agreements, see M. Ficsor, 'Collective Management: Voluntary? Extended? Obligatory? International Norms and the "Acquis Communautaires"' (2003), Eleventh Annual Conference on International Intellectual Property Law and Policy, Fordham University School of Law, New York City, 24–25 Apr. 2003.
78. *Sørensen and Rasmussen v. Denmark*, Application Nos 52562/99 & 52620/99, Eur. Ct. H.R. (2006) (Sørensen).
79. Convention for the Protection of Human Rights and Fundamental Freedoms, opened for signature 4 Nov. 1950, ETS No. 5 (European Convention), Art. 11.
80. Sørensen, *supra* n. 78, para. 36.

guaranteed in Article 11.[81] In reviewing this intervention, the ECHR considers whether the government has struck 'a fair balance . . . between the competing interests of the individual and of the community as a whole',[82] weighing the State's justification for permitting closed shop agreements against the extent to which they frustrate an employee's right to freedom of association.[83] In *Sørensen and Rasmussen*, the ECHR found that most States parties to the European Convention no longer support closed shop agreements, suggesting that the agreements were no longer 'an indispensible tool for the effective enjoyment of trade union freedoms'.[84] In light of this growing regional trend, the court found that Denmark's interest in maintaining closed shop agreements was insufficient to outweigh the harm to the employees' freedom of association.[85]

Although labour unions and CMOs are not directly analogous, the human rights concerns raised by compulsory membership in a labour unions may have repercussions for compulsory membership in CMOs. Both closed shop agreements and compulsory CMO membership affect a individual's livelihood. However, whereas closed shop agreements threaten the loss of employment for failure to join a union, mandatory membership in a CMO helps to ensure that creators receive revenue from the licensing of their works.

Nevertheless, there are strong arguments that mandatory membership in CMOs impermissibly interferes with freedom of association, at least in industrialized countries. In particular, compulsory membership rules are an overly broad means of advancing society's interest in facilitating access to creative works through a single licensing mechanism. The obvious efficiency gains of collective rights management will convince most rights holders to join CMOs voluntarily. These incentives are strong enough to enable CMOs to withstand the modest diminution of membership and revenue that would result from offering creators an exit option, a choice among multiple organizations or permitting individual or open-content licensing.[86]

The application of the ECHR's balancing test to mandatory CMO membership may differ, however, for developing countries with nascent creative industries. Many developing countries have only limited experience in encouraging creativity within their borders and in promoting the licensing of copyrighted works. As one commentator has explained:

---

81. *Ibid.*, at para. 57.
82. *Ibid.*, at para. 58.
83. *Ibid.*, at para. 58.
84. *Ibid.*, at para. 75.
85. *Ibid.*
86. Cf. D. Gervais, 'Collective Management of Copyright and Neighbouring Rights in Canada: An International Perspective', *Canadian Journal of Law and Technology* 1 (2002): 21 at 26, online: <cjlt.dal.ca/vol1_no2/pdfarticles/gervais.pdf>, 9 Sep. 2009. ('In the same way that rightsholders should be free to decide whether they want to be part of a collective scheme (except perhaps where individual management is impossible), they should be free to create new Collective Management Organizations.')

[T]he national cultural industries in these developing nations are frequently underdeveloped and the national repertoire underutilized. . . . From the government's perspective, and that of many creators as well, [initiatives to promote creativity] will be weakened to the extent that a significant number of national creators fail to participate in this collective effort. Furthermore, in many such countries, the number of creators involved is relatively small and so lacking in income that there is little potential for the native industry to develop without a coordinated comprehensive (and often subsidized) governmental effort.[87]

Mandating membership in CMOs is an appropriate response to these economic and social conditions. It centralizes public and private efforts to promote local culture and creativity in a single entity, enhancing their effectiveness. Such an approach is also consistent with a recognition of the special needs of developing countries that the ICESCR Committee emphasizes in its General Comment.[88] Admittedly, the freedom of choice and associational rights of individual creators are constrained by compulsory membership.[89] Under the conditions described earlier, however, in which collective management not only generates royalties but also helps to build the requisites of a national copyright culture, restrictions on the rights of individual creators can be justified under the stringent standard that the ICESCR Committee endorses as well as under the ECHR's balancing test in the *Sørensen and Rasmussen* case.[90] As economic and cultural conditions in developing countries improve, however, such restrictions will become increasingly difficult for governments to justify.

For many years, freedom of association concerns relating to mandatory CMO membership were of mostly theoretical interest.[91] As a practical matter, certain modes of exploiting protected works required collective action, and creators had little choice but to license these works collectively rather than individually. It thus made little difference whether the government formally mandated CMO membership.[92] Recently, however, two legal and technological developments have

---

87. Sinacore-Guinn, *supra* n. 1 at 291. See also E. Nwauche, 'Intellectual Property Rights, Copyright and Development Policy in a Developing Country: Options For Sub Saharan African Countries' (2003), Copyright Workshop, Zimbabwe International Book Fair, 30 Jul. 2003, at 10, <www.kopinor.org/content/download/1777/13422/file/zibf.pdf> (last visited: 9 Sep. 2009). ('Apart from South Africa where the collecting societies began operations in the sixties, most of the other [Sub-Saharan African] collecting societies are of a recent origin.')
88. See General Comment, *supra* n. 11 at para. 40.
89. The Covenant protects these associational rights expressly. See ICESCR, *supra* n. 2, Art. 8(1)(a) (recognizing the right 'of everyone to form trade unions and join the trade union of his choice . . . for the promotion and protection of his economic and social interests').
90. See General Comment, *supra* n. 11 at paras 22–23; Sørensen, *supra* n. 78, at para. 58; see also *supra*, Part I.B.
91. Sinacore-Guinn, *supra* n. 1 at 289 (stating that the issue of 'voluntary versus nonvoluntary collective affiliation' is 'rarely addressed directly in the legal literature or by governmental authorities').
92. World Intellectual Property Organization, 'Collective Administration of Copyright and Neighboring Rights' (1989), *Copyright* 309 at 342 (WIPO, *Collective Administration*).

increased the salience of analyzing mandatory participation from a human rights perspective.

The first development concerns online licensing of copyrighted works. Digital media and Internet technologies create new opportunities for exploiting protected works, opportunities that collective rights management can greatly facilitate. But the ease of digital communications, the pervasive labelling of works with rights management information, and the security provided by technological protection measures also enable creators to negotiate with users directly and to license their works themselves.[93]

The practical feasibility of issuing individual licenses substantially raises the stakes associated with CMO membership rules. Many, perhaps most, creators will continue to manage their works collectively. For these individuals, it may seem of little consequence whether membership is mandatory or permissive. But the collective enterprise as a whole may suffer if rights owners are not required to participate.[94] This is particularly true if global media companies that control large portfolios of protected works withdraw them from the system of collective licensing.[95] It is also a risk if popular creators or performing artists opt out of the collective to demand higher royalties than a CMO can negotiate on their behalf as part of a blanket license.[96] In either case, it is smaller and less well known individual creators who may suffer.[97]

Whether and to what extent these dark predictions come to pass affects whether state regulation of CMO membership rules is consistent with international human rights law. If a mass exodus of corporate rights owners or popular artists from the collective denies other creators the opportunity 'to enjoy an adequate standard of living' from their creative endeavours,[98] a human rights framework may require governments to favour exclusive participation in such organizations

---

93. See C. Graber, C. Govoni, M. Girsberger & M. Nenova (eds), *Digital Rights Management: The end of Collecting Societies?* (Berne: Staempfli Publishers Ltd., 2005), 251; Ficsor, *supra* n. 12 at 96–106; Gervais, *supra* n. 86 at 21.
94. A. Dietz, 'Legal Regulation of Collective Management of Copyright (Collecting Societies Law) in Western and Eastern Europe', *Journal of the Copyright Society of the U.S.A.* 49 (2002): 897 at 911 (noting arguments that 'an unduly rapid transition from collective management to individual management of rights [in digital networks] could disturb the established, socially balanced system of distribution').
95. Wallis, *supra* n. 75 at 21–22 (discussing the 'threat to the stability of collecting societies' from the withdrawal of multinationals' repertoires from collective administration).
96. See Ficsor, *supra* n. 12 at 97–98 (noting this possibility but arguing that it is counterproductive for individual creators and for the collective as a whole).
97. As one group of commentators recently stated:

> The threats [from recent challenges to CMOs] are greatest to those who earn modest royalties, especially from companies not linked with [major multinational conglomerates]. These artists . . . will find themselves squeezed twice. First, the collective agencies may ignore them, as their needs are costly to service. Second, the companies which represent them will have to be more aggressive if they are to survive.

Wallis, *supra* n. 75 at 25.
98. General Comment, *supra* n. 11 at para. 2.

and to refocus regulation on providing members with the means to hold CMOs accountable and to participate in CMO decisions that affect their interests.[99] These concerns could also justify government-mandated CMO membership rules under the ECHR's balancing test. On the other hand, individual and collective licensing may coexist harmoniously in certain media. Where they do, a human rights framework weighs strongly in favour of giving creators the freedom to decide whether to license their works individually or as part of the collective.

A second trend that may alter the calculus of whether CMO memberships should be mandatory or voluntary concerns the rise of Creative Commons and similar organizations that promote open content licensing of copyrighted works.[100] Open content licenses authorize third parties to exercise some or all of a creator's exclusive rights without remuneration for such uses. In doing so, they facilitate sharing of ideas, information and protected content between authors and users and directly promote 'the public interest in enjoying broad access to new knowledge' – two goals endorsed by Article 15 of the Covenant and by the ICESCR Committee.[101] Some advocates of open content licensing also make the more controversial assertion, that a limited relinquishing of exclusive rights promote creativity more effectively than existing proprietary models.[102]

Whatever the merits of this claim, there can be little doubt that open content licenses challenge the economic interests of CMOs.[103] They thus create potential conflicts between CMOs and their members that raise human rights concerns. One recent proposal would resolve these conflicts by allowing creators to assign all of their works to CMOs on a nonexclusive basis, thereby preserving the right to distribute those same works through open content licenses.[104] This approach accords with the diversity of arrangements (many of them nonexclusive) by which

---

99. *Ibid.*, at paras 18 and 34.
100. See, for example, 'Creative Commons', <creativecommons.org/> (last visited: 9 Sep. 2009); A Guide to Open Content Licenses, online: <pzwart.wdka.hro.nl/mdr/research/lliang/open_content_ guide/> (last visited: 9 Sep. 2009); Open Content, online: <opencontent.org/> (last visited: 9 Sep. 2009); Open Music, online: <openmusic.linuxtag.org/modules/freecontent/content/openmusic/> (last visited: 9 Sep. 2009).
101. ICESCR, *supra* n. 2, Art. 15(2) (requiring states parties to take steps 'necessary for the conservation, the development and the diffusion of science and culture'); General Comment, *supra* n. 11 at para. 35 (asserting that states parties must give 'due consideration' to 'the public interest in enjoying broad access' the production of authors).
102. See, for example, *A Guide to Open Content Licenses, supra* n. 100 (discussing models of collaborative production that are alternatives to copyright).
103. See Gervais, *supra* n. 86 at 28 and fn. 77 (reproducing statement by a Canadian collecting society urging authors to 'be prudent in granting free permissions', because the frequent grant of such permissions could be interpreted 'as a lack of support for the collective licensing system', and urging authors to forward all requests for free licenses to the CMO for processing).
104. See [A2k] Comments: Art. 8.1, <lists.essential.org/pipermail/a2k/2005-May/000360.html> (last visited: 9 Sep. 2009) (proposing for inclusion in new 'Access to Knowledge Treaty' a provision to 'ensure that copyright holders that are members of collecting societies are entitled to make available individual works outside of the framework of collecting societies').

creators currently transfer their rights to CMOs.[105] But it elides the difficulties that widespread open content licensing would engender for collectives and for the human rights benefits they produce for creators and users.[106]

More nuanced solutions are needed to balance the competing interests at stake. These could include requiring creators to transfer exclusive rights to the collective for an initial term of years or authorizing transfers on a work-by-work basis, thereby preserving some works for open content licensing. A more comprehensive solution might involve adapting the extended collective licensing system used in Scandinavian countries. Under this system, 'as soon as a substantial number of rights holders of a certain category agree to participate in a collective scheme, the scheme is automatically extended not only to other national rights holders in works of the same category, but to all foreign ones as well'.[107] Creators are not required to participate, however, and they may opt out of the collective system or veto the use of their works.[108] Such an approach places the burden on creators to exclude their works from the collective.

4.2   SHOULD CROS PROMOTE NATIONAL CULTURE?

In addition to collecting and distributing royalties on behalf of their members and enforcing their rights against licensees and infringers, many CMOs engage in a broad range of social, educational, and cultural activities. In the cultural field, these activities seek to 'promot[e] the creation of new works and the use of all national works' through grants to creators; competitions, awards and scholarships; workshops and educational programmes; and the promotion of works by local artists, creators and performers.[109] In some countries, these cultural activities are mandated by statute; in others they are permitted but not required by law; and in still others, cultural promotions are wholly private ventures.[110]

Commentators continue to debate the legality and wisdom of entrusting CMOs with the promotion of culture. Those who favour such a policy argue that cultural activities provide at least an indirect benefit to CMO members by encouraging public respect for creators and their works. Cultural promotions also provide additional incentives for creativity (especially by new or impecunious authors) and highlight classes of works that would otherwise go unnoticed or underappreciated by consumers.[111]

Opponents counter that authorizing CMOs to perform promotional activities conflicts with creators' exclusive rights and risks diminishing the public legitimacy of CMOs. As to the first issue, opponents claim that authors give only nominal

---

105. See Gervais, *supra* n. 86 at 27–32.
106. See *supra* Part 3.1.
107. Gervais, *supra* n. 86 at 29.
108. Sinacore-Guinn, *supra* n. 1 at 405 and 407.
109. *Ibid.*, at 479 and 484–485.
110. See Dietz, *supra* n. 94 at 912–913.
111. See *ibid.*, at 913; Sinacore-Guinn, *supra* n. 1 at 484–493.

consent for expenditures on cultural activities by joining an organization that already engages in such practices. As to the second issue, the monopoly licensing powers that CMOs possess already generate suspicion of collective entities in the eyes of user groups. 'In the face of such suspicion, it is appropriate that the collective only undertake to do that which is absolutely essential to its primary mission: the administration of creative rights.'[112]

To balance these competing perspectives, the amount deducted for cultural activities has remained generally 10% or less of royalties collected.[113] Within the last decade, however, some CMOs have urged their fellow organizations to reduce or even eliminate the deduction for cultural activities, both to maximize the distribution of royalties and to ensure that foreign authors do not subsidize the promotion of culture in other countries.[114] This trend has been most pronounced among CMOs operating in common law countries; it has made less headway in European collection societies.[115]

The cultural activities that CMOs perform – and the debates over their propriety – have never been assessed in human rights terms. Commentators analyzing the issue from an intellectual property perspective make a strong case that the promotion of culture by CMOs can weaken creators' exclusive rights. But a human rights framework proceeds from a very different premise. So long as CMOs perform their core functions and provide sufficient remuneration for authors 'to secure ... an adequate standard of living' from their creative endeavours, then the state – by assisting CMOs to perform these functions – has complied with Article 15(1)(c)'s mandate to protect creators' 'basic material interests'.[116]

Having satisfied this obligation, however, any additional royalties that the organizations collect need not be distributed to their members. Such royalties fall outside the zone of autonomy mandated by Article 15(1)(c) and within the scope of a state's discretion to weigh creators' private interests in receiving additional remuneration against other cultural goals that benefit the public at large.[117] It is a proper exercise of this discretion for States parties to delegate to CMOs a broad array of functions 'necessary for the conservation, the development and the diffusion of science and culture'.[118] Such functions undoubtedly include the promotional activities that CMOs already perform. And there is no reason – from a human

---

112. Sinacore-Guinn, *supra* n. 1 at 499.
113. WIPO, *Collective Administration, supra* n. 92 at 348.
114. See Competition Commission of the United Kingdom, 'Performing rights: A report on the supply in the UK of the services of administering performing rights and film synchronisation rights' (1 Feb. 1996) at 141, <www.competition-commission.org.uk/rep_pub/reports/1996/fulltext/378c9.pdf> (last visited: 9 Sep. 2009). The full version of the report can be viewed online: <www.competition-commission.org.uk/rep_pub/reports/1996/378performing.htm#full> (last visited: 9 Sep. 2009).
115. *Ibid.*
116. General Comment, *supra* n. 11 at para. 2.
117. See *supra* Part 2.2.
118. ICESCR, *supra* n. 2, Art. 15(2).

rights perspective, at least – why funding for such activities should be limited to 10% of royalties collected.[119]

Of course, nothing in the ICESCR requires states parties to appoint CMOs as their agents to conserve, develop and diffuse national culture. Many other options are available, including the creation of educational, not-for-profit or other specialized entities dedicated to studying, preserving and disseminating cultural products.[120] These activities may be undertaken by government agencies directly or by private actors operating with state support.

Alternatives that decouple the promotion of culture from CMOs' core functions have the advantage of respecting the wishes of creators who object to cultural subsidies but who are required, either by law or as a practical matter, to participate in the collective administration of their works.[121] However, such alternatives require governments to fund the promotion of culture from public revenues that are already overburdened. Officials may therefore be tempted to place the financial burden of promoting culture on CMOs rather than diminish the resources available for more pressing government programmes, including those implementing other social and economic rights protected by the Covenant.[122]

One final area of CMO cultural activities requires separate analysis – the promotion of national culture in developing countries with funds acquired from licensing the works of foreign creators. Commentators have long noted the tension between cultural promotion activities by CMOs and the national treatment rules of intellectual property treaties. Because foreign rights holders do not benefit from most cultural programmes undertaken in other nations, the argument goes, they do not receive same treatment that domestic rights owners enjoy.[123] Consequently, 'deductions for cultural activities are only allowed if ... foreigners, directly or indirectly (thought their representatives) approve them'.[124]

This issue continues to be debated in intellectual property circles. According to one influential report by the WIPO, the Berne and Rome Conventions categorically preclude Member States from imposing cultural deductions on foreign creators in their national laws, at least with respect to exclusive rights protected by

---

119. The more complex legal issues raised by funding cultural activities with the royalties collective on behalf of foreign creators are discussed in greater detail below.
120. See Sinacore-Guinn, *supra* n. 1 at 505–507 (discussing alternative methods for promoting culture by entities other than CMOs).
121. See *supra* Part 4.1.
122. ICESCR, *supra* n. 2, Art. 2(1) (requiring states parties to 'take steps ... to the maximum of [their] available resources' to fully realize the rights in the Covenant). See also S. Chavula, 'Cultural, Social and Economic Aspects of Authors' Rights: Legal and Practical Challenges in a Developing Country', Kopinor 25th Anniversary International Symposium, Oslo, Norway, 20 May 2005 at 5, <www.kopinor.org/content/download/2136/15475/file/Legal%20and%20practical%20challenges-kopinor.pdf> (last visited: 9 Sep. 2009) (stating that '[c]ulture is generally ... given very low priority in the national budget [of Malawi] as compared to health, agriculture and education').
123. Sinacore-Guinn *supra* n. 1 at 491 and 502; WIPO, *Collective Administration, supra* n. 92, at 348.
124. WIPO, *Collective Administration, supra* n. 92 at 348.

those treaties.[125] But a more recent WIPO study, written by a leading scholar of collective management of copyright and neighbouring rights, suggests a way to resolve the national treatment issue voluntarily in the case of developing countries. According to the study, the 'foreign partner organizations [of developing country CMOs] may find it appropriate to allow an even higher level of cultural and social deductions [than ten percent] in order to assist those organizations to establish an appropriate management system and copyright infrastructure and to encourage creativity'.[126]

A human rights framework favours this special solicitude for developing states and eschews an expansive interpretation of the national treatment rule. 'International assistance' from rich to poor nations is an important dimension of rights protection in the ICESCR.[127] More importantly, the Covenant provides special rules for developing countries, which 'with due regard to human rights and their national economy, may determine to what extent they would guarantee the economic rights recognized in the present Covenant to non-nationals'.[128]

At first glance, this text appears to conflict with the national treatment rule to the extent that it authorizes developing countries to enact legislation that mandates or permits public or private CMOs to discriminate against foreign creators and rights holders.[129] The Committee's interpretation of this provision, however, suggests that the creators' rights provisions of the Covenant apply both to foreigners and to a State's own nationals.[130] This interpretation also raises – but does not resolve – the more difficult question of how to resolve conflicts between a state's obligations under a human rights treaty and the commitments the state has undertaken by ratifying intellectual property conventions.[131]

---

125. *Ibid.* (unequivocally responding in the negative to the question whether 'any discrimination by collective administration organizations (or by legislation regulating their activities)" [is] permissible to the detriment of rights owners who are . . . foreigners').
126. Ficsor, *supra* n. 12 at 151.
127. ICESCR, *supra* n. 2, Art. 2(1).
128. *Ibid.*, Art. 2(3).
129. Of course, no treaty prevents foreign CMOs and their members from entering into agreements with CMOs in developing countries to authorize the withholding of foreign works royalties for cultural purposes in those countries. See Ficsor, *supra* n. 12 at 151. The plausibility of such voluntary contributions seems questionable, however. If, as noted earlier, rights holders are pressuring CMOs to reduce or eliminate domestic cultural promotions, it seems unlikely that they will support cultural deductions that provide benefits only in other countries.
130. General Comment, *supra* n. 11 at para. 21.
131. Perhaps surprisingly to intellectual property lawyers, the Committee has suggested that these conflicts should be resolved in favour of compliance with human rights treaty obligations. See Statement on Human Rights and Intellectual Property, *supra* n. 9 at para. 12 (emphasizing that 'any intellectual property regime that makes it more difficult for a State party to comply with its core obligations in relation to health, food, education, especially or any other right set out in the Covenant, is inconsistent with the legally binding obligations of the State party'). For an overview of the murky and unresolved rules for reconciling treaty conflicts, see L. Helfer, 'Constitutional Analogies in the International Legal System', *Loyola of Los Angeles Law Review* 37 (2003): 193 at 216–219.

5 CONCLUSION: THE PRACTICAL CONSEQUENCES OF
A HUMAN RIGHTS FRAMEWORK FOR THE
COLLECTIVE ADMINISTRATION OF COPYRIGHT

This chapter has explored how a human rights framework for creators' rights – as outlined by the ICESCR Committee in the General Comment on Article 15(1)(c) and in the Statement on Human Rights and Intellectual Property – intersects with the collective administration of copyright and neighbouring rights. Before concluding the analysis of these issues, it is worth considering two broader questions: first, what are the practical consequences of a human rights framework for the regulation of CMOs and, second, does that framework improve upon the existing legal and policy landscape?

In answering the first question, it bears re-emphasizing that the Committee's analysis of the interface between human rights and intellectual property is still in its early stages. In particular, the Committee has yet to publish general comments interpreting all of the subsections of Article 15, several of which protect the rights of the public. Until the Committee completes its analysis of all of the interrelated clauses of Article 15, a human rights framework will remain a work in progress, subject to revision and, possibly, contestation by states parties.

Recall too that the Committee's general comments are only non-binding, albeit highly persuasive, interpretations of the ICESCR. Given this soft law status, it remains open to governments to challenge the Committee's legal analysis. States have opposed previous general comments issued by other UN human rights treaty bodies.[132] And such opposition may be a plausible option for some industrialized countries if the Committee ultimately interprets Article 15 to give primacy to the Covenant's economic and social rights over the obligations of intellectual property treaties – a result suggested by its preliminary review of the human rights – intellectual property interface.[133]

Assuming, however, that most States parties endorse or at least acquiesce in the Committee's analysis, the general comments on Article 15 can serve more useful and less contentious functions. They can assist governments in reporting to the Committee on the steps they have taken, and the difficulties they have encountered, in implementing the treaty domestically.[134] The general comments

---

132. A decade ago, the United States objected to a general comment issued by the UN Human Rights Committee, the treaty body that monitors implementation of the International Covenant on Civil and Political Rights (ICCPR). See General Comments – Government Responses, *Observations on General Comment No. 24 (52), on Issues Relating to Reservations Made upon Ratification or Accession to the Covenant or the Optional Protocols Thereto, or in Relation to Declarations Under Article 41 of the Covenant, United States of America*, CCPR A/50/40/ Vol.1, Annex VI (1995) (contesting the authority of the UN Human Rights Committee to issue binding interpretations of the ICCPR), <www.bayefsky.com/general/a_50_40_vol._i_ 1995.php> (last visited: 9 Sep. 2009).
133. See Statement on Human Rights and Intellectual Property, *supra* n. 9 at para. 12.
134. ICESCR, *supra* n. 2, Arts 16–17 (setting forth reporting obligations of states parties to the ICESCR).

also can act as a catalyst for generating information about state practices concerning the human rights dimensions of intellectual property, including the regulation of CMOs.[135] From this fund of knowledge and experience, the Committee can then provide more detailed guidance to governments on how to balance the competing human rights concerns raised by the collective administration of copyright, including the issues discussed in this chapter.

The answer to the second question posed above – whether a human rights framework for intellectual property improves upon the existing legal and policy landscape – depends in part on whether affected parties believe that the current system is in need of reform. In the past, user groups have been the most frequent and vociferous critics of collective management of copyright.[136] But recent developments, such as the online distribution of protected works and the growing number of works controlled by corporate rights owners,[137] are increasing conflicts among actors who create and exploit intellectual property products – including tensions between individual and corporate rights owners and between CMOs and their members.[138] In this climate, a consensus may eventually develop on the need for change. If so, a human rights framework offers a possible focal point around which all parties can structure a revised regulatory regime.

It is unclear, however, whether all of the relevant actors will in fact endorse the approach to CMO regulation that is implied by the Committee's analysis. For one thing, not all countries are bound by the ICESCR. This includes, most significantly, the United States, which has signed the Covenant but shows no intention of ratifying it.[139] For another, the Committee has not yet provided a fully developed vision of how to regulate the collective administration of copyright consistently with international human rights law. These factors increase the risk of treaty conflicts and of applying different legal rules to different nation states. They also create an uncertain regulatory environment for private actors whose conduct transcends national borders.

The dangers of fragmentation and incoherence are real, but they are not insuperable. The creators' rights provisions in the Covenant and the UDHR have remained hidden in the shadows for far too long. In addition, the Committee has only recently begun the slow and difficult process of giving a more precise meaning to these provisions. To convince observers of the value of adopting a human rights framework for intellectual property, including collective management, the Committee must lead with the persuasive force of its reasoning. Only by demonstrating the values of this approach can the Committee hope to alter the behaviour of governments and, through them, private parties, and thereby affect the lives of the individuals and groups whose rights it is charged with protecting.

---

135. Given the many complex and contested issues that Art. 15 encompasses, however, the Committee will need to make a particular effort to discuss CMOs in its dialogues with government representatives during the state reporting process.
136. See Helfer, *supra* n. 59 at 113–119; Sinacore-Guinn, *supra* n. 1 at 238–39.
137. See Graber, *supra* n. 93; Jokhadze, *supra* n. 75; Wallis, *supra* n. 75.
138. See *supra* Part 3.2.
139. See D. Weissbrodt, J. Fitzpatrick and F. Newman, *International Human Rights: Law, Policy, and Process*, 3rd edn. (Cincinnati: Anderson Publishing, 2001), 1196 at 122 and 134–43.

Chapter 4

Multi-territorial Licensing and the Evolving Role of Collective Management Organizations

*Tanya Woods**

1   INTRODUCTION

The market has yet to produce an effective online copyright licensing system that transcends territorial limitations to meet the needs of copyright owners and content users.[1] This is not to suggest that nothing has been done. Indeed, many have tried, and continue to try, to find a solution to digital rights clearance issues. However, if we are to see a market solution come to fruition, we must stop and reflect on traditionally successful copyright licensing systems, while enhancing our understanding of the online environment and clarifying some guiding principles to achieve success going forward.

Harmonization on some level seems necessary. The current situation, often characterized by mass 'piracy', will only get worse if copyright continues to be

---

* B.A., LL.B., LL.M., LL.M. Parts of this chapter formed the basis for a previously published article: Tanya Woods, 'Working Toward Spontaneous Copyright Licensing: A Simple Solution for a Complex Problem', *Vanderbilt Journal of Entertainment and Technology Law* 11, no. 4 (2009): 1141–1168.
1. Lucie Guibault & Stef van Gompel (Ch. 5), 'Collective Management in the European Union', in *Collective Management of Copyright and Related Rights* (The Hague: Kluwer Law International, 2006), 117–153 at 137 [EU Collective Management].

Daniel Gervais (ed.), *Collective Management of Copyright and Related Rights*, pp. 105–133.
© 2010 Kluwer Law International BV, The Netherlands.

applied and viewed in ways that dismiss the unique nature of recent technological innovation, semiotic democracy[2] and users' increasing demands for interactivity and convergence. To combat this trend, the copyright challenges raised in the online environment must be approached in a pragmatic manner if copyright owners are to successfully preserve their rights in the virtual realm. Copyright owners are divided on how to manage their rights in the online environment.[3] Some have demonstrated an interest in exploring new licensing models such as Creative Commons (CC), while others – including most collective management organizations ('CMOs') – have yet to depart from their traditional ways.[4] As for the content industries, it appears that they are accepting globalization and seeking to harmonize their practices, and perhaps ultimately, copyright legislation where possible.[5]

CMOs operate globally through reciprocal agreements that affirm the territorial nature of collective management. In the past this may have worked because reproduction and distribution of content was not easy and rarely international in scope. Globalization and the perpetuation of a global information society have changed this. In fact, '[d]igital technology is fast rendering the old territorial system of managing intellectual property obsolete'.[6] The dilemma for CMOs is that they have an established network and clearance is still territory specific. For users, relying on this system for issuance of a global license is costly and the license nearly impossible to obtain. Nevertheless, while commercial users may be able to anticipate territorial clearance challenges, individual users will not – nor should they be expected to do so. Thus, the challenge for CMOs becomes finding an effective and efficient way to administer licensing agreements that meet users' needs and expectations and remains relevant.[7]

---

2. By semiotic democracy I am referring to the desire by individuals to give meaning to the content they experience on the Internet as first explained in John Fiske, *Television Culture* (London: Routledge, 1988).
3. The term 'copyright owner' is used broadly in this chapter and encompasses CMOs acting on behalf of authors through assignment and agency relationships.
4. This is not to say that they are standing still, as we will see this is not the case, but for the most part they have not been very experimental in how they have gone about licensing in the online environment.
5. For example, P. Bernt Hugenholtz & Ruth L. Okediji, 'Conceiving an International Instrument on Limitations and Exceptions to Copyright: Final Report' (6 Mar. 2008) available at, Open Society Institute, <www.soros.org/initiatives/information/articles_publications/publications/copyright_20080506> (last accessed: 5 May 2010).
6. Tilman Lueder, 'The Next Ten Years in EU Copyright: Making Markets Work', *Fordham Intellectual Property, Media & Entertainment Law Journal* 16 (2007): 1–60 at 47–48 [Next Ten], correctly notes that 'Digital technology is fast rendering the old territorial system of managing intellectual property obsolete.'
7. Gervais, 'The Evolving Role(s) of Copyright Collectives', in *Digital Rights Management: The End of Collecting Societies?* ed. C.B. Graber, C. Govoni, M. Girsberger & M. Nenova (Berne: Staempfli Publishers Ltd, 2005), 27–56 at 29 (footnotes omitted) [The End] at 30 (footnotes omitted).

2   CURRENT STATE OF PLAY

Internet technologies upset traditional notions of copyright law that are premised on discrete subject matter, territorial boundaries and the varied set of rights attached thereto.[8] Subsequently, copyright management systems long premised on these notions have also begun to unravel, leaving many to question how these systems will remain relevant in today's modern world. In short, traditional approaches to the management of copyright must be updated. When contemplating a new approach to copyright management it is important to identify and address one of the most fundamental challenges – long-standing collective management systems are being challenged by technological developments. As a result, right holders are not asking whether intermediaries are necessary but what kinds of intermediaries are necessary.[9]

2.1   COPYRIGHT LICENSING AND ITS TERRITORIAL ROOTS

CMOs are said to predate copyright.[10] Although they did not exist quite as they do today, authors' societies in France during the eighteenth century were seen as professional associations that combined the tasks of advocating for respect and recognition of authors and aspects of collective management.[11] It was in this spirit, that Beaumarchais, the author of the play 'The Marriage of Figaro', established a group to protect copyright in plays and operas around 1776, which later evolved into the Société des Auteurs et Compositeurs Dramatiques (SACD).[12] Following SACD in 1837, Honoré de Balzac, Alexander Dumas and Victor Hugo founded the Société des Gens de Lettres de France to represent literary authors.[13] In 1851, the Société de Auteurs, Compositeurs et Éditeurs de Musique (SACEM) was formed and is considered to be the first CMO to represent the 'match between a method of administration (i.e., collective rights

---

8. Marshall Leaffer, 'Protecting Authors' Rights in a Digital Age: From Gutenberg to Electronic Networks', *University of Toledo Law Review* 27 (1996): 1–12 at 7–8.
9. Michael W. Carroll, 'Creative Commons and the New Intermediaries', *Michigan State Law Review* (2006): 45–65 at 45 [Creative Commons].
10. David Sinacore-Guinn, *Collective Administration of Copyrights and Neighbouring Rights: International Practices, Procedures, and Organizations* (Boston: Little, Brown and Company, 1993), at 80 [International Practices]. Collective management if copyright is 'the exercise of copyright and related rights by organizations acting in the interest and on behalf of the owners of rights'. WIPO, 'Collective Management of Copyright and Related Right', <www.wipo.int/about-ip/en/about_collective_mngt.html#P46_4989> (last accessed: 5 May 2010).
11. Mihály Ficsor, *Collective Management of Copyright and Related Rights* (WIPO, 2002) [WIPO Rights] at 19 and Sinacore-Guinn, International Practices, *supra* n. 10 at 81–82.
12. See (SACD), <www.sacd.fr/en/societe/historique/index_dates.asp> and Sinacore-Guinn, International Practices, *supra* n. 10 at 82.
13. Sinacore-Guinn, International Practices, *supra* n. 10 at 83 and Ficsor, WIPO Rights, *supra* n. 11 at 18–19.

administration) and the rights and market being administered (i.e., non-dramatic musical performing rights)'.[14]

SACEM did not confine itself to territorial boundaries. In fact, it established branch offices in Belgium, Holland, Switzerland, Spain, Greece, Monaco, Portugal, Egypt, Romania, Syria and the United Kingdom.[15] CMOs continued to be established nationally;[16] however, the need for cooperation and harmonization was what prompted Romain Coolus, in 1925, to organize the Committee for the Organization of Congresses of Foreign Authors Societies to 'tackle insurmountable problems involving international issues'.[17] In 1926, the Confederation Internationale des Sociétés des Auteurs et Compositeurs (CISAC) was founded to strengthen and develop the international network of CMOs and later to devise standard terms of agreement between authors' societies, enhance the interoperability between CMOs and retain a central database allowing societies to exchange information efficiently.[18]

To ensure efficiency, most CMOs entered into reciprocal representation agreements with like CMOs in other jurisdictions, agreeing to represent the interests of the other within their respective territories.[19] These agreements are not the only, nor the primary, tool employed to build relationships between CMOs. As Sinacore-Guinn explains,

> such a process would be very expensive and difficult. To avoid these problems, collectives have forged a number of cooperative ventures to assist in creating and maintaining these international relationships through individual agreements or, more commonly, through the development of international associations that assist in developing methods, devices, and forums to promote international creative rights interests and the resolution of technical administrative problems.[20]

Many of the agreements formed between CMOs today in the field of musical works are based on the CISAC Model Contract, an agreement based on reciprocity, in which each contracting party undertakes to enforce the rights of the other party in

---

14. See SACEM, <www.sacem.fr/portailSacem/jsp/ep/channelView.do?channelId=-536882057& channelPage=ACTION%3BBVCONTENT%3B0%3B%2Fep%2FprogramView.do&page TypeId=536886881> (last accessed: 20 Sep. 2009); Catherine Kerr-Vignale, 'Lessons which may be learned from the French experience', in *Colloquium on The Collective Administration of Copyright* (Toronto: Ross Mayot, 1995), 127–135 at 127 and Sinacore-Guinn, International Practices, *supra* n. 10 at 84.
15. Sinacore-Guinn, International Practices, *supra* n. 10 at 84.
16. Stokes, Digital Copyright (London: Hart, 2005) at 163.
17. Gervais, The End, *supra* n. 7 at 29 (footnotes omitted).
18. CISAC, <www.cisac.org/CisacPortal/afficherArticles.do?menu=main&item=tab2&store=true> (last accessed: September 2009) [CISAC].
19. Sinacore-Guinn, International Practices, *supra* n. 10 at 48.
20. Sinacore-Guinn, International Practices, *supra* n. 10 at 48–49. The most important of these organizations according to Sinacore-Guinn are the Bureau International des Sociétés Gérant les droits d'Enrgistrement et de Reproduction Méchanique (BIEM), CISAC, The International Federation of Phonogram and Videogram Producers (IFPI), and IFFRO.

the territory within which it operates, among other obligations.[21] Like other CMOs, those managing the rights in musical works generally have reciprocal agreements with other CMOs in, and belong to, one of two main umbrella organizations – CISAC or the International Federation of Reproduction Rights Organizations (IFRRO).[22] CMOs base their operations on internal statutes and by-laws, which generally set out the competencies of the CMO and its relationship with its members.[23] These internal rules tend to vary by CMO, so a comprehensive description of these rules is difficult to provide.

The historical relationship between the early CMOs and copyright was somewhat reciprocal. Although CMOs are credited for being partially responsible for the development of copyright law, copyright law has helped to define the essential features of CMOs' management practices.[24] This is illustrated by the way that CMOs operate on the basis of copyright fragments, which in turn fragment the management of copyright.[25]

The bundle of rights afforded to the author or owner of copyright material have traditionally been monetized by being split up according to a particular type of use. For example, the reproduction rights in a song may be held by the songwriter, but the performance rights may belong to the performer, who may not be the songwriter. If both right owners entrust a CMO to manage these rights, they may find that they are dealing with two different CMOs – one that manages reproduction rights and another that manages performance rights. Thus, both types of rights are attached to a particular work but owned by different people and subsequently managed by different CMOs. Further adding to the fragmentation is the possibility that there may be more than one CMO in any territory administering the same type of rights; there may be more than one copyright owner of a particular fragment right (e.g., reproduction); and, to clear a use that spans multiple territorial jurisdictions, each territory will likely require its own license(s). The problems created by this complex fragmentation of copyright and its management makes the rights clearance process particularly difficult to maneuver, even for trained industry professionals.[26]

---

21. Ficsor, WIPO Rights, *supra* n. 11 at 42–43, in reference to Art. 3(1) of the CISAC Model Agreement. In Ch. 5, Professor Guibault further explains the nature of these agreements in Europe.
22. Gervais, EU Collective Management, *supra* n. 1 at 20. See also CISAC, *supra* n. 19 and IFRRO, <www.ifrro.org> (last accessed: 5 May 2010).
23. Thomas Vinje & Ossi Niiranen, 'The Application of Competition Law to Collecting Societies in a Borderless Digital Environment' (2005), EU Competition Law and Policy Workshop/ Proceedings, European University Institute, <www.eui.eu/RSCAS/Research/Competition/ 2005(papers).shtml> (last accessed: 5 May 2010) [EU Competition] at 2. These internal rules tend to vary by CMO so a comprehensive description of these rules is difficult to provide.
24. Sinacore-Guinn, International Practices, *supra* n. 10 at 80.
25. I use the word fragmentation as it was defined in D. Gervais & A. Maurushat, 'Fragmented Copyright, Fragmented Management: Proposals to Defrag Copyright Management', *Canadian Journal of Law and Technology* 2, no. 1 (2003): 15–33: 'Fragmentation is a term we use . . . to refer to the lack of cohesion, standardization and, to a certain extent, effective organization of both copyright law and collective management per se.'
26. For a thorough explanation of the problem, see Gervais & Maurushat, Fragmented Copyright, *supra* n. 25.

Although multi-territorial licensing (MTL) does not eliminate fragmentation entirely, it does enable the removal of one of the most costly aspects of the clearance process – the acquiring of multiple territorial licenses. As we will see, in the global online environment, these licenses are necessary to ensure that content lawfully travels beyond territorial borders. The difficulties that may arise in relation to the numerous territorial licenses required must not be understated because:

> one of the strongest factors that may preclude consistency between licences on an international level is the terminological differences between national copyright laws. This may actually hinder individual jurisdictions from creating licences that can be attached to works and mixed with licensed works from other jurisdictions, potentially fracturing the commons.[27]

Thus, a degree of interoperability (or compatibility) between territorial licenses is essential in the online environment. Provided that this consideration is accounted for, MTL offers the necessary means to ensure that users in any territory can access copyright content.

2.2   TECHNOLOGY AND ITS UNCANNY ABILITY TO UPROOT TRADITION

In looking at MTL as one facet of a larger global solution for digital licensing challenges, one should acknowledge points of tension between traditional copyright law and the evolving technological capabilities that influence users' demands.

Traditional copyright is premised on notions of fixation; however, there is nothing necessarily fixed or static about Internet content. The difference is that while a static work may exist within one country, one city or one venue, digitized works are generally not bound by territorial constraints.[28] This general lack of fixation coupled with the incredible ease to reproduce and distribute works online[29] often results in users implying that permission is not necessary or has been sought. This potentially false assumption is problematic to copyright owners that want to monetize their rights, and it signals that the actual degree of permission required before use needs to be clearer so that users can construct a more accurate picture of which uses are lawful and which require permission to be sought.

One would be remiss not to mention that when users focus on passing along the work, and not necessarily on passing along credit to the author or copyright owner, important copyright information may detach from the work and be lost in

---

27. Catherine Bond, 'Simplification and Consistency in Australian Public Rights Licences' (July 2007) UNSW Law Research Paper No. 2007-51, available at SSRN, <http://ssrn.com/abstract=1003691> (last accessed: 5 May 2010) at 16–17.
28. I say generally because technology does exist, and is used, to block access to certain types of works being accessed in different locations. One example is geo-blocking.
29. This 'ease' is made possible by the technology, which does not always signal to a user that his or her actions (or 'uses' in copyright language) are illegal; hence, the confusion!

cyberspace.[30] When this happens, copyright owners and authors may become unidentifiable or unlocatable. The resulting effect is that permission seeking becomes close to impossible for future users because they have no idea who to contact for permission.[31] However, to avoid liability for copyright infringement, online content providers need to be able to seek permission. This problem is not necessarily unique to the online context,[32] but it is exacerbated by lack of control copyright owners are able to exert and the speed at which works are distributed amongst users. Technical protection measures (TPMs) and digital rights management (DRMs) tools may be of assistance in partially resolving this issue and should be considered as complementary to any successful MTL regime.[33]

The online environment embodies certain characteristics that create a unique experience for users relating to copyright material.[34] First, users' experiences online tend to be interactive, as opposed to passive, enabling them to manipulate or change content from one form to another, to readily add new elements to existing content and to change the meaning of content to suit their own semiotic preconditions. Second, users' relationship with content in this new medium is increasingly participatory as opposed to being one-dimensional or strictly consumable. The ability to personalize one's experience with content is novel in contrast to content

---

30. This is a common problem in relation to younger new users that tend to focus on convenience and interactivity as opposed to ownership. See Terry McBride & Brent Muhle, 'Meet the Millennials: Fans, Brands and Cultural Communities' (Executive Summary), (2008) Music Tank, <www.musictank.co.uk> at 3 (last accessed: 5 May 2010) [Millennials].

31. The following observation adds context to this statement. In some cases, trying to use a work '[. . .] "beyond initial contact" (which is usually only listening, viewing or reading all or part of the work) is more difficult unless already allowed under the terms of the license or subscription agreement or as an exception to exclusive rights contained in copyright laws around the world. While in some cases this is a result of the copyright owners' unwillingness to authorize use – a priori a legitimate application of their right to prohibit –, there are several other cases where it is the unavailability of adequate licensing options that makes authorized use impossible. Both copyright owners and users are losers in this scenario: copyright owners because they cannot provide authorized (controlled) access to their works and lose the benefits of orderly distribution or their works, and users because there is no easy authorized access to the right to reuse digital material. In other words, this inability to "control" their works means that these works are simply unavailable (legally) on the Web.' See Gervais, EU Collective Management, *supra* n. 1 at 21 and 19.

32. The problem of orphan works has plagued many countries for quite some time. The US is currently working on finding a solution, Canada is in the process of releasing a study on its regime and studies are ongoing in Europe and elsewhere.

33. This would include watermarking, finger printing, etc. However, a full weighing of the advantages and drawbacks of DRM and TPMs is beyond the scope of this chapter. See John T. Mitchell, (Ch. 8) 'DRM: The Good, The Bad, and the Ugly', 116–182 in Publications in Librarianship No. 57, *Colleges, Code, and Copyright: The Impact of Digital Networks and Technological Controls on Copyright and the Dissemination of Information in Higher Education* (Association of College and Research Libraries, 2005) and Ariel Katz, 'The Potential Demise of another Natural Monopoly: New Technologies and the Future of Collective Administration of Copyrights', University of Toronto Law and Economics Research Paper No. 04-02, available at SSRN, <http://ssrn.com/abstract=547802> [Demise].

34. Tanya Alpin, *Copyright Law in the Digital Society: The Challenges of Multimedia* (London: Hart, 2005), 1–15.

typically distributed in a pre-packaged format. Now, skins can be added around streamed video, avatars can be designed in a person's own likeness and music can be downloaded on a per song basis as opposed to users having to buy entire albums. Third, users are now able to interact with content in a non-linear way. This means that users are not prevented from buying music after hours, then watching a film and reading a book all in the same online session. In other words, there is no set path to take because there are virtually no boundaries.[35] These characteristics facilitate a number of interesting results. Essentially, users are free to easily reproduce and transmit content, transform and adapt content and use different types of content, which traditionally attached to different media all in the same medium.[36] The result of this technological evolution is that users' expectations for content and its distribution have changed dramatically, and CMOs are forced to focus less on traditional distribution models and more on the uses made of individual works online by users.

The most prevalent uses are prima facie, reproduction, translation,[37] adaptation, communication and making available – depending, of course on the territory in which one is standing.[38] Indeed, unlike traditional works (e.g., a painting), digital content cannot be viewed or used without being reproduced (whether transitory or permanent copies). According to Stokes, this has two consequences: first, traditional copyright cannot effectively regulate the digital environment, and second, users will be required to enter into binding licenses with right owners in order to be permitted to access and use digital content – the great risk being an over-extension of copyright via contracts.[39]

2.3   FORGING NEW PATHS TO MEET EVERYONE'S NEEDS

It is no secret that many individual users of online content thrive on instant gratification. The 'millennials' user group – one of the largest user groups online, comprising individuals born after 1981 – illustrates this point through their persistent demands that content (largely copyright-protected content) be made available simultaneously across multiple formats, portals and territories.[40] Not only are these individuals less likely to venture into the licensing labyrinth, they are more

---

35. Of course, the exception being technological limitations. Even legal boundaries do not really prevent users from doing what they want. In this case, there may be repercussions but that is often after the fact.
36. Stokes, Digital Copyright, *supra* n. 16 at 9.
37. In the context of the Internet, taking a work in analogue form and making it visible or 'accessible' in digital form requires a translation of the physical work into digital language (1s and 0s). See Antonio Mille, 'Intellectual Property Issues in the Creation and Uses f Digital Images', in *Exploiting Images and Image Collections in the New Media: Gold Mine or Legal Minefield?*, ed. Barbara Hoffman (The Netherlands: Kluwer Law International, 1999), at 1–20.
38. Stokes, Digital Copyright, *supra* n. 16 at 9.
39. *Ibid.*
40. McBride & Muhle, Millennials, *supra* n. 30 at 3.

technologically savvy and in turn more likely to seek out alternative, although not necessarily lawful, means to achieve their desired end.

Online commercial content providers have one important preoccupation that individual users tend to be less concerned with – liability for infringement. As mentioned, this user group cannot ignore copyright because to do so may increase their liability for infringement and risk the complete failure of their model.[41] The problem for these users, particularly new content providers, is that much of their business is driven by consumer demand, and so they are not particularly interested in trading off popularity for legality.[42] As a result, this group is more likely to resort to finding alternative licensing solutions that may or may not involve CMOs.[43] The other main concerns for this user group are search costs (time and money) to locate copyright owners, the volume of licenses that must be negotiated and the risk for 'coordination failures upstream'.[44] When providing mass amounts of copyright content online the costs of seeking out each individual copyright owner, in each territory, for each protected use and then negotiating transactional licenses can be overwhelming. Traditionally, this is where CMOs have thrived because they have access to a large number of copyright owners in many territories, can negotiate blanket licenses and have the infrastructure to simplify the rights clearance process for users. The volume of requests made by online content providers to CMOs may risk a 'clog in the pipes' and slow down the licensing process, which is problematic when businesses are competing for popularity. The other concern is that there will be coordination failures or inefficiencies upstream that will result in an excessively high fee charged to downstream users.[45] To account for these concerns, CMOs may rely on their traditionally efficient licensing processes; although, they will

---

41. As has been demonstrated in the P2P music distribution models (e.g., Grokster, Morpheus, Gnutella, etc.).

42. David Trouve & Will Page, 'Should societies pursue equity?' (21 May 2008) 9 *MCPS-PRS Economic Insight*, <www.mcps-prs-alliance.co.uk/monline/research/Documents/Economic%20Insight%209.pdf> (last accessed: June 2008) at 2 [Equity]. ZML.com is a good example of an online commercial user of content that has opted to prioritize popularity. ZML.com grabbed the attention of Hollywood's major movie studios earlier this year when it proved that people are willing to pay for downloads from a pirate site. See 'Hollywood and the internet' (21 Feb. 2008) *The Economist*, <www.economist.com/world/na/displaystory.cfm?story_id=10723360> (last accessed: 5 May 2010).

43. One of the more interesting examples of rights owners and users finding an alternative solution is the 'breakthrough' licensing deal signed between Google and EMI Group in May 2007. Essentially, the agreement was designed to enable users to incorporate videos and performances from EMI artists into their user-generated content on You Tube and will rely on YouTube's content management tools to track EMI content and compensate its artists. See Stephanie Olsen, 'You Tube, EMI sign breakthrough licensing pact' (31 May 2007) CNet News.com, <http://news.cnet.com/YouTube,-EMI-sign-breakthrough-licensing-pact/2100-1030_3-6187759.html> (last accessed: 5 May 2010).

44. Reiko Aoki & Aaron Schiff, 'Promoting Access to Intellectual Property: Patent Pools, Copyright Collectives and Clearinghouses' (6 Apr. 2007), available at SSRN, <http://ssrn.com/abstract=976852> (last accessed: 5 May 2010) at 7–8 [Promoting Access].

45. Aoki & Schiff, Promoting Access, *supra* n. 44, at 7–8.

nevertheless have to factor in the very real possibility that they risk alienating users if the licensing costs end up outweighing the benefits.

CMOs and individual copyright owners share a common goal – to monetize and/or legitimize unlawful online uses of their rights.[46] Although some creators of digital content do so purely for non-economic purposes (i.e., 'art for art's sake'), there are others that rely on the monetization of their copyrights to enable them to continue to create. For this latter group, an effective licensing system must enable and facilitate the exchange of money and licenses. This exchange is crucial to any evolving rights management model. Indeed, technology is capable of supporting individual copyright owners interested in managing their own rights without the assistance of CMOs.[47] However, most authors do not see technology as a replacement for CMOs. Rather, new technologies (e.g., DRMs and TPMs) alleviate some of the concerns related to the inefficiency of individual licensing, collecting and enforcement of copyright.[48]

Copyright owners of content created for non-economic purposes may prefer to avoid representation by CMOs for the simple reason that they would maintain a greater amount of freedom to experiment with different licensing regimes. They may, for example, rely on evolving systems such as CC, which is known for facilitating the dissemination of royalty free speech and amateur-to-amateur communication.[49] Licensing in a 'some rights reserved' model allows individual content creators, in particular, to define the preferred level of exerted control. This makes for an excellent learning tool, but is not practically designed for professional content creators who seek compensation for uses of their economic rights. The value in studying systems such as CC is that they are creative, becoming more widely used, offer clear and accessible licensing models and have been deemed enforceable in some jurisdictions.[50] These attributes are well suited to an MTL regime, as we will see.

---

46. This concern is premised on the assumption that copyright owners and authors have made the content available to the public. If this is the case, then at the very least, one can assume that the copyright owner is prepared to allow browsing and potentially other common uses. See Daniel Gervais, 'Standard Internet Licensing Terms: A Proposal the World Intellectual Property Organization (WIPO)' (7 Nov. 2002), available at SSRN, <http://ssrn.com/abstract=506922> (last accessed: 5 May 2010) at 2 [SILTS].

47. See Katz, Demise, *supra* n. 33. For example, the major labels license their own catalogues to online content providers like iTunes which sells from a catalogue of over 1 million songs gleaned from 300 labels, including songs from each of the four major recording companies – Warner, Universal, Sony/BMG and EMI. See Michael A. Einhorn, 'Getting to Yes: How the Market Can Resolve Peer-to-Peer' (2005), available at Federal Trade Commission, <www.ftc.gov/os/comments/p2pfileshare/OL-100065.pdf> (last accessed: 5 May 2010) at 6 [Yes].

48. Gervais, The End, *supra* n. 7 at fn. 18, 30.

49. Carroll, Creative Commons, *supra* n. 9 at 47–48.

50. For example, the Netherlands and Spain.

3   COLLECTIVE MANAGEMENT AND
     MULTI-TERRITORIAL LICENSING

As discussed, neither copyright nor its administration was intended to manage multi-territorial uses in the way that technology now allows. Much effort is being expended by CMOs to manage rights for online uses, a truly international solution has yet to be achieved. Rather than surveying all of the efforts to date, which is deserving of a report on its own, this section will focus on one of the more well-known initiatives undertaken by international CMOs – the Santiago Agreement.[51]

Although predominantly focused on musical works, the Santiago Agreement ('the Agreement') offers valuable insight applicable to all CMOs regardless of the rights they administer. Not only was the Agreement international in scope, it was also applicable in common and civil law jurisdictions and tested by the complex regional laws of the European Union (EU). The lessons learned from the EU experience will no doubt serve as a guide for other countries and perhaps, as some have suggested, form the de facto legal framework for the Internet as the digital frontier continues to develop.[52] For these reasons, this section will look at the Agreement, highlight the learning points and address some of the challenges that arose and may arise again in the future.

3.1   THE APPROACH TO DATE

For some time now CMOs have had to respond to technological advancements. One of the first major adjustments arose from the capabilities of direct broadcasting satellites, which started transmitting programmes to multiple territories and countries.[53] A predominant issue at the time was determining,

> where the actual impact on the possibility of further exploitation of the works and objects of related rights concerned may be felt, and where the interests of certain rights owners – in particular, in those cases where the rights are territorially divided and the owner of rights in a country of footprint is not the same as in the country of emission – may truly be prejudiced.[54]

In 1987, CISAC attempted to respond to this concern by establishing the 'Sydney Addendum' (or principles) [hereafter 'the Addendum'].[55] The Addendum sought

---

51. Most of the activity in the field of collective management and multi-territorial licensing has occurred in the EU, and an overview of historical events and the current state of affairs is offered in Ch. 5 by Professor Guibault.
52. See Nancy Prager, 'If Elvis were a Digital Entrepreneur Today' (24 Jan. 2008) CNet News, <http://news.cnet.com/If-Elvis-were-a-digital-entrepreneur-today/2010-1025_3-6227396.html?part=rss&tag=2547-1023_3-0-5&subj=news> (last visited: 5 May 2010).
53. Ficsor, WIPO Rights, *supra* n. 11 at 111.
54. *Ibid.*
55. *Ibid.*

to achieve two goals: first, to offer a reasonable and workable licensing scheme to users; and second, to duly take into account the interests of, and the rights represented by, all the interested CMOs.[56] These objectives, while at times difficult to reconcile with one another,[57] remain at the forefront of solutions proposed today. The main difference is that now, an even more complex contractual system, with no less than global worldwide licenses, is needed because works transmitted through the Internet are made available to those individuals connected to the global network.[58]

In practice, the Addendum has acted as a model for some CMOs[59] but not all CMOs have treated it that way.[60] In fact, it has not been possible for all of CISAC's member societies to reach a general agreement about Sydney-type amendments to the CISAC Model Contract.[61] However, given that technological evolution does not stand still and problems of unauthorized uses remain, five CMOs[62] have attempted to develop a new licensing model[63] and adopted it in Santiago, Chile in 2001. It is commonly known as the Santiago Agreement.[64]

The Santiago Agreement was considered to be a new approach to multi-territorial and multi-repertoire licensing designed to facilitate the issuance of licenses for the exploitation of works and sound recordings on the Internet.[65] It introduced a non-exclusive licensing regime based on the MTL of authors' rights of online communication to the public and the 'making available' right in reference to the provision of music downloading or streaming;[66] but did not encompass the reproduction rights vested in these works[67] or the simulcasting

---

56. Ficsor, WIPO Rights, *supra* n. 11 at 113. A detailed overview of the Addendum is located at 113.
57. As will be explained later in this paper.
58. Ficsor, WIPO Rights, *supra* n. 11 at 113.
59. For example, those who proposed that the society of the country where the service provider is located, and from where the transmission emanates, should be authorized to grant global licenses, see Ficsor, WIPO Rights, *supra* n. 11 at 113–114.
60. Some societies wanted to take into account other criteria they regarded as better reflecting the actual place and impact of exploitation of works through the Internet, see Ficsor, WIPO Rights, *supra* n. 11 at 113–114.
61. Ficsor, WIPO Rights, *supra* n. 11 at 113–114.
62. BMI (United States of America), BUMA (Netherlands), GEMA (Germany), PRS (United Kingdom) and SACEM (France).
63. According to Fiscor, this was legally considered to be an 'amendment' to the existing contracts based on the CISAC Model Contract. Ficsor, WIPO Rights, *supra* n. 11 at 114.
64. Ficsor, WIPO Rights, *supra* n. x at 113–114 and Nathalie Piaskowski, 'Collective Management in France' (Ch. 5) in Gervais, Collective Management, *supra* n. x, 153–192 at 189 [France]. The Agreement was notified to the Commission in April 2001, see Notification of cooperation agreements European Communities, Notice 2001/C, <145/2 http://europa.eu.int/eur-lex/pri/en/oj/dat/2001/c_145/c_14520010517en00020002.pdf> (last visited: May 2008).
65. Piaskowski, France, *supra* n. 64 at 188.
66. Lueder, Next Ten, *supra* n. 6 at 49.
67. This was covered in the BIEM/Barcelona Agreement, European Communities, Notice OJ C 132/10, 4 Jun. 2002, (Case COMP/C-2/38.377 â€" BIEM Barcelona Agreements), PbEG 2002/C 132/10, <http://europa.eu.int/eur-lex/pri/en/oj/dat/2002/c_132/c_13220020604en00180018.pdf> (last visited: May 2008). This agreement dealt with mechanical reproductions in relation to

rights.[68] The Santiago Agreement included certain reporting requirements in relation to the licensees (e.g., they had to submit the name of the copyright owner and titles of works used)[69] and CMOs (e.g., when accounting to the other CMOs, they were required to supply a list of names, addresses and website domain names of each party to whom if had granted a license since the previous accounting period).[70] In practice, the Santiago Agreement was to serve as a template contract, allowing bilateral agreements between users and CMOs, whereby an Internet user would seek a worldwide license from the CMO in the territory in which the user's site is installed, thus enabling each CMO to offer the repertoires of third-party CMOs to users (or licensees).[71]

Although the Santiago Agreement seemed to be a step in the right direction, it was fraught with complex practical and legal problems. In May 2004, the European Commission formally objected to the fact that the certain provisions of the Santiago Agreement were anti-competitive and made it impossible for users to select their collective society of choice, and thus the local collective societies had preserved territorial exclusivity.[72] The Santiago Agreement expired at the end of 2004 and was not renewed, in large part because of the issues raised in the investigation by the European Commission.[73] Moreover, although various steps have

---

web-casting, on demand transmission by acts of streaming and downloading and was structured in largely the same manner as the Santiago Agreement.

68. This was covered in the IFPI Simulcasting Agreement, see IFPI, 'Major step forward for internet licensing: IFPI simulcast system wins European Commission approval' (8 Oct. 2002), <www.ifpi.org/content/section_news/20021008h.html> (last accessed: 5 May 2010). According to Mihály Ficsor, the European Commission accorded with the agreement because it felt that the single gateway was in the interest of promoters and the general public; however, two modifications were requested: (1) IFPI had to delete the notion of territorial exclusivity whereby users were obliged to go to the CMO in the territory in which their website was hosted and (2) the agreement had to include a limited form of price competition by showing the society's management fees in the applicable rate so that the promoter could choose the collective society with which he wanted to have a relationship. See Ficsor, WIPO Rights, *supra* n. 11 at 120.

69. Ficsor, WIPO Rights, *supra* n. 11 at 118. This in itself would likely have been problematic because, in the case of musical works, this information may be unknown, hence the phenomena of 'orphan works' or 'unlocatable copyright owners' as it is known in some jurisdictions.

70. Ficsor, WIPO Rights, *supra* n. 11 at 118 and for a detailed account of the Santiago Agreement see 114–120.

71. Piaskowski, France, *supra* n. 64 at 189.

72. Piaskowski, France, *supra* n. 64 at 189. See also, Summary of Commission Decision of 16 Jul. 2008 relating to a proceeding under Art. 81 of the EC Treaty and Art. 53 of the EEA Agreement (Case COMP/C-2/38.698 – CISAC), C(2008) 3435 final), 18 Dec. 2008, available at <http://eur-lex.europa.eu/LexUriServ/LexUriServ.do?uri=OJ:C:2008:323:0012:0013:EN:PDF> (last accessed: 5 May 2010).

73. Bennett Lincoff, 'Common Sense, Accommodation and Sound Policy for the Digital Music Marketplace', Journal of *International Media & Entertainment Law* 2, no. 1 (2008): 1–64 at 25–26 [Common Sense]. See also, 'European Commission Opens Proceeding into Collective Licensing of Music Copyrights for Online Use', (3 May 2004) IP/05/586, <http://europa.eu/rapid/pressReleasesAction.do?reference=IP/04/586&format=HTML&aged=0&language=EN&guiLanguage=en> (last accessed: 5 May 2010). For additional detail on the issues surrounding the Santiago Agreement see Lucie Guibault and Stef van Gompel, Collective Management in the European Union, Ch. 5 at 2.3.2.

been taken by the European Commission and CMOs since 2004, exceptional progress toward achieving a fully functional MTL regime in the EU, and for that matter anywhere else, remains to be seen.[74]

3.1.1 Benefits Derived from the Failure of the Santiago Agreement

Although the Santiago Agreement did not resolve the territorial online licensing issues, it is an excellent learning tool when contemplating how to proceed with the next generation of MTL regimes. First, it highlights the importance of closely considering national or regional laws that may hinder the success of an MTL regime.[75] These may relate to competition law, international treaties or privacy law, to name a few. Second, it demonstrates that the approach taken – building a new regime on inadequate foundation – is problematic. While reciprocal agreements exist between CMOs these agreements have not alone resolved the challenges that MTL aims to rectify. They are indeed familiar to CMOs, which provides a degree of comfort when negotiating terms and conditions for future agreements, but this does not in-and-of-itself guarantee that these agreements are suitable for the online environment. As such, one should consider importing existing agreements at the last stage of the discussion on how to effectively offer an MTL regime, particularly if one is aiming to be 'experimental'. Part III of this paper will elaborate on this point. Finally, the Santiago Agreement signals that there is an existing willingness by some CMOs to find a solution to the licensing and infringement issues via an MTL regime which is encouraging.

3.2 SELLING POINTS

Although CMO participation in MTL regimes to date has been the subject of much criticism, there are many advantages to facilitating online rights clearance through a mechanism that is multi-territorial and administered by CMOs. Not only do licensees benefit from the typical efficiencies of collective management, expertise (licensing 'know-how'), established practices for collection and distribution of

---

74. For an overview relating to Wuropean progress see Lucie Guibault & Stef van Gompel, Collective Management in the European Union, Ch. 5, in Daniel Gervais, *Collective Management of Copyright and Related Rights*, 2nd edn (Kluwer Law International, The Netherlands 2010).

75. The assumption here is that although the Internet is international in scope, a practical solution will have to account for national differences and if so, will result in optimal conditions for development. See WIPO, 'Report on the Online Forum on Intellectual Property in the Information Society, June 1–15, 2005' (19 Sep. 2005), <www.wipo.int/ipisforum/en/> (last visited: 5 May 2010) at 36. David Uwemedimo, 'WCT and WPPT: Opportunities and Challenges', <www.wipo.int/documents/en/meetings/2002/sccr/seminar_05/ppt/cisac_16-05-2002.ppt> (last visited: May 2008).

royalty fees, etc., but they also gain a degree of certainty, or insurance from liability, required to continue on with their content endeavours. Essentially, a global MTL regime administered by CMOs would increase the likelihood that prospective users would seek permission before use because the transaction costs to do so would be greatly reduced from what they are now.

3.2.1 Permission Requests

For both organizational[76] and individual users, MTL increases the likelihood of permission being sought by users.[77] Rather than seeking permission from each CMO in each territory, permission need only be sought from the CMO(s) in one territory. Although MTL does not resolve the problems of fragmentation outlined earlier, it does simplify the most costly aspect of the rights clearance process by creating a one-stop-shop (or perhaps, for the time being, better labelled 'one-territory-shop'). In turn, this may lead to efficiency gains for copyright owners and commercial users alike.[78] What is not necessarily resolved is the fact that these users still need to determine which CMO to approach for what use. Moreover, once determined, users may have to approach a number of CMOs and could require more than one license, as explained in the explanation in Part I regarding fragmentation.[79] This is where the idea of bundled licenses to facilitate a truly one-stop-shop clearance process becomes attractive. This solution should be explored in depth in the future.[80]

3.2.2 Certainty

In general, contracts provide certainty; hence their popularity in the evolving digital marketplace. With certainty, users may carry on their business knowing when they are shielded from liability for copyright infringement and knowing

---

76. For the sake of simplicity, this category would include commercial users, non-profit organizations, etc. Although their needs differ to some extent (e.g., royalty fees may be more of an issue for one than the other), generally they have common interests.
77. Gervais, EU Collective Management, *supra* n. 1 at 27.
78. Mary Mutoro, Laura Donoso, Erla Skuladottir & Daniela Stefanov, 'Collective Right Management in the Digital Environment' (7 May 2007) Stockholm University, Department of Law at 6 [CRM].
79. Gervais, EU Collective Management, *supra* n. 1 at 27.
80. Not least because the 'greatest commercial potential seems to emerge when acquisition of the right is simultaneous with the acquisition of content'. See Daniel Gervais, 'Electronic Rights Management and Digital Identifier Systems', prepared for the advisory committee on management of copyright and related rights in global information networks, WIPO, 23 Nov. 1998, ACMC/1/1, available at the Journal of Electronic Publishing, <http://quod.lib.umich.edu/cgi/t/text/text-idx?c=jep;view=text;rgn=main;idno=3336451.0004.303> (last accessed: 5 May 2010) at 6 [DOI]. This realization would also support an MTL regime established between commercial users and CMOs since this particular user has the capacity to bundle the rights clearance and content for its individual users. In this sense, the MTL regime would have to enable the commercial user to license downstream users to be efficient and effective.

when they are not so as to enable them to conduct more accurate cost-benefit analysis. As a result, they may develop their business model and reap the benefits of the worldwide marketplace currently accessible on the Internet. The challenge these users face and the potential benefits that may result if resolved, have been succinctly described as follows:

> [T] requirement of territory-by-territory management [i]s an impediment to the roll-out of new cross-border online services. Rights-holders state that complications inherent in the licensing process deprive them of online revenue. Online retailers therefore require cross-border or trans-national copyright clearance in line with their international reach and clearance services. These services cannot be provided effectively or efficiently when copyright clearing services remain mostly national in scope. [...] Simple and efficient rights clearance not only enables online service providers to achieve economies and efficiencies of scale, but it also leads to market entry by innovators, the development of new online services and, most importantly, has the potential to increase the revenue stream that flows back to the right-holders.[81]

That said, contracts do not guarantee ultimate certainty or full control of what uses are made of protected content online. Licenses establish a contractual relationship between the licensee and the licensor for certain uses of copyright content; but, in the digital realm, where third party use is common (e.g., in mashups, sampling), these licenses may or may not be able to guarantee full control to the copyright owners or any significant reduction of liability for third party users. Therefore, to enhance certainty, the reality of third party uses should be accounted for in any online MTL regime.[82]

3.2.3 Acknowledging Copyright Owners' Interests

Although the first copyright owner could directly issue multi-territorial licenses, CMO administration is advantageous because the copyright owner need not preoccupy himself with administering his rights to numerous licensees. Transactional licensing can be burdensome and time-consuming, thus detracting from the copyright owners' other responsibilities. In addition, direct licensing may not result in the copyright owner receiving the same amount of remuneration or favourable licensing terms as could be achieved via a CMO. One of the most important advantages copyright owners must consider is in relation to enforcement. By utilizing a CMO to issue MTLs the copyright owner benefits from having an enforcer of his rights. In this case, it would be important to ensure that adequate enforcement measures are established and acknowledged between CMOs in different territories. Indeed, a large part of copyright owners' choice to join a CMO is influenced by the promise of reduced enforcement costs – 'If the institution lowers the cost of

---

81. Lueder, Next Ten, *supra* n. 6 at 19.
82. A further consideration may be the use of DRMs and TPMs to enhance certainty provided that they are applied in an appropriate manner that balances user and copyright owner interests.

exchange and enforcement, it makes sense to join. If not, it is better for each right holder to rely on private enforcement.'[83]

CMOs also benefit from MTLs, particularly because each CMO has the possibility to function as a one-stop-shop, granting a single MTL covering the repertoire of all other CMOs who are a part of the system. This benefit is truly realized when one considers that this licensing information could be used to create a global, centralized database of each CMO's repertoire.[84] This effectively expands the number of issued licenses possible and may help to reduce the number of orphan works in a given territory as more information becomes available.

3.3   DRAWBACKS

The challenges that have arisen, or that are anticipated to arise, for CMOs administering MTL regimes are not unlike those that generally come up in relation to copyright and the Internet. Considering how these issues may arise in the context of this discussion is important because it highlights a practical consideration that must be addressed if CMOs are to be successful in the long term. Perhaps the most effective way to approach this part of the discussion is to look at the shortcomings of the Santiago Agreement and to identify points to take away for subsequent MTL regimes.

Three dominant issues arose from the Santiago Agreement and are considered primary obstacles confronting MTL – the threat of bargain shopping, breaches of competition law and general enforcement issues. These issues naturally occur in the global context of private and possibly public international law; however, the competition issue is typically national or regional and would be of concern predominantly in the EU for the moment.

3.3.1   Bargain Shopping: The Race to the Bottom

In examining the Santiago Agreement one realizes that there was a degree of concern that licensing requests would gravitate toward the territories with the most favourable licensing climate. This is not explicitly stated in the agreement; however, certain provisions, particularly those that dictate in which territory a user must seek a license, seem to imply this to be the case. Professor Ginsburg has made a particularly helpful comment that is not aimed at addressing MTL but is nonetheless applicable and worth citing in full:

> Given the effects of digital communications, maybe the only fixed point in all of this is the Author. For example, we might address the country of origin

---

83.   Robert P. Merges, 'Contracting into Liability Rules: Intellectual Property Rights and Collective Rights Organizations', *California Law Review* 84, no. 5 (1996): 1293–1393 at 1324–1325.
84.   Efforts to achieve such a database have been underway for some time as demonstrated by CISAC's initiative to establish a Common Information System (CIS). See CISAC, 'Bringing Societies Onboard CIS-Net' (19 Mar. 2008) at, <www.cisac.org/CisacPortal/listeArticle. do?numArticle=855&> (last visited: May 2008) [CIS].

problem by making that country the country of the author's residence at time of the work's first public disclosure. We might make the law of the Author's residence competent to adjudicate claims of copyright ownership. And we might make that law the one that governs multi-territorial infringements. An obvious objection to this proposal is that it will promote a peculiar variant of what American conflicts scholars call the race to the bottom. That is, that persons subject to the law's regulation will seek the most forgiving jurisdiction possible, such as, in financial matters, the Cayman Islands. The variant here would be the opposite: authors will flock to the jurisdiction offering the most author favorable norms. Perhaps, but is that such a bad thing? Worse things could happen than that nation-states would compete to attract authors to their shores.[85]

Indeed, worse things could happen. Enabling potential licensees to approach any CMO in any territory for a license elevates the global level of competitiveness between CMOs. It may also lead to an increase in 'value-added' services in which, for example, licensees are offered a 'better deal' with more 'perks'. Such a system would certainly ensure that the business nature of CMOs was emphasized, although this may not be preferable because it could detract from the aura of natural justice that sometimes shrouds CMOs rooted in civil law traditions. Nonetheless, the allure of convenience and perks must not be underestimated because it seems unlikely that individual users would stray farther than need be to find the best licensing deals, whereas sophisticated commercial users may be more apt to do so. Yet there is an argument to be made that CMOs in national markets with linguistic barriers and limited size could suffer from serious competitive disadvantages and possibly dissolve or amalgamate with other CMOs in their territory.[86] This may not be a negative outcome, although rendering a definitive conclusion at this point would be presumptuous, is beyond the scope of this chapter and requires more careful social and economic analysis.

3.3.2   Enforcement

The ability to enforce MTL provisions is essential if an MTL regime is going to dissuade user infringement. MTL raises a number of enforcement issues, particularly because of the multi-jurisdictional nature of transmissions and uses online that exacerbate 'traditional conflict of laws problems and put to the test most of the frameworks of private international law adjudication'.[87]

---

85. Jane Ginsburg, 'Berne without Borders: Geographic Indiscretion and Digital Communications (Stephen Stewart Memorial Lecture, Intellectual Property Institute London U.K., Oct. 29, 2001)' (November 2001) Columbia Law School, Pub Law Research Paper No. 01-30, available at SSRN, <http://ssrn.com/abstract=292010> (last accessed: 5 May 2010) at 13 [Without Borders].
86. European Commission, Accompanying Document, *supra* n. 73 at 7.
87. Kimberly A. Moore and Francesco Parisi, 'Rethinking Forum Shopping in Cyberspace', *Chicago-Kent Law Review* 77, no. 3 (2002): 1325–1358, SSRN, <http://ssrn.com/abstract_id=297100> (last accessed: 5 May 2010) at 1326.

As Professor Goldstein explains, a country's prescriptive competence to enforce its laws ends at its borders.[88] For this reason,

> More nettlesome cases for the territoriality principle arise where acts of copyright infringement occur in more than one country, where one element of an infringement occurs in one country and another occurs in a second country, and where the extraterritorial acts bear not on infringement but on the existence of copyright.[89]

It has been suggested that a new international instrument, such as the Anti-Counterfeiting Trade Agreement (ACTA), might help with jurisdictional issues arising from different national copyright laws; however, this will not likely be achieved in short order.[90] Thus, CMOs, copyright owners and content users must manage enforcement issues in the existing system. This means that to facilitate the enforcement of multi-territorial license provisions, CMOs have one of two options. First they may do nothing, and leave questions of enforcement to be determined on a case-by-case basis according to private international norms and rules. In contrast, CMOs may decide to include specific provisions that establish which courts will have jurisdiction over enforcement issues, which country's legal rules will apply and how these judgments will be enforced in other jurisdictions.[91] Of course, they may also support international state efforts to enhance international copyright enforcement, but as a rule this takes time and may not result in the desired outcome.[92]

It is beyond the scope of this paper to offer an in-depth analysis on how private international law issues might be resolved; however, it is important that these issues are noted and given serious consideration when establishing an MTL regime.[93] Included in these considerations is the effect such provisions might have

---

88. Paul Goldstein, *International Copyright: Principles, Law, and Practice* (New York: Oxford University Press, 2001), at 65 [International Copyright]. Goldstein is, of course, referring to the territorial principle here.
89. Goldstein, International Copyright, *supra* n. 88 at 66.
90. Jane Ginsburg, 'International Copyright: From a "Bundle" of National Copyright Laws to a Supranational Code?' (June 2000) *The Journal of the Copyright Society of the United States*, available at SSRN, <http://ssrn.com/abstract=222508> (last accessed: 5 May 2010).
91. Private international law (i.e., conflicts of laws) is essentially concerned with three questions: (1) whether a court in one jurisdiction has the power to deal with a case at all; (2) What jurisdiction's legal rules will apply to courts deciding conflicts cases; and (3) how judgments in one jurisdiction will be enforced in another jurisdiction. See C.M.V. Clarkson & Jonathan Hill, *Jaffey on the Conflicts of Laws*, 2nd edn (London: Butterworths, 2002), at 1–3.
92. For more on enforcement, see Tanya Woods, 'Copyright Enforcement at All Costs?: Why Compliance Will Never Be Achieved This Way', *AIPLA Quarterly Journal* 37, no. 3 (Summer 2009): 347–393.
93. For in-depth analysis on conflicts issues relating to copyright material online, see Jane Ginsburg, 'Private International Law Aspects of the Protection of Works and Objects of Related Rights Transmitted Through Digital Networks (2000 Update)' WIPO Forum on Private International Law and Intellectual Property, 30–31 Jan. 2001, WIPO/PIL/01/2; Andre Lucas, 'Private International Law Aspects of the Protection of Works and Objects of Related Rights Transmitted Over Digital Networks' WIPO Forum on Private International Law and Intellectual

for users, particularly when CMOs are seeking out the most favourable terms to meet their own interests. A balanced solution having regard for both sets of interests is preferable, although perhaps not plausible. With this goal in mind, it is considered vital that MTL provisions provide alternative dispute resolution (ADR) mechanisms that are less litigious, thereby increasing the likelihood that an MTL regime remain user-friendly.

When considering how to apply MTL in the EU, the EC noted its preference for ADR because it was more flexible than going to court; better at meeting the needs of both consumers and professionals; and is cheaper, quicker and more informal than court proceedings, which means they are an attractive mechanism for consumers seeking redress.[94] In promoting the adoption of ADR, the EC has published two Recommendations (Recommendation 98/257/EC and the 2001 Commission Recommendation);[95] established a quality criterion that each ADR scheme should offer to its users; proposed a European Directive on Mediation in Civil and Commercial Matters that aims to ensure a sound relationship between the mediation process and judicial proceedings by establishing common EU rules on a number of key aspects of civil procedure;[96] and enabled the European Consumer Centres Network (ECC-Net)[97] to provide consumers with information and assistance in accessing an appropriate ADR scheme in another Member State.[98] ADR should not be expected to resolve all enforcement issues, and it may need to be supported by the application of other technical measures, but it is nevertheless important.

3.3.3 Competition

The reason for addressing this final challenge in an international context is two-fold: first, it informs us that a global strategy must be compatible with territorial or

---

Property, 30–31 Jan. 2001, WIPO/PIL/01/1; Graeme Austin, 'Private International Law and Intellectual Property Rights A Common Law Overview' WIPO Forum on Private International Law and Intellectual Property, 30–31 Jan. 2001, WIPO/PIL/01/5 (all available at, <www.wipo.int/meetings/en/details.jsp?meeting_id=4243> (last accessed: 5 May 2010); Jane Ginsburg, 'Extraterritoriality and Multiterritoriality in Copyright Infringement', *Virginia Journal of International Law* 37 (1996–1997): 587–602; and Ginsburg, Without Borders, *supra* n. 85.

94. European Commission, Accompanying Document, *supra* n. 73 at 28.
95. 'Commission Recommendation of 30 March 1998 on the principles applicable to the bodies responsible for out-of-court settlement of consumer disputes', 98/257/EC, <http://eur-lex.europa.eu/smartapi/cgi/sga_doc?smartapi!celexapi!prod!CELEXnumdoc&lg=EN&numdoc=31998H0257&model=guichett> (last accessed: 5 May 2010) and 'Commission Recommendation of 4 Apr. 2001, on the principles for out-of-court bodies involved in the consensual resolution of consumer Disputes', 2001/310/EC, <http://ec.europa.eu/consumers/redress/out_of_court/adr/acce_just12_en.pdf> (last accessed: 5 May 2010), respectively.
96. This proposal has now been upgraded to a Directive, which was passed on 23 Apr. 2008. See 'Mediation in civil and commercial matters', MEMO/08/263, Brussels, 23 Apr. 2008, <http://europa.eu/rapid/pressReleasesAction.do?reference=MEMO/08/263&format=HTML&aged=0&language=EN&guiLanguage=en> (last accessed: 5 May 2010).
97. Factsheet, January 2008, <http://ec.europa.eu/consumers/publications/factsheet-ECC-Net_en.pdf> (last accessed: 5 May 2010).
98. European Commission, Accompanying Document, *supra* n. 73 at 28.

regional legislation, and second, it highlights the importance of considering users and copyright owners' ability to have choices in an MTL regime.

Licensing, the primary activity of CMOs, is closely linked to and, when necessary, governed by competition law, particularly law in the EU.[99] In Europe, the EC and the European Court of Justice have consistently found that CMOs hold 'a dominant, if not monopolistic, position in the rights licensing market in their national territory'.[100] The CMOs themselves are considered to have created this system by dividing the market for rights management services territorially amongst themselves, by concluding with other collecting societies bilateral reciprocal agreements and by giving each other the right to grant in their territories licenses to the repertoire of the other.[101] However, in the past this system was justified, 'at least in the case of offline performing rights because they were seen as an effective means through which the use of licensed music in performing rights could be monitored and thus provided valuable protection'.[102]

In 2004, the EC expressed a number of concerns over the various clauses in the Santiago Agreement that were considered anti-competitive.[103] The 'economic residency' clause was particularly problematic because it required potential licensees to seek the multi-territorial license from the CMO in the country where the content provider has its actual economic location.[104] The European Commission's concern was that each national CMO maintains absolute exclusivity for its territory in respect of the granting of multi-territorial licenses for online music rights.[105] The application of EU competition law to CMOs has been criticized as being out of date, applicable in the analogue, non-networked environment, but not yet adapted to the realities of the new digital, networked environment.[106] Regardless, it resulted in a serious impediment to the implementation of a necessary MTL regime and emphasizes that it must be considered in future licensing models.

---

99. Mutoro, Donoso, Skuladottir & Stefanov, CRM, *supra* n. 77 at 12. The specific provisions of the EC Treaty relating to CMOs are Arts 81 and 82, European Union, Consolidated Versions of the Treaty on European Union and of the Treaty Establishing the European Community, OJ/ C321, 29 Dec. 2006, <http://eur-lex.europa.eu/LexUriServ/LexUriServ.do?uri=OJ:C:2006: 321E:0001:0331:EN:pdf> (last accessed: 5 May 2010) at 73–74.
100. Vinje & Niiranen, EU Competition, *supra* n. 23 at 4. See also, Frederic Jenny, 'EC Competition Law Enforcement and Collecting Societies for Music Rights: What Are We Aiming For?' (2005) European University Institute, Robert Schuman Centre for Advanced Studies, EU Competition Law and Policy Workshop/Proceedings, <www.eui.eu/RSCAS/Research/ Competition/2005(papers).html> (last accessed: May 2008). See also, Guibault & Gompel, Ch. 5, part 2.
101. Vinje & Niiranen, EU Competition, *supra* n. 23 at 4.
102. Mutoro, Donoso, Skuladottir & Stefanov, CRM, *supra* n. 77 at 12.
103. Margreet Groenenboom, 'Improving cross border licensing practices for online music stores', (27 Sep. 2005) Indicare Project, <www.indicare.org/tiki-read_article.php?articleId=139> (last accessed: 5 May 2010) [Improving].
104. Groenenboom, Improving, *supra* n. 103.
105. Groenenboom, Improving, *supra* n. 103.
106. Vinje & Niiranen, EU Competition, *supra* n. 23 at 1.

A final point of note arising from EU competition issues is not generated from the Santiago Agreement but from the *Daft Punk* case.[107] Daft Punk, a techno-music group, complained to the EC that SACEM was in breach of Article 82 by refusing to allow the group to retain some of their rights for individual management. In response, the Commission opined that due to technological advances, prohibitions on individual management rights were not 'absolutely necessary', and so infringed competition laws. SACEM subsequently modified its membership rules and made 'individual management of specific rights possible as a derogation from the general rule of collective management of all rights'.[108] The result of this case may be taken to emphasize the importance of allowing affiliated copyright owners to regain some control over their rights for the purpose of exploiting them when CMOs cannot meet their needs. This is an important consideration to account for if an MTL regime potentially stifles an affiliate's capacity to better exploit his rights.

4   MOVING FORWARD . . . CREATIVELY STEPPING OUTSIDE OF THE BOX

Historically, when a new medium for dissemination (e.g., radio, television, cable, satellite) entered the marketplace, copyright was not used to prevent use, but rather to regulate and organize markets.[109] The advent of the Internet marks perhaps the most significant establishment of a new medium, enabling vast uses of copyright works to date. The difference is that copyright law is not being used to organize the Internet market; rather, it is being, and has been for many years, used to simply to deny it.[110] For CMOs, the lack of a practical remedy has meant that they are increasingly perceived as part of the problem by inhibiting novel solutions.[111]

In reality, CMOs' efforts to find a MTL solution have not ceased since the abandonment of the Santiago Agreement. For example, in April, 2007, the International Federation for Phonographic Industry (IFPI) announced that it and various European-based sound recording rights collecting societies had put into place a framework for collective licensing of sound recordings for certain streaming and podcast services across several territories.[112] To date, however, there is still no satisfactory broad-scale resolution to the problems outlined thus far. This section aims to highlight important considerations that must be made going forward if CMOs are to achieve a practical resolution to their demonstrated incompatibilities with the digital environment. Thus, emphasis in the following section is

---

107. Commission Decision of 12 Aug. 2002, Case C2/37.219 *Banghalter & Honem Christo/ SACEM* [*Daft Punk*].
108. Vinje & Niiranen, EU Competition, *supra* n. 23 at 6–7 in reference to *Daft Punk, supra* n. x.
109. Gervais, EU Collective Management, *supra* n. 1 at 8.
110. *Ibid.*
111. Mutoro, Donoso, Skuladottir & Stefanov, CRM, *supra* n. 77 at 7.
112. IFPI, 'Major Step Forward in Cross Border Music Licensing Regime' (27 Apr. 2007), available at <www.ifpi.org/content/section_news/20070427.html> (last accessed: 5 May 2010).

placed on encouraging clarity, cooperation and creativity by relinquishing some control and aiming for consistent practices.

4.1   CLARITY

The first consideration that must be made when contemplating a new business model is to identify the target user. Until the early nineties, this would have been a simple task because copyright was seen largely as a commercial or professional issue. As technology advanced, the reach of copyright regulation expanded beyond the early book publishers to a broader category of users and authors, which may be one and the same.[113] The current challenges facing individual end-users results from the fact that copyright was not meant to exclude their uses. Moreoever, as we have seen, trying to make copyright fit that job description is unlikely to work and denatures the underlying policy.[114] For this reason, it is strongly suggested that an MTL regime build in third-party licensing provisions to reduce the likelihood that an individual end-user will have to seek a license for their uses. That said, excluding individual end-users in the licensing process is difficult given the level of interactivity online that enables these users to also be creators (and possibly copyright owners). Public policy makers are starting to consider ways to deal with user-generated content; however, no definitive solution has been implemented as of yet. For this reason, it should be assumed that this new user group is not as sophisticated or well versed in the complex intricacies of copyright as traditional commercial users might be. Relying on clear and simple language increases the likelihood of compliance simply by increasing the ability of users to understand and appreciate what they can and cannot do, thus supporting a conclusion that for any MTL regime (or any online licensing solution) to work it must be clear and easy to understand, in other words, user-friendly. As the Right Honourable Beverley McLachlin, Chief Justice of the Supreme Court of Canada, once said, 'it does not serve the courts, the public or the profession to persist with language that only lawyers can understand'.[115]

The effectiveness of a simplistic licensing process is demonstrated by the global success of CC licenses.[116] The CC user interface relies on clear

---

113. Lawerence Lessig, *Free Culture* (New York: Penguin, 2004), at 139. The regulation of users as authors is particularly apparent if one considers authors of derivative works and user-generated content. See also, Stephen M. Cherry, 'Getting Copyright Right' (February 2002) IEEE Spectrum at 47–55 at 47.

114. Daniel Gervais, (Ch. 18) 'Use of Copyright Content on the Internet: Considerations on Excludability and Collective Licensing', in *In the Public Interest*, ed. Michael Geist (Toronto: Irwin Law, 2005), 517–549 at 524–525, and in Gervais, Collective Management, *supra* n. 1 at 8. The policy being based on the 'fundamental nature of intellectual property' that balances 'social welfare and revenue generation with equally important objectives and rights, especially when access to knowledge, information and culture is at stake'.

115. The Right Honourable B McLachlin, 'Legal Writing: Some Tools', *Clarity* 51 (2004): 5, <www.clarity-international.net/journals/default.htm> (last accessed: 5 May 2010).

116. Creative Commons, <www.creativecommons.org> (last accessed: 5 May 2010).

terminology, basic symbols and plain language to explain the licensing process to both licensees and licensors. The CC model is compatible with many of today's digital uses and for this reason should be considered as an instructive starting point for CMOs considering adapting their practices to better suit individual commercial users. CC is not without faults, nor is it employable *holus bolus* for commercial uses, particularly because it is not designed as a commercial licensing model.[117] Similarly, the BBC Archives license, developed as a pilot project to offer BBC content online to UK residents at no cost, also exemplifies how one might clearly license uses of protected online content to individuals.[118] Both of these models have a common weakness, which is that they are territorially based and so would have to be modified for to accommodate an MTL regime. That said, they take the right approach for new media creators and users – they are clear, simple to understand and permit uses of copyright material to be made online by individuals.

4.2   COOPERATION

It has been said that 'innovation is the primary means through which both the creative rights and technology industries come to understand and benefit from increasing user demand'.[119] This mutual benefit would seem to suggest that copyright owners (or their representatives are well suited to have a relationship with copyright content distributors and that such a relationship promises to be mutually beneficial if carried out accordingly.

With respect to the availability of content in emerging online markets, 'stakeholders are expected to find innovative and collaborative solutions to exploit content online and prevent or remedy bundling, exclusivity or non-use of media rights'.[120] Some licensing solutions that have been designed and implemented to work with online technologies include direct licensing,[121] ISP level licensing[122] and open licensing.[123] Although these solutions have not been widely adopted,

---

117. Niva Elkin-Koren, 'Creative Commons: A Skeptical View of A Worthy Pursuit', in *The Future of the Public Domain*, ed. P. Bernt Hugenholtz & Lucie Guibault (The Hague: Kluwer Law International, 2006), <http://papers.ssrn.com/sol3/papers.cfm?abstract_id=885466> (last accessed: 5 May 2010).
118. BBC Archives, <http://creativearchive.bbc.co.uk/archives/for_download/> (last accessed: 5 May 2010).
119. Trouve & Page, Equity, *supra* n. 42 at 1.
120. European Commission, 'Communication from the Commission to the European Parliament, The Council, The European Economic and Social Committee and the Committee of the Regions on Creative Content Online in the Single Market', Brussels, COM (2007) 836 final, {SEC(2007) 1710} at 5 (footnotes omitted).
121. Direct licensing is when the content owner or provider licenses directly with the end user. Apple iTunes is an example of this. See <www.apple.com/itunes> (last accessed: 5 May 2010).
122. This is when copyright owners license ISPs to disseminate content to users. In this model the user would pay a fee to the ISP. Noank Media engages in this type of licensing. See <www.noankmedia.com> (last accessed: 5 May 2010).
123. An open license is a copyright license for computer software that makes the source code available under terms that allow for modification and redistribution without having to pay

they do indicate that there are feasible alternatives to the traditional licensing model with which CMOs are familiar. For this reason, CMOs must think like new media entrepreneurs and be creative and willing to abandon, at least in part, their traditional business models and political agendas to remain relevant.

Partnerships between CMOs and content providers appear to be a viable approach to help facilitate MTL. In 2006, MCPS-PRS Alliance announced that together with EMI they had arrived at an agreement to work toward the creation of a 'one-stop shop' to clear the rights of EMI's Anglo-American songs in Europe for mobile and online music.[124] In 2007, Radiohead released its album 'In Rainbows' in this one-stop-shop format.[125] The album was successfully downloaded more than one million times and has since inspired similar initiatives from other groups like Nine Inch Nails, Metallica and Coldplay.[126] Although the involvement of CMOs in these endeavours is not immediately obvious to downloaders, it is nonetheless essential for these projects to work, given that in many cases CMOs hold the exclusive rights. MTL on a project-by-project basis is not ideal because it requires a lot of time and is less efficient than a universal MTL regime would be. Nevertheless, the mentioned projects demonstrate that creative partnerships are feasible. In relation to the development of a successful online MTL regime, these partnerships are crucial, not least because they join new media 'know-how' with licensing expertise in a way that meets users' needs.

In attempting to create partnerships it may be determined that it is easier to license content providers rather than individual users. This point has been raised a few times throughout this paper. It is also a growing trend and is worthy of additional consideration, albeit somewhat off topic.[127] As we have seen, clearing rights for online content generally requires extensive licensing efforts. It appears to be

---

the original author. Creative Commons relies on this type of licensing (Wikipedia). Brian Fitzgerald, 'Copyright 2010: The Future of Copyright' *European Intellectual Property Review* 2 (2008): 43–49 at 47.

124. Mutoro, Donoso, Skuladottir & Stefanov, CRM, *supra* n. 77 at 11 (footnotes omitted).

125. Richard Driver, 'Warner Chappell launches custom licensing model for Radiohead's "In Rainbows"' (11 Dec. 2007), Blogging Stocks, <www.bloggingstocks.com/2007/12/11/warner-chappell-launches-new-licensing-model-for-radiohead-album/> (last accessed: 5 May 2010); David Byrne, 'David Byrne's Survival Strategies for Emerging Artists – and Megastars' (18 Dec. 2007) Wired, <www.wired.com/entertainment/music/magazine/16-01/ff_byrne?currentPage=4> (last accessed: 5 May 2010); 'Billboard Exclusive, Radiohead's One-Stop Solution' (15 Dec. 2007), available at Penny Distribution, <http://pennydistribution.wordpress.com/2008/01/06/radiohead-and-in-rainbows-pushing-the-boundaries-in-publishing-too/> (last accessed: 5 May 2010).

126. 'Metallica to do a Radiohead?: Band hint at a future Internet release' (25 Apr. 2008) *NME News*, <www.nme.com/news/metallica/36217> and Mimi Turner, 'Radiohead says no more music freebies' (Tuesday 29 Apr. 2008) *Reuters*, <www.reuters.com/article/entertainmentNews/idUSN2937610420080430> (last accessed: 5 May 2010). The latter article notes that Radiohead's album sales topped both the US and UK charts, despite the fact that it was offered as a free download before the release of the CD.

127. See 'WMG funds project to monetize file-sharing by offering blanket licences to ISPs' (18 Apr. 2008) 364 *Music and Copyright* at 1. Warner Music Group is funding Jim Griffen to investigate the possibility of making licensing agreements with ISPs and others in the chain of services that enable P2P file-sharing.

unreasonable to expect individual users to determine who they need permission from for the use of a particular fragment because the copyright system is not designed to meet their needs. Licensing to content providers directly reduces the burden on individual users and may be the most efficient way to ensure that individual uses are lawful. If not, copyright owners need to consider who will be the main point of contact for individual licensees – the content provider or CMOs.

4.3   CONTROL

Efficient online management will enable multiple licenses to be issued in a minimal amount of time. Effective licenses meet users' needs and allow them to use copyright content in the ways they want. This also means that copyright owners agree with these uses and are compensated accordingly. An efficient and effective licensing regime must take into consideration national exceptions and limitations to copyright, as well as other important legislative provisions such as the duration of copyright protection in different territories. This not only builds the credibility of the licensor but it also fosters the licensees' trust in the MTL system.

There is, however, mounting concern over the unwillingness to provide efficient and effective online licensing. This is problematic because,

> When rights holders refuse to make licenses available for digital uses of their works, or only authorize activities of a very limited scope, or are unable to make licenses available in a timely manner, or charge license fees that are beyond the means of all but the most highly financed service providers, compliance is only possible by those who either forego the use of copyrighted music or cease doing business altogether.[128]

Copyright owners, particularly CMOs, must be flexible and willing to accept a lesser degree of control in the online environment. Where affiliated authors belonging to a CMO wish to regain some control for the purpose of exploiting their rights in a new way a CMO should be obliging, particularly when the CMO cannot achieve the same results. Vinje and Niranen expand on this point noting that,

> Among the most harmful of collecting societies practices in the digital environment is the imposition by the societies of strict exclusivity requirements on their members"[129] In practice this means that "a member of collecting society is effectively prevented from managing on-line usage of his repertoire through several collecting societies, from self-managing his on-line rights, and from delegating on-line rights management to any entity other than a collecting society. This also means that on-line music providers have no source for

---

128. Lincoff, Common Sense, *supra* n. 73 at 22.
129. Vinje & Niiranen, EU Competition, *supra* n. 23 at 5.

on-line music rights other than collecting societies, which reduces significantly the opportunity for on-line music providers to obtain competitive and innovative licence terms.[130]

A final point of note is that many affiliation agreements were established before the digital age and thus often do not include provisions for online exploitation. Thus, where there is uncertainty as to whether a CMO has been assigned digital rights, the CMO should inform the copyright owners and allow them to choose whether they want the CMO to manage these rights. This act alone may be considered a step toward increased transparency of CMO administration – something that is often seen as lacking.[131]

4.4   CONSISTENCY

Establishing a successful MTL regime requires consistent practices between CMOs and online stakeholders. The problem MTL addresses is a global problem beyond the boundaries of territories, types of works and categorizations of rights. For this reason CMOs must work together if they are to regain control over copyright material online. In turn, they will be better able to assimilate their practices and enhance their collective ability to meet licensees' needs.

To achieve the utopic global one-stop-shop, CMOs managing rights for all types of works (artistic, musical, performance, literary) need to collaborate with one another and develop a common information database. Such a system has been conceptualized in the past and perhaps is closer to being realized than ever before.[132] This system would standardize the types of information required by CMOs to issue licenses. What results is a large database that can be relied upon to support an online MTL regime for all CMOs regardless of the territory where they are located. This system promises to resolve much of the traditional delay, provided that all CMOs or most CMOs agree to use it.

CISAC, in particular, has been working on the development of its Common Information System (CIS). CISAC's CIS project is designed to rectify the lack of sufficient standardization and the lack of an appropriate infrastructure for sharing rights management information. The project began in 1994, and by 2000 great progress had been made. It was this momentum that generated a 'Fast Track' alliance between five of the larger CMOs – SACEM (France), GEMA (Germany), SGAE (Spain), SIAE (Italy) and BMI (USA). The alliance connected the information of these societies in a decentralized but harmonized structure, guaranteeing that, along with pursuing common goals, the societies may still maintain their independence and special features corresponding to the legal and cultural traditions

---

130. *Ibid.*
131. Lincoff, Common Sense, *supra* n. 73 at 44–46 and 60; and Vinje & Niiranen, EU Competition, *supra* n. 23 at 14.
132. Gervais, DOI, *supra* n. 79 and CISAC, CIS, *supra* n. 83.

of their respective countries.[133] Other joint programmes of authors' societies have also been launched for the purpose of the development of electronic systems for exchange of information and joint databases such as LATINAUTOR and MIS@-ASIA.[134] However, these systems have not demonstrated the truly unified approach required to achieve global success with an MTL regime.

The creation of standardized Internet licensing terms would also enhance the consistency of MTL practices. If adopted, these terms would be flexible to accommodate copyright owners' needs and interests, but standardized enough to be of value to users by simplifying rights clearance, thus leading to a higher degree of copyright compliance.[135] The question is really who would establish these terms. The suggestion has been that this is a task for WIPO; however, a broader dialogue needs to be facilitated between all CMOs, copyright owners, content providers and, given the challenges addressed in Part II, willing state representatives.[136]

5   CONCLUSION

This chapter endeavours to demonstrate that the adoption of MTL by CMOs could simplify copyright licensing for both copyright owners and Internet users in a mutually beneficial way. As we know, neither copyright nor its administration was intended to manage multi-territorial uses in the way that technology now allows. For this reason, much work is being done at the international, regional and national levels to find a solution that practically resolves the challenges that have arisen from the use of copyright material online. Examining models such as the Santiago Agreement is important because they highlight essential considerations that need to be accounted for by CMOs, or any licensing body for that matter, if MTL is going to be successful in the future.

---

133. Ficsor, WIPO Rights, *supra* n. 11 at 104.
134. *Ibid.*
135. Gervais, SILTS, *supra* n. 46 at 3–4.
136. In this respect it should be noted that in the EU, Austria, Finland and Portugal arranged Presidency Conferences to address online issues in relation to audiovisual content and competition in the online environment. The Commission has also undertaken a number of initiatives including the i2010 Initiative, the High Level Group on Digital Rights Management (DRM), Film Online and Digital Libraries Initiative and has conducted a public consultation process in 2006 in response to its communication entitled 'Content Online in the Single Market', which generated more than 175 written contributions. See, respectively, European Commission, Accompanying Document, *supra* n. 73 at 4–6; Communication from the Commission to the Council, the European Parliament, the European Economic and Social committee and the Committee of the Regions – 'i2010 – A European Information Society for growth and employment' (COM(2005) 229 final) <http://ec.europa.eu/information_society/eeurope/2005/all_about/digital_rights_man/high_levelgroup/index_en.htm> (last accessed: May 2008). On 30 Sep. 2005, the European Commission adopted 'i2010: Digital Libraries' (COM(2005) 465 final), <http://ec.europa.eu/information_society/activities/digital_libraries/index_en.htm> (last accessed: 5 May 2010). Communication 'i2010: Digital Libraries' (COM(2005) 465 final).

Looking at the historical approach taken by CMOs in general, and specifically in relation to MTL, demonstrates that a new approach is necessary if copyright content is to be efficiently and effectively managed online. As we have seen, CMOs have a great depth of expertise, which is an asset when developing a new licensing model. However, it must not artificially distort the realities of the online environment – where users can and will prioritize popularity, participation and use over copyright.

Efforts must be made to balance online content providers' need for MTL and 'one-stop-shops' with the need for copyright owners to be allowed to fully realize the potential of their economic rights in relation to uses they deem acceptable. Thus, CMOs must expand their traditionally restrictive approach to licensing by injecting more clarity into the process, cooperating with users, finding creative or unconventional solutions, relinquishing some control over the way content is used and, perhaps above all else, abandoning their habit of not globally working together.

Chapter 5

Collective Management in the European Union

Lucie Guibault* and Stef van Gompel**

1 INTRODUCTION

With the rapid growth of the Internet and mobile telephone use, the market for legitimate music delivery services has literally exploded in recent years. Online music services are accessible across the European Union (EU); thus the need for multi-territorial licensing that spans throughout the European territory is more acute than ever. In the absence of such licensing schemes, online content providers must currently obtain a license from every collective rights management organization (CMO) in each territory of the EU in which the work is accessible, so as to avoid liability for copyright infringement. Rights clearance for the exploitation of non-domestic repertoire must therefore occur via a network of reciprocal representation arrangements between CMOs that in most cases occupy a monopoly position within their national territory. This system has been criticized as expensive and burdensome for online users of copyright protected material. Although the multi-territorial licensing of (online) music is at this time the most pressing issue at the European level, it emphasizes the need for a coherent system of collective

*   (LL.M. Montréal, LL.D. Amsterdam) Senior researcher at the Institute for Information Law (IViR), University of Amsterdam.
** (LL.M. *cum laude*, Amsterdam) PhD candidate at the Institute for Information Law (IViR), University of Amsterdam.

Daniel Gervais (ed.), *Collective Management of Copyright and Related Rights*, pp. 135–167.
© 2010 Kluwer Law International BV, The Netherlands.

rights management as a whole.[1] The role and functioning of CMOs in the exploitation of copyright-protected works in Europe therefore stands under the close scrutiny of European lawmakers and stakeholders with a view to developing solutions for the licensing of the aggregate repertoire of works administered by all European societies.[2]

To improve the flow of cross-border licensing of copyright-protected works, the idea has been put forward that the market for collective management of rights be liberalized for right owners and users. The proponents of this solution argue that the most effective model for achieving multi-territorial licensing of legitimate online music would be to enable right holders to authorize a CMO of their choice to manage their works across the entire EU. Similarly, users should also be able to obtain a license from any society within the EU, even if located outside of the user's territory of economic residency.[3] In principle, increased competition between CMOs should be beneficial for both authors and users because the organizations would have to compete on the basis of their economic efficiency, transparency and accountability.[4]

Whether such a liberalization of the market is indeed the best solution to the problems of cross-border licensing of copyright-protected works is a highly disputed issue. Some steps have been taken in this direction, however, most notably through the Recommendation on collective cross-border management of copyright and related rights for legitimate online music services[5] and the decision of the European Commission in the CISAC case.[6] These two documents have put the European market for the collective management of rights in turmoil, especially

1. See: *Commission Decision of 16 July 2008 relating to a proceeding under Article 81 of the EC Treaty and Article 53 of the EEA Agreement (Case COMP/C2/38.698 – CISAC)*, C (2008) 3435 final, Brussels, 16 Jul. 2008, online: <http://ec.europa.eu/competition/antitrust/cases/decisions/38698/en.pdf> (last visited: 5 Jan. 2010), also reported in: [2009] 4 *Common Market Law Reports* 12 [*CISAC* decision]; *Commission Decision 2003/300/EC of 8 October 2002 relating to a proceeding under Article 81 of the EC Treaty and Article 53 of the EEA Agreement (Case No COMP/C2/38.014 – IFPI 'Simulcasting')*, O.J. L. 107/58 of 30 Apr. 2003, online: <http://eur-lex.europa.eu/LexUriServ/LexUriServ.do?uri=OJ:l:2003:107:0058:0084:en:PDF> (last visited: 5 Jan. 2010) [*IFPI Simulcasting* decision].
2. L. Guibault, 'A quand l'octroi de licences transfrontières pour l'utilisation de droits d'auteur et de droits voisins en Europe?', *Les Cahiers de Propriété Intellectuelle*, vol. 16, 2004-HS (Hors série): 189–208.
3. European Commission, *Notice published pursuant to Article 27(4) of Council Regulation (EC) No 1/2003 in Cases COMP/C2/39152 – BUMA and COMP/C2/39151 SABAM (Santiago Agreement – COMP/C2/38126)*, O.J. C. 200/11 of 17 Aug. 2005, <http://eur-lex.europa.eu/LexUriServ/LexUriServ.do?uri=OJ:C:2005:200:0011:0012:EN:PDF> (last visited: 5 Jan. 2010).
4. For an article expressing doubt on this point, see P.B. Hugenholtz, 'Is concurrentie tussen rechtenorganisaties wenselijk?', AMI (2003): 203, at 205.
5. *Commission Recommendation 2005/737/EC on Collective Cross-Border Management of Copyright and Related Rights for Legitimate Online Music Services*, O.J. L. 276/54 of 21 Oct. 2005, <http://eur-lex.europa.eu/LexUriServ/site/en/oj/2005/l_276/l_27620051021en00540057.pdf> (last visited: 5 Jan. 2010) [Online Music Recommendation].
6. CISAC decision, *supra* n. 1.

because stakeholders cannot fall back on any harmonized rules on good governance of CMOs.

Although the creation at the European level of a level playing field for CMOs has been an item on the European Commission's agenda at least since the publication of the Green Paper of 1995,[7] the *acquis communautaire* regulating the activities of CMOs remains rather sparse. Up until recently, the core of the *acquis* was composed of the decisions rendered on the basis of the European rules on competition. Over time, the European Court of Justice (ECJ) and the European Commission have developed an impressive body of jurisprudence putting the alleged anti-competitive behaviour of CMOs to the test of the European competition rules.[8] These were previously laid down in Articles 81 and 82 of the EC Treaty (TEC) and are currently provided for in Articles 101 and 102 of the Treaty on the Functioning of the European Union (TFEU).[9] In addition to the European competition law jurisprudence, efforts toward the establishment of a regulatory framework for CMOs have intensified in the past years, as evidenced by a number of documents issued by the European Parliament and the Commission.[10] Whereas the initial intention was to establish principles of good governance within CMOs, the preoccupations of the European lawmakers have now moved towards resolving the issue of cross-border licensing of copyright protected works. All efforts have yet to lead to a binding set of rules, however.

---

7. European Commission, *Green Paper on Copyright and Related Rights in the Information Society*, COM (95) 382 final, Brussels, 19 Jul. 1995, <http://aei.pitt.edu/1211/01/copyright_info_society_gp_COM_95_382.pdf> (last visited: 5 Jan. 2010).

8. See *infra* para. 2.

9. The Treaty of Lisbon entered into force on 1 Dec. 2009, renaming the EC Treaty (TEC) to Treaty on the Functioning of the European Union (TFEU) and changing the numbering of the provisions. See Consolidated version of the Treaty on the Functioning of the European Union, O.J. C. 115/47 of 9 May 2008, <http://eur-lex.europa.eu/LexUriServ/LexUriServ.do?uri=OJ:C:2008:115:0047:0199:EN:PDF> (last visited: 6 Jan. 2010). Hereinafter, the text refers to the TFEU articles. The corresponding articles of the TEC are added in parentheses.

10. See: European Parliament, *Resolution on a Community framework for collective management societies in the field of copyright and neighbouring rights (2002/2274(INI))*, P5_TA(2004)0036, Strasbourg, 15 Jan. 2004, <www.europarl.europa.eu/sides/getDoc.do?type=TA&language=EN&reference=P5-TA-2004-0036> (last visited: 6 Jan. 2010) [Community Framework Resolution]; European Commission, *Communication from the Commission to the Council, the European Parliament and the European Economic and Social Committee – The Management of Copyright and Related Rights in the Internal Market*, COM (2004) 261 final, Brussels, 16 Apr. 2004, <http://eur-lex.europa.eu/LexUriServ/LexUriServ.do?uri=COM:2004:0261:FIN:EN:PDF> (last visited: 6 Jan. 2010) [Communication on the Management of Copyright in the Internal Market]; European Commission, *Communication from the President in agreement with Vice-President Wallström – Commission Work Programme for 2005*, COM (2005) 15 final, Brussels, 26 Jan. 2005, <http://eur-lex.europa.eu/LexUriServ/site/en/com/2005/com2005_0015en01.pdf> (last visited: 6 Jan. 2010) [Commission Work Programme for 2005]; European Commission, *Commission Staff Working Document – Study on a Community Initiative on the Cross-Border Collective Management of Copyright*, Brussels, 7 Jul. 2005, online: <http://ec.europa.eu/internal_market/copyright/docs/management/study-collectivemgmt_en.pdf> (last visited: 6 Jan. 2010) [Study on Cross-Border Collective Management of Copyright].

This chapter is divided in three main parts. First, the chapter describes the current state of the law concerning CMOs in Europe, as pronounced over the past few decades in decisions of the ECJ and the European Commission in competition matters. Second, the chapter discusses the recent efforts deployed by the European lawmakers toward the establishment of a legal framework governing the activities of CMOs in Europe, and more specifically the multi-territorial licensing of online music services. The third part analyses the actual and potential impact on the market for the cross-border collective management of legitimate online music services of the most recent measures adopted by the European bodies. The chapter concludes on the overall state of the law in Europe pertaining to CMOs.

2   CONTROL OF CMOs THROUGH COMPETITION LAW

In general, CMOs in the EU Member States are subject to control under the two basic provisions of Community competition law, Articles 101 and 102 TFEU (ex Articles 81 and 82 TEC). Article 101 TFEU (ex Article 81 TEC) prohibits agreements between undertakings and concerted practices that may affect trade between Member States and that have as their object or effect the prevention, restriction or distortion of competition within the common market. This can be the case, for example, with price-fixing agreements. Article 102 TFEU (ex Article 82 TEC) prohibits the abuse by one or more undertakings of a dominant position within the common market or in a substantial part of it insofar as it may affect trade between Member States. This can be the case, for example, where an undertaking imposes unfair trading conditions or where it applies dissimilar conditions to equivalent transactions with other trading parties.

CMOs occupy a dominant market position in at least two respects: first, toward the users of protected works who may have just one legitimate supplier of licenses and, second, toward the individual owners of protected works who may have no alternative provider of a rights administration infrastructure. Furthermore, CMOs may be engaging in practices in restraint of trade, contrary to Article 101 TFEU (ex Article 81 TEC), by reinforcing their competitive position on the national market through reciprocal representation agreements for the exploitation of their respective repertoires.

European case law has consistently held that Articles 101 and 102 TFEU (ex Articles 81 and 82 TEC) are applicable to CMOs. First, these organizations constitute 'undertakings' within the meaning of these provisions. By acting as agencies entrusted with the safeguard of the rights of copyright owners, they participate in the commercial exchange of services and are therefore engaged in the exercise of economic activities,[11] irrelevant of whether they make profit or

---

11. See *IFPI Simulcasting* decision, *supra* n. 1, at para. 59, with reference to, *inter alia*, the ECJ judgments in Case 127/73, *Belgische Radio en Televisie (BRT) v. SABAM*, (1974) E.C.R. 51 and 313 [*BRT v. SABAM*]; Joined Cases 55/80 and 57/80, *Musik-Vertrieb Membran GmbH v. GEMA*, (1981) E.C.R. 147; and Case 7/82, *GVL v. Commission*, (1983) E.C.R. 483 [*GVL v. Commission*].

not.[12] Second, as CMOs enjoy a (quasi)-monopoly in their field, they are deemed to have a 'dominant position' in the meaning of Article 102 TFEU (ex Article 82 TEC).[13] Note that whether undertakings occupy a dominant position is not a relevant factor for consideration of a complaint under Article 101 TFEU (ex Article 81 TEC) – undertakings are prohibited from setting up agreements and engaging in concerted practices irrespective of whether they enjoy a dominant position.[14]

An exhaustive account of the European case law on the subject of CMOs would go far beyond the objectives of this chapter. The following pages are therefore limited to giving a broad overview of the main elements of the European competition rules as applied to CMOs.[15] As discussed later, the intervention of the ECJ and of the European Commission has traditionally addressed three broad issues: (1) the relationship between CMOs and their members, (2) the relationship between CMOs and users and (3) the reciprocal relationship between different CMOs. In view of the increased legal and political importance recently taken by the issue of the multi-territorial licensing of works and in view of the impact it has on the Internal Market, greater attention will be paid in this section to the competition law aspects of the reciprocal relationship between CMOs than to the other two types of relationships.

2.1   RELATIONSHIP WITH MEMBERS

The relationship between CMOs and their members was the object over the years of a certain scrutiny under the rules of European competition law. The main aspects of the legal framework regarding the relationship between CMOs and their members are still laid down in the early decisions rendered by the European Commission involving the German collective management organization GEMA.[16] In the *GEMA I* case, the European Commission put the following points to the test of

---

12. See: *Commission Decision 81/1030/EEC of 29 October 1981 relating to a proceeding under Article 86 of the EEC Treaty (IV/29.839 – GVL)*, O.J. L. 370/49 of 28 Dec. 1981, online: <http://eur-lex.europa.eu/LexUriServ/LexUriServ.do?uri=CELEX:31981D1030:EN:HTML> (last visited: 6 Jan. 2010) [*GVL* decision], at para. 44.

13. *GVL v. Commission, supra* n. 11, at paras 41–45.

14. P. Sean Morris, 'The reform of Article 82 and the operation of competition principles upon the normal trading functions of copyright collecting societies', *Journal of Intellectual Property Law & Practice* 4, no. 8 (2009): 566–572, at 569.

15. For further reading, see I. Govaere, *The Use and Abuse of Intellectual Property Rights in E.C. Law* (London: Sweet & Maxwell, 1996), 337; D.G. Goyder, *EC Competition Law*, 4th edn (Oxford: Oxford University Press, 2003), 660; F.L. Fine, 'The Impact of EEC Competition Law on the Music Industry', *Entertainment Law Review* (1992): 6 at 11; E. Lui, 'The Eurovision Song Contest: A Proposal for Reconciling the National Regulation of Music Collecting Societies and the Single European Market', *Entertainment Law Review* (2003): 67 at 73; and K.J. Koelman, 'Collectieve Rechtenorganisaties en Mededinging – deel I', AMI (2004): 45 at 49–50.

16. *Commission Decision 71/224/EEC of 2 June 1971 relating to a proceeding under Article 86 of the EEC Treaty (IV/26 760 – GEMA)*, O.J. L. 134/15 of 20 Jun. 1971 [*GEMA I* decision].

Article 102 TFEU (ex Article 82 TEC): (1) the scope of the assignment of rights in favour of the CMO, (2) the distribution of income, (3) the membership of foreign right holders and (4) the member's ability to have recourse to courts to decide on disputes with the CMO.

The Commission made at least two important rulings. First, the obligation set by a CMO requiring its members to assign unduly broad categories of rights, for example, to exclusively assign all their current and future rights with respect to all categories of works worldwide, could constitute an abuse of a dominant position. This aspect of the decision was later confirmed by the ECJ in the *BRT v. SABAM* case.[17] In the Court's opinion, the decisive factor when examining the statutes of a CMO in the light of the European competition rules, is whether the statutes exceed the limits absolutely necessary for effective protection (the 'indispensability' test) and whether they limit the individual copyright holder's freedom to dispose of his work no more than necessary (the 'equity' test).[18] In the *SABAM* case, the Court ruled that 'a compulsory assignment of all copyrights, both present and future, no distinction being drawn between the different generally accepted types of exploitation, may appear an unfair condition, especially if such assignment is required for an extended period after the member's withdrawal'.[19]

Second, the European Commission stressed in the *GEMA I* case that CMOs may not discriminate among members in regard to the distribution of income.[20] The Commission held that GEMA had abused its dominant position by paying supplementary fees, from revenue collected from the membership as a whole, only to those members who had been ordinary members for at least three years. Also, the Commission ruled that CMOs may not refuse nationals of other EU Member States as members, nor impose discriminatory terms concerning their membership rights, for example, by preventing a foreign right holder to become an ordinary or extraordinary member (a voting member).[21] According to the Commission, such practices must automatically be regarded as an infringement of Article 102 TFEU (ex Article 82 TEC), as they run counter to the principle of equal treatment resulting from the prohibition of 'any discrimination on grounds of nationality' in Article 18 TFEU (ex Article 12 TEC). Moreover, the refusal to accept the membership of nationals of other Member States falls directly under the special prohibition of discrimination under Community competition law, as contained in Article 102(c) TFEU (ex Article 82(c) TEC). In this respect, the ECJ confirmed, in the *Phil Collins* case,[22] that domestic provisions containing reciprocity clauses cannot be relied upon to deny nationals of other EU Member States' rights conferred on national authors.

---

17. *BRT v. SABAM, supra* n. 11.
18. *Ibid.*, at paras 8–11.
19. *Ibid.*, at para. 12.
20. See, for example, Fine, *supra* n. 15, at 12; and L. Bently & B. Sherman, *Intellectual Property Law*, 3rd edn (Oxford: Oxford University Press, 2009), at 298.
21. See also: *GVL* decision, *supra* n. 12; and *GVL v. Commission, supra* n. 11.
22. ECJ judgment in Joined Cases C-92/92 and C-326/92, *Phil Collins and Patricia Im- und Export v. Imtrat and EMI Electrola*, (1993) I E.C.R. 5145.

Years later, the European Commission ruled in its *'Daft Punk'* decision[23] that where the statutes of a CMO contain a mandatory requirement according to which all rights of an author must be assigned, without distinction, the organization may be abusing its dominant position, given that such practice corresponds to the imposition of an unfair trading condition. In this case, the two Daft Punk members wished to individually manage their rights for exploitation on the Internet, CD-ROM, DVD, etc. The French collective management organization SACEM refused membership, arguing that it protected authors from unreasonable demands of the record industry and prevented a cherry-picking of the most valuable rights.[24] The Commission considered this refusal as a disproportionate curtailment of individual management of the rights in question contrary to Article 102 TFEU (ex Article 82 TEC). Although the Commission recognized the legitimacy for SACEM to retain the means to monitor which authors wish to manage certain rights individually, it accepted that SACEM may retain its rule against individual management, provided derogations could be granted. Each application must be examined by SACEM on a case-by-case basis, and its decisions must be reasoned and objective. Following the *Daft Punk* decision, SACEM modified its statutes, which now allow members to apply for partial withdrawal of the rights assigned.

2.2 RELATIONSHIP WITH USERS

The relationship that CMOs entertain with users falls also under the scrutiny of Article 102 TFEU (ex Article 82 TEC), for CMOs may be tempted to abuse their dominant position when issuing licenses for the use of works in their repertoire. Over the years, the ECJ and the European Commission have developed an important body of jurisprudence in this area, addressing issues such as (1) the CMOs' relationship with foreign users, (2) the practices of blanket licensing and (3) the CMOs' pricing policy. The seminal case in this area remains the ECJ's judgment in the *Tournier* affair.[25] In this case, French discothèque owners had complained that the fees charged by the French collective management organization SACEM were excessive, in particular because the discothèque owners mainly used popular dance music of Anglo-American origin while the SACEM's fees were calculated for the use of the worldwide repertoire. As a result, the discothèque owners attempted, without success, to obtain a license directly from the relevant foreign CMOs.

The *Tournier* decision delivered a ruling on at least three important points. First, the ECJ ruled that a national CMO may refuse to grant direct access to its own

---

23. *Commission Decision of 06.08.2002 in case COMP/C2/37.219 Banghalter / Homem Christo (Daft Punk) v. SACEM*, <http://ec.europa.eu/competition/antitrust/cases/decisions/37219/fr.pdf> (last visited: 6 Jan. 2010) [*Daft Punk* decision].
24. T. Toft, *Collective Rights Management In The Online World – A review of recent Commission initiatives*, Brussels, DG Competition, 8 Jun. 2006, <http://ec.europa.eu/competition/speeches/text/sp2006_008_en.pdf> (last visited: 6 Jan. 2010), 12.
25. ECJ judgment in Case 395/87, *Ministère public v. Tournier*, (1989) E.C.R. 2521 [*Tournier*].

national repertoire to users established in other EU Member States only for efficiency reasons. For example, if it would be too burdensome to organize its own management and monitoring system in these countries. However, if the refusal were the result of agreements or concerted practices between the national CMOs in the Member States in which the users are established, this would have the object or effect of restricting competition in the common market contrary to Article 101 TFEU (ex Article 81 TEC).[26]

Second, the Court considered whether CMOs could refuse to grant licenses for only parts of their repertoire.[27] Instead of a blanket license, the discothèque owners had asked SACEM to grant them licenses for only the part of its repertoire that they actually used (popular dance music of Anglo-American origin), but SACEM refused. The Court ruled that the refusal by a CMO to grant national users licenses for only a certain part of the foreign repertoire it administers would not be prohibited under Article 101 TFEU (ex Article 81 TEC), unless such practice could entirely safeguard the interests of the right holders without thereby increasing the costs of managing contracts and monitoring the use of protected works.[28]

Third, in relation to SACEM's tariffs, the Court observed that one of the most pronounced differences among CMOs in the Member States lies in the level of operating expenses. The discothèque owners complained that SACEM charged excessive, non-negotiable and unfair royalties. The Court considered that a national CMO imposes unfair trading conditions in the meaning of Article 102 TFEU (ex Article 82 TEC), if the royalties charged are appreciably higher than those charged in other Member States, unless the differences were justified by objective and relevant factors.[29]

More recently, in the *Kanal 5* case,[30] the ECJ examined a remuneration model applied by a CMO for the television broadcast of protected musical works, whereby the royalties are calculated as a percentage of the revenue of the broadcasting companies and according to the amount of the music broadcast. The Court ruled that such a remuneration model does not run counter to Article 102 TFEU (ex Article 82 TEC), unless another method enables a more precise identification of the use and audience of those works without incurring a disproportionate increase of management and supervision costs. The fact that the royalties due are calculated in a different manner depending on whether the broadcasting company is commercial or public may constitute an abuse if the CMO applies dissimilar conditions to

---

26. *Ibid.*, at paras 16–26. See also: ECJ judgment in Joint Cases 110/88, 241/88 and 242/88, *Lucazeau v. SACEM*, (1989) E.C.R. 2811 [*Lucazeau*], at paras 10–20.
27. See Hugenholtz, *supra* n. 4, at 205; Bently & Sherman, *supra* n. 20, at 301; and J.H. Spoor, D.W.F. Verkade & D.J.G. Visser, *Auteursrecht: auteursrecht, naburige rechten en databankenrecht* (Deventer: Kluwer Law International, 2005), at 466.
28. See *Tournier, supra* n. 25, at paras 27–33.
29. *Ibid.*, at paras 34–36. See also: *Lucazeau, supra* n. 26, at paras 21–33.
30. ECJ judgment in Case C-52/07, *Kanal 5 Ltd and TV 4 AB*, O.J. C. 32/2 of 7 Feb. 2009, <http://eur-lex.europa.eu/LexUriServ/LexUriServ.do?uri=OJ:C:2009:032:0002:0003:EN:PDF> (last visited: 6 Jan. 2010).

equivalent services and if it places the television companies at a competitive disadvantage without objective justification.

2.3   RECIPROCAL AGREEMENTS BETWEEN CMOS

The rights clearance for the exploitation of non-domestic repertoire occurs on the basis of a network of reciprocal representation arrangements between CMOs. Through reciprocal agreements, the parties give each other the right, on a non-exclusive basis, to exploit the copyrights on their respective repertoire in their respective territories. As the ECJ stated in the *Tournier* decision, the advantage of a system of reciprocal agreements is that it 'enables copyright-management societies to rely, for the protection of their repertoires in another State, on the organization established by the copyright-management society operating there, without being obliged to add to that organization their own network of contracts with users and their own local monitoring arrangements'.[31] To the extent that CMOs are or become actual or potential competitors in respect to their services, the agreements between them could lead to a restriction of competition, contrary to Article 101 TFEU (ex Article 81 TEC). According to settled jurisprudence, concerted action by national CMOs with the effect of systematically refusing to grant direct access to their repertoires to foreign users must be regarded as amounting to a concerted practice restrictive of competition and capable of affecting trade between the Member States.[32]

Early on, the European Commission held that the CMOs in the different Member States must compete against each other, at least in certain areas. In 1985, the Commission held that the practices of GEMA, who charged royalties on sound recordings manufactured in Germany even where the licensee had obtained a mechanical license from a CMO in another Member State, constituted an abuse of a dominant position.[33] According to the Commission,[34] a mechanical license granted by a CMO in a Community Member State is valid throughout the Community and authorizes manufacture of sound recordings in any Member State. In other words, once a mechanical license has been granted in a Community Member State, this exhausts the right of a CMO in a Member State where the sound recordings are imported to charge another licensing fee. As a consequence, CMOs in Europe now have to compete against each other for so-called 'Central European Licensing' deals, allowing any user to acquire a mechanical license from one CMO that is valid throughout the Community.[35]

---

31. *Tournier, supra* n. 25, at para. 19.
32. *Ibid.*, at para. 23.
33. See, for example, Fine, *supra* n. 15, at 8–9; and Koelman, *supra* n. 15, at 49.
34. Commission's Press Release of 6 Feb. 1985, 2 *Common Market Law Review* 1.
35. See M. Kretschmer, 'The Failure of Property Rules in Collective Administration: Rethinking Copyright Societies as Regulatory Instruments', *European Intellectual Property Review* 24 (March 2002): 126, 133, online: <www.cippm.org.uk/pdfs/kretschmer_eipr_032002.pdf> (last visited: 6 Jan. 2010).

In the *Tournier* and *Lucazeau* cases, the ECJ addressed the reciprocal relationship between CMOs and concluded that such reciprocal agreements did not, as such, fall under Article 101(1) TFEU (ex Article 81(1) TEC), provided no concerted action was demonstrated. The reciprocal representation agreements appeared in those days to be economically justified in a context in which physical monitoring of copyright usage was required.[36] With the advent of the digital network environment, the exploitation of copyright-protected works has taken a new turn – one that can simultaneously reach the entire world and be monitored at a distance. As discussed in the following section in the *IFPI Simulcasting* decision and the more recent *CISAC* decision, these technological developments emphasize the need for multi-repertoire/multi-territory licenses, or in absence of such broad licenses, for a solid and transparent network of reciprocal agreements between CMOs.

2.3.1   IFPI Simulcasting Decision

The *IFPI Simulcasting* decision involved the licensing of neighbouring rights for the simulcasting of phonograms, where 'simulcasting' is defined as the simultaneous transmission by radio and TV stations via the Internet of sound recordings included in their broadcasts of radio and/or TV signals. The right to license simulcast rights on the Internet, given that simulcasting necessarily involves the transmission of signals into several territories at the same time, was not covered by the mono-territory inter-society mandates resulting from the existing reciprocal representation agreements. According to the IFPI Simulcasting reciprocal agreement, which the participating CMOs had signed on an experimental basis until the end of 2004, each of the participating societies could issue multi-territorial licenses for the online use of copyrighted works of the repertoires of these societies only to online users established in their own territory.[37] Following similar statements of objection against two similar constructs, known as the Santiago[38] and BIEM-Barcelona agreements,[39] the European Commission issued a statement of objection against the IFPI Simulcasting agreement and put its terms to the test of the provisions of Article 101 TFEU (ex Article 81 TEC).

Referring to the *Tournier* and *Lucazeau* cases, the European Commission considered that the monitoring task of CMOs in the online environment could easily be carried out directly on the Internet and could therefore take place from a distance, which meant that the traditional economic justification for CMOs not to

---

36. *Tournier, supra* n. 25, at paras 34–46; and *Lucazeau, supra* n. 26, at paras 21–33.
37. See Guibault, *supra* n. 2, for more details about the competition aspects and the Commission's viewpoints of these agreements.
38. Notification of cooperation agreements (Case COMP/C2/38.126 – BUMA, GEMA, PRS, SACEM), O.J. C. 145/2 of 17 May 2001, <http://eur-lex.europa.eu/LexUriServ/LexUriServ.do?uri=OJ:C:2001:145:0002:0002:EN:PDF> (last visited: 6 Jan. 2010).
39. Notification of cooperation agreements (Case COMP/C-2/38.377 – BIEM Barcelona Agreements), O.J. C. 132/18 of 4 Jun. 2002, <http://eur-lex.europa.eu/LexUriServ/LexUriServ.do?uri=OJ:C:2002:132:0018:0018:EN:PDF> (last visited: 6 Jan. 2010).

compete in cross-border provision of services no longer applied in this context.[40] Moreover, the parties in this case must undertake to increase transparency in regard to the payment charged to the users of phonograms in their repertoire, by separating the tariff that covers the royalty proper from the fee meant to cover the administration costs.[41] This transparency in pricing would enable users to recognize the most efficient societies and to seek their licenses from the society that provides them at the lower cost. The Commission further stated that

> In the present case, the model chosen by the parties for the simulcasting licensing structure results in the society granting a multi-repertoire/multi-territory license being limited in its freedom as to the amount of the global license fee it will charge to a user.[42]

The Commission therefore held that where the IFPI Simulcasting agreement determined that each contracting party could charge users the license fees that apply in the territories into which the user simulcasts its services, it significantly reduced competition between CMOs in terms of price (Article 101 TFEU (ex Article 81 TEC)), because this practice resulted in tariffs that were to a large extent pre-determined.[43] On this point, at the request of the Commission during the proceedings, the parties undertook to split the copyright royalty from the administration fee such as to bring about an increased degree of transparency in the relationship between CMOs and users. This was meant to allow users (as well as members of the societies) to better assess the efficiency of each of the societies and have a better understanding of their management costs.

Before drawing its conclusion regarding the compatibility of the IFPI Simulcasting agreement with Article 101(1) TFEU (ex Article 81(1) TEC), the Commission considered whether the agreement could be exempted under paragraph (3) of the same Article.[44] As the Commission previously stated, in certain circumstances cooperation may be justified and can lead to substantial economic benefits, namely where companies need to respond to increasing competitive pressure and to a changing market driven by globalization, the speed of technological progress and the generally more dynamic nature of markets. The Commission noted first that the

---

40. *IFPI Simulcasting* decision, *supra* n. 1, at para. 61.
41. *Ibid.*, at para. 103.
42. *Ibid.*, at. para. 67.
43. *Ibid.*, at paras 62–78.
44. Article 101(3) TFEU (ex Art. 81(3) TEC) reads as follows: 'The provisions of paragraph 1 may, however, be declared inapplicable in the case of:

    – any agreement or category of agreements between undertakings,
    – any decision or category of decisions by associations of undertakings,
    – any concerted practice or category of concerted practices,

    which contributes to improving the production or distribution of goods or to promoting technical or economic progress, while allowing consumers a fair share of the resulting benefit, and which does not: (a) impose on the undertakings concerned restrictions which are not indispensable to the attainment of these objectives; (b) afford such undertakings the possibility of eliminating competition in respect of a substantial part of the products in question.'

IFPI Simulcasting agreement gave rise to a new product – a multi-territorial, multi-repertoire simulcasting license, covering the repertoires of multiple CMOs, enabling a simulcaster to obtain a single license from a single CMO for its simulcast that is accessible from virtually anywhere in the world via the Internet. Second, under the reciprocal simulcasting licenses system, broadcasters would benefit from the fact that by obtaining one simulcast license from a single CMO, they would be able to simulcast in any participating territory without fear of being sued for infringement of the relevant rights. Third, the system put in place through the IFPI Simulcasting agreement would also benefit consumers, for it provides them with easier and wider access to a range of music by means of available simulcasts.

The only point raising concerns in the eyes of the Commission, however, was the manner in which, pursuant to the IFPI Simulcasting agreement, the copyright-royalty element of the license tariffs remained pre-determined and unchangeable by the society granting a simulcasting license. Nevertheless, after thorough consideration of the tariffs structure, the Commission concluded that the pre-determination of national copyright royalty levels represented in the circumstances a guarantee without which the participating societies would not contribute with their individual inputs so as to create and distribute a multi-territory/multi-repertoire simulcasting license. Therefore, the Commission considered such restriction to be indispensable within the meaning of Article 101(3)(a) TFEU (ex Article 81(3)(a) TEC) and granted an individual exemption until the end of 2004 when the agreement expired.[45]

2.3.2 CISAC Decision

The model reciprocal agreement drawn up by the Confédération Internationale des Auteurs et Compositeurs (CISAC) became the object of a comparable inquiry under Article 101 TFEU (ex Article 81 TEC), as a result of two separate complaints from the radio broadcasting group RTL and Music Choice, an online music supplier in the United Kingdom. In 2006, the European Commission issued a statement of objection against the CISAC model contract itself and its bilateral implementation between the CMOs of the European Economic Area (EEA),[46] which contained territorial restrictions[47] creating an obstacle to obtaining a multi-territory/multi-repertoire license for the online use of music. The model contract at issue and the agreements deriving from it at bilateral level form the basis of collective copyright-management for all modes of performance of copyright-protected music to the public. It is important to note, however, that the

---

45. *IFPI Simulcasting* decision, *supra* n. 1, at para. 115. See also, C. Stothers, 'Copyright and the EC Treaty: Music, Films and Football', *European Intellectual Property Review* 31, no. 5 (2009): 272–282, at 280.
46. The EEA includes all Member States of the EU plus Iceland, Norway and Lichtenstein.
47. Sean Morris, *supra* n. 14, 566.

complaints related only to the exploitation of musical works on modern platforms, such as the Internet, satellite and cable.

The Commission identified two potentially restrictive clauses in the CISAC model contract and the reciprocal agreements concluded on its basis by the European CMOs:

- Article 11(II) of the CISAC model contract, which reads: 'While this contract is in force neither of the contracting Societies may, without the consent of the other, accept as a member any member of the other society or any natural person, firm or company having the nationality of one of the countries in which the other Society operates';
- Article 6(II) of the CISAC model contract, which reads: 'For the duration of the present contract, each of the contracting Societies shall refrain from any intervention within the territory of the other Society in the latter's exercise of the mandate conferred by the present contract.'[48]

Taken individually, such restrictions had already given rise to investigations by competition authorities, leading, for example, to the GEMA decision[49] and the GVL case,[50] regarding membership discrimination clauses, and to the *Tournier* decision,[51] regarding restrictions in the grant of licenses to users located in another country. It is therefore no surprise that the Commission, in its decision of 16 July 2008, declared the practices of 24 EEA CISAC members contrary to Article 101 TFEU (ex Article 81 TEC).[52]

Before assessing whether the clauses in the model contract were contrary to Article 101 TFEU (ex Article 81 TEC), the European Commission engaged in a very detailed analysis of the relevant product and geographical markets in relation to the activities of CMOs. The Commission identified three distinct product markets: the provision of copyright administration services to right holders, the provision of services to other CMOs and the licensing of public performance rights for satellite, cable and Internet transmissions to commercial users. With respect to this last point, the Commission noted that, contrary to the *Tournier* and *Lucazeau* cases, a local presence is no longer required to monitor the use of the license for Internet, satellite and cable broadcast. As a consequence, CMOs have the technical capacity to issue multi-territorial licenses, although the uniform and systematic territorial delineation precludes them from offering multi-repertoire and multi-territorial licenses to commercial users. Conversely, the geographical market for the provision of copyright administration services to right holders remains national.[53]

---

48. *CISAC* decision, *supra* n. 1, at para. 74.
49. *GEMA I* decision, *supra* n. 16.
50. See: *GVL* decision, *supra* n. 12; and *GVL v. Commission, supra* n. 11.
51. *Tournier, supra* n. 25, at para.19.
52. *CISAC* decision, *supra* n. 1.
53. M.M. Frabboni, 'Old Monopolies Versus New Technologies – The Cisac Decision In Context', *Entertainment Law Review* 20, no. 3 (2009): 76–81, at 79.

Putting the CISAC model contract to the test of Article 101 TFEU (ex Article 81 TEC), the Commission then enquired how the agreement affected competition within the EEA. It found that competition between CMOs was affected in two ways: first, in relation to their own services or repertoires, and, second, in relation to the offering of similar repertoires. With respect to the first form of restraint on competition, the membership restrictions in the model contract impeded the ability of an author from becoming a member of the CMO of his choice or to be simultaneously a member of different EEA societies in different EEA territories.[54] As the Commission opined:

> the membership restrictions contribute to bringing about clearly separated national repertoires since they make it more difficult for authors to become members of other collecting societies. Without the membership restriction this distinction by nationality is less likely to exist, and this would potentially render the repertoires more homogeneous in the long term.[55]

With respect to the second form of restraint on competition, the territorial delineation clause, the Commission considered that territorial restrictions were not explained by the territorial nature of copyright and that the need for a local presence did not justify the systematic delineation of the territory as the territory of the country where the CMO is established. According to the Commission, this clause 'effectively leads to national monopolies for the multi-repertoire licensing of public performance rights and has the effect of segmenting the EEA into national markets. Competition is restricted on two levels: (i) on the market for administration services which collecting societies provide to each other; and (ii) on the licensing market'.[56] As the Commission further stated:

> the mutually guaranteed territorial monopolies for the licensing of public performance rights ensure that each collecting society will be able to charge administration costs for the management of rights and the delivery of the license without facing competitive pressure on these fees from other collecting societies.[57]

The Commission concluded that, on the basis of the evidence presented, the territorial delineation clause could not be objectively explained and was not necessary for ensuring that EEA CISAC members grant each other reciprocal mandates. The model contract therefore amounted to a concerted practice in restraint of competition contrary to Article 101 TFEU (ex Article 81 TEC). Finally, the Commission was of the view that the model contract and its implementation by the EEA CISAC members did not meet any of the four cumulative conditions of Article 101(3) TFEU (ex Article 81(3) TEC) so as to justify an exemption.

---

54. *CISAC* decision, *supra* n. 1, at para. 125.
55. *Ibid.*, para. 126.
56. *Ibid.*, para. 207.
57. *Ibid.*, para. 210.

The Commission considered that the EEA CISAC members had acted in a concerted way to prevent any competition between themselves regarding the management of music distribution rights by Internet, cable and satellite and that these practices, by permitting the maintenance of national monopolies, were preventing the issue of pan-European licenses. Nevertheless, the decision did not fix any financial penalty, and allowed the CMOs to retain their current system of bilateral agreements, with a few modifications.[58] The companies therefore were given 120 days from the date of the decision to submit revised bilateral agreements to the European Commission.

In October 2008, CISAC filed for appeal of the Commission's decision before the Court of First Instance. It argued that the decision creates legal uncertainty for copyright holders and for users.[59] CISAC submitted that the Commission made an error by determining that the parallel territorial delineation resulting from the reciprocal representation agreements concluded by the EEA CISAC members constitutes a concerted practice. CISAC considers that the presence of a territorial delineation clause in all the reciprocal representation agreements concluded by its members is not the product of a concerted practice to restrict competition. Rather, this state of affairs exists because all the societies find it in the interest of their members to include such a clause in their reciprocal representation agreements. Alternatively, CISAC claims that if there were a concerted practice on territorial delineations, it would not be restrictive of competition within the meaning of Article 101 TFEU (ex Article 81 TEC) for two reasons. First, it thinks that the alleged concerted practice on territorial delineations is not illegal because it concerns a form of competition that is not worthy of protection. Second, even if the alleged practice were to be considered to restrict competition, it believes that it does not infringe Article 101(1) TFEU (ex Article 81(1) TEC) because it is necessary and proportionate to the legitimate objective pursued. At the time of writing, the appeal was still pending.

3   EUROPEAN REGULATORY FRAMEWORK
         RELATING TO CMOs

Over the last few years, the European Commission has gained the conviction that, next to the control ex post exercised over the activities of CMOs under the rules of European competition law, a level playing field of undistorted competition between CMOs will emerge only provided that appropriate legislative measures are adopted to support it. The discussions around the establishment of a European legal framework for CMOs have shifted over the past few years from the wish to harmonize rules on the good governance of CMOs to the need to solve the more

---

58. Frabboni, *supra* n. 53.
59. Action brought before the European Court of Justice on 3 Oct. 2008, Case T-442/08, *CISAC v. Commission*, O.J. C. 82/25 of 4 Apr. 2009, <http://eur-lex.europa.eu/LexUriServ/LexUriServ.do?uri=OJ:C:2009:082:0025:0026:EN:PDF> (last visited: 6 Jan. 2010).

pressing multi-territorial licensing issues.[60] The main reason advanced for this lies in the fact that the market has failed to produce effective structures for cross-border licensing and cross-border royalty distribution and that it has not rectified a series of contractual restrictions preventing authors or other right holders from seeking the best collective rights management service across national borders. The following sections describe the main policy documents that have paved the way to the adoption of the 2005 Recommendation on collective cross-border management of copyright and related rights for legitimate online music services, before examining the content of the Recommendation itself and the critique that it generated.

3.1   RESOLUTION OF THE EUROPEAN PARLIAMENT

The European Parliament's Resolution of January 2004 on the subject set out policy considerations, which the European Commission should take into consideration when the time comes to draw up the text of a directive.[61] At the outset, the European Parliament emphasized the importance of the cultural and social aspects of collective rights management and the traditional and still necessary role of CMOs.[62] The Parliament pointed out that in the area of copyright and related rights, a proper, fair, and professional system of collective rights management is crucial for financial as well as cultural success. Collective rights management can constitute an important factor in stimulating creativity and influencing the growth of cultural and linguistic diversity. Nevertheless, the Parliament was rather critical about the actual state of collective rights management in the EU It noted, for instance, the deficit in the internal democratic structures of CMOs, the lack of transparency in the financial policy of the societies and the absence of rapid dispute settlement mechanisms. In addition, the European Parliament observed that major structural differences existed in the regulation and efficiency regarding the external control of CMOs in the different Member States. Therefore, the European Parliament believed 'that a Community approach in the area of the exercise and management of copyright and related rights, in particular of effective collective rights management in the internal market, must be pursued'.

In this respect, the European Parliament presented several possible solutions,[63] one of which was the creation of common tools and of comparable parameters and the coordination of CMOs' areas of activity. With respect to the societies' internal democratic structure, a proposal was made to establish minimum standards for organizational structures, transparency, accounting and legal remedies. Furthermore, the European Parliament called for the adoption of provisions

---

60. Study on Cross-Border Collective Management of Copyright, *supra* n. 10, at 30.
61. Community Framework Resolution, *supra* n. 10.
62. See A. Dietz, 'European Parliament versus Commission: how to deal with collecting societies?', *International Review of Intellectual Property and Competition Law* (2004): 809 at 810–814.
63. *Ibid.*, at 819.

requiring the publication of tariffs, distribution keys, annual accounts, a listing of appropriate management costs and information on reciprocal representation agreements. A framework of minimum standards for the calculation of tariffs and of uniform coding standards for works should also be instituted to simplify the exercise of rights. With regard to the cooperation between CMOs, a call was made for an efficient exchange of information between the societies and the discontinuation of so-called 'B contracts' in reciprocal representation agreements.[64] Finally, the European Parliament made a general call for the establishment of efficient, independent, regular, transparent and expert control mechanisms and for comparable and compatible arbitration mechanisms in all EU Member States.

However, together with the introduction of equitable, transparent and balanced rules for CMOs, the European Parliament also appealed to the restriction of competition law to cases of abuse, in order to safeguard rights management effectively both now and in the future. According to the Explanatory Statement to the Resolution, a misguided insistence on competition would lead to further fragmentation of the markets, chaos in the clarification of rights and dumping tariffs. Furthermore, the European Parliament saw CMOs as an important safeguard in the world of media concentration. It stressed that the monopoly of CMOs should not be replaced by a monopoly of the media industry.

3.2   COMMUNICATION FROM THE COMMISSION

In contrast to the Parliament's Resolution, the European Commission's Communication of 2004 on the Management of Copyright and Related Rights in the Internal Market was a rather technically and legally oriented document.[65] The European Commission stated that to safeguard the functioning of collective rights management throughout the Internal Market and to ensure that it continues to represent a valuable option for the management of rights benefiting right holders and users alike, a legislative approach at Community level was required. Although the Commission recognized that competition rules remain an effective instrument for regulating the market and the behaviour of CMOs, it took the view that an internal market in collective rights management could be best achieved if the monitoring of CMOs under competition rules was complemented by the establishment of a legislative framework.

According to the Commission, complementary action was needed on those aspects of collective rights management that impede the full potential of the Internal Market in regard to the cross-border trade of goods and provision of services

---

64. See Community Framework Resolution, *supra* n. 10, at paras 45 and 56. In the current system of reciprocal representation agreements, there are two kinds of agreements. Under the 'A agreements' a reciprocal transfer of royalties collected is provided for, where under the 'B agreements', no money or data is transferred and each society collects and distributes royalties used in its territory only to its own right holders.
65. Communication on the Management of Copyright in the Internal Market, *supra* n. 10.

based on copyright and related rights. In this respect, the efficiency, transparency and accountability of CMOs were of particular importance. To improve the functioning of collective rights management in the Internal Market, the Commission intended to establish a level playing field in which general conditions for several features of collective rights management would be defined. These features were:

– Establishment and status of CMOs

The Commission wanted the establishment of CMOs to be subject to similar conditions in all Member States. These conditions would relate to the persons who may establish a society, the status of the latter, the necessary proof of efficiency, operability and accounting obligations and a sufficient degree of representativity. On the other hand, the Commission saw no need to bring uniformity in regard to the legal form of organization of CMOs, because it reasoned that the efficiency of a society is not linked to its legal form.

– Relationship with users

In their relation to users, the Commission deemed it necessary to safeguard the functioning of CMOs as one-stop shops for licensing. Common ground would therefore be required on the grant of licenses under reasonable conditions, the transparency in the pricing policy of the CMOs and the reasonableness of the tariffs. Furthermore, the Commission found it essential for users to be in a position to contest the tariffs before national courts or specially created mediation tribunals or with the assistance of supervisory authorities.

– Relationship with right holders

In the societies' relation to right holders, the Commission wished to achieve a level playing field in regard to the acquisition of rights (the mandate), the conditions of membership and the termination of membership. The mandate would offer right holders a reasonable degree of flexibility on its duration and scope. In principle, right holders should also have the possibility, in the light of the deployment of Digital Rights Management ('DRM') systems, to manage certain rights individually if they so desire. Moreover, the Commission wanted similar conditions to exist on the representation and the position of right holders within the society, for example, in regard to their influence on the decision-making process and their access to internal documents and financial records in relation to distribution and licensing revenue and deductions. In this respect, the leading principles must be the good governance, non-discrimination, transparency and accountability of the CMOs.

– External control of CMOs

Finally, the Commission wished to create a level playing field with respect to the external control of CMOs. The external control would cover such matters as the behaviour of CMOs, their functioning, the control of tariffs and licensing conditions and the settlement of disputes. The Commission wanted to see adequate external control mechanisms be established throughout the Community and, to that end, ensure that specific supervisory bodies (such as specialized tribunals, administrative authorities or arbitration boards) became available in all Member States. In addition, the Commission wished to establish common ground on the powers of these bodies, on their composition and on the binding or non-binding nature of their decisions.

When considering the possible options to achieve the objectives outlined in the Communication, the Commission expressly stated that it no longer seemed to be an option to abstain from legislative action. For the Commission, neither soft law nor codes of conduct agreed upon in the marketplace appeared as an adequate solution. Therefore, the Commission expressed the intention to propose a legislative instrument.

3.3   STUDY ON CROSS-BORDER COLLECTIVE MANAGEMENT
        OF COPYRIGHT

In 2005, the European Commission published a study on the cross-border collective management of copyright.[66] In this document, the Commission identified the main problem encountered in the cross-border collective management of copyright as flowing from the fact that the core service elements of the 'cross-border grant of licenses to commercial users' and 'cross-border distribution of royalties' did not function in an optimal manner and hampered the development of an innovative market for the provision of online music services. The study underlined the difficulties of establishing the necessary number of agreements and the problem of legal uncertainty that this has caused.

Three different policy options were put forward as a proposal for reform on collective administration of copyright in the online environment:

- Option 1: To abstain from Community action;
- Option 2: To eliminate territorial restrictions and discriminatory provisions in the reciprocal representation agreements concluded between CMOs;
- Option 3: To give right holders the choice to authorize a CMO of their choice to manage their works across the entire EU.

Option 2 would, according to the Commission, limit EU policy to improving the traditional way in which national CMOs in the Member States cooperate to ensure the cross-border management of copyright. It would introduce a single entry point and choice for commercial end-users, but it would not introduce increased choice at the level of right holders as to the CMO to which to entrust the management of their rights. This solution would also improve the way reciprocal agreements

---

66. Study on Cross-Border Collective Management of Copyright, *supra* n. 10.

function, by improving the way the affiliate society monitors use, collects royalties and transfers them back to the management society. In relation to licensing, this option would ensure that the territorial restrictions in classical reciprocity agreements that hinder the affiliate society from licensing the management society's repertoire beyond its own home territory are removed from all reciprocal representation agreements.[67] Moreover, reciprocal representation agreements would no longer provide that the affiliate society is restricted to granting a multi-territorial license to content providers whose economic residence is located in its 'home' territory.

By contrast, Option 3 would not rely on reciprocal representation agreements to give CMOs licensing authority over a homogeneous product. Instead, it would give all right holders across the EU the possibility to adhere to any CMO of their choice for the EU-wide exploitation of their online rights. Option 3 would effectively cut out the intermediary – the affiliate society – in favour of direct membership in a CMO who, by choice of the right holder, could receive an EU-wide mandate to manage this right holder's copyright protected works. Option 3 would therefore introduce choice and competition at the level between right holders and CMOs. The Commission expressed a strong preference for this option because it would offer the most effective model of cross-border management of copyright.[68] However, this option should first be adopted for rights clearance for online music, before being extended to the collective management of rights as a whole.

In setting forth Option 3 as the preferable long-term rights management model for cross-border copyright exploitation, the Commission emphasized that EU action should be based on the following core principles:

(1) Right-holders choice as to the online management society is based on the freedom to provide rights management services directly across borders. The freedom to provide cross-border management services by means of direct membership contracts will eliminate administrative costs inherent in channelling non-domestic right-holders royalties through reciprocal agreements between different societies;

(2) The principle that a right-holders' choice of a single EU rights manager should be exercised irrespective of residence or nationality of either the rights-manager or the right-holder;

(3) The principle that a collective rights society's repertoire and territorial licensing power would not derive from reciprocal agreements but from right-holder concluding contractual agreements directly with a society of their choice. Right-holders should be able to withdraw certain categories of rights (in particular categories of rights linked to online exploitation) from their national CRMs and transfer their administration to a single rights manager

---

67. *Ibid.*, at 34.
68. *Ibid.*, at 54. See also: M.M. Frabboni, 'Cross-border licensing and collective management: A proposal for the on-line context',. *Entertainment Law Review* 16, no. 8 (2005): 204–208, at 206.

of their choice. For that to work, these online rights must be withdrawn from the scope of reciprocal agreements as well;

(4) The principle that the individual membership contract will allow the right-holder to precisely define the categories of rights administered and the territorial scope of the society's authority. As the licensing authority would derive from the individual

membership contract, the collective rights manager of choice would not be limited to managing these rights in his home territory only, but throughout the EU;

(5) Individual membership contracts create a fiduciary duty between the collecting society and its members, obliging the former to distribute royalties in an equitable manner. The principle of equitable distribution obliges CRMs to treat domestic and nondomestic members alike with respect to all elements of the management service provided. The fiduciary duty enshrined in membership contracts is thus is a tool to maximise the royalties that accrue to right-holders;

(6) Membership cannot be refused to individual categories of right-holders who represent mainly non-domestic interests (e.g., music publishers). In addition, these right-holders should have a voice in how royalties are distributed that is commensurate to the economic value of the rights they represent;

(7) Non-discrimination as to the service provided and the fiduciary duty of the collective rights manager vis-à-vis its members introduces a culture of transparency and good governance as to how rights are collectively managed across EU borders.[69]

Contrary to the statement made in its 2004 Communication, according to which principles of good governance should be implemented through a legislative instrument, in its Staff Working Document, the Commission kept silent on the type of measure needed to put these principles into practice.

3.4   RECOMMENDATION OF 2005 ON CROSS-BORDER LICENSING OF ONLINE MUSIC SERVICES

Shortly after the publication of the Staff Working Document and at the close of a brief period of consultation with stakeholders, the European Commission issued on 18 October 2005 a Recommendation on collective cross-border management of copyright and related rights for legitimate online music services.[70] Despite its good

---

69. Study on Cross-Border Collective Management of Copyright, *supra* n. 10, at 56.
70. Online Music Recommendation, *supra* n. 5. See also: European Commission, *Commission Staff Working Document, Impact Assessment Reforming Cross-Border Collective Management of Copyright and Related Rights for Legitimate Online Music Services*, SEC (2005) 1254, Brussels, 11 Oct. 2005, <http://ec.europa.eu/internal_market/copyright/docs/management/sec_2005_1254_en.pdf> (last visited: 6 Jan. 2010).

intentions, this Recommendation was met with severe criticism, not least because stakeholders thought the process of adoption of the Recommendation had been rushed and that no one had sufficient opportunity to consider the implications of the proposal or the practical modalities for implementation of the new system. Before turning to these points of critique in the next section, let us first examine the content of the Recommendation.[71]

At the outset, the Recommendation falls short of the promises made in the 2004 Communication in two ways. First, it remains a non-binding document calling not only Member States but also all 'collective rights managers' involved in the cross-border licensing of rights to live up to its principles on a voluntary basis.[72] Although Article 2 of the Recommendation invites Member States 'to take steps necessary to facilitate the growth of legitimate online services in the Community by promoting a regulatory environment which is best suited to the management, at Community level, of copyright and related rights for the provision of legitimate online music services', it sets no deadline for doing so, nor does it involve any sanction for failure to do so.[73] It is therefore highly doubtful that all Member States will voluntarily implement the requirements set by the Recommendation so as to achieve a minimum level of harmonization.[74]

Second, the Recommendation applies only to the cross-border licensing of rights in the online environment, leaving the off-line licensing models unaffected. Although it is to be expected that the online business models will influence the manner in which licenses are granted off-line,[75] it may take some time before both areas actually follow similar forms of licensing. According to some commentators, it is not excluded that, with respect to off-line uses of their repertoire, CMOs will for a time persist with the traditional way of granting licenses applicable to their own national territory only, relying on reciprocal agreements for representation in other EEA countries. Where CMOs decide to observe the requirements of the Recommendation for the online licensing of rights, while maintaining the traditional practice for off-line licensing, a situation of legal uncertainty in the collective management of rights is bound to arise for both right holders and users.[76]

---

71. M.M. Frabboni, 'Online Music Licensing: The Calm after the Storm', *Entertainment Law Review* 17(2) (2006): 65–69.
72. J. Drexl, 'Le droit de la gestion collective en Allemagne après la recommandation européenne sur la gestion collective des droits en ligne dans le domaine musical', in *Impulse für eine europäische Harmonisierung des Urheberrechts: Urheberrecht im deutsch-französischen Dialog*, ed. R.M. Hilty, C. Geiger & V.-L. Benabou (Berlin: Springer, 2007), 399–430, at 400.
73. Member States and collective rights managers are merely invited to report to the Commission on a yearly basis, on the measures they have taken in relation to the Recommendation and on the management of copyright and related rights for the provision of legitimate online music services, so that the Commission can assess the need for further action at Community level. See: Art. 16 of the Online Music Recommendation, *supra* n. 5.
74. R. Matulionytė, 'Cross-Border Management and Principle of Territoriality', *Journal of World Intellectual Property* 11, no. 5–6, (2009): 467–497, at 478.
75. Drexl, *supra* n. 72, at 401.
76. Frabboni, *supra* n. 68, at 207.

Contrary to a directive, which is normally addressed to the Member States who are obligated to implement its rules in their national legal order, the Recommendation is addressed not only to the Member States, but also to all economic operators who are involved in the management of copyright and related rights within the Community. Some provisions contained in the Recommendation, however, are directed specifically to Member States. Article 2, for example, invites Member States 'to take the steps necessary to facilitate the growth of legitimate online services in the Community by promoting a regulatory environment which is best suited to the management, at Community level, of copyright and related rights for the provision of legitimate online music services'. But most provisions are aimed at 'collective rights managers', who are defined as persons who provide to several right holders management services of copyright and related rights for the provision of legitimate online music services at Community level. Such management services include the grant of licenses to commercial users, the auditing and monitoring of rights, the enforcement of copyright and related rights, the collection of royalties and the distribution of royalties to right holders.[77]

With respect to multi-territorial licensing of rights, the Commission decided to favour Option 3, as announced in its Staff Working Document, that is, to give right holders the choice to authorize a CMO of their choice to manage their works across the entire Union. The Recommendation incorporates the seven principles enumerated in the Staff Working Document. Article 3 of the Recommendation emphasizes that right holders should have the right to entrust the management of any of the online rights necessary to operate legitimate online music services, on a territorial scope of their choice, to a collective rights manager of their choice, irrespective of the Member State of residence or the nationality of either the collective rights manager or the right holder. This provision introduces competition among collective rights managers at the level of right holders, because they are no longer compelled to join exclusively the CMO in their country of residence.

According to the Recommendation, right holders should be able to determine the online rights to be entrusted for collective management as well as the territorial scope of the mandate of the collective rights managers. Right holders should also, upon reasonable notice of their intention to do so, have the right to withdraw any of the online rights and transfer the multi-territorial management of those rights to another collective rights manager, irrespective of the Member State of residence or the nationality of either the manager or the right holder. This principle directly addresses the situation encountered in the *Daft Punk* decision,[78] in which the authors wanted to withdraw their online rights from SACEM's management to exercise them individually (*supra*, text). This entails that where a right holder has transferred the management of an online right to another collective rights manager, without prejudice to other forms of cooperation among rights managers, all collective rights managers concerned should ensure that those online rights are

77. Article 1a of the Online Music Recommendation, *supra* n. 5.
78. *Daft Punk* decision, *supra* n. 23.

withdrawn from any existing reciprocal representation agreement concluded among them.

The Recommendation further sets out principles with respect to the good governance of collective rights managers. Collective rights managers are therefore urged to inform right holders and commercial users about the repertoire they represent, any existing reciprocal representation agreements, the territorial scope of their mandates for that repertoire, the applicable tariffs and any changes to these. Collective rights managers are invited to abide by the principle of non-discrimination in the grant of licenses to commercial users as well as in their relationship with right holders. Royalties should be distributed according to principles of equity and fairness. Collective rights managers should operate in a transparent manner and report regularly to all right holders they represent on any licenses granted, applicable tariffs and royalties collected and distributed. In particular, they should specify vis-à-vis all the right holders they represent the deductions made for purposes other than for the management services provided. With respect to the establishment of a dispute settlement mechanism, Member States are invited under the Recommendation to provide for effective solutions in particular in relation to tariffs, licensing conditions, entrustment of online rights for management and withdrawal of online rights.[79]

3.5 REACTIONS OF THE EUROPEAN PARLIAMENT

Among the most critical reactions to the Commission's Recommendation on the cross-border licensing of legitimate online music services was that of the European Parliament. The Parliament felt the need to issue two resolutions in respect to this recommendation, a first one on 13 March 2007[80] and a second one, on 25 September 2008.[81] The first and foremost point of critique voiced by the European Parliament concerns the Commission's failure to undertake a broad and thorough consultation process with interested parties and with the Parliament before adopting the Recommendation, as well as the Commission's omission to involve Parliament formally, particularly in view of Parliament's previously mentioned resolution of 15 January 2004, given that the Recommendation clearly goes further than merely interpreting or supplementing existing rules. The Parliament found it

---

79. Frabboni, *supra* n. 71, at 68.
80. European Parliament, *Resolution of 13 March 2007 on the Commission Recommendation of 18 October 2005 on collective cross-border management of copyright and related rights for legitimate online music services (2005/737/EC)*, P6_TA(2007)0064, Strasbourg, 13 Mar. 2007, online: <www.europarl.europa.eu/sides/getDoc.do?pubRef=-//EP//TEXT+TA+P6-TA-2007-0064+0+DOC+XML+V0//EN&language=EN> (last visited: 6 Jan. 2010).
81. European Parliament, *Resolution of 25 September 2008 on collective cross-border management of copyright and related rights for legitimate online music services*, P6_TA(2008)0462, Brussels, 25 Sep. 2008, online: <www.europarl.europa.eu/sides/getDoc.do?pubRef=-//EP//TEXT+TA+P6-TA-2008-0462+0+DOC+XML+V0//EN&language=EN> (last visited: 6 Jan. 2010).

unacceptable that a 'soft law' approach was chosen without prior consultation and without the formal involvement of Parliament and the Council, thereby circumventing the democratic process, especially as the initiative taken had already influenced decisions in the market to the potential detriment of competition and cultural diversity.

The Parliament further emphasized the important role played by national CMOs in providing support for the promotion of new and minority right holders, cultural diversity, creativity and local repertoires, which presupposes that they retain the right to charge cultural deductions. In this regard, the Parliament said to be concerned about the potentially negative effects of some provisions of the Recommendation on local repertoires and on cultural diversity, given the potential risk for favouring a concentration of rights in the bigger CMOs. Any initiative for the introduction of competition between rights managers in attracting the most profitable right holders must therefore be examined and weighed against the adverse effects of such an approach on smaller right holders, small and medium-sized CMOs and cultural diversity.

Consequently, the Parliament invited the Commission to make it clear that the 2005 Recommendation applied exclusively to online sales of music recordings. It also wished to see a genuine legislative procedure, for which the interested parties would be closely consulted, producing, as soon as possible, a proposal for a flexible directive under the co-decision procedure with a view to regulating the collective management of copyright and related rights in the online music sector. In the Parliament's view, such a proposal ought to take into account the special features of the digital era while safeguarding European cultural diversity.

In its 2008 Resolution, the European Parliament reiterated its opinion that the Commission's refusal to legislate – despite various European Parliament resolutions – and the decision to try to regulate the sector through a recommendation had created a climate of legal uncertainty for right holders and for users. It stressed that the effect of the CISAC decision would be to preclude all attempts by the parties concerned to act together to find appropriate solutions, such as a system for the clearing of rights at European level. In its view, the decision also left the way open to an oligopoly of large CMOs linked by exclusive agreements to publishers belonging to the worldwide repertoire. The Parliament was convinced that the result would be a restriction of choice and the extinction of small CMOs, to the detriment of minority cultures. Finally, it asked to be involved effectively, as co-legislator, in the initiative on Creative Content Online, in which the multi-territory licensing of creative content has been identified as one of the main areas requiring EU action.[82]

---

82. Creative Content Online initiative, <http://ec.europa.eu/avpolicy/other_actions/content_online/index_en.htm> (last visited: 6 Jan. 2010).

4   IMPACT OF RECENT MEASURES ON THE MARKET
              FOR CROSS-BORDER LICENSING OF RIGHTS

Even if the European Commission's 2005 Recommendation is a non-binding instrument, its effect on the market for cross-border licensing of rights should not be underestimated. Within four years since its adoption, the Recommendation has brought severe legal uncertainty by putting the market for collective management of rights in turmoil, which was only aggravated by the Commission's decision in the CISAC case. As shall be seen below, the multi-territorial licensing of rights in Europe experiences tremendous difficulty in moving from a system of reciprocal representation agreements between CMOs to a 'one-stop shop' system based on the freedom of choice of the right holders, as called for by the Recommendation. At this time, neither form of system is fully functional and some of the concerns expressed against the Recommendation by the European Parliament and legal commentators seem to be materializing.[83]

Among the biggest concerns is the fear that the implementation of the Recommendation will lead to the emergence of monopolies or regional oligopolies for the management of online music rights which, in the long term, could have a negative effect on the cultural diversity.[84] By allowing right holders to assign their online rights to the CMO of their choice, competition will arise at the level of the repertoires, which leads to a segmentation of the market, favouring the establishment of monopolies and the appearance of network effects. As a result, CMOs will develop a specialized repertoire[85] and competition will be possible only between CMOs with substitutable repertoires.[86]

Competition at the repertoire level therefore means that CMOs will tend to build up a repertoire containing only the most popular works among online users. Authors of less popular works may find themselves at a disadvantage if they can assign their rights to only one CMO active in a niche market for a specialized music genre. This is not unlikely, because, although there is no obligation on CMOs to accept them as members, their requests can simply be ignored by CMOs administering popular repertoire who find their repertoire too unprofitable to be administered. This may especially be so if CMOs start collaborating with large music

---

83. A. Porcin, 'The quest for pan-European Copyright Licensing Solutions: A Series of Unfortunate Events', *Concurrences* 4-(2009): 57–64, at 60.
84. Frabboni, *supra* n. 53, at 81. See also: P. Tuma, 'Pitfalls and Challenges of the EC Directive on the Collective Management of Copyright and Related Rights', *European Intellectual Property Review* 28, no. 4 (2006): 220–229, at 228; and M. Ricolfi, 'Individual and Collective Management of Copyright in a Digital Environment', in *Copyright law: a handbook of contemporary research*, ed. P. Torremans (Cheltenham: Edward Elgar Publishing, 2007), 283–314, at 297.
85. This was also foreseen by the Commission, which concludes: 'Option 3 would allow CRMs [i.e., CMOs] to build up attractive genre-specific repertoires. The increasing diversity of online music services will create a demand for cross-border genre-specific licenses. Option 3 would give CRMs to specialise in line with this demand and compete for right-holders that complement their existing genre repertoires.' See Study on Cross-Border Collective Management of Copyright, *supra* n. 10, at 36.
86. Drexl, *supra* n. 72, at 417.

publishers to offer EU-wide licenses for online use that exclusively apply to their repertoire.[87] As will seen later, signs of such collaborations are currently already manifesting in the area of cross-border collective management of rights.

Under the system recommended by the Commission, therefore, the repertoire of right holders for which online users may seek a multi-territorial license will be dispersed among different CMOs. Despite the Commission's hope that the European repertoire will be split among a small number of CMOs,[88] it is possible that the number of CMOs offering EU-wide licenses will increase if the not too profitable local repertoire continues to be administered by the existing national CMOs (which, given the local differences in Europe is not unlikely to occur), while the management of specific repertoire, most presumably the popular repertoire, is concentrated in a few newly established CMOs that dominate the market of cross-border collective management of copyright.

The Recommendation may therefore not have the desired outcome for online users. Although they will no longer need to obtain licenses from the CMOs in the twenty-seven EU Member States to cover the entirety of the European territory, they will still need to obtain licenses from different CMOs to cover the breadth of the repertoire they wish to use.[89] Especially if online users wish to obtain a blanket EU-wide license covering the entire music repertoire, the proposed system requires them to acquire licenses from all the European CMOs offering such licenses, unless these CMOs again conclude reciprocal representation agreements among themselves (which, however, is not likely to be expected if the licensing models are based on administering the rights of competing music publishers). Users may very well find this too burdensome and choose rather to obtain licenses from the few CMOs in which the popular repertoire is concentrated. This implies that the local repertoire would remain highly unrepresented in the online environment, which would be very detrimental for European cultural diversity.

A tendency toward a concentration of the market can already be felt as the European Commission itself reports on the appearance of a number of initiatives where major publishing and record companies together with selected CMOs are bundling their efforts to act as a one-stop shop for the licensing of online rights.[90] CELAS, a joint venture between EMI Music Publishing and two of the larger national CMOs in Europe, GEMA and PRS, is one such example for the multi-territorial licensing of online and mobile uses of EMI Music Publishing's repertoire in forty European countries. Warner/Chappell Music, GEMA, MCPS-PRS, and STIM have teamed up to offer EU-wide digital licenses for Warner's entire repertoire. Universal Music Publishing Group, another publishing giant, has signed

---

87. To the extent that a CMO exclusively administers the repertoire of a single music publisher, it arguably can be maintained that it no longer concerns collective licensing but rather individual licensing disguised as collective licensing.
88. Study on Cross-Border Collective Management of Copyright, *supra* n. 10, at 41.
89. Porcin, *supra* n. 83, at 61.
90. European Commission, *Monitoring of the 2005 Music Online Recommendation*, Brussels, 7 Feb. 2008 [Online Music Recommendation Monitoring Report], <http://ec.europa.eu/internal_market/copyright/docs/management/monitoring-report_en.pdf> (last visited: 6 Jan. 2010).

an agreement with SACEM that will allow SACEM to administer EU-wide licenses covering Universal Music Publishing's repertoire.[91]

The consequence of such a restructuring of activities of the CMOs involved in these initiatives is that the music publishers have withdrawn their online rights from all other CMOs in Europe that are not part of the deal. These are often the smaller European CMOs that attract a rather local repertoire. The economic impact on the CMOs that are left out is significant, for these CMOs may lose an important portion of their revenues. Assuming that the aggregate administration costs of these societies remain the same (and arguably will become even higher in the future), the remuneration that individual right holders who are represented by these CMOs receive from the use of their works will be lower than in the situation before. This may negatively affect the creation of works by local authors and therefore once more jeopardizes European cultural diversity. Also, if the financial situation of these CMOs worsens dramatically or even reaches the point that they have to end their operations, who will engage in the promotion of local talent?

Interestingly, on 25 June 2009, in the case *MyVideo v. CELAS*, the District Court of Munich invalidated the license system set up by CELAS for use of content on the Internet.[92] After a period of unsuccessful negotiations between MyVideo, which hosts a streaming website for user-provided video content, and CELAS and foreseeing the possibility that CELAS institute proceedings against it for copyright infringement, MyVideo filed for a declaratory judgment, saying that CELAS had no injunction claim against it concerning the reproduction of copyright protected works for online uses. CELAS, on the other hand, claimed that MyVideo infringed the mechanical reproduction rights for online uses of the EMI repertoire that it administers. CELAS invoked no rights of making its repertoire available to the public, because it confirmed that these rights were managed by national CMOs, such as GEMA.[93]

MyVideo's main argument was that CELAS was not mandated for the management of the mechanical reproduction rights for online uses of the EMI repertoire, because the management of these rights had not been validly transferred and therefore remained in the hands of the GEMA.[94] Moreover, even if the rights had been validly transferred, it argued that the separate management of mechanical reproduction rights for online uses was unlawful because these rights are inseparably connected with the right of making available to the public.[95] This argument

---

91. *Ibid.*, at 6.
92. *MyVideo Broadband S.R.L. v. CELAS GmbH*, District Court of Munich *(Landgericht München)*, No. 7 O 4139/08 (25 Jun. 2009), <http://openjur.de/u/31093-7_o_4139-08.html>, last visited: 6 Jan. 2010 (for an English language summary, see M. von Albrecht & J.N. Ullrich, 'Munich District Court Holds Pan-European Copyright Licensing Model of Joint Venture CELAS Invalid', 20 Jul. 2009, <www.klgates.com/newsstand/Detail.aspx?publication=5793>, last visited: 6 Jan. 2010). This decisions was confirmed by the Court of Appeal of Munich, 29 U 3698/09, 29 Apr. 2010, unpublished, on file with the authors.
93. *Ibid.*, no. 36.
94. *Ibid.*, no. 42.
95. *Ibid.*, no. 46.

was upheld by the Munich court. It considered that, in general, the making available of copyright-protected works online cannot technically take place without making a reproduction. In such a case, in which the acts in relation to copyright-protected works cannot be clearly separable and constitute no economically and technically autonomous and unitary use, German copyright law does not allow a splitting of online rights into rights of making available to the public and rights of mechanical reproduction.[96] If this were allowed, it could lead to significant legal uncertainty for online users.[97] As a consequence, the court ruled that EMI could not have validly transferred only the mechanical reproduction rights for online uses to CELAS while leaving the making available rights with GEMA. CELAS therefore had no right to prohibit reproductions of the EMI repertoire for online uses in Germany.

Also as a consequence of the adoption of the Recommendation, CMOs are heavily engaged in litigation against each other, thus impeding progress toward a competitive market for the cross-border licensing of online rights. CMOs are not unanimous about the preferred licensing model and, in some instances, question other societies' mandate to license their repertoire on an EU-wide basis.[98]

The Dutch CMO Buma/Stemra was involved in such litigation following its decision, announced on 21 July 2008, to grant the US-based online electronic music retailer Beatport a pan-European license allowing the latter to offer the entire worldwide repertoire of music online throughout the EU.[99] Buma/Stemra's initiative followed by less than a week the European Commission's decision in the CISAC case. It was the only CMO for music copyright so far to issue such a pan-European license. The license model offered by Buma/Stemra provided online music service providers with a one-stop shop for authors' rights for music for 27 European countries. The licensing model was based on retaining the world's music repertoire for every European CMO for music copyright. According to the press-release of Buma/Stemra, the royalty rates applied through this multi-territorial license were the tariffs set in the country where the copyright was to be exploited.

> In other words, music used in Germany will be accounted for on the basis of the tariffs in use in Germany; music used in Spain will be subject to royalty payments on the basis of the tariff in use there. The advantage of this model is that competition between collecting societies offering multi-territorial licenses takes place on the basis of the costs and services of the music copyright organisations and not on the royalty rates paid to rightsholders. The income of authors, composers and music publishers is thus safeguarded from any downward pressure which might occur in the case of unbridled competition.

---

96. *Ibid.*, nos 54 and 65 et seq.
97. *Ibid.*, no. 71.
98. Online Music Recommendation Monitoring Report, *supra* n. 90, at 7.
99. Buma/Stemra Press Release, 'Buma/Stemra issues Beatport.com a Pan-European License', Amsterdam/Denver (CO), 21 Jul. 2008, online: <www.bumastemra.nl/en-US/Pers/Persberichten/Beatport_press+release.htm> (last visited: 6 Jan. 2010).

Other European CMOs were not pleased with Buma/Stemra's action. The British PRS instituted a court proceeding before the District Court of Haarlem in the Netherlands to stop Buma from applying its pan-European license.[100] PRS argued that pursuant to the reciprocal representation agreement it had concluded with Buma, Buma had not obtained any rights to the repertoire of works administered by PRS beyond Dutch territory. Accordingly, it had no right to grant licenses the territorial scope of which was not limited to this territory. Buma argued that the territorial restriction clause as to the rights granted did not apply to online music sales, because these have by definition a cross-border reach, and that such a clause should therefore not be taken into account. In addition, Buma argued that considering the date when the reciprocal agreement was signed, neither party could have envisaged the grant of a license on online rights. According to Buma, the agreement therefore could not be interpreted as applying territorial restrictions to online rights. On this point, the judge stressed that a reasonable interpretation of the agreement leads to the conclusion that the reciprocal agreement in its entirety is not applicable to online rights and that the parties need to come to a new agreement in this matter.

Buma also relied on the European Commission's invalidation of reciprocal agreements as a result of the CISAC decision. Here, the judge emphasized the fact that the CISAC decision did not invalidate territorial restriction of licenses per se, but rather concerted practices between CISAC members which de facto lead to a situation where only a single CMO in each EU Member State is able to offer multi-repertoire licenses. Finally, Buma pleaded that both PRS and Buma had continued the business practice of cross-border licensing for online exploitation, which they had agreed upon in the framework of the yet expired Santiago Agreement (i.e., a trial reciprocal agreement permitting the participating societies to issue multi-territorial licenses of music performing rights for online use). However, since Buma could by no means substantiate that PRS had licensed Buma's repertoire outside of the United Kingdom, this argument also failed. The preliminary injunction granted in the Dutch ruling thus orders Buma to refrain from granting, concluding or executing license agreements for the online exploitation 'outside of the Netherlands' of musical works administered by PRS. The order precludes Buma from offering such licenses to online music stores that are accessible from outside the Netherlands.[101] This ruling was affirmed on appeal.[102]

---

100. *The Performing Rights Society Limited v. Vereniging BUMA*, District Court of Haarlem (*Rechtbank Haarlem*), 148418/KG ZA 08-410 (19 Aug. 2008), LJN: BE8765, <www.rechtspraak.nl/ljn.asp?ljn=BE8765>, last visited: 6 Jan. 2010 (for an English language translation of the case, made available by Pauline Kuipers (Bird & Bird), see <www.boek9.nl/index.php?//Prs+vs.+Buma////20609/>, last visited: 6 Jan. 2010; B9 7021).
101. K. Neefs, 'Collecting Societies Collide over pan-European Online Music Licensing', *Journal of Intellectual Property Law and Practice* 3, no. 12 (2008): 758–759.
102. *Vereniging BUMA v. The Performing Rights Society Limited*, Court of Appeal of Amsterdam (*Gerechtshof Amsterdam*), 200.016.122/01 KG (19 Jan. 2010), LJN: BL4289, <www.rechtspraak.nl/ljn.asp?ljn= BL4289>, last visited: 4 May 2010.

The same set of facts also gave rise to a court ruling in Germany. On 25 August 2008, the District Court of Mannheim granted an interim injunction against both the online electronic music retailer Beatport and Buma/Stemra. The injunction prohibits Beatport from making musical works that are administered by GEMA available to the public over the Internet in the territory of Germany without having obtained prior consent from GEMA. Buma/Stemra is prohibited from issuing such licenses for the German territory.[103] From GEMA's perspective, Buma/Stemra is not entitled to grant EU-wide licenses of its repertoire, because it had granted Buma/Stemra the right to license the GEMA repertoire for uses only within Buma/Stemra's own administrative territory.[104]

What all these recent developments show is that, despite the Recommendation of 2005 and the CISAC decision, the path to multi-territorial multi-repertoire licenses in Europe is still a long way ahead.

5   CONCLUSION

In summary, the collective management of rights at the European level is in a state of chaos. Instead of cooperating through bilateral agreements to optimize the licensing of copyright at the international level, as they previously did, national CMOs in Europe are currently involved in litigation to prevent each other from issuing pan-European licenses of their respective repertoires. Moreover, under the system proposed by the 2005 Recommendation, small CMOs are threatened to be overrun by a few big conglomerates of CMOs administering the online rights of major music publishers for the European territory. This may affect the income of individual right holders who are represented by these small CMOs, puts the online availability of local repertoire at risk and jeopardizes cultural diversity in Europe. A well-functioning system of multi-territory, multi-repertoire licensing at the European level, which online content providers in Europe languish for and which the 2005 Recommendation has aimed to achieve, has not yet been established.

Remarkably, the European Commission states, in its monitoring report prepared by DG Internal Market, that the Recommendation seems to have produced an impact on the licensing marketplace and is endorsed by a number of collective rights managers, music publishers and users. Therefore the Commission sees no immediate need to intervene in the market for cross-border licensing of rights or for the introduction of clear and binding rules of good governance. The

---

103. *Gema v. Beatport and Buma/Stemra*, District Court of Mannheim (*Landgericht Mannheim*), No. 7 O 224/08 (25 Aug. 2008), <http://lrbw.juris.de/cgi-bin/laender_rechtsprechung/document. py?Gericht=bw&GerichtAuswahl=Landgerichte&Art=en&Datum=2008-8&nr=11180&pos =3&anz=8> (last visited: 5 Jan. 2010).

104. GEMA Press Release, 'Interim injunction against Buma/Stemra and beatport', Munich, 10 Sep. 2008, <www.gema.de/en/press/press-releases/press-release/browse/16/?tx_ttnews% 5Btt_news%5D=756&tx_ttnews%5BbackPid%5D=73&cHash=68709ff6b5> (last visited: 5 Jan. 2010).

Commission merely proposes to follow further developments and to repeat the monitoring, should a clear need to do so arise.

Meanwhile, the question is far from settled. Given the strong criticism expressed by both the European Parliament and various stakeholders in the field, it seems that there is ongoing pressure on the European legislator to come up with adequate solutions to address the problems in the field of cross-border collective management of rights. What such solutions might encompass and what legal instrument would be most suitable to implement them is still unclear. So far, a clear policy cannot be detected. Nevertheless, several departments within the Commission are studying the issue. At this time, the responsibility for the regulation of issues relating to collective rights management seems to lie with DG Internal Market, who has adopted a 'wait-and-see' approach to the issue. By contrast, DG Competition keeps a close eye on the collective management and licensing of rights in music and audiovisual content because licensing practices can obstruct the development of cross-border services on the Internet, radio and television. Moreover, any legislative measure or policy to be elaborated in this area must comply with the European rules on competition law.

To support the cross-border delivery of online content, DG Information Society has launched the 'Creative Content Online in the Single Market' initiative.[105] This initiative aims to enhance the availability of online content and ensure that all players in the value chain receive adequate revenues. The multi-territory licensing of creative content has thereby been identified as one of the main areas requiring EU action. In the short term, these goals may be realized through pragmatic solutions, but the Commission is examining whether, in the medium term, regulatory intervention is needed.[106] The Commission is also preparing a Second Commission Communication on Creative Content, in which the findings and results of the Creative Content Online initiative will be summarized and analysed. Moreover, it shall define a set of principles for action by stakeholders and public authorities and offer a continuing framework for discussions with stakeholders. Finally, the Commission has mandated a study on multi-territory licensing of audiovisual content, the results of which are expected in early 2010.[107]

Studying the issue alone is not enough, however: Action is needed! In the absence of a coherent framework for the multi-territorial multi-repertoire licensing of works supported by binding rules on good governance applicable to CMOs, legal uncertainty will persist in the market for cross-border licensing of works. Where stakeholders are not competing on a level playing field because of the lack of uniform rules governing CMOs' activities, the risk is that the market crystallizes in its current form or takes an undesirable direction. The negative impact of such a

---

105. *Supra* n. 82.
106. European Commission, *Final Report on the Content Online Platform*, May 2009, online: <http://ec.europa.eu/avpolicy/docs/other_actions/col_platform_report.pdf> (last visited: 6 Jan. 2010).
107. S. van Gompel, 'European Commission Final Report on the Content Online Platform', IRIS 6, no. 4/4 (2009).

situation would be felt not only by right holders but also by users of copyright protected material.

Hence, the cross-border rights clearance remains a problematic issue. Online environments such as the Internet and mobile services by definition allow content services to be made available across the single European market. However, the lack of multi-territory copyright licenses – allowing the use of content in several or all EU Member States – makes it difficult for online services to be deployed across Europe and to benefit from economies of scale. Although it is first for right holders to appreciate the potential commercial benefits of multi-territory licensing, there is an underlying need, also from a consumer perspective, to improve existing licensing mechanisms.

Chapter 6

Collective Management in France

*Nathalie Piaskowski**

1   INTRODUCTION

The issues related to collective management are not framed in the same terms as
they were ten years ago. And yet, some have condemned collective management a
bit too quickly.[1] The history of the emergence of collective societies contains in
itself the reasons for their existence. The oldest date back more than a century, and
they either accompanied or actually preceded the creation of copyright. It is true
that they may appear to have remained unchanged for some time. This stasis was
not a problem in itself, because all means of consumption of works and other
protected objects were known and controlled and the works were materialized and
thus easily identifiable. Each new discovery and technological advance put the
industries concerned at risk. Instead of using collective societies as constructive
and aggressive tools, these industries used them as defensive weapons whose main
role was to channel the development and consumption of works. Only in the last
few years has the approach seemed more constructive and open, but it is already
very late. The music industry in France has seen its volume of physical sales drop
by 65% in about eight years,[2] mainly as a result of the development of pirate

---

* Consultant.
1. A. Bertrand, *La Musique et le Droit de Bach a Internet* (Paris: LITEC, 2002), 216 at 87–115.
2. Source: Syndicat National de l'Edition Phonographique. The phonographic industry lost about
   696 millions euros since 2002.

Daniel Gervais (ed.), *Collective Management of Copyright and Related Rights*, pp. 169–213.
© 2010 Kluwer Law International BV, The Netherlands.

downloading of electronic files, which has followed the technical evolution and expanded exponentially. What in the analogue era was the preserve of just a few experts has become a common practice, facilitated by the spread and improved performance of high-speed Internet access. One no longer needs to be a computer scientist or a technician to build a tailor-made, low-cost music or video library. This structural modification of piracy has had a definite impact on collective management and its place in the evolution of copyright and the consumption of culture. Despite the recent adoption in 2009 of an act entitled Hadopi, it does not seem that it will be able to stamp out the phenomena on the long term.

These environmental transformations have also had an impact on the status of collective societies and on how they are overseen. As long as their role was limited to the management of a few well-identified uses, the public authorities were content with a fairly superficial oversight, but as they have begun to manage greater numbers of uses and increasing amounts of money, there has been a strong demand for close supervision of these activities. Collective societies have thus been subjected to new laws more strictly prescribing the conditions for their collection and distribution activities. Today, one of the crucial problems in copyright is the issue of the individual allocation of remuneration.[3]

The second part of this chapter will describe the nature of collective management in France, through the history of how the societies were formed. The third section will examine more in depth how these societies work and look at modalities of oversight of collective societies. Finally, this chapter will attempt to sketch out the issues and future prospects for these societies.

2   HISTORY AND NATURE OF COLLECTIVE MANAGEMENT IN FRANCE

In France, collective societies are called royalty collection and distribution societies (RCDS), a term used in the Act of 11 March 1957, which was modified by the Act of 3 July 1985.[4] This section gives a short history of collective societies, then an overview of the categories of main RCDS and the sectors and rights covered by collective management.

2.1   HISTORY OF COLLECTIVE SOCIETIES IN FRANCE

Collective management was born in France. Its evolution paralleled the development of copyright. Discussion of authors' societies and societies managing

---

3. T. Paris, *Le droit d'auteur: l'ideologie et le systeme* (Paris: Presses Universitaires de France, 2002), 232 at 25–26.
4. Law No. 85-660 of 3 Jul. 1985 concerning copyright and the rights of performers, phonogram producers and audiovisual communication enterprises; available in French at <http://admi.net/jo/loi85-660.html> (last visited: 7 Nov. 2005).

neighbouring rights will be done separately, because the latter notion developed only in the second half of the twentieth century.

2.1.1 The Birth of Copyright Collective Societies

The history of copyright began under the *Ancien Régime*. At the time, the term used was not copyright, but 'property of the product of genius'. This term, far from being insignificant, influenced the approach to copyright protection throughout its history.[5]

Playwright Pierre Augustin Caron de Beaumarchais created the first ever collecting society. At the time, actors, not authors, were all-powerful within the *Comédie Française*. This theatre in effect held a monopoly on the performance of plays, and it pressured authors to abandon their rights. Beaumarchais refused to accept this situation and maintained that if a work has an economic life, its author must be associated with the revenues that it generates.

On 3 July 1777, Beaumarchais and twenty of his fellow writers met at the *Hôtel de Hollande* and created a bureau of theatre legislation, which quickly formed a collection agency, Agence Framery, named after the man authorized by notarized deed to collect copyright fees throughout France. This agency later became the *Société des Auteurs et Compositeurs Dramatiques* (SACD), when Beaumarchais engaged in a strike and stopped writing for three years. He won his battle – he succeeded in establishing that the basis for calculation of copyright would be clearly determined and that the purchase of plays for a lump sum would be forbidden.[6] A large body of jurisprudence on protection of copyright was compiled over the years based on what Beaumarchais had achieved. A statute enacted on 21 July 1793 and the ensuing decree on 3 September of that year laid the foundation for all modern legislation on intellectual property by extending protection of the property rights of all types to music composers, painters and draughtsmen.[7]

It was in this context that the second collective society, *Société des Auteurs Compositeurs et Éditeurs de Musique* (SACEM), was born. One evening in 1847, the composer Ernest Bourget went to a concert café called Les Ambassadeurs. He ordered a glass of sugar water and when his bill arrived, he was indignant that he had to pay extra for having listened to his own composition while he was drinking his glass of sugar water. He therefore refused to pay the inflated bill and sued. The business court of the Seine ruled in favour of Bourget, forbade Les Ambassadeurs to play his pieces and sentenced the manager to pay damages to the composer,

---

5. I. Inchauspé & R. Godeau, *Main basse sur la musique: enquete sur la Sacem* (Paris: Calmann-Lévy, 2003), 239 at 140–155.
6. A decision by the Conseil du Roi dated 9 Dec. 1780 provided that 'the author must preserve for himself and his descendants in perpetuity the privilege of publishing and selling his works'.
7. Ministère de la Culture, 'La mise en œuvre du droit d'auteur et des droits voisins en France: leur gestion en 1990 et 1991 par les sociétés de perception et de répartition' (March 2003), report presented by the sub-directorate of legal affairs of the directorate of general administration of the Ministère de la Culture, Paris, 1993.

although the manager objected and repeated the banned activity. The decision established jurisprudence with regard to protection of musical works.

With this success under his belt, Bourget formed a union with Victor Parizot and Paul Henrion, two playwrights, with the financial support of a publisher, Jules Colombier. In 1850, the union began to collect payments from café owners for all public performances of musical pieces, under the name *Agence Centrale pour la Perception des droits des Auteurs et Compositeurs de Musique*; it was renamed SACEM on 28 February 1851.

A fraternal conception of the body corporate was behind the creation of the first collective societies,[8] and it endured through the years that followed. A group of writers led by Victor Hugo formed the *Société des Gens de Lettres* (SGDL), which then gave rise to the *Société Civile des Auteurs Multimédia* (SCAM), to manage the rights for new audiovisual processes. In 1935, music authors and composers created the *Société pour l'administration du Droit de Reproduction Mécanique* (SDRM) an outgrowth of the performing rights society, the SACEM, to collect fees for reproduction using modern processes. In the 1950s, graphic artists created the *Société des Auteurs des Arts Visuels* (SPADEM) and the *Société des Auteurs Dans les Arts Graphiques et Plastiques* (ADAGP).[9]

Then, new collective societies were formed as new rights were created – sometimes, even before they were created. SOFIA, for instance, was created in 1999 by publishers of printed works, on the initiative of the SGDL, which had actively lobbied for the implementation of royalties for library lending, as set out in the European Communities' Rental Directive[10]; these royalties came into being with a law enacted on 18 June 2003.[11] This process led to the development of societies for collective management of neighbouring rights.

2.1.2 The Birth of Collective Societies for Neighbouring Rights

The Act of 3 July 1985 introduced neighbouring rights to copyright into French legislation for the first time, by applying the *Rome Convention for the Protection of Performers, Producers of Phonograms and Broadcasting Organizations*, which France had signed in 1961 and then ratified on 3 April 1987.[12] However, the

---

8. P.Y. Gautier, *Propriété Littéraire et Artistique*, 5th edn (Paris: Presses Universitaires de France, 2004), 864 at 755.

9. In the graphic arts sector, these two societies, which resulted from a split, were competitors. This rivalry was resolved when SPADEM was dissolved in 1996.

10. EC, *COUNCIL DIRECTIVE 92/100/EEC of 19 November 1992 on rental right and lending right and on certain rights related to copyright in the field of intellectual property* (2002), O.J. L. 346/61 [Rental Directive], <http://europa.eu.int/smartapi/cgi/sga_doc?smartapi!celexapi!prod! CELEXnumdoc&lg=EN&numdoc=31992L0100&model=guichett> (last visited: 18 Oct. 2005).

11. Law No. 2003-517 of 18 Jun. 2003 concerning the remuneration for library (public) lending and reinforcing the social protection of authors, available in French at <www.culture.gouv.fr/culture/dll/droit-pret/texte_loi.html> (last visited: 7 Nov. 2005).

12. Law No. 85-660 of 3 Jul. 1985 on Authors' Rights and on the Rights of Performers, Phonogram and Videogram Producers and Audiovisual Communication Enterprises (O.J. of 7 Mar. 1985).

1985 statute did not create neighbouring rights, but simply affirmed a long history of jurisprudence that obliged public and private radio organizations to obtain permission from artists and producers for all broadcasts of their performances and sound recordings.

While this statute introduced neighbouring rights for producers of sound recordings and performers, in the form of both exclusive rights and legal licenses, it also brought the need to form organizations to collect and distribute royalties in order to implement some of the rights that had been created. Until 1985, the *Syndicat National de l'Edition Phonographique* (SNEP) collectively managed some of the producers' rights. For instance, the public radio network, Radio France, had paid royalties to SNEP from 1946 to 1974. In 1984, record producers gave the society a mandate that resulted in a contract with the television network Canal Plus authorizing the network to broadcast SNEP members' music videos.

In 1985, two collective societies were created: the *Société Civile des Producteurs de Phonogrammes* (SCPP), which represented mainly, but not exclusively, multinational record companies, and the *Société des Producteurs de Phonogrammes en France* (SPPF), which represented 'independent' record producers. At the same time, two performers' societies were created: the *société pour l'Administration des Droits des Artistes et Musiciens Interprètes s* (ADAMI), to manage the rights of solo artists and audiovisual artists, and the *Société de Perception et de Distribution des Droits des Artistes Interprètes de la Musique et de la Danse* (SPEDIDAM), to manage other musicians' rights.

When the 1957 statute was first enacted, and even more in 1985,[13] France had a large number of collective societies, although there were not yet the 27 that exist today. It was thus important to set up a legal environment that would regulate how these societies were created and operated.

2.2   EXISTING COLLECTIVE SOCIETIES

It is not easy to determine an appropriate typology for the existing collective societies. However, there are several categories found in the annual report of the *Commission Permanente de Contrôle des SPRD,*[14] which are particularly interesting in that they cover two different realities of collective management. Primary management collective societies are in direct contact with their members and often take on other missions, such as defence of their members' legal and economic interests. Intermediary societies respond to a concern with rationalization of collection and are a sort of 'common gateway' for one category of rights or works. Generally, the objective of these societies is limited to collection of royalties and their distribution to their member primary management collective societies.

---

13. See *supra* n. 4.
14. *Rapport Annuel de la Commission Permanente de Contrôle des SPRD,* June 2004.

2.2.1 Primary Management Collective Societies

For the purposes of brevity, this chapter will discuss only the main authors' societies and the neighbouring rights societies in the various cultural sectors.

2.2.1.1 Authors' Societies

In the music sector, collective societies were created in light of the types of rights that they had to manage. As in many countries, the most complete rights-management systems were created to manage 'small rights', or rights of execution in certain musical categories (notably, songs).[15] 'Grand rights' are rights having to do with musical-theatre works (plays, operas, etc.) and are usually managed individually. All of these authors' societies were originally created to manage rights in the context of voluntary collective management. They were then used to manage rights under mandatory collective management, such as remuneration for private copying, for lending rights, for reprography and for simultaneous, complete, unchanged cable retransmission of television programmes.

2.2.1.1.1 SACEM

As mentioned previously, SACEM is one of the oldest collective societies in the world. Its mandate is to operate and administer, in all countries, all rights involving public execution, public performance, mechanical reproduction and, notably, the collection and distribution of royalties arising from the use of these rights.[16] SACEM's repertoire is made up of musical compositions, documentary works dealing with exclusively musical subject matter, most poems and sketches (SACEM, SCAM and SACD all accept them), excerpts from dramatic and musical-theatre works shorter than twenty minutes for television and twenty-five minutes for radio, dubbing and subtitles for foreign films and audiovisual productions that apply to the works in the SACEM repertoire (notably music videos). SACEM manages the rights of its members worldwide on the basis of exclusive assignment for a renewable ten-year period. It distributes the royalties that it collects for public performance and mechanical reproduction to its members and to foreign authors' societies with which it has concluded reciprocal representation contracts. Through these contracts, it is mandated to manage the repertoire of all of these foreign societies within its territory of activity (mainly France, Luxembourg and Monaco). However, those contracts were seriously challenged and threatened by the recent European Decision of 16 July 2008 condemning collecting societies, among them SACEM, for these reciprocal agreements in the field of music online exploitation and satellite and cable retransmission.

Royalties collected are first allocated to works and then shared among the respective right holders. SACEM represents more than 128,000 authors and

---

15. M. Ficsor, *Collective Management of Copyright and Related Rights* (Geneva: WIPO, 2002), 165 at 37–49.
16. Article 4 of SACEM's corporate statutes.

manages a worldwide repertoire of 37 million works. In 2008, the society collected Euro (EUR) 755.8 million and redistributed EUR 616 million. It also devoted EUR 14.6 million to assistance to creation, distribution of live shows, and training of artists.[17] Royalties are distributed as one third each for the composer, the lyricist and the publisher.

2.2.1.1.2   SACD

The *Société des Auteurs et Compositeurs Dramatiques* (SACD) was founded in 1777. It has three categories of members: authors and composers, heirs and lega- tees and assignees admitted as members. The society manages adaptation and performance rights for the plays of its members and their right to authorize and forbid communication of their works to the public by any method whatsoever, other than dramatic performance, as well as reproduction by any method and use for publicity or advertising purposes. SACD's repertoire is made up of dramatic works such as plays, musical-theatre works (operas), choreographed works, pan- tomimes and audiovisual works such as cinematographic, television, multimedia and radio works. SACD is one of the few societies to have incorporated a form of individual management within its collective management activities.[18]

In 2008, SACD collected EUR 179.5 million, of which 67.6% concerned audiovisual works and 32.3% live shows. EUR 3.9 million was devoted to cultural assistance.

2.2.1.1.3   SCAM

Members of the *Société Civile des Auteurs Multimédia* are authors of multimedia works other than plays and musical works. SCAM's repertoire is made up of documentary audiovisual works, audio works that are neither musical nor dra- matic, written works, still images and documentary interactive works. Members may contribute their rights in management or in property for the lifetime of the society. Acting with contributions in property, SCAM manages, in whole or in part, the reproduction and performance rights for works in its repertoire as well as translation rights for published books and the right to authorize or forbid publica- tion of these works. When works are contributed for management only, SCAM's mission is limited to overseeing executions of contracts concluded by the author (notably the collection of sums due, thanks to such executions and their payment to the author). Nevertheless, if the author has so specified, SCAM is also authorized to negotiate and conclude contracts with users on the author's behalf concerning exploitation of his works.

In 2008, SCAM collected EUR 74 million and distributed EUR 67.8 million.

2.2.1.1.4   ADAGP

The *Société des Auteurs Dans les Arts Graphiques, Plastiques et Photographiques* long shared management of graphic-art works with another society, SPADEM,

---

17. Source: SACEM.
18. See para. 3.2.1, below.

from which it split. The two societies competed fiercely until SPADEM folded in 1996. ADAGP's sphere of activity is the visual arts and thus involves paintings, sculptures, architecture, computer graphics, photographs, illustrations and so on. The members assign their rights to ADAGP, which provides collective management of the performance, reproduction and 'droit de suite' for the works in its repertoire.

Nevertheless, individual management has been a part of the society's operations since it was founded. Thus, members are consulted and give their prior agreement for the publication of books, for separate reproductions, for media involving a transformation of the work, for three-dimensional reproduction and for reproduction for advertising purposes.

2.2.1.1.5 SOFIA

SOFIA was created in 1999, on the initiative of the *SGDL,* later joined by the *Syndicat National de l'Édition,* to collect the new rights created by the Act of 18 June 2003 on library lending rights and by the Act of 17 July 2001[19] making authors the beneficiaries of the royalties for private copying on digital media of their works.[20] SOFIA began to collect these royalties and, since it was approved by public authorities on 14 March 2005, has collected remuneration for library lending rights on behalf of writers and publishers. It is administered on a parity basis by authors and publishers of books exclusively.

SOFIA's management is based on mandatory assignments with regard to lending rights and remuneration for digital private copying. On the other hand, management of new rights to come from exploitation of works on digital networks is based on optional mandates.

2.2.1.2 Neighbouring Rights Societies

Unlike authors' societies, most societies that manage neighbouring rights were created to fulfil a mission of mandatory collective management attached to the non-voluntary licensing system implemented for exploitation of sound recordings. Only over time have these societies developed an increasingly greater share of voluntary collective management, upon request of their members.

2.2.1.2.1 The Sound Recording Producers' Societies (SCPP and SPPF)

The SCPP was created in 1985, and SPPF was created in 1987, when the Act of 3 July 1985,[21] implementing the measures of the Rome Convention, came into force. The members of these two societies are right holders from the same category, with the small distinction that SPPF members are exclusively 'independent'

---

19. Article 15 and foll. of the Law No. 2001-624 of 17 Jul. 2001 concerning various social, educational and cultural matters (O.J. No. 164 of 18 Jul. 2001 page 11496) available in French at <www.legifrance.gouv.fr/WAspad/UnTexteDeJorf?numjo=MESX0100056L> (last visited: 7 Nov. 2005).
20. Measure implemented by decision No. 4 of the *Commission Copie Privée,* 10 Jun. 2003.
21. See *supra* n. 4.

producers, whereas SCPP's members are both independent producers and multinational record companies, thus representing more than 80% of the rights of French producers. The repertoire of these societies comprises sound recordings published for commercial and music-video purposes. The societies manage the same kinds of rights; they both distribute the royalties collected by Société pour la Perception de la Rémunération Equitable (SPRE) for mandatory collective management of rights arising from the broadcasting of sound recordings and their communication in public places, as well as royalties collected by Société pour la Rémunération de la Copie Privée Sonore (SORECOP) for private copying. In addition, over time, they have developed a large share of voluntary collective management for broadcasting of music videos on television networks and for use of excerpts of sound recordings, whether on the Internet, for mobile telephones, or for on-demand listening in points of sale. Many types of uses remain under individual management by the producers themselves. When a new use emerges and producers wish to entrust management to their society, the society institutes optional mandates that can be revoked without the member having to resign, which allows the impact of the mode of management of the new use to be measured in terms of remuneration. With this flexible and open approach, not only have few mandates been revoked but a growing number are entrusted to these societies.

There is another difference between these two societies: SCPP is authorized to give permission for use only within France, whereas SPPF has a worldwide mandate for a great number of uses. This is explained by the difference in the structure of right holders that belong to each society. SCPP involves mainly, though not exclusively, international record companies, which have subsidiaries in each European country and in almost every region of the world. Each subsidiary belongs to the collective society in the country in which it operates and can thus easily control the management of its rights in each territory. SPPF involves only independent producers, many of which are small companies that do not have the resources to control the use of their catalogues abroad. It is thus more rational for these companies to provide their collective society with a mandate that is territorially broader than if they had subsidiaries in each national territory.

Unlike ADAGP and SPADEM in the past, SPPF and SCPP do not compete fiercely. They coexist in a climate of mutual trust and sometimes pool their collected funds (particularly for collection for the use of sound recordings for telephone call waiting) and coordinate some of their distribution rules for greater homogeneity to avoid double payments. In any case, these steps toward harmonization are taken in utter respect for the national and European competition rules and are proof that two societies may coexist and manage similar rights while responding to different expectations by right holders even though those right holders are of the same category. SCPP and SPPF joined very early (in 1987) within a joint society, Société Civile des Producteurs Associés (SCPA), which represents them in organizations that allocate to categories of right holders the product of fair remuneration and private copying. It also pools collection for some uses arising from exclusive rights in the context of voluntary collective management (use of sound recordings for telephone call waiting).

Aside from its rights-management mission, SCPP delivers to its producer members an International Standard Recording Code (ISRC) number that identifies all sound recordings and music videos.

In 2008, SCPP collected EUR 69.8 million and distributed EUR 59 million. It devoted EUR 9.7 million to cultural assistance.

2.2.1.2.2   Performers' 'Societies (ADAMI and SPEDIDAM)

ADAMI, created in 1955, is the main society for collection and distribution of neighbouring rights for performing artists; it began as a professional association affiliated with the union of performing artists. SPEDIDAM was created in 1959 by the *Syndicat National des Musiciens.* The membership in these two societies is divided as follows: ADAMI represents performing artists, variety artists and solo singers, dancers and musicians, known as 'label artists' (an artist is presumed to be a 'label artist' when his or her name figures in the credits or on the label of the sound recording), and SPEDIDAM manages the rights of performing artists whose names do not appear in the credits or on the label of sound recordings. Both societies collect the same types of remuneration – that from non-voluntary licenses and from management of exclusive rights on secondary uses of the artists' performances – according to a distribution formula set out by arbitration concluded between the two parties on 11 July 1987. Divergences of interpretation that arose concerning the arbitration ruling led to a long dispute, which finally ended on 28 June 2004, when ADAMI and SPEDIDAM concluded a framework agreement that led to the creation of a joint society, the *Société des Artistes Interprètes,* on 29 November 2004. Under this framework, the new society makes joint distributions on the basis of distribution formulas agreed to between ADAMI and SPEDIDAM.

In 2008, SPEDIDAM collected EUR 29 million and distributed EUR 17 million. It dedicated EUR 9.4 million to cultural assistance. In regard to ADAMI, it collected approximately EUR 53 million and distributed about EUR 35 million. The dedication to cultural assistance amounted to EUR 11.8 million.

2.2.1.2.3   Audiovisual Producers' Societies (ANGOA and PROCIREP)

For audiovisual works, the principle is that of individual management. Nevertheless, when it comes to rights for simultaneous and complete retransmission by cable and remuneration for private copying, the French law sets out obligatory collective management in compliance with the cable and satellite directive. Two societies have been created for this purpose: ANGOA and PROCIREP.

Association Nationale de Gestion des Œuvres Audiovisuelles (ANGOA) was created in 1981. It manages simultaneous, complete, unchanged retransmission of audiovisual works through cable network, ADSL and satellite platforms. It collects and distributes royalties on behalf of French and foreign producers registered with *Association de Gestion Internationale Collective des Œuvres Audiovisuelles* (AGI-COA), and it exists only because management of cable retransmission rights must be collective under Article 8 of the Satellite and Cable Directive.[22] By majority will of the producers, audiovisual collective management constitutes an exception and usually comes into effect only when it is made mandatory by the law.

The *Société Civile pour la Perception et la Répartition des droits de Représentation Publique des films Cinématographiques* (PROCIREP) was created in 1964 to provide collective management of audiovisual producers' royalties for private copying and for educational uses of their works by schools and universities. Aside from the producers that it represents, PROCIREP also has a mandate from the *Institut National de l'Audiovisuel* (INA), which manages the audiovisual archives of French television channels and the legal deposit for audiovisual works and broadcasters. In 2008, the PROCIREP collected EUR 32.4 million from the private copies levy and distributed EUR 20.7 million. It dedicated EUR 7.9 million to cultural assistance.

2.2.2 Intermediary Collective Societies

These societies are 'intermediary' because they constitute an extra layer in the flows of remuneration. Characteristically, their members are primary collective societies. These common-law companies are designed to realize economies of scale. With the exception of SDRM and SESAM, they also fall within the framework of obligatory collective management.

2.2.2.1 SDRM

The SDRM was founded in 1935 and manages the mechanical reproduction rights of authors, composers and publishers of music. Its members are SACEM, SACD and SCAM, linked to SGDL; and Association des Editeurs pour l'Exploitation des Droits de Reproduction Mécanique (AEEDRM), a publishers' group association. SDRM issues authorizations to fix to a medium and to reproduce from this recorded medium the works in the repertoires managed by its member societies. The royalties due for reproduction of sound recordings are calculated as a function of the sale price of the sound recording at 8% of retail price or 11% of the wholesale price published to retailers. The royalties for music use on television and radio amounts to 5% of television's exploitation receipts and 6% of radio's receipts. The royalties collected by SDRM are then distributed among the member societies on a basis of 25% for the author, 25% for the composer and 50% for the publisher.

SDRM also receives from SORECOP and COPIE France the share of remuneration for private copying due to authors and distributes these monies among the authors' societies, which then distribute the payments among their members.

---

22. EC, *COUNCIL DIRECTIVE 93/83/EEC of 27 September 1993 on the coordination of certain rules concerning copyright and rights related to copyright applicable to satellite broadcasting and cable retransmission* (1993), O.J. L. 248/15 [Satellite and Cable Directive], online: <http://europa.eu.int/eur-lex/lex/LexUriServ/LexUriServ.do?uri=CELEX:31993L0083:EN:HTML> (last visited: 18 Oct. 2005).

Nevertheless, SDRM does not have true management autonomy. It functions essentially through SACEM's operational system.

2.2.2.2 SESAM

This society was founded in 1996 and groups together authors' societies (SACD, SACEM, SCAM, ADAGP). It manages rights linked to production of multimedia programs (i.e., when more than two pre-existing works are used). SESAM has always been viewed in France as the first experiment with a 'common gateway' for authors, in that it was asked to manage complex requests for licenses concerning multimedia productions that use several types of works (music, still and animated images, texts, graphics, etc.). SESAM does not have its own repertoire; rather it has a mandate from its member societies' members to manage their repertoire. It is competent as long as the use of a protected content involves at least two repertoires for an interactive use. It has access to the databases of its member societies in order to fulfil its mission.

2.2.2.3 COPIE FRANCE and SORECOP

COPIE France (the *Société pour la Rémunération de la Copie Privée Audiovisuelle*) was created in 1986 to collect remuneration for the reproduction of works on video media reserved strictly for the private use of the person who produces them. Copie France's board of directors includes representation from SDRM, ADAMI, SPEDIDAM, PROCIREP and SCPA.

SORECOP (*Société pour la Rémunération de la Copie Privée Sonore*) is the counterpart to Copie France for private copying of sound recordings. SDRM, ADAMI, SPEDIDAM and SCPA are members of SORECOP.

Copie France and SORECOP are the only societies authorized under the management mandates provided to them by their member societies to collect and distribute royalties for authors, performers and producers or their assignees, for the reproduction for private use of sound or video recordings.

The remuneration for private copying is paid by importing manufacturers or entities that make intra-community acquisitions of usable recording media for the private reproduction of sound or video recordings. It is being updated by an administrative committee created for this purpose by the CPI, for both analogue and digital media.

The Act of 17 June 2001 instituted remuneration for authors and publishers of written works and still images, while the system in place up to then included only musical and audiovisual works. Following a decision by the administrative committee on 10 June 2003, this category of right holders became part of the authors' category.

2.2.2.4 CFC

The *Centre Français d'exploitation du droit de Copie* (CFC) was created in 1996 with the mission of administering, under a legal license, the reprography rights mandated or assigned to it by authors or their right holders. Its members are authors and authors' societies and newspaper and book publishers. Distribution is done on a parity basis between author and publisher with regard to book publishing. It is determined by an ad hoc committee for newspaper publishing. The CFC collected in 2008 EUR 37.8 million and distributed EUR 29.7 million to its members.

2.2.2.5 SPRE

The *Société Civile pour la Perception de la Rémunération Équitable* groups two societies of performing artists (ADAMI and SPEDIDAM) and SCPA (which groups the two sound-recording-producer societies, SCPP and SPPF). SPRE has the mandate of collecting a 'fair' remuneration with regard to certain forms of public communication of sound recordings provided for in Article L.214-1 of the *Code de la Propriété Intellectuelle* (Intellectual Property Code or CPI), namely broadcasting and cable retransmission,[23] and performance in public places provided the recording is not being used as part of a show. Concretely, SPRE collects directly from radio and television networks and from discothèques. However, since 1990, SPRE has mandated SACEM to collect from sites with P.A. systems. The law provides for that this remuneration is calculated in most cases according to the users' operating income.

On the other hand, SPRE, which, according to its statutes, should be authorized to collect sums related to use of sound recordings in shows on behalf of performing artists, uses for which the members must have given prior authorization, has proved to be not very active in this area because of the long conflict between ADAMI and SPEDIDAM. Thus, theatre operators must deal separately with these two societies.

3 COLLECTIVE MANAGEMENT AND OVERSIGHT OF COLLECTIVE SOCIETIES IN FRANCE

Section 3 of this chapter describes how collective societies work, in three regards: their legal establishment, royalty-collection operations and the process of distributing the royalties collected. It also examines the oversight of collective societies.

3.1 Constitution and Status of Royalty Collection and Distribution Societies

The Act of 3 July 1985, slightly amended on those points by the 2006 Act, DADVSI, devoted an entire chapter to 'RCDS' in the CPI.

---

23. The provision of Art. L.214-1 of the CPI has been amended by a law enacted in 2006, extending the scope of the compulsory license in the field of broadcasting although the different concerned parties still do not share the same interpretation of this new text.

3.1.1 Legal Form

Article L.321-1 of the CPI states that all RCDSs, whether they are administering copyright or neighbouring rights, must be established as civil-law companies whose members are the holders of the copyright or neighbouring rights, depending on the case. The following Article (Article L.321-2) draws the logical conclusion, in conformity with French corporate law, that 'Contracts concluded by the civil law societies of authors or of owners of neighboring rights, in implementation of their purpose, with the users of all or part of their repertoire shall constitute civil law instruments.' One author has called attention to the fact that this capacity is a sort of 'guarantee of civil quality' made to the members, themselves physical persons,[24] excepting, of course, producers and publishers, which are usually businesses.[25] If one examines the preparatory work for the act, it seems quite obvious that the legislature intended to place all of the management of literary and artistic property rights under the aegis of civil law.[26]

This determination has a number of consequences. First, the courts with juris-diction if there is a dispute are the common-law civil courts. Second, collective societies are not supposed to make a profit and must be content with pooling their resources to serve their members. Third, collective societies are not subjected to taxation or to commercial legislation, which is reserved for businesses. Their civil character does not allow them to evade competition law, as a case brought before the *Cour de Cassation* (High Court) regarding SDRM has shown.[27] Finally, RCDSs, as civil-law companies, fall under Article 1845 for civil-law companies, but only insofar as set out by the CPI.

3.1.2 Legal Bases for Activity

A collective society may, in principle, act freely as long as the government ministry of culture has not demanded its dissolution by court.[28] However, for certain types of collection expressly set out in the CPI, a collective society must obtain approval from public authorities. Once it is established, it must obtain from its members the right to collect royalties on their behalf.

3.1.2.1 Approval

Collective societies in certain collection sectors are subject to specific authorisa-tion, which is issued or withdrawn by the Minister of Culture. This procedure is still quite rare, because the principle remains that there is freedom of establishment and

---

24. Gautier, *supra* n. 8 at 757.
25. B. Edelman, *Droits d'auteurs et droits voisins: droit d'auteur et marche* (Paris: Dalloz, 1993), 360.
26. Senate Report, 4 Apr. 1985, JO Sénat CR 5 Apr. 1985, at 162.
27. Chambre Commerciale de la Cour de Cassation, 5 Nov. 1991, Dalloz, 1993, 63, note Daverat.
28. See para. 3.4.2.1, below.

collection when societies are duly mandated by their member right holders. Approval is implemented mainly for copyright and neighbouring rights under mandatory collective management. Currently, approval must be issued in three categories of exploitation. The first is collective management of the reprography right, for which Act 95-4 of 3 January 1995 set out approval according to the criteria of professional qualification of the officers, the human and material resources proposed, and the equitable nature of the proposed means of distribution. Another statute, Act 97-283 of 27 March 1997, sets out an approval procedure for societies charged with management of rights for simultaneous, complete, unchanged retransmission in France of works broadcast on television in one of the EU Member States. This approval has to be renewed every five years. Finally, a more recent act, dated 18 June 2003, requires approval for societies managing remuneration for library book lending, according to the same criteria as those discussed earlier. Approval requires that the conditions for performing the activity under consideration be fulfilled, but it also requires that these conditions be respected over time, or the society may have its approval withdrawn. To date, none of the approvals issued by the ministry of culture have been withdrawn. On the other hand, some approvals have still not been issued, which is keeping some societies from proceeding with collection. This is the case, in particular, for neighbouring rights societies, which, until recently, did not have approval by the ministry to collect royalties for simultaneous cable retransmission of programmes from EU Member States because of a legal dispute between producers and performers. From January 2010, the Ministry of Culture shall be obliged to issue on a yearly basis the list of the collecting societies to which the agreement has been granted.

3.1.2.2 Assignment or Mandates

Members of RCDSs are not members like others. Aside from corporate members, such as film producers, record producers and publishers of printed works, most members are individuals. It is in fact in the spirit of collective management to place at the service of a group of individuals the means to negotiate for and collect royalties that they would not be able to collect individually. It therefore follows that the contributions used to constitute the capital will very rarely be cash inputs. Usually, collective societies ask a prospective member to pay in a symbolic right representing one or several (depending on the case) capital shares. The contribution made by members is thus usually a contribution in kind, often – but not always (e.g., societies representing corporations such as record producers) – a transfer of property for current and future rights from the member to the collective society.[29]

---

29. For example, Arts 1 and 2 of SACEM's corporate statute stipulate that its members contribute to it the right to authorize or forbid the public performance and the mechanical reproduction of their works as created, to permit the society to achieve its goal. For SACD, the contribution is limited to the right to authorize or forbid audiovisual distribution. In other societies, the contribution is limited to certain types of use expressly provided for in their statutes. However, some collecting societies recently amended their by-laws in a more flexible way allowing their

183

Nevertheless, and this is what creates the particularity and the infringement in common law by civil-law companies, these contributions of rights are not of the same nature as contributions to companies set out by the Civil Code. In effect, they are considered assignments on a fee basis[30] and are not incorporated into the capital.[31] Similarly, members do not share in the profits as a function of the society's results but collect a royalty that is a function of the use that is made of their works.

3.1.2.2.1 Assignment Contributions

With regard to these contributions, some have evoked Article L.131-1 of the CPI, according to which 'total transfer of future works shall be null and void'. Of course, the directors of SACEM appeal to the spirit of the statute, which is to protect authors from overly committing themselves under pressure from the users of their works, and they maintain that this provision thus cannot apply to relations between authors and their collective society – the *raison d'être* of which is to protect the authors against distributors of their works. The jurisprudence is unanimous in validating the legal basis of SACEM's activities. However, ambiguity remains because there is no consensus on what these contracts should be called. The Civil Division of the Cour de Cassation terms them fee-based transfers,[32] whereas the Criminal Division tends to call them simply management mandates.

Nevertheless, an analysis of these contributions seems convincing that they resemble a fiduciary operation,[33] in that the collective societies manage the rights that have been contributed to them not on their own behalf, but on behalf of their members. There is indeed a property transfer, but a member may take his rights back from the collective society when he leaves without having to pay to repurchase them.[34] This concept is equivalent to a trust deposit by the member in his collective society. The contribution formula presents the advantage for the societies that use it for facilitating infringement actions, notably by providing proof of ownership of rights of the members whom they represent.

3.1.2.2.2 Mandates

The other legal basis for the activity of collective societies is the mandate. In copyright management, the usual legal basis of rights management is the assignment; with regard to neighbouring rights, however, the mandate is mentioned expressly in

---

members to make partial contribution according to types of rights and to facilitate partial withdrawal of their rights.

30. T. Desurmont & J.-C. Desurmont, *Propriété Littéraire et Artistique*, Fasc. 1574, No. 8.
31. In this regard, Art. 2*ter* of SACEM's corporate statute specifies that patrimonial rights contributed to it are not used in the formation of its capital.
32. Three decisions by Cour de Cassation, 1ère chambre civile of 1 Mar. 1988. See André Lucas. 'Lettre de France', 12 *Cahiers de propriété intellectuelle*, available at <www.robic.ca/cpi/Cahiers/12-1/12-1%2012LucasAndre.htm>.
33. A. Lucas & H.-J. Lucas, *Traite de la propriete litteraire et artistique*, 2nd edn (Paris: Litec, 2001), 1132 at 699; Gautier, *supra* n. 8 at 405.
34. See, however, the corporate statute of SCAM, which has rights for certain exploitations contributed to it in a limited list for the lifetime of the society.

legal texts. Might one therefore deduce that this provision of the CPI requires neighbouring-rights societies to use the mechanism of the mandate to represent their members? Some think that this may not be the case, insofar as the legislature cannot interfere in the relations between societies and their members, and the chapter in which this Article is included is aimed at all RCDSs.[35] This is not the opinion expressed in this chapter, however, because this provision is aimed expressly at societies managing the rights of sound-recording producers and performing artists, and therefore the adage *specialis generalibus derogant* may very well apply. In addition, one may greet with scepticism the idea that the legislature may not meddle in the relationship between members and their society because it has already interfered in this relationship, notably with regard to information on members.

Mandates are, by nature, revocable. Revocability presents the limitation that it leads ipso facto to the member withdrawing from the collective society.[36] Mandates also give members greater control over their society's activity and provide an important means of pressuring the society to be more transparent. There are two main types of mandates: mandatory exclusive mandate and optional mandate. Although members may not, in principle, select the works they wish to have administered, they may determine which rights they wish to have administered or assigned to their society. For instance, DG IV of the European Commission has asked SCPP to change its 'music videos' mandate, authorizing it to collect royalties from television stations broadcasting music videos of its members in such a way that it is no longer either exclusive nor a requirement.

One drawback of the mandate, however, is that it reduces the certainty of the repertoire available to users, which can weaken the society's negotiating position. Another is that it makes infringement suits more complex because the collective society must prove that it is mandated by its members, notably when it represents foreign right holders, to pursue the case in the court and demonstrate that they are in fact holders of the rights infringed.

Whereas the sound-recording producers' societies manage the rights of their members solely on the basis of exclusive or optional mandates (for some uses on the Internet), artists' societies sometimes resort to the technique of assignment of rights.[37]

3.2   COLLECTION OF REMUNERATION

Collection of remuneration is the reason that collective societies exist. A study of the modalities of collecting remuneration reflects the relations that the collective

---

35. A. & J. H. Lucas, *supra* n. 33 at 709.
36. Nevertheless, see the optional mandates of SCPP with regard to interactive uses of the photographs in its repertoire. All members who have given this mandate to SPCC may revoke it and remain a member of SCPP, for up to at least one year.
37. SPEDIDAM changed its statutes in 1994 so that it would hold the exclusive right to authorize and forbid the reproduction and communication to the public of artists' performances.

societies maintain with the users of protected works or objects. In this context, it is useful to distinguish whether one is talking about copyright or neighbouring rights. On the one hand, the applicable provisions show clear differences related to the fact that the legislation on copyright predates that on neighbouring rights; on the other hand, neighbouring rights are governed, exceptionally, by a legal license system, which has a certain impact on modalities of collection, even though copyright is also subjected to mandatory management for certain uses, as we have seen above.

3.2.1   Collection of Copyright Royalties

Collective management of copyright in France takes a contractual approach,[38] in that uses are protected by exclusive rights (except for copying for the private use of the copier and lending royalties, which fall under legal licenses). The nature of these contracts is regulated by the CPI. Article L.321-2 of the Code provides that contracts concluded with users by civil-law companies of authors in implementation of their objective for all or part of their repertoire are civil acts. This specificity seems superfluous given that the RCDSs are civil-law companies, but it was designed to decisively shield the statutes of the societies from other constraining legislation applying to commercial statutes. Article L. 132-18 also defines the nature of the contracts that authors' societies are authorized to conclude with users. For instance, 'representation' contracts are those 'under which a professional body of authors grants to an entertainment promoter the right to perform, for the duration of the contract, the existing or future works constituting the repertoire of such body under the conditions stipulated by the author or his successors in title'.

Under these contracts, the user may be a single party who may collect a specific authorization from each right holder. What exactly is the legal nature of the subject of the contract? Is it a royalty paid in exchange for authorization?[39] Or is it only a precarious authorization to use with no transfer of property?[40] There appear to be stronger arguments in favour of the latter despite these contracts having been challenged in court by certain categories of promoters on the charge of abuse of dominant position.[41]

For SACD, contracts with users take a different form in that playwrights wish to preserve the possibility of negotiating directly with theatre operators the financial conditions for performance of their play. This is why SACD has concluded a

---

38. A. & J. H. Lucas, *supra* n. 33 at 688.
39. *Ibid.*, at 706.
40. Gautier, *supra* n. 8 at 344. The author supports his thesis by citing the express infringement on the interdiction on global assignment of future works, which is not legally possible unless there is no transfer of property.
41. Discothèque operators attacked SACEM and its representation contracts in a lawsuit that lasted more than ten years and was resolved in favour of the society in a decision of 3 Dec. 1985. For a complete discussion of this case, see T. Desurmont, 'La Sacem et le droit de la concurrence', *Revue international du droit d'auteur* 140 (1989): 117, and A. Françon, 'Le conflit entre la Sacem et les discothèques devant la Cour de Justice des Communautés Européennes', *Revue internationale du droit d'auteur* 144 (1990): 51.

framework agreement with theatre operators or their association defining the general conditions for use of works, but leaves to each right holder the possibility to negotiate royalties. These royalties are nevertheless paid out to SACD, which will be responsible for then paying them out to the member concerned.

The nature of remuneration for use of the subject of the contract may vary. It may consist of a percentage of the user's receipts, as is the case for the general contracts concluded by SACEM[42] with radio broadcasters or take the form of a lump-sum payment.

The problem of compatibility of collective contracts with individual contracts has been raised regarding contracts concluded by SACD with television networks. In effect, movie producers are legally the beneficiaries of a presumption of assignment of the rights of authors and thus pay remuneration to them. However, these authors have, at the same time, assigned their rights to SACD. The television networks thus contested what they considered to be a double payment, one of which had no basis. The courts decided in favour of the SACD, ruling that the basis was materialized by the services provided by the society.[43] It is true that the contribution of audiovisual rights to SACD is statutorily submitted to the reservation that the society collects the royalties for authors from broadcasters.

3.2.2 Collection of Neighbouring Rights

3.2.2.1 Collection of Royalties Arising from Exclusive Rights

Article L.321-10 of the CPI determines the means for collection of neighbouring rights.[44] What is particularly interesting in this provision is that the contract through which the collective society represents its members is no longer termed a 'general representation contract' but is called a 'general contract of joint interest'; this refers directly to the notion of mandate, because, indeed, the mandate's main characteristic is that it is of joint interest. It seems that this change in terminology is linked to problems that SACEM encountered with the discothèques. The expressly mentioned goal of these contracts, 'improving the dissemination of' videos and sound recordings and 'promoting technical or economic progress', is aimed at giving collective societies a way out of being accused of abuse of dominant

---

42. For authors, the CPI requires as a principle, although there are limited exceptions, that the remuneration be proportionnal to the exploitation incomes of the work.
43. TGI Paris 28 Jan. 1987, *Revue internationale du droit d'auteur* 77; TGI Paris, 23 Sep. 1992, *Revue internationale du droit d'auteur* 257.
44. 'The societies that collect and distribute the royalties of phonogram and videogram producers and performers shall have the faculty, within the limits of the instructions given to them by all or part of the members, or by foreign bodies having the same purpose, to collectively exercise the rights afforded by Articles L213-1 and L215-1 by concluding general contracts of joint interest with the users of phonograms or videograms for the purpose of improving the dissemination of the latter or of promoting technical or economic progress'.

position. Some consider, however, that the scope of this provision cannot be limited to societies managing neighbouring rights, because there is no justification for a difference in treatment between copyright and neighbouring rights, especially if this distinction goes against the interest of the former.[45] In any case, this provision is not strong enough to exempt collective societies, pure and simple, from the French and European competition rules. It means only that the conclusion of a contract between a collective society, representing all of its members and users, does not constitute in itself an abuse of dominant position. If other elements characterizing such abuse accumulate, however, the collective society will not be exempt from application of the relevant positive law.

As they do for copyright, all contracts for neighbouring rights concluded with users require the users to send declarations of use, without which the royalties collected cannot be distributed among right holders. This aspect is considered by jurisprudence to be a fundamental obligation, which users must respect. This is the case mainly in collection of fair remuneration from radio organizations, because the modalities for calculating these royalties were set out in the Act of 20 July 1993[46] and a decision by the Administrative Committee on 22 December 1993, modified by a decision of 15 October 2007.[47] Because the rate of broadcast of sound recordings in radio programmes constitutes an element in the calculation of royalties, supplying broadcast declarations becomes a legal obligation and the failure to do so legally actionable.[48]

Users have the right to know the list of members of RCDSs. They may consult it on the premises of the society or ask for a copy. In the latter case, the collective society has the right to invoice the cost of the copying.

The CPI sets out few constraints with regard to collection in the framework of voluntary collective management. It does, however, oblige collective societies to arrange for a reduction in remuneration for associations on the ground of joint interest.[49] Although this provision figures in the statutes of all collective societies,

---

45. C. Joubert, 'Les sociétés de perception et répartition des droits', *Revue internationale du droit d'auteur* 128 (1986): 185.
46. Act No. 93-924 of 20 Jul. 1993 setting the terms for calculating remuneration due to performing artists and sound-recording producers by private broadcast services (O.J. of 21 Jul. 1993).
47. Décision du 22 décembre 1993 de la Commission créée par l'article L.214-4 du Code de la Propriété Intellectuelle complétant la décision du 9 septembre 1987 (O.J. of 4 Jan. 1994), <www.spre.fr/radios_bareme.asp#22dec> (last visited: 7 Nov. 2005).
48. Sentencing of Radio France in 2000. Nevertheless, the case ended with a transaction, with Radio France agreeing to pay a lump-sum royalty for the past. The collective societies for sound-recording producers had come to agreement with Radio France on a statement format for the future.
49. Article L.321-8 of the CPI:

> The statutes of the royalty collection and distribution societies shall lay down the conditions under which associations of general interest shall enjoy, in respect of events for which no entrance fee is charged, a reduction on the amount of authors' royalties and of the royalties of performers and phonogram producers which they are required to pay.

overall it has not been much applied by some societies, notably because it is not easy to define precisely what 'associations of general interest' means.[50] The law does not set the rate of this reduction, leaving collective societies free to determine it.

3.2.2.2 The Collection of Remuneration from Non-voluntary Licenses

3.2.2.2.1   Collection of 'Fair Remuneration'

Fair remuneration is the royalties due for direct communication of a recording in a public place, when it is not used in a show, on a radio or television broadcast[51] or in the simultaneous and complete cable retransmission of this broadcast. The institution of the legal license was accompanied by the obligation to set up collective management – moreover, joint collective management – because Article L.214-1 of the CPI sets out not only the basis for the remuneration, which must be based on the user's operating receipts or assessed on a lump-sum basis, but also the distribution formula at half each to artists and producers. The producers and performing artists entrusted this task to SPRE.

Another administrative committee, created by Article L.214-4 of the CPI, is responsible for determining the schedules for 'fair remuneration'. This committee has set the applicable schedules for various categories of broadcasters.[52] Although these decisions have given a certain basis for collection, they have not quelled the numerous court cases with users, to the point that the legislature has sometimes been compelled to intervene so that SPRE is able to collect remuneration under a decision whose term has expired.[53]

For fair remuneration in public places with a P.A. system, it is again SACEM that does the collecting, on its own behalf and for SPRE. However, users pay two separate invoices: SACEM's and SPRE's. SACEM then pays SPRE a global remuneration sum and invoices it for its intervention.

---

50. See T. Des Moines, 'La gestion collective des droits', in *Lamy Droit des Medias et de la Communication* (Paris: Éditions Lamy, 2002).
51. The precise determination of what a legal license covers in the broadcasting field has generated cumbersome and complex litigation between rights holders and users. See, notably, *SPRE v. M6 and Canal Plus* on broadcasting of music videos. The decision of the Cour de Cassation of 16 Nov. 2004 ended a case that had lasted more than twelve years by ruling that a video recording incorporating a sound recording constitutes a distinct work submitted to the exclusive right to authorize by producers and performing artists. See also above n. 23.
52. Decision of 9 Dec. 1987, modified 22 Dec. 1993 and then 15 Oct. 2007 for private radio stations and 30 Nov. 2001 for discothèques. The new fee schedule for radios substitute to the uniform former rate of 4.25% a new progressive rate from 4% to 6% of the operating income of the private radios. This decision is available at <www.spre.fr/radios_bareme_2007.asp>.
53. In the private radio sector, the schedule, applicable until 31 Dec. 1993, had to be validated by Parliament in the Act of 20 Jul. 1993.

3.2.2.2.2   Collection of Remuneration for Private Copying

The system is different for the collection of remuneration for private copying. This remuneration falls under a non-voluntary license, because the act of copying for the private use of the copier was not controllable at the time it was instituted. The modalities of collection and the remuneration schedule, payable by makers of blank tapes, were determined by the CPI and again by decisions by an ad hoc administrative committee.

The royalties are collected in the framework of joint collective management by two societies, SORECOP for private copying of sound recordings and Copie France for private audiovisual copying. The Private Copying Committee, which had determined the schedule for analogue private copying in 1987, met again in 2000 and then in 2007 to determine the schedules for private copying done on various digital media.[54]

3.3   DISTRIBUTION OF REMUNERATION

3.3.1   Sums Distributed

3.3.1.1   The Distribution Formulas

Distribution of remuneration, except for under legal licenses, is not regulated by law; Article L.214-4 of the CPI provides that fair remuneration will be shared half and half between sound-recording producers and performing artists. With regard to private copying, Article L.311-7 determines the distribution formula between categories of right holders.

Remuneration for private copying of sound recordings goes half to authors, one-quarter to performing artists and one-quarter to record producers. Within the body of artists, distribution is done according to the provisions of a 1985 arbitration decision that remuneration would be awarded in totality to SPEDIDAM when the label does not bear an artist's name and in totality to ADAMI when the names of all the performers appear on the label.[55]

Within the body of sound-recording producers, distribution of remuneration for private copying of sound recordings was done on a lump-sum basis at the rate of 75% for the SCPP and 25% for the SPPF up to 1995. After this date, it was agreed between the two societies that it would be done 'reflecting reality', which means, for example, that for 2002, 86.4% went to SCPP and 13.6% to SPPF.

Remuneration for private copying of audiovisual material goes in equal thirds to authors, producers and artists.

---

54. Commission Copie Privée, Decision No. 1 of 4 Jan. 2001; Decision No. 3 of 4 Jul. 2002; Decision No. 11 of 17 Dec. 2008.
55. See Pierre Allaeys. *La ventilation des repertoires entre sociétés de gestion collective*. Mémoire, at 21, <www.u-paris2.fr/adipdeux/dea/promo_2003/memoire_allaeys.pdf> (last visited: 7 Nov. 2005).

Finally, remuneration for private copying of books goes half each to authors and publishers.

Outside of these specific cases, the terms for distribution of remuneration collected are set out in detail in the general regulations of the respective collective society – regulations that are, as previously mentioned, submitted to the ministry of culture for scrutiny of their formulation and modification. Thus, depending on the right holders and the uses, the distribution formulas will be very different from one society to another. Many collective societies, notably authors' societies, have set up schedules that classify the works and sometimes even the authors.

When the declarations of use are too imprecise to use or do not exist, some societies (record producers' societies) proceed by sampling or surveys.

In all cases, each society expects its members to declare their work, their production or their performance so that it has the elements necessary to identify the protected object in the declarations of use provided by users, unless it uses the database of another collective society.[56]

3.3.1.2   Levies on Monies Collected

Management fees are levied on the remuneration allocated to right holders. These fees vary widely from society to society and depending on the use. The nature and rate of the levy on collection, which is used to fund management costs, are set by the decision-making bodies of the respective societies (board of directors and annual general meetings). In 2004, on average, the percentage of the levy for all collective societies in France was approximately 15%,[57] but this figure does not mean much because it covers situations that are very different from one society to another. In general, it is observed that the levies charged by intermediary collective societies are lower than those charged by primary societies. For instance, SCPA, SORECOP and Copie France had a levy rate of less than 1.5% in 2002, whereas artists' and producers' societies had a rate of below 10%.

The rates for primary collecting societies widely vary. In 2008, SACEM claims a rate of 15.5%, SACD a rate of 15.7%, SCAM 12.9%, SCPP 8.4% and SPEDIDAM 11.5%. A low rate does not mean that the management charges are low; it means only that the society has other means of financing its activities. ADAMI, for example, made the policy decision to reduce the levy rate on collections from 16.5% to 6.1% in 2002, although its management charges grew by 9%. In 2008, however, the rate rose to 23.7%. The levy rate does not necessarily remain stable over the long term. Its depends very much on parameters such as the amount of collected remuneration from one year to another, whereas the RCDS has to undertake fixed structural costs.

In this regard, a representative of the *Commission Permanente de Contrôle* noted that the levy rates announced by the RCDSs did not correspond to reality in

---

56. This is the case for ADAMI, which uses SCPP's database.
57. Commission permanente de contrôle des sociétés de perception et de répartition des droits, annual report, June 2004, 33.

the sense that 'the money sometimes transits through several RCDSs and what is levied on the financial products does not necessarily appear in the accounts: the figure is thus closer to 25%–35%. For all societies together, the average is 23%'.[58] Even if it is still very difficult to compare all of these figures, it nevertheless seems that the global trend shows a slight decrease in those rates.

3.3.2 Sums That It Was Not Possible to Distribute

French law requires RCDSs to devote part of the monies collected to assistance to creation. These are monies that the societies were not able to distribute. First, this section will look at the nature of the undistributed funds and, second, at how they are used.

3.3.2.1 The Nature of Undistributed Funds

Here, we must distinguish between sums allocated by law to activities of general interest and those that are allocated by the conventional route, even if they are legally framed. These undistributable funds have their basis in Article L.311-2 of the CPI.[59]

3.3.2.1.1   The Undistributed Sums Collected under a Legal License
The CPI provides that French collective societies shall use for assistance to creation, dissemination of live shows, and training of artists, 25% of the sums from remuneration for private copying and all of the sums from 'fair remuneration' that could not be distributed whether because of initial agreements or because the right holders could not be identified. There is a similar provision for sums collected for authors under reprography rights.

These sums are collected for works or sound recordings not published or recorded in France or the EU, which the exclusionary clauses of France at the time of the signature of the International Conventions kept from being distributed to right holders. The 25% levied on private copying is a lump-sum evaluation corresponding to these situations.

Many authors have criticized this legal appropriation, without the consent of right holders, of remuneration that belongs to them,[60] and, what is more, for purposes that do not represent an 'immediate general interest'.

---

58. 'Les droits d'auteur, un système "opaque" et d'un fonctionnement trop cher', interview with Jean-Pierre Guillard and Marie-Thérèse Cornette-Artus, president and rapporteur, respectively, of the Commission Permanente de Contrôle, *Le Monde*, 9 Jul. 2005.
59. 'On the basis of international agreements, the right to remuneration mentioned at Article L.214-1 [fair remuneration] and in the first paragraph of Article L.311-1 [remuneration for private copying] is distributed between the authors, the performing artists, the sound-recording or video producers for sound and video recordings fixed for the first time in France.'
60. A and J.H. Lucas, *supra* n. 33 at 562; M. Ficsor, *supra* n. 15 at 147–149.

3.3.2.1.2   Undistributed Sums Collected under Obligatory Management
Similarly, the CPI provides that French collective societies shall use for assistance
to creation all of the copyright and neighbouring rights royalties collected for the
simultaneous, complete, and unchanged retransmission of programmes broadcast
from another Member State of the European Union that could not be distributed,
either under the international conventions to which France is a signatory or because
the recipients could not be identified or found before the expiration of a ten-year
period from the date of collection.

3.3.2.2   Appropriation of Sums That It Has Been Impossible to Distribute

Before the Act passed on 1 August 2000,[61] certain collective societies had interpreted Article L.321-9 as establishing two categories of undistributable sums:[62]

- Undistributable sums in the strict sense – that is, sums that have been
  collected but that it has been impossible to distribute because they were
  not due under the Rome Convention (performing artists or producers not
  from a member country of the EU or a signatory to the Rome Convention or
  for transcription of the sound recording outside of the EU and the Rome
  Convention).
- 'Undistributable' funds collected under the right to fair remuneration and
  the right to remuneration for private copying, which were due because they
  belonged to right holders eligible for distribution under the law but whom it
  had not been possible to identify or find.

The old version of Article L.321-9 left some of the undistributable sums unallo-
cated, which enabled collective societies to fund their management costs with these
sums, in conformity with the regulations. The Act of 1 August 2000[63] ended this
practice in the sense that there is no longer any distinction between the two categories of sums collected. Referring to sums 'that could not be distributed' either
because of international conventions or because the right holders could not be
identified, the act allocates these funds in totality to assistance to creation.
In addition, the allocation of these sums is controlled, as we shall see below, by
the *Commission Permanente de Contrôle*.

All other sums that could not be distributed for other reasons (public domain,
for example, as well as sums due from the exercise of exclusive rights) are outside
the scope of this chapter. It seems that at the end of the prescribed period of time,

---

61. Article 11 and foll. of the Law No. 2000-719 of 1 Aug. 2000 amending Law No. 86-1067 of
    30 Sep. 1986 concerning the freedom of communication (O.J. No. 177 of 2 Aug. 2000), avail-
    able in French at <http://admi.net/jo/20000802/MCCX9800149L.html> (last visited: 7 Nov.
    2005).
62. For a discussion of the situation before the Act of 1 Aug. 2000 and the questions that this system
    is already raising, see A. Latreille, 'Droits voisins: la notion de sommes non répartissables',
    Légipresse 163 (1999): 97.
63. See *supra* n. 59.

some societies distribute the funds allocated to unidentified right holders to existing right holders according to a formula identical to the initial distribution.

The collective societies wondered about the scope and nature of the assistance to creativity actions targeted by the CPI's new Article L.321-9, but the State Council gave these actions a very restrictive interpretation in its decision of 8 December 2000,[64] in which it specifies that the assistance to creation mentioned in Article L.321-9 should not be understood as 'the use of funds for the support of activities, operations, or manifestations which would not have the direct objective of the creation of works'. Given the confusion raised by this decision, the French government gave a more detailed description of the nature of operations authorized by Article L.321-9 in a decree dated 6 September 2001,[65] which reiterates the State Council's restrictive interpretation. It must be noted that in 2006 the French Court of Appeal recognized to a collecting society representing performers the right to use these sums to finance its trade union activities.[66]

This scheme very nearly got challenged when the new Act of 2006 was discussed as some French parliamentarians wanted to limit further the scope of use of these sums but finally the amendments were deleted.

3.3.3 Prescription of Actions in Payment

In principle, the prescription applicable to royalties for rights was that in the common law – thirty years – but the Act of 27 March 1997[67] made this regime more flexible. Nevertheless, the system adopted by French regulators does not stand out for its clarity. As one author has remarked, the prescription applicable to remuneration that has not been claimed should be the same as that applicable to periodic claims – that is, five years.[68] But the CPI sets out a two-track prescription:

- One provision in the CPI sets the prescription for payment of remuneration collected by collective societies at ten years, starting from the date of collection.
- But elsewhere in the statute, the sums that cannot be distributed may be used for assistance to creation at the end of the fifth year following their being made available for distribution, and this, the CPI specifies, 'without prejudice to claims for payment of non-statute-barred royalties'.

In other words, at the end of a five year term, the collective society may use the royalties collected that it has not been able to distribute to a specific right holder for

---

64. Conseil d'Etat, 8 Dec. 2000, Nos 202076 and 203626, association 'protection des Ayants Droit' and others.
65. Decree No. 2001-809 of 6 Sep. 2001 modifying Art. R.321-9 of the Code de la Propriété Intellectuelle (O.J. Numéro 208 du 8 Septembre 2001), available at <www.admi.net/jo/20010908/MCCB0100470D.html> (last visited: 7 Nov. 2005).
66. Court of Appeal, 4th Ch. 18 janvier 2006, Communication Commerce Electronique 2006, comm. 63, note C. Caron.
67. Law No. 97-283 of 27 Mar. 1997 implementing in the Intellectual Property Code provisions from European Community Directives No. 93/83 of 27 Sep. 1993 and 93/98 of 29 Oct. 1993.
68. Gautier, *supra* n. 8 at 766.

the purpose of 'assisting creators'. But if this right holder turns up in the five years following the use of these sums, the collective society will be required to reimburse the sums due. This provision creates a legal insecurity that is incompatible with the management of such large sums. In addition, it accentuates the concern that often weighs over the use of sums belonging to right holders for purposes of general interest. One may hope that the legislature will provide a bit more clarity and, especially, more simplicity.

In this regard, a recent decision by the Court of Appeal specified that 'fair remuneration, like remuneration for private copying, is independent of any membership in a collective society', and that because a society's payments consists notably of having payment of this remuneration depends on a declaration of sales, payment cannot be refused to a member for the period before joining, because the collective society is required to reserve its portion of the member's royalties throughout the period of legal prescription.[69]

The complex organization of collection and distribution of copyright and neighbouring rights royalties is today the object of oversight by the public authorities. This oversight has evolved clearly in the last ten years into a completely separate tool serving the ministry of culture as the 'trusteeship authority' over collective societies.

3.4   OVERSIGHT OF COLLECTIVE SOCIETIES

The system for monitoring collective societies has not always been the way it is today. Until about ten years ago, it was small and not very restrictive for collective societies. A socialist senator, Michel Charasse, led a movement that resulted in a major reform of the system for monitoring the operations of collection and distribution societies. There are both internal oversight systems and external types of monitoring.

3.4.1   Internal Oversight

There are two types of internal oversight systems: monitoring performed by the members of their society, and the audit performed annually by the statutory auditor.

3.4.1.1   Monitoring by the Members

Before 1 August 2000, Article L.321-5 of the CPI set out a short list of documents that members could obtain in the context of their right to communication. The 1985 Act[70] thus did not provide for a direct application of Article 1855 of the Civil Code, which sets up permanent access to information for members by authorizing

---

69. *P. Gaviglio v. SCPP* (2003) [published] (Cour d'Appel de Versailles, 1ère chambre, 1ère section.).

70. See *supra* n. 4.

them to ask questions about corporate management in writing to the directors of companies. In this sense, Article L.321-5 of the CPI overrides the common law of civil-law companies.[71] This is explained by the fact that many collective societies have large numbers of members and express concern with protecting these societies against abusive and untimely requests. But the Act of 1 August 2000[72] modified this approach greatly by providing that 'the right to communication provided for in Article 1855 of the Civil Code shall apply to RCDS, but without a member being able to obtain communication of the amount of royalties distributed on an individual basis to any other right holder than himself'.

A decree dated 17 April 2001[73] described the right to communication of all members of RCDSs. The right to information has a permanent aspect and a recurrent aspect.

- Under the permanent right to communication, the member may ask the society of which he is a member, at any time, to communicate the list of company managers; a table showing over a five-year period the annual amounts collected and distributed and the levies for management fees and other levies; a document describing the applicable distribution rules; the total royalties due to him over the last twelve months; and a description of the manner in which this product is determined.

- The right to recurrent communication may be exercised only during annual general meetings – thus, once a year. It is provided that before the annual general meeting at which the accounts are approved, any member has the right to see a certain number of documents to which members of civil-law companies must have access under common law. This right may be exercised during the two months preceding the annual general meeting. However, the member must make the request in writing to the society specifying the documents that he wishes to see. The collective society may organize to have documents consulted on its premises, without the member being able to make a copy. This is a simple right to consultation. Aside from these documents linked to collective management, the decree extends the right of communication to documents of common law such as annual accounts, the text of resolutions at the annual general meeting, the directors' reports, the amount of the five or ten highest pay-outs, the list of investments with their yield rate, a table of organizations in which the

---

71. This in effect is what a decision by the Chambre Civile of Cour de Cassation of 9 Oct. 1991 stated: 'In listing four series of documents about which the members of collection societies have the right to obtain communications, Article L.321-5, which transposes to collection and distribution societies the rules [of commercial law], has the objective of overriding, by these particular provisions, the provision of Article 1855 of the Civil Code.' (see comment above) *Revue internationale du droit d'auteur* 291.
72. See *supra* n. 59.
73. Decree No. 2001-334 of 17 Apr. 2001 'portant modification de la partie Réglementaire du code de la propriété intellectuelle et relatif au contrôle des sociétés de perception et de répartition des droits' (O.J. No. 91 of 18 Apr. 2001), available at <http://admi.net/jo/20010418/MCCB0100181D.html> (last visited: 7 Nov. 2005).

society has shares, and a statement of the main categories of users and the amount of royalties paid during the year.

Any member who is refused communication may appeal to a special committee composed of at least five members elected at the annual general meeting from among those who are not corporate officers. Every year, this committee must make a report and transmit it to the ministry of culture.

The decree sets out another precaution to ensure that the member's right to communication is respected: an officer of a collective society that refuses to communicate the list of items mentioned in the pertinent Articles is liable for the fines set out for third-class infractions.

The decree also set out limits to the right of communication with a view to protecting collective societies against demands that could put them at risk. For instance, this right could be exercised only within the limits of the rules of confidentiality and commercial confidentiality with regard to third parties. In addition, the member could not have access to personal information, documents made in preparation for decisions by corporate bodies, or documents related to an ongoing court case. Similarly, a collective society confronted with repetitive and abusive demands would be well founded in refusing access to the maker of these demands. However, this provision was in large part squelched by the State Council, which left as a single firewall the protection of collective societies against repetitive and abusive demands.[74]

In general, both before and after the Act of 1 August 2000[75] came into effect, disputes between members and collective societies have been quite rare. Among the few examples are the disputes between ADAMI and a collective of performing artists,[76] a dispute that put SACEM's statutes into question, and a dispute between SCPP and one of its producer members concerning an ongoing court case. In this last case, the SCPP had refused to communicate a certain number of items to a member who had requested them because the court case had not been decided and the production of these documents would have put SCPP's legal strategy in peril. It is regrettable that the provisions of the decree limiting this type of request were deleted.

Before the Act of 1 August 2000 was passed, some emphasized that the rarity of these disputes could be interpreted as a sign either that members were totally satisfied with the provision of information to them or that they were completely

---

74. Decision by the State Council of 25 Oct. 2002. This decision deemed that in setting out the limits to the right to information of members other than those resulting from the act (the member could not obtain information on distributions made to a member other than him), the authors of the decree did not set the terms for exercising the right to communication but defined its extent and thus ignored the provisions of the act.

75. See *supra* n. 59.

76. The Cour d'Appel de Paris, 4ème chambre, referred 21 Jan. 1998, unpublished, had refused the members of ADAMI the right to require adding to the agenda of an annual general meeting a question regarding conditions and terms of laying off an officer of a society because 'the rights to information and communication recognized for members are specifically defined by the provision of the *Code de la propriété intellectuelle* and in particular by Article L.321-5'.

ignorant of their rights.[77] It seems that the latter interpretation prevailed, given the cumbersome system in place. It is true that the level of information set out before the Act of 1 August might have seemed insufficient. However, from this observation, the diametrically opposed conclusion was reached; this had the effect of mobilizing large numbers of staff within collective societies, with corresponding budgets, and it nevertheless did not really protect collective societies against untimely demands. It may have been possible to envisage a middle road between the two alternatives.

Aside from these provisions, the CPI allows members to force the designation of a minority expert. This faculty is inspired by the system for corporations and was already present in the statutes of some collective societies[78] in various forms. As stated at the end of Article L.321-6, paragraph 1, 'Any group of members representing at least one-tenth of the membership may take legal action for the designation of one or more experts to be entrusted with submitting a report on one or more administrative operations.' The same provision gives the equivalent power to the public prosecutor.

This internal oversight is accompanied by oversight by the statutory auditor. The CPI is, however, less specific about how this fits with the legal status of collective societies as civil-law companies.

3.4.1.2   Oversight by Statutory Auditors

The provisions concerning the appointment of auditors are taken from the Act on commercial businesses and are not remarkable. Article L.321-4 of the CPI states, 'The royalty collection and distribution societies shall be required to appoint at least one auditor and one alternate' from an official list. This text also subjects the auditors to penal provisions in the business act that crack down on non-revelation of tortious facts and the confirmation of false information.

Alongside elements of internal auditing required by law are external auditing structures, which have become much more complex and in depth since the Act of 1 August 2000.[79]

3.4.2   Mechanisms for External Audit

There are two types of external audit measures. First, audits are conducted by the ministry in charge of culture (and, incidentally, by the legal system) through a right to information. Second, after 1 August 2000, a permanent audit committee (la Commission Permanente de Contrôle) was set up dedicated to ongoing monitoring of the activities of collective societies.

---

77. F. Mariani Ducray, J. F. de Canchy, M. Lê Nhat Binh & M. C. Vitoux, 'Les sociétés de perception et de répartition des droits d'auteur et droits voisins' (February 2000), available from the Ministère de la Culture, at 114.
78. SACEM, ADAMI, PROCIREP, SACD.
79. See *supra* n. 59.

3.4.2.1   Audit by Public Authorities

Before the Act of 1 August 2000, there was only one type of external audit, along with, of course, the audit by the judge who intervened to sanction, if necessary, an improperly held meeting, questionable distributions, or any other behaviour subject to credit guarantee. But this type of audit is self-evident in any legal system with a minimum of organization.

The government had, and still has, an audit power that is manifested in two ways: first, it benefits from a right to information that enables it to intervene in the case of irregularities, and, second, it intervenes indirectly in the process of formulating certain types of remuneration.

3.4.2.1.1   Audit through the Right to Information
In the bill that was to become the Act of 3 July 1985, it was proposed that RCDSs would be subjected to the approval of the minister of culture if certain elected representatives felt that the collective societies were exerting a monopoly resembling a de facto monopoly.[80] However, this approach was not selected. The mechanism adopted was the following: the minister in charge of culture may require an audit of RCDSs when they are formed and at certain key times in their existence.

3.4.2.1.2   When RCDSs Are Formed
In general, the minister of culture does not have an active audit power at the time that a collective society is formed. The CPI accords the minister a right to intervene *a posteriori*. In fact, when a collective society is formed, it must send its draft statutes and general rules to the Minister of Culture, who may, within a month after receiving them, demand that a civil-law judge dissolve them if he feels that there are real, serious obstacles (such as obvious illegalities) to the creation of the society. The criteria for evaluation are essentially linked to the professional qualifications of the society's founders and the human and material resources that they propose to implement to ensure recovery of royalties and exploitation of the repertoire. This power has been used by the government only twice in twenty years, when the Minister of Culture appealed to a civil-law judge on the occasion of the constitution of PASA France and of JAPAS. The first represented American artists, the second Jamaican artists, and 90% of the remuneration collected in France on behalf of these artists was not distributed to them.[81] With regard to JAPAS, its creation was rejected by the high court because the society being formed had no material or human resources. It is indisputable that rejection of this society was well founded. It is regrettable, however, that the message that came out, conveyed by adversaries of collective management, was that foreign collective societies could not be established in France because of the de facto monopolies held by French collective societies.

---

80. Hearing of Jack Lang before the Commission spéciale du Sénat, Rapport Jolibois, No. 212, Vol. 1, at 89.
81. A. Bertrand, *supra* n. 1 at 96.

This power seems a bit disproportionate to be truly effective and put pressure on negligent directors. For instance, as previously mentioned, the Minister of Culture may issue or withdraw approval for certain societies responsible for mandatory collective management of certain rights.[82] However, approval applies only to French RCDSs because it was considered that the public authorities could not impose approval on RCDSs of the EU States as a result of the community law principles of freedom of service delivery and freedom of establishment.[83]

3.4.2.1.3   At Key Times in the Life of a Collective Society

This oversight mechanism enables the Minister of Culture to ensure that there have been no irregularities during the life of the society, notably at the time of the annual general meetings, when RCDSs approve the annual accounts and modify their statutes. RCDSs must send their annual accounts to the Minister and inform the Minister at least two months before the annual general meeting studies any plan to modify their statutes or their rules for collection and distribution (usually set out in their general rules). The Minister may also request that RCDSs submit all documents regarding collection and distribution of royalties and a copy of the agreements made with third parties. The minister may collect these documents on the premises.

On the basis of this provision, the Minister of Culture, with the authorization of the Minister of Finance, had an audit of the management of ADAMI conducted in a joint inspection by the Inspector General of Finance and the Inspector General of Administration of Cultural Affairs, and a report was issued in February 1997. A conflict of an internal nature between a group of members and the officers of ADAMI had provoked very heavy criticism of the society's management. The report led to a strengthening of the right to information for the Minister in charge of culture and the members of collective societies, implemented by a decree dated 18 November 1998.[84]

No sanction was defined until 2006 for a situation in which a collective society does not respect the obligation to inform the Minister of Culture. It seems that the only tool the minister would have is the threat of seizure by the court because the society would have been found guilty of these infractions and would no longer fulfil the conditions for administration of the rights for which it is responsible,[85] but this would not seem very credible. Nevertheless, Article L.321-11 of the CPI provides that if the law is violated, the court may forbid a society from continuing with its collection activities in one sector or for one mode of exploitation. This

---

82. See s. 3.1.2.1, above.
83. Rapport Lafitte, made for the Commission des affaires culturelles du Sénat on the bill on transposition of directives No. 93/83, of 27 Sep. 1993, and No. 93/98, of 29 Oct. 1993, No. 240, appended to the minutes of the session of 21 Feb. 1996, at 27.
84. Decree No. 98-1040 of 18 Nov. 1998 amending the Regulations under the CPI (O.J. No. 268 of 19 Nov. 1998), <www.admi.net/jo/19981119/MCCB9800751D.html> (last visited: 6 May 2010).
85. The first degree tribunal decided on 21 Oct. 2008 the dissolution of the collecting society Grace (European performers collecting society) set up in 1996.

faculty has never been implemented to date by the French courts, because the sanction is excessive for the minor nature of the infractions. Maybe for those reasons, the new Act of 2006, DADVSI (Droit d'Auteur et Droits Voisins dans la Société de l'Information), completed the procedure in allowing the Ministry of Culture to seize the tribunal 'pour demander l'annulation des dispositions des statuts, du règlement general ou d'une décision des organes sociaux non conformes à la règlementation en vigueur dès lors que ses observations... n'ont pas été suivies d'effet dans un délai de deux mois'.

For approved societies, the threat of withdrawal of approval would probably be also an effective means of pressure in that it does not put the very existence of the society at risk. Nevertheless, this type of oversight, which the public authorities have refused to call 'trusteeship',[86] is clearly not meant to meddle in the affairs of collective societies, which manage private property rights. It is intended simply to regulate activities for which the financial stakes are growing year by year.

3.4.2.1.4 Surveillance of the Formulation of Certain Kinds
of Remuneration

This aspect of the involvement of the public authorities in the activities of collective societies is special. It consists of surveillance and of assistance with the formulation of certain types of remuneration linked to non-voluntary licenses or to obligatory collective management. The CPI provides for the creation of administrative committees with the mission of determining the amount of remuneration and the terms of collection. This determination is made through extensive consultation with representatives of the right holders concerned, paying users, the state, and, if necessary (with regard to private copying), consumers.

To date, two committees have been created. They have met to update the remuneration that they originally set:

– The Commission *pour la fixation des montants de rémunération équitable pour la communication de phonogrammes du commerce dans les lieux publics ou leur radiodiffusion*. This committee was originally a committee by default and was to meet only if there was no agreement between right holders and users. Today, it is the tool for determining and modifying fair remuneration for communication of commercial sound recordings in public places and broadcasting. This committee is chaired by a magistrate and composed of a member of the State Council, a qualified person appointed by the Minister of Culture, and representatives of the right holders and users concerned.
– The *Commission pour la détermination de la rémunération au titre de la copie privée*. This committee is chaired by a government representative,

---

86. Rapport Mariani Ducray, *supra* n. 77 (?) at 133: 'It is definitely not trusteeship in the sense that a person placed under the trusteeship of another may not in general make strategic or management decisions except with authorization or approval for each decision by the trustee.' See also the report Assemblée Nationale 2235 by M. Alain Richard of 26 Jun. 1985: 'The creation of the state's right of review over these societies in no way has the objective of creating a trusteeship over their activities.'

and its members are representatives of right holders (50%), media manufacturers and importers (25%) and consumers (25%). Its mandate is to determine, for private copying, the types of media, the remuneration rates and the terms of payment.

This type of involvement does not approach the oversight by public authorities of how RCDSs manage themselves. It is, however, an example of intervention in the essential process of negotiations over remuneration and modes of collection. Recourse to the committees system is closely linked to obligatory collective management.

The major reform in the last ten years with regard to oversight of RCDSs has been the creation of the *Commission Permanente de Contrôle*.

3.4.2.2   La Commission Permanente de Contrôle

Article L.321-13 of the CPI, introduced through the Act of 1 August 2000,[87] created the *Commission permanente de contrôle des sociétés de perceptions et de répartitions des droits*. This committee's five members, appointed by decree for a five-year term, are magistrates from the *Cour des Comptes*, the *Cour de Cassation* and the State Council and one member each of the *Inspection générale des finances* and the *Inspection générale de l'administration des affaires culturelles*. The committee draws a large share of its status from the *Cour des Comptes*.

The committee's mission is to oversee the accounts and the management of RCDSs. It examines the internal audit procedures; the use of sums for assistance to creation, which constitutes a particularly important aspect of its oversight; the statutes; and, for the largest societies, the distribution procedures. A decree describes the details of its operating terms.[88] The officers of collective societies are required to cooperate with the committee, or they may be taken to court for obstruction or refusal to respond to the committee; if convicted, they may be sentenced to one year of prison and to pay a fine of EUR 15,000.

The committee has a very broad right of access, ranging from any document necessary to the execution of its mission to computer data and software used by the society to make its distributions. It also has the right to ask for a transcription of the computer data by any appropriate processing means so that the data are directly usable in the context of its mission. In addition, it may question the society's auditors, who are then released from their obligation of professional confidentiality, for any information on the societies that it investigates. For the sake of a greater transparency, the 2006 Act provides that the accounting rules applicable to the RCDSs are established in the conditions set up by the Committee of Accounting Regulation (*Comité de la Règlementation Comptable*).

The committee makes an annual report, which it sends to the societies concerned under the adversary principle. The societies make observations on the part of the report that concerns them. The observations are appended to the

---

87. See *supra* n. 59.
88. Articles R.325-1 to R.325-4 of the CPI, recently modified by a decree of October 2009.

final report, which is then presented to Parliament, to the government and to the annual general meetings of the societies.

It is important to note that despite its broad investigatory powers, the committee has no decision-making power and its objective is not to meddle in the management of the societies. Its mission, like that of the *Cour des Comptes,* is to exercise an oversight of legality and not of opportunity.[89]

From this point of view, the approach has not changed much since the preparatory work mentioned earlier. The objective is to strengthen oversight of collection and distribution operations (notably the destination and use of the portions of the remuneration collected that are to be used for assistance to creation) and make collective management more transparent, less complex and more harmonized.

Although the committee has the ability to present a report, it audits the accounts of RCDSs only every two years, and it has published, to date, five reports (2002, 2004, 2006, 2007, 2008[90]). In each report, the Commission picks up a few collecting societies for scrutiny and focuses on different aspects of the collective management in France. These reports are particularly useful in that they give an overall view of collective management in France and possible ways for improvements.

4   CHALLENGES AND ISSUES FOR COLLECTIVE
         MANAGEMENT IN FRANCE

The evolution of the uses of protected works or objects due to the advent of Internet communication, which has raised problems and questions that remain unresolved has led to a questioning of collective management. One of the main issues that must be decided concerns collection of royalties for cross-border uses, that is, the internationalization of copyright.

The problem posed today, in fact, is how to deal with the multiplication and rapidity of uses. Collective management must be sufficiently responsive to react to massive requests for uses and to adapt to their innovative character to stem piracy. If piracy continues to exist in a stable market, *a fortiori* the absence of an appropriate response to the new requests for use, or rejections of them pure and simple, will inevitably lead to and intensify the impact of this phenomenon. This is what has happened in the music sector, in which French record producers have seen the volume of sales drop significantly.

At the same time that they become more responsive, collective societies must keep in mind that they are above all at the service of their members, the right holders. It means that they must implement very precise distribution scheme, a sort of 'nanodistribution system' of very small amount of money accruing from individualized downloading.

---

89. Gautier, *supra* n. 8 at 774.
90. The 2008 report is available at <www.ccomptes.fr/fr/CPCSPRD/documents/divers/SPRD-Rapport-2008.pdf> (last visited: 6 May 2010).

These two requirements are sometimes difficult to reconcile, because certain categories of right holders wish, for legitimate reasons, to hold back the collective management of certain uses and manage other types of exploitation – notably the new forms – individually.

A third factor very recently came into play with the European Commission's decision in the CISAC matter to sentence twenty-four authors societies, including SACEM,[91] because of the reciprocal agreements they had entered into with respect to online use, satellite broadcasting and cable retransmission systems. The Commission has requested that they review the territorial limits of these bilateral agreements. This decision has already had a considerable impact on the agreements of societies of authors that are in the process of developing paneuropean licenses with major music publishers.

A fourth factor involves the mandate assigned, in September 2009, by the Minister of Culture to Patrick Zelnik, a sound recording producer to develop proposals designed to improve legal access to music and movies on the Internet as well as the remuneration paid to creators. Mr Zelnick published his report on 6 January.[92] The report includes several proposals that could have a direct effect on the evolution of collective management in France.

Finally, another development will likely further enhance the role of collective societies in the digital management of rights – the processing of orphan works, which, in November 2009, the French government has pledged to legislate on.

4.1   Life without Reciprocal Agreement?

4.1.1   Cancellation of the Santiago Agreement

Besides the existing bilateral, reciprocal performance agreements between societies of authors permitting them to be represented mutually on their respective home territories, SACEM[93] and its foreign counterparts concluded a new type of multi-territorial and multi-repertoire agreement in Santiago, Chile, in September 2000. This was in fact a frame contract, the goal of which was to allow bilateral agreements between users and collective societies. The Internet user made a contract for a world license with the collective society in the territory on which the user's site was installed. Each society is thus able to offer to users the repertoire of third-party collective societies. In May 2004, the European Commission, which had found out about these agreements, made a grievance to SACEM in which it objected to the fact that it was impossible for users to select the collective society of their choice and that the local collective societies therefore had territorial exclusivity.[94] The European

---

91. 16 Jul. 2008 decision of the European Commission.
92. <www.culture.gouv.fr/mcc/Actualites/A-la-une/Remise-du-rapport-de-la-mission-creation-et-internet> (last visited: 6 May 2010).
93. Thierry Desurmont, 'Les accords de Santiago', *Auteurs et Médias* (2002): 135–139.
94. Notification de l'accord de coopération in O.J. C145/2 of 17 May 2001, case COMP/C 2/38.126, and press release IP/04/586 by the Commission dated 3 May 2004.

Commission in the CISAC matter put an end to this kind of agreement. Instead and in compliance with the 2005 Commission recommendation,[95] paneuropean licenses developed between major collecting societies and major publishing companies.

4.1.2 Development of Paneuropean Licenses

The new development of paneuropean licenses in Europe pursuant to the previously mentioned European Commission recommendation is currently limited to the management of music license fees contemplated by the recommendation. This explains why only SACEM has set up paneuropean agreements, as did its European counterparts, such as GEMA in Germany. SACEM, for instance, recently signed an agreement with music publisher Universal Publishing, which is referred to as DEAL, (agreement for the licensing and administration of rights related to multi-territorial uses in Europe in the field of Internet and mobile phone). SACEM has therefore become stakeholder of the online rights of the Anglo-American Universal repertoire in Europe. SACEM has already signed a large number of paneuropean licenses with renowned users. In 2008, SACEM had also entered into an agreement with Warner Music Publishing to represent online its Anglo-American repertoire.

Meanwhile and under pressure from the European Commission, SACEM has agreed to the idea of mandating other collective societies to grant paneuropean licenses on its territory and of acting as the administrator of non-exclusive rights for publishers and for other collective societies.

These recent developments that challenged the basis of reciprocal agreements have been perceived as disturbing and worrisome by some of the stakeholders in the music industry, in that the acquisition of rights worldwide has become more complex with the elimination of the idea of one-stop service and, in the long run, the likely demise of small collective societies in favour of much larger ones.

4.2 CSPLA'S WORKS RELATING TO COLLECTIVE MANAGEMENT

The *Conseil Supérieur de la Propriété Littéraire et Artistique* (CSPLA), which has now been in existence for more than ten years, has been involved in several activities which had a direct or indirect impact on the collective management of rights. We shall focus in this review on two of the most relevant working groups.

4.2.1 CSPLA Working Group on Simplification of Collective Management

CSPLA, created on 10 July 2000, instituted a special committee to investigate the implementation of a common gateway. The committee's mission letter stated, 'The current complexity of the search to identify the respective right holders makes it

---

95. European Commission Recommendation of 18 Oct. 2005 on collective cross-border management of copyright and related rights for legitimate online music services.

necessary, to formulate a simplified management mechanism that will contribute to broader exploitation of works and to richer and more diversified production.'

The committee envisaged two formulas: true joint management of all societies' repertoires and a pooling of all available information that would allow works or objects and right holders to be identified. During the committee's deliberations, the participating collective societies emphasized that it would be difficult to implement a 'single gateway' because of divergences between the different categories of right holders, which would reduce the effectiveness of such a structure. On the other hand, the societies concerned were more in favour of a common gateway system for certain categories of right holders.

Finally, the committee issued a statement[96] in which its recommendation was:

> to favour, over the long term, the implementation of an information and orientation platform common to all royalty collection and distribution societies that will ensure, by the interconnection of databases of the different societies, identification in a single consultation of the sought protected works or objects listed in the repertoires of these societies, their right holders, and the nature of the rights that can be acquired on them. Users will be directed electronically to the right holders, from which they may acquire online rights.

In other words, it was much ado about nothing, especially because this recommendation had no long-term follow-up, although, as previously noted, the streamlining of collective management in France is one of the main concerns of the *Commission permanente de contrôle*.

4.2.2 CSPLA Working Group on Orphan Works

The emergence in the past several years of a large scanning project now highlights more than ever the importance of the issue of orphan works, that is, works for which right holders cannot be identified or located. There are currently a large number of these orphan works in France that are being held up because they are not subject to any applicable laws or rules. This is why in 2007 the CSPLA set up a working group to review the issue. This working group is made up of representatives of collective societies and users of copyright works. The working group's report, which was issued in April 2008, had interesting conclusions, such as stressing the importance of giving collective societies a meaningful role and of encouraging them to further develop their databases and thus help find a long-term solution to the problem. The report recommends a sector-wide approach to the problem and focuses exclusively on the writing sector, where it suggests incorporating the notion of orphan works into the CPI and making mandatory the collective management of these works. The collective societies or users (to be determined) would be required to conduct serious, authentic studies to ensure the orphan character of the work. The remuneration lost by the management society would be held during a period to be determined in order to enable any identified right holders to be compensated. This

---

96. Advice of CSPLA 2002-2 regarding implementation of a common gateway.

example underscores the extent to which the increasingly individualized nature of digital use requires collective management, but also the establishment of reliable databases that may be networked via technical harmonization. The French government announced at the Commission on Orphan Works hearing, held on 26 October 2009, that it was now ready to implement the recommendations of the CSPLA concerning the writing sector and that it was really looking forward to the upcoming enactment of a document regarding this.

4.3 ZELNIK REPORT

In its recommendations regarding the improvement of legal music and movie offers on the Internet as well as the remuneration paid to artists, the Zelnik report submitted proposals on collective management. It stressed, as it has often done in the past before the *Commission permanente de contrôle,* the complexity resulting from the various categories of right holders, with each having its own system of rights negotiations and several categories of rights being negotiated separately according to their own distribution key. The report finally noted that the completion of the rights negotiation process does not necessarily give access to some of the contents, such as musical content. It also referred to the confusion and the disastrous consequences ensuing from the European decision in the CISAC matter in July 2008.

The report therefore submitted the following three proposals relating to the French collective management system:

- that, with regard to web casting, the equitable remuneration plan under the legal broadcasting license of sound recordings be extended and be under mandatory collective management;
- that, with regard to other interactive access services, all professionals involved be given the option to select voluntary collective management, failing which, at the end of 2010, public authorities would require compulsory collective management of exclusive rights;
- that these proposals to limit the free exercise of exclusive rights include remuneration conditions that would:
  (a) on the one hand, upgrade the equitable remuneration and;
  (b) on the other hand, set up mechanisms to enable right holders to track the income derived from the use of what has been distributed.

Although the scope of the report appears wide (music, movies, audiovisual systems and books), its recommendations really affect only online music use. There have already been, however, negative reactions to the report. It is now up to the Ministry of Culture to follow up on this report.

5 CONCLUSION

Collective management, often burdened by several layers of management, has become more complex over the years, making the system difficult to understand for right holders and users. The report by Ms. Mariani-Ducray[97] presents the architecture of the collection system in France in a fairly meaningful way:

- For mechanical reproduction, there are two levels of management between the first collecting society and the final beneficiary right holders.
- For fair remuneration, there are two or three levels.
- For private copying, there are, for almost every category of right holders, three levels between the collecting society and the right holder receiving the royalty (see also appendix 4).

Prospects for mergers exist over the medium and long terms. Some societies are tending to group together in joint societies to achieve economies of scale in the context of identical distribution and to be able to present users with a single interlocutor. It is much too early to say with certainty whether these groupings will turn into mergers, but the trend is very much in the air.

Another trend in recent years is sharper questions about the right to competition. On the one hand, on the French level, the *Direction Générale de la Concurrence, de la Consommation et de la Répression des Fraudes* (DGCCRF), which is a directorate of the Ministry of Finance, whose mission is to ensure respect for the rules of competition, is increasingly more often appealed to by mistrustful and often ill-informed users. On the other hand, at the European level, the European Commission intervenes quite frequently, as has been the case over the five last years in initiatives developed by collective societies arguing that these may have effects on competition in domestic markets.

Although, collective management does not appear at all threatened by the rapid development and constant innovation of uses, it goes without saying that the societies will have to adapt, become more responsive (at least, some of them) and more truly transparent than they are today. This will happen when French collective societies accept regulation of collective management at the European level, which they have always opposed vigorously. This systematic opposition has been effective, since to date there still is no proposal for a directive on the issue (though the recent report by the *Internal Market Directory* on cross-border management of rights may augur a rapid change). In any case, societies find themselves today in a situation in which their activity is regulated case by case by administrative jurisprudence (the *IFPI Simulcasting* case and the *CISAC* case); the complexity of this activity requires, above all, a global approach or it may give rise to unrealistic solutions, as mentioned earlier.

Collective management is, and will remain, indispensable to the management of rights in the context of new uses. However, it will have to evolve to take account of different, probably more refined and harmonized forms at least at a national level.

---

97. Mariani-Ducray, Les Sociétés de perception et de répartition des droits d'auteur et de droits voisins, February 2000, <www.culture.gouv.fr/culture/actualites/rapports/mariani/sommaire. htm> (last visited: 7 Nov. 2005).

French Collecting Societies

Acronym	Full name	Year	Members and (Member of)	Collected Royalties	Payments to
ADAGP	Société des Auteurs dans les Arts Graphiques et Plastiques	1953	– Authors of plastic and graphic arts (*member of SESAM and AVA*)	– Author's exclusive rights – Mechanical, private copying and multimedia rights via SACEM, SDRM and SESAM	– Individual right holders
ADAMI	Société pour l'Administration des droits des Artistes et Musiciens Interprètes	1955	– Credited performers (*member of SPRE, SORECOP, COPIE France*)	– Neighbouring rights: 'equitable remuneration' through SPRE and private copying through SORECOP and COPIE France	– Individual right holders
ANGOA	Agence Nationale de Gestion des Œuvres Audiovisuelles	1981	– Audiovisual producers	– Simultaneous cable retransmission (a large part collected via the European association AGICOA)	– Individual right holders – ARP
ARP	Société Civile des Auteurs Réalisateurs et Producteurs	1987	– Authors-directors-producers	– Audiovisual private copying (via PROCIREP)and cable retransmission (via ANGOA)	– Individual right holders
AVA	Société des Arts Visuels Associés	2001	– ADAGP, SAIF, SCAM	– Rights on works including visual arts works	– Individual right holders

French Collecting Societies (contd)

Acronym	Full name	Year	Members and (Member of)	Collected Royalties	Payments to
CFC	Centre Français d'Exploitation du droit de Copie	1984	– Authors' societies – Book publishers – newspaper Publishers	– Reprography rights, contracts with users (news services, national education system)	– Individual right holders
COPIE France	Société pour la Rémunération de la Copie Privée Audiovisuelle	1986	– SDRM, ADAMI, SPEDIDAM, SCPA, PROCIREP	– Audiovisual private copying (from manufacturers and importers of blank supports)	– SDRM, ADAMI, SPEDIDAM, PROCIREP
Extra-Media		2001	– PROCIREP and SACD	– Use of exerts from audiovisual works in multimedia programmes	– No royalties collected yet
PROCIREP	Société Civile pour la Perception et la Répartition des droits de Représentation Publique des films Cinématographiques	1961	– Audiovisual producers *(member of COPIE France and EXTRA-MEDIA)*	– Audiovisual private copying	– Individual right holders – ARP and SCPA
SACD	Société des Auteurs et Compositeurs Dramatiques	1777	– Authors and composers	– Dramatic authors' exclusive rights – Mechanical and private copying rights (via SDRM)	– Individual right holders
SACEM	Société des Auteurs Compositeurs et Éditeurs de Musique	1850	– Authors, composers and music publishers *(member of SDRM and SESAM)*	– Authors' exclusive rights – Mechanical and private copying rights (via	– Individual right holders

SAI	Société des Artistes Interprètes	2005	– ADAMI and SPEDIDAM	– Repartition of royalties collected for all performers by ADAMI and SPEDIDAM	– Individual right holders
SAIF	Société des Auteurs de l'Image Fixe	1999	– Authors of fixed pictures	– Private copying (via ADAGP) – Reprography	– Individual right holders
SAJE	Société des Auteurs de Jeux	1999	– Game authors	– Audiovisual private copying	– Individual right holders
SCAM	Société Civile des Auteurs Multimédia	1981	– Authors *(member of SDRM, SESAM, AVA)*	– Authors' exclusive rights – Mechanical and private copying rights (via SDRM)	– Individual right holders
SCELF	Société Civile des Éditeurs de Langue Française	1960	– Publishers as assignees of rights	– Secondary rights on books either directly (audiovisual producers) or through SCAM, SACEM/SDRM, SACD)	– Authors through publishers according to individual contracts
SCPP	Société Civile des droits des Producteurs Phonographiques	1985	– Phonogram producers (independent and majors) *(member of SCPA)*	– Private copying and equitable remuneration of phonogram producers' rights – Exclusive rights for public communication of phonograms and music videos	– Individual right holders

French Collecting Societies (contd)

Acronym	Full name	Year	Members and (Member of)	Collected Royalties	Payments to
SDRM	Société pour l'Administration du droit de Reproduction Mécanique	1935	– SACEM, SACD, SCAM, ADAGP (*member of SESAM, SORECOP, COPIE France*)	– Mechanical rights – Private copying via SORECOP and COPIE France	– SACEM, SCAM, SACD, ADAGP
SEAM	Société des Éditeurs et Auteurs de Musique	1988	– Music authors' and composers' unions (SNAC and UNAC) – Independent authors and composers – Music publishers' trade associations (CEMF and CSDEM) – GIE SECLI (religious music)	– Reprography rights of music scores	– Individual right holders
SESAM		1996	– SACEM, SDRM, SACD, SCAM, ADAGP	– Inclusion of protected works in multimedia products (collected from multimedia producers)	– SDRM, ADAGP
SOFIA		1999	– Société des Gens de Lettres (SGDL) – Publishers' national association – Authors and publishers	– Direct rights brought by its members – Collective rights on written works, public lending, video private copying	– Individual right holders

SORECOP	Société pour la Rémunération de la Copie Privée Sonore	1986	– SDRM, SCPA, SCPP, SPPF, ADAMI, SPEDIDAM	– Sound private copying (from manufacturers and importers of blank supports)	– SDRM, ADAMI, SPEDIDAM, SCPA
SCPA	Société Civile des Producteurs Associés	1988	– SCPP and SPPF *(member of SORECOP, COPIE France, SPRE)*	– Act as an intermediary between SPRE, SORECOP, PROCIREP for the rights of phonogram producers and collects directly for music use in telephone call waiting	– SCPP ET SPPF
SPEDIDAM	Société de Perception et de Distribution des droits des Artistes Interprètes de la Musique et de la Danse	1959	– Non-credited performers *(member of SPRE, SORECOP, COPIE France)*	– Neighbouring rights: 'equitable remuneration' through SPRE and private copying through SORECOP and COPIE France	– Individual right holders
SPPF	Société Civile des Producteurs de Phonogrammes en France	1986	– Phonogram and videogram independent producers *(member of SCPA)*	– Private copying and equitable remuneration of phonogram and music videos producers' rights	– Individual right holders
SPRE	Société pour la Perception de la Rémunération Equitable SPEDIDAM,SCPA	1985	– ADAMI, SPEDIDAM, SCPA, SCPP, SPPF	– Royalties for public communication of phonograms (radio, television, discos, public places)	– ADAMI,

Source: Adapted from the 2008 Annual Report of the Commission Permanente de Contrôle.

Chapter 7

Collective Rights Management in Germany

Prof. Dr Jörg Reinbothe

1   INTRODUCTION

Corresponding to the continental European traditions and principles, copyright protection in Germany has always focused on, and has its origin in, strong rights for authors. For centuries, authors of music, literature and art have been synonymous for German cultural and societal values. To safeguard the economic interests of authors in Germany, authors' societies have developed as collective organizations of authors and have served as intermediaries between authors and users for more than hundred years. As the authors' trustees, such societies were originally designed and founded by the authors themselves and their music publishers to effectively control and collectively manage their rights and to defend their interests in general.

Today, with more than 80 million inhabitants, Germany has the largest population of all European Union (EU) Member States. It is at present the biggest domestic market for copyright-based goods and services in Europe. A significant proportion of the German economy is therefore closely related to, if not based on, copyright protection – be it in the area of music, print media, broadcasting or film.[1]

---

1. See the study on the economic importance of copyright in Germany of Marlies Hummel, *Die volkswirtschaftliche Bedeutung des Urheberrechts* (Berlin/Munich, 1989). See also Commission of the European Communities, 'Communication from the Commission: The Management of

Daniel Gervais (ed.), *Collective Management of Copyright and Related Rights*, pp. 215–250.
© 2010 Kluwer Law International BV, The Netherlands.

Collective rights management carried out by collective management organizations (CMOs) has been for many decades a well-established tool for the effective enforcement and management of copyright protection in Germany, and CMOs form an indispensable part of the German copyright system.

Apart from their more technical rights management functions, the history and origin of German authors' and performers' CMOs, that is, those that represent creative natural persons, implies a strong element of solidarity among all the rightholders, whose rights are represented irrespective of their status or reputation. From the German rightholders' perspective, particularly among authors and performers, both famous and less known, this element of solidarity has traditionally had a similar weight as the enhanced economies of scale and efficiency inherent in the joint management of their rights. At the same time, collective rights management offers significant advantages to users, too, because they can obtain a bundle of rights from the CMO as a one-stop shop, without the need to address and negotiate with each author individually.

In the following section, the origins and the history of collective rights management will be explained, followed by a presentation of the German law on collective rights management and some perspectives on the future.

2   THE HISTORY OF COPYRIGHT COLLECTING
          SOCIETIES IN GERMANY

2.1   THE ORIGINS

In Germany, like in other countries, particularly of continental Europe, the collective or centralized management of authors' rights and related rights has had a long tradition. Like the protection of authors as such, it has its roots in France.[2]

Collective rights management, and hence CMOs, occurred as a consequence of the development and further evolution of copyright protection. At the outset, copyright protection or authors' rights consisted of the right to authorize or prohibit the copying and distribution of works, which, at least in principle, could be administered, that is, controlled and made available individually. However, individual control and rights management became much more difficult, if not to say impossible in practice, when authors began to enjoy other rights to control exploitation, notably the public performance of their works (the right to control the public performance of dramatic works, first protected in France in the late eighteenth century, could best be managed collectively).

Copyright and Related Rights in the Internal Market' (16 Apr. 2004), COM (2004) 261 final at 5, fn. 1, <http://eur-lex.europa.eu/LexUriServ/LexUriServ.do?uri=COM:2004:0261:FIN:EN:PDF> (last visited: 7 Jun. 2010).

2.   This is not to deny the importance of *The Statute of Queen Anne*, 8 Anne, c. 19 (1710), which can be considered a first step in the direction of recognizing intellectual property.

As a consequence, the establishment of the first collective rights management organizations *Société des Auteurs et Compositeurs Dramatiques* (SACD) and *Société des Auteurs, Compositeurs et Éditeurs de Musique* (SACEM) in France, in 1829[3] and 1851[4] respectively, was at the origin of, and served as a model for, the founding of CMOs in other European countries, including Germany. From the outset, SACD rather efficiently safeguarded the interests of French composers of dramatic music. However, foreign authors could benefit only if their works were printed or first performed in France. In other words, works of German origin, which had first been performed and printed in Germany, were not protected through SACD against publication or performance in France, despite the particular popularity of German operas and classical music in France. Later, SACEM also represented several German composers, such as Robert Schumann, Richard Wagner, Johannes Brahms and Max Bruch. However, their influence in SACEM was limited. Moreover, though SACEM became increasingly active outside France, it did not distribute the remuneration that it had collected for German works to German authors as long as performances of French compositions in Germany did not result in payments to SACEM.[5]

First initiatives for a collective protection of authors in Germany date back to the end of the eighteenth century.[6] Later, in the 1820s, German composers, including Ludwig van Beethoven, submitted initiatives for legislative action toward author protection. They were determined to meet the challenge of the French law in general and SACEM in particular regarding authors' rights and their collective management.[7]

In 1837, the first German copyright law was enacted. It provided protection for the performance of dramatic musical works and notably operas.[8] In 1871, German authors and composers of operas founded the *Deutsche Genossenschaft dramatischer Autoren und Komponisten* to protect and manage their rights. In those days, however, the law and practice of rights management in Germany still focused to a limited extent only on the protection of performances of non-dramatic works of music (concerts).

---

3. In March 1829, the 'Bureau de Perception des droits d'auteurs et compositeurs' (established in 1791) and another society merged to found the 'Société des Auteurs et Compositeurs Dramatiques (SACD)'. See the chapter on collective management in France.

4. The first CMO for composers of non-dramatic musical works, SACEM ('Société des Auteurs, Compositeurs et Éditeurs de Musique') was established in 1851. See *ibid.*

5. M. Kufferath, *Les abus de la Société des Auteurs, Compositeurs et Éditeurs de musique* (Brussels, 1897), in A. Dümling, *Die Musik hat ihren Wert – 100 Jahre musikalische Verwertungsgesellschaft in Deutschland* (Regensburg: ConBrio Verlagsgesellschaft, 2003), at 26.

6. C. Thamasius, *Praktische Beyträge zur Geschichte der Musik* (Leipzig, 1778), in A. Dümling, *ibid.*, at 19.

7. K. Benyovszky & J. N. Hummel (Preßburg, 1934), 306, in A. Dümling, *ibid.*, at 20.

8. 'Gesetz zum Schutze des Eigenthums an Werken der Wissenschaft und Kunst in Nachdruck und Nachbildung' of 11 Jun. 1837, Kingdom of Prussia; cf. R. Kreile & J. Becker, Verwertungsgesellschaften, in A. Moser & A. Scheuermann, *Handbuch der Musikwirtschaft*, 6th edn (Starnberg & Munich: Keller-Verlag, 2003), 1460 at 593.

The Austrian copyright law of 1885 also protected non-dramatic works of music.[9] Upon the initiative of music publishers, the Austrian CMO ACM (later AKM) was founded on 5 December 1897.[10] It took several years until, on 19 June 1901, the German copyright law was enacted, which granted all composers comprehensive public performance rights.[11] This law finally laid the foundation for the establishment of CMOs in Germany.

Subsequently, upon the initiative of the composer Richard Strauss, the *Gesellschaft Deutscher Tonsetzer* (GDT) and *Anstalt für musikalisches Aufführungsrecht* (AFMA) were founded in 1903 as the first German CMOs. Their repertoire mainly consisted of derivative public performance rights of music publishers.

2.2   THE DEVELOPMENTS FROM 1903 TO 1965

After the establishment of those first two CMOs, other societies appeared fairly quickly. In 1909, *Anstalt für mechanisch-musikalische Rechte* (AMMRE) was founded to claim rights of authors and music publishers from the sound recording industry. In 1915, the CMO *Gesellschaft zur Verwertung musikalischer Aufführungsrechte* (GEMA) was established. The Austrian CMO AKM (representing authors, composers and music publishers) had already existed since 1897.[12] As a result, in the 1920's, partial competition regarding rights management on German territory occurred between the three CMOs GEMA, GDT (both German) and the Austrian AKM. To terminate this situation, they formed the Association for the Protection of Music in 1930 *(Verband zum Schutze musikalischer Aufführungsrechte für Deutschland)*.[13]

On 4 July 1933, the first German law dealing specifically with CMOs was enacted. It submitted the activities of CMOs regarding the 'management by agents of rights on the public performance of musical works with or without text' to prior authorization. The underlying objective of the law was to create an officially authorized CMO with a monopoly on the collective management of musical performance rights. Consequently, GEMA and GDT merged in September 1933 to form the State-authorized Society for the Management of Musical Authors' Rights (STAGMA; *Staatlich genehmigte Gesellschaft zur Verwertung musikalischer Urheberrechte*). In 1934, STAGMA obtained official monopoly status. The STAGMA legislation of 1933–1934, through making collective management subject to prior authorization, created a legal monopoly for STAGMA.

---

9. *Law on the Protection of Copyright* (Gesetz über den Schutz des Urheberrechts) of 1885; see A. Dümling, *supra* n. 5, at 26.
10. 'Gesellschaft der Autoren, Componisten und Musikverleger'
11. *Law Concerning the Copyright on Works of Literature and Music* (Gesetz betreffend das Urheberrecht an Werken der Literatur und der Tonkunst, LUG) of 19 Jun. 1901.
12. See *supra* n. 10.
13. R. Kreile & J. Becker, *supra* n. 8.

In addition, it obliged police and other public authorities to assist STAGMA in its control tasks. This obligation largely facilitated STAGMA to fulfil its functions and added significantly to its credibility and legitimacy. The STAGMA legislation also introduced a dispute settlement mechanism in the form of an arbitration board. Its mandate was to settle disputes about tariffs between STAGMA and the music users' association.

In 1945 – after the Second World War – STAGMA changed its name to GEMA *(Gesellschaft für musikalische Aufführungs- und mechanische Vervielfältigungsrechte)* and resumed its activities with the approval of the British Military Administration. Although both the obligation to seek prior authorization for collective management and the legal monopoly of STAGMA were declared void by Allied legislation, all other provisions of the STAGMA legislation of 1933–1934 remained in force. In 1954, they were approved of by the German Supreme Court, which confirmed that these provisions were politically neutral.[14]

Once STAGMA/GEMA had lost its legal monopoly, the door was open again for other CMOs to appear in the German market. Other CMOs were established in Germany, and notably, for the first time, in copyright areas outside of music. The very first CMO of authors of literature, *Gesellschaft zur Verwertung literarischer Urheberrechte* (GELU), went bankrupt in 1955; since 1958, *Verwertungsgesellschaft* (VG) WORT manages the rights of authors of literary works and their publishers. Around the same time, *Gesellschaft zur Verwertung von Leistungsschutzrechten* (GVL) was founded to represent in particular (neighbouring) rights of performing artists and phonogram producers; it is still the most important German CMO for the management of neighbouring rights. Later, other CMOs for the management of different work categories or rights followed, such as Bild-Kunst, which manages the rights of authors and agencies in the area of fine arts, photography and graphic design. GEMA continues to exist in the form of a non-profit association and remains the most important CMO in Germany in terms of turnover and membership.[15]

2.3   THE DEVELOPMENTS AFTER 1965

2.3.1   Collective Rights Management in the German Copyright Reform of 1965

The year 1965 marks the beginning of a new era in German copyright law. The ratification of the Brussels Revision of the Berne Convention of 1948[16] and of the Rome Convention of 1961[17] had to be prepared. Moreover, German copyright law

---

14. Decision of the German Supreme Court of 30 Nov. 1954, BGHZ 15, 338/350 et seq. ('Indeta').
15. See s. 2.3.2 below.
16. *Berne Convention for the Protection of Literary and Artistic Works* (as revised at Brussels on 26 Jun. 1948) [Berne Convention].
17. *International Convention for the Protection of Performers, Producers of Phonograms and Broadcasting Organisations* [Rome Convention].

had to be adapted to new developments in technology and in the marketing of copyright works, reaching from television to public lending and home taping. This led to the most comprehensive revision in the history of German copyright law and a total reform of the German Copyright Act *(Urheberrechtsgesetz)*.[18] The new German Copyright Act of 1965 made a clear distinction between authors' rights and neighbouring rights; it introduced new rights and exceptions, spelled out moral rights for authors and reinforced their contractual position.[19]

In this context, the German legislator held that a new and comprehensive regulation of collective rights management was an indispensable part of the copyright reform package – in the interest of both rightholders and users. There were mainly three reasons underlying this approach.

Firstly, the German legislator wanted to explicitly recognize the role of CMOs, which it considered to be key for the smooth functioning in practice of the German copyright system. In fact, the legislative documents of the 1965 Copyright Reform extensively elaborate on the functions and nature of CMOs, for all CMOs that had been previously established in Germany entered into limited long-lasting contracts with rightholders.[20] The mandate of the societies was to claim such rights on behalf of the rightholders, but in their own name vis-à-vis users or their associations. Subsequently, they were to administer and redistribute the revenues to rightholders according to specific criteria and distribution schemes. Because of the large number of their rightholders/members, CMOs traditionally enjoyed a considerable degree of discretion. They functioned as trustees of rightholders. The German legislator confirmed that CMOs were much more than just private agents; their activities were clearly considered to be in the public interest and located in the neighbourhood of State agencies or the Unions.[21]

Secondly, and against this background, the German Copyright Act of 1965 deliberately recognized and reinforced further the economic and cultural position and the importance of CMOs by entrusting them with additional tasks. In several instances, the new German Copyright Act introduced rights to equitable remuneration and made them subject to mandatory collective management by CMOs: the remuneration for the artists' resale right (Article 26), for rental and lending rights (Article 27), private copying (Article 53) or mechanical licensing (Article 61) could only be claimed jointly by CMOs.

Finally, the German legislator had become increasingly aware of the interface between collective rights management and competition law. It is important to note in this context that in 1957, the first comprehensive German antitrust law, the

---

18. *Law on Copyright and Neighbouring Rights of September 9, 1965,* Bundesgesetzblatt, Teil I, 1965, 1273 [German Copyright Act of 1965].

19. M. Vogel, in G. Schricker & U. Loewenheim, eds, *Urheberrecht, Kommentar,* 4th edn (Munich: Beck Juristischer Verlag, 2010), at Einleitung Notes 107–117.

20. Explanatory Memorandum of the Government Bill, in Parliamentary Document 'Bundestags-drucksache', IV/271, at 9 and ff. [Explanatory Memorandum].

21. J. Reinbothe, in *Urheberrecht, Kommentar, supra* n. 19, Vor § § 1 and following LACNR, Note 6.

Antitrust Act GWB *(Gesetz gegen Wettbewerbsbeschränkungen)*, had been enacted.[22] It drew upon the US Sherman Act and its concept of antitrust regulation. The fact that CMOs usually hold a dominant position in their respective field of activity was amply demonstrated by GEMA and the other CMOs that had been founded after the War. In the view of the German copyright legislator of 1965, CMOs hold dominant positions in their field of activity according to their very nature; each copyright work is unique and not replaceable and thus a monopoly in itself that results in a monopoly position of its author.[23] The CMO holds many, if not all such monopoly rights of a certain category and may thus even acquire a 'world monopoly' of rights for its territory of operation. Such a dominant position based on the bundling of the rights of all rightholders was considered to be both inevitable and desirable, as being beneficial for rightholders and users alike and a condition for the efficient management of rights at low cost. At the same time, the legislator wanted to take into account this dominant position by creating a legal basis for a copyright-specific State control over CMOs so as to prevent CMOs from abusing their position with users or rightholders.

On the whole, the German copyright reform of 1965 built upon functioning collective rights management organizations and increased even further their exclusive competencies and influence. Moreover, the legislator recognized that, when fulfilling their legal, societal, cultural and social functions, CMOs in Germany discharge the State from those tasks that it would normally have to fulfil itself to safeguard the functionality of copyright. From this perspective, the only possible consequence was to give the rights and duties of CMOs in Germany an explicit and comprehensive legal basis through the Law on the Administration of Copyright and Neighbouring Rights (LACNR),[24] which was enacted simultaneously with the new German Copyright Act on 9 September 1965.

2.3.2 Existing Collecting Societies in Germany

At present, thirteen CMOs exist in Germany and have been authorized to engage in collective rights management.[25]

The oldest and biggest German CMO is the already mentioned GEMA <www.gema.de>, which has its headquarters in Berlin and Munich. GEMA collectively manages mainly reproduction rights and communication to the public rights of composers, text authors and music publishers on works of music.

---

22. *Law on Restrictions to Competition* (Gesetz gegen Wettbewerbsbeschränkungen, GWB), of 15 Jul. 2005, Bundesgesetzblatt Teil I, 2005, 2114 [German Antitrust Act].
23. Explanatory Memorandum, *supra* n. 20 at 9 and 17.
24. *Law on the Administration of Copyright and Neighbouring Rights (Urheberrechtswahrnehmungsgesetz) of 9 September 1965*, Bundesgesetzblatt, Teil I, 1965, 1294 [LACNR].
25. For the statutes of these societies see H.-P. Hillig, *Urheber – und Verlagsrecht*, 11th edn (Munich: Beck Juristischer Verlag, 2008), 223.

Rights of authors of literary works and their publishers are managed collectively by VG WORT r.V. <www.vgwort.de> in Munich. Among others, VG WORT administers the rights of communication to the public, public lending rights and reproduction rights for press clippings for six categories of rightholders: (1) authors and translators of literary works of fiction and drama; (2) journalists, authors and translators of literary works of non-fiction; (3) authors and translators of literary works of science and research; (4) publishers of literary works of fiction and non-fiction; (5) publishers of dramatic works (for performance on stage); and (6) publishers of literary works of science and research.

The CMO Bild-Kunst r.V. <www.bildkunst.de> represents three categories of rightholders: (1) authors of fine art (paintings, sculptures, etc.); (2) photographers, photo journalists, photo agencies, graphic designers and photo designers; and (3) film, television and audiovisual. Bild-Kunst administers, among others, public lending rights, reproduction rights for press clippings and (for authors of fine art) the artists' resale right *(droit de suite)*.

The most important CMO for the management of neighbouring rights is GVL <www.gvl.de> with headquarters in Hamburg. GVL was founded jointly by the German Association of Orchestras *(Deutsche Orchestervereinigung)* and the German section of International Federation of Phonogram and Videogram Producers (IFPI). It administers remuneration rights for broadcasting and communication to the public for performing artists, phonogram producers, film producers, video producers and organizers of public performances.

VG Musik-Edition r.V. <www.vg-musikedition.de> administers neighbouring rights regarding scientific editions and editions of posthumous works, mainly in the area of music, for scientific authors and publishers as well as reproduction rights for sheet music.

Gesellschaft zur Übernahme und Wahrnehmung von Filmaufführungsrechten mbH (GÜFA) <www.guefa.de> has its seat in Düsseldorf. It collectively manages remuneration rights for public performance and communication to the public of erotic films for the authors and producers of such films.

Verwertungsgesellschaft der Film- und Fernsehproduzenten mbH (VFF), Munich <www.vffvg.de>, administers in particular rights of communication to the public and reproduction for independent film producers, broadcasters and their advertising companies.

Also, *Verwertungsgesellschaft für Nutzungsrechte an Filmwerken mbH* (VGF) Wiesbaden <www.vffvg.de>, deals with film rights. It administers rights in the video sector for film producers and distributors.

Gesellschaft zur Wahrnehmung von Film- und Fernsehrechten mbH (GWFF) Munich <www.gwff.de>, administers remuneration rights of public performance, communication to the public and reproduction for film, television and video producers.

AGICOA Urheberrechtsschutz-Gesellschaft mbH (Association de Gestion Internationale Collective des Oeuvres Audiovisuelles (AGICOA)) <www.agicoa.de> exclusively administers remuneration rights of non-German film producers in the redistribution by cable.

VG Media Gesellschaft zur Verwertung der Urheber- und Leistungsschutz-rechte von Medienunternehmen mbH (VG Media) <www.vgmedia.de>, formerly *VG Satellit Gesellschaft zur Verwertung der Leistungsschutzrechte von Sendeun-ternehmen mbH* (VG Satellit), is owned by several commercial broadcasters and administers in particular their rights in the redistribution by cable of their broadcasts.

Another CMO, *VG Werbung und Musik mbH* <www.vg-werbung.de>, was established in March 2004. It intends to administer rights in the field of music with respect to the exploitation of works connected with advertising. To date, however, prospects for this CMO are unclear because it does not seem to have generated significant, if any, income, and its membership appears to be instable.

The *TWF Treuhandgesellschaft Werbefilm mbH* (TWF) <www.twf-gmbh.de> was registered as the youngest CMO in February 2008. It intends to manage the collective rights of producers of advertising films.

A number of other societies exist in Germany that also collect copyright-based remunerations, such as *Zentralstelle für private Überspielungsrechte* (ZPÜ), *Zen-tralstelle Bibliothekstantieme* (ZBT), *Zentralstelle Fotokopieren an Schulen* (ZFS), *Zentralstelle Videovermietung* (ZVV), *Zentralstelle für die Wiedergabe von Film- und Fernsehwerken* (ZWF) and *Arbeitsgemeinschaft Drama* (ARGE DRAMA). However, these companies do not qualify as CMOs. They are joint foundations of CMOs for the actual collection of revenues and pass the revenues directly on to the CMOs, who distribute them to their rightholders. These 'cashing' companies, as they are called in German,[26] are technically only revenue collectors; they have no direct contacts with rightholders and no trustee functions toward them. The same goes for the one-stop shops for EU-wide licensing that were more recently established as joint ventures of several German and other CMOs, such as the Centralised European Licensing and Administration Service (CELAS) by the German CMO GEMA and MCPS/PRS from the United Kingdom.

Traditionally, CMOs in Germany are organized as economic non-profit asso-ciations *(rechtsfähiger wirtschaftlicher Verein, r.V.)*. This continues to be the case for the classical authors' society such as GEMA, VG WORT and others. The more commercial CMOs have the status of an Ltd. Company *(Gesellschaft mit bes-chränkter Haftung, GmbH)*.

Most of the thirteen German CMOs generate considerable revenues each year. In 2007, these revenues totalled around EUR 1.3 billion, with GEMA having the lion's share of more than EUR 850 million, followed by GVL (almost EUR 160 million), VG WORT (almost EUR 94 million), VG Bild-Kunst (more than EUR 60 million) and VG Media (almost EUR 30 million).[27]

---

26. 'Inkasso' companies; cf. G. Schulze, in T. Dreier & G. Schulze, (eds), *Urheberrechtsgesetz, Kommentar*, 3rd edn (Munich: Beck Juristischer Verlag, 2008), at Vor § 1 UrhWG, 1675–1676.
27. German Patent and Trade Mark Office ('GPTO'), Annual Report 2008, at 53.

3   TODAY'S REGULATORY FRAMEWORK FOR
COLLECTING SOCIETIES

3.1   THE GENERAL PRINCIPLES ENSHRINED IN THE GERMAN LAW ON
COLLECTIVE RIGHTS MANAGEMENT (LACNR)[28]

The LACNR provides a comprehensive legal framework for collective rights management and the activities of CMOs in Germany. The law is based on several fundamental principles. It is driven by, and based on, the understanding that:

- protecting and fostering creativity is an important function of copyright;
- collective rights management is particularly required for protecting the creativity and defending the rights of natural persons, notably of authors and performers, through CMOs as their trustees;
- collective rights management by CMOs is useful and beneficial for all parties, notably rightholders and users, as well as for culture and society at large in many sectors of copyright (authors' rights and neighbouring rights);
- collective rights management is therefore an indispensable part of the German copyright system; and
- collective rights management can function well only on the basis of a reasonable balance of all rights and interests.

The LACNR to some extent strengthens the position of CMOs with users and competition law. However, the LACNR does not grant any CMO a legal monopoly nor does it oblige rightholders to join a CMO. At the same time, the LACNR recognizes and accepts the de facto dominant position of CMOs and takes account of the potential to abuse this position against users or rightholders.

On the basis of these principles, the LACNR contains the following provisions:

- Chapter 1 ('Authorization for Doing Business') on the establishment of CMOs subject to prior authorization;
- Chapter 2 ('Rights and Obligations of the CMO') on rights and obligations, and on the Arbitration Board and access to the Courts;
- Chapter 3 ('Supervision over the CMO') on the control over CMOs;
- Chapter 4 ('Transitional and Final Provisions').

3.2   THE PROVISIONS OF THE LACNR

3.2.1   Chapter 1: The Authorization/Establishment of Collecting Societies (Articles 1–5 of the LACNR)

The LACNR deliberately did not follow the approach of the STAGMA legislation and did not grant any CMO a legal monopoly. At the same time, the legislator in

---

28. See *supra* n. 24.

1965 clearly identified the advantages of CMOs having a dominant position in their field of activity for both rightholders and users. It saw no benefit in competition between CMOs. The law has therefore sought to limit the number of CMOs, with a view to safeguarding their sustainable operation. The State was determined to make sure that those CMOs that existed were reliable trustees for rightholders and reliable partners for users. At the same time, the law seeks to avoid raising any unjustified barriers for the establishment of CMOs, not least in the light of Article 12 of the German Constitution and the EU Treaty provisions on the freedom of establishment.[29]

3.2.1.1 Article 1 of the LACNR (Requirement of Prior Authorization)

Article 1 of the LACNR provides that engaging in the collective management of authors' rights or neighbouring rights is dependent on prior authorization *(Erlaubnis)*.

Collective rights management is defined in Article 1(1) as 'managing exploitation rights, exclusive rights or remuneration rights granted under the Copyright Act . . . jointly and for joint exploitation on behalf of several authors or holders of neighbouring rights'. The LACNR covers only collective rights management, which is a regular business activity; occasional or short-term collective rights management does not qualify (Article 1(2) of the LACNR). Moreover, agents or other cashing companies may qualify as CMOs only if they function as trustees, that is, with direct links to their rightholders and to users. It should also be noted that the authorization requirement applies to any CMO as defined in Article 1(1), whether German or not, as long as it provides for collective rights management, as defined, in the German territory.

Anyone who engages in collective rights management (as defined), without having prior authorization to do so, is not entitled to claim any of the rights under the Copyright Act, even if rightholders have entrusted him with rights management, Article 1(3) of the LACNR.

The entire LACNR clearly envisages collective rights management by CMOs as defined in Article 1(4), namely 'a legal person or community of persons' that engages in collective rights management as previously defined in Article 1(1). Nevertheless, Article 1(4) of the LACNR also allows natural persons to engage in such collective rights management, and all provisions of the LACNR also apply to a one-person collective rights manager. So far, however, collective rights management by a natural person has remained only a theoretical possibility in Germany.

---

29. Article 12 of the German Constitution grants the freedom of profession; *Constitution for the Federal Republic of Germany* (Grundgesetz für die Bundesrepublik Deutschland) of 23 May 1949, Bundesgesetzblatt, Teil III, 100–101 [German Constitution]; EU, Treaty On the Functioning of the European Union (TFEU), (2008) OJ C 115/47 at 67, Art. 49 grants the right of establishment. However, competition among collecting societies is not considered a desirable option; cf. G. Schulze, in *Urheberrechtsgesetz, Kommentar, supra* n. 26 at 1679.

3.2.1.2 Article 2 of the LACNR (Application for Authorization)

According to Article 2 of the LACNR, the application for authorization as a CMO has to be filed in writing with the supervisory authority, which according to Article 18(1) of the LACNR, is the German Patent and Trade Mark Office (GPTO)[30] in Munich. The application has to include the statutes of the society, the names, addresses and citizenship of its representatives, as well as a declaration about the number of represented rightholders and the number and economic importance of the rights, whose management the society is entrusted with.

The GPTO grants the authorization in agreement with the Federal Antitrust Office *(Bundeskartellamt),* Article 18(3) of the LACNR. This underlines the impact of competition law on collective rights management.

3.2.1.3 Article 3 of the LACNR (Denial of Authorization)

Only on a limited number of grounds can the authorization be denied. Article 3 of the LACNR includes an exhaustive list of possible reasons for such denial. The authorization can be denied only if the statutes of the CMO do not comply with the provisions of the LACNR; if there are reasonable grounds to expect that representatives of the CMO are not sufficiently reliable; or if the economic basis of the CMO is so weak that no effective management of the rights that the society is entrusted with can be expected. This would be the case, in particular, if the applying society would not represent a sufficient number of rightholders so as to achieve reasonable economies of scale for both rightholders and users. However, if none of these shortcomings occur, the authorization must be granted.

A denial of the authorization has to be in writing and accompanied by reasons. As a decision by a public authority (the GPTO), the denial may be appealed before the Courts.

3.2.1.4 Article 4 of the LACNR (Repeal of the Authorization)

To date, all applications for authorization under Article 1 of the LACNR have been granted. This reflects the generally open and constructive approach of the GPTO on authorization. However, the GPTO disposes of a rather effective tool to correct this if needed: it can repeal the authorization. So far, no authorization has been repealed. However, particularly the development of the recently established CMO VG Werbung und Musik (see section 2.3.2 above) is being closely scrutinized by the GPTO.

The authorization is to be repealed if any of the reasons for a denial of the authorization occurs or becomes known after the authorization was granted. However, the CMO has to be given the opportunity to improve on the respective shortcoming within a certain delay.

---

30. Its German name is Deutsches Patent-und Markenamt (DPMA).

3.2.1.5   Article 5 of the LACNR (Publication of the Authorization)

According to Article 5 of the LACNR, any authorization made under Article 1 of the LACNR, as well as any repeal of an authorization under Article 4 of the LACNR, is to be published in the Official Journal. This provision confirms once more the importance that the German legislator attaches to collective rights management and CMOs and the public attention paid to them.

3.2.2   Chapter 2 (First Part): The Rights and Obligations of Collecting Societies (Articles 6–13c of the LACNR)

The second Chapter of the LACNR (Articles 6–17a) deals with the rights and obligations of CMOs. The provisions contained in Articles 6–8 refer directly to the relation between CMOs and rightholders. Article 9 contains accounting obligations of CMOs, which are relevant both for rightholders and the public. Articles 10–13c deal with the relation between CMOs and users.

3.2.2.1   Article 6 of the LACNR (Rights Management Obligation toward Rightholders)

Article 6 of the LACNR is the key provision for rightholders who seek the collective management of their rights through a CMO. Article 6 establishes the obligation for CMOs to administer rights; in other words, the CMO is not allowed to reject a rightholder's request to engage in the collective management of his or her rights. It is 'obliged to manage, on equitable conditions, the rights and claims belonging to its field of activity upon request of the rightholder, if the rightholder is a German, a citizen of an EU Member State or the European Economic Area (EEA) or has his regular residence in Germany and if an effective management of his rights or claims is otherwise not possible'.[31]

The rather complex wording of this provision contains important elements and conditions for its application.

First, the CMO is only obliged to manage rights that belong 'to its field of activity', but not other rights or categories of works or subject matter that are outside of its usual scope. However, although the rightholder, if this condition is met, has a right toward the society to get his or her relevant rights administered, Article 6 does not grant the rightholder the right to become a full member of the CMO. The statutes of many societies make full membership dependent on certain conditions (e.g., the amount of revenues). As long as these conditions are objective and not discriminatory, they remain valid and are not altered by Article 6 of the LACNR.[32]

---

31. Article 6, *supra* n. 24 (translations provided by the author).
32. For those rightholders, whose rights are managed by the CMO without being its ordinary members (usually because they only generate little revenues), Art. 6(2) contains a specific safeguard clause: the CMO is obliged to establish a special common representation of those rightholders and to reflect rules of their representation in its statute.

Second, only those rightholders who are German, citizens of another EU or EEA Member State or have their permanent residence in Germany may invoke the obligation under Article 6. If the rightholder is a company, its headquarters are equivalent to the permanent residence of a natural person. This set of conditions corresponds to the habitual provisions regarding the beneficiaries of copyright protection: in principle, only German residents or citizens enjoy protection under the German Copyright Act and related laws including the LACNR. In its *Phil Collins* decision, the European Court of Justice confirmed that the general non-discrimination clause contained in Article 12 of the EC Treaty (now Article 18 TFEU – Treaty on the Functioning of the European Union) results in the obligation of all Member States of the EU to grant each others' citizens unconditional national treatment on all intellectual property rights.[33] The Agreement on the European Economic Area extends this obligation to all its Member States, which are, besides the EU Member States, Norway, Iceland and Liechtenstein, that is, all European Free Trade Association (EFTA) States with the exception of Switzerland. This condition of Article 6 of the LACNR is therefore an explicit repetition of the generally applicable rules under German and international law.

Third, the collective rights management obligation under Article 6 of the LACNR applies only if no other effective rights management would be possible – in other words, if the collective rights management by the CMO in question is a precondition for the effective management of the rightholder's rights. It is the rightholder who has the burden of proof in this respect. However, proving that there is no viable alternative option to the rights management by one particular German CMO should not be overly difficult, provided the society in question is the main, if not the only society in Germany that administers the rights in question. For instance, that a composer with residence in Germany can oblige GEMA to engage in the collective management of his or her remuneration rights of the type that GEMA also administers for other composers, should almost go without saying and hardly requires any specific proof from the side of the composer.

Article 6 of the LACNR obliges the CMO to manage rights for rightholders 'on equitable conditions'. This term is crucial for the relation between the rightholder and the CMO – the CMO has to offer the rightholder fair contractual conditions for the management of his or her rights. The contractual conditions are fair, and thus adequate, if the society does not charge exaggerated administrative fees (German CMOs usually charge and deduct around 10% from the revenues for administrative purposes); the CMO does not impose undue 'packaging' conditions for the bundling of certain rights; it leaves the rightholder sufficient flexibility to cancel the rights management contract; and rightholders have sufficient say within the CMO on the way it operates.

Article 6 of the LACNR, and specifically Article 6(2), with its provisions on the representation of rightholders in the society, confirms once more how the German legislator sees CMOs – not as independent economic entities, but rather

---

33. Joint cases C-92/92 and C-326/92, *Phil Collins v. Imtrat Handelsgesellschaft mbH* and *Leif Emanuel Kraul v. EMI Electrola GmbH*, 1993 C.M.L.R. 773; ECR 1993, I-5145.

as the rightholders' 'own' organizations that function as their trustees and under their close control.

3.2.2.2 Article 7 of the LACNR (Distribution of Revenues)

One of the most important aspects of collective rights management from the rightholders' perspective is certainly the redistribution of collected revenues. The general principle of fair redistribution of revenues to rightholders cannot already be derived from the 'equitable conditions' requirement in Article 6 of the LACNR; the distribution of revenues is not a condition of rights management; rather is it the result of the latter. Article 7 of the LACNR contains specific rules on the distribution itself and on the principles of the distribution schemes.[34]

The first sentence of Article 7 obliges every CMO to establish an explicit distribution plan *(Verteilungsplan)* with clear rules on how, and according to which criteria, the distribution is to take place. The purpose of this provision is, as the law states, to 'exclude any distribution at random', and to provide for transparency. Accordingly, the principles of the distribution plan must be laid down in a society's statutes (third sentence, Article 7).

The second sentence in Article 7 contains a rule, which highlights again the particular responsibility that CMOs carry in the view of the legislator: 'The distribution plan should comply with the principle that culturally important works or [neighbouring rights] subject matter are to be promoted.' This provision entrusts CMOs with the promotion of culture through their distribution keys. In other words, while the distribution should follow transparent rules and not be done at random (first sentence of the same Article), it may, and is encouraged to, deliberately differentiate to the extent that this is appropriate for the promotion of culturally important works or subject matter.

However, this provision does leave some question marks: which works or subject matter have a higher cultural value than others? Which measure should be applied to differentiate within the distribution keys for the sake of promoting culture? German CMOs have found an answer. In the area of music, for example, composers or performers of classical music or jazz obtain a proportionally higher share of the revenues than their pop music colleagues. Another example is literary works, for which authors of scientific or research books or articles obtain a higher share than their fellow authors of fiction. In addition, CMOs regularly promote concerts or other projects of young authors and artists.

In any event, the principles of distribution, as well as the distribution plan itself, are subject to the approval by the rightholders, whose rights are represented by the CMO, through the representative bodies of the society, including the regular assembly meetings.

---

34. J. Reinbothe in *Urheberrecht, Kommentar, supra* n. 19, § 7 LACNR, Note 5.

3.2.2.3   **Article 8 of the LACNR (Social Assistance and Funding)**

Article 8 of the LACNR reflects the social function of CMOs and is, like the entire law, based on the idea that they are rightholders' trustees and bound to practice loyalty among them.

Article 8 of the LACNR states that 'the CMO should establish mechanisms of social security and support for the owners of the rights or claims that they administer'. Though this provision establishes no strict obligation for the societies, it has been implemented at least by all of the German CMOs that administer rights for authors or performers as natural persons.[35] Socially disadvantaged authors or performers receive welfare or other forms of support from 'their' CMO. As a general rule, it can be said that CMOs spend up to 10% of their revenues on such social purposes; this amount is considered to be appropriate.[36]

In any case are these social funding activities of CMOs of course subject to approval by their representative bodies, including the assemblies, and therefore by their own rightholders represented therein.

3.2.2.4   **Article 9 of the LACNR (Accounting Rules)**

Articles 9(1) through (7) of the LACNR lay down detailed accounting rules for CMOs. The degree of detail and the rather severe nature of these rules demonstrate the desire of the German legislator to safeguard the good governance of German CMOs.

Regarding the contents of Article 9, it may suffice to mention that each CMO has to establish every year its annual account *(Jahresabschluß)*, indicating in a clear and transparent manner the income, payments and losses. In addition, it has to submit an annual report *(Jahresbericht)* describing the activities of the society and an evaluation of its situation.

The annual account and the annual report have to be assessed by recognized accountants in compliance with the law and the society's statute. Within eight months after the end of the reporting year, the CMO has to publish the annual account and the annual report with the approval of the accountants in the German Federal Gazette *(Bundesanzeiger)*.

---

35. G. Schulze in *Urheberrechtsgesetz, Kommentar, supra* n. 26 at 1706–1707; naturally, this applies to a lesser extent or not at all to CMOs that represent legal persons. When a study paper from the services of the European Commission describes 'social and cultural, promotional and funding activities' as 'other services . . . which are not linked to the collective management of copyright', it does not differentiate between these different kinds of CMOs; cf. Commission of the European Communities, 'Study on a Community Initiative on the Cross-Border Collective Management of Copyright', (Brussels: 7 Jul. 2005), at 7, cf., <http://ec.europa.eu/internal_market/copyright/copyright/docs/management/study-collectivemgmt_en.pdf> (last visited: 7 Jun. 2010).
36. J. Reinbothe in *Urheberrecht, Kommentar, supra* n. 19, § 8 LACNR, Note 3; cf. M. Ficsor, *Collective Management of Copyright and Related Rights* (Geneva: World Intellectual Property Organization, 2002), 165 at 149 and ff.

3.2.2.5   Article 10 of the LACNR (Right of Information)

Article 10 is the first of six provisions that govern the relationship between CMOs and users. It obliges the CMO 'to provide anyone upon written request with information as to whether it administers rights on a specific work or [neighbouring rights] subject matter for a specific author or rightholder'.

Article 10 of the LACNR thus intends to facilitate the exploitation of a protected work or subject matter: anyone, including any potential user, is entitled to obtain relevant information from all CMOs in Germany. At the same time, the provision works both ways: it deprives users of any possible excuse that it was too difficult to find out if a work or subject matter was protected and who managed the respective rights.

The message is clear – in the case of any doubt about the existence or allocation of rights, potential users should knock at the door of CMOs. They are entitled to get an answer.

**3.2.2.6   Article 11 of the LACNR (Obligation to Grant
                Exploitation Rights)**

Article 11 of the LACNR is for users what Article 6 is for rightholders. From the perspective of users, Article 11 of the LACNR contains, no doubt, the key provision of the entire Collective Rights Management Law. Article 11(1) obliges the 'CMO, on the basis of the rights it administers, to grant anyone upon request exploitation rights on equitable conditions'.

This means, first, that the CMO cannot, as a matter of principle and subject to very few exceptions defined by the Courts, refuse granting a license. This is true even if it administers exclusive rights (to authorize or prohibit exploitation). This obligation to allow exploitation *(Kontrahierungszwang)* enshrined in Article 11 is the price for the dominant position that a CMO usually holds in its field of activity.

Second, the CMO is obliged to grant the users 'equitable conditions'. The same term is used in Article 6 of the law for the relationship between CMOs and rightholders. In the context of the exploitation of rights and in relation to users, it basically means equity: the conditions of exploitation, particularly the license fee, the frequency and the kind of use of protected works or subject matter, have to be in balance; they have to be appropriate – not too much, and not too little. What is an equitable condition may vary and can be assessed only on a case-by-case basis.[37]

At first sight, the obligation under Article 11(1) of the LACNR seems to have two important, negative consequences for the CMO: the society has no means to prevent the potential user from going ahead with the intended exploitation, and it is deprived of any negotiating power as far as the license fee is concerned.

---

37. J. Reinbothe in *Urheberrecht, Kommentar, supra* n. 19, § 11 LACNR, Note 5, with further references.

However, CMOs are better off than it seems. Article 11(2) of the LACNR provides:

> If no agreement can be reached on the remuneration for granting the exploitation rights, the rights are considered to be granted as soon as the amount of the licensing fee recognised by the user is paid to the collecting society, and the additional part of the licensing fee as claimed by the collecting society is paid to the collecting society under reservation or deposited to its benefit.[38]

True, also under Article 11(2), the CMO must, in principle, grant any request for exploitation provided it holds the rights in question. But the potential user must first pay. Moreover, the user cannot go ahead with the exploitation simply and only on the basis of the license fee that he or she is ready to pay (and thus determined unilaterally by him or her). In turn, the CMO cannot bypass its obligation under Article 11(1) of the LACNR (to allow the exploitation of rights) through setting the licensing fee too high. Article 11(2) achieves this by splitting the license fee claimed by the CMO in two parts: the part, which is not contested, has to be paid to the society, whereas the part of the fee, which is in dispute, has to be paid under reservation or to a deposit. The CMO can dispose of this latter part only to the extent that the dispute is settled in its favour.[39]

Article 11(2) of the LACNR compensates for the CMO's inherent loss of negotiating power and, at the same time, serves users by giving them the possibility to exploit and contest the amount of the license fee asked by the CMO. Another significant advantage for CMOs is that they receive immediate – though sometimes in their view too modest – payment for each act of use. In many other countries, CMOs do not receive any payment until the successful conclusion of (sometimes lengthy) litigation, though the act of exploitation has already taken place.

In any case, Article 11 of the LACNR requires the potential user to turn to the CMO and ask for permission. Acts of exploitation that have not been registered with the CMO in question are not covered by Article 11 and remain illegal.

3.2.2.7 Article 12 of the LACNR (Umbrella Agreements with Users)

Article 12 of the LACNR obliges the CMO:

> to conclude, on equitable conditions, umbrella agreements on the rights and claims that it administers with associations whose members exploit works or subject matter protected, or are obliged to pay equitable remuneration, under the Copyright Act, unless the collecting society cannot reasonably be expected

---

38. See *supra* n. 24.
39. Access to the Courts and to the Arbitration Board remains open in any case; see s. 3.2.3.1.1 below (on the mandate of the Arbitration Board, Art. 14(1) of the LACNR) and 3.2.3.4 (on Art. 16 of the LACNR, dealing with access to justice).

to conclude such an agreement, in particular because membership of the association is too small.[40]

Whereas Article 11 is designed to facilitate for individual users the exploitation of rights administered by CMOs on the basis of individual agreements, Article 12 of the LACNR focuses on framework or umbrella agreements, to which users' associations are a party. In fact, umbrella agreements between CMOs and associations of users are common practice in Germany and often the only way for an effective collective rights management of the numerous rights of the numerous rightholders with a large number of users. Such agreements have obvious advantages for both parties. They are beneficial for CMOs; it is much easier, for example, to collect the remuneration for acts of private copying from producers of blank recording material on the basis of a framework agreement with their association than to conclude agreements with each producer individually. Umbrella agreements are beneficial for users, too, because they usually pay reduced license fees that were negotiated by their association as part of the umbrella deal.

There is one exception to the obligation of CMOs to enter into such umbrella agreements. It is stated in the last part of Article 12 – CMOs may refuse an umbrella agreement with associations that do not have enough members to provide the CMO with the economies of scale usually inherent in such agreements.

Like Article 11 of the LACNR, Article 12 provides that the conditions of the agreement have to be 'equitable'. This term has a very similar meaning as in Article 11 – there should be a balance of what both parties give and take. The conditions of the umbrella agreement have to be appropriate – what each party, the CMO and the users' association provide should not be too much or too little in relation to each other. What is considered an equitable condition may vary and can be assessed only on a case-by-case basis.[41]

3.2.2.8 Article 13 of the LACNR (Tariffs)

Another obligation that CMOs have vis-à-vis users in particular, and toward the public in general, relates to the transparency and fairness of the tariffs. Article 13 of the LACNR contains several specific rules in this respect, under Articles 13(1) and (2) focusing on transparency and Article 13(3) on fairness. In addition, specific parameters for the fairness of tariffs for private copy and reprography levies were inserted into Article 54 of the German Copyright Act in 2008 side by side with a new Article 13a LACNR that provides for the mechanisms to agree on those tariffs (see section 3.2.2.9. below).

It has to be clear from the outset, however, that the rules contained in Article 13 on tariffs relate only to the tariffs requested by the CMO and are without prejudice to their validity. In other words, although the CMO establishes its tariffs unilaterally, they become valid only if and when agreed upon with the user(s).

---

40. See *supra* n. 24.
41. See *supra* n. 37.

3.2.2.8.1 Rules on Tariff Transparency
The first sentence of Article 13(1) spells out the general obligation that 'the CMO has to establish tariffs on the remuneration that it asks on the basis of the rights and claims it administers'. The second states that 'to the extent umbrella agreements have been concluded, the remuneration agreed upon therein is considered to be tariffs'. It is in the own interest of CMOs to have a transparent framework of tariffs. The obligation under Article 13 of the LACNR corresponds therefore to general practice. All CMOs have detailed tariffs for the different rights and acts of use. For example, GEMA's tariff framework includes more than eighty different tariffs. Likewise, CMOs distinguish individual tariffs from those based on umbrella agreements. The latter are usually more beneficial to users.

Under Article 13(2), CMOs have to publish their tariffs without delay in the *German Federal Gazette (Bundesanzeiger)*. All CMOs do anyway provide potential users with information leaflets on their tariffs upon request. However, because of the obligation to publish all tariffs in the *Federal Gazette,* the latter is the most comprehensive source of tariffs of all German CMOs and therefore particularly useful for potential users and their associations. It goes without saying that the *Federal Gazette* is also available online. In addition, all CMOs in Germany have published their tariffs on their respective websites (see section 2.3.2. above).

3.2.2.8.2 Rules on the Fairness of Tariffs
Article 13(3) contains general rules on the fairness of the tariffs and on how they are in general to be calculated. However, these are recommendations rather than strict obligations.

According to Article 13(3): 'the basis of calculation of the tariffs should, as a general rule, be the financial benefits that are generated by the use . . . or a different basis, if it provides indications of the benefits, which can be assessed with a reasonable amount of effort'. In any event, the CMO, when establishing its tariffs, should take due account of the share of the exploitation of the protected work in relation to the entire act of use (Article 13(3), third sentence). Finally, the fourth sentence of Article 13(3) provides that both the tariffs of the CMO and the collection of the remuneration should 'take due account of the religious, cultural and social interests' of the users, including 'aspects of the promotion of young people'. On the whole, Article 13(3) of the LACNR thus calls upon the fairness and the particular cultural and societal responsibilities of CMOs. If users are the 'weaker part', CMOs should take this into account not only in the calculation of their tariffs, but also in their methods of collecting the remuneration – and they actually do; in such cases, CMOs regularly offer reductions or flexible methods of payment.

3.2.2.9 Article 13a of the LACNR (Tariffs for Recording Equipment and Storage Devices)

Like Article 13, Article 13a of the LACNR relates to the fairness of tariffs. However, Article 13a deals with only rather specific tariffs, namely, tariffs for the levies on recording equipment and storage devices *(Geräte und*

Speichermedien). This provision has rather recently been added to the LACNR.[42] It relates to the payment of equitable remuneration for acts of private copying and photocopying by producers of recording equipment and storage devices (*Geräte und Speichermedien*, Articles 54 and 54a of the German *Copyright Act*). Whereas, before 2008, the German Copyright Act contained statutory tariffs for these levies in an annex to Article 54d, the German legislator now leaves it to the parties – the CMOs on the one hand and the producers of recording equipment and storage devices on the other – to agree on such tariffs themselves.

To this end, the statutory tariffs were replaced in 2008 by two sets of provisions. First, the amended Articles 54 and 54a of the German Copyright Act now provide for some general criteria for the calculation of the levies, the 'equitable remuneration', such as the reasonably expected use and the storage capacity of the equipment/devices. Furthermore, these provisions state that for the calculation of the levies it should be taken into account 'to what extent technological protection measures under Article 95a [of the] German Copyright Act [protection of technological measures] are being applied on the respective works or [neighbouring rights] subject matter', and thus address the relation between the payment of the levies and the application of technological protection measures (DRM or Digital Rights Management systems).[43] Most elements of these provisions were formerly contained in Article 13(4) of the LACNR.[44]

The second set of provisions, however, is to be found in the LACNR: with a view to enabling the parties to agree on the levies among themselves (by way of self-regulation instead of the previously applied statutory tariffs), Article 13a LACNR as well as some other newly inserted provisions of the LACNR now provide the parties with the mechanisms for reaching an agreement on the tariffs.

While explicitly referring to the previously mentioned criteria for the equitable remuneration under Articles 54 and 54a of the Copyright Act, at the outset, Article 13a LACNR obliges the CMOs to negotiate with the representatives of the producers (of recording equipment and storage devices) both the level of the equitable remuneration and the conclusion of an umbrella agreement within the meaning of Article 12 LACNR. But even if the negotiations on an umbrella agreement have failed, the CMO cannot unilaterally establish the levy tariffs: it has to

---

42. Article 13a was added to the LACNR by the German Second Law on the Regulation of Copyright in the Information Society (Zweites Gesetz zur Regelung des Urheberrechts in der Informationsgesellschaft) of 26 October 2007, Bundesgesetzblatt, Teil I, 2007, 2513.
43. On the protection of DRM systems and its origin in the WCT and WPPT, see J. Reinbothe & S. von Lewinski, *The WIPO Treaties 1996: The WIPO Copyright Treaty and the WIPO Performances and Phonograms Treaty: Commentary and Legal Analysis* (London: Butterworths, 2002), 581, Art. 11 WCT, Note 10 and following; cf. J. Reinbothe in E. Becker, W. Buhse, D. Günnewig & N. Rump, (eds), *Digital Rights Management – Technological, Economic, Legal and Political Aspects*. (Berlin/Heidelberg, 2003), 805 at 410 and following; on the (claimed) risk of double payment see T. Dreier in *Urheberrechtsgesetz, Kommentar, supra* n. 26 at 893 with references.
44. See 1st edition, s. 3.2.2.8.2.

establish the 'relevant use' under Article 54a(1) Copyright Act [45] through empirical studies *(empirische Untersuchungen)*.[46]

3.2.2.10 Article 13b of the LACNR (Obligations of Users and Organizers)

Whereas Articles 10–12 of the LACNR constitute obligations of CMOs in relation to users, Articles 13b and 13c present certain obligations with which users have to comply. Both provisions were inserted into the law in 1985. They reflect the desire of the German legislator to further help CMOs to fulfil their tasks accurately.

In principle, it should go without saying that potential users have to contact the CMO before they engage in an act of exploitation of protected works or subject matter.[47] However, this may be less obvious in the case of rights of equitable remuneration, where no exclusive right to authorize or prohibit use is involved. It was consequently deemed appropriate by the German legislator to insert an obligation of organizers of public performances into the law with a view to facilitating the control of CMOs over public performances of works. Article 13b(1) of the LACNR therefore states explicitly that 'organisers of public performances of copyright protected works have to seek permission of the CMO administering the exploitation rights on such works before the event'.

Moreover, under the first sentence of Article 13b(2), the organizers have to provide the CMO after the event with a listing of all used works. It should be noted, however, that the second sentence of the same Article exempts from this obligation organizers of 'a communication to the public of a work from a recording, a communication to the public of a broadcast of a work, and organizers of events, where regularly works in the public domain or insignificantly modified works are performed'. This means, in short, that the obligation to send listings of the used works under Article 13b(2) applies mainly to live performances.

Article 13b(3) includes a specific obligation of broadcasters vis-à-vis CMOs – again, with a view to facilitating the operations of the latter, in particular regarding the distribution of the collected revenues to rightholders:

> To the extent that, for the distribution of revenues from the management of rights of communication to the public of broadcasts, information from the broadcasters is needed, these broadcasters are obliged to provide the collecting society with this information against payment of the costs involved.[48]

---

45. Article 54a(1) Copyright Act reads: 'It is essential for determining the level of the equitable remuneration to what extent the recording equipment and storage devices have actually been used as types for private copying within the meaning of Article 53(1) to (3) Copyright Act'.
46. For details see J. Reinbothe in *Urheberrecht, Kommentar, supra* n. 19, § 13a LACNR, Note 5.
47. See also s. 3.2.2.5 above, on Art. 10 of the LACNR (Right of Information), and s. 3.2.2.6, on the obligation to allow exploitation (Art. 11 of the LACNR).
48. See *supra* n. 24.

The provision is designed to help the CMO with one of its own and most genuine tasks – redistribution of the revenues to rightholders; thus it seems only fair that the society has to reimburse the broadcaster for its costs in this respect.

3.2.2.11 Article 13c of the LACNR (Presumption of Legitimacy)

Article 13c of the LACNR establishes presumptions for the legal standing of the CMO regarding two types of claims of CMOs vis-à-vis users: rights of information (Article 13c(1)) and rights of equitable remuneration (Article 13c(2) to (4)). The underlying idea is that users should not be able to undermine any such claims by casting doubts on whether the CMO exercising them does in fact represent all relevant rightholders. In practice, each CMO in Germany has a dominant position, if not a monopoly, in its area of activity. A few exceptions apart, it cannot be doubted that each CMO does represent all rightholders in its area and often even the world repertoire based on agreements with its foreign sister societies. Article 13c, therefore, basically confirms reasonable practice and addresses possible cases of doubt as well as the treatment of outsiders.

For the purpose of this brief description of the LACNR, it may suffice to summarize, in short, the four paragraphs of Article 13c.

Article 13c(1) provides that 'if the CMO claims a right of information that can only be exercised through a CMO, it is presumed to represent the rights of all rightholders'. In fact, exercising a right of information cannot be made dependent on how many rightholders the CMO actually represents. Moreover, a CMO that does not represent at least a significant number of rightholders would not obtain the authorization to engage in collective rights management in the first place.[49]

The first sentence of Article 13c(2) of the LACNR provides that:

> if the collecting society claims a right of equitable remuneration under Articles 27 [public lending right], 54 (1) [private copying], 54c(1) [reprography], 77(2) [reproduction and distribution of recorded performances], 85 (4)[reproduction, distribution and making available to the public of sound recordings], 94(4) [reproduction, distribution, public performance and making available of films] or 137l(5) [transitional provisions for new forms of use] Copyright Act, it is presumed to represent the rights of all rightholders.[50]

This presumption is qualified in the second sentence of the Article, which states that, if more than one CMO is entitled to claim such rights of equitable remuneration, 'the presumption only applies, if all entitled CMOs present their claims together'. (This is regularly being done in the case of private copying, where all entitled CMOs in Germany operate and present their claims of equitable remuneration together under the heading of ZPÜ.)[51] Finally, the third sentence of the Article obliges the CMO that benefits from the presumption to keep the user

---

49. See ss 3.2.1.1–3.2.1.4 above, on Arts 1–4 of the LACNR.
50. See *supra* n. 24.
51. On the ZPÜ see s. 2.3.2 above, third to last paragraph.

from whom the remuneration is collected, free of possible claims from those rightholders that the society actually does not represent.

Article 13c(3) and (4) of the LACNR deal with a very specific issue, namely the collection of remuneration rights for cable redistribution under Article 20b of the *Copyright Act*. Under the latter, the authors' right of equitable remuneration for acts of cable redistribution can be administered only by a CMO, except if a broadcaster claims the remuneration right in relation to its own broadcasts. In combination with the presumption of ownership or representation in Article 13c(2) of the LACNR, several issues may occur between CMOs and broadcasters, among CMOs, and between CMOs and authors that do not want to be represented by a CMO (so-called outsiders).

Article 13c(3) and (4) of the LACNR offer detailed solutions to these situations. These provisions basically implement Article 9 of the EU Satellite and Cable Directive.[52] Article 13c(3) creates a fiction of entitlement: if an author has not assigned his remuneration right for cable redistribution under Article 20b(1) of the Copyright Act to any CMO, the CMO that usually administers rights of this kind is considered to be entitled to also administer the rights of the said 'outsider'. If more than one CMO is dealing with such rights, they are considered to be entitled together; if the author chooses the society himself, only this one is considered to be entitled to exercise his rights. However, these rules do not apply to rights held by the broadcaster whose broadcasts are redistributed by cable. Article 13c(4) concerns the relation between the 'outsider' and the CMO. It states that, as a consequence of the presumptions contained in Article 13c(3), in principle authors have the same rights and obligations in relation to the CMO as if they had actually assigned their rights to the CMO.

3.2.3   Chapter 2 (Second Part): The Arbitration Board and Access to the Courts (Articles 14–17a of the LACNR)

Like the Articles 6–13c of the LACNR, the provisions contained in Articles 14–17a belong to Chapter 2 of the LACNR entitled 'Rights and Obligations of the Collecting Society'. They do not form part of a separate subsection, and yet they are special. Articles 14–17 of the LACNR deal with the Arbitration Board *(Schiedsstelle)* and access to the Courts, and the recently inserted Article 17a addresses voluntary arbitration between the conflicting parties.[53] Apart from the latter, these provisions created in 1965 a new and comprehensive mechanism for copyright litigation involving CMOs. The German legislator rightly assumed that, while copyright litigation is already something for experts and not easily accessible to general Courts, cases involving CMOs and their sometimes complex dealings with

---

52. EC, Directive 93/83/EEC of 27 Sep. 1993 on the coordination of certain rules concerning copyright and rights related to copyright applicable to satellite broadcasting and cable retransmission (1993), O.J. L. 248/15 [EU Satellite and Cable Directive], <http://eur-lex.europa.eu/LexUriServ/LexUriServ.do?uri=CELEX:31993L0083:EN:HTML> (last visited: 7 Jun. 2010).

53. See s. 3.2.3.6 *infra*.

users are even more complicated. In particular, assessing the economic impact of an umbrella agreement under Article 12 of the LACNR between the CMO and an association of users on rights of remuneration for private copying, rights of communication to the public or public lending rights may be easiest for the parties themselves with the assistance of neutral experts. Hence, the idea to establish an institutionalized public arbitration board, the *Schiedsstelle*, was born.[54] Articles 14–17 include detailed provisions on the mandate of the Arbitration Board, its composition, the nature and consequence of its decisions and the role of the proceedings before the Arbitration Board in relation to access to the Courts.

3.2.3.1 Article 14 of the LACNR (Arbitration Board)

3.2.3.1.1 The Mandate of the Arbitration Board
The mandate of the Arbitration Board is set out in Article 14(1) of the LACNR.
Under Article 14(1)1, each of the parties may turn to the Arbitration Board:

for disputes to which a collecting society is a party if
a) the disputes concern the exploitation of works or subject matter protected under the Copyright Act,
b) if the disputes concern the equitable remuneration under Articles 54 or 54c of the Copyright Act,[55] or
c) if the disputes concern the conclusion or modification of an umbrella agreement.[56]

The Arbitration Board is hence involved in all of the most relevant disputes between CMOs and users, be it in the context of individual agreements under Article 11, in the context of disputes about private copying or reprography levies or in the context of umbrella agreements under Article 12 of the LACNR. Parties to such disputes are the CMO on the one side and individual users or user associations on the other. In the context of disputes about the levies, the parties concerned are the CMO on the one side and producers' (of recording equipment and storage devices) associations on the other – though the latter are, strictly speaking, not 'users' of rights.

Under Article 14(1)2, each of the parties may turn to the Arbitration Board 'for disputes to which a broadcaster and a cable re-distributor is a party, if the disputes concern the obligation to conclude an agreement on the redistribution by cable'.

This provision was added to Article 14 of the LACNR in 1998, when the right of cable redistribution was introduced in Article 20b of the Copyright Act. It implements Article 11 of the EU Satellite and Cable Directive.[57] Although the

---

54. On the nature of the Arbitration Board as an administrative body see J. Reinbothe, *Schlichtung im Urheberrecht* (Munich: Beck Juristischer Verlag, 1978), 188; A. Strittmatter, *Tarife vor der urheberrechtlichen Schiedsstelle* (Berlin: Berlin Verlag, 1994), 202; G. Schulze in *Urheberrechtsgesetz, Kommentar, supra* n. 26 at 1770.
55. This provision was inserted into the LACNR in 2008 as part of the amendments regarding the new structuring of agreements on the levies; cf. s. 3.2.2.9 *supra* and Note 42.
56. See *supra* n. 24.
57. See *supra* n. 52; J. Reinbothe in *Urheberrecht, Kommentar, supra* n. 19, § 14 LACNR, Note 1.

disputes described in Article 14(1)2. do not involve CMOs and are, strictly speaking, not about the collective management of rights, the German legislator wanted to make available and apply the proven mechanism of the Arbitration Board also to such disputes.

Article 14(1) of the LACNR grants all parties a right to initiate the proceedings before the Arbitration Board – in writing, as Article 14(5) requires. Of course, they are not obliged to do so; however, at least in principle, none of the kind of disputes mentioned in Article 14(1) can be brought before the Courts without prior proceedings before the Arbitration Board having taken place.[58] Moreover, agreements on private arbitration board settlements for future disputes must not prejudice the right of each party to invoke the proceedings before the Arbitration Board and to seek a decision by the Courts (Article 14(7)). Therefore, de facto, the proceedings before the Arbitration Board are some sort of a first instance before Court proceedings on matters described in Article 14(1) and have precedence over private settlement agreements. This is confirmed by Article 14(8) of the LACNR, which states that initiating proceedings before the Arbitration Board has the same effect of interrupting prescription as initiating Court proceedings. Moreover, the settlements before the Arbitration Board are enforceable under the law of civil procedure (second sentence of Article 14(6)).

The first sentence of Article 14(6) describes the mandate of the Arbitration Board in very general terms: it is 'to promote an amicable settlement of the dispute'.

3.2.3.1.2   The Composition of the Arbitration Board
According to Article 14(2) of the LACNR, the Arbitration Board is established 'at the supervisory authority (Article 18 (1))', that is, the German Patent and Trade Mark Office (GPTO). It is composed of three members, including the chairperson, who must have a complete legal education with the qualification to become a judge.

The Federal Ministry of Justice appoints the three members of the Arbitration Board for an initial (and renewable) term of at least one year. The recently added Article 14(3) provides for the possibility of establishing several Chambers of the Arbitration Board with a view to making it more efficient. Article 14(4) of the LACNR explicitly states that the members are independent and not subject to instructions.

3.2.3.1.3   Consideration of Economic Facts and Stakeholders' Views
It follows from the important role of the Arbitration Board that it always had to take account of the economic circumstances of the dispute in question, as well as of the interests of the parties. Nevertheless, in 2008 two provisions were inserted into Article 14 that are to reinforce these elements, especially in the context of disputes about the equitable remuneration for private copying and reprography.

To this end, Article 14(5a) obliges the Arbitration Board to establish the 'relevant use' of recording equipment or storage devices for private copying within

---

58. For details see s. 3.2.3.4 below (on Art. 16 of the LACNR).

the meaning of Article 54a(1) Copyright Act through empirical studies *(empirische Untersuchungen).*[59] Moreover, under Article 14(5b), certain consumer associations are now entitled to submit comments on disputes about the equitable remuneration within the meaning of Article 54 Copyright Act.

3.2.3.2 Articles 14a, 14b, 14c, 14d and 14e of the LACNR (Proposal for Agreement)

The general mandate and composition of the Arbitration Board according to Article 14 of the LACNR gives the impression that it functions like a first instance peace judge. In fact, the original Arbitration Board of 1965 did have a similar function. Originally, only the chairperson was appointed by the public authority (each party appointed one additional member) and the judgments of the Arbitration Board were binding on the parties. But this model met with little acceptance by the copyright world; the 'old' Arbitration Board was hardly ever used, and where it was, it took years to arrive at a decision.[60]

For these reasons, the structure of the Arbitration Board, and in particular its decision making power were completely revised in 1985. The Articles 14a, 14b, 14c and 14d of the LACNR contain the main elements of the 1985 revision. They focus on the content and the effects of the Arbitration Board's decisions. Article 14e was added in 2008 to make the procedure more efficient in case several disputes are pending before the Arbitration Board (see section 3.2.3.2.5 below). The Arbitration Board of today may still look like a first instance peace judge tribunal – but, in fact, it is not. The Explanatory Memorandum of the 1985 government proposal describes the Arbitration Board as an administrative body established at the supervisory authority.[61] The Arbitration Board nowadays really focuses on what it was always meant to be – a body that facilitates amicable agreements between the parties.[62]

3.2.3.2.1 Article 14a of the LACNR

The acceptance and success of the Arbitration Board is mainly due to the nature of its decisions. According to Article 14a, the Arbitration Board does not issue judgments. With the simple majority of its (three) members, it adopts a decision and submits it to the parties as a 'proposal for an agreement' (Article 14a (1) and (2)). If the proposal is not contested by any of the parties within one month (for disputes

---

59. See s. 3.2.2.9 *supra* and n. 46.
60. On the original Arbitration Board of 1965 see J. Reinbothe in *Urheberrecht, Kommentar, supra* n. 19, Vor § 14 LACNR, Note 2, with further references; GPTO, Annual Report 2004, at 50 (where it states that between 1998 and 2004, the 'new' Arbitration Board received 270 requests, presented 167 decisions and handled in total 222 requests). According to the GPTO Annual Report 2008, at 136, between 2005 and 2008 the Arbitration Board received 306 requests, presented 222 decisions and concluded in total 316 requests.
61. Explanatory Memorandum of the Government Bill, in: Parliamentary Document (Bundestags-drucksache) 10/837, at 20.
62. GPTO, Annual Report 2008, at 56.

about cable redistribution rights, three months), the proposal is considered accepted by the parties and becomes the valid settlement of their dispute (Article 14a(3)).

In the context of the amendments to the LACNR introduced in 2008, an obligation for the Arbitration Board was added to Article 14a(2) to submit its proposal for an agreement within one year after the procedure has been initiated.[63] This new deadline, like several other provisions introduced in 2008, is designed to shorten the arbitration procedure. However, the deadline can be extended if both parties to the dispute agree.

3.2.3.2.2 Article 14b of the LACNR

Article 14b of the LACNR provides the Arbitration Board with an important exception to its rather comprehensive mandate under Article 14(1)1.a) of the LACNR regarding disputes between CMOs and individual users.[64] If, in the context of such disputes, the application and appropriateness of the tariff (Article 13 of the LACNR) as well as other facts are contested, the Arbitration Board may limit its proposal for an agreement to the application and appropriateness of the tariff – which is, in fact, its genuine mandate. Following the same logic, if the tariff itself is not contested at all, the Arbitration Board may even refrain from submitting any proposal for an agreement.

3.2.3.2.3 Article 14c of the LACNR

Article 14c deals with the content and effect of the Arbitration Board's decisions regarding disputes in the context of umbrella agreements under Article 12 of the LACNR between CMOs and users' associations. Article 14c(1) provides that, for such disputes under Article 14(1)1.c) of the LACNR,[65] the Arbitration Board proposes the contents of the umbrella agreement. Umbrella agreements are usually of a longer duration; thus the Arbitration Board may also, upon request of a party, propose provisional measures (Article 14c(2)). In practice, however, this provision has not become relevant. Furthermore, Article 14c(3) of the LACNR takes into account the potential effects of umbrella agreements on competition by providing that the Arbitration Board has to keep the German Federal Antitrust Office *(Bundeskartellamt)* informed about the proceedings.

3.2.3.2.4 Article 14d of the LACNR

Article 14d reflects the additional mandate that the Arbitration Board obtained in 1998 for disputes between broadcasters and cable re-distributors under Article 14(1)2. of the LACNR.[66] The legislator held that agreements on cable redistribution are more similar to umbrella agreements than to individual user

---

63. See *supra* n. 42.
64. See s. 3.2.3.1.1. *supra.*
65. See *ibid.*
66. *Ibid.*

agreements. Therefore, the same rules apply to such disputes before the Arbitration Board as to disputes on umbrella agreements.

3.2.3.2.5 Article 14e of the LACNR

This provision was inserted into the LACNR in 2008.[67] It addresses the relation between a CMO's use or remuneration disputes with individual parties under Article 14(1) 1.a) or b) and disputes about umbrella agreements under Article 14(1)1.c).

If such parallel disputes are pending, the Arbitration Board may put the individual dispute(s) on hold until it has proposed the contents of the umbrella agreement. It is clear that, through this provision, the legislator wanted to stress the importance of, and its preference for, umbrella agreements and give them priority over individual agreements.

3.2.3.3 Article 15 of the LACNR (Rules of Procedure of the Arbitration Board)

Under Article 15 of the LACNR, the Federal Minister of Justice has the competence to regulate on the rules of procedure before the Arbitration Board on the compensation for its members and on its fees. The Regulation on the Arbitration Board for Copyright Disputes of 1985 contains detailed provisions on how to initiate the proceedings and on the previously mentioned issues.[68]

3.2.3.4 Article 16 of the LACNR (Access to the Courts)

Article 16 clarifies the relation between the proceedings before the Arbitration Board and access to the Courts in copyright disputes. The provision confirms that, as a matter of principle, there is always access to the Courts in copyright matters, even in those cases in which Article 14(1) of the LACNR entrusts the Arbitration Board with a particular mandate.

However, Court proceedings have to be preceded by proceedings before the Arbitration Board in four cases: first, for disputes between CMOs and individual users according to Article 14(1)1.a) of the LACNR, if 'the application or the equitability of a tariff is contested'; second, for disputes about the equitable remuneration for private copying or reprography according to Article 14(1)1.b); third, for disputes between CMOs and users' associations about umbrella agreements according to Article 14(1)1.c); and fourth, for disputes about cable redistribution rights according to Article 14(1)2. of the LACNR.

---

67. See *supra* n. 42.
68. Order Concerning the Mediation Body for Copyright Disputes (Urheberrechtsschiedsstellen-verordnung) of 20 Dec. 1985, *Bundesgesetzblatt,* Teil I, 1985, 2543 and as amended in Teil I, 24 Jun. 1994, 1325.

3.2.3.5   Articles 16(4) and 17 of the LACNR (Competent Court)

The LACNR contains two specific provisions on the competent Court. According to Article 16(4), for all disputes regarding the equitable remuneration for private copying or reprography, umbrella agreements and cable redistribution agreements under Article 14(1)1.a), b) and 2, respectively, of the LACNR the Munich Court of Appeals is the competent Court of First Instance. As mentioned above, in these cases prior proceedings before the Arbitration Board are mandatory.[69]

Article 17 of the LACNR provides that complaints of CMOs regarding the alleged infringement of their rights or claims can be filed with the Court only where the infringement took place or where the infringer has his or her residence.

3.2.3.6   Article 17a of the LACNR (Voluntary Arbitration)

As stated before, the amendments of the LACNR introduced in 2008[70] were designed to streamline and shorten the procedures before the Arbitration Board in general and to provide the parties with better means to agree on the levies for private copying and reprography[71] in particular.

For the same reason, and equally in 2008, the legislator introduced the entirely new provision of Article 17a. It confirms that the parties of a dispute over the levies may seek voluntary arbitration – something they were always free to do – and provides them, on top of this confirmation, with the specific and structured assistance of the Federal Ministry of Justice in this regard; if the parties want to turn to private arbitration instead of applying to the Arbitration Board, the Ministry may nominate a mediator and determine the procedure upon request of, and in agreement with, the parties. In any case and at any point in time, however, the parties maintain the right to turn to the Arbitration Board.

There is little experience yet with this type of assisted voluntary arbitration. It remains to be seen if it really is a viable alternative option to the procedure before the Arbitration Board. However, the Article 17a model is another proof of the intention of the German legislator to arrive quickly and in a non-bureaucratic manner at agreements on the payment of levies.

3.2.4   Chapter 3: The Control over Collecting Societies (Articles 18–20 of the LACNR)

One of the main motives behind the LACNR was to submit CMOs to comprehensive State control so as to cope better with the potential risks that result from their dominant position and their function as trustees. This specific State control, which is contained in Chapter 3, Articles 18–20 of the LACNR, applies side by side with the control by the German Federal Antitrust Office *(Bundeskartellamt)* and other

---

69.   See s. 3.2.3.4. *supra.*
70.   See *supra* n. 42.
71.   See s. 3.2.2.9 *supra.*

forms of supervision by the State, depending on which organizational structure the CMO has chosen.[72]

In general, CMOs may therefore be subject to three different forms of supervision. However, only the supervision spelled out in Articles 18–20 is copyright-specific and, so to speak, tailor-made for the functions of CMOs. The LACNR takes account of the possible interfaces between these different forms of control over CMOs.

3.2.4.1   Article 18 of the LACNR (Supervising Authority)

The supervisory authority for CMOs is the GPTO, the German Patent and Trade Mark Office (*Deutsches Patent- und Markenamt* (DPMA)) in Munich (Article 18(1)). The GPTO can take its two most important decisions, namely, on the granting (Article 1 of the LACNR) and the repeal (Article 4 of the LACNR) of the authorization, only if the German Federal Antitrust Office agrees (Article 18(3) of the LACNR). In this respect, the GPTO depends on the latter. Public authorities that exercise other forms of control over CMOs because of their organizational structure, for example, under company law, have to coordinate with the GPTO (Article 18(2)).

3.2.4.2   Article 19 of the LACNR (Supervision)

The main substance of the supervision is outlined in Article 19 of the LACNR. It draws upon the German State control over banks and insurance companies,[73] but contains several specific features with reference to collective rights management.

First of all, the GPTO is obliged to safeguard compliance of the CMOs with their obligations under the LACNR (Article 19(1)) and may take all appropriate measures to this effect (Article 19(2)). This is of particular importance for users[74] and also for the rightholders[75] that are represented in a CMO. For the latter, the supervision by the GPTO has a particularly protective function. It includes the control over the appropriate influence of the rightholders in the society. In the view of most scholars, and apparently also the GPTO, rightholders are directly entitled to claim appropriate action from the GPTO.[76] Foreign rightholders benefit from this right, too, in accordance with international law.

Under Article 19(3) and (4) of the LACNR, the GPTO has an extensive right of information vis-à-vis CMOs and can attend their Assemblies and meetings.

---

72. See s. 2.3.2 *supra*.
73. J. Reinbothe in *Urheberrecht, Kommentar, supra* n. 19, § 18 LACNR, Note 1.
74. Cf. the obligations under Arts 10, 11, 12 and 13 of the LACNR, *supra* n. 24.
75. Notably regarding the obligations under Arts 6, 7 (first sentence) and 9 of the LACNR, *supra* n. 24.
76. J. Reinbothe in *Urheberrecht, Kommentar, supra* n. 19, § 18 LACNR, Note 2, with further references.

Furthermore, it can require the removal of representatives who are not deemed sufficiently reliable (Article 19(5)).

3.2.4.3   Article 20 of the LACNR (Procedural Obligations of Collecting Societies)

With a view to facilitating the GPTO's tasks, Article 20 obliges CMOs to provide it regularly, and on their own initiative, information about any change in the executive staff, the statute, the tariffs, umbrella agreements, agreements with foreign CMOs, decisions of the Assemblies, the supervisory board and all committees, the annual report, the annual account, and, upon request of the GPTO, all decisions of Courts and public authorities, to which they were a party.

3.2.5   Chapter 4: The Transitional and Final Provisions (Articles 21–28 of the LACNR)

Most of the transitional and final provisions contained in Articles 21–28 of the LACNR have become obsolete over the years and are not worth mentioning here; after all, on 1 January 2006, the LACNR had been in force for forty years.

Nevertheless, one provision deserves to be highlighted. It is the former Article 24 of the LACNR, which had inserted a specific provision on the control of CMOs under competition law into the German Antitrust Act, the *Gesetz gegen Wettbewerbsbeschränkungen* (GWB) of 1957.[77] Under this provision, CMOs were explicitly exempted from the prohibition of horizontal and vertical agreements and of pricing arrangements. At the same time, CMOs continued to be subject to the control of a possible abuse of their dominant position under competition law.[78]

Over the years, this specific exemption for CMOs under the German Antitrust Act has been modified and adapted to the jurisprudence of the Court of Justice of the European Union (CJEU) on the same subject. In fact, the CJEU has tackled on several occasions the issue of abusive behaviour of CMOs under Article 82 of the EU Treaty (now Article 102 TFEU).[79] More recently, the German legislator decided to remove the exemption for CMOs altogether from the GWB in the implementation of the obligation under EC Regulation 1/2003[80] to remove any

---

77. See *supra* n. 22.
78. J. Reinbothe in *Urheberrecht, Kommentar, supra* n. 19, § 24 LACNR (§ 102a/30 GWB), Note 2.
79. Cf. F. Gotzen, 'A new perspective for the Management of Copyright and Competition Law in the Internal Market', in *Perspektiven des Geistigen Eigentums und Wettbewerbsrechts, Festschrift für Gerhard Schricker zum 70. Geburtstag*, ed. A. Ohly, T. Bodewig, T. Dreier, P. Götting, M. Haedicke, M. Lehmann, (Munich: Beck Juristischer Verlag, 2005), 944 at 299 with references; Court of Justice of the European Union, judgment of 11 Dec. 2008, case C-52/07 (Kanal 5 Ltd.), OJ C 32/2 [<http://eur-lex.europa.eu/LexUriServ/LexUriServ.do?uri=OJ:C:2009:032:0002:0003:EN:PDF>]. (last visited: 7 Jun. 2010).
80. EC, Council Regulation (EC) No. 1/2003 of 16 Dec. 2002 on the implementation of the rules on competition laid down in Arts 81 and 82 of the Treaty (2002), O.J. L. 1/1 [EC Regulation 1/2003], <http://eur-lex.europa.eu/LexUriServ/LexUriServ.do?uri=OJ:L:2003:001:0001:0025:EN:PDF> (last visited: 7 Jun. 2010).

explicit sector exemptions from the antitrust legislation.[81] Apart from the obligation under the EC Regulation, the reasoning for this step is plausible: it is not contested that CMOs fulfil legitimate functions and are, as such, not cartels. No specific exemption is needed, therefore, from the application of those provisions of the GWB that refer to horizontal or vertical agreements and pricing arrangements, because they do not apply in the first place. By the same token, abuse control has always applied and will continue to do so.

3.3   Conclusions

The LACNR provides solutions for all copyright-related issues regarding collective rights management in Germany:

- It contains rules on who may establish a collecting society under which conditions (Articles 1–5);
- it regulates the relation between collecting societies and rightholders, including the obligation of societies to administer rights, the principles of the distribution of the revenues and of accounting and reporting (Articles 6–9);
- the LACNR provisions on the relation between collecting societies and users include obligations of collecting societies to provide information, grant licenses and conclude umbrella agreements under equitable conditions, and to publish tariffs that are transparent and based on fair criteria (Articles 10–13c);
- detailed provisions deal with the Arbitration Board and access to justice (Articles 14–17a);
- specific provisions of the LACNR (notably Articles 13a, 14, 14e, 16 and 17a) provide the parties with mechanisms for, and guidance on, how the equitable remuneration for private copying and reprography under Articles 54 et seq. of the German Copyright Act can be agreed on; and
- the LACNR provides for the supervision of collecting societies by the GPTO, which constantly examines whether the conditions for granting the authorization to engage in collective rights management continue to exist and ensures that the collecting societies fulfil their duties under the LACNR.[82]

The LACNR reflects in a comprehensive manner the economic, cultural and societal functions of collective rights management in Germany. The law leaves the

---

81. *Seventh Law on the Amendment of the Law on Restrictions to Competition (Siebtes Gesetz zur Änderung des Gesetzes gegen Wettbewerbsbeschränkungen) of 7 July 2005*, Bundesgesetzblatt, Teil I 2005, 1954. Cf. Explanatory Memorandum of the Government Bill (in preparation of the Law of 7 Jul. 2005 amending the Antitrust Act GWB), in: Parliamentary Document ('Bundestagsdrucksache') 15/3640 of 12 Aug. 2004 at 49–50; cf. EC Regulation 1/2003, *ibid.*
82. Cf. GPTO, Annual Report 2008, at 52.

establishment of CMOs and their operations to a large extent to the market. However, through its provisions, it has succeeded in ensuring the good governance of CMOs. The LACNR has made sure that CMOs are reliable trustees for rightholders and reliable partners for users. Also, it has provided for the general acceptance of collective rights management in Germany today.

On the whole, the LACNR has achieved its purpose and passes the practice test continuously. It has, in fact, safeguarded the pragmatic and sustainable operation of collective rights management and CMOs as an important element of the German copyright system.

Indeed, the LACNR almost seems to be a model for successful regulation in this field. The concepts chosen in 1965 have been reasonably future-proof. They have already worked for more than four decades and have been accepted by all players. Basically, only four sets of amendments had to be applied over the years: one in 1985, to improve on the functioning and acceptance of the Arbitration Board; one in 1998, to implement the EU Satellite and Cable Directive;[83] one in 2003 to implement the EU Directive on Copyright in the Information Society,[84] and one in 2008 to better adapt the LACNR to helping CMOs and their contracting parties agree on the equitable remuneration for private copying and reprography (the levies).[85]

4 FUTURE PERSPECTIVES FOR COLLECTIVE RIGHTS MANAGEMENT IN GERMANY

The environment of intellectual property is changing. The digital revolution and notably the Internet and new digital products and services have had the highest impact on copyright protection ever – comparable only to the appearance of commercial printing (copying) and certainly much more radical than the appearance of new forms of exploitation based on new technology in the early twentieth century.

The digital revolution and its effects on the economy, on communication habits and on culture has done at least two things to copyright: it has changed the perception of copyright protection, and it has further stimulated the move of copyright away from authors' rights to producers' rights. The discussions about the so-called private copy levies and the role of DRM systems are, at the same time, testimony, proof and catalyst of these developments.

The issues are authors' rights or producers' rights; individual rights management by producers and publishers or collective rights management by CMOs; and DRM systems or equitable remuneration schemes. And they all directly affect the mandate and function of CMOs and collective rights management. Governments and legislators are called upon to tackle these issues without delay.

---

83. See *supra* n. 52.
84. See *supra* n. 42.
85. See *supra* n. 42 and s. 3.2.2.9.

In countries without a particular history and tradition of collective rights management, these issues may raise no specific problems. They do raise problems, however, in most E U Member States, including and in particular Germany, with a long and successful tradition of collective rights management and its comprehensive legal framework, the LACNR.

As far as the LACNR is concerned, it continues to function in the new environment of digital services. So far, only a few adjustments, because of the new features of the Information Society, had to be applied, mainly in 2008,[86] and the regular reporting of the control authority confirms that collective rights management continues to function well, to the benefit of all players.[87]

At the same time, the changes that were introduced in 2008 and mainly designed to employ the mechanisms of the LACNR for arriving at agreements on the payment of the equitable remuneration for private copying and reprography, have not passed the practice test yet. They have arguably led to a stagnation, if not reduction of the income of CMOs and thus of rightholders, in spite of a boom of private copying, especially in the Internet environment, and a rather slow take-off of DRM-driven payments that may not equally benefit all rightholders.[88]

Developments in Germany will have to be seen in the EU context. And while the LACNR is an inextricable part of the German Copyright Act and the underlying concepts of continental European copyright protection that is based as a matter of principle on the strong protection of authors and creativity as such, the recent signals at EU level about collective rights management in its relation to competition and the EU Internal Market seem to indicate that there is no particular focus on the specificities that the mandate and function of CMOs are based on in the cultural context. In the understanding of the LACNR, collecting societies and collective rights management as such is beneficial for both the individual rightholders (because many of their rights cannot be managed individually) and for users (because CMOs provide them with a one-stop shop for, and thus easy access to, the world repertoire). A European Commission Communication of 2004[89] highlighted the position of CMOs as trustees; however, a paper issued by the European Commission's services in July 2005[90] seemed to confirm that they see little if any difference between CMOs and other service providers such as banks and insurance companies. Moreover, when focusing almost exclusively on the

---

86. See s. 3.2.2.9. *supra* and n. 42.
87. GPTO, Annual Report 2008, at 22.
88. J. Reinbothe in *Urheberrecht, Kommentar, supra* n. 19, § 27 LACNR, Note 2, with further references.
89. 'Communication from the Commission: The Management of Copyright and Related Rights in the Internal Market', *supra* n. 1, at 14.
90. 'Study on a Community Initiative on the Cross-Border Collective Management of Copyright', Commission Staff Working Document of 7 Jul. 2005; cf. BNA Patent, Trademark & Copyright Journal, Vol. 70, 22 Jul. 2005, No. 1729, at 367. EC, 'Commission Recommendation of 18 October 2005 on collective cross-border management of copyright and related rights for legitimate online music services' (2005), O.J. L. 276/54, <http://eur-lex.europa.eu/LexUriServ/LexUriServ.do?uri=OJ:L:2005:276:0054:0057:EN:PDF> (last visited: 7 Jun. 2010).

objective to create one-stop shops for EU-wide licensing, the advantages of the existing one-stop shops on the (in most cases, world) repertoire may be over-looked.[91] Of course, it is mainly up to EU Member States and to the European Parliament to decide on the appropriate way forward for collective rights management, at least as far as EU legislation is concerned. Against the background of the principles enshrined in the LACNR and its vast experience in this field, Germany may be expected to have an influential voice, when the EU legislative institutions want to define together the future of collective rights management in the EU.

---

91. For details on developments at EU level, see above Ch. 5, Collective Management in the European Union; for the discussion in Germany, see J. Reinbothe in *Urheberrecht, Kommentar, supra* n. 19, Vor § § 1 and following LACNR, Note 16, with further references.

Chapter 8

Collective Management in the United Kingdom (and Ireland)

*Prof. Dr Paul L.C. Torremans**

1 INTRODUCTION

One does not need to dwell here on the fact that it is in many circumstances virtually impossible for an individual owner of an intellectual property right to police all potentially infringing uses. This gave, as we know, rise to the idea of collective licensing,[1] whereby rights are assigned to a society or such a society is given the right to grant licenses on behalf of the right owner. The society is also given the right to enforce those rights against infringers.[2] This essay will look at collective licensing,[3] mainly in the United Kingdom, but also in the Republic of Ireland. Before this essay focuses on these societies and the way in which they are regulated, it will first provide a historic overview of their development within the United Kingdom.

---

* Professor of Intellectual Property Law, School of Law, University of Nottingham, UK.
1. See R. Arnold, *Performers' Rights*, 4th edn (London, Sweet & Maxwell, 2008), 550 at 121.
2. See K. Garnett, G. Harbottle & G. Davies, (eds), *Copinger and Skone James on Copyright*, 15th edn (London: Sweet & Maxwell 2005), at 1540–1541.
3. See, in general terms, P. Torremans, *Holyoak and Torremans: Intellectual Property Law*, 5th edn (Oxford: Oxford University Press, 2008), 608 at 284–285; L. Bently & B. Sherman, *Intellectual Property Law*, 2nd edn (Oxford: Oxford University Press, 2004), 1231 at 267–269 and W. Cornish & D. Llewelyn, *Intellectual Property: Patents, Copyright, Trade Marks and Allied Rights*, 5th edn (London: Sweet & Maxwell, 2003), 895 at 481–482.

Daniel Gervais (ed.), *Collective Management of Copyright and Related Rights*, pp. 251–281.
© 2010 Kluwer Law International BV, The Netherlands.

2   HISTORY AND NATURE OF
           COLLECTIVE MANAGEMENT

2.1   HISTORY

Collective licensing in the United Kingdom started early in the twentieth century.
The *Copyright Act 1911* gave the impetus, and even before the Act was adopted the
Mechanical Copyright Licences Company Ltd (MECOLICO) was formed to collect and distribute mechanical royalties from the gramophone companies.[4] Soon
afterwards, in 1914, the Performing Rights Society Ltd (PRS) saw the light of day.
Its specific aim was the collective administration of public performance rights in
musical works.[5]

The next phase in the development of collective licensing was prompted by the
Cawardine case.[6] In this case, it was established that the *Copyright Act 1911* gave
full copyright to sound recordings. There was therefore a new need to administer
the public performance rights in sound recordings, and this is what Phonographic
Performance Ltd (PPL) set out to do from its creation in 1934 onwards.[7]

For a while this seemed to be the end of developments in this field, and among
themselves the three collecting societies seemed to cover the whole area of
collective licensing. So comprehensive seemed the coverage at the time that the
review of copyright undertaken by the Gregory Committee led to a mention in a
1952 report[8] that the PPL and PRS were effectively quasi-monopolies. The emphasis therefore shifted to the regulatory aspect. The Gregory Committee saw the need
for the establishment of a tribunal that could, if necessary, revise and review the
tariffs and conditions that the quasi-monopolists PRS and PPL imposed. The
Copyright Act 1956 followed up that recommendation and created the Performing
Right Tribunal, which is now known as the Copyright Tribunal.[9]

Technological developments and the emergence of inexpensive copying techniques brought the next phase in the development of collective licensing, which
started in the late 1970s.

A first new phenomenon that needed to be dealt with was the extent of photocopying that was being carried out in educational institutions such as schools and
universities. When this problem was considered by the Whitford Committee[10] as

---

4. *Copyright Act, 1911*, 1 & 2 Geo. V., c. 46.
5. See H. Laddie, P. Prescott & M. Vitoria, *The Modern Law of Copyright and Designs*, 3rd edn
   (London: Butterworths, 2000), at 943–944.
6. *Gramophone Co. Ltd v. Stephen Cawardine & Co.* [1934] Ch 450. See Cornish, *supra* n. 3 at 351.
7. See Garnett, *supra* n. 2 at 1545–1546.
8. Copyright Committee, Report of the Copyright Committee, (Chairman H.S. Gregory), Cmnd
   8662, Board of Trade, 1952, at paras 136 and 146.
9. *Copyright Act, 1956*, 4 & 5 Eliz. II, c. 74.
10. Committee to consider the Law on Copyright and Designs (Whitford Committee), Report of the
    Committee to consider the Law of Copyright and Designs, (Chairman the Honourable
    Mr Justice Whitford), CMD 6732, HMSO, 1977, Ch. 4.

part of its review of copyright, all parties involved saw collective licensing as the only feasible solution. What emerged as a solution was a system of negotiated blanket licenses that were to be administered by a collecting society. Despite the fact that the Committee's recommendations were not followed to the letter, the scheme eventually went ahead. A number of publishers' and authors' associations took the initiative in 1982 to create the Copyright Licensing Agency Ltd (CLA). The CLA then opened negotiations with the representatives of schools and universities with the aim to come to a system of blanket licenses. Some of the members of the CLA backed these negotiations up with well-publicized copyright infringement actions. As a result, the schools and universities on the other side of the table were made acutely aware of the risk and the extent of their potential liabilities for this form of widespread copyright infringement. What emerged was a first set of three-year blanket licenses, and over the years the CLA and its system of blanket licenses have gone on to cover the whole educational sector. The extensive coverage of the scheme and monopoly position of the CLA have meant that the *Copyright, Designs and Patents Act 1988* (CDPA) has expanded the jurisdiction of the Copyright Tribunal to include the CLA schemes.[11] The Act also provides a legal framework to ensure the smooth operation of the schemes.[12]

Schools and universities did not only engage in photocopying, however. The increased use of recording equipment, such as tape recorders and video recorders, also led to widespread recording of radio and television broadcasts, with the aim of using them for educational purposes. Because of the multitude of right holders involved, it was once more not practicable to negotiate individual licenses for each such recording. The *CDPA* therefore contains an incentive to come to some form of compulsory collective licensing scheme.[13] It does so by making the off-air recording by educational establishments for educational purposes free of charge until a certified licensing scheme is put in place. To receive compensation, right holders needed to come up with an acceptable licensing scheme. Eventually, two schemes were developed and have been in place since 30 May 1990. The first is operated by the Educational Recording Agency Ltd (ERA) and the second by Guild Sound and Vision Ltd. The latter has since been replaced by Open University Educational Enterprises Ltd.[14]

---

11. *Copyright Designs and Patents Act 1988*, c. 48, <www.opsi.gov.uk/acts/acts1988/ UKpga_19880048_en_1.htm> (last visited: 10 May 2010) [*CDPA*].
12. See, for example, *ibid.*, s. 36.
13. *Ibid.*, ss 36 and 143.
14. See Copyright (Certification of Licensing Scheme for Educational Recording of Broadcasts) (Guild Sound and Vision Limited) (Revocation) Order 1990, Statutory Instrument 1990/2007, <www.opsi.gov.uk/si/si1990/Uksi_19902007_en_1.htm> (last visited: 10 May 2010) (revoking the Guild Sound and Vision scheme) and Copyright (Certification of Licensing Scheme for Educational Recording of Broadcasts) (Open University Educational Enterprises Limited) Order 1990, Statutory Instrument 1990/2008 (certifying the Open University Educational Enterprises scheme), <www.opsi.gov.uk/si/si1990/Uksi_19902008_en_1.htm> (last visited: 10 May 2010).

Later in the 1990s the emphasis moved to performers. They were for the fist time given property rights in relation to their performances by means of the Copyright and Related Rights Regulations 1996,[15] which made changes to the relevant sections of the *CDPA*.[16] These property rights can be transferred much like copyright, and it is therefore logical that the performers can also transfer them to a society that will enforce them on their behalf. Rental rights provide a stark example of this. The performer can transfer the rental right in a sound recording or film to the producer, but even then the performer retains a right to equitable remuneration for the rental. That right to equitable remuneration is not assignable *inter vivos*, with one exception. That exception is indeed the assignment of the right to a collecting society with the aim to enforce the right on behalf of the performer.[17]

For the sake of completeness, one should also refer to the publication right in this respect. This right gives a copyright style property right to those publishing for the first time an unpublished work once the copyright protection in the work has expired. All of the provisions on collective licensing also apply to such a publication right, as if a proper copyright was involved.[18]

On the basis of this very brief historic overview, this chapter now examines each of the societies that operate under the regulatory framework. Afterward, it will consider the regulatory framework for collective licensing, as it is currently in place in the *CDPA*.

2.2   EXISTING COLLECTING SOCIETIES IN THE UNITED KINGDOM

This section will describe the current collective licensing landscape in the United Kingdom from the perspective of the collecting societies that are active there. As will be shown, there are now quite a number of them and to simplify the task, they will be divided into the following categories:[19]

- reprographic rights societies;
- mechanical rights societies;
- licensing bodies for off-air recording;
- performing rights societies;
- multi-purpose collecting societies.

---

15. The Copyright and Related Rights Regulations 1996, Statutory Instrument 1996/2967, <www. opsi.gov.uk/si/si1996/Uksi_19962967_en_1.htm> (last visited: last visited: 1 May 2010).
16. *CDPA, supra* n. 11, ss 182–184 and 182A–182C.
17. *CDPA, supra* n. 11, ss 191G(1), (2) and (6).
18. See The Copyright and Related Rights Regulations 1996, *supra* n. 15, Regulations 16 and 17.
19. See Laddie, *supra* n. 5 at 952–976.

2.2.1   Reprographic Rights Societies

2.2.1.1   The Copyright Licensing Agency Ltd

The CLA[20] was established in April 1982 and deals generally with the copying from books, journals and periodicals. Its board contains an equal number of representatives from author's associations and publishers' associations.

The CLA grants licenses for the copying of works contained in books, journals and periodicals. To grant these licenses, the CLA obtains mandates from authors and publishers, whose interests it represents. The mandates grant the CLA a non-exclusive right in relation to all literary works in which all concerned authors and publishers have an interest in the copyright. In this respect, the CLA works with the Authors' Licensing and Collecting Society Ltd (ALCS) and the Publishers Licensing Society (PLS). The latter two effectively grant (sub-) licenses to the CLA in respect to the reproduction of the works by reprographic means. In return, the CLA distributes to the PLS and the ALCS their share of the license fees, minus its administrative fee, as well as the relevant information to allow the PLS and the ALCS to distribute the income to those members whose works have been copied. It is also noteworthy that artistic works are licensed under an agency agreement with DACS.

The first main aspect of the CLA's activity consists of a licensing scheme for educational establishments. Under the terms of these licenses, teachers are free to copy up to 5% of a book. One short story or poem in a collection may also be copied in its entirety if it does not exceed ten pages. For universities,[21] the scheme allows the copying of 5% of a book, a single chapter or a single article out of a periodical. There is a list of excluded works – typically newspapers, printed music, maps, charts and photographs, but some literary works and also works published in some countries other than the United Kingdom are included in the scheme. There is also a rapid clearance centre 'CLARCS' for staff who wish to produce course packs that involve copying on a larger scale than permitted by the license.

The licenses that are granted by the CLA are typically blanket licenses that enable the licensee, within the permitted limits, to copy anything from CLA-controlled works without having to seek prior permission. Typically these licenses do not include scanning and electronic storage and reproduction, but since 1999, separate digitization licenses are available. At the time of writing, these still require the use of the CLARCS system on each occasion, but it is understood that negotiations for a proper blanket scanning license are all but complete.

The second main aspect of the CLA's activity focuses on similar reproduction licenses for other major users of copyrighted works. These include charities, local

---

20. See <www.cla.co.uk/> (last visited: 10 May 2010). See also Garnett, *supra* n. 2 at 1576–1577 and Laddie, *supra* n. 5 at 952–956.
21. See the decision of the Copyright Tribunal in relation to this scheme: *Universities UK v. CLA and DACS* [2002] RPC 36 and [2002] EMLR 35.

and central government as well as businesses. Again, a combination of blanket licenses and the CLARCS system is an option.

The CLA mainly works with a blanket license or collective user arrangement. In this case, a global level of copying is assumed and a global fee is paid. In certain cases though, the CLA can also offer a transactional user arrangement. For these there is no global fee; instead, fees are paid per copied page at a fixed rate. In both cases, licensees are to supply information on the works that are copied. This is straightforward for the transactional arrangements and for the collective user arrangements, a rotating sampling system has been put in place. The information thus collected allows the CLA to distribute the fees among the right holders by using the PLS and ALCS as intermediaries.

Finally, it is important to keep in mind that the CLA license schemes effectively replace, in most cases, section 36 of the *CDPA*. The latter has a restrictive maximum of 1% that can be copied, and it is specifically provided that that system will operate only in the absence of a licensing scheme.

2.2.1.2   The Music Publishers' Association Ltd

This is really the trade association of the main music publishers in the United Kingdom. As such, the Music Publishers' Association (MPA) is not concerned with licensing schemes and is not a licensing body.[22] The MPA is, however, indirectly involved because it has acquired ownership of the Mechanical Copyright Protection Society Ltd (MCPS), which collects the mechanical royalties on behalf of most of its members.

It is important to note, however, that the MPA does not at present run a licensing scheme for the reprographic copying of sheet music. All that is in place currently is a code of practice that allows copying in certain circumstances, for example, when the work is out of print or when the original copies have not been supplied on time.[23] Infringements outside the code are prosecuted by the MPA and its members. Individual licenses obtained from the individual publishers are therefore still the norm in this area.

2.2.1.3   Design and Artists Copyright Society Ltd

The Design and Artists Copyright Society Ltd deals with works of visual art and negotiates and collects revenue from their exploitation. Membership of the Design and Artists Copyright Society (DACS) is open to all visual artists.[24] This group includes illustrators, designers, printmakers, animators, photographers, sculptors, architects and craftsmen, as well as painters and obviously for all of them their successors in title. The society gets an exclusive mandate to collect fees in the

---

22. See also Laddie, *supra* n. 5 at 956.
23. See <www.mpaonline.org.uk/> (last visited: 10 May 2010).
24. See <www.dacs.org.uk/> (last visited: 10 May 2010). See also Garnett, *supra* n. 2 at 1577–1578 and Laddie, *supra* n. 5 at 957–959.

United Kingdom from its members, but the artists remain free to make their own individual arrangements.[25] In its dealings with users of the works, DACS licenses the reproduction of the artistic works of its members and the right to issue copies of these works to the public. The members are free to impose restrictions on the use that can be authorized; for example, it is often the case that the artists exclude the use of their work in the context of advertising.

DACS works with standard licenses and fee scales that are independent of the fame of the artist concerned. Licenses can be granted for a one-off use or as a blanket license. On top of this form of collective licensing, DACS also handles primary licensing on behalf of its members, that is, licensing of rights that are exercisable individually. DACS also administers the Artist's Resale Right, which entered into force in 2006.

In relation to the photocopying of its works by educational establishments, DACS had appointed the CLA as its agent. These establishments therefore no longer have to deal separately with DACS, and the DACS license can be included in their CLA license.

2.2.1.4   The Artists' Collecting Society

The Artists' Collecting Society (ACS) was formally established as a collecting society in June 2006 to collect the artist's resale right on behalf of artists in the United Kingdom. ACS was set in up in response to requests from artists and from their dealers via the British Art Market Federation (BAMF) and the Society of London Art Dealers (SLAD) for artists to be provided with a choice of collecting society for the management of artists' resale right. Its members are effectively artists that are represented by BAMF or SLAD. The society is run on a not-for-profit basis,[26] and it shares the artists' resale right market with DACS.

2.2.1.5   The Newspaper Licensing Agency Ltd

The copying of newspaper articles is, as discussed earlier, not included in the standard CLA license. Instead, the licensing of the making of copies of newspaper articles is a matter for the Newspaper Licensing Agency (NLA).[27] Newspaper publishers assign the copyright in the typographical arrangement of the published editions of any of their works, as well as the copyright in the literary and artistic works that appear in the newspaper to the NLA. Following the House of Lords' decision in *NLA v. Marks & Spencer*[28] the NLA concentrates its efforts on enforcing its literary and artistic copyrights rather than the copyright in the typographical arrangements of the newspapers of its members. The system also covers those

---

25. They should notify DACS though.
26. See <www.artistscollectingsociety.org.uk> (last visited: 10 May 2010).
27. See <www.nla.co.uk/> (last visited: 10 May 2010). See also Garnett, *supra* n. 2 at 1581–1582 and Laddie, *supra* n. 5 at 959–962.
28. *Newspaper Licensing Agency Ltd v. Marks & Spencer plc* [2001] 3 WLR 290.

works in which the newspaper publishers themselves only have a license. For these, the publisher agrees to indemnify the NLA if a license it grants is unduly wide and amounts to unauthorized licensing. The licenses that are granted to users cover the making of copies of articles insofar as the whole or a substantial part of the newspaper is copied.[29]

Press cutting agencies are the major users of the NLA licenses. Its clients can in turn make further copies for internal use. They will then need a license from the NLA. The NLA can require press cutting agencies to assist in persuading infringers to obtain a license and to notify the NLA if one of their clients does not have a license.[30] For its other licensees, the NLA offers three types of licenses. These enable the licensees to make copies from newspapers for internal management purposes and to distribute these copies within their organization by means of photocopies or faxes. External use is not permitted under the licenses. For the Variable license the fee is based on the total volume of estimated cuttings in a twelve-month period. The estimate is determined using actual cuttings in an average two-week period. This is then multiplied by twenty-six (the number of fortnights in a year) and by the number of staff who receive the cuttings. This license is suitable for low-use clients. Medium-use clients are better served by the Fixed option, the fee for which is based on the number of recipients of an electronic service and the organization's headcount. This option has an annual cuttings volume cap of EUR 500. Clients who receive cuttings via a media monitoring agency will not need to complete a survey of use, and the agency's returns will be used to calculate the client's volume of use. The client will need to complete an NLA survey only if it systematically scans cuttings as well. Finally, there is a Universal option for high volume clients. The fee for this option is based on the total number of personnel in the client's company and the standard fee is based on a maximum of an average of twenty cuttings per day based on a two-week survey the licensee is required to complete. For even higher use the fee will be multiplied in function of the volume of use. This license provides unlimited access to newspaper cuttings.

Special types of licenses exist for schools in which the normal admission age is 16 years or under and persons in professional practice who as part of their service provide clients with copies from newspapers. All copies made under any of the licenses also need to carry a copyright notice. The basic licenses can be extended to electronic use to allow the licensee to distribute electronic copies for the permitted purposes or to archive the cuttings in an electronic database.

---

29. See *Newspaper Licensing Agency Ltd v. Marks & Spencer Plc* [2003] 1 A.C. 551, [2001] 3 W.L.R. 290, [2001] 3 All E.R. 977.
30. *Romeike & Curtice Ltd v. Newspaper Licencing Agency Ltd* [1999] E.M.L.R. 142. The Copyright Tribunal held that it was reasonable to include these conditions in a license granted to a newspaper cutting agency.

2.2.2 Mechanical Rights Societies

2.2.2.1 The Mechanical Copyright Protection Society Ltd

The MCPS deals with mechanical copyright, that is, according to its membership agreement the right to make sound-bearing copies of musical works, and it covers a wide range of uses of works through its activities.[31] These include the recording of music for audio and video recordings, films, television and radio programmes and radio and television commercials. The society is the only surviving society in this field and was created through mergers with societies over the years in the twentieth century. It is a subsidiary of the Music Publishers' Association Ltd and is now part of the MCPS-PRS Alliance.[32] Under the alliance, both societies and the rights vested in them remain separate, but both societies are managed by a single limited company which is jointly owned by them. The MCPS's members are composers, authors and arrangers of music, as well as music publishers.

Unlike many other societies, the MCPS does not take an assignment or license of the copyright of its members. Instead, the society acts as an agent for its members in granting licenses and in collecting revenue.

A major part of the MCPS's business is found in its dealing with record companies. Its licenses and tariffs for these purposes changed dramatically once the *CDPA* entered into force, and they were finally settled by the Copyright Tribunal in *British Phonographic Industry Ltd v. Mechanical Copyright Protection Society (No 2) and Composers' Joint Council (Intervener).*[33] Three standard licenses are available. The standard starting point is a blanket license to record any musical work within the MCPS scheme, but it excludes first recordings unless these have been granted directly by the MCPS or a right owner who is a member of the MCPS. All formats of recording, such as CDs, tapes, digital audio tapes, etc., are covered, and a standard 8.5% royalty rate applies. Within the limits imposed by moral rights, record companies may make those modifications to the works they consider necessary in relation to the recording product they want to make. The AP1 version of the license requires royalties to be paid on sales, in arrears and on a quarterly basis. Under it, the record company also needs to inform the MCPS in advance of any product it intends to manufacture. The AP2 version of the license requires payment in advance on actual pressings. The MCPS then hold on to the money, and payments to members can take place only on the basis of notification of actual sales on a regular basis by the record company involved. Finally the AP2A version of the license allows the record company to defer payment for a stated period. This version is mainly used for smaller record companies to protect their position.

---

31. See also Garnett, *supra* n. 2 at 1580–1581 and Laddie, *supra* n. 5 at 962–964.
32. See <www.mcps-prs-alliance.co.uk/aboutus/> (last visited: 10 May 2010).
33. *British Phonographic Industry Ltd v. Mechanical Copyright Protection Society (No 2) and Composers' Joint Council (Intervener)* [1993] E.M.L.R. 86.

There are also other licenses available for other users and other uses. These include use in relation to films, videos and TV programmes. Blanket licenses are in place for the major broadcasters. Under these licenses, unrestricted use of works is permitted even if arrangements and parodies are restricted somewhat, but in exchange the broadcasters need to keep records that will allow the MCPS to distribute the fees to the appropriate right holders. Video licenses require the payment of a fee within a stated time limit, and only those works specifically listed by the licensee can be used. These licenses are normally also limited in their territorial scope to the United Kingdom.

2.2.3 Licensing Bodies for Off-Air Recording

2.2.3.1 The Educational Recording Agency Ltd

ERA deals with off-air recordings of television and radio broadcasts by schools and other educational establishments.[34] The Copyright Designs and Patents Act 1988 has an exemption to copyright infringement that exempts such recordings insofar as they are made for educational purposes until a certified licensing scheme is brought into existence.[35] The ERA and its licensing scheme was created in 1989 to use the latter option.[36] On the licensor side, the ALCS, the DACS, the British Phonographic Industry, the MCPS, the Musicians' Union, Equity, the Incorporated Society of Musicians, the Independent Television Network Ltd, the DPRS, the Association of International Collective Management of Audiovisual Works and the major broadcasters (BBC, Channel Four Television, Channel 5 Broadcasting, S4C), as well as the Performing Rights Society Limited, Phonographic Performance Limited and Sianel Pedwar (Cymru) are members of the ERA. Under the licensing scheme, schools and educational establishments can make off-air recordings of anything broadcast by members of ERA, with the exception of those broadcasts produced by the Open University. However, recent changes mean that the rights licensed will cover not only the making of recordings of broadcasts off-air for educational purposes, but also the 'communication' of such recordings to students and teachers within the premises of licensed educational establishments. This extended use helps to reflect increased use of computers

---

34. See <www.era.org.uk> (last visited: 10 May 2010). See also Garnett, *supra* n. 2 at 1579–1580 and Laddie, *supra* n. 5 at 964–965.
35. *CDPA, supra* n. 11, s. 35.
36. The initial scheme was first replaced by a new one in 2005, and the current version was put in place in 2007, see SI 2007/266, the Copyright (Certification of Licensing Scheme for the Educational Recording of Broadcasts) (Educational Recording Agency Ltd) Order 2007, <www.opsi.gov.uk/si/si2007/uksi_20070266_en_1> (last visited: 10 May 2010), SI 2008/211, the Copyright (Certification of Licensing Scheme for Educational Recording of Broadcasts) (Educational Recording Agency Limited) (Revocation and Amendment) Order 2008, <www.opsi.gov.uk/si/si2008/uksi_20080211_en_1> (last visited: 10 May 2010) and SI 2009/20, the Copyright (Certification of Licensing Scheme for Educational Recording of Broadcasts) (Educational Recording Agency Limited) (Amendment) Order 2009, <www.opsi.gov.uk/si/si2009/uksi_20090020_en_1> (last visited: 10 May 2010).

for access to material stored on school servers and the use of white boards for presenting material in classrooms. Since August 2007, ERA also offers the ERA Plus License, which allows for ERA Recordings to be accessed by students and teachers online, whether they are on the premises, at home or working elsewhere in the United Kingdom.

The recordings that are made may be kept and archived, and additional copies for educational purposes within the establishment may be made. Editing of the recordings, however, is not permitted. The license fee is calculated on a per-capita basis and depends on the type of establishment.

2.2.3.2 Open University Educational Enterprises Ltd

As mentioned earlier, Open University productions are excluded from the ERA licensing scheme. An off-air recording licensing scheme for these productions is operated by Open University Educational Enterprises Ltd for the benefit of schools and educational establishments.[37] Under the terms of the scheme, off-air recordings can be made for educational purposes in exchange for a fee that is payable on a per-programme basis and that depends on the type of educational establishment concerned.

2.2.4 Performing Right Societies

2.2.4.1 The Performing Right Society Ltd

The membership of the Performing Right Society (PRS) comprises composers, authors and publishers of music.[38] The society aims to protect music from unauthorized exploitation, and it administers the performing rights in musical works[39] (and the film synchronization right in musical works). It does so by taking an assignment of its members from the public performance right and the broadcasting right, plus in the case of writers, the film synchronization right in any work that is composed primarily for the purpose of being included in the soundtrack of a particular film.[40] The PRS, however, is not concerned with the right to control the presentation of a musical work in dramatic form, when the work was originally written for a dramatico-musical work or a ballet. This right remains vested in the author or the publisher, who deal with it independently of the PRS.

The PRS collects practice license fees for the public performance and broadcast of the musical works of its members.[41] It does so as part of an alliance it has formed with the MCPS. That MCPS-PRS alliance manages common activities, services both societies and is jointly owned by them.

---

37. See <www.open.ac.uk/foi/subsidiary-companies/p9.shtml> (last visited: 10 May 2010). See also Laddie, *supra* n. 5 at 965.
38. See also Garnett, *supra* n. 2 at 1583–1585 and Laddie, *supra* n. 5 at 966–970.
39. That is, the right to perform musical works in public, to communicate them to the public and to authorize others to do the same.
40. *Music Gallery Ltd v. Direct Line Insurance plc* [1998] E.M.L.R. 551.
41. See <www.prs.co.uk/> (last visited: 10 May 2010).

PRS licenses are normally granted as blanket licenses to the proprietors of premises in which public performances take place. Under such a license, the licensee can perform or authorize the performance in public of the entire PRS repertoire. The PRS rarely deals directly with the performers of copyright music. Individual licenses are also possible. The license fees are based on a series of tariffs depending on the type of licensee, for example, in relation to the basis for the calculation of the tariff.[42] Licenses are granted annually and are renewed automatically. A sophisticated sampling system based on itemized returns of some licensees is put in place to guarantee a fair distribution of the fees that are collected.

2.2.4.2 Phonographic Performance Ltd

According to the Phonographic Performance Ltd (PPL) website[43]:

> PPL is the UK collecting society for record companies and performers.
>
> PPL licenses radio stations, TV stations and other broadcasters who use sound recordings (records, tapes, CDs etc) in their transmissions. PPL also licenses clubs, shops, pubs, restaurants and thousands of other music users who play sound recordings in public.
>
> The licence fees that PPL collect are then distributed to the rightful owner of the sound recording copyright – usually the record company responsible for creating the track – and also the performers who played on the track.[44]

The PPL is an association of the record companies, which operates as a limited company. On their behalf, the PPL takes an assignment of and administers the performing and broadcasting rights in the sound recordings for its members.[45] In relation to the Internet, the PPL is deploying an increasing number of options for online radio and television in its various formats.

The PPL operates standard tariffs. In principle, licensees are given blanket licenses, the terms of which allow use of the recordings in the repertoire of the society. Licenses are available for one-off events or on an annual basis.[46]

Most licensees are direct users, but there are also licenses for those companies that provide music systems hardware and/or software.

For broadcasters, individually negotiated licenses are the norm, but the commercial radio licenses follow a common pattern as a result of the *AIRC* case.[47] Its rates are based on a percentage of advertising revenue.

---

42. See *British Airways plc v. The Performing Right Society Ltd* [1998] E.M.L.R. 556, [1998] R.P.C. 581, *The Performing Right Society Ltd v. Boizot* [1999] E.M.L.R. 359 (CA).
43. See also Garnett, *supra* n. 2 at 1585–1586 and Laddie, *supra* n. 5 at 970–973.
44. See <www.ppluk.com/> (last visited: 10 May 2010).
45. See Arnold, *supra* n. 1 at 122.
46. See *British Sky Broadcasting Ltd and Another v. The Performing Right Society* [1998] E.M.L.R. 193, [1998] R.P.C. 467.
47. *Association of Independent Radio Companies Ltd (AIRC) v. Phonographic Performances Ltd* [1994] R.P.C. 143, [1993] E.M.L.R. 181.

On the distribution side, the PPL works with a computerized return from the major licensees to structure the distribution of revenues. The return sets out the extent of playing time for each recording during the licensed period. For those licensees that do not produce returns, figures are produced by matching them up with comparable licensees that did produce returns.

One should add, however, that some outlets do not need a PPL license. Indeed, public performance through the showing or playing of a broadcast including the sound recordings to a non-paying audience is not an infringing act, and no license is therefore required, for example, for playing a radio in a restaurant or pub.[48]

In 2006, PPL incorporated PAMRA and AURA. In turn, PPL works with VPL on a basis of two separate companies with a centralized management.

2.2.4.3 The Performing Artists Media Rights Association/The Association of United Recording Artists

The emergence of the Performing Artists Media Rights Association (PAMRA) was intricately linked with the introduction of a right to equitable remuneration.[49] More specifically, the collecting society dealt with the right to equitable remuneration of performers whenever a commercially published sound recording is included in a broadcast or is played in public.

Membership of PAMRA was open to all performers whose performances have been included in a commercially published sound recording.[50] The society operated by taking an authorization from its members to collect the performers' share of the equitable remuneration and to enter into negotiations with organizations of performers and producers to obtain remuneration. PAMRA was authorized by its members to operate a licensing scheme that could include blanket licenses.

In practice, the PPL collected the fees and PAMRA received a share. Income generated from the broadcast of commercially released recordings was therefore collected from broadcasters and public performance venues by the record labels' collecting society, the PPL, and shared between the record companies and the performers who have contributed to the recordings. In 2006 PAMRA merged with PPL and PAMRA itself went into voluntary liquidation.[51]

The Association of United Recordings Artists (AURA) was founded in 1995 by featured performers as their exclusive agent to collect equitable remuneration from the exploitation of sound recordings embodying their performances and their right to remuneration in respect of blank tape levy, rental, public performance and communication to the public. The rights were collected

---

48. See *CDPA, supra* n. 11, ss 19(3) and 72.
49. See <www.ppluk.com/> (last visited: 10 May 2010). See Laddie, *supra* n. 5 at 973–975.
50. Foreign performers can become associate members. PAMRA will then collect their remuneration arising in the United Kingdom only.
51. See Arnold, *supra* n. 1 at 122.

through PPL. In 2006, AURA merged with PPL and AURA itself went into voluntary liquidation.[52]

2.2.4.4 The British Equity Collecting Society Ltd

The principal object of the British Equity Collecting Society Ltd (BECS)[53] is to collect, distribute and administer performers' remuneration. It effectively represents audiovisual performers. The remuneration it collects includes income arising from the rental of a sound recording or film, income from blank tape levies and similar levies and income from cable retransmission of programmes including the performers' performances. BECS acts in this respect as the agent of its members.

2.2.5 Multi-purpose Collecting Societies

2.2.5.1 Authors' Licensing and Collecting Society Ltd

The ALCS administers the secondary rights in literary, dramatic, musical and artistic works.[54] These secondary rights include the reprographic right, the cable retransmission right, the blank tape levies collected abroad, the educational off-air recording rights (it does so as a member of ERA), the lending right, the rental right and the German public lending right. ALCS acts on behalf of its members, who are the authors of the works concerned, and the Society of Authors, as well as the Writers' Guild. A lot of the licensing work is franchised out to the CLA.

2.2.5.2 Video Performance Ltd

Video Performance Ltd (VPL) deals exclusively with music videos or rather with certain rights in the latter.[55] Its membership is made up of the makers of music videos and the owners of the public performance rights in them, the owners of the rights to broadcast music videos and the owners of the right to dub these videos. These members assign to VPL their public performance and related dubbing rights, and they grant VPL a non-exclusive license of the broadcasting and related dubbing rights. VPL then operates a licensing scheme for these rights.[56] VPL effectively operates in tandem with PPL as separate companies with a centralized management.

---

52. *Ibid.*
53. See <www.equitycollecting.org.uk> (last visited: 10 May 2010). See also Garnett, *supra* n. 2 at 1575.
54. See <www.alcs.co.uk> (last visited: 10 May 2010). See also Garnett, *supra* n. 2 at 1573–1575 and Laddie, *supra* n. 5 at 975.
55. See also Garnett, *supra* n. 2 at 1586 and Laddie, *supra* n. 5 at 976.
56. See <www.vpluk.com> or <www.ppluk.com> (last visited: 10 May 2010).

2.2.5.3   Directors UK

Until June 2008 Directors UK was know as the Directors' and Producers' Rights Society (DPRS). Just as DPRS Directors UK is the collecting society that represents British film and television directors.[57] It collects and distributes money due to directors for the exploitation of their work. Its main sources of income are found abroad. Throughout the European Union (EU), and in several other countries, film and television directors are legally recognized as being authors of their work. This right of authorship may give directors an entitlement to receive payment for certain uses of their work, such as cable retransmission, private copying and video rentals. Apart from its work as a collecting society, Directors UK also represents the interests of British film and television directors.

Directors UK collects these fees for its member directors through an international network of authors' collecting societies. Directors UK has for this purpose concluded agreements with societies in over twenty countries.

Traditionally the position of directors has been weaker in the UK, but under the terms of the Directors' Rights Agreement agreed with broadcasters and independent producers in 2001, Directors UK receives an annual payment to compensate freelance television directors for the secondary use of their work.

Directors UK is also charged by its members with the responsibility of devising, implementing and administering a scheme for the distribution of payments to individual directors. This takes account of the type of programme and the length and form of the secondary use. The scheme is based on information supplied by broadcasters.

2.2.5.4   Compact Collections Ltd

Compact Collections Ltd collects secondary television royalties for film and television content owners. It acts in the UK and abroad on behalf of its clients, among which one finds many production and distribution companies. It deals essentially with the cable and satellite retransmission right, the private copying right and the educational off-air recording right in their respective forms in the respective countries. Compact Collections provides a complete administration service from registering the audiovisual works of its clients with the relevant collecting societies through to the distribution of the money that has been collected. Its clients assign the relevant rights to Compact Collections, while retaining all other rights.[58]

---

57.   See <www.directors.uk.com/> (last visited: 10 May 2010). See also Garnett, *supra* n. 2 at 1578–1579.
58.   See <www.compactcollections.com> (last visited: 10 May 2010); see also Garnett, *supra* n. 2 at 1575–1576.

3   THE CURRENT REGULATORY FRAMEWORK

3.1   LICENSING SCHEMES AND LICENSING BODIES IN GENERAL

The *CDPA* starts its approach to copyright licensing by setting out a series of provisions on licensing schemes and licensing bodies.[59] Section 116 deals with definitions in the following way:

> (1) In this Part a 'licensing scheme' means a scheme setting out –
>> (a) the classes of case in which the operator of the scheme, or the person on whose behalf he acts, is willing to grant copyright licences, and
>> (b) the terms on which licences would be granted in those classes of case;
>>> and for this purpose a 'scheme' includes anything in the nature of a scheme, whether described as a scheme or as a tariff or by any other name.
> (2) In this Chapter a 'licensing body' means a society or other organisation which has as its main object, or one of its main objects, the negotiation or granting, either as owner or prospective owner of copyright or as agent for him, of copyright licences, and whose objects include the granting of licences covering works of more than one author.

In a first set of provisions, contained in sections 118–123 *CDPA*, these licensing schemes are regulated insofar as they are operated by licensing bodies, cover works of more than one author and relate to licenses for:

> (a) copying the work;
> (b) rental or lending of copies of the work to the public;
> (c) performing, showing or playing the work in public; or
> (d) communicating the work to the public.[60]

The first situation that is envisaged in these provisions is that in which a group of persons claims that they may require licenses. An organization claiming to represent such persons is then given the right to refer to the Copyright Tribunal the terms of a proposed licensing scheme that is to be operated by a licensing body. The users of the works to be covered by the scheme can therefore take the initiative to create a licensing scheme, rather than remain dependant on individual licenses. The Copyright Tribunal will first check that the reference is not premature. If this is not the case, the Tribunal will consider the request and may confirm or modify the proposed scheme. Its final decision, which may put a scheme in place, requires the form of an Order of the Tribunal.[61]

A second situation envisaged arises when a licensing scheme is in operation. A conflict may indeed arise between the operator of the scheme and a person who

---

59. See, in general terms, Torremans, *supra* n. 3 at 284–285 and Arnold, *supra* n. 1 at 123–124.
60. *CDPA, supra* n. 11, s. 117.
61. *CDPA, supra* n. 11, s. 118. The effects of such an Order on the licensing scheme are dealt with in detail in s. 123 of the *CDPA*.

claims he or she requires a license or an organization representing such persons. The latter have the power to refer the conflict to the Copyright Tribunal. The Tribunal will hear the case and will resolve the conflict by means of an order. Such an order may either confirm the terms of the scheme or make changes to it.[62]

A third situation that is envisaged deals with the refusal to grant a license. The straightforward scenario is that in which, in a case covered by the scheme, a person claims that the operator of the scheme has refused to grant a license in accordance with the scheme or has failed to grant such a license within a reasonable time after being asked. This case is straightforward because it deals with a case that is covered by the licensing scheme. A more difficult scenario arises when one is concerned with a case that is excluded from the licensing scheme. This will, for the current purpose, be the case on the one hand where the scheme provides for the grant of licenses subject to terms excepting matters from the license and the case falls within such an exception, or on the other hand, where the case is so similar to those in which licenses are granted under the scheme that it is unreasonable that it should not be dealt with in the same way. In either of these situations, the person also needs to demonstrate that it is unreasonable in the circumstances that a license should not be granted. One may also be concerned with a case in which the potential licensee claims that the operator of the licensing scheme proposes terms for a license that are unreasonable. In both scenarios the persons affected may apply to the Copyright Tribunal. If the Tribunal, upon examination, finds the claim to be well founded, it will make an order by which it declares that the applicant is entitled to a license; the Tribunal may also determine the terms of such a license.[63]

A second set of provisions, contained in sections 125–128 of the *CDPA*, applies to licenses that are granted by a licensing body otherwise than in pursuance of a licensing scheme and cover works of more than one author. It does so insofar as these licenses authorize:

(a) copying the work;
(b) rental or lending of copies of the work to the public;
(c) performing, showing or playing the work in public; or
(d) communicating the work to the public.[64]

The applicant for such a license may refer the terms of the proposed license to the Copyright Tribunal. The Tribunal may, if it decides to take up the matter, confirm or alter the terms of the license by means of an order.[65] Similarly, 'a licensee under a license which is due to expire, by effluxion of time or as a result of notice given by the licensing body, may apply to the Copyright Tribunal on the ground that it is unreasonable in the circumstances that the license should cease to be in force'.[66]

---

62. *CDPA, supra* n. 11, s. 119.
63. *CDPA, supra* n. 11, s. 121.
64. *CDPA, supra* n. 11, s. 124.
65. *CDPA, supra* n. 11, s. 125.
66. *CDPA, supra* n. 11, s. 126.

There is also a specific provision that imposes a notification obligation in respect to licenses or a licensing scheme for excepted sound recordings. Section 128A, which was introduced in 2003, applies solely to a proposed license or licensing scheme that will authorize the playing in public of excepted sound recordings included in broadcasts in those circumstances in which, by reason of the exclusion of excepted sound recordings from section 72(1) *CDPA*, the playing in public of such recordings would infringe their copyright. Any proposed license or licensing scheme for these excepted sound recordings must be referred to the Secretary of State before it comes into operation.[67]

A different set of provisions of a more general nature are set out as factors that are to be taken into account by the Copyright Tribunal in making its determinations. First of all, the concept of reasonableness appeared on several occasions in the foregoing paragraphs. The Act now offers the following indications on unreasonable discrimination.

In determining what is reasonable on a reference or application under this chapter relating to a licensing scheme or license, the Copyright Tribunal shall have regard to –

   (a) the availability of other schemes, or the granting of other licenses, to other persons in similar circumstances; and
   (b) the terms of those schemes or licenses, and shall exercise its powers so as to secure that there is no unreasonable discrimination between licensees, or prospective licensees, under the scheme or license to which the reference or application relates and licensees under other schemes operated by, or other licenses granted by, the same person.[68]

Second, the Act contains specific provisions on specific factors that are to be taken into account in relation to:

   – licenses for reprographic copying;[69]
   – licenses for educational establishments in respect of works included in broadcasts;[70]
   – licenses to reflect conditions imposed by promoters of events;[71]
   – licenses to reflect payment in respect of underlying rights;[72] and
   – licenses in respect of works included in re-transmissions.[73]

A final set of provisions deals with the use as of right, but against payment, of sound recordings in broadcasts. Such use takes place outside a license or licensing scheme, but payments need to be made to the licensing body.[74]

---

67. *CDPA, supra* n. 11, s. 128A.
68. *CDPA, supra* n. 11, s. 129.
69. *CDPA, supra* n. 11, s. 130.
70. *CDPA, supra* n. 11, s. 131.
71. *CDPA, supra* n. 11, s. 132.
72. *CDPA, supra* n. 11, s. 133.
73. *CDPA, supra* n. 11, s. 134.
74. *CDPA, supra* n. 11, ss 135A-H.

3.2   PROVISIONS ON SCHEMES AND LICENSES FOR
                       REPROGRAPHIC COPYING

Here the aim is to cover as many as possible of the works that are available for licensing. That comprehensive coverage is coupled with the fact that a licensee does then not need to seek prior permission for each individual act of copying. The licensee is entitled to rely on the license and to assume that it covers all works controlled by the licensing body, unless he or she receives a specific notification to the contrary, for example, by means of a notice placed on top of the photocopier. The assumption takes as a starting point that the publishers that are part of the scheme do indeed own the copyright in all the works that are part of the scheme. This, however, is not necessarily the case, and in certain cases the copyright in the work may be owned by the author or authors of the work. This undermines the assumption and inadvertently puts the licensee at risk for an infringement action by the author or authors that have retained the copyright in the work. Because the latter was not assigned to the publisher, the latter could not assign it to the licensing body, which in turn had no right to license it to its licensee in respect of such a work. This loophole could affect any such scheme significantly, and the government therefore moved to close it. The result of the matter is that section 136 of the *CDPA* now provides an implied indemnity in favour of the licensee whenever the latter made copies within the scope of the scheme or license.

It is important to precisely determine the exact scope of this implied indemnity. It applies to those licensing schemes that cover the reprographic copying of published literary, dramatic, musical or artistic works, as well as the typographical arrangements of published editions and to licenses granted for such copying by licensing bodies. This application is conditional on the fact that the scheme or license does not specify the exact works to which it applies with such a specificity that it enables the licensee to determine whether an individual work falls within the scheme or license by means of a simple inspection of the scheme or license on the one hand and the work on the other hand.[75] The effect of the implied indemnity is that it implies into each scheme or license an undertaking by the operator of the scheme to indemnify a person granted a license under the scheme and by the licensor to indemnify the licensee against any copyright liability whenever the copy was made within the apparent scope of the scheme or license. The indemnity covers, obviously, any sums payable in respect to the infringement, as well as costs that are reasonably incurred by the licensee. The procedural operation of the indemnity, such as the deadlines by which it is to be invoked and the conduct of any subsequent proceedings, can be stipulated within the bounds of reason in the rules of any particular licensing scheme.[76]

---

75. *CDPA, supra* n. 11, s. 136(1).
76. *CDPA, supra* n. 11, ss 136(2)–(5) and The Copyright and Related Rights Regulations 1996, *supra* n. 15, Regulation 17.

3.3   REPROGRAPHIC COPYING BY EDUCATIONAL ESTABLISHMENTS

Once again, comprehensive coverage in terms of works is the major strength of the CLA scheme. However, in principle, nothing stops an individual right holder or any group of right holders from not joining the existing scheme and from instead setting up their own scheme. The *CDPA* addresses this potential problem by giving the Secretary of State the power to extend the coverage of existing licensing schemes and by giving the Secretary of State the power to impose a statutory license if no scheme exists and if no voluntary scheme has been created following a recommendation by an inquiry.[77]

3.4   THE POWER TO EXTEND THE COVERAGE OF A SCHEME

This power of the Secretary of State to extend the coverage of a licensing scheme is the next instrument, after the implied indemnity, which needs to be analysed in a bit more detail. This instrument is first of all concerned with licensing schemes that are operated by licensing bodies or with licenses that authorize the making by or on behalf of educational establishments for the purposes of instruction of reprographic copies of published literary, dramatic, musical or artistic works that cover the works of more than one author or of the typographical arrangements of published editions or in the case of the publication right, the works of more than one publisher. Second, it must appear to the Secretary of State that works that conform to a description that is very similar to those that are covered by the scheme or license are excluded from its scope without a good reason. If, additionally, it would appear to the Secretary of State that making these works subject to the scheme or license would not conflict with the normal exploitation of these works or would not unreasonably prejudice the legitimate interests of the copyright holders or the owners of the publications, the Secretary of State may make an order under section 137 of the *CDPA* by which it is provided that the scheme or license shall extend to these works. Whenever such an order is envisaged, there is an obligatory consultation exercise that needs to be completed before an order can be made and that involves all interested parties. These parties then have a right to make representations before an order is made, and once an order is made, it is obviously subject to appeal to the Copyright Tribunal. In practice this is very much a tool that is not designed to be used. Its very presence in the Act seems to deter all interested parties from creating the very problem it is supposed to address. In that sense, section 137 is very effective even though no order has yet been made under it.[78] Section 138 of the *CDPA* adds the opportunity to vary or discharge any order. The procedural aspects of such a variation or discharge are similar to those for putting an order in place.

---

77.   *CDPA, supra* n. 11, ss 137–141 and The Copyright and Related Rights Regulations 1996, *supra* n. 15, Regulation 17.
78.   See Laddie, *supra* n. 5 at 948.

3.5   IS A NEW SCHEME OR A NEW LICENSE REQUIRED?

Despite its obvious advantages, section 137 of the *CDPA* does not cover all scenarios, for example, because its conditions refer explicitly to works that contain the
works of more than one author. This means that in some situations one is still left
with the basic proposition of the current legislative framework that it is up to the
interested parties themselves to take the initiative to set up a scheme or a license.
There may be various reasons why this may not work in a particular case, though.
The *CDPA* recognizes the problem and addresses it by granting the Secretary of
State a right of initiative. The situation one becomes concerned with here is one
that is outside the scope of section 137 and where it appears to the Secretary of
State that certain descriptions of published literary, dramatic, musical or artistic
works or the typographical arrangement of published editions are not covered by an
existing licensing scheme or by a general license. In such a situation, the Secretary
of State may appoint a person to inquire whether a new licensing scheme or general
license is needed to authorize educational establishments or someone on their
behalf to make copies of those works or arrangements.[79] The Secretary of State
will then take regulations to set out the procedure for the inquiry.[80] It must include
notice being given to all interested parties, both on the side of the right holders and
on the side of the educational establishments, and these parties must also be given
the opportunity to make oral and written representations.[81] The inquiry may only
recommend the creation of a new licensing scheme or general license if two
requirements are found to be met. On the one hand, there must be evidence that
it would be an advantage for educational establishments to be authorized to make
reprographical copies of the works involved. On the other hand, there must also be
evidence that the grant of a general license or the establishment of a licensing
scheme would not conflict with the normal exploitation of the works involved or
would not unreasonably prejudice the interests of the copyright or publication right
holders.[82] The inquiry will also need to suggest the terms of such a licensing
scheme or general license,[83] but the charges payable are left for the parties
involved to negotiate. The parties have essentially one year to act upon the recommendation and to agree upon the charges of such a licensing scheme or general
license. In the absence of an agreement after the expiration of the one-year period,
the Secretary of State may make an order by which the making of reprographic
copies by educational establishments in accordance with the inquiry's recommendations shall be treated as licensed.[84] This effectively puts a fair amount of pressure
on the right holders to come to an agreement because any license imposed by the

---

79. *CDPA, supra* n. 11, s. 140(1) and The Copyright and Related Rights Regulations 1996, *supra*
     n. 15, Regulation 17 for the publication right.
80. *CDPA, supra* n. 11, s. 140(2).
81. *CDPA, supra* n. 11, s. 140(3).
82. *CDPA, supra* n. 11, s. 140(4).
83. *CDPA, supra* n. 11, s. 140(5).
84. *CDPA, supra* n. 11, s. 141 and The Copyright and Related Rights Regulations 1996, *supra* n. 15,
     Regulation 17 for the publication right.

Secretary of State will be royalty-free. As with section 137, section 140 has until now not been put into practice.[85] The interested parties have always been able to take the initiative themselves, but section 140 clearly plays a role in inciting them to agree voluntarily.

3.6   THE CERTIFICATION OF LICENSING SCHEMES

The current regulatory framework relies heavily on the private initiatives that are taken by the parties, as discussed already, but in the absence of a licensing scheme or a general license there are some very limited statutory copyright exemptions that have been put in place by the *CDPA*:

- section 35 deals with the recording of broadcasts by educational establishments;
- section 60 deals with the making and issuing of copies to the public of abstracts of scientific or technical articles published in a periodical;
- section 66 deals with the licensed lending to the public of copies of literary, dramatic, musical or artistic works, sound recordings or films pursuant to an order of the Secretary of State;
- section 74 deals with the provision of subtitled copies of television broadcasts by certain designated bodies.

These activities may later form the subject of a licensing scheme or an agreed general license. The legislator felt that it would clearly not be advisable to have both an agreed licensing scheme or general license in place between parties that have signed up to it and a statutory scheme of minimal exemption that was being relied upon by those that had not become part of the licensing scheme or of the general license. Specifically, on the enforcement side, this would have caused a fair amount of confusion.

Such confusion is avoided through the use of the certification mechanism that is put in place by section 143 *CDPA*. This section gives the Secretary of State the power to certify a licensing scheme or a general license, and when that is done the minimal exemptions provided for in the relevant sections of the Act referred to earlier lapse. Anyone performing any of these previously statutorily exempted acts will then infringe copyright unless he or she has a license under the licensing scheme or is covered by the general license.

Additionally, there is the possibility for the Secretary of State to certify under section 143 a licensing scheme for the reprographic copying of published works by educational establishments. For the licensing body there is a dual advantage. First, the scheme or license is given publicity and the parties concerned that have not yet signed up to it are encouraged to do so, and second, the imposition of a royalty-free statutory license in application of section 141 *CDPA* is avoided.

---

85. See Laddie, *supra* n. 5 at 949.

The certification mechanism is mechanical in nature. The Secretary of State will not examine, let alone approve the terms of the licensing scheme or the general license. Any judgment on the reasonableness of such a licensing scheme or license is left to the Copyright Tribunal. According to section 143(2) of the *CDPA*:

> The Secretary of State shall by order made by statutory instrument certify the scheme if he is satisfied that it –
>
> (a) enables the works to which it relates to be identified with sufficient certainty by persons likely to require licences, and
> (b) sets out clearly the charges (if any) payable and the other terms on which licences will be granted.

But it is the case that the mechanism of certification enables the interested parties to make such a reference to the Copyright Tribunal.

As far as performers' rights are concerned, the opportunity to apply for certification is limited to licensing schemes that relate to the lending to the public of sound recordings or films.[86] Anyone who operates or proposes to operate such a scheme can apply to the Secretary of State to have it certified, which has as its main advantage that in case of certification, the Secretary of State is precluded from treating the rental of the sound recordings or films that are covered by the scheme as sound recordings or films licensed by the performer subject only to the payment of a reasonable royalty as foreseen in paragraph 14A(1) of Schedule 2 of the *CDPA*. Obviously, certification does not flow automatically from the application. But if the licensing scheme clearly sets out any charges that are payable, as well as the terms on which the licenses will be granted, *and* the Secretary of State is satisfied that the scheme enables the works included in it to be identified with sufficient certainty by any person that may require a license, then certification of the scheme will follow.[87] The certification can be revoked if it appears to the Secretary of State that the licensing scheme is no longer operated or if it is no longer operated according to its terms.[88]

4 COLLECTIVE MANAGEMENT IN THE REPUBLIC OF IRELAND

4.1 THE LEGAL FRAMEWORK

The *Copyright and Related Rights Act, 2000* contains extensive provisions dealing with collective management and licensing schemes.[89] These provisions show a lot of similarities with the provisions in the United Kingdom that were discussed

---

86. *CDPA, supra* n. 11, Sch. 2 at para. 14A.
87. *CDPA, supra* n. 11, Sch. 2 at para. 16.
88. *CDPA, supra* n. 11, Sch. 2 at para. 16(5).
89. *Copyright and Related Rights Act, 2000*, number 28 of 2000, <www.irishstatutebook.ie/ZZA28Y2000.html> (last visited: 10 May 2010) [*CRRA*].

earlier. In Ireland, the Controller of Patents, Designs and Trade Marks fulfils the role of the Secretary of State though and appeal against the decisions of the Controller can be brought in the High Court, but in general, only appeals on points of law are permitted.[90]

A licensing scheme can be created by means of a reference of its proposed terms to the Controller, who will then rule on the proposed scheme by means of an order. Or, as section 151 of the *CRRA* puts it:

> (1) The terms of a licensing scheme proposed to be operated by a licensing body may be referred to the Controller by an organisation which claims to be representative of persons who claim that they require licences in cases of a description to which the scheme would apply.
>
> [...]
>
> (4) Where the Controller decides to consider a reference under *subsection (1)*, he or she shall consider the subject matter of the reference and make an order, either confirming or varying the proposed scheme, as the Controller may determine to be reasonable in the circumstances.[91]

Similarly, disputes concerning licensing schemes that are in operation can be referred to the Controller, who may then, if necessary, vary the scheme by means of an order. Section 152 enables this in the following terms:

> (1) Where a licensing scheme is in operation and a dispute arises with respect to the scheme between the operator of the scheme and –
>   (a) a person claiming that he or she requires a licence in a case of a description to which the scheme applies, or
>   (b) an organisation claiming to be representative of such persons, that operator, person or organisation may refer the scheme to the Controller in so far as it relates to cases of that description.
>   [...]
> (4) The Controller shall consider the matter referred to him or her and shall make an order, confirming or varying the scheme, as the Controller may determine to be reasonable in the circumstances.[92]

A person who has been refused a license can also appeal to the Controller, who may then grant the license by order when appropriate, as set out in Section 154 of the *CRRA:*

> (1) A person who claims, in a case to which a licensing scheme relates, that the operator of the scheme has refused to grant or to procure the grant to him or her of a licence in accordance with the scheme, or has failed to do so within a reasonable period, may apply to the Controller for an order under *subsection (4)*.

---

90. *Ibid.*, s. 366.
91. See also *ibid.*, s. 267 in relation to rights in performances.
92. See also *ibid.*, s. 268 in relation to rights in performances.

(2) A person who claims, in a case excluded from a licensing scheme, that the operator of the scheme –

    (a) has refused to grant or to procure the grant to him or her of a licence, or has failed to do so within a reasonable period and that in the circumstances it is unreasonable that a licence should not be granted, or

    (b) proposes terms for a licence that are unreasonable, may apply to the Controller for an order under *subsection (4)*.

[...]

(4) Where the Controller is satisfied that a claim under this section is well-founded, he or she shall make an order declaring that in respect of the matters specified in the order, the applicant is entitled to a licence on such terms as the Controller may determine to be applicable in accordance with the scheme, or as the case may be, to be reasonable in the circumstances.[93]

Until now the discussion has dealt mainly with licensing schemes, but similar mechanisms are in place for licenses. Section 158, for example, deals with references to the Controller of the terms of proposed licenses and section 159 with references to the Controller of expiring licenses.[94] The Controller may then vary the terms of the license or extend the term of the license by means of an order.

All these provisions, like their UK counterparts, refer to the concept of reasonableness. Section 162 of the *CRRA* then goes on to clarify how the Controller is to use and interpret this concept and criterion:

(1) In determining what is reasonable, on a reference or application under this Chapter relating to a licensing scheme or licence, the Controller shall have regard to –

    (a) the availability of other schemes, or the granting of other licences, to other persons in similar circumstances, and

    (b) the terms of those schemes or licences,

and shall exercise his or her powers so as to ensure that there is no unreasonable discrimination between licensees, or prospective licensees, under the scheme or licence to which the reference or application relates and licensees under other schemes operated by, or other licences granted by, the same person.

(2) *Subsection (1)* shall not affect the obligation of the Controller in any case to have regard to all relevant circumstances.[95]

Additional sections of the Act then list further factors the Controller shall take into account in relation to licenses for various types of works.[96]

Licensing schemes can also be certified by the Minister for Enterprise, Trade and Employment upon application by the society operating the scheme concerned. The Minister will only issue an order satisfying the scheme if he or she is satisfied

---

93. See also *ibid.*, s. 270 in relation to rights in performances.
94. See also *ibid.*, ss 274 and 275 in relation to rights in performances.
95. See also *ibid.*, s. 278 in relation to rights in performances.
96. *Ibid.*, ss 163–166.

on the one hand that the licensing body in charge of the scheme is representative of a substantial number of right holders in the category of works to which the scheme is designed to apply and on the other hand that the scheme sets out clearly the charges payable and the other terms and conditions on which licenses are to be granted.[97]

Finally, a register of copyright licensing bodies is established by the Controller. Section 175 of the *CRRA* sets out how this is to be done:

(1) The Controller shall establish and maintain a register of copyright licensing bodies in such form and manner and containing such particulars as the Minister may prescribe to be known as the 'Register of Copyright Licensing Bodies' and referred to in this Part as the 'Register'.

(2) The Controller shall keep the Register in such form so that the Register is capable of being used to make a copy of any entry in the Register.

(3) The Register shall be kept at such place as may be prescribed by the Minister and, subject to the payment of such fee as may be prescribed by the Minister with the consent of the Minister for Finance –

   (a) the Register shall be made available for inspection by a person at such times and in such manner as may be prescribed by the Minister, and

   (b) where a request is made to the Controller for a certified or uncertified copy of, or extract from, an entry in the Register, the Controller shall issue a copy of the entry or extract to the applicant.

(4) An application for registration or renewal of a registration of a licensing body shall be made to the Controller in such form and manner as may be prescribed by the Minister and shall be subject to the payment of such fee as may be prescribed by the Minister with the consent of the Minister for Finance.

(5) The Controller shall register an applicant or renew a registration where the Controller is satisfied that –

   (a) the applicant complies with the definition of a licensing body specified in section 38 or 149, and

   (b) the applicant has provided such information and satisfied such conditions as may be prescribed by the Minister for the purposes of registration. [...]

Before we turn to the Irish collecting societies, it is worth noting that Ireland has very recently put in place a Public Lending Right by means of the *Copyright and Related Rights (Amendment) Act 2007* that enabled the scheme that was brought in on 31 December 2008 in the form of a Regulation.[98] Payment will now be paid to living authors who are registered and resident in the European Economic Area in respect to books registered with the PLR and loaned by public libraries authorities. The scheme excludes publishers, audio books and sound recordings, but it applies

---

97. *Ibid.*, s. 173.
98. SI 597/2008, <www.attorneygeneral.ie/esi/2008/B26672.pdf> (last visited: 10 May 2010).

to authors, illustrators, photographers, editors and translators.[99] The scheme is run by the Library Council.[100]

4.2   THE IRISH MUSIC RIGHTS ORGANISATION

The Irish Music Rights Organsiation (IMRO) deals with performing rights in copyright music. Its website summarizes its activities and role as follows:

> IMRO is a national organisation that administers the performing right in copyright music in Ireland on behalf of its members – songwriters, composers and music publishers – and on behalf of the members of the international overseas societies that are affiliated to it. IMRO's function is to collect and distribute royalties arising from the public performance of copyright works. IMRO is a not-for-profit organisation.
>
> Music users such as broadcasters, venues and businesses must pay for their use of copyright music by way of a blanket licence fee. IMRO collects these monies and distributes them to the copyrightsholders involved. The monies earned by copyrightsholders in this way are known as public performance royalties. [. . .]
>
> IMRO issues licences to those wishing to use copyright music in public and in the on-line environment.
>
> IMRO's tariff setting policy is based on negotiating agreements with trade bodies representing the various sections of the music using public in Ireland. It has been singularly successful in this policy and all of the bodies representing the main music users in the country have now agreed tariffs with IMRO – the Irish Hotels Federation, the Restaurant Owners Association of Ireland, the Licensed Vintners Association, the Vintners' Federation of Ireland, the Association of Independent Radio Stations, Radio Teilifís Éireann and so on.[101]

IMRO takes an assignment of the performing right from its members for the purposes of issuing licenses and collecting fees on behalf of its members. Concerning these licenses the IMRO website provides the following details:

> IMRO licences are in the form of contracts which run from year to year until cancelled by either party. They are blanket licences, authorising the public performance of any of the millions of works which IMRO controls on behalf of both of its members and of the members of its affiliated societies throughout the world. The royalties payable under IMRO licences vary as the nature or extent of music usage changes in the premises concerned. The general nature of the licence contract is that it authorises the licensee to perform, or to cause

---

99.   If these are named on the title page of the book concerned.
100.   The An Chomhairle Leabharlanna.
101.   See <www.imro.ie/about/what_we_do.shtml> (last visited: 10 May 2010).

or authorise the performance of IMRO's copyright repertoire, in consideration for which the licensee undertakes to pay the appropriate royalty. Naturally, it does not oblige the performance of all or any part of IMRO's repertoire. The extent to which that repertoire is performed, within the terms of the licence, is the licensee's choice entirely. It would obviously be quite impracticable for IMRO to monitor every performance given by each of its licensees, just as it would be intolerable for most licensees to keep a precise check on the nature and extent of all performances in their premises. Therefore, IMRO must be told immediately of any reduction of music usage if it is to agree to a corresponding reduction in the royalty. Similarly, increased music usage must be promptly notified.

IMRO's licences cover both 'live' performances and performances by mechanical means, i.e., juke boxes, radio and television, video, record, CD and tape players, and so on. Licences are in issue for numerous categories of premises, including cinemas, clubs, concert halls, discos, town halls, church halls, public houses, restaurants, shops, factories, universities, ships, aircraft, sports stadia, theatres and many others. Nearly 30,000 establishments are covered by the IMRO licence in Ireland.

In certain cases, permits are issued for the use of IMRO's repertoire, or sometimes for specified works, either at a single performance or at a short series of performances at premises not licensed for those occasions. If a copyright musical work is performed in public without the copyright owner's consent then the copyright owner has a claim against not only the promoter of the performance but also the proprietor of the premises (unless he can show that he had no reason to believe that infringement would take place) and the performers. It is not IMRO policy to grant licences to performers (other than to brass and military bands as such, for performances in public places). IMRO normally issues its licence to the proprietor of the hall or other premises concerned, so relieving the promoter of a musical entertainment there from having to apply for a special permit. Promoters should make a point, when hiring premises for a function involving music, of ensuring that the proprietor holds an IMRO licence which will cover the occasion.[102]

4.3   THE MECHANICAL-COPYRIGHT PROTECTION SOCIETY
             (IRELAND) LTD

The Mechanical-Copyright Protection Society (Ireland) (MCPSI) deals with mechanical royalties. Its membership comprises composers and music publishers, and its income is generated from the recording of music onto many different

---

102. See <www.imro.ie/node/757> (last visited: 10 May 2010).

formats. It shows strong similarities with MCPS in the United Kingdom. Starting 1 February 2009 it has outsourced the collection of its royalties to IMRO.[103]

4.4 THE IRISH COPYRIGHT LICENSING AGENCY

The Irish Copyright Licensing Agency (ICLA) is Ireland's reproduction rights organization.[104] Under Irish copyright law, a license is mandatory for any educational establishment wishing to make multiple copies of a variety of copyright-protected works and ICLA operates the only scheme in Ireland whereby such a license can be obtained. ICLA also licenses users in business, industry and the professions to photocopy extracts from books, journals and periodicals, particularly by means of a blanket license to businesses wishing to make multiple copies of copyright material for distribution to members of staff. ICLA's licenses do not impose a strict record keeping obligation. Instead surveys are carried out every three years on a rotational basis.

ICLA is a non – profit-making organization, and all license fees with a deduction for administrative expenses go to the authors and publishers whose works have been copied.

4.5 THE IRISH VISUAL ARTISTS RIGHTS ORGANISATION

The Irish Visual Artists Rights Organisation (IVARO)[105] is a non-profit organization that aims to protect and promote the copyright and related rights of artists, visual creators and their heirs. It also acts as a collecting society for visual artists by collecting royalties that are due to artists for the use of their works. IVARO is a membership organization that is owned and controlled by the artists and copyright heirs that make up the membership.

Arguably the main task of IVARO is the collection and distribution of the Artist's Resale Right in Ireland since it entered into force in 2006. IVARO also mandates ICLA to include copying (photocopying) of visual works in the licenses it grants. Under that agreement ICLA pays IVARO a percentage of its gross income.

4.6 PHONOGRAPHIC PERFORMANCE IRELAND

Phonographic Performance Ireland (PPI) controls the public performance rights and broadcasting rights of record labels and operates licensing schemes and a total

---

103. See <www.imro.ie/content/mcpsi-outsources-its-irish-operations-imro> (last visited: 10 May 2010).
104. See <http://icla.ie> (last visited: 10 May 2010).
105. See <http://ivaro.ie> (last visited: 10 May 2010).

of fifty-seven different tariffs[106] depending on the type and size of user in its dealings with the owners of premises and the promoters of events. It also deals with the rights of performers in this respect. Its websites summarize its role as follows:

> Whenever a sound recording (CD, Tape, LP) or music video is played in public, broadcast on the radio or carried over a cable service (TV), a royalty must be paid to the company that produced the recording. Playing a radio or television for your customers is treated exactly the same as if you are playing recorded music.
>
> Phonographic Performance (Ireland) Limited was established in 1968 to act as a central administrator of record company rights in the public performance, broadcasting and reproduction of their recordings. PPI is owned by its members – Irish and multinational record companies – and membership is open to all record companies, big & small.
>
> Record companies have a right to be paid whenever their recordings (CDs, tapes, LPs, etc) or music videos are played in public. Performers have a right to be paid when sound recordings they have contributed to are played in public.
>
> PPI collects both of these payments in one single licence fee and then distributes the money to record companies and performers through Recorded Artists And Performers Ltd.
>
> PPI's members consist of record companies including all the well-known multinational and major Irish record companies. All of PPI's income (less administration charges) is distributed every year to its members and to performers signed to member record companies.[107]

5   CONCLUSION

The preceding overview has demonstrated that collective management and collective licensing has become highly organized and structured in both the United Kingdom and the Republic of Ireland. Complex provisions have been put in place in the copyright acts of both countries to regulate this part of copyright, and it is quite remarkable that a lot of these provisions are administrative in nature in the sense that they involve to a large extent the intervention of government ministers and administrative tribunals such as the Copyright Tribunal in the United Kingdom.

---

106. See, for example, the decision of the Irish High Court in a case opposing the Irish Nightclub Industry Association (INIA) and the Irish Hotels Federation (IHF) on the one hand and the Phonographic Performance (Ireland) Limited (PPI) on the other hand. See <www.hg.org/articles/article_1175.html> (last visited: 10 May 2010).
107. See <www.ppiltd.com> (last visited: 10 May 2010).

In practice, the system of collective management seems to work well, covering the relevant areas of copyright almost comprehensively. One can of course have doubts on whether the system can collect all fees due, whether the distribution of the fees really gives to each right holder what he or she is due or whether the societies operate effectively without deducting too much for costs and overhead, but this is a matter that has been addressed in more depth in various other chapters of this book.

It is likely that the system of collective management in the United Kingdom and the Republic of Ireland will continue to grow in the foreseeable future. There are already signs of expansion to include Internet use of copyright works in the operation of the societies, but this development is still in its infancy and the territorial restrictions on the scope of operations of the societies seriously hinder this development. More international interaction and cooperation among societies will be required, and the societies will also have to find their place in the broader European-wide framework that the European Commission has started to put in place. Further developments are therefore guaranteed, even if the shape of things to come is not yet exactly clear.

Chapter 9

Collective Management in the Nordic Countries

*Tarja Koskinen-Olsson**

1   INTRODUCTION

All of the Nordic countries – Denmark, Finland, Iceland, Norway and Sweden – are relatively small countries. They have a long-standing tradition of working together in copyright matters, based on similar legislation since the early 1960s.

A high degree of organization and cooperation among various groups of right holders are two typical features. This has over the years proven to be necessary to answer adequately to ever-varying user needs. One of the guiding principles has been to provide lawful access for users in an efficient and cost-effective manner.

Legislators have paid special attention to the position and legal security of users. A special legal technique that combines exclusive rights and voluntary licensing with legal certainty is called an 'extended collective license' (ECL). Its origins stem from the beginning of the 1960s when primary broadcasting was at stake. In the 1970s and 1980s, reprography and re-transmission of

---

*   Tarja Koskinen-Olsson currently works as International Adviser in intellectual property rights matters. From 1987 to 2003, she served as the Chief Executive Officer of KOPIOSTO (Joint Finnish Copyright Organization). From 1972 to 1986, she held several posts in TEOSTO (the Finnish Composers' Copyright Bureau). In 1993, she was elected as Chairman of the International Federation of Reproduction Rights Organizations (IFRRO), which she held until 1999. She has served as Honorary President of IFRRO during the years 2001–2009.

Daniel Gervais (ed.), *Collective Management of Copyright and Related Rights*, pp. 283–306.
© 2010 Kluwer Law International BV, The Netherlands.

broadcasts called upon swift licensing solutions, and the ECL proved to be a balancing factor. With the national implementations of the EU Copyright Directive,[1] the Nordic countries added new ECL provisions to address digital uses, in particular in educational establishments and libraries. Denmark explores a general applicability of an ECL provision with its 2008 amendment of the Danish Copyright Act.

This chapter describes how collective management organizations (CMOs) function in the Nordic countries, with a special emphasis on the ECL that is also referred to as the 'extended repertoire system (ERS)'. This legal technique addresses the issue of fully covering licenses. Although various legal techniques exist to safeguard the user's position in collective licensing, the ECL has proven its applicability and flexibility as a viable solution.

2   HISTORY AND SHORT OVERVIEW OF COLLECTIVE MANAGEMENT

The scope and coverage of main CMOs in the Nordic countries are described in this chapter sector by sector. In some sectors, licensing is supported by an ECL provision, either in part or in whole. Special emphasis lies on the implementation of the Copyright Directive and new licensing possibilities inherent therein. This implementation took place in Denmark in 2002, in Finland, Norway and Sweden in 2005 and in Iceland in 2006.

2.1   PERFORMING AND MECHANICAL RIGHTS OF MUSICAL WORKS

In comparison with Europe, Nordic CMOs in the field of music are semi-old; most of them were established in the 1920s. The organizations are KODA (Denmark), STEF (Iceland), STIM (Sweden), TEOSTO (Finland) and TONO (Norway). Nordisk Copyright Bureau (NCB) originally started as a Danish performing rights organization, but now works with mechanical rights covering the Nordic countries and the Baltic States (Estonia, Latvia and Lithuania).

The ECL was introduced as an answer to technological developments long before we knew anything about digital technologies. In the late 1950s, broadcasting organizations demanded adequate solutions to their copyright concerns in primary broadcasting. As a real mass use situation, it would be practically impossible for a broadcaster to clear rights individually for all literary and musical works that are broadcast over time. Collective management is thus the only feasible solution. Nordic broadcasters paid attention to the representativity issue and

---

1. EC, *Directive 2001/29/EC of the European Parliament and the Council of 22 May 2001 on the harmonisation of certain aspects of copyright and related rights in the information society* (2001), O.J. L. 167/10 [Copyright Directive], <http://eur-lex.europa.eu/pri/en/oj/dat/2001/l_167/l_16720010622en00100019.pdf> (last visited: 7 Oct. 2009).

wanted safeguards from the legislators. As a consequence, ECLs were established in all Nordic countries for broadcasting of literary and musical works.

The challenge was to combine the exclusive rights of authors and the demands of broadcasters to get a waterproof license without needing to face possible claims from outsiders, irrespective of their country of origin. Whereas the global coverage of performing rights organizations is today fairly extensive,[2] that was not the case in the late 1950s. And even though the need for special legislative measures may be smaller today, Nordic broadcasters have continuously pleaded for the maintenance of an ECL for primary broadcasting.

2.2   RELATED RIGHTS IN THE FIELD OF MUSIC

Current Nordic copyright laws stem from the beginning of the 1960s, when related rights were introduced. Performers and phonogram producers established new CMOs to correlate adequately with new legislation. Joint organizations for performers and phonogram producers exist in all Nordic countries except Sweden. The organizations are GRAMEX (Denmark and Finland), GRAMO (Norway) and SFH (Iceland). In Sweden, SAMI[3] and the Swedish Group of IFPI work in close cooperation. Collection of remuneration rights for broadcasting and other public performances forms the core activity of CMOs representing holders of related rights.

Over time, discussions have taken place to change remuneration rights of performers and phonogram producers to exclusive rights with an ECL as a support mechanism. Related right holders have demonstrated on several occasions that the mere existence of a compulsory license radically weakens their bargaining power and gives an undue advantage to users.

In Sweden and Denmark, the right of making available to the public was changed already in the middle of the 1990s so that related rights have a status similar to authors' rights. The exclusive right, however, is subject to a compulsory license in the case of broadcasting and other public performances. Thus, as yet, related right holders do not benefit from an ECL.

2.3   VISUAL ARTS AND PHOTOGRAPHY

Visual authors and photographers have CMOs in all Nordic countries, established in 1970s and 1980s. The organizations are BONO[4] (Norway), BUS[5] (Sweden),

---

2. The international organization CISAC has 225 members in 118 countries (October 2009), <www.cisac.org> (last visited: 7 Oct. 2009).
3. The Swedish Artists and Musicians Interest Organization, <www.sami.se> (last visited: 7 Oct. 2009).
4. Norwegian Visual Artists Copyright Society, <www.bono.no> (last visited: 7 Oct. 2009).
5. Pictorial Art, Copyright in Sweden, <www.bus.se> (last visited: 7 Oct. 2009).

Copydan Pictorial Art[6] (Denmark), KUVASTO (Finland) and MYNDSTEF[7] (Iceland). In most of the countries, a major part of remuneration comes from resale right.

The use of works of art is common in exhibition catalogues and similar materials. The Copyright Directive allows an exception or limitation in certain cases.[8] However, the narrow scope of the permitted exception has led to the introduction of new ECLs in some Nordic Countries, to facilitate reproduction and dissemination of works of visual art and photography.

2.4 RIGHTS IN LITERARY WORKS

Specialized CMOs for literary authors are a relatively recent phenomenon in the Nordic countries. Established in 1995, ALIS[9] in Sweden is the oldest, followed by similar organizations in Norway (LINO[10]) and Finland (SANASTO[11]). Literary works are frequently used in broadcasting, covered by the original ECL provisions concerning literary and musical works.

2.5 REPROGRAPHY AND CERTAIN DIGITAL USES

Reprography posed a critical mass use situation and challenge to rights management in the late 1960s and the early 1970s. The first country to react was Sweden, with the establishment in 1973 of a specialized CMO called BONUS.[12] It negotiated a voluntary contract with the Government to cover photocopying in schools and universities.

A joint Nordic law revision process was underway in the 1970s. The solution based on an ECL was reinvented and introduced to cover widespread photocopying for educational purposes. Finland went one step further, and the 1980 amendment to the Copyright Act[13] introduced an ECL that covers photocopying not only in schools and universities, but also in administration and businesses. The other Nordic countries widened the scope of the ECL in later amendments.

New organizations (RROs[14]) emerged in the 1970s and the early 1980s. They are coalitions or umbrellas representing various groups of authors and

---

6. Part of Copydan, the Joint Collecting Society, <www.copydan.dk> (last visited: 7 Oct. 2009).
7. Established in 1991, Myndstef is the representative organization in the field of visual arts and photography, <www.myndstef.is> (last visited: 7 Oct. 2009).
8. Copyright Directive, *supra* n. 2, Art. 5.3 (j): 'use for the purpose of advertising the public exhibition or sale of artistic works, to the extent necessary to promote the event, excluding any other commercial use'.
9. The Administration of Literary Rights in Sweden, <www.alis.org> (last visited: 7 Oct. 2009).
10. Established in 1996; the activities will be terminated at the end of 2009 and administered by the writers' organization and KOPINOR, subject to the case.
11. Established in 2005, <www.sanasto.fi> (last visited: 7 Oct. 2009).
12. Bonus-Presskopia sine 1999, <www.bonuspresskopia.se> (last visited: 7 Oct. 2009).
13. Act 897 of 19 Dec. 1980 amending the Copyright Act (Law No. 404 of 8 Jul. 1961).
14. In the field of reprography, CMOs are called Reproduction Rights Organizations (RROs); they are members of The International Federation of Reproduction Rights Organizations (IFRRO), <www.ifrro.org> (last visited: 7 Oct. 2009).

publishers: BONUS-PRESSKOPIA (Sweden), Copydan Writing (Denmark), FJÖLIS[15] (Iceland), KOPIOSTO[16] (Finland) and KOPINOR[17] (Norway). Their scope of activity was originally photocopying, but with technological developments many digital uses are now licensed. Denmark was the first Nordic country to introduce an ECL to cover digital copying for educational purposes in 1995.[18] With the implementation of the Copyright Directive, many new ECL stipulations cover digital uses. In Chapter 5, the scope of these provisions is described in some detail.

2.6   SECONDARY USE OF AUDIOVISUAL WORKS

Off-air recording of television programmes for educational purposes presents a similar copyright clearance challenge as reprography. In Finland, legislation was amended in 1984 and a new ECL was introduced to cover off-air recording of television programmes for educational purposes.

During the same time, another real mass use situation, re-transmission of broadcasts, was discussed jointly in the Nordic countries. Neighbouring countries' television programmes had long been popular in spillover areas and demands to distribute these programmes wider either by re-broadcasting or by wire (cable) was actively promoted by the viewing public.

Clearing copyright programme-by-programme for re-transmission is a factual impossibility because one television channel includes some 10,000 individual programmes during a year. In the middle of the 1980s, an ECL was found to be a workable solution also for re-transmission of broadcasts. Thus, the Nordic countries solved copyright clearance far earlier than the Satellite and Cable Directive[19] of the European Union (EU). In Denmark, a compulsory license was introduced in 1985 to cover simultaneous and unchanged re-transmission by cable. In 1996, this provision was changed into a voluntary system based on an ECL,[20] as a response to the Satellite and Cable Directive stating the following:

(1) Member States shall ensure that when programmes from other Member States are retransmitted by cable in their territory the applicable copyright and related rights are observed and that such retransmission takes place on the

---

15. See <www.fjolis.is> (last visited: 7 Oct. 2009).
16. See <www.kopiosto.fi> (last visited: 7 Oct. 2009).
17. See <www.kopinor.no> (last visited: 7 Oct. 2009).
18. Copyright, Act, Law No. 395 of 14 Jun. 1995.
19. EC, *COUNCIL DIRECTIVE 93/83/EEC of 27 September 1993 on the coordination of certain rules concerning copyright and rights related to copyright applicable to satellite broadcasting and cable retransmission* (1993), O.J. L. 248/15 [Satellite and Cable Directive], <http://eur-lex.europa.eu/LexUriServ/LexUriServ.do?uri=CELEX:31993L0083:EN:HTML> (last visited: 7 Oct. 2009).
20. With the effect from 1 Jan. 1998.

basis of individual or collective contractual agreements between copyright owners, holders of related rights and cable operators;

(2) Notwithstanding paragraph 1, Member States may retain until 31 December 1997 such statutory licenses systems which are in operation or expressly provided for by national law on 31 July 1991.[21]

Coalition organizations were needed to clear re-transmission rights because many different groups of right holders are involved. In Denmark and Finland, the existing coalitions (Copydan Cable TV and KOPIOSTO) extended their activities to cover cable re-transmission, whereas in Norway and Sweden new coalitions (NORWACO[22] and COPYSWEDE[23]) were established. These coalitions cover all relevant authors and performing artists and in some countries also producers of phonograms and films. Cooperation agreements with broadcasters, either through their collective body (Union of Broadcasting Organizations[24]) or individually with each broadcaster, secure to the users fully covering licenses.

Producers of films have either established their own CMOs; alternatively, they are represented directly in the previously mentioned coalitions.

2.7   Private Copying Remuneration

Iceland and Finland were among the five first countries in the world to introduce special compensation for widespread private copying. In 1984, both countries introduced remuneration in the price of blank audio and video recoding media, known redundant, at that time as a blank tape levy. Denmark introduced a similar system in 1993. Sweden and Norway had a tax law–based system, but changed their systems in 1999 and 2005, respectively. In Norway, compensation is paid from budgetary funds and not collected in the price of media and equipment.

Collection of revenue is done by one of the existing CMOs: TEOSTO in Finland, Copydan Blank Tape in Denmark and COPYSWEDE in Sweden. In Iceland, IHM has a special arrangement with the customs authorities who are in charge of the collection. Distribution of revenue takes place by the relevant sector-specific CMOs. In Norway, NORWACO receives the budgetary allocation and distributes it through its member organizations. These private copying remuneration schemes have been extended to cover digital media and equipment.

---

21. Article 8, Satellite and Cable Directive, *supra* n. 21.
22. See <www.norwaco.no> (last visited: 7 Oct. 2009).
23. See <www.copyswede.se> (last visited: 7 Oct. 2009).
24. See <www.ubod.dk> (last visited: 7 Oct. 2009).

2.8   Summary of Main Nordic Collective
        Management Organizations

The main characteristics in Nordic rights management are:

- well-organized authors, performing artists, publishers and producers;
- high degree of representation in CMOs;
- high degree of cooperation among various CMOs;
- joint agreements with users.

This provides a good ground for legislators to consider support mechanisms, such as ECLs, for collective licensing. The very essence of an ECL lies in good representativity, with direct representation of most right holders whose works are used in a given area.

A summary[25] of the main Nordic CMOs is presented in Table 9.1.

Table 9.1 Main Nordic CMOs

Scope	Denmark	Finland	Iceland	Norway	Sweden
Music performing rights	KODA	TEOSTO	STEF	TONO	STIM
Music mechanical rights	NCB	NCB	NCB	NCB	NCB
Music related rights	GRAMEX	GRAMEX	SFH	GRAMO	SAMI (performers) IFPI (producers)
Visual authors	Copydan Pictorial Art	KUVASTO	Myndstef	BONO	BUS
Literary authors		SANASTO		LINO	ALIS
Reprography and certain digital uses	Copydan Writing	KOPIOSTO	FJÖLIS	KOPINOR	BONUS-PRESSKOPIA
Secondary use of audiovisual works COPYS WEDE	Copydan Cable TV	KOPIOSTO	IHM[26]		NORWACO
Producers of audiovisual works		TUOTOS			FRF

---

25. This list is not all inclusive, but summarizes the areas and organizations mentioned in this chapter.
26. Primarily active in private copying remuneration, but also coordinates cable retransmission licensing.

3   MAIN ELEMENTS OF AN EXTENDED
           COLLECTIVE LICENSE

An ECL means provisions in the law giving an extension effect to clauses in a collective licensing agreement in specific areas of the copyright and related rights. This extension applies to right holders who are not members of the contracting organization.

3.1   HISTORY OF THE SYSTEM

The first ECL provisions came as a result of the revision of the copyright laws in the Nordic countries in the early 1960s. Revision committees had been working in Denmark, Finland, Norway and Sweden, with Iceland also participating. They proposed the first ECL in the field of broadcasting of literary and musical works. Over the years, the system was deemed successful and as a result, it was extended to new areas. The legislative amendments related to the implementation of the Copyright Directive have resulted in a substantial number of new ECL provisions. The latest amendment of the Danish Copyright Act in 2008[27] opens new possibilities to use an ECL in various kinds of contracts. One of the driving forces in this law revision was the desire to obtain balance between the rights of right holders and interests of users.

Essentially, the same structure exists in all the Nordic countries. However, there are differences both with regard to the scope and certain elements in the system itself. These will be briefly described below; a detailed approach would not serve non-Nordic readers.

Provisions on ECL were originally designed to apply to literary and musical works for use in sound radio and television broadcasts. The application of the system has since been extended to, among others, the following areas (at a different pace in the each of the Nordic countries[28]):

- reprographic reproduction of printed material for educational purposes and for internal information in administration and businesses;
- off-air recording of radio and television programs for educational use;
- re-transmission of broadcast programs by re-broadcasting or by wire;
- certain library uses;
- use of works of visual art;
- use of works in broadcasting companies' archives.

During the implementation process of the Copyright Directive, there were demands to apply collective licensing in new fields. In Sweden, for instance, broadcasters requested such a system for the exploitation of material in their archives and for the making available in on-demand services of literary and artistic

---

27. Law No. 231 of 8 Apr. 2008.
28. Some of the examples are not in force in all Nordic countries.

works and commercial sound recordings used in sound radio or televisions programmes. The Government, however, did not want to address those proposals in the implementation process, but has promised to discuss them at a later date. In Denmark, however, such a provision does exist.[29]

3.2   RATIONALE AND BASIC ELEMENTS

ECL is a support mechanism for freely negotiated licensing agreements, based on exclusive rights. In cases of mass uses, it is seldom the case that a single right holder could draw full benefit from exclusive rights by negotiating alone. Collective management organizations represent authors and other right holders and negotiate on their behalf.

Once an agreement is reached in free negotiations between a representative CMO and a user, and both are satisfied with the terms and conditions, an ECL mechanism comes into effect. For a user, it is important to know that the license is fully covering and this is exactly what the ECL addresses – the issue of fully covering licenses in cases of mass uses.

In mass use situations, a CMO and a user, or in most cases a representative of a large user group, negotiate and, sometimes after long negotiations, conclude an agreement. Once the agreement is concluded, it is made legally binding on non-represented right holders as well. This is the so-called extension effect.

A prerequisite is that the organization is representative in its field, that is, represents by mandate a substantial number of right holders on whose behalf it negotiates. If that is the case, it is unlikely that an individual could obtain a better licensing deal by acting alone.

Once an agreement with the extension effect is concluded, the user may legally use the materials covered by the agreement and does not run the risk to get a claim, either legal or financial, from a non-represented right holder. These non-represented right holders have, directly on the basis of the law, a right to individual remuneration and in most cases a right to opt out (so-called veto right).

In summary, the basic elements of an ECL[30] are:

– the organization and the user conclude an agreement on the basis of free negotiations;
– the organization has to be representative[31] in its field;
– the agreement is made legally binding on non-represented right holders;
– the user may legally use all materials without needing to meet individual claims by outsiders and criminal sanctions;
– non-represented right holders have a right to individual remuneration;

---

29. Section 30a of the Danish Copyright Act, Law No. 231 of 8 Apr. 2008.
30. J. Liedes, H. Wager, T. Koskinen & S. Lahtinen, 'Extended Collective Licence' (June 1991), leaflet prepared by the Ministry of Education, Finland [Collective Licence Leaflet].
31. The criterion was originally national representation, but this has been changed in Denmark, Finland and Norway.

– non-represented right holders have in most cases a right to prohibit the use of their works.

An ECL can be supplemented by mediation, arbitration, tribunal procedures or other similar legal arrangements in case the negotiating parties disagree regarding the terms and conditions of the agreement.

3.3   BENEFITS

The system benefits both right holders and users and society at large.

The right holders' benefits lie in the fact that individuals are not able to control all of the hundreds of thousands of uses that are made of their works. Collective management is therefore needed to safeguard the rights that copyright law intends to give to the authors and other beneficiaries. This is equally true in the digital environment, where new products and services are being offered.

The users' benefits are that they can obtain fully covering licenses and can trust that their exploitation would not be hindered or affected by unexpected claims from non-represented right holders.

The need to ensure that exploitation is possible in certain important areas, such as educational establishments and libraries, lies in the interest of the society. The ECL strikes a balance between the rights of the right holders and the interests of the users, providing easy access in a lawful manner.

3.4   ALTERNATIVES TO AN EXTENDED COLLECTIVE LICENSE

The problem of outsiders has been approached in different ways, and alternatives to the Nordic ECL solution exist in various countries.[32] In all of these alternatives the aim is the same – to ensure a fully covering license to users of copyright material.

One alternative is to incorporate into an agreement an indemnity clause by which the organization assumes the liability for the payment of remuneration to a non-represented right holder. This alternative, however, does not make the use of non-represented works permissible, but only eliminates financial liability under civil law. Agreements cannot transfer liability under criminal law; the user is always responsible for any infringements committed. This alternative does not therefore fully safeguard the position of the user.

Another alternative is to incorporate into the law provisions by which a CMO is given a general authorization to represent right holders or it is presumed that the organization has such right. The practical effects of this alternative hardly differ from those of an ECL, which, however, does not give the organization a general

---

32. Collective Licence Leaflet, *supra* n. 30

right of representation, but only extends an agreement concluded by the organization to cover non-represented right holders.

A third alternative is compulsory collective management,[33] where management of an exclusive right is a voluntary act, but right holders cannot make claims on an individual basis. In 1995, the legislation in France introduced for the first time the concept of compulsory collective management in the area of reprographic reproduction rights. This safeguards the position of users, because an individual right holder cannot make claims against them. Besides reprography, compulsory or obligatory collective management is used in some licensing areas, such as cable retransmission rights in some European countries.

A fourth alternative would be to incorporate into the law a legal license, as either a compulsory or statutory license, when permitted by international conventions. In both cases, the consent of right holders for the use of protected works is not needed, but they have a right to remuneration. A non-voluntary license significantly weakens the negotiating position of right holders.

4   EXTENDED COLLECTIVE LICENSES AND GOVERNMENT OVERSIGHT

The ECL is a support mechanism for freely concluded agreements. Government supervision or oversight consists of provisions concerning representativity of the CMO and the position of non-represented right holders. Different forms of mediation or arbitration and government approval also fall under this topic.

4.1   REPRESENTATIVENESS CRITERION

The CMO that grants the rights through an agreement supported by an ECL must be a representative one. It must be truly representative of the right holders whose rights are licensed through the agreement. The requirement of representativity is expressed in various ways.

In most Nordic countries, the representativity criterion concerns a substantial number of authors of works that are used in the country. The Common Provisions on ECL in the Danish Copyright Act[34] states the following in section 50:

> Extended collective licence according to sections . . . may be evoked by users who have made an agreement on the exploitation of works in question with an organization comprising a substantial number of authors of a certain type of works which are used in Denmark.

---

33. T. Koskinen-Olsson, *Collective Management in Reprography* (Geneva: WIPO/IFRRO, 2005), 60, <www.wipo.int/freepublications/en/copyright/924/wipo_pub_924.pdf> (last visited: 7 Oct. 2009).
34. See *supra* n. 29: reference is made to s. 1 of para. 50.

This provision has been in force since 2001. Norway and Finland introduced a similar criterion in the implementation of the Copyright Directive in 2005. In Sweden, the representativity criterion means that the contracting organization must represent a substantial number of national right holders.

4.2   GUARANTEES FOR NON-REPRESENTED RIGHT HOLDERS

The need for guarantees for non-represented right holders applies to situations in which outside right holders are not satisfied with their works being used in a foreign country on conditions that they are not familiar with or to which they have not agreed. It is thus important that there are certain guarantees for foreigners. Legislators in the Nordic countries have considered this to be a particularly important aspect and have incorporated legislative provisions to that effect.

Such guarantees could be of two kinds:[35]

- a right to prohibit the use of their works (opt out);
- a right to claim individual remuneration.

The right to opt out or the 'veto right' is designed and applied somewhat differently in the different countries. For example, in Sweden a right to file a prohibition applies in the case of ECL in the following fields:

- copying for information purposes within enterprises, organizations, etc. (Article 42b);
- copying for educational purposes (Article 42c);
- libraries' and archives' possibility to communication to the public and distribution of works in digital form (Article 42d); and
- primary sound radio and television transmissions (Article 42e).

In the latter case, sound radio and television transmission on the basis of the ECL must also not take place even if there is no formal prohibition but if the broadcasting organization has, because of the circumstances in the case, a special reason to assume that the author would object to the transmission.

In the first three above-mentioned cases, the prohibition may be filed with any of the contracting parties. With regard to the fifth ECL in Sweden, that is, retransmission of broadcasts (Article 42f), the author has no right to file an individual prohibition. This is in accordance with the Satellite and Cable Directive.

As to a guaranteed right to remuneration, provisions in the law apply to right holders who are not members of the contracting organization. The organization has

---

35. H. Olsson, 'The Extended Collective License as Applied in the Nordic Countries' (2005), paper presented at the Kopinor 25th Anniversary International Symposium, Oslo, 20 May 2005, <www.kopinor.org/hva_er_kopinor/kopinor_25_ar/kopinor_25th_anniversary_international_symposium/the_extended_collective_license_as_applied_in_the_nordic_countries> (last visited: 7 Oct. 2009).

to see to it that those non-members actually receive remuneration. For instance, in Article 42a in the Swedish law it is prescribed:

> The author shall, as regards remuneration according to the agreement and benefits from the organizations that essentially are funded from the remuneration, be treated in the same way as the authors who are represented by the organization.

There may be, however, situations in which such outsiders are not satisfied with the conditions concerning remuneration that are prescribed in the agreement. One such situation may occur when the contracting organization has decided to use the remuneration for collective purposes. In such cases the non-represented right holders are entitled to the same treatment as the members. Moreover, most ECL provisions contain a clause that, regardless of the possibility to take part in such collective arrangements, a non-represented right holder always has the right to claim individual remuneration. The claim can be directed only toward the contracting organization, and such claims have to be made within a certain period of time, in most cases within three years from the year in which the exploitation took place.

4.3   MEASURES TO ENSURE THAT COLLECTIVE
           AGREEMENTS ARE CONCLUDED

In most Nordic countries, there are measures based on mediation, arbitration or both. Section 52 of the Danish Copyright Act includes detailed provisions on mediation, which each party may demand in the absence of any results in negotiations on agreements based on ECL provisions. The demands for mediation shall be addressed to the Ministry of Culture. This option, however, has been rarely used. That is why the latest law revision, in 2008,[36] offers a possibility to take the disagreement to an Arbitration Body[37]; its decisions are administratively binding, but can be taken to court.

In Sweden,[38] there has always been a considerable political resistance against any form of compulsory measures when difficulties arise in the negotiations concerning an ECL agreement. The Swedish law contains no provisions on arbitration or similar compulsory measures, but the Government and the Parliament have preferred to have confidence in the good will of the parties to reach a settlement. When the Satellite and Cable Directive was implemented, this approach was put to a test, because Article 11 of that Directive obliges the EU Member States to have a system of mediation in case negotiations fail. In Sweden, this resulted in a specific provision on a mediation process, based on the provisions in labour law.

---

36. See *supra* n. 29.
37. A special arbitration for licensing tariffs, called *Ophavsretslicensnævnet*.
38. Olsson, *supra* n. 35.

4.4   APPROVAL BY PUBLIC AUTHORITIES

It is a matter for national consideration whether there is a need for an approval by the public authorities (e.g., the Ministry of Culture) in order for an organization to conclude an agreement that could form the basis for an ECL.

For instance, in Finland, the Ministry of Education and Culture needs to approve all organizations that conclude agreements supported by ECLs. This requirement was added to the copyright law in conjunction with the implementation of the Copyright Directive in 2005.

Authorization by relevant authorities takes place also in Denmark, Iceland and Norway. Sweden remains the only Nordic country with no requirement of an authorization from public authorities.

5   PRACTICAL EXAMPLES FROM NORDIC COUNTRIES

Although legislation lays down the necessary prerequisite for right holders to enjoy and benefit from their rights, enforcement and management are necessary elements. Together, they form the three pillars of a well-functioning copyright system.

How to assess the functioning today? A few case studies will be offered, each describing a particular licensing area supported by an ECL, to enable the reader to judge the practical implications of the system. These examples put an emphasis on digital uses and they are chosen from different Nordic countries.

5.1   BROADCASTING IN FINLAND

An ECL was adopted in Nordic copyright legislation for the first time in the field of primary broadcasting. The Finnish provision dates back to 1961.[39] The aim was to solve the broadcasters' problem in trying to reach all right holders of the content used in daily programming. This provision, which has served as a model of further ECL, was originally written as follows:

> A broadcasting organization that has the right to broadcast works by virtue of an agreement concluded with an organization representing a large number of Finnish authors in a certain field may also broadcast a work in the same field by an author not represented by the organization. The provisions of this paragraph do not however apply to dramatic works, cinematographic works or even other works if the author has prohibited the broadcasting thereof.[40]

---

39. Copyright Act (Law No. 404 of 8 Jul. 1961).
40. *Ibid.*, Art. 25f.

The main motivation was a practical consideration.[41] Because it is practically impossible to reach all right holders and to secure all licenses before the actual use, broadcasting music in this case, the user may want to take full advantage of the blanket license offered by TEOSTO. In practice, this means that the broadcasting organization does not need to know whether an author is represented by the organization or not.

Taking into account good national representation and solid foreign representation through reciprocal representation agreements with similar CMOs in other countries, the extension effect has a relatively small application. Customarily some 2% to 3% of broadcast revenue is allocated to non-represented right holders. However, measured by the number of individual right holders whose works are performed, a lot more falls into the category of non-identified right holders.[42] Thus, an ECL is a safety net also in primary broadcasting, which today is in the main in digital format.

The copyright legislations of the other Nordic countries include similar ECL provisions. In Denmark and Norway, the provisions cover not only literary and musical works, but all works except dramatic works and films.

All Nordic CMOs in the field of creative music represent a substantial number of national right holders; more than 118,000 right holders have given a mandate to the Nordic organizations. In 2008, total domestic performing rights collection was EUR 194 million,[43] and broadcasting revenue represents a major part of that collection.

5.2   REPROGRAPHY AND CERTAIN DIGITAL USES IN DENMARK

In the late 1970s and early 1980s, the ECL was found to be the proper solution to copyright questions concerning reprography. Later on with technological development, digital uses have been added to the scope of application.

The Danish example shows a gradual development of the system. Copydan Writing is the CMO that has been approved by the Danish Ministry of Culture to enter into agreements on the exploitation of works with users pursuant to sections 13, 14 and 16b and to section 50[44] of the DCA. These areas of application are described in the following section.

---

41. V. Verronen, 'Extended Collective License in Finland: A Legal Instrument for Balancing the Rights of the Author with the Interests of the User', *Journal of the Copyright Society of the USA* 49 (2002): 1149.

42. In Finland, TEOSTO allocated 3.1% of the broadcasting revenue to non-represented rightsholders in 2004, which represented 6,275 individual right holders of the total of 48,198 right holders.

43. The revenue does not include remuneration received from foreign CMOs.

44. General provisions on extended collective license.

5.2.1 Reproduction in Educational Activities

The ECL in the Danish Copyright Act, section 13, concerns reproduction of published works for the purpose of educational activities, both public and private. When the ECL provision was introduced in 1985, it covered only analogue reproduction. However, in light of technological developments, the ECL provision was broadened in 1998 to include all forms of reproduction, hereunder scanning and downloading and other types of digital reproduction.

All Danish educational establishments have an agreement. According to the framework agreement, every institution may choose the rights that they need in their activities. The basic structure in the agreements is the same, and variations occur only in the scope of rights and price. When it comes to digital reproduction, Copydan Writing offers a license that includes use of digital presentation tools, such as Microsoft PowerPoint and digital boards. It further offers a license that includes scanning of published works in hard copy. Practically all institutions have acquired a permission that includes scanning. Reproduction for course-packs may take place only by reprographic reproduction.

One of the novelties is a pilot agreement with the Legal Faculty of Copenhagen University that allows the production of digital course-packs, in collaboration with an e-commerce service.[45]

Digital uses are thus well incorporated into the agreements in the educational market.

5.2.2 Reproduction by Institutions, Organizations and Business Enterprises

Section 14 of the DCA concerns reproduction of descriptive articles in newspapers, magazines and collections, of brief excerpts of other published works of a descriptive nature, of musical works and of illustrations reproduced in association with the text for internal use within public or private institutions, organizations and business enterprises.

Contrary to section 13 of the DCA, section 14 covers only analogue reproduction. When extending the scope of section 13 in 1998 to cover digital reproduction, the Danish Ministry of Culture also proposed the same extension for section 14. However, this proposal met strong opposition from the publishers, mainly the Danish Newspaper Publishers' Association. It was their opinion that at that time the proposal would cause serious harm to the development of their digital publishing. Subsequently, a majority in the Danish Parliament voted against extending section 14 to cover digital reproduction on the basis that, within a foreseeable future, newspaper publishers and journalists would be capable of clearing copyright on an individual basis in relation to the digital exploitation of their works.

Consequently, Copydan's standard licensing agreement on reproduction for administrative purposes covers only photocopying from paper to paper, including

---

45. See <www.ebog.dk>, 7 Oct. 2009.

photocopying of print-outs, for example, from the Internet, and transmission through fax.

A press clipping service[46] offers access to published articles, based on voluntary individual licensing by participating rightsholders.

5.2.3   Reproduction in Public Libraries

In 2002, an ECL provision was introduced under section 16(a) (currently section 16b) of the DCA in light of technological developments. The aim of the provision is to facilitate public libraries' copyright clearance in relation to digital reproduction of copyright protected works for inter-library loans. An inter-library loan is the process by which a library requests material from or supplies material to another library. The purpose of this is to enable a library user to obtain material not available in the user's library.

Pursuant to section 16b of the DCA, public libraries and other libraries that are financed in whole or in part by public authorities may upon request reproduce articles and other short excerpts. The public libraries, however, must respect any limitations that the right holders and libraries have agreed upon concerning grant of access to works. Furthermore, the library user who has ordered and received the scanned material is not allowed to re-distribute the work in digital form.

The provision supplements the exception in section 16 of the DCA, pursuant to which public libraries can make single copies of works on specified conditions to be used for the purpose of their activities, if this is not done for commercial purposes.

A framework licensing agreement on reproduction for the purpose of inter-library loans ('Lib-agreement') was negotiated between the Danish National Library Authority on behalf of the public research libraries and Copydan Writing; the agreement was concluded in 2004.

According to the agreement the research libraries are permitted to scan scientific journals in hard copy. The service[47] now includes some 30,000 periodicals and magazines. Whereas the already scanned articles are at disposal immediately, a few days are needed for material that is not yet scanned.

5.2.4   Situation in Other Nordic Countries

In Finland, KOPIOSTO has concluded agreements that cover education, state and municipal administration, church administration, associations and business enterprises. The evolution of the ECL provisions is as follows:

- 1980: General provision covering all areas of use by reprographic reproduction;

---

46.   See <www.infomedia.dk> (last visited: 7 Oct. 2009).
47.   See <www.bibliotek.dk> (last visited: 7 Oct. 2009).

- 2005: Reproduction of work for educational activities and scientific research by other means than reprography (Article 14);
- 2005: Reproduction of articles with accompanied illustrations and their transmission for internal information purposes by authorities, businesses and other persons, also by digital technology (Article 13a[48]).
- 2005: Use of works in archives, libraries and museums (Article 16d).

In Iceland, FJÖLIS is the relevant organization. The Icelandic Copyright Act has evolved as follows:

- 1992: Reprographic reproduction in general activities (Article 15a(1);
- 2006: Reproduction of certain types of works in libraries (Article 12(2).

In Norway, KOPINOR is the relevant organization that has concluded agreements in all areas of reprography and many digital uses. The ECL provisions have evolved as follows:

- 1979: Reprographic reproduction in educational activities;
- 1995: Reprographic reproduction for internal purposes in enterprises;
- 2005: Educational use extended to cover also digital uses (Article 13b);
- 2005: Internal information in enterprises extended to cover all forms of reproduction (Article 14).
- 2005: Use of works in archives, libraries and museums (Article 16a).

In Sweden, BONUS-PRESSKOPIA is the relevant organization, and the development of the ECL provisions is as follows:

- 1980: Reprographic reproduction in educational activities;
- 2005: The Parliament, decision-making municipal assemblies, governmental and municipal authorities as well as enterprises and organizations, for information purposes, by means of reprographic reproduction (Article 42b);
- 2005: Educational activities, including digital copying[49] (Article 42c);
- 2005: Archives and libraries to communicate the work to the public (Article 42d).

In summary, all Nordic countries have in recent years introduced new ECL provisions to cover digital uses. An ECL provision in the law, however, is only enabling legislation, on the basis of which right holders and users can negotiate agreements. It normally takes some time before agreements are concluded and the enabling provisions are used in the marketplace.

Representativeness of coalition organizations is fairly extensive in all Nordic countries. Moreover, bilateral agreements with similar organizations in other countries enlarge the organization's representation. For example, in Finland, KOPIOSTO has forty-four member organizations. They have individual mandates

---

48. The right holders have a right to prohibit such reproduction and transmission;
49. Unless the author has filed a prohibition against the reproduction with any of the contracting parties.

from 47,000 right holders, each in their field of activity. Member organizations transfer these mandates to KOPIOSTO when they consider collective management to be a proper way to manage the rights.

In 2008, domestic collection for reprography and some digital uses in the Nordic Countries totalled EUR 86 million.

5.3   Retransmission of Broadcasts in Norway

In the latter half of the 1980s, it was noted that collective management was the most expedient alternative regarding re-transmission rights. The re-transmission of broadcasts – by wire or other means or by re-broadcasting – in practice requires collective management of rights. Operators[50] must obtain fully covering licenses, because they cannot themselves influence the contents of the programmes to be re-transmitted; they can decide only whether to distribute the programmes. Many countries' legislation reduces the right to a mere right to remuneration. This was the case also in Denmark until 1998. Today, right holders in all Nordic countries enjoy exclusive rights, supported by an ECL.

Because of the complexity of copyright clearances of re-transmission rights, the EU Satellite and Cable Directive[51] opted for compulsory collective manage-ment in 1993. According to the Directive, the organization is deemed to be man-dated also vis-à-vis non-represented right holders. The Nordic solution based on an ECL is in conformity with the Directive.

5.3.1   Retransmission in Norway

In Norway, an agreement between an operator and NORWACO[52] binds all Norwegian and foreign right holders, including film producers, and thus provides full indemnity against claims by outsiders. In principle, right holders can be grouped into three main groups: authors and performing artists, producers of films and phonograms and broadcasters. NORWACO represents altogether thirty-four right holders' organizations: twenty-two authors' organizations, seven performing artists' organizations and six producers' organizations. NORWACO has been approved by the Ministry of Culture and Church Affairs.

The agreement concerning re-transmission of broadcasts is concluded between NORWACO and thirty-two broadcasting organizations as members of UBON[53] on one hand and the operator on the other hand. In 2009, the agreement covers 105 channels and most of them may be used in analogue and digital form.

---

50. The term operator is used for cable operators and distributors who use IP-net, Internet and equivalent.
51. See *supra* n. 21.
52. NORWACO has thirty-four member organizations, see <www.norwaco.no> (last visited: 7 Oct. 2009).
53. Union of Broadcasting Organizations in Norway.

The agreements cover 1.1 million households connected to a network in Norway, of the total 2.1 million households.

The agreement includes detailed provisions on prohibition of the re-transmission of certain programmes. Such a prohibition may take place only in special cases and needs to be notified in advance. Thus, the Norwegian agreement recognizes the possibility to prohibit the use of certain programmes despite the law not containing a provision to that effect.

If the parties are unable to agree on the terms and conditions and the remuneration, either party may submit the terms and conditions to a specific committee.[54] In 2004, the Committee settled a case initiated in 2003 by NORWACO and UBON against seven cable networks that did not conclude an agreement for their re-transmission. The reason for refusal was remuneration for Norwegian channels. The Committee concluded in its decision of 2004 that national channels are to be remunerated irrespective of their possible 'must carry' status and further that the claimed remuneration was considered to be reasonable. This decision was confirmed in a new case decided in April 2009.[55]

5.3.2 Situation in Other Nordic Countries

Retransmission by wire or by re-broadcasting is licensed by joint copyright organizations also in other Nordic countries. In Denmark, film producers are members of Copydan Cable TV, whereas in Sweden and Finland they have their own CMOs, FRF[56] and TUOTOS,[57] respectively, working in cooperation with COPYSWEDE and KOPIOSTO.

In 2008, remuneration for re-transmission collected in the Nordic countries totalled EUR 88 million. Whereas the main part of the revenue comes from distribution by cable, other distribution channels, such as IP-net and Internet, are on the increase.

6 CHALLENGES AND POSSIBILITIES

6.1 APPLICABILITY OF THE ECL IN THE DIGITAL ENVIRONMENT

When the Copyright Directive was negotiated, the Nordic delegations were conscious about the status of the ECL system in the context of a closed list of

---

54. Cable Council ('Kabeltvistnamnda').
55. Decision of the Cable Council in 29 Apr. 2009.
56. The Swedish Film Producers' Rights Federation (FRF), <www.frf.net.se> (last visited: 21 Oct. 2005).
57. Copyright association for audiovisual producers in Finland, <www.tuotos.fi> (last visited: 21 Oct. 2005).

possible exceptions that the Directive prescribes in its Articles 5.2 and 5.3. The end result of these deliberations is documented in Preamble 18, which states that:

> This Directive is without prejudice to the arrangements in the Member States concerning the management of rights such as extended collective licenses.[58]

This makes it clear that the nature of an ECL is a modality concerning rights management. The statement in the Preamble is seen as a general statement that applies not only to already existing ECL provisions but also leaves a freedom to establish new ones.

The implementation of the Copyright Directive has widened the scope of the ECL provisions in particular in two areas: digital copying in education and library uses. Legislation is now in place in all Nordic countries and many new agreements have been concluded.

6.2   DANISH NOVELTY[59]

Denmark made a reform of its ECL system in 2008. The foundation lies in the fact that the ECL system has been a success because of its facilitating role in areas in which it had been practically impossible to conclude fully covering licenses. Practice had shown that there were constantly new areas in which an ECL would be of assistance. On the other hand, the legislator needs to consider carefully every new ECL provision, and examine whether individual rights management would be an option.

The Danish Copyright Act contained sector-specific ECL provisions and general conditions to all of them (section 50). With a new provision (section 50(2)), a general possibility to conclude agreements with the extension effect was added to the law. Within the framework of this provision a user can negotiate with an organization representing a substantial number of right holders in the specific field, and if parties so decide, they can apply for the extension effect to the agreement that they have negotiated.

The added-value of this general provision lies in the following:

- it is flexible and can be applied in any field in which there is a need to clear rights for a large group of right holders;
- there is no need for a legislative change every time such a need arises;
- the general provision can function as a 'fill-in' mechanism in cases in which there already exists an ECL provision, but its limits are too restricted for the use in question.

---

58. See *supra* n. 2.
59. Based on an article by Martin Kyst, Kromann Reumert, in NIR (Nordiskt Immateriellt Rätts-kydd), vol. 1, 78 (2009) <www.nir.nu> (last visited: 7 Oct. 2009).

The general provision can also function in cases in which the problem of 'orphan works'[60] is dominant. Such orphan works are particularly common when older materials are used. Large digitization programmes of cultural heritage encounter with this challenge.

It is an essential premise that the general ECL provision is only applied in cases in which rights cannot be cleared by individual rights management.

Right holder organizations that wish to conclude agreements with the extension effect are subject to the approval of the Ministry of Culture. It is clearly stipulated in the law that outside right holders have a possibility to opt-out, that is, the veto right. The opting-out needs to take place personally and individually. In case in which an organization wishes to opt-out, it needs to be duly mandated by the right holders to do so. The possibility to opt-out ensures that the provision is in line with international treaties and EU Directives.

In October 2009, the Ministry of Culture has approved one agreement in the audiovisual sector. A number of further agreements are being submitted to the Ministry. Some of them deal with digitization programmes in which publishers' individual management is combined with authors' collective management with the support of an ECL.

6.3   ORPHAN WORKS

The problem of orphan works has been extensively discussed over the last couple of years. In particular in large digitization projects, cultural institutions may encounter works for which rights cannot be effectively cleared.

There are in principle two ways to settle the problem:

– license-based approach; and
– exception based approach.

The ECL falls within the license-based option. In this category, there are two options. In some countries, for instance in Canada,[61] a public authority can issue a non-exclusive, time-limited license to use an orphan work, after a user has conducted 'diligent search' in trying to find the right holder. The ECL provision in the Nordic countries settles the issue of orphan works in areas in which this provision is applicable. Mass digitization projects among others in libraries can benefit from collective agreements with an extension effect.

It is outside the scope of this article to elaborate on the pros and cons of various alternatives to settle the issue of orphan works. However, it is important to recognize that the ECL is a viable option that has already been tried out in the Nordic Countries.

---

60. Works of unidentified right holders or works whose right holders cannot be located.
61. The Canadian Copyright law includes a possibility for the Copyright Board to issue a license.

6.4   LIBRARY DIGITIZATION PROJECT IN NORWAY

Traditionally, libraries are used to base their activities on free use provisions. Usages have been limited to cases in which the law allows storage, archiving and conservation by traditional means of copying. Libraries have been keen, however, to develop new services to their customers. New digital copying instances and network usages will presuppose a license from the right holders. An ECL can facilitate rights clearance, if right holders and libraries negotiate new licensing agreements.

A landmark agreement was concluded in April 2009 in Norway. The Norwegian National Library started the web service <www.bokhylla.no> (in English 'Bookshelf'). Through the service, all Norwegian web users have access to 12,000 books under copyright. More books will be introduced in 2009–2010, and the project will continue until the end of 2011.

The service makes all Norwegian books from the 1690s, 1790s, 1890s and 1990s available on the Internet. All titles from the 1990s and some titles from the 1890s, together approximately 50,000 books, are under copyright. These books will not be prepared for print or download, but will be made available in full text to Norwegian IP-addresses. KOPINOR and the National Library of Norway are the contracting parties. The agreement[62] is in accordance with the ECL provision in the Norwegian Copyright Act.

6.5   BROADCASTERS' ARCHIVES AVAILABLE IN DENMARK

Not only libraries hold treasures of cultural heritage, but so do broadcasting organizations. In 2008, the agreement between the Danish Broadcasting Organization, DR,[63] and the Danish coalition Copydan Archive opened up a possibility to make major parts of archival material available on the net. Furthermore, a new agreement concluded in September 2009 enables the inclusion of old archival material into new niche channels that DR will launch in November 2009. This is a new area in which the applicability of an ECL provision opens the possibility to use archival material, to the benefit of viewers. Negotiations are pending also in Norway concerning the use of archival material (covered by paragraph 32), between NORWACO and the Norwegian Broadcasting Corporation.

6.6   RADIO AND TELEVISION CHANNELS GO MOBILE IN FINLAND

In October 2009, the Finnish collective management organizations KOPIOSTO and TEOSTO concluded an agreement with the company DNA[64] concerning

---

62. An English version of the agreement is available, <www.kopinor.org/nationallibrary> (last visited: 7 Oct. 2009).
63. Danmarks Radio, <www.dr.dk> (last visited: 7 Oct. 2009).
64. See <www.dna.fi> (last visited: 11 Nov. 2009).

mobile TV transmission in the DVB-H network. This groundbreaking agreement opens the possibility to follow Finnish broadcasting channels also in mobile TV. The new agreement is based on an ECL and shows its applicability in the new technological environment.

7   CONCLUDING REMARKS

The system of giving extension effect to collective agreements in certain areas is a typical Nordic way of finding copyright solutions to complex situations of mass use of protected works and other subject matter.

The system presupposes that there exists a well-developed network of organizations and that such organizations represent a substantial number of right holders in their field. It presupposes in other words that the 'copyright market' is well organized and disciplined. If such is the case, the system is likely to function very well and experience in the Nordic countries has proven that.

Finding a proper balance between the rights of right holders and the legitimate interests of users is a much debated topic these days. Everybody seems to share the common goal – finding a balance. Views may differ on how the balance can be achieved.

The task of a CMO is to facilitate the possibilities to use works in a legal manner. In the Nordic countries, the ECL plays an important role as it addresses the crucial issue of legal certainty for users. At the same time, it generates remuneration for right holders. It is thus a balancing factor in the trade.

Chapter 10

Collective Management in Commonwealth Jurisdictions: Comparing Canada with Australia

Mario Bouchard*

1   INTRODUCTION

The Canadian Copyright Act[1] (CCA) dates from 1921 and was largely based on the 1911 UK legislation. Yet, Canadian copyright policy is not as firmly rooted in British tradition as some[2] appear to think. Canada was the first Commonwealth jurisdiction to expressly recognize the moral rights of authors,[3] to regulate collective management of copyright otherwise than through generally applicable competition legislation[4] or to offer a comprehensive regulatory scheme for all

*   General Counsel, Copyright Board Canada. The views expressed in this paper are my own and may not reflect those of the Copyright Board or of the Government of Canada. My sincere thanks go to Franny Lee for her assistance in researching and writing the second edition of this paper. Tony Tesoriero, then Secretary to the Copyright Tribunal, helped me to keep my Australian facts straight in the first edition; Dennis Pearce and Chris Creswell helped me hone my understanding of the situation in 2010 for the second edition.
1.   R.S.C. 1985, c. C-42, as amended [CCA].
2.   Including the Supreme Court of Canada: see *Théberge v. Galerie d'Art du Petit Champlain Inc.* 2002 SCC 34, [2002] 2 S.C.R. 336.
3.   Within three years of moral rights being incorporated in the Berne Convention: Copyright Amendment Act, 1931, 22–23 George V, c.8, s. 5.
4.   *Ibid.*, s. 10.

Daniel Gervais (ed.), *Collective Management of Copyright and Related Rights*, pp. 307–337.
© 2010 Kluwer Law International BV, The Netherlands.

dealings between collective management organizations (CMOs) and users of their repertoires.[5] Collective management in Canada is both prevalent and varied. This is due in part to the power of the Copyright Board of Canada to regulate the relationships of all CMOs with their users and to the manner in which the Board has chosen to exercise that power.

Until the 1980s, Australian copyright legislation closely tracked developments in the United Kingdom. In 1912, Australia adopted en bloc the UK Copyright Act of 1911. The current Australian statute[6] originally reflected the underlying principles of the British legislation of 1956. Until the 1970s, the ACA left Australian CMOs unregulated. Until 2006, there existed no comprehensive regulatory scheme for dealings between CMOs and copyright users. Furthermore, when the Australian Copyright Tribunal had the power to intervene, the extent to which it could do so appeared more limited than for its Canadian counterpart. Recent amendments[7] would appear to have reversed the situation and to endow the Tribunal with much more comprehensive powers. However, opinions in this respect remain mixed; the president of the Tribunal at the time when the Amending Act came into effect 'would not describe the amendments as fundamental'.[8] It seems too soon to really assess the impact of these recent changes.

Having compared the situation in both jurisdictions, this writer is left with a somewhat counter-intuitive impression. In Canada, the presence of a specialized authority able to supervise all dealings between CMOs and copyright users has helped collective management to expand and to gain legitimacy. In Australia, by contrast, the absence of such an authority (at least until 2006) might help to explain the fragmentation of supervision, stifled growth and continued mistrust that seem characteristic of collective management in that country. Outlining some of the similarities and differences between the two jurisdictions might sufficiently whet the interest of scholars in pursuing the matter.

2   A BRIEF HISTORY OF COLLECTIVE MANAGEMENT IN CANADA AND AUSTRALIA

The British Performing Rights Society (PRS) set up the Canadian Performing Rights Society (CPRS) in 1925. Starting in 1931, the CCA was amended to require that the CPRS file its statements of royalties; Cabinet could modify the statements following an investigation and report by a commissioner of inquiry.[9] In 1936,

---

5. Through the introduction of ss 70.1 and ff., CCA, *supra* n. 1, in 1988.
6. Copyright Act 1968 (Cth), Act No. 63 of 1968 [ACA].
7. Copyright Amendment Act 2006 (Cth), Act No. 158 of 2006. (Amending Act)
8. Justice Kevin Lindgren, 'The Jurisdiction of the Copyright Tribunal of Australia: the 2006 Amendments' (2007), <www.fedcourt.gov.au/aboutct/judges_papers/speeches_lindgrenj2.html> (last visited: 10 Feb. 2010), at 21.
9. Copyright Amendment Act, 1931, *supra* n. 3, s. 10.

following a recommendation of a Commission,[10] the CCA was further amended so that performing rights tariffs would have to be certified by a new administrative agency, the Copyright Appeal Board, before coming into force.[11] The Board issued its first decision within six months. In 1940, BMI Canada emerged as a result of the battles that were then being waged over the use of music on American commercial radio.[12] The evolution of collective management over the next fifty years could be described as slow, quiet and not always successful. In 1971, as soon as record manufacturers secured from the Board a tariff for the public performance of 'mechanical contrivances', the underlying right was abolished.[13] In 1975, the Canadian Musical Reproduction Rights Agency (CMRRA) started acting as an agent for the mechanical licensing of musical works. A few French CMOs installed beachheads in the province of Québec; their presence played a small but significant role in the evolution of collective management in Canada. The *Union des écrivains et écrivaines du Québec* (UNEQ) began administering reprographic rights in 1982 and signed its first license with the Québec Ministry of Education in 1984. That same year, the Video Music Licensing Agency started issuing licenses for the reproduction and exhibition of music videos; in 1989, the names changed to AVLA Audio-Video Licensing Agency Inc. (AVLA) to reflect the fact that the collective could now issue licences for the reproduction of mechanical contrivances by commercial users. In 1985, The *Société du droit de reproduction des auteurs, compositeurs et éditeurs au Canada* (SODRAC) started to administer the reproduction right in musical works. In 1988, CanCopy began managing reprographic rights outside Québec. Uncertainty surrounding the status of CMOs under competition law explained in part the somewhat timid growth of collective management, as did the release of reports that were in part critical of CMOs in other Commonwealth jurisdictions.[14]

The year 1989 represented something of a watershed for Canadian CMOs. The CCA was amended in two important respects. First, the Copyright Appeal Board was replaced by the Copyright Board. The Board was empowered to supervise dealings between collectives and individual users or groups of users in areas others than music performing rights; collective management was legitimized and its relationship with competition law was somewhat clarified. Second, the use of protected works in retransmitted distant radio and television signals was subjected to a compulsory licensing scheme according to which right holders could seek remuneration only through a CMO; for the first time, collective management became the only legally available course of action.[15]

---

10. 'Report of the Parker Commission' (1935).
11. An Act to Amend the Copyright Act, 1931, (1936) 1 Edw. VIII c. 28 s. 2. The Canadian Board predates the British Performing Rights Tribunal by some twenty-one years.
12. See L. Allen, 'The Battle of Tin Pan Alley', *Harper's Magazine*, October 1940.
13. An Act to Amend the Copyright Act, 1970–71–72 S.C., c. 60.
14. See, for example, 'Merger and Monopolies Commission, Collective Licensing: A report on certain practices in the Collective Licensing of Public Performance and Broadcasting Rights in Sound Recordings' (Dec. 1988), Cm 530.
15. Composers have never been legally required to join a collective society.

In 1997, as a result of other amendments to the CCA, collective management received further recognition. The basic framework created in 1989 was expanded. Under the general regime, CMOs were no longer limited to dealing with users on a case-by-case basis; they could secure tariffs that would apply to all current and future users. Even more significantly, Parliament used collective management as the tool of choice in dealing with areas in which access had to be guaranteed in exchange for a form of compensation, including music neighbouring rights,[16] educational uses of television programmes,[17] private copying[18] and some forms of ephemeral recordings and transfer of format.[19] These developments led to a further increase in the number of collectives, and to a significant expansion of the role the Copyright Board was asked to play in regulating the relationship between collectives and users.[20]

The evolution of Australian CMOs followed a somewhat different path. The Australian Performing Right Association (APRA), was created in 1926, again by the British PRS. In 1933, a commission of inquiry recommended the creation of a copyright tribunal;[21] that recommendation was not followed because of fear that the compulsory arbitration of disputes might not be consistent with the Berne Convention. CMOs were essentially left to their own devices until the late 1970s. In 1968, following a comprehensive review of copyright legislation[22] which led to the adoption of the ACA, the Copyright Tribunal was established, largely in response to the perceived need to control CMOs that administered rights in the public performance or broadcast of musical works or sound recordings.[23] The Tribunal issued an advisory report in 1979; its first decision was issued in 1981. Growth in collective management apparently was driven to a large extent by the imposition of a significant number of statutory licenses,[24] some of which require that only 'declared' societies be active in the relevant market. Amendments to the ACA starting in the 1980s resulted in a progressive expansion of the jurisdiction of the Copyright Tribunal; still, that jurisdiction, though extensive, was not

---

16. CCA, *supra* n. 1, s. 19(2)(*a*).
17. CCA, *ibid.*, ss 71–76.
18. CCA, *ibid.*, ss 79–88.
19. CCA, *ibid.*, ss 30.8(8), 30.9(6); pursuant to these provisions, exceptions that allow broadcasters to make ephemeral and transfer of format copies do not apply if a CMO offers a license for the use of the relevant work, performance or sound recording.
20. See C. Craig Parks, 'Copyright Management in the Canadian Music Industry' ['Music Industry Report'], *Department of Canadian Heritage* (January 2008), <www.pch.gc.ca/pc-ch/org/sectr/ac-ca/pda-cpb/publctn/2008/080317-eng.pdf> (last visited: 10 Feb. 2010).
21. Hon. Mr Justice Owen, 'Report of the Royal Commission on Performing Rights' (1933), [Owen Report].
22. 'Report of the Committee Appointed by the Attorney-General of the Commonwealth to Consider What Alterations are Desirable in the Copyright Law of the Commonwealth' (1959), [Spicer Committee Report].
23. Copyright Law Review Committee, 'Jurisdiction and Procedures of the Copyright Tribunal Final Report' (2000), para. 1.05, [CLRC Jurisdiction Report (2000)].
24. Lahore puts their number at fifteen: see J. Lahore, *Copyright and Designs*, 3rd edn (Sydney: Butterworths, 1996), para. 28,005.

comprehensive. Throughout that time, collective management of copyright attracted considerable attention on the part of government[25] and competition authorities.[26]

3   CANADIAN CMOs: MARKETS, STRUCTURES, PRACTICES

This part provides an overview of the areas in which Canadian CMOs are currently active and of their various organizational and other characteristics. Some comparisons with the Australian situation are offered.

3.1   SPHERES OF ACTIVITY

It is difficult to present Canadian CMOs in a fashion that is both systematic and useful. The manner in which right holders arrange their affairs is, to a large extent, left unregulated. More than one CMO may be active in a given market; conversely, a collective may be active in more than one market. For the purposes of this paper, it is probably most useful to present Canadian collectives according to the types of rights they administer.[27]

3.1.1   Music

Collective management of musical rights offers a vivid illustration of how diverse the organization of CMOs can be in Canada. Collective management is divided not only according to rights (performance/communication, reproduction) or subject-matter (work, performance, sound recording), but also to a right holder's craft (musician, singer, backup artist) and linguistic background.

---

25. Owen Report (1933), *supra* n. 21; Spicer Committee Report, *supra* n. 22; Australian Government Publishing Service, 'Report of the Copyright Law Committee on Reprographic Reproduction' (1976), Canberra (Franki Report); Report of the Copyright Convergence Group, 'Highways to Change : Copyright in the New Communications Environment' (1994), Canberra; S. Simpson, 'Review of Australian Copyright Collecting Societies, a Report to the Minister for Communications and the Arts and the Minister for Justice' (1995) [Simpson Report (1995)]; Standing Committee on Legal and Constitutional Affairs, 'Don't stop the music! A report of the inquiry into copyright, music and small business' (1998) (Don't Stop the Music); CLRC Jurisdiction Report (2000), *supra* n. 23; Final report by the Intellectual Property and Competition Review Committee, 'Review of Intellectual Property Legislation under the Competition Principles Agreement' (2000), (Ergas Report).

26. *Re Applications by Australasian Performing Rights Association* (1999), 45 I.P.R. 53. *[Re Applications']*

27. An expanded description of the collectives can be found on the website of the Canadian Copyright Board. See also D. Gervais, 'Collective Management of Copyright and Neighbouring Rights in Canada: an International Perspective', *Canadian Journal of Law and Technology* 1 (2002): 21, at 42, <http://cjlt.dal.ca/vol1_no2/pdfarticles/gervais.pdf> (last visited: 10 Feb. 2010).

The Society of Composer, Authors and Music Publishers of Canada (SOCAN) administers the right to perform or to communicate musical works. Created in 1990 by the merger of its two predecessors, its origins date back to 1925. SOCAN has some 80,000 members, of which about one-third receive royalties every year. As with most performing rights collectives, its network of foreign affiliations is extensive. SOCAN can collect royalties only pursuant to a tariff certified by the Copyright Board.[28] In 2008, it collected Canadian Dollar (CAD) 255.7 million and distributed CAD 198.2 million.

On April 1, 2010, the Neighbouring Rights Collective of Canada became Re:Sound. It is the only CMO currently authorized to collect royalties for the equitable remuneration of performers and makers for the performance or communication of sound recordings of musical works. Created in 1997, Re:Sound is an umbrella organization; it has no individual members, but five member collectives. The American Federation of Musicians (AFM) and the Alliance of Canadian Cinema, Television and Radio Artists (ACTRA) Performers' Rights Society (ACTRA PRS) receive royalties for the benefit of most performers, while Artisti manages the rights of some 1,600 performers (mostly singers) from the province of Québec. The makers' share of royalties is paid to Québec Sound and Video Collective Society for the Rights of Makers of Sound and Video Recordings (SOPROQ) and AVLA, which are described later. Re:Sound can collect royalties only pursuant to a tariff certified by the Copyright Board. In 2008, Re:Sound collected some CAD 19.8 million and distributed CAD 14.4 million. Another society, the *Société de Gestion des droits des Artistes-Musiciens* (SOGEDAM), formerly acted for a small number of Canadian musicians as well as for at least one foreign collective. Partly as a result of a decision of the Copyright Board that deprived it of any direct source of income, it became largely inactive in late 1999 and has since wound up.

Two collectives administer the right to reproduce musical works, including the so-called mechanical and synchronization licenses.[29] CMRRA acts both as a centralized licensing and a collecting agency, for Canadian and American publishers who control approximately 75% of the music recorded and performed in Canada. With some exceptions,[30] licensing is done on a per-use basis. SODRAC was created by the French *Société des auteurs, compositeurs et éditeurs de musique* (SACEM) and by *La Société professionnelle des auteurs et des compositeurs du Québec* (SPACQ), an association acting for some successful French-Canadian authors. It represents some 6,000 members, mostly from the province of Québec; it also acts in Canada for sixty or so foreign societies. SODRAC offers per-use and blanket licenses; it also administers some tariffs certified by the Copyright Board. In 2008, SODRAC collected some CAD 15.5M and distributed CAD 11.6 million.

---

28. This is true in law but incorrect in practice: see, *infra* n. 82.
29. Christian Copyright Licensing Inc., an American corporation, licenses the reproduction of some religious music.
30. Such as the reproduction of musical works by radio stations, online music services and satellite radio, for which CMRRA, jointly with SODRAC, asked for tariffs.

Two collectives administer rights in sound recordings and music videos. SOPROQ represents mostly Francophone independent record labels, artists and producers from Canada and abroad. AVLA acts for the major record companies and for many independent labels, artists and producers. Together, these CMOs can license more than 90% of all musical audio recordings and music videos produced and/or distributed in Canada. Both collectives administer the copyright in master audio and music video recordings. Both license the exhibition and reproduction of music videos and the reproduction of audio recordings for commercial use. Both receive a part of the makers' share of neighbouring rights royalties and private copying levies. They recently filed with the Copyright Board a joint proposed tariff for the reproduction of published sound recordings of musical works by radio stations.

In 2006, twenty Canadian-owned independent sound recording labels, in partnership with the Canadian Independent Record Production Association, received funding from the Ontario provincial government to create the Independent Digital Licensing Agency (IDLA), whose purpose was to offer a comprehensive 'one-stop source' for collective licensing and delivery of Canadian independent music content to new and emerging digital music services in Canada and worldwide.[31] IDLA reports that its current membership now includes more than thirty Canadian independent labels,[32] to which it provides services such as digital asset delivery to digital music services, royalty collection and administration, copyright enforcement and collective licensing of neighbouring rights and private copying royalties for independent Canadian labels and artists.[33]

Artisti, AFM and Actra PRS administer some exclusive rights that the CCA grants to performers over the reproduction of their performances. They have filed proposed tariffs for reproductions made by commercial radio stations.

3.1.2 Reprography

There are two reprographic rights organizations in Canada. Access Copyright (formerly CanCopy) was created in 1988. It represents some 8,000 writers, publishers and other creators. It licenses uses in all provinces except Québec. Until recently Access Copyright negotiated only comprehensive licenses with user groups, such as schools, colleges, universities, governments and corporations. It has now obtained its first tariff from the Copyright Board, targeting so-called K to 12 schools.[34] In 2008, it collected CAD 36.8 million and distributed CAD 30.1 million. The *Société québécoise de gestion collective des droits de*

---

31. See Entertainment and Creative Clusters Partnerships Fund Recipient Information, Ontario Media Development Corporation, <www.omdc.on.ca/Page5409.aspx> (last visited: 10 Feb. 2010).
32. Copyright Consultations, Submissions regarding copyright (5 Oct. 2009), Geoff Kulawick (IDLA), <www.ic.gc.ca/eic/site/008.nsf/eng/02250.html> (last visited: 10 Feb. 2010).
33. *Ibid.;* see also <www.idla.ca> (last visited: 10 Feb. 2010).
34. *Access Copyright Elementary and Secondary School Tariff, 2005–2009*, <www.cb-cda.gc.ca/tariffs-tarifs/certified-homologues/2009/20090626-b.pdf> (last visited: 10 Feb. 2010).

reproduction (COPIBEC) (replacing UNEQ), administers the reproduction right in literary works, including books, magazines, newspapers and digital reproduction. It represents more than 18,000 Québec authors and publishers as well as foreign right holders through reciprocal agreements. In 2008–2009, it collected CAD 13.5 million and distributed CAD 12 million. Access Copyright and COPIBEC act for each other in their respective territory.

3.1.3　　　Retransmission of Distant Radio and Television Signals

Nine CMOs act for a variety of right holders in retransmitted radio and television programmes. Each gets a share of the royalties set out in a single tariff certified by the Board.[35] Collectives act for broadcasters (Border Broadcasters' Inc., Canadian Broadcasters Rights Agency (CBRA), Canadian Retransmission Right Association (CRRA), Canadian Retransmission Collective (CRC)), American and other film and programme producers (Copyright Collective of Canada, CRC), infomercial producers (Direct Response Television Collective), sports leagues (FWS Joint Sports Claimants, Major League Baseball Collective of Canada) and music composers (SOCAN). Each CMO receives a percentage of television royalties; only CBRA, CRRA and SOCAN share in the radio royalties. Total royalties collected in 2008 were approximately CAD 90 million. Television retransmission royalties have grown over the past few years as a result of factors such as the increase in the tariff rate per subscriber and organic growth within broadcasting distribution undertakings. Because most of these CMOs do not publish financial results, it is impossible to determine how much of the collected amounts were distributed to right holders.

3.1.4　　　Private Copying

The Canadian Private Copying Collective (CPCC) was created in 1999. An umbrella collective, it collects the private copying levy pursuant to a tariff certified by the Copyright Board, for the benefit of other collectives, who in turn, have secured the right to represent eligible authors, performers and makers of sound recordings of musical works: CMRRA, SODRAC, SOCAN and Re:Sound. In 2008, CPCC collected approximately CAD 29.3 million, of which CAD 27.6 million was available for distribution. Collections are expected to diminish rapidly as the market share of recordable CDs dwindles.

3.1.5　　　Audiovisual and Multimedia

The website of the Board lists seven entities as CMOs dealing in audiovisual and multimedia rights. The Directors Rights Collective of Canada (DRCC) acts for

---

35. See 'Retransmission of Distant Television and Radio Signals 2004–2008' (13 Dec. 2008), <www.cb-cda.gc.ca/tariffs-tarifs/certified-homologues/2008/20081213-s-b.pdf> (last visited: 10 Feb. 2010).

film and television directors. The Producers Audiovisual Collective of Canada (PACC) collects 'secondary rights' royalties on behalf of Canadian right holders in audiovisual works, including the sale of blank audiovisual media, the rental and lending of video recordings, exhibition or public performance, educational copying and performance. Royalties are mostly from foreign sources. The *Société civile des auteurs multimédia*, a French collective with offices in Canada, administers two types of rights for screenwriters and filmmakers of documentary works: communication to the public by telecommunication and reproduction. The Canadian Screenwriters Collection Society (CSCS) acts for film and television writers. The other entities mentioned on the website of the Board are non-theatrical film distributors. For example, Christian Video Licensing International is an independent copyright licensing organization that offers a public performance license for the exhibition of motion pictures and other licensed programmes.

3.1.6 Off-Air Programme Taping

Two collectives license off-air taping of television and radio programmes. The Educational Rights Collective of Canada (ERCC), established in 1998, collects royalties pursuant to a tariff that is set by the Copyright Board for the off-air taping and public performance of television and radio programmes by educational institutions.[36] CBRA licenses the use of programmes owned by Canadian private television and radio broadcasters by media monitoring firms and by government entities that operate in-house monitoring services, pursuant to a combination of individual licenses and a tariff set by the Copyright Board. The amounts collected pursuant to that tariff are unknown.

3.1.7 Collective Management in Other Areas

A variety of other CMOs play a role in distributing royalties collected in Canada or elsewhere. CSCS collects secondary use levies for private copying of audiovisual works, videocassette rental and cable retransmission of broadcast signals payable to film and television writers under Canadian and foreign copyright legislation.[37] The Playwrights Guild of Canada (formerly Playwrights Union of Canada), a service organization for professional playwrights, also acts as agent for the distribution of amateur rights and collection of royalties. *Société des auteurs et compositeurs dramatiques*, a French collective with offices in Canada, represents Canadian and foreign authors, composers and choreographers of dramatic and audiovisual works. *Société québécoise des auteurs dramatiques* (SoQAD) redistributes to playwrights whose works are performed in pre-school, primary and

---

36. It would appear that ERCC's collections are very low. Educational institutions apparently prefer to deal with specialized distributors, who supply pre-recorded videocassettes along with the right to perform the underlying work in the classroom, rather than to make use of the tariff set by the Board.
37. CSCS receives domestic retransmission royalties through CRC, CBRA and CRRA.

secondary schools, royalties (approximately CAD 100 per performance and CAD 90,000 in total) agreed to with the Ministry of Education of the Province of Québec.

Currently, two collectives deal in visual arts. The *Société des droits d'auteur en arts visuels* closed its doors in 2008, leaving the administration of visual arts copyrights to the Canadian Artists' Representation Copyright Collective (CARCC) and SODRAC. CARCC was established in 1990, and negotiates terms for copyright use and licenses users of works of visual and media artists. SODRAC's Visual Arts and Crafts Department grants licenses for the public exhibition, communication to the public by telecommunication and reproduction of foreign and Canadian works on any media, including audiovisual and multimedia.

3.2   CHARACTERISTICS AND PRACTICES OF CANADIAN CMOs

In Canada, a CMO is a 'collective society', a term defined since 1997 as:

> a society, association or corporation that carries on the business of collective administration of copyright or of the remuneration right conferred by section 19 [neighbouring rights] or 81 [private copying] for the benefit of those who, by assignment, grant of licence, appointment of it as their agent or otherwise, authorize it to act on their behalf in relation to that collective administration, and
>
> (a) operates a licensing scheme, applicable in relation to a repertoire of works, performer's performances, sound recordings or communication signals of more than one author, performer, sound recording maker or broadcaster, pursuant to which the society, association or corporation sets out classes of uses that it agrees to authorize under this Act, and the royalties and terms and conditions on which it agrees to authorize those classes of uses, or
>
> (b) carries on the business of collecting and distributing royalties or levies payable pursuant to this Act;[38]

That definition is very broad. There are no conditions regarding the corporate structure of a CMO, the manner in which it secures the repertoire it administers or the nature of its relationship with right holders or users. Not surprisingly, then, practices vary considerably, and interactions between CMOs are sometimes complex.

3.2.1   Corporate Structure and Business Practices

Most CMOs are not-for-profit corporations. Some (e.g., SoQAD) are for-profit corporations. The corporate structure of a CMO can change over time; SODRAC, originally a for-profit corporation whose shares were held by SACEM and SPACQ,

---

38. CCA, *supra* n. 1, s. 2.

has been moving to a not-for-profit, membership-based corporate structure since 2004.

Voting structures also vary according to the corporate model adopted. Most collectives operate according to a multiple vote system based on a member's revenues in the previous years, up to a maximum number of votes. SODRAC's founding members, SPACQ and SACEM, each retain the power to appoint one of the eleven members of the Board, even though that CMO has opted for a membership-based corporate structure.

Membership also varies considerably. SOCAN follows the traditional *société de droit d'auteur* model – its members are right holders (authors and publishers), as now are SODRAC's. Members of COPIBEC and Access Copyright are organizations representing publishers and creators; right holders are affiliates and have no voting rights. CMRRA acts only for music publishers. Umbrella collectives (Re:Sound, CPCC) have other collectives as members, and no direct contacts with individual right holders. Finally, some CMOs (e.g., performers' collectives) limit membership to creators or their assignees.

3.2.2   Nature and Extent of the Repertoire

A CMO can secure its repertoire 'by assignment, grant of license, appointment . . . as . . . agent or otherwise'. All of these approaches are used. SOCAN secures exclusive assignments for its members' public performance and communication rights and staunchly opposes any form of 'back licensing'. COPIBEC secures exclusive licenses for reprography and non-exclusive licenses for digital reproduction. SODRAC, which used to secure exclusive assignments, now allows authors to retain rights for certain territories and for the Canadian advertising and feature film markets. AVLA administers its repertoire on a non-exclusive basis. CMRRA acts as an agent in the synchronization rights market, licenses directly some Internet uses and secures exclusive assignments of the right to authorize radio broadcasters, satellite radio services and online music services to reproduce musical works.[39] Access Copyright' mandate is exclusive for reprographic uses and non-exclusive for digital uses.

The nature of the rights secured by related CMOs in the same market also varies. SODRAC administers all aspects of the non-paper reproduction of musical works, whereas CMRRA administers only certain aspects of it. Increasingly, collectives manage, directly or through an umbrella collective, a variety of rights, usually (but not always) in the same copyright subject matter. AVLA and SOPROQ both receive from umbrella collectives a part of the makers' share of neighbouring rights royalties and private copying levies. SODRAC's repertoire includes artistic as well as musical works. SOCAN not only administers the public performance and telecommunication rights, but also receives for the benefit of some of its members a share of the private copying levy.

---

39.   This was done in order to facilitate the certification of a tariff by the Copyright Board.

The extent to which CMOs represent the available repertoire varies considerably. Only SOCAN and Re:Sound can claim to represent anything close to the world's eligible repertoire.[40] CMRRA and SODRAC together also probably can make such a claim, at least with respect to the reproduction of musical works by radio stations. AVLA and SOPROQ should be in the same situation in regard to certain forms of exploitation of music videos and sound recordings. As for ERCC, the retransmission collectives and CPCC, they collect royalties for all of the eligible repertoires as designed for under their respective regimes.

3.2.3 Pricing Practices, Administrative Expenses and Royalty Distributions

The public availability of terms and conditions of licenses varies considerably. A tariff certified by the Copyright Board is public. For most CMOs, the essential terms of licensing schemes and industry-wide agreements usually are available over the Internet. Some users are able to negotiate terms that are either better adapted to their business models or, because of their bargaining power, more favourable than for smaller users. The results of these negotiations rarely become public unless they are filed with the Board, either pursuant to the general regime[41] or in the context of tariff proceedings. Some grids and scales are not readily available, unless requested. Individual licensing agreements often are kept confidential.

Information concerning revenues and expenses is altogether a different matter. SODRAC, SOCAN, Access Copyright and COPIBEC willingly disclose them. CMRRA and AVLA do not divulge their revenues, but do publicize their administrative fee structure. In its annual report, SOPROQ provides no financial information whatsoever. By contrast, although it is easy to infer how much royalties each retransmission collective receives, it is impossible to determine the expenses of those that are privately held.

CMOs account for their expenses in a variety of ways. SOCAN, Access Copyright, CPCC, Re:Sound and SODRAC pay their expenses before allocating royalties for distribution. CMRRA, COPIBEC and AVLA generally charge a straight commission, something that is truly possible only when individual transactions are tracked.[42] Expense-to-revenue ratios vary considerably, from as low as 5% to 20% or even more. Although lower overhead costs can often be explained by the phenomenon of economies of scale, some smaller collectives manage to

---

40. Still, NRCC's repertoire is considerably smaller than that of SOCAN given that the right of remuneration for sound recording performances does not extend to nationals of countries that do not recognize this right (such as the US): see C. Craig Parks, 'A Report of the Copyright Collectives Operating in Canada' [Collectives Report], *Department of Canadian Heritage* (October 2006) at 11, <http://dsp-psd.pwgsc.gc.ca/collection_2007/ch-pc/CH44-125-2007E.pdf> (last visited: 10 Feb. 2010).
41. See Part 4.B, *infra*.
42. Thus, what CMRRA's practice may be with respect to royalties collected pursuant to a tariff of the Copyright Board remains to be determined.

operate at the low end of the spectrum whereas larger ones might operate toward the higher end. Overhead costs are at least as much a function of the kind of right being administered, licensee diversity and sophistication and the size of the collective's repertoire, as it is a function of administrative efficiency. How meaningful reported ratios are also varies – some CMOs compare gross expenses to gross revenues, but SOCAN uses its 'net administrative expenses' (gross expenses offset by investment and rental income), which reduces the declared expense-to-revenue ratio.

CMOs are not required to use any particular methodology when distributing royalties. Distribution can be based on census (music performing rights on television), surveys (music performing rights on radio), be work-by-work (mechanical rights) or rely on a combination methodologies (radio play and CD sales in the case of private copying). The manner in which monies are allocated when more than one person is entitled to share in the distribution also is left to individual CMOs. At SOCAN, the publisher's share cannot exceed 50% unless an executed agreement or a court order directs otherwise. SODRAC apportions royalties according to the shares agreed upon by the author and the publisher. A non-member publisher can license the publisher's share of a work that is in SODRAC's repertoire; if the publisher is a member, only SODRAC can issue a license. Since 2009, SODRAC's publisher members can issue synchronization licenses under certain circumstances. Re:Sound divides its distributions into two equal parts (representing the performers' and makers' shares), whose individual proportions are determined according to sound recording use information such as frequency of artist or song play, weighting by audience size and eligibility of the recording for remuneration.[43] Access Copyright distributes royalties according to a set grid that gives publishers any amount from 0% to 100% of the royalties. As for CMRRA, because it acts only for music publishers, it pays nothing directly to creators.

The speed at which each CMO distributes royalties to its right holders varies. Some collectives, such as CMRRA, have initiated electronic licensing and are encouraging users to adopt a common licensing protocol for electronic licensing. Such measures may help to diminish 'distribution lag', because the delay between usage and payment should decrease given lower human intervention requirements.[44]

3.2.4 Interaction between CMOs

Canadian CMOs often form strategic alliances. Sometimes, these are dictated by the structure of the regulatory regimes – this explains in part the creation of CPCC and Re:Sound as umbrella collectives.[45] Others respond to the structure of the market. It is considerably easier for CMRRA and SODRAC to jointly seek a tariff

---

43. Music Industry Report, *supra* n. 20, at 11.
44. Collectives Report, *supra* n. 40, at 16 and 26.
45. The neighbouring rights regime, under which NRCC operates, requires a single payment for the use of a given sound recording: CCA, *supra* n. 1, s. 68(2)(a)(iii). The private copying regime,

for commercial radio stations because the use of their respective repertoires varies considerably between French- and English-speaking stations. This resulted in the creation of CMRRA/SODRAC Inc. (CSI), which has since obtained tariffs for the reproduction of musical works by commercial radio stations, satellite radio services and online music services. It is also easier for Access Copyright and COPIBEC to act for each other in their respective 'home territories'. Other alliances probably are perceived by the relevant CMOs as shotgun weddings, because the Copyright Board imposes them by certifying a single tariff for two or more collectives.[46]

Alliances between CMOs can be used to prevent the Copyright Board from dealing with an issue. When two performing rights societies merged to form SOCAN, the need to allocate royalties among them disappeared. By filing a single tariff that applies to commercial radio stations, irrespective of their relative use of their respective repertoires, CMRRA and SODRAC are free to apportion between them as they see fit the royalties collected pursuant to the tariff certified by the Board. By creating CPCC, CMRRA, SODRAC and SOCAN removed from the Board the determination of their individual share of music creators' remuneration for private copying.

Right holders also can bring to the table divergent points of view, either through the relevant CMOs or the associated industry associations. Record producers opposed a request by CMRRA and SODRAC for a tariff that applies to the licensing of online music services on a number of legal and business grounds. The variety of Canadian retransmission collectives is explained in part by the fact that some right holders wished to convince the Board to attribute a higher value for the viewing of certain programmes than to others.[47] One CMO, representing script writers, even filed a proposed tariff with the intention of having the Board determine the share of a television program's royalties that should be paid to the program's scriptwriter.[48]

---

under which CPCC operates, requires that a single body be designated to collect the levy: CCA, *ibid.*, s. 83(8)(d).

46. 'Statement of Royalties to be Collected by SOCAN and NRCC in Respect of Commercial Radio (Tariff 1.A – 2003–2007)' (23 Feb. 2008), Supplement Canada Gazette, Part I, online: <www.cb-cda.gc.ca/tariffs-tarifs/certified-homologues/2008/20080223-m-b.pdf> (last visited: 10 Feb. 2010); 'Statement of Royalties to be Collected by SOCAN and NRCC in Respect of Pay Audio Services (2003–2006)' (26 Feb. 2005), Supplement Canada Gazette, Part I, <www.cb-cda.gc.ca/tariffs-tarifs/certified-homologues/2005/20050226-m-b.pdf> (last visited: 10 Feb. 2010); 'Statement of Royalties to Be Collected by SOCAN, NRCC and CSI in Respect of Multi-Channel Subscription Satellite Radio Services' (11 Apr. 2009), Supplement Canada Gazette, Part I, <www.cb-cda.gc.ca/tariffs-tarifs/certified-homologues/2009/20090411-m-b. pdf> (last visited: 10 Feb. 2010).

47. These attempts have thus far been unsuccessful: *FWS Joint Sports Claimants Inc. v. Border Broadcasters Inc.* (2001), 16 C.P.R. (4th) 61 (F.C.A.) *[FWS (2001)]*.

48. See 'Statement of Proposed Royalties to be Collected by CSCS for the Retransmission of Distant Television Signals, in Canada, in 2002 and 2003' (14 Apr. 2001), Supplement Canada Gazette, Part I, <www.cb-cda.gc.ca/tariffs-tarifs/proposed-proposes/2001/20010708-s-b.pdf> (last visited: 10 Feb. 2010); the issue was eventually settled between the association representing script writers and the CMO of which they previously had been members.

3.3   CANADIAN AND AUSTRALIAN CMOS: SOME COMPARISONS

There are eight main Australian CMOs. APRA administers performing and broad-casting rights in musical works. The Australasian Mechanical Copyright Owners' Society (AMCOS), whose day-to-day operations APRA now manages, deals in mechanical rights in musical works. The Phonographic Performance Company of Australia (PPCA) licenses performing and broadcasting rights in sound recordings and music videos.[49] APRA and PPCA operate in similar ways, having *de facto* monopolies in their repertoires and offering non-exclusive licences. However, APRA owns the rights it administers; PPCA does not. Copyright Agency Ltd (CAL) is the declared collective for the copying and communication of print material by educational institutions, by those assisting persons with certain dis-abilities and by government agencies; it also issues voluntary licenses for other forms of copying and communication of literary and artistic works. The Audio-visual Copyright Society (Screenrights) is the declared CMO for the educational taping and communication of television and radio broadcasts, the use of works in assisting persons with certain disabilities, government copying of radio and tele-vision programmes and retransmission of free-to-air broadcasts. The Visual Arts Copyright Collecting Agency (Vi$copy) acts for visual artists. The Australian Screen Directors Authorship Collecting Society (ASDACS) acts for film and tele-vision directors and the Australian Writers Guild Authorship Collecting Society (AWGACS) for screenwriters, mostly in respect to royalties payable under foreign legislation.

For the most recent year available, revenue and distribution data for Australian CMOs are as follows: APRA and its controlled subsidiary entities collected Aus-tralian Dollar (AUD) 156 million and distributed AUD 140 million; AMCOS and its controlled subsidiary entities collected AUD 49 million and distributed AUD 42 million; PPCA collected AUD 20 million and distributed AUD 14.5 million; CAL collected AUD 114 million from licensing fees, 86.3% of which was avail-able for distribution; Screenrights collected AUD 34 million and distributed AUD 25.6 million; Vi$copy collected AUD 2.43 million and distributed AUD 1.55 million; AWGACS collected AUD 925,818 and distributed AUD 776,851. ASDACS is the other Australian CMO with an income that has yet to reach $1M.

As can be expected, Canadian and Australian CMOs are at the same time similar and different. Some distinctions are a function of cultural factors. Others flow from differences in the legislative approach to the regulation of collectives in each jurisdiction.

Each Australian collective has one (or more) Canadian counterpart. Virtually none competes with another CMO in the Australian market (there may be a slight overlap between CAL and Vi$copy in the area of licensing the reproduction of artistic works). Canada often knows at least two language-based collectives; eight

---

49.   ACA, *supra* n. 6, ss 108 and 109.

collectives currently receive a share of retransmission royalties. Consequently, the number of CMOs is much higher in Canada than in Australia.[50]

Contrary to their Canadian counterparts, all Australian CMOs operate under similar (and significant) organizational or structural constraints. Declared CMOs are subject to statutory[51] and regulatory[52] requirements concerning corporate structure, membership and distribution of funds to members and non-members. In 2002, following a recommendation to that effect[53] and after APRA was the subject of a fairly detailed examination of its business practices by the Australian Competition Tribunal,[54] all CMOs subscribed to a voluntary code of conduct.[55] The code addresses issues such as membership, dealings with licensees, distribution of royalties, administrative expenses and dispute resolution; in it, voluntary collectives agree to comply with the Attorney General's Guidelines for Declared Collecting Societies.[56] As a result, the corporate structure and business practices of Australian CMOs are much more similar than those of their Canadian counterparts. All Australian collectives are not-for-profit corporations. All have right holders as members. None are as secretive with respect to their revenues, expense or licensing terms than some of their Canadian counterparts: for example, the annual reports of every Australian CMO are available on the Internet. Finally, all of them provide mechanisms for the resolution of disputes with users, something that does not appear to exist in Canada.[57]

Larger Australian CMOs tend to be de facto monopolies more than Canadian collectives, again partly because, in Canada, there tends to be one collective operating in each official language. Two Australian CMOs – CAL and Screenrights – also are de jure monopolies.[58] There is no de jure monopoly in Canada.

---

50. See *supra* n. 27. Not too much should be read into this, however. The Canadian definition of 'collective society' includes entities that would not be considered CMOs in Australia. Some collectives only receive royalties through a 'collective of collectives', such as NRCC and CPCC, and do not deal directly with users. The fact that more than one CMO administers a specific right is of little practical impact for users if all CMOs are subject to a single tariff (as is the case for all retransmission collectives) or if each collective acts for the others in a given territory (as do Access Copyright and COPIBEC). See also Collectives Report, *supra* n. 40, at 45.
51. ACA, *supra* n. 6, ss 135P(3), 135 ZZB(3) and 135ZZT(3).
52. *Copyright Regulations 1969*, (Cth) regs 23J, 23JM, 23L.
53. Simpson Report (1995), *supra* n. 25.
54. *Re Applications, supra* n. 26.
55. 'Code of Conduct for Copyright Collecting Societies' (2002, amended May 2007, confirmed Feb. 2008), <www.apra-amcos.com.au/downloads/file/About%20APRA/CodeofConduct_2008.pdf> (last visited: 10 Feb. 2010). Don't Stop the Music, *supra* n. 25 and the Ergas Report, *supra* n. 25 almost certainly played a role in the immediate impetus for the Code.
56. 'Declaration of Collecting Societies, Guidelines' (June 1990, revised April 2001), <www.ema.gov.au/www/agd/rwpattach.nsf/VAP/(CFD7369FCAE9B8F32F341DBE097801FF)~Guidelines.pdf/$file/Guidelines.pdf > (last visited: 10 Feb. 2010). (Guidelines)
57. SOCAN provides an internal appeal process for distributions. Access Copyright has appointed an ombudsman to deal with internal matters. Issues with users are not addressed. See Collectives Report, *supra* n. 40, at 19.
58. See *infra*, text accompanying n. 109.

In Canada, ERCC, CPCC and the retransmission CMOs taken together collect royalties for the entire repertoire, including works or other subject matters owned by non-members. The same is true of 'declared' Australian CMOs. However, the way in which each jurisdiction deals with moneys collected on behalf of non-members is significantly different. In Canada, non-members can collect royalties from the relevant collective without becoming a member, within a fixed period of time.[59] In Australia, moneys collected by a declared collective on behalf of non-members must be held in trust for a period of at least four years set out in the collectives' by-laws; however, the ACA requires only that distributions be made to members and nothing specifies what is to happen to moneys collected on behalf of non-members at the end of the trust period.[60] The Guidelines, which bind declared collectives and to which all other CMOs voluntarily adhere, provide the answer: the amounts are added to the next general revenue for distribution.[61]

Interactions between CMOs are of a different nature. The need for strategic alliances in the same market between collectives does not exist in Australia, simply because either by choice (as is the case with APRA) or through a society being 'declared', there always is only one collective active for a given set of rights in a given market. Indeed, when one compares the situation with respect to retransmission royalties, it seems that Canadian right holders can express their dissatisfaction with an existing collective's view of what their rights are worth much more readily than is the case with an Australian 'declared' society – all they have to do is to secede, form a new collective, file a new tariff and force the issue to be addressed by the Copyright Board; Australian right holders would have to apply for a cancellation of the collective's declaration, something that has never even been tried to this writer's knowledge.[62]

Other comparisons also could be interesting. For example, the role played by the emergence of compulsory and statutory licenses in the creation of new CMOs seems to have been more important in Australia than in Canada. Finally, it might be helpful to determine why, with respect to the compulsory license granted to educational institutions to copy and use broadcast materials, ERCC collects so little royalties, whereas Screenrights collects so much.[63]

---

59. CCA, *supra* n. 1, ss 76, 83(11) and 83(13).
60. See Lahore, *supra* n. 24, at para. 28,375.
61. *Supra* n. 56, at para. 18.
62. In theory, nothing would stop rights holders from forming a rival CMO in areas where societies are not declared.
63. One possible explanation may be that the Copyright Board wanted to certify a tariff that would 'coexist with the existing distribution market [for educational videos], and not act as a substitute for it': *Statement of Royalties to be Collected by ERCC From Educational Institutions in Canada, for the Reproduction and Performance of Works or Other Subject-Matters Communicated to the Public by Telecommunication for the years 1999–2002* (2002), 23 C.P.R. (4th) 352, at 357 (Cop.Bd.), <www.cb-cda.gc.ca/decisions/2002/20021025-e-b.pdf> (last visited: 10 Feb. 2010).

4   GOVERNMENT OVERSIGHT OF CANADIAN CMOs

Canadian CMOs are overseen by competition law authorities and by the Copyright Board.[64] This part outlines these oversight mechanisms and compares them, in several respects to the mechanisms used to regulate the activities of Australian CMOs.

4.1   OVERSIGHT BY COMPETITION LAW AUTHORITIES[65]

In Canada, pursuant to the Competition Act,[66] the Commissioner of Competition and the Competition Tribunal oversee business practices in general, including those of CMOs. The application of the regulated conduct defence[67] limits the matters that can attract the attention of Canadian competition authorities; they would not review the royalties and related terms and conditions set by the Copyright Board.[68] This limits competition oversight essentially to dealings between collectives and right holders; historically, however, the level of involvement of these authorities has been minimal in the area of copyright law generally, and almost non-existent in the area of collective management in particular.

4.2   OVERSIGHT BY THE COPYRIGHT BOARD

The Copyright Board can oversee virtually any dispute between a CMO and its users. This part of the paper outlines the structure of the Board and the regimes under which collectives operate, as well as the procedures the Board follows and the powers it exercises.

4.2.1   The Structure of the Copyright Board[69]

The Copyright Board is an independent administrative tribunal. It consists of not more than five members, appointed by the government for a set term of up to five years. Members can serve either full time or part time; to date, all members but our, except the Chairman, have served full-time. The Board has a small permanent staff

---

64. There is no ministerial oversight of CMOs in their activities as collective societies. This paper does not deal with any forms of oversight that ordinary courts of law may exercise.
65. For an excellent introduction to the subject, see S. Gilker, 'Statut des ententes négociées hors du processus de la Commission', in *Copyright Administrative Institutions*, ed. Y. Gendreau (Montreal: Yvon Blais, 2002), 678 at 142–156 [Gilker (2002)].
66. R.S.C. 1985, c. C-34.
67. See Competition Bureau Canada, 'Technical Bulletin on "Regulated" Conduct (Draft)' (June 2006), <http://competitionbureau.gc.ca/eic/site/cb-bc.nsf/eng/02141.html> (last visited: 10 Feb. 2010).
68. Gilker (2002), *supra* n. 65, at 152.
69. CCA, *supra* n. 1, ss 66–66.5.

that includes a Secretary General, a General Counsel and a Director of Research and Analysis.

The Board presents two singular characteristics for a Canadian regulatory agency. First, for historical rather than practical reasons,[70] the Chairman must be a sitting or retired judge of a superior court. Second, because the Chairman invariably serves part time, the Board's direction is two-headed: the Chairman directs the work of the Board, but the Vice-Chairman is its Chief Executive Officer.

4.2.2   Regulatory Regimes Administered by the Board

The Board regulates Canadian CMOs through one of four regulatory regimes. One applies in the absence of another regime. A second targets performing rights in musical works and sound recordings of musical works. A third provides the framework for two compulsory licenses. The fourth concerns the levy for private copying of sound recordings of musical works. Each regime imposes a different level of constraint on a collective's relations with those who use its repertoire. Those that operate as compulsory licensing schemes as a matter of law or practice impose limits on the ability of right holders to decide how to administer their rights and determine some aspects of the relationship of right holders with the relevant CMOs.

The residual, or general regime,[71] applies to all CMOs that operate 'a licensing scheme, applicable in relation to a repertoire of works of more than one author, pursuant to which the society sets out the classes of uses for which and the royalties and terms and conditions on which it agrees to authorize the doing of' a protected act.[72] This includes virtually every form of voluntary collective management of any protected use of works, performers' performances, sound recordings or broadcast signals, unless another regime applies.[73] This regime is the most flexible; collectives can deal with users in one of four ways.

CMOs and users are free to agree on the terms of a license. They then have the option to file the agreement with the Copyright Board. If they do not, the Board cannot review the terms of the agreement; the contract is enforceable before the ordinary courts of law and is subject to all relevant provisions of the Competition Act. If the agreement is filed with the Board, however, certain provisions of the Competition Act no longer apply. Instead, the Commissioner of Competition may

---

70. When the Copyright Appeal Board was set up in 1936, it was a fairly common practice in Canada to ask a judge to preside over the deliberations of administrative tribunals. This is no longer the case.
71. CCA, *supra* n. 1, ss 70.1–70.6.
72. CCA, *ibid.;* s. 70.1.
73. According to one author, some forms of collective management may escape that definition: '[a] company that licenses the use of the works of multiple authors to users can avoid the application [of the general regime] . . . if that company does not deal with users on a general tariff basis but negotiates each use individually'. See P. Grant, 'Competition and the Collectives in Canada: New Developments in the Relationship between Copyright and Antitrust Law', *Media and Communications Law Review* 1 (1990-1): 191, at 199. Also, because a collective society is a 'society, association or corporation', it would appear that a natural person who would set up shop as a CMO (nothing appears to prevent this) would remain unregulated.

ask the Board to examine the agreement if the Commissioner is of the view that it is contrary to the public interest. The Board then sets the royalties payable under the agreement, as well as the related terms and conditions. The Board has never been asked to examine an agreement pursuant to this aspect of the general regime.

If a CMO and a user fail to agree on the terms of a license, either party can ask the Copyright Board to fix the royalties and the related terms and conditions. The Board will do so unless it is advised before issuing a ruling that an agreement was reached.[74] Uptake of this aspect of the regime has been slow. To date, the Board has issued only one arbitration decision.[75] Currently, however, several hearings have been scheduled to deal with such applications. The extent to which the Board can force a collective to issue a license pursuant to this arbitration scheme remains unclear. Some are of the view that a CMO always can refuse to issue a license to a recalcitrant user. Others argue that once a CMO offers licenses for a certain type of use to a certain category of users, it no longer can refuse to issue a license for that use to a user within that category and must accept the Board's jurisdiction.[76]

A final option offered to CMOs pursuant to the general regime is to file proposed tariffs that, once certified, apply to all users who have not reached a separate agreement with the collective.[77] The process leading to the certification of these and other tariffs is examined later. To date, the Board has certified tariffs pursuant to this aspect of the general regime for the reproduction of radio and television programmes for the purpose of media monitoring; for the reproduction of musical works by radio stations, online music services, satellite radio services and distributors of video copies of feature films; and for the reprographic reproduction of literary works by educational institutions. Further proposed tariffs target the reproduction of musical works in other contexts, the reproduction of sound recordings and performers' performances by commercial radio stations and the reprographic reproduction of literary works by provincial governments.

The second regime concerns the performance or telecommunication of musical works and sound recordings of musical works.[78] This regime currently targets SOCAN and Re:Sound. In theory, those who own rights in musical works can avoid the application of the regime by managing their rights on their own; that option is not open to performers and record producers, because only a collective can collect royalties for the performance or telecommunication of sound recordings of musical works.[79] In practice, there is no difference, because SOCAN's

---

74. The agreement as such does not have to be filed: CCA, *supra* n. 1, s. 70.3(1).
75. See *Society for Reproduction Rights of Authors, Composers and Publishers in Canada v. MusiquePlus Inc.* (2000), 10 C.P.R. (4th) 242 (Cop. Bd.), <www.cb-cda.gc.ca/decisions/2000/20001116-a-b.pdf> (last visited: 10 Feb. 2010).
76. For a detailed demonstration of the proposition, see D. Gervais, 'Essai sur le fractionnement du droit d'auteur', *Cahiers de Propriété Intellectuelle* 15 (2002): 501, at 517–524.
77. Tariffs do not apply to matters covered in individual agreements: CCA, *supra* n. 1, s. 70.191.
78. CCA, *ibid.*, ss 67–69.
79. CCA, *supra* n. 1, s. 19(2)(a). The remuneration right for the performance or telecommunication of other sound recordings can be paid to either the performer or the record producer: CCA, s. 19(2)(b).

repertoire includes virtually every musical work communicated or performed in Canada. This regime operates in most respects as a compulsory license. All tariffs must be certified by the Copyright Board before they can be enforced. CMOs who do not file proposed tariffs for a given use or market are no longer allowed to seek legal redress for that use or market.[80] A user who offers to pay the appropriate tariff cannot be prosecuted for violation of copyright, even if the CMO refuses to issue a license.[81] Agreements between a collective and a user probably are null and void as a matter of public policy.[82]

A third regime sets a non-voluntary, statutory license for the retransmission of distant radio and television signals as well as for the reproduction and public performance by educational institutions, of radio or television programmes, for educational or training purposes.[83] No royalties can be collected except pursuant to a tariff certified by the Copyright Board; all royalties must transit through one or more CMOs, each of which collects a share set by the Board in the tariff. The only right of copyright holders who have not authorized a collective to act on their behalf is to be paid royalties by the collective designated by the Board to that effect; right holders are then entitled to the same royalties as if they had authorized the society to collect royalties on their behalf.

Finally, the CCA sets out a compensation scheme for the private copying of published sound recordings of musical works.[84] The scheme replicates the retransmission regime in all but two relevant respects. First, the levy must be collected through a single collecting body designated by the Board.[85] Second, rather than apportioning royalties among collectives, the Board sets the share of the levies to which all eligible authors, eligible performers and eligible makers (or record producers) are entitled;[86] how these shares are then divided within each college of right holders is up to the relevant collectives.

---

80. Absent a tariff, an action may be commenced with the permission of the relevant Minister: CCA, ibid., s. 67.1(4). In practice, however, that permission has never been sought, and, barring exceptional circumstances, would not be granted.
81. CCA, *ibid.*, s. 68.2(2). SOCAN still can enjoin a person who does not conform to the tariff from using its repertoire: see, for example, *Society of Composers, Authors and Music Publishers of Canada v. Kicks Roadhouse Inc. (c.o.b. How-Dee's)* 2005 FC 528, at para. 27, <http://decisions.fct-cf.gc.ca/en/2005/2005fc528/2005fc528.html> (last visited: 10 Feb. 2010).
82. Gilker (2002), *supra* n. 65, at 140–141. In practice, SOCAN does have agreements with a variety of users. They clarify which tariffs apply to certain uses, offer discounts on the rates set out in the tariffs or even set prices for uses that are outside any of the tariffs certified by the Board.
83. CCA, *supra* n. 1, ss 71–76.
84. CCA, *ibid.*, ss 79–88.
85. CCA, *ibid.*, s. 83(8)(d).
86. CCA, *ibid.*, s. 84.

4.2.3 Procedures before the Copyright Board

The procedure leading to the certification of a tariff is similar in all regimes.[87] A proposed tariff is filed on or before 31 March of the year preceding the year in which the tariff is to come into effect. The Board publishes the proposal in the *Canada Gazette*. Prospective users or their representatives[88] may object to the proposal within sixty days of the publication. The Board then issues a directive on procedure and sets a timetable for the proceedings.[89] The CMO and objectors are given the opportunity to argue their case in a hearing before a panel, usually constituting three members.[90] The Chairman presides over the panel if present; if not, the Vice-Chairman does so. The nature of the evidence offered varies considerably. The Board is not bound by the rules of evidence;[91] participants make liberal use of hearsay. After deliberations, the Board certifies the tariff, publishes it in the *Canada Gazette* and provides written reasons for its decision. A tariff comes into effect on 1 January following the date by which the proposed tariff was filed and is effective for one or more calendar years.[92]

The process is essentially the same when a request for arbitration is made pursuant to the general regime;[93] however, the effective period of an arbitration decision need not be a period of one or more calendar years.

4.2.4 The Powers of the Board

As with any administrative tribunal, the Copyright Board has powers of a substantive and procedural nature. Some are expressly granted; others are implicit. Thus, the CCA grants the Board the power to issue interim decisions, to vary earlier decisions, to make regulations governing its procedure and to cause the publication and distribution of notices.[94] The Board also enjoys some of the powers of a superior court of record;[95] for example, it can compel the production of evidence or the appearance of witnesses. The Board even can formulate its own objections to proposed tariffs.[96] However, contrary to most Commonwealth copyright tribunals,

---

87. CCA, *ibid.*, ss 67.1, 68 (performing rights regime); 70.13–70.15 (general regime, tariffs); 71–73 (statutory licenses); 83(1)–83(10) (private copying).
88. In the private copying regime, anyone is entitled to object.
89. The Board's model directive is available, <www.cb-cda.gc.ca/about-apropos/directive-e.html> (last visited: 10 Feb. 2010). The Board has the power to adopt rules of procedure, but has not exercised it.
90. Exceptionally, no hearing will be held if proceeding in writing accommodates a small user or if the issues at hand do not warrant a hearing. The hearing is also dispensed with on most preliminary, interlocutory or interim issues.
91. Indeed, any Canadian administrative tribunal that blindly follows the rules of evidence illegally fetters its discretion: *Université du Québec à Trois-Rivières v. Larocque* [1993] 1 S.C.R. 471.
92. CCA, *supra* n. 1, ss 67.1(3), 70.14, 71(4), 83(5).
93. CCA, *ibid.*, ss 70.2–70.4.
94. CCA, *ibid.*, ss 66.51, 66.52, 66.6 and 66.71, respectively.
95. CCA, *ibid.*, s. 66.7(1).
96. CCA, *ibid.*, ss 68(1), 70.14, 72(2), 83(7).

the Board does not have the power to award costs. The Board has some implicit powers, such as to regulate its proceedings, to decide questions of law that are necessarily incidental to the exercise of its core function[97] and even to set royalties at a higher rate than what a CMO requested or to refuse to certify a tariff even though the existence of a protected use was proven to exist.[98]

The Board's powers are constrained by the CCA, regulations, general principles of administrative law and court decisions. The CCA provides that performing rights tariffs must not place broadcasters at a financial disadvantage because of linguistic or content requirements imposed pursuant to the Broadcasting Act,[99] that the neighbouring rights royalties must be made in a single payment, that the private copying levy must be collected by a single body and that small cable systems are entitled to preferential rates.[100] The government can, by regulation, issue policy directions to the Board and establish general criteria that the Board must apply or take into consideration.[101] Decisions of the Federal Court of Appeal set other limits; for example, the Board cannot blindly rely on its earlier decisions.[102]

The Board does not directly determine which CMOs are active in a market, nor does it supervise their operations. Subject to the intervention of Canadian competition authorities, right holders are free to organize their affairs as they wish; even when a compulsory licensing scheme applies, nothing forces them to join a given collective or to organize CMOs along predetermined rules; as a result, nine retransmission CMOs, some of which administer similar rights, receive a share of the royalties directly from copyright users. The Board does have two obligations that influence the ability of a CMO to enter a market; as noted earlier, it must ensure that the payment of royalties for the performance or communication of sound recordings of musical works is made in a single payment and that the private copying levy is collected by a single collecting body.

The Board has made ample use of its power to certify royalties and their related terms and conditions 'with such alterations . . . as the Board considers necessary'[103] to influence the structure of CMO markets. It has carved new tariffs out of existing ones to suit the purposes of certain groups of users, imposed reporting requirement, authorized audits and imposed interest on late payment.[104]

---

97. *Canadian Cable Television Association v. Canada (Copyright Board)* [1993] 2 F.C. 138 (C.A.).

98. *Canadian Private Copying Collective v. Canadian Storage Media Alliance (F.C.A.)* [2005] 2 F.C.R. 654, at para. 167 and ff.; *Society of Composers, Authors and Music Publishers of Canada v. Bell Canada* 2010 FCA 139.

99. S.C. 1991, c.11.

100. CCA, *supra* n. 1, ss 68(2)(a)(iii) (single payment), 83(8)(d) (single collecting body) and 68.1(4), 74(1) (preferential rate).

101. CCA, *ibid.*, s. 66.91. The CCA speaks of 'having regard to'. That power has been exercised only once, with respect to retransmission royalties: see *Retransmission Royalties Criteria Regulations*, SOR/91-690, 28 Nov. 1991.

102. *FWS (2001)*, *supra* n. 47, at para. 14.

103. For example, CCA, *supra* n. 1, ss 68(3) and 70.15(1).

104. See, for example, *Statement of Royalties to be Collected for Performance or Communication in Canada of Dramatico-musical Works in 1992, 1993 and 1994* (1994), 58 C.P.R. (3d) 79, 83–87

The Board is allowed to develop a tariff structure that is completely different from the one proposed by the collective or the users[105] – in the first retransmission proceedings, the Board set aside eleven separate proposals to adopt a single tariff based on a tariff formula that it developed.[106] The Board has imposed identical tariff structures on separate collectives; in the case of the performing rights tariff for commercial radio, for example, until SOCAN became the sole collective, an overall rate was set and then apportioned, instead of dealing with each collective's tariff separately. The Board has even certified single tariffs for the combined use of two or more repertoires.[107] The same author who correctly predicted that the Board would merge tariffs filed pursuant to separate regimes also offered the view that the Board could impose a single payment rule in retransmission.[108]

4.3   Comparing CMO Oversight in Canada and Australia

The Australian approach to supervising collective management is different and more complex than in Canada. It involves at least four authorities that, taken together, exert significant influence on every aspect of the operations of CMOs.

The first authority is the Attorney-General, who, by declaration, can entrust to specific CMOs the administration of statutory licensing schemes such as educational copying of broadcasts, reprographic and electronic reproduction by educational institutions, retransmission of free-to-air broadcasts and government uses of materials protected by copyright.[109] A declaration grants to the relevant collective a monopoly either for all rights involved (for educational copying of broadcasts) or for any given class of copyright holders.[110] The Attorney-General has also adopted guidelines to be applied before declaring collectives.[111] Among other things, the

---

(Cop. Bd.) (new tariff); *Maple Leaf Broadcasting Company Limited v. CAPAC* [1954] S.C.R. 624 (audits); *FWS Joint Sports Claimants v. Canada (Copyright Board)* [1992] 1 F.C. 487 (C.A.) (interests).

105. *Canadian Broadcasting Corp. v. Copyright Appeal Board* (1986), 17 C.P.R. (3d) 460. (F.C.A.).
106. *Re Royalties for Retransmission Rights Of Distant Radio and Television Signals* (1990), 32 C.P.R. (3d) 97 (Cop. Bd.).
107. *Re Statement of Royalties to be Collected by SOCAN and by NRCC for Pay Audio Services (Tariff 17.B)* (2002), 19 C.P.R. (4th) 67 (Cop. Bd.); *Neighbouring Rights Collective of Canada v. Society of Composers, Authors and Music Publishers of Canada* (2004), 26 C.P.R. (4th) 257 (F.C.A.); *SOCAN Statement of Royalties, Satellite Radio Services Tariff (SOCAN: 2005–2009; NRCC: 2007–2010; CSI: 2006–2009) (Re)* (2009), 74 C.P.R. (4th) 399 (Cop.Bd.).
108. Gervais, *supra* n. 76, at 532–533.
109. ACA, *supra* n. 6, ss 135P, 135ZZB and 135ZZT. In the case of government use, the power of declaration is entrusted to the Copyright Tribunal: ACA, *ibid.*, ss 153F and 153J. The Minister can now refer the declaration power in all cases to the Copyright Tribunal: ACA, *ibid.*, ss 135P, 135Q, 135ZZB and 135ZZC, among others.
110. *Audio-visual Copyright Society Ltd v. Australian Record Industry Association Ltd* (2000) 47 OPR 40.
111. Declaration of Collecting Societies, Guidelines, *supra* n. 56.

guidelines set out fundamental objectives, including that each society collect all the money to which it is entitled, and none to which it is not, that it operate efficiently, that it distribute royalties fairly and that it treat evenly current and future beneficiaries. The guidelines also provide that any element of cross-subsidy between the operation of the scheme for which the society has been 'declared' and any other activities be kept to a minimum.

The second authority is the Australian Competition and Consumer Commission (ACCC), overseen by the Competition Tribunal. The interest of competition authorities in collective management seems as intense in Australia as it seems timid in Canada. Input arrangements of CMOs (i.e., their dealings with right holders) can constitute a contravention of Part IV of the Trade Practices Act.[112] A collective can avoid being in contravention of these provisions by subjecting these arrangements to the scrutiny of the ACCC. CMOs have attempted to use this mechanism several times in the past. One attempt resulted in a thorough examination of APRA's operations; in the end, the Competition Tribunal refused to authorize APRA's input arrangements until they allowed for a non-exclusive license-back scheme and included a dispute resolution mechanism.[113] The Competition Tribunal even offered its views on the ability of the Copyright Tribunal to regulate APRA's dealings with users.[114]

The Amending Act increased the role of the ACCC over copyright collective licensing. It requires the Copyright Tribunal, at the request of a party, to have regard to any relevant guidelines issued by the ACCC and gives the Tribunal the discretion to admit the ACCC as a party to tribunal proceedings.[115] The ACCC states that it will seek to become a party to Copyright Tribunal proceedings only when it considers the intervention would be in the public interest, as assessed on a case-by-case basis.[116] It was made a party to two references by PPCA for an increase in the royalties payable for electronic downloading of sound recordings (the matter settled without a decision) and for a Fitness Class Licensing Scheme.[117]

---

112. Trade Practices Act 1968 (Cth) Act No. 51 of 1974.
113. *Re Applications, supra* n. 26.
114. *Re Applications, ibid.*, at 113. ACCC interest in CMOs has not extended to declared societies acting as such, because their monopoly position derives entirely from the provisions of the ACA conferring that status on them. This is the Australian equivalent of the Canadian regulated industry defence.
115. ACA, *supra* n. 6, ss 157A, 157B.
116. See Australian Competition & Consumer Commission, 'Copyright Licensing and Collecting Societies: A Guide for Copyright Licensees (Draft for Comment)' (November 2006), <www.accc.gov.au/content/item.phtml?itemId=824094&nodeId=c1d738595ff48e c74ecf68d24b17dd80&fn=A+draft+guide+for+COPYRIGHT+licensees.pdf> (last visited: 10 Feb. 2010). Submissions from interested parties and stakeholders regarding the ACCC's draft guidelines can be found online at: <www.accc.gov.au/content/index.phtml/itemId/ 824095> (last visited: 10 Feb. 2010).
117. ACCC's participation in this instance was sufficiently active to attract concerns on the part of PPCA and an apparent invitation on the part of the Tribunal to limit future interventions: *Phonographic Performance Company of Australia Limited under section 154(1) of the Copyright Act 1968* [2010] ACopyT 1 at paras 315–323. [*PPCA Fitness*]

The third authority is the Copyright Tribunal of Australia.[118] It is composed of a President and of an indeterminate number of Deputy Presidents and members, appointed by the Government for one or more set terms of up to seven years. The President must be a judge of the Federal Court, and Deputy Presidents must be current or past judges of the Federal Court or of a State or territorial Supreme Court. Matters are heard by the President or a Deputy President, unless a party requests a panel, in which case the matter is heard by two or more persons, including the President or a Deputy President. The Tribunal has no permanent staff – its Registrar is a registrar of the Federal Court.

The Copyright Tribunal oversees statutory license schemes as well as non-statutory (or voluntary) licenses where these are offered by a CMO. The Tribunal intervenes only upon request; a licensing scheme, including a statutory scheme, can operate without the Tribunal being asked to examine it. Generally speaking, license schemes continue operation pending order of the tribunal.[119]

Until 2006, the Copyright Tribunal determined rates and certain other conditions of statutory licenses and certain other music licenses administered by copyright collecting societies, but did not oversee all forms of licensing; for example, it had no jurisdiction over non-statutory licenses issued by CAL. The Amending Act extended the Tribunal's jurisdiction to cover all licenses and licensing schemes administered by collecting societies.[120] The Copyright Tribunal's new powers include the power to:

> declare or revoke the declaration of a collecting society; make determinations regarding all licences administered by collecting societies; entertain applications made by collecting societies, or members of those societies, for review of the arrangements for allocating and distributing remuneration; and more generally, make determinations on 'any question that is necessary or convenient to help an administering body of an educational or other institution or the collecting society to comply in the future with the requirements of the statutory licences'.[121]

The ACA usually specifies who can participate in an application before the Tribunal. The Act sometimes adds that an organization cannot file or be party to an application unless the Tribunal is convinced that it is reasonably representative of the class of persons that it claims to represent or that it has a substantial interest in

---

118. ACA, *supra* n. 6, ss 138 and ff.
119. ACA, *ibid.*, s. 158.
120. Australian Copyright Council Copyright, 'Information Sheet: Copyright Amendment Act 2006' (April 2007) at 5–6, <www.copyright.org.au/pdf/acc/infosheets_pdf/g096.pdf> (last visited: 10 Feb. 2010). An awkward situation arose when the Tribunal concluded that it had the power to review the communication license for ringtones, but not the reproduction license required for the same ringtones: see *Reference by Powercom Interactive Media Pty Ltd* [2003] ACopyT 1. The amendment remedies the situation.
121. Kimberlee Weatherall, 'Of Copyright Bureaucracies and Incoherence: Stepping Back from Australia's Recent Copyright Reforms' (2007), 31 Melbourne U. L.R. 967, at 1015, fn. 281. See also Lindgren, *supra*, n. 8.

the matter.[122] The Tribunal appears to have applied a fairly rigorous test in this respect.[123]

The fourth authority is the collectives themselves. As noted earlier, all collectives now subscribe to a voluntary code of conduct that deals with membership, relations with licensees, distribution of royalties, administrative expenses and dispute resolution and even provides that voluntary collectives agree to comply with the Attorney General's guidelines for declared societies. The collectives went as far as to ask a former President of the Copyright Tribunal to act as independent reviewer of the Code of conduct and its application.[124]

The Canadian and Australian approaches to overseeing collective management offer interesting contrasts. Australian controls are greater on issues such as corporate organization, areas of activity, internal operations, membership, dealings with right holders, collection practices, cross-subsidization of operations, dispute resolution and transparency, among others; the imposition of severe constraints on the operation of statutory licenses by declared societies plays a significant role. On the other hand, the Canadian regime allows for almost unlimited control over the structure of all licensing schemes, voluntary or not. *Ex ante* controls take different forms. In Australia, liberal use is made of statutory licensing schemes, coupled with declaration mechanisms, to control market entry and to impose stringent operational requirements. In Canada, any collective can enter the market, but the requirement in some regimes for a certified tariff before any royalties are collected is a form of control over the nature and extent of the collective's dealings before it can start its activities.

Comparisons between the Canadian Board and the Australian Tribunal also are instructive. The Canadian Board has a small permanent infrastructure that provides it with some research capacity; the Copyright Tribunal, having no research capacity, must rely on the parties' evidence and analysis. Dealing with matters in a timely fashion is not an issue, however; the Tribunal is situated within the Federal Court and can call upon its staff. If anything, the Tribunal's record in that respect is better than the Board's; in 2000, the average time taken to finalize matters was approximately twenty-two months.[125]

In Australia, all hearings are presided over by a judge or heard by a judge alone. In the past, the tendency was for matter to be heard by a single judge, which might have had the effect of 'judicializing' the process.[126] Recently, however, requests for panels that include lay members have become more common. By contrast, over the past fifteen years, several hearings of the Canadian Board have been chaired by one of three Vice-Chairmen, including a non-lawyer, rather than

---

122. See, for example, ACA, *supra* n. 6, ss 155(3) and 155(4).
123. *Universal Music Australia v. EMI Music Publishing Australia Pty Ltd* [2000] ACopyT 3 (14 Mar. 2000).
124. See <http://copyright.com.au/assets/documents/Report%20of%20Review%202009.pdf> (last visited: 10 Feb. 2010).
125. CLRC Jurisdiction Report (2000), *supra* n. 23, para. 5.05.
126. Even though s. 164(c) of the ACA, *supra* n. 6, requires that the Tribunal proceed with as little formality as possible.

by one of three judicial Chairmen. With respect to the participation of 'strangers', the Canadian Board's policy has been extremely liberal. It has made full use of its ability to control its own proceedings to allow interventions from persons or groups who are not directly interested but who are likely to provide a useful point of view. Nothing seems to indicate that the Australian Tribunal has followed a similar path.

The Copyright Tribunal's jurisdiction appears more limited than that of the Copyright Board in a number of respects. The Canadian Board's jurisdiction clearly extends to all licensing schemes; the Amending Act so extends the Australian Tribunal's jurisdiction, but there appears to have been little or no use of these new powers to date, possibly because the jurisdiction remains application-driven. In Australia, licensing schemes can operate without the Tribunal's intervention if the collective and its users come to an agreement; in Canada, it is often impossible for a CMO to collect royalties without a decision of the Board. While the rates the Board sets are the price, 'the licence fee fixed by the Tribunal . . . is a maximum fee. There is nothing to prevent a collecting society charging its licensees a lower fee'.[127] The extent to which changes can be made to proposed licensing schemes, which used to be vastly different, may be less so now. The Canadian Board's discretion in this respect appears to be virtually unlimited. By contrast, until 2006, the Australian Tribunal could vary or confirm a scheme put forward by the collecting society, but could not adopt an altogether different one.[128] The Amending Act changed this, though the extent of the change seems ambiguous and may be limited.[129] Finally, while the Tribunal's orders regarding voluntary licences take effect from the time they are issued, the Board's decisions often operate retrospectively as a result of a tariff being certified after its proposed commencement date.[130]

The manner in which issues can be raised also differs significantly. The Australian Tribunal acts only on application, which can be withdrawn[131]; it would seem that, as a result, parties more or less control the agenda. In tariff matters, the Canadian Board can raise its own objections, regardless of whether users take issue with the collective's proposal. In some cases, withdrawing a tariff results in giving access to the repertoire for free. The Board sometimes is required to take

---

127. *PPCA Fitness, supra* n. 117 at para. 8.
128. *Reference By Australasian Performing Right Association Limited Re Australian Broadcasting Corporation* (1985), 5 UPR 449.
129. ACA, *supra* n. 6, ss 155(4), 155(5) and others. It may be that the power is not a power at large, that the Tribunal can only substitute another scheme if it is proposed by one of the parties and that the Tribunal cannot vary or amend a proposed substitute scheme but must take or leave the proposed substitute as a whole. In its most recent decision, the Australian Tribunal appeared to conclude that while it could modify an alternative scheme proposed by a participant, it still could not opt for an altogether different scheme of its own: *PPCA Fitness, supra* n. 117 at paras 282, 286.
130. By contrast, since a user can act pursuant to a statutory license under the ACA without a determination by the Tribunal, such a determination, when sought, can be expressed to apply to prior activity.
131. ACA, *supra* n. 6, s. 155(7).

agreements into account,[132] but always remains free to ignore them. Finally, as was noted earlier, the Commissioner of Competition can ask the Board to modify an agreement that has been filed with the Board over the objection of the parties.

The costs of proceedings also play a different role. In Australia, both sides have choices to make; they each must ask themselves whether it is worth their while to refer the matter to the Tribunal; the possibility of an award for costs must also have some influence. In Canada, the same question arises, but somewhat differently. Some CMOs have no choice but to apply for a tariff; it is also clear that the inability of the Board to award costs has sometimes resulted in it having to deal with matters that could have been addressed more expeditiously.

The fact that some Canadian CMOs must obtain a tariff from the Board before collecting any royalties seems to have had other significant effects. This sometimes has accelerated the process leading to the effective implementation of a collective in a market. In Canada, a retransmission tariff was in place less than ten months after royalties became payable.[133] The requirement also has allowed the emergence of a form of continuing supervision that does not appear to exist in Australia; for example, the Board can ensure a certain level of uniformity in the terms and conditions of the various tariffs without having to wait for a dispute to arise between a collective and its users.

Finally, the manner in which each agency perceives its role appears to be somewhat different. The fundamental rationale for the Copyright Tribunal remains to counterbalance the potential monopoly position of collecting societies through the arbitration of disputes in the absence of agreement.[134] Two decades or so ago, the Copyright Board redefined its role – to regulate the balance of market power between copyright holders and users.[135] When called upon to determine equitable remuneration, the Australian Tribunal appears to seek to act as a substitute to a non-functioning market and to reflect the price that would be arrived at by 'a willing, but not anxious, licensor, and a willing, but not anxious, licensee' or some other hypothetical bargain.[136] Only if neither of these approaches is appropriate will the

---

132. *Retransmission Royalties Criteria Regulations*, SOR/91-690, 28 Nov. 1991, s. 2(c).
133. Collectives subject to the general regime have even started to use the filing of a proposed tariff as a tool to enter a market and force recalcitrant users to the bargaining table: see *Statement of Royalties to be Collected by CBRA for the Fixation and Reproduction of Works and Communication Signals, in Canada, by Commercial Media Monitors for the Years 2000–2005 and Non-commercial Media Monitors for the Years 2001–2005* (2005), 39 C.P.R. (4th) 152 (Cop. Bd.), <www.cb-cda.gc.ca/tariffs-tarifs/certified-homologues/2005/20050326-mv-b.pdf> (last visited: 10 Feb. 2010).
134. The (then) President of the Tribunal has offered the view that decisions should be fair to both sides : Justice Kevin Lindgren, 'Market power, collecting societies and the role of the Copyright Tribunal', *The Australian Law Journal* 79 (2005): 561, 584.
135. *Re Statement of Royalties to be Collected for Performance in Canada of Dramatico-musical or Musical Works in 1990, 1991, 1992 and 1993* (1993) 52 C.P.R. (3d) 23, at 34 (Cop.Bd.) [*SOCAN Tariff 2.A, 1993*]; approved by *Canadian Association of Broadcasters v. SOCAN* (1994), 58 C.P.R. (3d) 190, at 196 (F.C.A.).
136. *Copyright Agency Limited* v. *Department of Education (NSW)* (1985), 4 IPR 5, 15–16. This is similar to the approach of the American rate court, which has interpreted 'reasonable' rates as

Tribunal resort to 'judicial estimation' based on such factors as previous agreements, earlier negotiations, comparison with foreign rates or with rates in other Australian copyright markets, capacity to pay, administrative costs and the general public interest. By contrast, the Canadian Board has asserted not only that a market price is only one of several possible rational bases for a tariff, but that in certain circumstances, public policy would lead it to ignore market considerations altogether.[137]

5   CONCLUSION

This author's lack of familiarity with the day-to-day realities of Australian CMOs and the yet undetermined impact of the Amending Act on their overall operations make it difficult for him to speculate on the future of collective management in that jurisdiction. Australian right holders still appear to be less likely than Canadians to resort to collectives as a means of obtaining compensation for the use of their protected works and other copyright subject matters. Several factors may explain this. One is the perception that collective management, while sometimes useful, poses risks and that the first function of government oversight of collectives is to prevent those risks from materializing. Another may be the size of the Copyright Tribunal, which may prevent it from acting as catalyst for the promotion of collective management (assuming that Australian public policy is to promote collective management). A third could be a continued fear of involvement on the part of competition authorities.

In Canada, the growth of collective management is difficult to measure, owing in part to the presence of private collectives whose financial data remains unavailable. Still, that growth has been significant, as is the number of areas in which CMOs operate, especially for a common law jurisdiction. This seems to be the result of deliberate policy choices on the part successive Canadian governments, combined with the ability of the Copyright Board to develop the tools that would allow it to best implement those choices. In effect, it would seem that the evolution of collective management in Canada has been intimately linked to the emergence, in the CCA, of mechanisms to overview the relationship between collectives and copyright users.

The growing importance of digital rights and Internet offer CMOs as much a challenge as an opportunity. Some believe that technology makes individual copyright administration possible in instances in which until now, only collective action made sense.[138] In practice, however, there seems to be no Holy Grail on the

---

market rates: see *SOCAN Tariff 2.A, 1993, ibid.*, at 35. The American Copyright Royalty Tribunal applies similar principles.

137. *SOCAN Tariff 2.A, 1993, ibid.*, at 34 b–c, 39 c–d.
138. Ariel Katz, 'The Potential Demise of Another Natural Monopoly: Rethinking the Collective Administration of Performing Rights', *Journal of Competition Law and Economics* 1 (2005): 541, <http://papers.ssrn.com/sol3/papers.cfm?abstract_id=547802> (last visited:

horizon. Still, CMOs will have to strive to adapt to this new environment if they wish to remain relevant. New CMOs are emerging, the nature and scope of repertoires are changing and alliances are being struck. Trusted third parties, including digital music delivery services, are offering a measure of competition. Given commercial realities, and the practical limitations of individual licensing of digital rights, collective licensing regimes could become an increasingly attractive option for copyright management. Dylan, Springsteen and those others who already administer rights in the physical world that others prefer to hive off to a CMO may also succeed to do so in the digital world. For most, however, resort to some clearinghouse, whether it be a traditional collective or some other entity, seems inevitable.

The challenges facing collective management in Canada are varied. It takes time to gather a repertoire that is large enough to enter a market, especially when the uses involved are modest and the users dispersed. Addressing that issue may require the implementation of mechanisms such as extended collective licensing.[139] Proceedings before the Copyright Board are generally perceived as expensive, even though the Board has demonstrated an ability to tailor its process to the importance of the issues. Some collectives are fractioning their tariff applications for strategic, not practical, reasons, thereby forcing multiple hearings before the Board, where one or two might have proven sufficient; others use the process to obtain information on users' business practices that would not be available in the context of a normal negotiation or to force recalcitrant users to come to the bargaining table. Users have started to complain. It may well be another decade before one can say with some certainty that the future of collective administration in Canada is ensured.

---

10 Feb. 2010); Ariel Katz, 'The Potential Demise of Another Natural Monopoly: New Technologies and the Administration of Performing Rights', *Journal of Competition Law and Economics* 2 (2006): 245, <http://papers.ssrn.com/sol3/papers.cfm?abstract_id=1183672> (last visited: 10 Feb. 2010).

139. See D. Gervais, 'Application of an Extended Collective Licensing Regime in Canada: Principles and Issues Related to Implementation' (2003), Report prepared for Heritage Canada, <http://aix1.uottawa.ca/~dgervais/publications/extended_licensing.pdf> (last visited: 10 Feb. 2010).

Chapter 11

Copyright Collectives and Collecting Societies: The United States Experience

*Glynn Lunney**

1   INTRODUCTION

In the United States, as technology and markets have developed to make possible the widespread and dispersed infringement of copyrights, collective management organizations (CMOs) have developed in response. These organizations attempt to deal with specific instances of widespread copyright infringement by obtaining licenses from large numbers of copyright owners. These licenses authorize the CMO to act as the copyright owner's agent with respect to certain types of infringement. Armed with a portfolio of licensed works, the collective assumes the responsibility for enforcing, or assisting with the enforcement of, copyrights against certain types of infringement, eliminating the need for duplicative infringement actions. They also provide a single source or clearinghouse for licensing the specific use at issue and thereby eliminate the need for individually negotiated licenses from each copyright owner. By reducing the transaction costs associated with enforcing, on the one hand, and licensing, on the other, they help convert widespread infringement into markets.

---

* McGlinchey Stafford Professor of Law, Tulane University School of Law.

Daniel Gervais (ed.), *Collective Management of Copyright and Related Rights*, pp. 339–382.
© 2010 Kluwer Law International BV, The Netherlands.

Although CMOs can reduce transaction costs in order to create markets, there is a key distinction between a copyright collective and a collecting society. With a copyright collective, the pricing and licensing terms for the portfolio of copyrights licensed to the collective are set by the collective to maximize the revenue of the portfolio as a whole. Competition in pricing or access terms for individual copyrights within the portfolio is, if not altogether absent, severely lacking. In contrast, under the collecting society model, pricing and licensing terms are set by the individual copyright owners. The collecting society does not set those terms itself; it merely enforces and collects the licensing fees due, given the licensing terms set by the individual copyright owners for the use at issue.

In the United States, three CMOs that follow the copyright collective model: the American Society of Composers, Authors and Publishers (ASCAP), Broadcast Music Industry (BMI) and SESAC.[1] All three CMOs developed to address the unauthorized public performance of musical works – a problem too widespread, with each individual infringement of too small a scale, to be addressed effectively by individual copyright owners. All three CMOs have obtained licenses from large numbers of copyright owners that authorize the CMOs to license specific musical works for public performance. With their respective license portfolios in hand, all three CMOs, in turn, offer public performance licenses covering their respective portfolios to radio stations, restaurants and other businesses that engage in the public performance of music.

In the United States, these CMOs are viewed as something of a necessary evil. By reducing the transaction costs entailed in enforcing and licensing the public performance of musical works, they create a market in which otherwise there would be only infringement. But they do not merely reduce the transaction costs associated with the public performance right, they also eliminate competition between the individual copyright owners over public performance licensing terms and pricing. Because of this anti-competitive potential, copyright collectives in the United States have faced recurring litigation over whether their licensing practices violate the anti-trust laws.

The first such lawsuit was initiated by the Department of Justice in the early 1930s. In the lawsuit, the Department of Justice alleged that ASCAP was an unlawful combination, in the vein of Standard Oil. In the 1940s, the Department of Justice initiated a second set of lawsuits against both BMI and ASCAP, alleging that the collectives' licensing practices unreasonably restrained trade. The parties settled the litigation in 1941 and entered into consent decrees[2] that have governed the licensing practices of ASCAP and BMI ever since.[3] Over the years, the terms of

---

1. SESAC used to stand for the Society of European Stage Authors and Composers, but has since been renamed to SESAC.
2. 'A consent judgment is "an agreement of the parties entered into upon the record with the sanction and approval of the court".' *New York ex rel. Spitzer v. St. Francis Hosp.*, 289 F. Supp. 2d 378, at 383-84 (S.D.N.Y. 2003) (quoting *Schurr v. Austin Galleries of Ill., Inc.*, 719 F.2d 571, at 574 (2d Cir., 1983)).
3. See *United States v. American Society of Composers, Authors and Publishers*, 1941 Trade Cas. (CCH) para. 56,104, 1941 U.S. Dist. Lexis 3944 (S.D.N.Y. 1941) [*US v. ASCAP*];

the consent decrees have been adjusted to reflect the developments of new technologies and new markets. Yet, although their precise terms have varied over time, their thrust has remained consistent. In essence, the consent decrees validate the essential role of the collectives in creating a workable market in the public performance right, and then attempt to regulate their pricing and licensing terms in order to limit the collective's anti-competitive potential. It is, at best, an imperfect solution.

More recently, an alternative model for collective enforcement of copyrights has developed in response to the widespread use of copying machines to make photocopies of written works. Like the public performance issue that had developed half a century earlier, the use of photocopying machines led to unauthorized copying both too widespread, and individually of too small a scale, to be policed effectively by individual copyright owners. From the copyright owners' perspective, this problem called again for a collective rights management solution. Yet, rather than begin with a fundamentally anti-competitive collective and add an overlay of government regulation intended to make the structure act as if it were competitive, an alternative collective management structure developed to solve the widespread photocopying problem. The Copyright Clearance Center (CCC) allows copyright owners to register their works with the CCC and to set their own terms and prices on which photocopying will be allowed. Once the terms are set by the copyright owners, the CCC makes those terms known to potential copiers and arranges for the collection of the appropriate licensing fees.

The CCC thereby solves, as much as a collective would, the transaction costs problem otherwise entailed in enforcing copyrights against widespread photocopying, yet, unlike a collective, it does so without eliminating competition between copyright owners over licensing terms and pricing. Because it does not set price or licensing terms, it is not a collective in the sense that ASCAP, BMI and SESAC are, but is merely a collecting agent of the copyright owner. So long as CCC allows the individual copyright owners to set their own licensing terms, the anti-competitive potential of the collecting society model is minimal. As a result, CCC is not, as yet, and appears unlikely to be, subject to a consent decree or other limitations on its licensing practices as a result of the antitrust laws.

The United States' experience with collective rights management thus reveals two distinct models: a copyright collective and a collecting society. Both act as agents of individual copyright owners and reduce the transaction costs associated

---

United States v. Broadcast Music Industry, 1940–1943 Trade Cas. (CCH) para. 56,096 (E.D. Wis. 1941) [*US v. BMI*]. Perhaps because of its relatively smaller size, the Department of Justice has not pursued antitrust claims against SESAC, and SESAC's operations are not (as yet) governed by a consent decree. Nevertheless, the omnipresent threat of antitrust litigation likely constrains SESAC's behaviour to a considerable degree. On 11 May 2005, Congress conducted an oversight hearing regarding BMI, SESAC and ASCAP and considered testimony by ASCAP and BMI representatives that the lack of a consent decree governing SESAC's operations gave SESAC an unfair advantage over ASCAP and BMI. See Oversight Hearing on 'Public Performance Rights Organizations', Hearing before the House Subcommittee on Courts, The Internet, and Intellectual Property, 11 May 2005, <http://judiciary.house.gov/Oversight.aspx?ID=157>, 5 Dec. 2005.

with the enforcement and licensing of copyrights for particular uses. Both thereby create markets where otherwise there would be only infringement. Yet, despite these similarities, the copyright collective, because it sets prices and licensing terms for the individual copyright owners it represents, threatens competition in a way that the collecting society, which allows the individual copyright owners to dictate those terms, does not.

To be sure, the Department of Justice has worked hard to incorporate flexibility into the consent decrees that govern ASCAP and BMI and has also attempted to update the decrees to reflect changing technologies and markets. But at the end of the day, the copyright collective model remains fundamentally anti-competitive. As a result, all of the ingenuity that the profit motivation can generate is directed not at developing more flexible and creative licensing options for the benefit of copyright owners and consumers alike, but toward exploiting the loopholes in, and working around, the consent decrees to achieve the anti-competitive result that will always remain the copyright collective's true goal. For that reason, attempting to impose some semblance of competition onto the CMOs through the consent decrees has been and will likely remain a constant struggle.

Despite this essential flaw, for years, Americans have tolerated copyright collectives as necessary, provided that adequate restraints, such as those in the consent decrees, are in place. Yet, with the development of the CCC and its alternative model of collective rights management, it is apparent that the evils of the copyright collective are not necessary. The market can solve the transaction cost problem that particular instances of widespread copyright infringement create without the need for a uniform price, collectively set. Given the proven viability of the collecting society model, the question thus becomes: How long will the copyright collective model be permitted to endure?

To get some sense for the likely answer to this question, this essay will explore the United States' experience with collective copyright management, beginning with the copyright collectives.

2   THE COPYRIGHT COLLECTIVES: ASCAP, BMI AND SESAC

As discussed, there are presently three major copyright collectives in the United States: ASCAP, BMI and SESAC. All three CMOs provide a method by which the owners of copyrights in musical works[4] can license their work for public

---

4. Like most countries, the United States differentiates the protection provided to the underlying musical composition, which is known as the 'musical work', and a particular artist's rendition of the composition, which is known as a 'sound recording' See 17 U.S.C. § 102(a)(2), (7) (separately recognizing 'musical works' and 'sound recordings' as works of authorship eligible for copyright protection). However, unlike many other countries, the United States protects both the musical work and the sound recording under its Copyright Act. Yet, the US Copyright Act does not provide the same protection for musical works and sound recordings. Under US law, sound recordings receive protection only against exact duplication of the 'actual sounds fixed in the

performance and provide would-be public performers with a practical method for obtaining public performance licenses for a wide variety of copyrighted musical works.[5] The following sections provide: (1) a brief description of each of the CMOs, (2) a discussion of the legal right they enforce and (3) a discussion of the antitrust litigation and resulting consent decrees that have shaped the licensing practices of the collectives.

2.1　A Brief Description of the Collectives

2.1.1　ASCAP

ASCAP was founded in 1914 to protect right holders from the unauthorized non-dramatic performances of music in restaurants, bars and hotels. It is a non-profit, private company that is owned by its members.[6] To protect its members, ASCAP sues establishments that perform material in the ASCAP repertory without a license. As technology has evolved, these licenses have been issued for radio broadcasters, television broadcasters, movie and television show producers and webcasters.

Currently, ASCAP has over 200,000 members.[7] The license fees generated by ASCAP in 2007 reached United States Dollar (USD) 864 million (compared to USD 786 million in 2006), and distributions reached USD 741 million (USD 680 million in 2006).[8] According to ASCAP's information, it distributes 86 cents

---

recording' (17 U.S.C. § 114(b)) and receives only limited protection, and that only recently received, against public performances. See 17 U.S.C. §§ 106(6) (recognizing the copyright owners exclusive right to 'perform [a sound recording] publicly by means of a digital audio transmission), 114(d) (effectively limiting the sound recording public performance right to a very narrow category of performances, such as interactive digital transmissions over the Internet). The principal opponents of a broader public performance right for sound recordings remain musical work copyright owners, who rightly fear that licensing fees for a broader public performance right for sound recording would come out of their pockets in the form of reduced licensing fees for the musical work public performance right. Congress tried to prohibit such a direct redistribution of licensing revenues when it recognized the limited public performance right for sound recordings (17 U.S.C. § 114(i)), but if a radio station is already paying the profit-maximizing license fee for a public performance to ASCAP for the musical work performance right, there is simply no other fee that can be charged that would increase the total public performance licensing fees collected in a way that would allow sound recording rightsholders to receive a public performance fee without diminishing that paid to the musical work rightsholders'.

5. See <www.ascap.com/about/> (last visited: 5 Dec. 2005). ('ASCAP protects the rights of its members by licensing and distributing royalties for the non-dramatic public performances of their copyrighted works.')
6. See Hoover's Inc., Hoover's Company Records – Basic Record for American Society of Composers, Authors and Publishers (2005), <www.hoovers.com> (last visited: 5 Dec. 2005) (Hoover ID: 51047).
7. See <www.ascap.com/about/> (last visited: 5 Dec. 2005).
8. ASCAP 2007 Annual Report, <www.ascap.com/about/annualReport/annual_2007.pdf> (last visited 1 Feb. 2009).

of every dollar collected to its members.[9] It is worth noting in that respect that one cannot compare directly the collection and distribution numbers for a given year because the collection and distribution calendars overlap only in part. There is a (normal) delay between collection, processing of usage data and distribution. This is referred to as Royalty Months Outstanding. The normal range is a few months (typically 4 to 8), but some CMOs and some royalties have much longer lag times.

2.1.2 BMI

BMI was founded in 1939 by members of the broadcast industry to create an alternative to ASCAP. BMI also is a private, non-profit company that offers the same service as ASCAP, but with a different library. At the time of BMI's formation, ASCAP held the rights to more than 80% of the music that was played on the radio. Dissatisfied with the licensing terms and prices set by ASCAP, the broadcast industry and the formation of BMI provided radio with an alternative play-list that enabled radio broadcasters to boycott ASCAP in 1940.

Originally envisioned as a competitor to ASCAP that would force ASCAP to offer its licenses at reasonable rates and to deal more fairly with its members, BMI has proven more redundancy than competitor. With ASCAP and BMI both having developed their own large catalogues of copyrighted popular music, would-be public performers today typically obtain blanket licenses from both ASCAP and BMI.[10] As a practical matter, instead of being part of the solution to the monopolistic excesses of ASCAP, BMI today simply adds another monopoly to the mix and has become part of the problem.

BMI's membership is currently over 300,000.[11] BMI's website states that earnings for 2008 were approximately USD 900 million in revenue. Approximately USD 790 million of the revenue was in the form of royalties for members.

2.1.3 SESAC

Often, the forgotten sibling because of their limited repertory,[12] SESAC is the second oldest of the CMOs, founded in 1930. It is a privately held, for-profit organization, as opposed to ASCAP and BMI. As a further difference from the

---

9. See <www.ascap.com/about/ascapadvantage.html> (last visited: 30 Jan. 2009).
10. See, for example, *United States v. American Society of Composers Authors and Publishers* (Application of Muzak, LLC), 309 F. Supp. 2d 566 at 569 (S.D.N.Y. 2004) *[ASCAP (Application of Muzak, LLC)]* ('Applicants state that, as a practical matter, they are required to obtain licenses with both ASCAP and BMI because each organization has a distinct large and diverse repertory of works necessary for their programming.'); *United States v. American Society of Composers, Authors and Publishers*, 586 F. Supp. 727 at 730 (S.D.N.Y. 1984) (noting that obtaining blanket licenses from both ASCAP and BMI 'is the practice all three networks have followed until now').
11. See <www.bmi.com/about/backgrounder.asp> (last visited: 5 Dec. 2005).
12. See Hearing before the House Subcommittee on Courts; The Internet, And Intellectual Property Committee On The Judiciary, 11 May 2005, <http://judiciary.house.gov/Oversight.aspx?ID= 157>, (last visited: 5 Dec. 2005).

other two, SESAC operates without a consent decree. Originally, SESAC was short for the Society of European Stage Authors & Composers, but now SESAC is the official name. Membership numbers are not available for SESAC, though they are estimated to have the fewest members of the performing rights organizations.

SESAC does not share its sales figures, but it is estimated that SESAC had between USD 52 million and USD 92 million in revenue annually for the years 2001 through 2003.[13]

2.2   THE LEGAL RIGHT AT ISSUE: PUBLIC PERFORMANCES UNDER UNITED STATES' LAW

In the United States, Congress first extended copyright protection to 'musical compositions' in 1831,[14] but initially protected musical composition solely against unauthorized copying.[15] It was not until 1897 that Congress prohibited others from 'publicly performing' a copyrighted musical composition without the copyright owner's permission.[16] In the 1897 Act, Congress prohibited unauthorized public performances generally.[17] It did not limit the prohibition to those performances that were 'for profit', though it did provide additional criminal penalties for unauthorized public performances that were 'willful and for profit'.[18]

In the Copyright Act of 1909, however, Congress retained a prohibition on unauthorized public performances of musical compositions, but limited the prohibition to those done 'for profit'.[19] In the Act, Congress further limited the public performance right by excluding from its reach: (1) public performances by 'public schools, church choir, or vocal societies' done 'for charitable or educational purposes and not for profit'[20]; and (2) public performances by 'coin-operated machines . . . unless a fee is charged for admission to the place where such reproduction or rendition occurs' – the so-called 'jukebox' exception.[21]

Although these express exemptions narrowed the public performance right somewhat, the key legal question that arose initially was over the meaning of the phrase 'for profit'. Within a decade of the 1909 Act's enactment, the question came up in a pair of cases in which copyright owners sued restaurant owners who had hired bands or orchestras to publicly perform copyrighted musical compositions

---

13. See Company Briefs-Gale Group, 2004 (estimating USD 92 million in sales); Hoover's Inc., Hoover's Company Records – Basic Record for SESAC (2005), <www.hoovers.com> (last visited: 6 Dec. 2005) (Hoover ID: 55695) (estimating $52 million in sales).
14. Act of 5 Feb. 1831, Ch. 16, § 1, 21st Cong., 2nd Sess., 4 Stat. 436 at 436.
15. *Ibid.*, § 7, 4 Stat. at 438.
16. Act of 6 Jan. 1897, Ch. 4, 54th Cong., 2nd Sess., 29 Stat. 481 at 481–82.
17. *Ibid.*
18. *Ibid.*, 29 Stat. at 482.
19. *Ibid.*
20. *Ibid.*, § 28, 33 Stat. at 1082.
21. *Ibid.*, § 1(e), 33 Stat. at 1076.

for the entertainment of their patrons.[22] Because there was no separate charge for the musical entertainment and because there was no door or cover charge for simply entering the restaurants, the defendants in the cases contended that their performances were not 'for profit' within the meaning of the Act. Although the Second Circuit agreed with the defendants, the Supreme Court rejected the notion that there must be some separate, specifically identifiable charge for the musical performance in *Herbert v. Shanley Co.* in 1917.[23]

As Justice Holmes explained in his sparse, but elegant prose:

> The defendants' performances are not eleemosynary. They are part of a total for which the public pays, and the fact that the price of the whole is attributed to a particular item which those present are expected to order, is not important. It is true that the music is not the sole object, but neither is the food, which probably could be got cheaper elsewhere. The object is a repast in surroundings that to people having limited powers of conversation or disliking the rival noise give a luxurious pleasure not to be had from eating a silent meal. If music did not pay it would be given up. If it pays it pays out of the public's pocket. Whether it pays or not the purpose of employing it is profit and that is enough.[24]

Having successfully persuaded the Court to adopt a broader interpretation of 'for profit', right holders established a correspondingly broad need for public performance licenses – a need that initially ASCAP and then the other CMOs attempted to satisfy.

For more than half a century following the *Herbert* decision, the basic legal rule continued to require a license for essentially any public performance of a copyrighted musical composition by a profit-oriented commercial enterprise. The only exceptions to this general rule were the statutory exemptions in the 1909 Act for certain charitable performances and for jukeboxes. As technology evolved, however, another key legal issue developed: What constitutes 'publicly performing' a musical composition? Given the Court's decision in *Herbert*, hiring a band or orchestra to play a song for a restaurant's patrons clearly constituted such a performance, but what if a restaurant owner merely turned on the radio. The issue was presented to the Supreme Court in *Twentieth Century Fox v. Aiken* in 1975.[25]

As the Supreme Court recounted the facts, Aiken owned a small 'fast-service' chicken restaurant in downtown Pittsburgh, Pennsylvania.[26] Although Aiken did not hire a band or orchestra to play for his customers, he did have a radio receiver connected to four speakers in the restaurant's ceiling. During the business day,

---

22. See *Herbert v. Shanley Co.*, 242 U.S. 591 (1917) *[Herbert]*; *John Church Co. v. Hilliard Hotel Co.*, 221 F. 229 (2d Cir., 1915). The name plaintiff in *Herbert v. Shanley Co.*, Victor Herbert, was a founding member of ASCAP, and brought the case as a test case to establish a broader scope for the right of public performance.
23. *Herbert, ibid.*, at 594.
24. See *Herbert, ibid.*
25. *Twentieth Century Fox v. Aiken*, 422 U.S. 151 (1975) *[Aiken]*.
26. *Aiken, ibid.*, at 152.

Aiken would turn on the radio, so that he, his employees and his customers could listen to whatever the radio station was broadcasting, whether that happened to be 'music, news, entertainment, [or] commercial advertising'.[27] When Aiken refused to take an ASCAP license for his restaurant, two ASCAP members sued him for copyright infringement when their musical compositions were played by the radio station to which Aiken was listening. The copyright owners contended that *Herbert* controlled. Aiken countered by arguing that he was not 'performing' the musical compositions; he was merely receiving the radio station's performance.[28] By a 7–2 vote, the Court agreed with Aiken, holding that Aiken's actions did not constitute 'publicly performing' the musical compositions within the meaning of the 1909 Act.[29]

In agreeing with Aiken, the Court worried that finding Aiken liable 'would result in a regime of copyright law that would be both wholly unenforceable and highly inequitable'.[30] Such a rule would be unenforceable, in the Court's view, because even a collective, such as ASCAP, only reduces the transaction costs of licensing – it does not eliminate them. Even with very low transaction costs, licensing every business with a radio would prove impractical.[31] The Court also believed that such a rule would be inequitable for two reasons. First, even a business that took an ASCAP license would have no way of policing the radio station's airplay to ensure that no performances of non-ASCAP works occurred. Second, allowing ASCAP to charge a public performance licensing fee to both radio stations and businesses playing the radio would lead to double-monopoly exactions and their associated inefficiencies,[32] because the CMOs would charge a profit-maximizing and monopolistically priced license fee first to the radio stations and then a second similarly priced license fee to businesses such as Aiken's.[33]

---

27. *Ibid.*, at 153.
28. The radio station held a license from ASCAP for its broadcast of the musical compositions at issue. *Ibid.*
29. *Ibid.*, at 162–163.
30. *Ibid.*, at 162.
31. As the Court observed: 'One has only to consider the countless business establishments in this country with radio or television sets on their premises – bars, beauty shops, cafeterias, car washes, dentists' offices and drive-ins – to realize the total futility of any evenhanded effort on the part of copyright holders to license even a substantial percentage of them.' See *Aiken, ibid.*, at 162. In a footnote, the Court went on: 'The Court of Appeals observed that ASCAP now has license agreements with some 5,150 business establishments in the whole country, noting that these include "firms which employ on premises sources for music such as tape recorders and live entertainment". As a matter of so-called "policy" or "practice," we are told, ASCAP has not even tried to exact licensing agreements from commercial establishments whose radios have only a single speaker.' *Ibid.*, at 162, fn. 12.
32. For a general discussion of the double-monopoly problem, please see H. Varian, *Intermediate Microeconomics: A Modern Approach,* 5th edn (New York: W.W. Norton, 1999), 600 at 463–465.
33. *Ibid.*, at 162–163. ('[T]o hold that all in Aiken's position "performed" these musical compositions would be to authorize the sale of an untold number of licenses for what is basically a single public rendition of a copyrighted work.')

A year after the Court decided *Aiken,* Congress enacted the Copyright Act of 1976.[34] This was Congress's first wholesale revision of the copyright statutes since the Copyright Act of 1909 and was intended to update US law both to reflect technological changes since the 1909 Act and to bring US law closer to the norms reflected in the Berne Convention in anticipation of the United States' subsequent decision to join that Convention in 1988. But the 1976 Act did little to change the applicable rules governing public performances. Although the 1976 Act did away with the 'for profit' language of the 1909 Act, the *Herbert* Court's interpretation of 'for profit' to incorporate any indirect commercial advantage had rendered the 'for profit' limitation largely irrelevant in any event. Similarly, although the 1976 Act specifically defined 'performance' broadly enough to incorporate Aiken's conduct, Congress expressly exempted from copyright liability 'the public reception of [a transmission embodying a performance of a work] on a single receiving apparatus' where no separate charge was made to see or hear the transmission.[35] The 1976 Act thus overturned the 'not a performance' reasoning of the *Aiken* decision, but reaffirmed the ultimate result that Aiken's conduct did not constitute copyright infringement. The 1976 Act also specifically carried forward the statutory exemptions for various charitable and educational performances[36] and provided a compulsory licensing mechanism for jukeboxes.[37] Yet, if the 1976 Act did not broaden the effective reach of the public performance right, it did not narrow it significantly either.[38] Congress's continued recognition of the public performance right thus ensured that a large number of businesses, including radio stations, entertainment venues, retailers, bars and restaurants, would continue to need the public performance licenses that the copyright collectives, ASCAP, BMI, and SESAC, provided.

2.3   THE ANTITRUST CHALLENGES TO THE COLLECTIVES AND
        THE RESULTING CONSENT DECREES

With the recognition of the right of public performance, and its broad reading in *Herbert,* the CMOs were in business. For roughly a quarter century, ASCAP was

---

34. Act of October 19, 1976, Pub. L. No. 553, 94th Cong., 1st Sess., 90 Stat. 2586, codified as amended at 15 U.S.C. §§ 1-1332 (2005).
35. *Ibid.,* at § 110(1), (2), (3), (4), (6), (8), (9), codified as amended 15 U.S.C. § 110(1), (2), (3), (4), (6), (8), (9) (2005).
36. *Ibid.,* at § 110, codified as amended 15 U.S.C. § 116 (2005).
37. *Ibid.,* at § 116, codified as amended 15 U.S.C. § 116 (2005). Congress amended this provision in 1988 to provide for voluntarily negotiated jukebox licenses in order to bring United States' law into compliance with the Berne Convention. Act of October 31, 1988, Pub. L. No. 568, § 4(a)(4), 100th Cong., 1st Sess., 102 Stat. 2853, 2855–2857.
38. See *Broadcast Music, Inc. v. Columbia Broadcasting System, Inc.,* 441 U.S. 1 at 18–19 (1979) *[BMI v. CBS].* ('Furthermore, nothing in the Copyright Act of 1976 indicates in the slightest that Congress intended to weaken the rights of copyright owners to control the public performance of musical compositions. Quite the contrary is true.')

the single source for public performance licenses covering a broad catalog of musical compositions. Rather than compete with each other on price and licensing terms, copyright owners assigned their public performance rights to ASCAP, and ASCAP set the price and licensing terms for the pooled rights collectively. During the 1920s, as music moved to broadcast radio, ASCAP became the dominant source for licensing music on the radio,[39] licensing some 80% of all music played on the radio, and its licensing revenues increased substantially.[40] Had it been any other industry, the use of such a combination to set prices and access terms for the industry's products would quickly have brought antitrust scrutiny. As it was, it took the Department of Justice two decades before it finally filed suit in 1934 against ASCAP for violation of the Sherman Antitrust Act.[41]

In its initial lawsuit, the Department of Justice took the position that ASCAP was itself an unlawful combination, in the vein of Standard Oil, and should therefore be dissolved. But after a two-week trial, the Department of Justice obtained a continuance in the case and essentially dropped its attempt to abolish ASCAP.[42] Instead, when it filed a second set of antitrust claims, this time against both ASCAP and BMI, the Department of Justice targeted particular business practices of the collectives, rather than the collectives themselves.[43]

At the time of this second set of suits, both ASCAP and BMI issued only blanket licenses. Blanket licenses provide the licensee with the authority to publicly perform all copyrighted musical compositions in either ASCAP or BMI's catalogue for the specified license period, but they are priced as a fixed percentage

---

39. The *Herbert* principle was extended and applied to radio airplay by the Sixth Circuit in 1925. See *Jerome H. Remick & Co. v. American Auto. Accessories Co.*, 5 F.2d 411 at 412, cert. denied, 269 U.S. 556 (6th Cir., 1925); see also *M. Whitmark & Sons v. L. Bamberger & Co.*, 291 F. 776 (D.N.J.1923) (reaching the same conclusion that radio airplay constitutes publicly performing the musical composition for profit).

40. Michael A. Einhorn, 'Intellectual Property and Antitrust: Music Performing Rights in Broadcasting', *Columbia-V.L.A. Journal of Law & the Arts* 24 (2001): 349 at 355.

41. *United States v. American Society of Composers Authors and Publishers*, Equity No. 78-388 (S.D.N.Y., filed 30 Aug. 1934).

42. See *BMI v. CBS, supra* n. 38 at 10 (1979). ('A criminal complaint was filed in 1934, but the Government was granted a midtrial continuance and never returned to the courtroom.') Lionel Sobel has suggested that the Department of Justice asked for the continuance because the broadcasters and ASCAP reached a five-year compromise agreement during the trial. See L. Sobel, 'The Music Business and the Sherman Act: An Analysis of the "Economic Realities" of Blanket Licensing', *Loyola of Los Angeles Entertainment Law Journal* 3 (1983): 1 at 5; see also *United States v. American Society of Composers Authors and Publishers (Application of Buffalo Broadcasting Co.)*, Copy. L. Rep. (CCH) para. 27,088, 1993-1 Trade Cas. (CCH) para. 70,153, 1993 U.S. Dist. LEXIS 2566, at *13 *[ASCAP (Application of Buffalo Broadcasting Co.)]*. ('As recounted by its long-time General Counsel, Herman Finkelstein, Esq., the Department of Justice filed a criminal antitrust action against ASCAP in this district in 1934, which led to a hearing the next year. Although the hearing was subsequently adjourned, the Government and ASCAP ultimately agreed to the entry of a civil Consent Decree. The Consent Decree was premised on the filing of a civil suit in 1941, which was followed a few months later by court approval of the Decree.')

43. See *US v. ASCAP, supra* n. 3; *US v. BMI, supra* n. 3.

of the licensee's revenue regardless of the quantity of copyrighted music that the licensee actually used.[44] Once the license fees are collected, ASCAP and BMI then distribute them to their respective members (ASCAP) or affiliates (BMI) based on sampling of the licensees' public performances.

Blanket licenses were convenient not only for the CMOs, but also for many of the licensees. Variety shows, rather than corporate-dictated play-lists, dominated radio airplay at the time. The blanket license therefore provided a convenient fit with the somewhat random and spontaneous nature of radio airplay.

Because the Department of Justice no longer challenged their very existence, BMI and ASCAP both negotiated consent decrees with the Department of Justice to resolve the Department's antitrust lawsuits. These initial consent decrees tried to address four issues. First, it tried to establish some realistic alternative to the blanket license system by: (1) prohibiting the CMOs from obtaining an exclusive assignment of the public performance rights from their members and affiliates, and thus allowing, at least in theory, direct licensing between the copyright owners and the public performance licensees[45]; and (2) requiring the CMOs to offer per-program licenses as an alternative to the blanket licenses.[46] Second, it prohibited the CMOs from discriminating in prices or terms between similarly situated licensees.[47] Third, the consent decree prevented BMI and ASCAP from charging local radio broadcasters for programmes performed on network radio broadcasts.[48] One license issued to the network must cover the simultaneous broadcast of a programme containing licensed material. Such 'downstream' or 'through-to-the-audience' licenses eliminated the need for the local re-broadcaster to obtain a license and prevented ASCAP from charging two license fees for the same performance. Fourth, the consent decree also attempted to ensure an equitable distribution of the collected royalties through provisions governing the internal structure of the CMOs, such as the composition of the Board of Directors and their electoral process[49] as well as the revenue distribution procedures.[50]

The decree provides for the Department of Justice to 'secure compliance with [the] decree'.[51] The Department of Justice is provided with the ability to enforce the decree through access to the records of ASCAP, as well as employees of ASCAP. ASCAP also consented to the retention of jurisdiction by the Second Circuit for 'orders and directions ... in relation to the construction' or modification of the decree, as well as punishment for violation of the decree.[52]

---

44. The collectives vary the percentage for different classes of licensees. For example, radio stations pay a higher percentage of their revenue than restaurants, presumably because music plays a more central role in the earning power of a radio station than it does for a restaurant.
45. *US v. ASCAP, supra* n. 3. at *3.
46. *Ibid.,* at *6.
47. *Ibid.,* at *4–5.
48. *Ibid.,* at *7–8.
49. *Ibid.,* at *10–11.
50. *Ibid.*
51. *Ibid.,* at *12–13.
52. *Ibid.,* at *14.

Yet, these initial consent decrees were not the end of the collectives' antitrust troubles. Only a year later, in 1942, in *Alden-Rochelle, Inc. v. ASCAP*,[53] one hundred sixty-four cinema owners sued ASCAP for violating sections 1 and 2 of the Sherman Antitrust Act[54] because ASCAP required movie producers to distribute their films only to movie theaters with ASCAP licenses.[55] At the time, movie producers secured rights for using the music in their movies – the so-called synchronization right – directly from the copyright owner of the musical composition at issue. However, the agreements between the CMOs and the right holders precluded the latter from licensing the public performance right directly to the movie producer.[56] As a result, to play the movies, the theaters had to obtain a public performance license from ASCAP. The theater owners asserted that the pooling of public performance rights effectively precluded competition between the individual right holders and therefore constituted an antitrust violation. In a second case, *M. Whitmark & Sons v. Jensen*,[57] filed a few years later, the same antitrust issues were raised, but in a slightly different procedural context. In *M. Whitmark & Sons*, the right holders initiated the litigation, suing theater owners for copyright infringement based upon the showing of a movie containing copyrighted music, without an ASCAP license. In response to these claims of copyright infringement, the theater owners asserted the antitrust claims as a defence.[58]

Both district courts found that the pooling of the public performance rights constituted a violation of the antitrust laws.[59] As the court explained in *Alden-Rochelle*:

> Although each member of ASCAP is granted by the copyright law a monopoly in the copyrighted work, it is unlawful for the owners of a number of

53. *Alden-Rochelle, Inc. v. American Society of Composers, Authors and Publishers*, 80 F. Supp. 888 (S.D.N.Y. 1948) *[Alden-Rochelle]*.
54. See 15 U.S.C. §§ 1 (prohibiting agreements in restraint of trade) and 2 (prohibiting monopolization) (2005).
55. See *Alden-Rochelle, supra* n. 53.
56. *Alden-Rochelle, supra* n. 53 at 893. ('The producer does not acquire the performing rights from ASCAP members, because they are prohibited by their arrangement with ASCAP from licensing the performing rights to motion picture producers.') This provision arguably violated the terms of the initial consent decree which prohibited ASCAP 'with respect to any musical composition, [from] acquir[ing] or assert[ing] any exclusive performing right'. *US v. ASCAP, supra* n. 3 at *3.
57. *M. Whitmark & Sons v. Jensen*, 80 F. Supp. 843 (D. Minn. 1948), appeal dismissed, *sub nom. M. Whitmark & Sons v. Berger Amusement Co.*, 177 F.2d 515 (8th Cir., 1949) *[M. Whitmark & Sons]*.
58. See *ibid.*, at 844.
59. See *Alden-Rochelle, supra* n. 53 at 893 ('Almost every part of the ASCAP structure, almost all of ASCAP's activities in licensing motion picture theatres, involve a violation of the anti-trust laws.'); *M. Whitmark & Sons, supra* n. 57 at 849–850. ('It cannot be denied, therefore, that plaintiffs and their associates, acting in concert through ASCAP, fix prices and completely control competition and thereby restrained trade in violation of Section 1 of the Sherman Anti-Trust Act which declares illegal "every contract, combination in the form of trust or otherwise, or conspiracy, in restraint of trade or commerce among the several States". Moreover, it seems

copyrighted works to combine their copyrights by any agreement or arrangement, even if it is for the purpose of thereby better preserving their property rights.[60]

Or as Judge Nordbye wrote in *M. Whitmark & Sons:*

Instead, therefore, of having a single monopoly of a particular piece of copyrighted music and the benefits which that might afford, every copyright owner of music in ASCAP obtains the added economic power and benefit which the combined ASCAP controls gives to them and their associates. Obviously, no one copyright owner would have the monopolistic power over the motion picture industry which ASCAP now enjoys.[61]

Partially in response to these two cases, and partially in response to the development of, and increase in popularity of television, the Department of Justice negotiated amendments to the consent decree with ASCAP in 1950 (known as the Amended Final Judgment).[62] The new consent decree provided television stations with the same rights that were negotiated for radio stations in the 1941 decree: 'through to the audience' licenses for television networks and producers of shows,[63] mandatory non-exclusive license upon request without discriminating between similar situated users[64] and the availability of per-programme licenses as an alternative to the blanket license.[65] The new consent decree provided similar changes in ASCAP's dealings with movie producers and theaters. The decree prohibited ASCAP from collecting performance fees from movie theaters for performances in the movie.[66] The decree required ASCAP to issue a performance license to movie producers upon request and not to seek further performance licenses for the movie.[67] Finally, it prohibited ASCAP members from granting synchronization or recording rights without granting performance rights for movies.[68] As a result, theaters were no longer required to obtain licenses for movies that contained ASCAP material.

Affecting all participants, section IV made it clear that any member of ASCAP could issue licenses directly to users. This provided, at least in theory, for the possibility of competition between ASCAP members by allowing public

inescapable on this record that plaintiffs, through ASCAP, have achieved monopolistic domination of the music integrated in the sound films in the motion picture industry and have effectively monopolized that part of trade and commerce in violation of Section 2 of the Sherman Anit-Trust Act.')

60. *Alden-Rochelle, ibid.*
61. *M. Whitmark & Sons, supra* n. 57 at 848.
62. *United States v. American Society of Composers, Authors and Publishers,* 1950–1951 Trade Cas. (CCH) para. 62,595, 1950 U.S. Dist. LEXIS 4341 (S.D.N.Y. 1950) *[US v. ASCAP 2].*
63. *Ibid.,* at *7.
64. *Ibid.,* at *9 and *11 (§ VI and VIII).
65. *Ibid.,* at *10–11 (§ VII).
66. *Ibid.,* at *4 (§ IV(E)).
67. *Ibid.,* at *7–8 (§ V(C).
68. *Ibid.,* at *16 (s. XVI(B)).

performance licensees to go to the copyright owners directly, rather than to ASCAP. Moreover, the decree provided that the revenue earned by those licenses could go directly to the owner and did not have to be handed over to ASCAP for pooling.[69] This was a change from the original decree, in favour of increasing competition and alternatives in the market for licenses.

Moreover, in an important innovation, section IX of the consent decree amendment provided that if ASCAP and the applicant could not agree on a fee, the applicant could apply to the US District Court for the Southern District of New York to set a 'reasonable' fee for the license.[70] Under the consent decree, ASCAP has the burden of proof in establishing that the fee it seeks is reasonable.[71] By authorizing a third party to set a reasonable fee, the consent decree removed one of the most important weapons available to ASCAP in its negotiations with licensees. ASCAP could no longer unilaterally threaten to deny a public performance license and thereby expose a potential licensee to the ruinous damages available for copyright infringement as a tactic for pressuring licensees to accept higher priced licenses.

Although BMI was not a party to the 1950 decree, in 1966, the Justice Department amended the consent decree with BMI to mirror ASCAP's amended decree.[72] But it was not until 1994 that the consent decree was modified to designate the Southern District of New York as the Rate Court for BMI as well.[73]

As with the earlier consent decree, the 1950 ASCAP decree did not end the antitrust litigation. But taken together, the limitations established in the consent decrees, along with the Justice Department's continued endorsement of a legitimate role for the CMOs, began to take hold with the courts and served to shield the collectives from antitrust liability.[74] Thus, in *K-91, Inc. v. Gershwin Publishing Corp.*,[75] a copyright owner sued a radio station for copyright infringement for

---

69. *Ibid.*, at *5. (s. IV(B) 'Defendant ASCAP is hereby enjoined and restrained from: Limiting, restricting, or interfering with the right of any member to issue to a user non-exclusive licenses for rights of public performances.') As Michael Einhorn has noted: 'After signing the [1941] Decree, ASCAP immediately moved to require that all direct license revenues be pooled, thereby negating any writer incentive to pursue the alternative licenses that the Department had envisioned.' See Einhorn, *supra* n. 40 at 355.

70. *Ibid.*, at *12–13.

71. *Ibid.*

72. See *United States v. Broadcast Music, Inc.*, 1966 Trade Cas. (CCH) para. 71,941, 1966 U.S. Dist. LEXIS 10449 (S.D.N.Y. 1966).

73. *United States v. Broadcast Music, Inc.*, 1996-1 Trade Cas. (CCH) para. 71,378, 1994 U.S. Dist. LEXIS 21476 (S.D.N.Y. 1994).

74. As a legal matter, the consent decrees are not binding on persons who were not parties to them, and hence are not a legal defence to antitrust claims brought by such a non-party. See *Sam Fox Publishing Co. v. United States*, 366 U.S. 683 at 690 (1961) *[Sam Fox Publishing]*; see also *BMI v. CBS, supra* n. 38 at 13. Nevertheless, in evaluating the potential antitrust liability of the collectives, 'it cannot be ignored that the Federal Executive and Judiciary have carefully scrutinized ASCAP and the challenged conduct, have imposed restrictions on various of ASCAP's practices, and by the terms of the decree, stand ready to provide further consideration, supervision, and perhaps invalidation of asserted anticompetitive practices'. *Ibid.*

75. *K-91, Inc. v. Gershwin Publishing Corp.*, 372 F.2d 1 (9th Cir., 1967), *cert. denied*, 389 U.S. 1045 (1968) *[K-91, Inc.]*.

publicly performing a musical composition without an ASCAP license. As in *M. Whitmark & Sons,* the defendant asserted antitrust allegations as a defence. But in *K-91, Inc.,* the Ninth Circuit rejected the defendant's antitrust defence and held that ASCAP had not violated the antitrust laws. In reaching that conclusion, the Ninth Circuit pointed to the Amended Final Judgment and specifically, its re-delegation of the power to fix prices from ASCAP to the Rate Court.[76]

In 1979, the Supreme Court finally had its opportunity to consider application of the antitrust laws to CMOs. In *BMI v. CBS,*[77] CBS asserted that both ASCAP's and BMI's blanket licenses constituted illegal price-fixing in violation of the antitrust laws. When the Second Circuit agreed and found a per se[78] violation of the antitrust laws,[79] the Supreme Court granted certiorari to review the case and reversed.[80] In the Court's view, CMOs were necessary to protect and license the right of public performance effectively.[81] And the blanket license offered by CMOs differed from the individual use licenses that individual copyright owners could offer sufficiently to avoid characterization as a form of horizontal price-fixing by competitors that would be subject to per se liability under the antitrust laws.[82] Rejecting the per se characterization, the Court remanded for consideration of whether the blanket license constituted a violation of the antitrust laws under the so-called rule of reason.[83]

---

76. *K-91, Inc., ibid.,* at 4 ('ASCAP cannot be accused of fixing prices because every applicant to ASCAP has a right under the consent decree to invoke the authority of the United States District Court for the Southern District of New York to fix a reasonable fee whenever the applicant believes that the price proposed by ASCAP is unreasonable, and ASCAP has the burden of proving the price reasonable. In other words, so long as ASCAP complies with the decree, it is not the price fixing authority.'); see also *Buffalo Broadcasting Co. v. American Society of Composers, Authors and Publishers,* 744 F.2d 917 at 927 (2d Cir., 1984) (also pointing to the consent decrees and the Rate Court in rejecting antitrust claims against the collectives) *[Buffalo Broadcasting v. ASCAP]; Broadcast Music, Inc. v. Moor-Law, Inc.,* 527 F. Supp. 758 (D. Del. 1981) (applying a rule of reason analysis and rejecting antitrust claims asserted against BMI) *[BMI v. Moor-Law],* aff'd without opinion, 691 F.2d 490 (3d Cir., 1982).
77. See *supra* n. 40.
78. Under United States antitrust law, '[t]here are ... two complementary categories of antitrust analysis. In the first category are agreements whose nature and necessary effect are so plainly anticompetitive that no elaborate study of the industry is needed to establish their illegality – they are "illegal per se". In the second category are agreements whose competitive effect can only be evaluated by analyzing the facts peculiar to the business, the history of the restraint, and the reasons why it was imposed'. *National Society of Professional Engineers v. United States,* 435 U.S. 679 at 692 (1978) *[Professional Engineers].*
79. *Broadcast Music, Inc. v. Columbia Broadcasting Systems, Inc.,* 562 F.2d 130 at 134 (2d Cir., 1977).
80. *BMI v. CBS, supra* n. 38.
81. *Ibid.,* at 19 ('Otherwise, the commerce anticipated by the Copyright Act and protected against restraint by the Sherman Act would not exist at all or would exist only as a pale reminder of what Congress envisioned.'), and at 22–23. ('ASCAP, in short, made a market in which individual composers are inherently unable to compete fully effectively.')
82. *Ibid.,* at 21–24.
83. *Ibid.,* at 24. ('[W]e cannot agree that [the blanket license] should automatically be declared illegal in all of its many manifestations. Rather, when attacked, it should be subjected to a more discriminating examination under the rule of reason.')

Under the rule of reason, an antitrust plaintiff must demonstrate that the agreement or conduct at issue restrains trade, and that such anti-competitive effects outweigh its pro-competitive effects.[84] On remand, the District Court concluded, and the Second Circuit agreed, that the blanket license had no anti-competitive effects because CBS could negotiate public performance licenses directly with individual copyright owners (or, at least, CBS failed to prove that such individually negotiated licenses were not feasible).[85] Subsequently, other courts applying the rule of reason to CMOs and their blanket licenses have reached similar conclusions.[86] As a result, while antitrust claims have continued to be asserted against the collectives, they have, since *BMI v. CBS,* been unsuccessful, at least so far.

Yet, if the Amended Final Judgment therefore limited the role of private antitrust litigation in regulating CMOs, it created avenues for judicial resolution of two other areas of dispute. First, it carried forward and expanded the rules from the 1941 consent decree regarding ASCAP's internal structure and its methods for distributing the royalty pool to its members.[87] Second, it created the Rate Court and thereby established a procedure for judicial review of ASCAP's licensing fees.[88]

With respect to ASCAP's internal operations, although ASCAP was a membership-based organization and therefore supposedly inherently representative, as part of the antitrust claims leading to the 1941 ASCAP consent decree, the Department of Justice had:

> alleged restraint of competition among the Society's members *inter sese,* resulting from the asserted domination of the Society's affairs by a few of its large publisher members who, it was claimed, were able to control the complexion of the Board of Directors and the apportionment of the Society's revenues.[89]

As a result, the 1941 consent decree set forth the procedures by which the Board was to be elected and the royalty pool distributed.[90] More extensive rules concerning ASCAP's internal structure and the distribution of the royalty pool were added when the consent decree was amended in 1950. Yet, concerns regarding ASCAP's treatment of its own members persisted. So in 1960, the Department of Justice returned to court for a modification to the Amended Final Judgment.[91]

---

84. See, for example, *Professional Engineers, supra* n. 78 at 687–692.
85. *Columbia Broadcasting System, Inc. v. American Society of Composers, Artists and Publishers,* 620 F.2d 930 at 936-39 (2d Cir., 1980), cert. denied, 450 U.S. 970 (1981) *[CBS v. ASCAP].*
86. See *Buffalo Broadcasting v. ASCAP, supra* n. 76; *BMI v. Moor-Law, supra* n. 76.
87. *US v. ASCAP 2, supra* n. 62 at *15, 16–17 (§§ 11, 13).
88. *Ibid.,* at *6–14 (§§ V, VI, VII, VIII, IX).
89. *Sam Fox Publishing, supra* n. 74 at 685–686.
90. See *US v. ASCAP, supra* n. 3 at *10–11.
91. See *United States v. American Society of Composers, Authors and Publishers,* 1960 Trade Cas. (CCH) para. 69,612, 1960 U.S. Dist. LEXIS 4967 (S.D.N.Y. 1960) *[US v. ASCAP 3]; US v. ASCAP 2, supra* n. 62.

In its petition leading to the 1960 modification, the Department of Justice alleged that:

> at present complete control over votes and revenues is in the hands of the Board of Directors [of ASCAP], who are a self-perpetuating body, as they are elected by those members with the greatest number of votes which number is in turn determined by the share in revenues, which is determined by rules of distribution enacted by the Board.
>
> The alleged result is that less than 5 percent of the writer-members and less than one percent of the publisher-members have the power to elect all the directors.[92]

The net result was, in the Department of Justice's view, 'seniority considerations and the will of the "controlling" group are emphasized as to members, songs and performance credit averaging to such a degree that young writers and publishers are being discouraged from writing and publishing new songs'.[93]

To address these concerns, the 1960 modification to the Amended Final Judgment attempted to impose a royalty-distribution system based more heavily on actual performances, as measured by scientifically valid surveys. Less or no weight was to be given to a writer's seniority in allocating the royalty pool, and ASCAP's discretion to vary the distribution by weighting some performances, such as feature performances, more heavily than others, such as background or commercial performances, was limited somewhat.[94]

---

92. *US v. ASCAP 3, ibid.*, at *6.
93. *Ibid.*, at *3.
94. See *ibid.*, at *5. ('The great fluctuation in credit given to different songs performed in the same manner was one of the major grievances brought to the attention of the Justice Department. In the past, it was possible for credit to fluctuate as much as 1000 to 1 on the performance of different compositions as themes, jingles, background, cue or bridge music. Under the new system, this ratio has been cut in most instances to at most 10 to 1 and in isolated instances to no more than 100 to 1. The test used to qualify compositions for the 10 to 1 ratio has also been changed to allow more for the performance record of the piece and less for the discretion of the board.') The ASCAP royalty pool is divided based upon performance credits. Performance credits are given based upon the number of times a particular work is performed, as measured by the surveys, but in allocating performance credits, one minute of airtime is not necessarily worth one minute of airtime. In allocating performance credits, performances are weighted based on broadcast type, time of day, and usage category (feature, background, theme, advertising, and promotional). The weights assigned to different music uses are based upon entirely subjective judgments of relative worth. The most valued performance is a feature performance and the ratio of feature performances to commercial performances which are least valued is 1:1 in the United Kingdom, 3:1 in France, 4.5:1 in Germany, and 33.3:1 under ASCAP. M. Holden, 'ASCAP and BMI Usage Weightings – Out-of-Step with the World?', *Film Music Magazine* 3 (2000): 345. Feature music includes compositions that are the primary focus of audience attention, theme music is used to open and close programmes, background music is used to complement screen action, and commercial music includes advertising jingles, public service announcements and promotional music that pitch other programmes.

Still not satisfied with their treatment by ASCAP, a group of small publishers sought to intervene, as of right, in the antitrust 'litigation'[95] between the United States and ASCAP, so that they could protect their interests directly. In *Sam Fox Publishing*,[96] the Supreme Court considered the small publishers' claims and held that they could not intervene as of right.[97] In so concluding, the Court argued that a Catch-22 situation precluded intervention as of right for the small publishers. The Department of Justice had brought its antitrust claims against ASCAP, both as an entity and as a representative of all the Society's members.[98] The small publishers, as members of ASCAP, were therefore class defendants. However, 'the judgment in a class action will bind only those members of the class whose interests have been adequately represented by existing parties to the litigation'.[99] To intervene as of right, on the other hand, the small publishers had to show that they would be bound by any judgment in the litigation, yet were not adequately represented. From these two rules, the Court framed its Catch-22 dilemma: If the small publishers were not adequately represented by ASCAP, then they could not intervene as of right because, despite their nominal status as class defendants, they would not be bound by any resulting judgment. If the small publishers were adequately represented by ASCAP, then they could not intervene as of right because their interests were already adequately represented.[100] Given this logical conundrum, the Supreme Court rejected the small publishers' motion to intervene as of right.[101]

These attempts to regulate ASCAP's internal operations (as it were) were largely abandoned by the Department of Justice in 2001, when the Department of Justice and ASCAP reached agreement on amending (again) the final judgment

---

95. There was, in truth, no active litigation, but the consent decrees gave the district court continuing jurisdiction over the initial antitrust lawsuits. This allowed the district court to amend the final judgment and approve amendments and modifications to the consent decrees in 1950, 1960 and again in 2001.
96. See *supra* n. 76.
97. *Ibid.*, at 695.
98. *Ibid.*, at 691.
99. *Ibid.*
100. *Ibid.* In explaining its decision, the Court went on to differentiate the adequacy of ASCAP's representation with respect to the government's two types of antitrust claims. With respect to ASCAP's external dealings with its licensees, the interests of ASCAP and the small publishers were sufficiently aligned so that ASCAP adequately represented the small publishers and hence the small publishers were bound by the aspects of the consent decree governing ASCAP's external dealings. However, with respect to ASCAP's internal dealings with its own members, the interests of ASCAP and the small publishers were not aligned. As a result, ASCAP did not adequately represent the small publishers and the small publishers were not bound by the provisions of the consent decree dealing with ASCAP's internal operations. *ibid.*, at 692.
101. See also *United States v. American Society of Composer, Authors and Publishers (Application of Metromedia, Inc.)*, 341 F.2d 1003 (2d Cir.) (applying *Sam Fox Publishing* to a would-be ASCAP licensee and holding that because Metromedia was not a party to the consent decree, it did not have standing to enforce its provisions through contempt motion), cert. denied *sub nom. Metromedia, Inc. v. American Society of Composers, Authors and Publishers*, 382 U.S. 877 (1965).

(the Second Amended Final Judgment [AFJ2]).[102] Apparently believing that competition between BMI and ASCAP for affiliates/members would adequately protect copyright owners from the CMOs' 'monopsonistic' buying power,[103] the provisions respecting the collectives' internal structure and election procedures were removed from the consent decrees.[104] Similarly, the provisions respecting the collectives' royalty distribution procedures were loosened to provide the CMOs with more discretion in allocating their respective royalty pools.

The establishment of a procedure for judicial review of ASCAP's licensing rates has also proved a fertile ground for litigation. In addition to the straightforward judicial review of whether ASCAP's rates for its blanket licenses were reasonable, would-be licensees also tried to use the Amended Final Judgment to push for more flexible licensing options. Thus, in *United States v. American Society of Composers, Authors and Publishers (Application of Shenandoah Valley Broadcasting, Inc.)*,[105] a group of television stations, following the procedure set forth in section 11 of the Amended Final Judgment, requested a blanket license from ASCAP that would exclude programmes obtained either from a television network or from independent film producers.[106] In essence, the local television stations were trying to avoid the same double-licensing problem that led to the *Alden-Rochelle* and *M. Whitmark & Sons* litigation by getting the public performance license issue resolved at the time the independent film producer obtained the synchronization license. When ASCAP refused to quote a rate for the proposed license, the local television stations petitioned the Southern District of New York to establish a reasonable rate for the proposed license. In support of their petition, the television stations pointed to the language of section IX of the Amended Final Judgment, which provided:

> Defendant ASCAP shall, upon receipt of a written application for a license for the right of public performance of any, some or all of the compositions in the ASCAP repertory, advise the applicant in writing of the fee which it deems reasonable for the license requested.[107]

But the Second Circuit rejected the television stations' arguments. Although the Second Circuit acknowledged that 'a strictly literal reading of [section IX] would [. . .] require ASCAP to quote a fee for any license requested', it felt that such a

---

102. See *United States v. American Society of Composers,* Authors and Publishers, 2001–2002 Trade Cas. (CCH) para. 73,474, 2001 U.S. Dist. LEXIS 23707 (S.D.N.Y. 2001) *[US v. ASCAP 4]*.
103. See Einhorn, *supra* n. 40 at 364–366.
104. See *US v. ASCAP 4, supra* n. 102.
105. *United States v. American Society of Composers, Authors and Publishers (Application of Shenandoah Valley Broadcasting, Inc.)*, 331 F.2d 117 (2d Cir.) *[ASCAP (Application of Shenandoah Valley)]*, cert. denied *sub nom. Shenandoah Valley Broadcasting, Inc. v. ASCAP*, 377 U.S. 997 (1964).
106. *ASCAP (Application of Shenandoah Valley), ibid.*, at 121.
107. *Ibid.*

reading would 'ignore [. . .] both context and good sense'.[108] The Second Circuit therefore read section IX as requiring ASCAP to quote a rate only for the two types of licenses otherwise required by the Amended Final Judgment: (1) the blanket license required by section VI and (2) the per-programme license required by section VII(b).[109] Through this restrictive reading of the rate review provisions, the Second Circuit sharply limited the flexibility that a literal reading of section IX would otherwise have incorporated into the Amended Final Judgment.

Despite this setback, ASCAP licensees have also used the rate review provisions in a more straightforward manner: (1) to limit the rates for ASCAP's blanket licenses and (2) to push for per-programme license rates that make such licenses a realistic and practical alternative to blanket licenses. In the first appellate decision on these issues, *American Society of Composers, Authors and Publishers v. Showtime/The Movie Channel, Inc.*,[110] the Second Circuit laid out the basic approach. As a general matter, the court stated that a 'reasonable' rate must reflect the 'fair market value' of the blanket license, and defined '[f]air market value [. . . as] the price that a willing seller and a willing buyer would agree to in an arm's length transaction'.[111] Despite its imprecise phrasing, this standard does not mean that whatever historical prices ASCAP had managed to charge for its blanket licenses conclusively established a 'reasonable' rate. After all, the transactions between a monopolist and those who purchase its goods involve willing parties, on both sides, in an arm's length transaction.[112] Yet, the very point of regulating a monopolist's rates is to reduce the prices that willing parties would otherwise have to pay for the monopolist's goods.[113] As a result, the Second Circuit held that historical licensing fees, while relevant if otherwise comparable,[114] were not controlling, and could be

---

108. *Ibid.*
109. *Ibid.*, at 122. ('We construe the sentence as relating to requests for licenses which some other portion of the Judgment required ASCAP to grant.')
110. *American Society of Composers, Authors and Publishers v. Showtime/The Movie Channel, Inc.*, 912 F.2d 563 (2d Cir., 1990) [*Showtime/The Movie Channel*].
111. *Ibid.*, at 569.
112. In *Buffalo Broadcasting v. ASCAP, supra* n. 76, the Second Circuit missed this point. In analyzing whether the price ASCAP had set for per-programme licenses was reasonable, the court asked whether 'the price for such a license, in an objective sense, is higher than the value of the rights received'. *ibid.*, at 926. But, as discussed, even a monopolist will price its goods so that some consumers value them more than the price. Otherwise, the monopolist will not sell any of its goods.
113. See, for example, *United States v. American Society of Composers, Authors and Publishers (Application of Turner Broadcasting System, Inc.)*, 782 F. Supp. 778 at 790 (S.D.N.Y. 1991) [*ASCAP (Application of Turner Broadcasting System, Inc.)*] ('This language explicitly confirms the obvious – that the Decree was designed to limit ASCAP's ability, by pooling copyrights for large amounts of music used in radio broadcasting, to extract unreasonable fees for performance of the music.'), aff'd *per curiam*, 956 F.2d 21 (2d Cir.), cert. denied, 504 U.S. 914 (1992).
114. See *Showtime/The Movie Channel, supra* n. 110 at 566–567 (noting differences between ASCAP's relationship with two other pay cable services, HBO and Disney, and its relationship with Showtime in discounting weight given to terms of ASCAP's licenses with HBO and Disney in setting the proper rate for Showtime license).

properly discounted to the extent they were artificially inflated by ASCAP's market power or by licensees' perception of such power.[115]

Yet, if the lack of a competitive market for ASCAP licenses means that market comparables is not the answer, it is a little difficult to see what sort of factual evidence a court should rely upon in setting a reasonable rate.[116] In the prototypical case of monopoly rate regulation involving utilities, the rate is set so as to ensure the utility a reasonable return on its investment given its operating costs.[117] There is quite simply no way to apply that standard to blanket, or even individual, performance licenses for music.[118] Alternatively, if we tried to define the socially optimal fee, we would begin by recognizing that a higher fee will re-distribute somewhat more of society's wealth to musical work copyright owners and will perhaps encourage the creation of somewhat more, or better quality, works; a somewhat lower fee will re-distribute somewhat less. Ideally, then, the fee should be set precisely at the point where the additional works a higher fee would encourage are less valuable to society than the alternative goods or services to which the resources would otherwise be devoted.[119] Although perfectly sound as a theoretical

---

115. *Ibid.*, at 570. ('Nor did the Magistrate commit legal error in regarding ASCAP's market power as a relevant consideration in diminishing the weight of the ASCAP licenses to HBO and Disney as comparable sales. The rate court was established as a component of the settlement of the Government's antitrust challenge to ASCAP's licensing practices. Though the rate court's existence does not mean that ASCAP has violated the antitrust law, the court need not conduct itself without regard to the context in which it was created. The opportunity of users of music rights to resort to the rate court whenever they apprehend that ASCAP's market power may subject them to unreasonably high fees would have little meaning if that court were obliged to set a "reasonable" fee solely or even primarily on the basis of the fees ASCAP had successfully obtained from other users.')

116. Because of these difficulties, Professor Cirace has suggested that the question is not, in fact, an economic one, but a political one: How much of society's wealth should be redistributed to music composers through what, in effect, is a public performance tax? See Prof. Cirace, 'CBS v. ASCAP: An Economic Analysis of a Political Problem', *Fordham Law Review* 47 (1978): 277 at 298.

117. See, for example, *In re Permian Basin Area Rate Cases*, 390 U.S. 747, 754–755 (1968) (reviewing application of FPC price-setting formula based on costs of extraction of natural gas and prescribed rate of return).

118. See *ASCAP (Application of Buffalo Broadcasting Co.)*, *supra* n. 42 at *59. ('Not surprisingly, given the nature of the business, we also have no evidence directly relating to the musical equivalent of "costs of production" or reasonable rates of return.') Moreover, any rate of return approach would inevitably become circular. Any given fee level will generate a certain level of revenue for copyright owners, and if copyright owners are rational, they will continue to invest in creating additional works until they reach the marginal work – the one for which expected revenue precisely equals the author's reservation price. A higher fee level means more revenue for any given work, but it remains true that copyright owners will continue to invest in additional works until the last work just breaks even.

119. See G. Lunney, 'Reexamining Copyright's Incentives-Access Paradigm', *Vanderbilt Law Review* 49 (1996): 483 at 487–492 and 576–579. ('If we broaden copyright, we increase the economic return on any given authorship investment. We can thereby lure resources, in the form of labour and capital, away from other productive endeavors into the production of copyrighted works and lead the market to produce additional works. But to create these additional works, we must strip the resources from other sectors of the economy. As a result,

standard, trying to identify such an 'ideal' rate in practice would inevitably require so much guesswork, uncertainty and relative valuation of different productive activities that it is fairly characterized more as a question of policy for the legislature, than a question of fact for the courts.

Rather than approach it from a rate regulation perspective or attempting to define a theoretically ideal rate, courts have defined the 'reasonable' blanket fee as the price that would be charged in a competitive market for blanket licenses.[120] Yet, such a competitive market does not exist. That is precisely why judicial rate setting is necessary in the first place. Nevertheless, given the absence of any other factual basis for setting a 'reasonable' rate, courts have been forced to rely on ASCAP's historical prices, discounting them more or less, depending on the court's own sense for the potential influence of undue market power, and adjusting them for differences in circumstance.[121] Often, the exercise seems little more than baby-splitting,[122] picking a license fee somewhere between a low fee proposed by the licensee and a high fee proposed by ASCAP.[123]

In any event, having pretended to set a 'reasonable rate' for the blanket license, the next task for the courts was setting a reasonable rate for the per-programme

---

broadening copyright imposes a second critical cost: the lost value society would have associated with the alternative investments to which these resources would otherwise have been devoted.')

120. See *ASCAP (Application of Buffalo Broadcasting Co.), supra* n. 42 at *57–58. ('Since we are looking at a market for certain types of licenses, the theoretical "competitive market" that we seek to recreate, in concededly imprecise ways, is not that of competing composers seeking to license their compositions to public performers who are free to choose among available musical offerings. Rather, it is a market of competing licensors capable of offering the type of protection and benefits provided now by ASCAP in the form of its blanket and per-programme licenses.')

121. See *United States v. Broadcast Music, Inc. (Application of Music Choice, Inc.),* 316 F.3d 189 at 194 (2d Cir., 2003); *Showtime/The Movie Channel, supra* n. 110 at 566–568; *United States v. American Society of Composers, Authors and Publishers (Application of Capital Cities/ABC, Inc.),* 831 F. Supp. 137 at 144–145 (S.D.N.Y. 1993) (noting that determination of reasonable rate may consider previously negotiated agreements 'as well as changed circumstances that make prior benchmarks outdated measures of fair value'.); *ASCAP (Application of Buffalo Broadcasting Co.), supra* n. 42 at *60. ('Accordingly, both in prior cases and in this proceeding, the parties and the court have focused principally on agreements voluntarily arrived at by the same or comparably situated parties contracting for the same or comparable rights.')

122. The inevitable arbitrariness of the rate set undoubtedly contributes to the undue time and expense associated usually associated with rate setting proceedings. For a discussion of the time and expense associated with rate settings, please see 'Memorandum of the United States in Support of the Joint Motion to Enter Second Amended Final Judgment, United States v. ASCAP, No. 41-1395' at 29 and 33 (S.D.N.Y. 2000), <www.usdoj.gov/atr/cases/f6300/6395.pdf> (last visited: 6 Dec. 2005) [AFJ2 Memo]. ('Rate court proceedings under the AFJ have been protracted and costly for music users, ASCAP, and the Court. Indeed, some proceedings have lasted a decade or longer, even though the purpose of the proceedings was to determine license fees to be charged during a five-year period.')

123. See *Showtime/The Movie Channel, supra* n. 110 at 566 (setting a blanket license rate of USD 15 per subscriber where Showtime asked for a rate of USD 8 per subscriber and ASCAP sought a rate of USD 25 per subscriber).

licenses. The Amended Final Judgment stated that the fee for per-programme licenses was to be set so that radio and television broadcasters 'shall have a genuine choice between per program and blanket licenses'.[124] Yet, when the proper rate for per-program licenses was initially litigated in *ASCAP (Application of Buffalo Broadcasting Co.)*, ASCAP proposed to set the percentage-of-revenue for programme licenses at a fourfold multiple of any blanket fee amount, and wanted to add an unspecified increment to cover additional expenses that it would have incurred in administering and monitoring the programme.[125] In his report, Magistrate Judge Doniger rejected this proposal. In his view, 'ASCAP's current proposal for a per-program license [was] plainly geared to making it unusable for most, if not virtually all, of the television stations.'[126]

Instead, Magistrate Judge Doniger designed the per-programme license so that a typical local television station would pay ASCAP the same amount under either the blanket or per-programme license alternatives, exclusive of additional administration costs. To achieve this equality, Magistrate Judge Doniger found as a factual matter that the typical local station needed an ASCAP programme license to cover roughly 75% of its programming. The remainder consisted of network or other programme for which the public performance right was already cleared. As a result, Magistrate Judge Doniger set the percentage-of-revenue in the programme license at a 1.33 multiple of the blanket rate to ensure 'revenue equivalence' between per-programme and blanket license fees for the typical station.[127] Magistrate Judge Doniger also added a 7% increment to the per-programme rate to compensate ASCAP for the additional inefficiencies and administrative costs inherent in per-programme licensing.[128] Subsequently, the parties agreed to add a 10% increment to the per-programme license for a 'miniblanket' to cover a local broadcaster's incidental use of ASCAP music in commercials.[129]

---

124. *US v. ASCAP 2, supra* n. 62 at *11–12 (§ VII(B)(3)).
125. *ASCAP (Application of Buffalo Broadcasting Co.), supra* n. 42 at *169–170. ('[O]nce again citing prior agreements, [ASCAP] argues that the per-program license fee should be set at a percentage-of-revenue rate that is four times the effective percentage-of-revenue rate of each station's blanket license fee, together with a separate, undetermined fee designed to cover all of ASCAP's expenses of administering the license. Since the starting revenue base that ASCAP seeks for the per-program license is the same as the revenue base for the blanket license, under this proposal the ceiling for the per-program fee for each station would be 400 percent of its blanket license fee.')
126. *Ibid.*, at *189.
127. *Ibid.*, at *230 fn. 111. ('We presume, in very rough terms, that if twenty-five percent of the station's programs contain no ASCAP music, the station's per-program fee at that point – without further changes – will be about 75 percent of the fee ceiling. For this fee to equal the station's blanket license fee, the ceiling must be set at about 133 percent of the blanket fee.')
128. *Ibid.*, at *246–247. ('Based on the foregoing [discussion of the additional administrative expenses a per-program license will entail], the per-program fee will be calculated on the basis of a ceiling set at 140 percent of each station's blanket license fee.')
129. See Einhorn, *supra* n. 40 at 360. Magistrate Judge Doniger had added a 7.5% increment to the per-programme license fee to cover such incidental uses, but that aspect of his decision was overturned on appeal. See *United States v. American Society of Composers, Authors and Publishers (In re Capital Cities/ABC, Inc.)*, 157 F.R.D. 173 at 204 (S.D.N.Y. 1994). In a

Given the additional administrative fees associated with a per-programme license, as well as the additional administrative expense that a licensee would itself incur to keep track of its music usage, Magistrate Judge Doniger acknowledged that '[f]or most stations, the blanket license is likely, in the end, to be less expensive'.[130] Nonetheless, the magistrate hoped that the availability of per-programme licenses could become 'a bridge to source or direct licensing over time'.[131] With the guaranteed availability of a per-programme license, a station could begin the process of negotiating direct licenses with confidence that, if it should prove unable to license all of the musical works at issue, it could cover the remaining performances through a per-programme license.

In June 2001, the Department of Justice and ASCAP reached an agreement on amending the final judgment (referred to as the AFJ2).[132] As with previous amendments, this decree was adjusted for changes in technology since the last agreement. In addition to television and radio broadcasters, it addressed cable, satellite and Internet broadcasting, and unlike earlier decrees also included language to cover not yet developed performance technologies.[133] For two classes of music users, foreground/background music services and online music users, AFJ2 required ASCAP to issue 'per-segment' licenses very similar to the per-programme licenses required for more traditional radio and television broadcasters.[134]

In section VIII, AFJ2 sided with Magistrate Judge Doniger's interpretation of the fee level required for per-programme licenses to offer a 'genuine choice'.[135] As the Department of Justice explained in its Memorandum in Support of AFJ2:

> Section VIII(b) thus is intended to clarify that a representative user has a 'genuine choice' between a per-program or per-segment license and a blanket

---

subsequent case, the Rate Court approved the use of such an increment for radio per-programme licenses. See *United States v. American Society of Composers, Authors and Publishers (Application of Salem Media of California, Inc.)*, 981 F. Supp. 199 at 219-20 (S.D.N.Y. 1997).

130. *ASCAP (Application of Buffalo Broadcasting Co.)*, *supra* n. 42 at *232; see also *ibid.*, at 231 fn. 112 (noting that under the interim regime license, with a somewhat narrower gap between the per-programme and blanket license fees, less than one-third of stations took the per-programme license option).

131. *Ibid.*, at *225.

132. See *US v. ASCAP 4*, *supra* n. 102.

133. *Ibid.*, at *4 (§ II(F)). Because earlier consent decrees were often written to apply specifically to a given distribution technology, questions had arisen as to whether they applied to new distribution technologies. See, for example, *ASCAP (Application of Turner Broadcasting Co.)*, *supra* n. 113 at 781 (considering and rejecting ASCAP's arguments that because cable channels were not specifically mentioned in the 1950 consent decree they were not covered by the decree's requirements).

134. *US v. ASCAP 4*, *supra* n. 102 at *13–14 (§ VII(A)(2)). In *ASCAP (Application of Muzak LLC)*, *supra* n. 10, two foreground/background music services argued that the 'per segment' license provisions required ASCAP to issue licenses for portions (or segments) of its music catalog. The court rejected such a construction of 'segment' and held that a 'segment' refers to a cohesive unit of the licensee's performance, similar to the unit 'program' found on more traditional radio or television broadcasts. *Ibid.*, at 568.

135. *Ibid.*, at *15–16 (§ 8).

license only if it would pay roughly the same total license fee under the per-program or per-segment license that it would have paid under the blanket license (excluding any added administration cost), assuming it did not reduce or directly license any of its performances of ASCAP music.[136]

However, AFJ2 went a bit further by ensuring that the per-programme or per-segment license fee would be effectively reduced to reflect any ASCAP material directly licensed from the copyright owner.[137] In section VII(A), AFJ2 also incorporated into per-programme or per-segment licenses a 'miniblanket' license that would cover 'ambient and incidental uses' and prohibited ASCAP from burdening its licensees with the obligation to monitor or keep records of such uses.[138]

Following AFJ2, in *United States v. Broadcast Music, Inc. (Application of AEI Music Network, Inc.)*,[139] the Second Circuit addressed the issue of whether the Rate Court could consider per-piece or direct licenses a licensee had otherwise obtained in determining the 'reasonable' fee for a blanket license. Predictably, the collective opposed the proposal, because it would provide licensees with an incentive to seek out and obtain public performances directly from the right holders. BMI argued that the licensees were seeking a new type of 'carve out' license – a license to perform all of BMI's repertoire, except those works otherwise directly licensed. Such a license, BMI continued, was not required by the consent decree and was foreclosed by the Second Circuit's earlier decision in *Shenandoah*.[140] But the Second Circuit rejected BMI's arguments. In the court's view, '[t]he only modification Applicants have proposed to the traditional blanket license is in the way the fee is calculated, which is, of course, exactly what is contemplated in the rate court provision'.[141] The court therefore remanded the case for an order directing BMI to issue a blanket license with 'a fee structure that reflects per piece and direct licenses' otherwise obtained.[142]

In *ASCAP (Application of Muzak, LLC)*,[143] a similar gloss was added to AFJ2.[144] Yet, in a subsequent clarification, the *Muzak* court undermined even the trivial incentive toward direct licensing[145] that such a reduction in the blanket

---

136. AFJ2 Memo, *supra* n. 122 at 29–30.
137. *US v. ASCAP 4, supra* n. 102 at *16 (In relevant part, § VIII(B) provides: 'it shall be assumed for the purposes of this Section VIII(B) that all of the music user's programs or segments that contain performances of ASCAP music are subject to an ASCAP fee'.).
138. *US v. ASCAP 4, ibid.*, at *13 (§ VII(A)(1), (2)).
139. *United States v. Broadcast Music, Inc. (Application of AEI Music Network, Inc.)*, 275 F.3d 168 (2d Cir., 2001). Broadcast Music was not governed by the terms of AFJ2, as they applied only to ASCAP, but was bound to a similar consent decree. *United States v. Broadcast Music, Inc., supra* n. 72; *United States v. Broadcast Music, Inc., supra* n. 73.
140. 275 F.3d at 176–177. For a discussion of *[ASCAP (Application of Shenandoah Valley)]*, please see text accompanying nn. 107–111 *supra*.
141. *Ibid.*, at 176.
142. *Ibid.*, at 177.
143. See *supra* n. 10.
144. *Ibid.*, at 578–579.
145. In truth, allowing even one-for-one discounts from the blanket license fee for previously negotiated direct licenses leaves a music user with no savings over simply paying for the blanket license until the user has acquired so many direct licenses that it no longer requires the

license fee would provide. In its clarification, the court explained that while it would consider 'direct licensing relationships already in existence at the time of trial in determining a reasonable blanket licensing fee', it would not establish a fee mechanism 'that provides credits or discounts for direct licensing arrangements that applicants may enter into during the term of the license'.[146] Given the long-term nature of the typical public performance license, this interpretation means that a licensee might have to wait years before direct licensing would bear fruit in a blanket license fee reduction.

2.4   THE NEW CMO ON THE BLOCK: SOUNDEXCHANGE

Although US copyright law has long protected the composers of musical works, it has only recently begun protecting the performers or producers of those works. In the Sound Recording Copyright Act of 1971, Congress formally extended copyright protection to an artist's rendition of a musical work, recorded on a phonogram as a sound recording.[147] However, the United States is not party to the 1961 Rome Convention. Thus, although the Sound Recording Act gave the owners of sound recording copyrights control over the reproduction of their record-ings, it did not give sound recording copyright owners a right to control their public performance. As a result, US law did not provide for the remuneration of perfor-mers and/or producers of phonograms (sound recordings) when their phonograms were publicly performed. Performers and producers of sound recordings have long argued that they too should have a performance right, just as the composers of musical works do. Musical work copyright owners have strenuously opposed the recognition of a public performance right for sound recordings, however. They have feared (rightly) that any licensing revenue from a sound recording public performance right would come primarily not from additional licensing fees from the public performance venues, but from a split of the existing public performance licensing fees already being paid to the musical work copyright owners.[148]

---

blanket license at all. Nonetheless, the change is certainly an improvement over the previous rule under which music users who obtained direct licenses had to pay twice for the music – once to the direct licensor and once to the relevant CMO.

146.   *ASCAP (Application of Muzak, LLC), supra* n. 10 at 592–593. Although this may seem arbi-trary, the court felt constrained by its authority under AFJ2 not to issue a new type of license, but only to set a reasonable fee for a blanket license.

147.   See Sound Recording Copyright Act, Pub. L. No. 92-140, 85 Stat. 391 (1971) (incorporated as an amendment to the 1909 Act). When the United States enacted the Copyright Act of 1976, it retained this recognition of sound recordings as a type of copyrightable work. See 17 U.S.C. § 102(7) (2009).

148.   Presumably, ASCAP, BMI and SESAC are already charging these venues a profit-maximizing licensing fee for the public performance of their musical works. That necessarily means that attempting to charge a higher fee would reduce the revenue to ASCAP, BMI and SESAC, as the higher fee would drive enough potential consumers away that a higher fee would prove unprofitable. Creating the need for a second license for the same effective right will not increase the value to the venues of publicly performing music. As a result, it will not increase

In the Digital Performance Right in Sound Recordings Act of 1995, Congress enacted a limited digital public performance right for sound recordings.[149] As codified in section 114 of the Copyright Act, the sound recording digital public performance right does not apply to historically paradigmatic public performances, such as a non-subscription broadcast transmissions, such as radio or television, the re-transmission of such a broadcast, through, for example, a cable provider, or to the performance of a sound recording within a business establishment.[150] Rather, it applies only (1) to a limited category of non-subscription and subscription transmissions, such as certain webcasters, and (2) to interactive transmissions that enable a member of the public to receive, on request, a transmission of a particular sound recording or a programme specially created for the recipient.[151] With respect to the first category, Congress narrowed the digital public performance for sound recordings further by providing a compulsory license.[152] Moreover, the Copyright Act expressly tasked the US Copyright Office with designating a CMO for these compulsory or statutory licenses, which it did, naming SoundExchange, Inc. as the CMO for this right.[153] With respect to the second, no CMO has yet emerged,

---

the profit-maximizing total licensing fee for the public performance right. Recognition of a public performance right for sound recordings, and the requirement of a separate license, thus creates two possibilities. First, the CMOs for the two rights jointly set the profit-maximizing fee. In this case, the existing licensing fees do not change, but are now simply split between the musical work composers and the sound recording artists – exactly as the composers feared. Or, second, the sound recording artists could force public performance venues to pay a second licensing fee on top of the existing licensing fees. To the extent the existing licensing fee was already properly set at the profit-maximizing rate, however, such a double license fee will necessarily reduce the revenue for the musical work performance license, thus cutting into the public performance royalties of the composers indirectly.

149. 104 Pub. L. No. 39, 109 Stat. 336 (1995).
150. 15 U.S.C. § 114(d)(1)(A), (B), and (C) (2009).
151. In *Arista Records, LLC v. Launch Media, Inc.*, the Second Circuit considered the question whether a music service that tailored a music stream to each of its consumers based upon their individually expressed preferences constituted an interactive transmission. 2009 U.S. App. LEXIS 18843 (2d Cir., 2009). The plaintiffs argued that it did because the user's preferences influenced the music the user heard. The court, however, rejected that argument and emphasized that the line between an interactive and non-interactive service must reflect Congress's concern that an interactive service would allow a user to pick the songs she wanted to hear and thus vitiate any need to purchase those songs. Finding that the defendant's Launchcast did not provide that level of interactivity, the Second Circuit held as a matter of law that Launchcast was not interactive. *Ibid.*, at *40. ('Based on a review of how LAUNCHcast functions, it is clear that LAUNCHcast does not provide a specially created program within the meaning of § 114(j)(7) because the webcasting service does not provide sufficient control to users such that playlists are so predictable that users will choose to listen to the webcast in lieu of purchasing music, thereby – in the aggregate – diminishing record sales.')
152. 15 U.S.C. § 114(d)(2), (f)(2) (2009); see also *Bonneville Int'l Corp. v. Peters,* 347 F.3d 485, (3d Cir., 2003) (affirming Copyright Office's decision to require a compulsory license for simultaneous transmission of a radio station's broadcast through the Internet).
153. See Notice of Designation As Collective Under Statutory License filed with the Licensing Division of the Copyright Office in accordance with Copyright Office regulation 270.5(c), 37 C.F.R. § 270.5(c).

leaving such interactive services to negotiate licenses with each individual copyright owner.

In addition to giving the Copyright Office the right to designate the CMO, the Act also gave the Copyright Office the authority to set rates and licensing conditions for the statutory licenses. The Act thus moved from an antitrust regulation model to a specialized regulatory model. Rather than rely on judicial rate-setting proceedings and the consent decree mechanism, as was done with musical works, the Act authorizes the US Copyright Office to designate a CMO, to set the rates and licensing terms and to set a distribution key. Under this key, SoundExchange distributes 50% of the revenues to the sound recording copyright owners, 45% to the featured artists and 5% to an independent administrator to distribute to non-featured artists and vocalists.

Within the Copyright Office, rates for compulsory and statutory licenses are now set by Copyright Royalty Judges (CRJs),[154] possibly as an attempt to render the process more specialized and 'professional'. This follows reforms of the rate-setting process, from the Copyright Royalty Tribunal (CRT) of the 1976 Act, to the Copyright Arbitration Royalty Panel (CARP) system, to the current Copyright Royalty Board and its CRJ system.[155] The CRJs are full-time employees in the Library of Congress who are appointed by the Librarian of Congress for six-year terms with an opportunity for reappointment.[156] It will be interesting to see whether, and if so, how the CRJs broaden their regulatory purview beyond the dollar amounts of rates and use the power to impose related terms and conditions as a way to regulate the operation of the CMOs active in their field of jurisdiction.

---

154. 17 U.S.C. §§ 801–805 (2009).
155. 'With the enactment of the Copyright Royalty and Distribution Reform Act of 2004 [see below] on Nov. 30, 2004, the Copyright Arbitration Royalty Panel (CARP) system that had been part of the Copyright Office since 1993 was phased out. The Act replaced CARP (which itself replaced the CRT in 1993) with the Copyright Royalty Board (CRB), which determines rates and terms for the copyright statutory licenses and makes determinations on distribution of statutory license royalties collected by the Copyright Office.' <www.copyright.gov/carp> (last visited: 31 Jan. 2009). See also Copyright Royalty Tribunal Reform Act of 1993, Pub. L. No. 103–198, 107 Stat. 2304 (amending, *inter alia*, Ch. 8, title 17, United States Code), enacted 17 Dec. 1993; and Copyright Royalty and Distribution Reform Act of 2004, Copyright Royalty and Distribution Reform Act of 2004, Pub. L. No. 108–419, 118 Stat. 2341 (revising Ch. 8, title 17, United States Code, in its entirety), enacted 30 Nov. 2004.
156. See 17 U.S.C. § 801(a). ('The Librarian shall appoint 3 full-time Copyright Royalty Judges . . . after consultation with the Register of Copyrights.') Questions have been raised as to whether this method of appointing CRJs is consistent with the Constitution's Appointment Clause. See *Intercollegiate Broadcast Sys., Inc. v. Copyright Royalty Bd.*, 2009 U.S. App. LEXIS 17674 (D.C. Cir., 2009). The Appointments Clause requires that 'inferior officers', such as the CRJs, be appointed by the President, or by a court, or by a 'Head of Department'. The key legal question is whether the Librarian of Congress is a Department Head. If not, this raises two issues. First, prospectively, the power to appoint CRJs will need to move from the Librarian to a Department Head, such as the Secretary of Commerce. Second, if the appointments were unconstitutional, that raises questions regarding the legitimacy of the decisions reached by the unconstitutionally appointed CRJs.

Although conducted within an administrative rather than judicial setting, the CRJs generally focus on the same types of considerations in setting the statutory license fees for the sound recording performance right that we see in the judicial rate setting for the musical work performance right. As one court explained:

> In delegating authority [to set rates to the CRJs], Congress required the Judges to follow certain statutory guidelines. The schedule of rates and terms must 'distinguish among the different types of eligible nonsubscription transmission services then in operation and shall include a minimum fee for each such type of service'. *Id.*, § 114(f)(2)(B). Rates should 'most clearly represent the rates and terms that would have been negotiated in the marketplace between a willing buyer and a willing seller'. *Id.* 'In determining such rates and terms,' the Judges must 'base [their] decision on economic, competitive and programming information presented by the parties.' *Id.* Specifically, they must consider whether 'the service may substitute for or may promote the sales of phonorecords' or otherwise affect the 'copyright owner's other streams of revenue'. *Id.*, § 114(f)(2)(B)(i). The Judges must also consider 'the relative roles of the copyright owner and the transmitting entity' with respect to 'relative creative contribution, technological contribution, capital investment, cost, and risk'. *Id.*, § 114(f)(2)(B)(ii). Finally, '[i]n establishing such rates and terms,' the Judges 'may consider the rates and terms for comparable types of digital audio transmission services and comparable circumstances under voluntary license agreements described in subparagraph (A)'. *Id.*, § 114(f)(2)(B). Identical statutory language applies to 'reasonable rates and terms' for ephemeral recordings. *Id.*, § 112(e).[157]

Whether moving the issue from the judicial, consent-decree arena into an administrative forum will change the substantive outcomes, however, remains to be seen.

The Copyright Royalty Board's first attempts at royalty-setting does not provide much reason for optimism, though. In 2007, the Board retroactively set the royalty rates for webcasting at USD 0.08 per performance in 2006, increasing to USD 0.19 per performance in 2010.[158] To ensure that the royalties were paid, the Board required each webcaster to pay a USD 500 advance for each stream a webcaster expected to transmit.[159] Webcasters protested the rates.[160] Even Sound Exchange expressed surprise that the Board had accepted its proposed rates outright.[161] Following the Board's decision, simulcasting radio stations have

---

157. *Intercollegiate Broadcast Sys., Inc. v. Copyright Royalty Bd.*, 2009 U.S. App. LEXIS 17674 (D.C. Cir., 2009).
158. Digital Performance Right in Sound Recordings and Ephemeral Recordings, Docket No. 2005-1, 125, <www.loc.gov/crb/proceedings/2005-1/rates-terms2005-1.pdf>.
159. *Ibid.*, at 88.
160. For a general discussion of the issue in the context of the Internet music webcaster, Pandora, see Aurelia J. Schultz, *Escaping from the Box: Bringing Pandora Back to Global Access* (Spring 2009).
161. *Ibid.*, at 13.

successfully negotiated, and webcasters are trying to negotiate lower rates with SoundExchange.[162]

In the meantime, SoundExchange, Inc., which was established in 2003, remains the designated CMO in this area. It currently represents more than 3,600 sound recording copyright owners and over 31,000 featured artists.[163] Thus far, it has distributed approximately USD 90 million (as of the third quarter 2007) and processed over USD 1.8 billion performances (as of third quarter 2007).[164] Its 18-member Board has representatives of producers and featured and non-featured artists. It has thirty staff members and posted an administrative rate (in percentages) of 12.3% in 2007.[165] In that year, it collected approximately USD 140 million.[166]

2.5   CONCLUSION: TRYING TO CAGE THE BEAST

The story of the CMOs in the United States is thus largely a cautionary tale. Whereas competitive markets generally work well, monopolistic markets do not. CMOs, although they create markets that allow copyright owners to be paid for the public performance of their works, create monopolistic markets. Also, we have spent more than seventy years unsuccessfully trying to reign in the collectives' monopolistic excesses. Rates, at least for ASCAP and BMI, are now regulated, but they are often set based upon earlier unregulated rates. Such an approach to rate setting may prevent ASCAP and BMI from exploiting their market power to a greater degree than they had in the past, but it does little to improve the situation. If, at the end of the day, the excuse for such an approach is that there is no sensible legal or factual basis for determining a reasonable fee, we should acknowledge as much, admit that determining a reasonable fee is a policy question not susceptible to judicial resolution and turn the matter over to the legislature. Perhaps, the move to an administration regime for the sound recording digital performance right represents a step in this direction.

Similarly, the effort to encourage direct licensing through the consent decrees has also proven uneven and largely unsuccessful. This lack of success comes despite the nearly wholesale shift away from the spontaneous performances that justified a blanket license in the early days of television and radio. Even where the consent decrees have tried to encourage direct licensing, too often, amendments to the decrees have focused on a specific problem facing a specific industry at a specific time without considering how the same problem could arise more generally. Thus, in response to the double licensing issue in *Alden-Rochelle* and

---

162. *Ibid.*, at 13–14.
163. See <www.soundexchange.com/> (last visited: 30 Jan. 2009).
164. See *Ibid.*
165. See *Ibid.*
166. See SoundExchange Annual Report (2007), <www.soundexchange.com/assets/download_forms/2007AnnualReport-PDF-3-31-08-PRE_AUDIT.pdf> (last visited: 30 Jan. 2009).

M. Whitmark & Sons, the 1950 Amended Final Judgment required direct licensing of both the synchronization and public performance right. After all, where a synchronization license has to be obtained from the copyright owner directly in any event, separating the public performance right and then using a CMO to enforce and license it increases, rather than decreases, the transaction costs involved. Yet, the AFJ required direct licensing only for movies and for network programmes, and although the AFJ thus corrected the problem in those cases, the same problem arose and has long persisted for non-network television programmes and commercials.

Moreover, it is not just a matter of getting a perfect consent decree. Even if that were possible, industry conditions are constantly changing. Instead of adapting and responding to the market, the CMOs often resist adopting more efficient licensing options until forced to do so by yet another set of amendments to the consent decree.[167]

At the end of the day, the argument nonetheless remains that we have to accept the collectives and the problems they create because there is no other practical option for licensing of public performance rights. Recent developments suggest that there may be another way, however, and it is to the much briefer story of the copyright collecting society that we now turn.

3 THE COPYRIGHT COLLECTING SOCIETY: THE CCC

3.1 A BRIEF DESCRIPTION OF COPYRIGHT COLLECTING SOCIETIES

Formed in 1978, the CCC is a non-profit corporation that enables authors and publishers of work to collect fees for the photocopying of their works, and a centralized location for potential licensees to obtain licenses.[168] Publishers and authors register their works with the CCC, delineating the works they are licensing and the fee for photocopying the works. The CCC provides licenses that grant permission to the licensee to reproduce works that are listed with the CCC. The CCC offers two forms of licenses to users: an annual blanket license with a fee set by CCC and a per-copy license with the fees set by the individual copyright owners.

Unlike ASCAP and BMI, the CCC has not been the target of antitrust claims by either individuals or the government. It has obtained a review letter from the antitrust division of the Department of Justice. In Fiscal Year 2007, CCC collected USD 175 million and distributed USD 123 million.[169]

---

167. See, for example, AFJ2 Memo, *supra* n. 122 at 24–25. ('In addition, ASCAP has refused to offer a per-program license or per-program-like license to users other than those named explicitly in the decree, although, over time, such licenses would be practical for more and more types of users.')
168. Corporate Overview, <www.copyright.com> (last visited: 7 Dec. 2005).
169. CCC Annual Report, 2007, <www.copyright.com/media/pdfs/AR_CCC_07_Spreads.pdf> (last visited: 31 Jan. 2009). Royalty Months Outstanding stood at five months.

3.2   OF CHICKENS AND EGGS, MARKETS AND RIGHTS

Ordinarily, as was the case for the other CMOs, one thinks of the legal right coming first, followed by the development of the market. But that is not how it worked in the United States with respect to unauthorized photocopying of scientific journal articles. Instead, the courts did not recognize photocopying as copyright infringement until after a means to license such reproductions had developed.

The issue whether unauthorized photocopying constituted copyright infringement first arose in 1973 in *Williams & Wilkins v. United States*.[170] In the case, a publisher of scientific and medical journals, Williams & Wilkins, sued the United States for copyright infringement. Williams & Wilkins alleged that Department of Health, Education and Welfare, through the National Institute of Health (NIH) and the National Library of Medicine (NLM), had infringed by making unauthorized photocopies of its copyrighted medical journal articles.[171] The government conceded that it was making unauthorized copies. The NIH, for example, 'filled 85,744 requests for photocopies of journal articles (including plaintiff's journals), constituting about 930,000 pages' in 1970 alone – all of which were for its own in-house researchers.[172] Similarly, in 1968, the NLM '[filled] about 120,000 of the requests [for interlibrary loans] [. . .] by photocopying single articles from journals, including plaintiff's journals'.[173]

Despite conceding extensive unauthorized copying, the government contended that the photocopying constituted a fair use under US copyright law and was not therefore copyright infringement. On appeal, the Court of Claims[174] agreed.[175] At the time, there was no licensing mechanism for photocopying. As a result, in analysing the impact of the photocopying on the market value of the works at issue, the copyright owners had to prove that the photocopying reduced subscriptions for their journal. But the available evidence did not demonstrate any such reduction. As the court explained, 'the photocopying shown here had not

---

170. *Williams & Wilkins v. United States*, 487 F.2d 1345 (Ct. Claims 1973) *[Williams & Wilkins]*, aff'd by an equally divided Court, 420 U.S. 376 (1975). After Justice Blackmun recused himself, the remaining Justices of the Supreme Court were split 4–4. Such a disposition affirms the results of the case as between the parties, but does not affirm the reasoning of the lower court.
171. *Ibid.*, at 1346–1347.
172. *Ibid.*, at 1348.
173. *Ibid.*, at 1349.
174. At the time, the Court of Claims had both trial and appellate jurisdiction over patent and copyright infringement claims asserted against the federal government. In 1982, the appellate jurisdiction of the Court of Claims and that of the Court of Customs and Patent Appeals were merged in creating the new Federal Circuit. See Federal Courts Improvement Act of 1982, Pub. L. No. 97-164, § 127, 96 Stat. 25, 37 (1982), codified as amended at 28 U.S.C. 1295 (2005).
175. *Williams & Wilkins, supra* n. 170 at 1362. ('Fusing these elements together, we conclude that plaintiff has failed to show that the defendant's use of the copyrighted material has been "unfair", and conversely we find that these practices have up to now been "fair". There has been no infringement.')

damaged plaintiff, and may actually have helped it'.[176] On the other hand, a finding of infringement would clearly impair the flow of information to medical and scientific researchers.[177] Together with other factors, the court found that the balance weighed in favour of allowing the use to consider, and as a result, the court labelled the copying 'fair':

> While, as we have said, this record fails to show that plaintiff (or any other medical publisher) has been substantially harmed by the photocopying practices of NIH and NLM, it does show affirmatively that medical science will be hurt if such photocopying is stopped. Thus, the balance of risks is definitely on defendant's side – until Congress acts more specifically, the burden on medical science of a holding that the photocopying is an infringement would appear to be much greater than the present or foreseeable burden on plaintiff and other medical publishers of a ruling that these practices fall within 'fair use'.[178]

The court noted that 'Plaintiff's answer is that it is willing to license the libraries, on payment of a reasonable royalty, to continue photocopying as they have.'[179] But in the absence of a viable license system already in place, or of any statutory authority for the court to create one, the court was unwilling to entrust medical research to the mere possibility that some copyright owners might be willing and could find a way to license their works for photocopying.[180]

Thirty years later, the photocopying issue came before the courts a second time in *American Geophysical Union v. Texaco, Inc.*[181] The facts pertaining to the unauthorized copying were very similar to those in *Williams & Wilkins Co.* Like the NIH, Texaco would circulate copies of the tables of contents from various scientific journals and allow its researchers to request photocopies of particular articles for their own files. But this time, the Second Circuit rejected the fair use argument and determined that the photocopying of articles from a scientific journal constituted copyright infringement.[182] A few other differences between the cases[183]; however, the principal one appeared to be the existence of the

---

176. *Ibid.*, at 1358.
177. *Ibid.*, at 1356. ('There is no doubt in our minds that medical science would be seriously hurt if such library photocopying were stopped. We do not spend time and space demonstrating this proposition. It is admitted by plaintiff and conceded on all sides.')
178. *Ibid.*, at 1359.
179. *Ibid.*, at 1360.
180. *Ibid.*
181. *American Geophysical Union v. Texaco, Inc.*, 60 F.3d 913 (2d Cir., 1994), writ dismissed, 516 U.S. 1005 (1995) [*American Geophysical Union*].
182. *Ibid.*, at 931.
183. The most prominent other distinction appears to be that Texaco was a for-profit entity, whereas the NIH and the NLB were both non-profit, government agencies. It is also worth noting that *Williams & Wilkins* was decided under the 1909 Act, whereas *American Geophysical Union* was decided under the 1976 Act. This change should not have been material, however, because the 1976 Act did not change the applicable legal rules with respect to the photocopying issue. Although the 1976 Act formally codified the fair use doctrine in section 107, Congress expressly stated that in doing so, it intended to 'restate the present judicial doctrine of fair

CCC.[184] Although it remained the case that there was not a market for the 'direct sale and distribution of individual articles', the CCC provided a mechanism for licensing articles for photocopying.[185] Given the existence of a practical means to license the photocopying, what had been fair became unfair. As the court explained: 'it is sensible that a particular unauthorized use should be considered "more fair" when there is no ready market or means to pay for the use, while such an unauthorized use should be considered "less fair" when there is a ready market or means to pay for the use'.[186]

Thus, because a market for the photocopying of journal articles had developed, the court recognized a corresponding legal right.

4   A NEW CMO RISING: THE GOOGLE
        BOOK SETTLEMENT

In 2004, Google began digitizing books, all kinds of books, including books in copyright and books out of copyright, books in print and books out of print. Google's goal is to create a searchable database containing the vast majority of works ever written. Google obtains these books either directly from publishers, through its Partner Program, or from university and other libraries, through its Library Project. In either case, once a work is digitized, it becomes part of the Google Book Search database.

A consumer can search the database for particular phrases or quotes, and obtain a list of works that contain the search terms. A user can then click on any of the works listed. What happens next depends on the nature of the work. For books digitized through the Partner Program, the right holder decides how much of the work Google can display. Some right holders allow extensive previews; others permit very little. For out-of-copyright (or public domain) works digitized through the Library Project, a user can browse online or download a PDF copy of the entire work. For works digitized through the Library Project that are still copyrighted, Google provides a brief excerpt of the text surrounding the search terms.

Neither the digitizing and display of the public domain works, nor the authorized use of works through the Partner Program, presented any systematic risk for copyright infringement claims.[187] The digitizing and display of copyrighted works,

---

use, not to change, narrow, or enlarge it in any way'. H.R. Rep. No. 94-1476 at 66 (1976), quoted in *Campbell v. Acuff-Rose Music, Inc.*, 510 U.S. 569 at 577 (1994).

184. *American Geophysical Union, supra* n. 181 at 929–931.
185. *Ibid.*, at 930.
186. *Ibid.*, at 931.
187. Even for these uses, there remained some risk that Google would misidentify the public domain status of a work or that it would obtain permission from someone who turned out not to be the right holder with respect to the work.

without the consent of the right holder, did, however. In 2005, two lawsuits claiming infringement on the basis of Google's use of these works were brought. Moreover, they were brought as class actions, purporting to represent the interests not only of the named plaintiffs, but of all similarly situated right holders whose copyrighted works had been digitized and included in the Google Book Search database. In response to these lawsuits, Google asserted that its actions constituted a fair, and hence non-infringing, use under US copyright law.

Rather than litigate the fair use issue, the parties negotiated a settlement to this class action litigation, and at the time of this writing, the court has given preliminary approval to the settlement. A final hearing on the fairness of the proposed settlement is still pending, however, and is scheduled for 7 October 2009.

Although complex, the settlement addresses two basic issues. First, with respect to Google's past conduct of digitizing and displaying works, Google will make a one-time payment of approximately USD 110 million.[188] Of this, up to USD 30 million will go to the plaintiff's lawyers, and another USD 34.5 million will go the administrative costs of distributing payments to right holders. The remaining USD 45 million will go to right holders, with cash payments of USD 60 for each book and USD 15 for essay or articles, digitized without the right holder's permission. Because the case is a class action, this settlement effectively immunized Google from any claims of copyright infringement that arose before the opt-out date of 4 September 2009. Moreover, even if a right holder opts out of the settlement agreement in a timely fashion, that will not remove the right holder's works from the Google Book Search database. Rather, opting out will provide the right holder only with the legal right to pursue a separate copyright infringement lawsuit against Google for its conduct.

Second, the settlement would grant Google, going forward, a non-exclusive license to digitize and display 'all Books and Inserts obtained by Google from any source'.[189] In return, Google agrees to pay over to right holders 63% of its Net Revenues from Google Book Search.[190]

To facilitate the identification and representation of right holder, the plaintiffs agree in return to establish a Book Rights Registry. Pursuant to the settlement, the Registry will be authorized to act on behalf of all right holders, will maintain a database of rights information for books and other written works and will attempt to locate right holders with respect to books and other written works.[191] The Registry will also receive on behalf of the right holders the agreed payments from Google and will be responsible for distributing those payments to right holders who have registered their works with the Registry.

---

188. Settlement Agreement, Art. V, *Author's Guild, Inc. v. Google Inc.*, No. 05-8136 (S.D.N.Y. October 2008), available at <www.googlebooksettlement.com/r/view_settlement_agreement> (last visited: 3 Sep. 2009) (hereinafter 'GBS Settlement').
189. See GBS Settlement, *supra* n. 188, Art. 3.1(a), at 21.
190. GBS Settlement, *supra* n. 188, Arts 1.86, 1.87, 4.5(a)(i) and (ii), at 11, 56.
191. GBS Settlement, *supra* n. 188, Art. 6.1, at 65.

The settlement agreement thus will establish, if approved, a new CMO, the Book Rights Registry. Unlike long-standing CMOs, such as ASCAP, BMI and CCC, this CMO will not arise from individual right holders choosing to license a CMO to represent them – the classic 'opt in' model. Rather, by virtue of the class action nature of the settlement, the Book Rights Registry will become the right holders' representative with respect to Google's Book Search Project unless a right holder expressly opts out of the settlement. By switching from an 'opt in' to an 'opt out' model, use of the class action settlement thus enables Google to obtain a license to digitize works for so-called 'orphan' works, where the right holder cannot reasonably be found or identified. Of importance, however, the settlement is binding only on members of the settlement class that includes 'all Persons that, as of the Notice Commencement Date, have a Copyright Interest in one or more Books or Inserts'.[192] As a result, future authors are not bound by the settlement agreement and the Book Rights Registry will not become their authorized representative absent express consent.

Like ASCAP and BMI before them, the Book Rights Registry, and the Google Book Settlement that creates it, raise serious antitrust issues. By letter dated 2 July 2009, the Department of Justice notified the District Court considering the settlement that it has opened an antitrust investigation into the settlement.[193] Like these earlier CMOs, the Book Rights Registry creates a horizontal agreement among right holders, which may have anti-competitive consequences. Absent the Registry, right holders might compete with each other by offering more favourable licensing terms for digital uses of their works. With the Registry, there may be less or no such competition between right holders.

Similar to the CCC model, the settlement agreement leaves right holders some room to compete with each other by setting their own terms for the digital use of their work, but it is not clear how effective this leeway will be at constraining prices. For example, the settlement agreement expressly authorizes Google to sell consumers the right to view, copy and paste, and print pages of a book.[194] Under the settlement, an individual right holder retains the right to set the price for such access. However, the default rule is that, unless the right holder expressly set the price, Google will set the price for her.[195] Moreover, under the original proposed settlement, Google would do so using an algorithm that finds 'the optimal . . . price for each Book, and accordingly . . . maximize[s] revenue for each Rightsholder'.[196] An algorithm that seeks to maximize revenue for any given book, however, will necessarily consider the impact of the pricing of other books and will eventually reach the monopolist's conclusion that the best way to maximize revenue for any given book is to raise prices for all books. Thus, rather than compete with each

---

192. *Ibid.*, Art. 1.142, at 17.
193. *Authors Guild v. Google, Inc.*, 2009-1 Trade Cas. (CCH) para. 76,666, 2009 U.S. Dist. LEXIS 63081 (S.D.N.Y. filed 2 Jul. 2009).
194. GBS Settlement, *supra* n. 188, Art. 4.2(a), at 48.
195. *Ibid.*, Art. 4.2(b)(iii), at 49.
196. *Ibid.*, Art. 4.2(b)(i)(2), at 49.

other, enough right holders may delegate pricing decisions to Google to create effectively a price-fixing cartel. In the amended proposed settlement agreement filed November 9, 2009, the parties have tried to address this concern.[197] Under the GBS Amended Settlement, Google will set a book's price 'to maximize revenues for the Rightholder for such book and without regard to changes to the price of any other Book',[198] so that prices mimic prices in 'a competitive market, that is, assuming no change in the price of any other Book'.[199] Whether Google's pricing algorithm will prove successful in mimicking a competitive market, in the absence of a competitive market to use as a benchmark for prices, or whether the ability of right holders to defect and set their own, lower price will ensure competitive prices,[200] remains to be seen.[201]

In other areas, the originally proposed settlement left no room for competition between right holders at all. For example, some right holders may be more interested in the widespread dissemination of their work than in potential royalties and so desire to license the digital use of their works for free under a Creative Commons or other open access license. The original settlement provided no mechanism for implementing such a preference. The GBS Amended Settlement provides at least one mechanism to honor such an open access preference. Specifically, the GBS Amended Settlement expressly allows a right holder to 'direct the Registry to make its Books available at no charge pursuant to one of several standard licenses',[202] such as a Creative Commons license. However, even under the Amended Settlement, institutional subscriptions cover either the full Google Search database or a discipline-based collection,[203] but the settlement does not permit Google to offer a lower priced subscription specifically for those works right holders choose to designate open access. For these uses, under the settlement, if a right holder designates her work open access, there is no change in the subscription fees, or the advertisements associated with her work, nor is there any change in the percentage of revenue Google must pay the Registry. The only difference is that an open access right holders' share of that revenue will go to someone else, whether the Registry itself, other right holders, or the Registry's favoured charities.[204]

The potential for reduced competition among right holder is thus a serious issue, but it is also a familiar one from seventy years of antitrust-based regulation of

---

197. Amended Settlement Agreement, Art. 4.2(b)(i)(2), 4.2(c)(ii)(2), *Author's Guild, Inc. v. Google Inc.*, No. 05-8136 (S.D.N.Y. October 2008), available at <www.googlebooksettlement.com/agreement.html> (last visited: 9 Nov. 2009) (hereinafter 'GBS Amended Settlement').
198. *Ibid.*, Art. 4.2(b)(i)(2).
199. *Ibid.*, Art. 4.2(c)(ii)(2).
200. James Grimmelmann, 'How to Fix the Google Book Search Settlement', *Journal of Internet Law* 12 (2009): 1, 13.
201. See Randal C. Picker, 'The Google Book Search Settlement: A New Orphan-Works Monopoly?', at 16–17, <www.ssrn.com> (last visited: 24 Aug. 2009).
202. GBS Amended Settlement, *supra* n. 197, Art. 4.2(a)(i).
203. GBS Settlement, *supra* n. 188, Art. 4.1(a)(v), at 42–43.
204. *Ibid.*, Art. 6.3(a)(i), at 66–67.

CMOs. Perhaps more worrisome, however, is the fact that the underlying Google Book Search project also creates the potential for a monopoly in a second market – that for a comprehensive database of digitized literary works. This threat is unlike anything that we have seen with prior CMOs. When ASCAP brought right holders together to license the public performance of musical works, this did not lead to a monopoly in the venues for public performances. Both before and after the consent decrees, we had a wide array of competing radio stations, dance halls, restaurants and the like. Yet, the Google Book Search project creates the risk for precisely that sort of monopoly – a single comprehensive source for digitized books.

To a large extent, this threat of monopolization does not arise directly from the settlement or the Registry. Rather, it arises from the fact that only Google is presently engaged in this sort of mass digitization project. Whether the settlement is approved or sent back to the drawing board, Google will likely still be first to the market with its Google Book Search database and will likely still likely be the only source for this type of product for some time to come. For that reason, one could argue that the settlement and the Registry's licensing of Google's use does not raise any particular antitrust concerns. The Registry's licensing of Google is no more an antitrust violation than if ASCAP licensed public performances at a stadium, where that stadium is the only public performance venue in town.

We should not dismiss the antitrust issues with respect to this second market too readily, however, for three reasons. First, the Registry's revenue from the license is tied directly to Google's. As a result, while the settlement expressly provides that the digitization license to Google is non-exclusive, leaving the Registry formally free to license would-be Google competitors,[205] it will likely be contrary to the Registry's self-interest to do so. Because the Registry is to receive a fraction of Google's net revenue from Google Book Search, the decision to license a second digitization project would entail a trade-off between reduced licensing revenue from Google versus the additional licensing revenue from the new competitor. Given the low marginal costs involved in the distribution of digital works, there is a strong likelihood that the Registry will maximize its total payments by licensing only Google. A refusal to license others will maintain Google's monopoly in the market for a comprehensive database of digitized literary works, maximize the available net revenue from that market and thereby maximize the Registry's revenue as well.

Second, even if the Registry wanted to license a would-be competitor, it would likely have trouble inducing competitors to enter the market at issue. The very high fixed costs and the low marginal costs of a project such as Google Book Search, as well as the associated network effects for this type of database, are likely to make competitive entry into the market for a comprehensive database of digitized literary works naturally difficult. To induce entry, the Registry might need to offer the newcomer more favourable license terms. Otherwise, Google's cost and network advantages would overwhelm the newcomer. Yet, the originally proposed

---

205. *Ibid.*, Art. 3.1(a), at 21.

settlement agreement contained a most-favoured nation clause that would prevent the Registry from offering a would-be competitor more favourable terms.[206]

For these reasons, commentators have argued that the District Court should not approve the settlement unless the most-favoured nation clause is removed.[207] In response to these and other concerns, the parties filed an amended, proposed settlement agreement on November 9, 2009, and in that agreement, the most-favoured nation clause has been removed.[208] Some have suggested going a step further to require the Registry to offer the same license to others on the same 63% of net revenue terms as have been offered to Google.[209] However, there is another, potentially more serious problem.

If the action is settled as a class action, the settlement will cover Google's digitization of orphan works. Indeed, even in the absence of a settlement, a final dismissal will resolve all claims class members did assert or could have asserted against Google based upon its digitization project. It is not clear, however, that the settlement either does or could give the Registry the legal right to license works to Google's would-be competitors going forward. Of course, over time, some right holders will come forward and register their works with the Registry, and as part of that process may authorize the Registry to license their works. As more right holders authorize the Registry to do so, the Registry will have an ever larger bundle of works that it may turn around and license to would-be Google competitors. However, not all right holders will so authorize the Registry, and indeed for orphan works in particular, almost by definition, no such express authority is likely to be given. As a result, even if all other right holders expressly authorized the Registry to license digitization of their works, this would still leave Google with the exclusive right to digitize the orphan works.

Although some of the language in the settlement might be read as an attempt to authorize the Registry to license orphan works to third parties,[210] it is not clear that either the parties or the court, in resolving this litigation would have the authority to grant the Registry the right to represent orphan works right holders going forward. That the plaintiffs necessarily have the authority to bind such right holders to the settlement of the dispute with Google is an inevitable consequence of the class action nature of the lawsuit. But Article III limits every federal court's power to an actual 'case or controversy'.[211] Under Article III, the settlement may resolve the parties' dispute, perhaps even to the extent of binding absent class members with respect to future uses by Google. Yet, the excuse of the class action will not empower the plaintiffs or the Registry to license works for uses that are not part of the case or controversy before the court.

---

206. *Ibid.*, Art. 3.8(a), at 37 (requiring Registry to offer same terms to Google as it offers to another licensee for period of ten years following the settlement).
207. See Grimmelmann, *supra* n. 200, at 15; Picker, *supra* n. 201, at 22–25.
208. GBS Amended Settlement, *supra* n. 197, at Art. 3.8.
209. See Grimmelmann, *supra* n. 200, at 15.
210. See Picker, *supra* n. 193, at 21 ('It seems possible that the settlement agreement intends for the Registry to be able to issue new licenses for the orphan works going forward.').
211. U.S. CONST., Art. III.

This leaves would-be competitors two options to obtain a license for the use of orphan works. First, they can press Congress for orphan works legislation. Second, they can follow the same path as Google. They can begin digitizing copyrighted works, hope to get sued, hope that the suit is a class action and then hope that whoever ends up as class representatives will prove as amenable to settlement as the plaintiffs in the *Google* litigation. In short, when it comes to competition with Google Book Search, all we may have is hope.

5   CONCLUSION: SOME NORMATIVE THOUGHTS ON
         COLLECTIVE RIGHTS MANAGEMENT

A normative evaluation of collective rights management should focus on two issues: (i) the normative desirability of the particular legal right at issue and (ii) the relative normative desirability of the differing models for collective rights management. In the United States, the primary purpose of copyright is neither to protect the natural or moral rights of authors nor to reward right holders. Rather, the primary purpose of copyright is to ensure the public an adequate supply of creative works.[212] Moreover, the point is not to maximize the incentive for the production of such works. Increasing copyright protection entails two significant costs. First, more production of copyrighted works must come at the expense of some other productive activity. Once we acknowledge that these other productive activities would likely have generated positive spillovers as well, the question of where to allocate society's resources becomes an extremely difficult one. Second, more protection means less access to existing works.

If one were to try to determine whether recognition of either a broad right of public performance or a right to control photocopying under the circumstances presented in *Williams & Wilkins* or *American Geophysical Union* would increase social welfare, the normative claim for either right is relatively weak. Recognizing a broad right of public performance will likely re-distribute somewhat more of society's wealth toward songwriting and, by offering a higher return for any given work, may well attract additional resources into the production of songs. It is even possible that these additional resources will lead to more or better musical works. But even were one to accept all of that as true, there is still no reason[213] to believe that the additional works created thereby would be more valuable to society than

---

212. See, for example, *Sony Corp. v. Universal City Studios, Inc.*, 464 U.S. 417 at 429 (1984). ('The monopoly privileges that Congress may authorize are neither unlimited nor primarily designed to provide a special private benefit. Rather, the limited grant is a means by which an important public purpose may be achieved. It is intended to motivate the creative activity of authors and inventors by the provision of a special reward, and to allow the public access to the products of their genius after the limited period of exclusive control has expired.')

213. At least, there is no reason once we put aside the unrealistic assumptions that all other markets are complete (i.e., no positive or negative externalities) and perfectly competitive. Creativity is the resource we are attempting to allocate through the copyright laws, and wherever creativity is allocated in our economy, it will almost certainly create positive spillovers.

the alternative endeavours to which those resources would otherwise have been devoted.[214] Recognizing the photocopying right is even more problematic. In that industry, the journal authors – the scientists, doctors and other researchers – typically assign their copyrights to the journal publishers, yet receive no monetary royalties in return. As a result, recognizing the photocopying right will likely redistribute resources from those doing the science to those publishing the science. From a social welfare perspective, there is no clear way in which this might prove desirable. As I have explained elsewhere, '[i]ncreasing the revenue of publishers at the expense of the authors and their underlying research scarcely seems likely "to promote the Progress of Science", as the Constitution requires'.[215]

Yet, the working assumption seems to be that once Congress has recognized a legal right, such as the right of public performance, its market value must be recognized as well, and whatever steps are necessary to ensure a working market for the right are therefore justified.[216] Perhaps where Congress has spoken clearly, such an assumption can be justified. For the rights at issue in this essay, however, Congress's intent was not so clear. Instead, the courts took general language with respect to 'publicly performing a work for profit' or the 'reproduction' of a work, and applied it to circumstances, such as radio or television airplay, or the photocopying of scientific journal articles, that Congress had not expressly considered. Although the suggestion may offend those with a strong sense for the procedural niceties, there may be some exclusive rights, formally recognized as belonging to the right holder, that ought nonetheless to be left unenforceable. Thus, before we rush to embrace collective rights management or to apply it to new areas, we ought to consider seriously whether the potential market at issue ought to remain outside the scope of the copyright monopoly. With public goods, such as copyrighted works, just because we can convert existing activity into a paying market, through a copyright collective or otherwise, does not mean that we should.[217]

Assuming that we have determined that a given right should be enforced and assuming further that the value of the use at issue is less than the transaction costs of individually negotiated licenses so that some model of collective rights management is required, the second issue is the relative normative desirability of the two models of collective rights management: the copyright collective and the copyright collecting society. Between these two models, the advantages of the collecting society model are clear. Allowing (or requiring) individual copyright

---

214. See A. Plant, 'The Economic Aspects of Copyright in Books', *Economica* 1 (1934): 167 at 170; see also B. Kaplan, *An Unhurried View of Copyright* (New York: Columbia University Press, 1967), 142 at 75 ('Magnify the headstart and you may conceivably run the risk of attracting too much of the nation's energy into the copyright-protected sectors of the economy.'); R. Hurt & R. Schuchman, 'The Economic Rationale of Copyright', *American Economic Review* 56 (1966), 421 at 425 and 430; Lunney, *supra* n. 119 at 488–489 and 629–653.
215. G. Lunney, 'Fair Use and Market Failure: Sony Revisited', *Boston University Law Review* 82 (2002): 975 at 1022.
216. See, for example, *ASCAP (Application of Buffalo Broadcasting Co.), supra* n. 42 at *56 ('Thus, ASCAP is entitled to be paid for those [public performance] licenses').
217. See Lunney, *supra* n. 119 at 991–996.

380

owners to determine the prices for the use at issue with respect to their own works replicates the model that we have adopted for distributing copyrighted works to the public generally. Book publishers are not allowed to get together and agree on a blanket license, under which consumers could read, copy, publicly perform or prepare derivative works from any book they wanted in return for a set percentage of their income.[218] Despite the transaction costs savings such a blanket license might entail, we nonetheless require these right holders to make their own decisions as to the form in which their respective work will be published, hardbound or paperback, its price and the terms on which they will license their work for copying, public performance or the preparation of derivative works.[219] Although copyright may grant each author some degree of market power over her own work, they still must pit their 'little' monopolies against each other in the marketplace.

It is only because we thought such a system of individually priced licenses unworkable that we tolerated collective licensing of the public performance right.[220] Yet, the CCC demonstrates that it is practical to offer both individual licenses at prices set by the individual right holders and a blanket license at a price set by a CMO. Although not all users have the ability to track and monitor their performances of copyrighted works, some do.[221] Requiring members of ASCAP or affiliates of BMI to state their rate for individual public performance licenses as a requirement for joining such a CMO would give users a genuine choice as to which works to use and how much to pay – the same choice consumers face in the market for copies of works generally. And the forces of competition would work on such individual pricing decisions directly, just as they do (at least to some extent) on pricing decisions for copies of works. The ready availability of competitively priced individual licenses could thus become an effective check on the market power of the CMOs as well as a ceiling on the reasonable rate for a blanket license. Moreover, if we require the collectives to provide a clear listing of individual license prices, as set by their members or affiliates, a given user's decision to go with the blanket license would necessarily reflect the efficiency advantages of a blanket license, rather than the lack of a practically available alternative.

It would also allow individual right holders to set their own rates to maximize their individual expected utility – something that cannot be done easily with the

---

218. And if we were to adopt such a system, we would certainly want the fee setting to be done by a competent government authority and not the pool of copyright owners themselves. The idea of such a tax-based compensation scheme is not as far-fetched as it might sound. Indeed, the use of levies on blank recording media and recording technology to compensate copyright owners for instances of private copying represents a similar system.

219. See *CBS v. ASCAP, supra* n. 85. ('Trade is restrained, frequently in an unreasonable manner, when rights to use individual copyrights or patents may be obtained only by payment for a pool of such rights.')

220. See, for example, *BMI v. CBS, supra* n. 38 at 20 ('Individual sales transactions in this industry are quite expensive, as would be individual monitoring and enforcement, especially in light of the resources of single composers. Indeed, as both the Court of Appeals and CBS recognize, the costs are prohibitive for licenses with individual radio stations, nightclubs, and restaurants . . .').

221. See, for example, *ASCAP (Application of Muzak, LLC), supra* n. 10 at 569.

current CMOs. For example, if an individual right holder decides to set the price for licensing her work for photocopying to zero to increase access to and the distribution of her work, that result is easily and directly achieved in the collecting society model. The copyright owner simply states her terms to the CCC, and the CCC reports those terms to potential users accordingly. In contrast, under the copyright collective model, a similar result for the public performance right is not so easily achieved. Although the consent decrees that govern ASCAP and BMI leave individual copyright owners formally free to license their works for public performances, a radio station or other user could not take advantage of such a 'free' public performance offer without obtaining performance licenses covering a large number of other performances as well. Because of the difficulties facing a radio station looking to clear all of the music it wants to play, copyright owners who would like more airplay[222] have not typically offered a discount on their public performance license fee. Instead, they have had to work around the CMOs and their blanket licenses by paying radio stations directly for more airtime – hence, the recurring payola scandals in radio.[223]

More generally, for individual licenses to become an effective competitive alternative, it will take more than sporadic or idiosyncratic offering of 'free' or low-cost public performance licenses by individual copyright owners here and there. Instead, what we need is a systematic listing of all the works available for public performance and their corresponding prices. Fortunately, the consent decrees provide a convenient means for imposing such a requirement. By amending the decrees to require that each ASCAP member or BMI affiliate identify his or her own performance license price(s) for each of his or her works, we can take a real step toward the creation of a competitive alternative to the current CMOs.1

---

222. Because of the popularity of networks inherent in the consumption of certain forms of entertainment, increased airtime leads to increased album sales and sales of other complements, such as concert tickets and merchandise. Copyright's division of music into the musical work copyright and the sound recording copyright, and the differing rights attached thereto, may lead to conflicts between the two copyright owners. Because the musical work copyright owner receives the public performance royalty, but only a relatively low mechanically licensing fee for phonorecord sales, the musical work copyright owner will not be as willing to trade-off a lower public performance royalty for increased album sales. The sound recording copyright owner, on the other hand, receives nothing from the public performance royalty (except for limited digital public performances), but is entitled to the full profit on phonorecord sales (less the mechanical royalty) as well as the profit on concerts and merchandize.

223. R. Caves, *Creative Industries: Contracts between Art and Commerce* (Cambridge, MA: Harvard University Press, 2000), at 286–296 (discussing payola in various industries); Ralph Blumenthal, 'Charges of Payola over Radio Music' (25 May 2002), *New York Times* at B7.

Chapter 12

Collective Management of Copyright and Neighbouring Rights in Japan*

*Koji Okumura***

1   INTRODUCTION

In this chapter, the collective management of copyright and neighbouring rights in Japan is discussed. In section 2, an overview of the history of collective management is given. In section 3, the current legal framework for collective management is introduced. In section 4, the key points of regulations on collective management organizations are explained. In section 5, the major collective management organizations are introduced. Finally, in section 6, issues relating to collective management in Japan are introduced and considered, to an extent.

---

 * The literature cited in this chapter is in Japanese unless otherwise noted.
** Associate Professor of Law, Faculty of Business Administration, Kanagawa University, Japan. In writing this Chapter, I wish to express my gratitude to my mentor, Mr Zentaro Kitagawa, Professor Emeritus of Kyoto University and Doctor of Law. In particular, the concept of the contract approach and Copymart in s. 6.4 owes much to the writings of Professor Kitagawa.

Daniel Gervais (ed.), *Collective Management of Copyright and Related Rights*, pp. 383–407.
© 2010 Kluwer Law International BV, The Netherlands.

2 HISTORY OF COLLECTIVE MANAGEMENT

2.1 WHIRLWIND OF PLAGE

When discussing the history of collective management of copyright in Japan, we have to mention the 'Whirlwind of Plage'.[1]

Japan, which joined the Berne Convention in 1899, declared its reservations regarding Article 9(3) (a provision permitting the free performance of musical works provided that there is no indication to the effect that performance is prohibited) of the original Berne Convention when ratifying the Berlin Act. When ratifying the Rome Act, however, Japan abandoned its reservations and revised its Copyright Act in 1931. Therefore, performers were required to get the permission of lyricists and composers for the public performance of foreign musical works that had been freely performed until the revision. Furthermore, because the revised Copyright Act created the right to broadcast by radio, broadcasting organizations were required to obtain the permission of lyricists and composers for radio broadcasting.

In the same year, Dr Wilhelm Plage, a German, opened an office in Tokyo and started to act as an agent for European right holders of musical works. Dr Plage demanded royalties from *Nippon Hôsô Kyôkai* (Japan Broadcasting Corporation (NHK)) and performers. These royalties were higher than those charged by domestic right holders at that time. Moreover, he took the attitude that he would not hesitate to file suits. Because of this, some performers discontinued using musical works managed by him. Even NHK stopped using musical works under his management in its radio programmes after the breakdown of negotiations with him.

This confusion among broadcasters and performers caused by the activities of Dr Plage is called the 'Whirlwind of Plage' because of the animosity felt toward him.

2.2 ENACTMENT OF THE ACT ON INTERMEDIARY BUSINESS CONCERNING COPYRIGHTS

The backlash against the Whirlwind of Plage peaked when he began to expand his business to the management of the copyright of Japanese authors.

---

1. For the details of the Whirlwind of Plage and the enactment of the Intermediary Business Act, see Shigeo Ohie, *Nippon Chosakuken Monogatari: Purâge Hakase no Tekihatsu-roku* (literally, Japanese Copyright Story: Dr Plage's Revelation), 2nd edn (Kanagawa: Seizansha, 1999). See also *Chosakuken Hôrei Kenkyû-kai* ed., *Chikujô Kaisetsu Chosakuken-tô Kanri Jigyô-hô* (literally, Article-by-Article Guide of the Act on Management Business of Copyright and Neighbouring Rights), (Tokyo: Yûhikaku, 2001), at 2–3 (hereinafter referred to as 'Article-by-Article Guide') and Fumio Sakka, *Shôkai Chosakuken-hô* (literally, Detailed Guide to the Copyright Act), 3rd edn (Tokyo: Gyôsei, 2004), at 56–58.

As a result, in 1939, the Japanese government enacted *Chosakuken ni kansuru Chûkai Jigyô-hô* (literally, the Act on Intermediary Business concerning Copyrights, hereinafter Intermediary Business Act), which strongly regulated the copyright management business. Under this Act, Dr Plage needed a license from the government to continue his business. However, because his application for a license was not accepted, Dr Plage was excluded from the intermediary business in Japan.

2.3   OUTLINE OF THE INTERMEDIARY BUSINESS ACT

A brief outline of the Intermediary Business Act is considered because the Act has already been abolished.[2]

2.3.1   Regulated Business

The Intermediary Business Act, as its title suggests, regulated *Chûkai Jigyô* (literally, the intermediary business, hereinafter the same). Intermediary business was defined by the Act as the business of acting as an agent or intermediating on behalf of copyright holders with regard to contracts for the exploitation of works.[3] Under the Act, the business of managing works on behalf of copyright holders with the copyrights being entrusted by them was deemed to be the intermediary business.[4]

However, the Act was applicable only to intermediary businesses handling works of types designated by imperial ordinance (the imperial ordinance designated novels, scripts, lyrics accompanied by a musical composition and musical compositions[5]). Or, to put it the other way around, intermediary businesses for other types of works were not regulated by the Intermediary Business Act.

2.3.2   License

Under the Intermediary Business Act, any person or organization who intended to conduct intermediary business was obligated to determine the scope and method of business and obtain a license from the Commissioner of the Agency for Cultural Affairs.[6] Any person or organization who engaged in intermediary business without a license faced a criminal penalty.[7]

Although the Intermediary Business Act did not provide licensing criteria, the Commissioner, as an operational principle, granted a license only to one person or

---

2. See Article-by-Article Guide, *supra* n. 1 at 3–4 and Sakka, *supra* n. 1 at 762–763.
3. See Intermediary Business Act, Art. 1(1).
4. See Intermediary Business Act, Art. 1(2).
5. Imperial Ordinance No. 835 of 1939.
6. See Intermediary Business Act, Art. 2.
7. Any person or organization who engages in intermediary business without a license was punished by a fine not more than JPY 20,000 (Art. 10 of the Intermediary Business Act and Art. 2(1) of *Bakkin-tô Rinji Sochi-hô* (literally, the Act on Temporary Measures concerning Fines).

organization for each type of work. For example, if the Commissioner licensed an organization to conduct intermediary business for novels, the Commissioner would not license any other person or organization for intermediary business for novels.[8]

Every *Chûkai-nin* (literally, a licensed intermediary, hereinafter the same) was obligated to obtain the approval of the Commissioner for its tariff.[9] Every licensed intermediary was also obligated to obtain the approval of the Commissioner for any changes in its scope of business, method of business or tariff.[10]

2.3.3 Supervision, Etc.

Licensed intermediaries had to submit a business and accounting report to the Commissioner of the Agency for Cultural Affairs annually.[11] On the other hand, the Commissioner had the authority to require licensed intermediaries to give such reports at any time.[12] The Commissioner was also authorized to inspect the business and financial status of licensed intermediaries and, if necessary, order a change of business methods.[13] With regard to licensed intermediaries that disobeyed such orders, the Commissioner was authorized to order the rescission of their license or the partial or complete suspension of their business.[14]

Together with the power of licensing and approving described in section 2.3.2, the Intermediary Business Act granted the government wide administrative and supervisory powers over licensed intermediaries.

2.3.4 Licensed Intermediaries

Because of the legal system and practical custom, the number of intermediaries who were able to obtain licenses was extremely limited. Licensed intermediaries that were in existence immediately before the abolition of the Intermediary Business Act were as follows:[15]

- Musical compositions and lyrics: *Shadan-hôjin Nihon Ongaku Chosakuken Kyôkai* (Japanese Society for Rights of Authors, Composers and Publishers, (JASRAC)).
- Novels: *Shadan-hôjin Nihon Bungei Chosakuken Hogo Dômei* (literally, Japan Literary Copyright Protection Association).
- Scripts: *Kyôdô-kumiai Nihon Kyakuhonka Renmei* (Writers Guild of Japan) and *Kyôdô-kumiai Nihon Shinario Sakka Kyôkai* (Japan Writers Guild).

---

8. For scripts, two organizations were eventually granted a license.
9. See Intermediary Business Act, Art. 3(1).
10. See Intermediary Business Act, Arts 4 and 3(1).
11. See Intermediary Business Act, Art. 5.
12. See Intermediary Business Act, Art. 6.
13. See Intermediary Business Act, Arts 7 and 8.
14. See Intermediary Business Act, Art. 9.
15. See Article-by-Article Guide, *supra* n. 1, at 4–5.

2.4   Review of the Intermediary Business Act

2.4.1   1967 Copyright Council Recommendation

In 1963, when the revision project of the Copyright Act was in progress, *Chosa-kuken Shingi-kai* (literally, the Copyright Council) began its deliberations on the review of the Intermediary Business Act. In 1967, the Council recommended that the scope of application of the Act should be narrowed.[16] However, the government did not revise the Act.

**2.4.2   Report by the Collective Right Management
Subcommittee of the Copyright Council**

Chosakuken Shingi-kai Kenri no Shûchû-kanri Shô-iinkai (literally, the Collective Right Management Subcommittee of the Copyright Council) began considerations related to a review of the Intermediary Business Act to cope with changes in the usage of copyrighted works accompanying progress in digitalization and networking and to relax unnecessary governmental regulations; it released a report (hereinafter, Subcommittee Report) in 2000.[17]

The Subcommittee Report accepted that collective management is beneficial to both right holders and users and presented the following five basic viewpoints for considering what collective management business should be:

(1) respect for the intent of copyright holders;
(2) responding to changes in the forms of exploitation of works;
(3) securing the confidence of both authors and users in copyright management organizations and their management business;
(4) securing the transparency of copyright management organizations and their management business; and
(5) enhancing the function of providing copyright information.

In light of these basic viewpoints, the Subcommittee Report considered the Intermediary Business Act and suggested five points to be reviewed in it. The five points are summarized as follows:

(1) The scope of application of the Act is narrow; thus review is necessary because the forms of exploitation of works are expected to further diversify.
(2) So that the intent of copyright holders will be respected, they should be given the freedom to choose a copyright management organization. The licensing system under the Act needs to be reviewed to allow multiple

---

16. See Article-by-Article Guide, *supra* n. 1, at 21–25.
17. See <www.cric.or.jp/houkoku/h12_1b/h12_1b.html> (last visited: 5 May 2010). See also Article-by-Article Guide, *supra* n. 1, at 32–41.

     copyright management organizations to be established for each type of work.

(3) The system for approving tariffs should also be reviewed in addition to relaxing the restrictions on entry into the intermediary business. In this case, it is necessary to introduce a simple and quick system for settling disputes.

(4) It is necessary to establish provisions for securing the transparency of copyright management organizations and their management business.

(5) The provisions of the Act giving broad discretion to the competent government agency should be reviewed in line with the trend for administrative reform.

Based on these points, the Subcommittee Report concluded that it was necessary to establish a new legal framework for collective management as soon as possible by extensively revising the Intermediary Business Act.

3   CURRENT LEGAL FRAMEWORK FOR COLLECTIVE MANAGEMENT

In this section, I first give an overview of *Chosakuken-tô Kanri Jigyô-hô* (literally, the Act on Management Business of Copyright and Neighbouring Rights, hereinafter the Management Business Act).[18] The following subsections explain the legal framework for the collection and management of secondary use fees and remuneration for rental for commercial phonograms and the legal framework for the collection and management of compensation for private sound and visual recording.

3.1   OUTLINE OF THE MANAGEMENT BUSINESS ACT

Based on the conclusion of the Subcommittee Report, the revision project of the Intermediary Business Act was advanced, leading to the 2000 enactment of the Management Business Act. The Management Business Act came into effect on 1 October 2001, on which date the Intermediary Business Act was abolished.

3.1.1   Regulated Business

The Management Business Act regulates *Chosakuken-tô Kanri Jigyô* (literally, the management business of copyrights, etc., hereinafter the same). The management business of copyrights, etc., means any business that, under *Kanri Itaku Keiyaku*

---

18. This article gives a brief outline of the Management Business Act. For full and accurate details, readers should consult the original Japanese texts of the Act. See also Article-by-Article Guide, *supra* n. 1, at 44–144 and Sakka, *supra* n. 1, at 767–777.

(literally, a management commission contract, hereinafter the same), authorizes the exploitation of works,[19] performances, phonograms, broadcasts or cable broadcasts (hereinafter, works, etc.) or otherwise manages copyrights or neighbouring rights (hereinafter, copyrights, etc.).[20,21] However, certain cases in which there is a close personal or capital relationship between the parties of a management commission contract (further details are provided in the Ordinance of the Ministry of Education, Culture, Sports, Science and Technology) are excluded from the management business of copyrights, etc.[22]

A management commission contract is one of the following two types of contract.[23] One is a trust contract by which a trustor transfers its copyrights, etc., to a trustee who authorizes the exploitation of its works, etc., or otherwise manages the copyrights, etc. The other is a mandate contract by which a mandator empowers a mandatary to both act as its agency or agent to authorize the exploitation of its works, etc., and manage its copyrights, etc., in connection with the function of agency or agent.

However, cases in which a trustor or mandator (hereinafter, trustor, etc.) has the power to determine the amount of royalties due when the exploitation of its works, etc., is authorized are not included in management commission contracts.

3.1.2 Registration

The Management Business Act prohibits any person or organization from conducting the management business of copyrights, etc., without registration with the Commissioner of the Agency for Cultural Affairs.[24] Furthermore, only juridical persons (including associations without juridical personality), whether profit-making or non-profit-making, may make such registrations.[25]

Items to be registered include the names of the applicant and officers, the name and address of the office, the types of works, etc., to be managed and the manner of exploitation of such works, etc.[26] The Commissioner must be notified of any changes to these registered items.[27]

The Commissioner must refuse registration if the application for registration includes any false statements or fails to meet statutory requirements.[28] Or, to put it another way, restrictions on entry into the copyright management business have been significantly relaxed compared to those of the Intermediary Business Act.

---

19. Unlike the Intermediary Business Act, the Management Business Act does not limit the types of works.
20. Whereas the Intermediary Business Act regulated only copyrights, the Management Business Act regulates neighbouring rights as well as copyrights.
21. See Management Business Act, Art. 2(2).
22. See Management Business Act, Art. 2(2).
23. See Management Business Act, Art. 2(1).
24. See Management Business Act, Arts 3 and 29.
25. See Management Business Act, Art. 6(1)(i).
26. See Management Business Act, Art. 4(1).
27. See Management Business Act, Art. 7(1).
28. See Management Business Act, Art. 6(1).

A registered juridical person under this Act is referred to as *Chosakuken-tô Kanri Jigyô-sha* (literally, an operator of management business of copyrights, etc., hereinafter, an operator of management business).[29]

3.1.3   Notification

Every operator of management business, prior to commencing its business, must notify the Commissioner of its tariff and general conditions of its management commission contract.[30] This also applies when an operator of management business changes its tariff or general conditions of its management commission contract (see section 4.1(2) and 4.2.2 for the period during which the enforcement of a tariff is prohibited).

3.1.4   Other Major Regulations

Every operator of management business must explain to an owner of copyright, etc., who intends to conclude a management commission contract the details of the general conditions. [31] Any operator of management business shall not conclude a management commission contract with a trustor, etc., without complying with the notified general conditions of its management commission contract.[32] A trustor, etc., may make a request for inspection or copying of the financial statements of an operator of management business.[33]

No operator of management business is allowed to charge royalties higher than those prescribed in its notified tariff and, without justifiable grounds, to refuse to authorize the exploitation of works, etc., under its management.[34]

Every operator of management business must publish its tariff and the notified general conditions of its management commission contract[35] and endeavour to provide users with the titles and other information of works, etc., under its management.[36]

Any operator of management business that meets statutory requirements is subject to further regulations as a designated operator of management business (See section 4.2 for further details).

3.1.5   Supervision, Etc.

The Commissioner of the Agency for Cultural Affairs may require operators of management businesses to report their business or financial status if the

---

29. See Management Business Act, Art. 2(3).
30. See Management Business Act, Arts 11(1) and 13(1).
31. See Management Business Act, Art. 12.
32. See Management Business Act, Art. 11(3).
33. See Management Business Act, Art. 18(2).
34. See Management Business Act, Arts 13(4) and 16.
35. See Management Business Act, Art. 15.
36. See Management Business Act, Art. 17.

Commissioner deems it necessary.[37] The Commissioner may also have its officials conduct an on-site inspection of the offices of operators of management businesses.

The Commissioner may order operators of management businesses to improve their business operations if the Commissioner finds any fact harmful to the interests of a trustor, etc., or a user in their business operation.[38] Furthermore, the Commissioner may rescind the registration of any operator of management business that disobeys such an order or has neither started nor conducted its business for more than one year.[39]

3.1.6 Current Operators of Management Businesses

There were only four licensed intermediaries under the Intermediary Business Act, but there are thirty-seven operators of management businesses under the Management Business Act (as of 5 May 2010).

The increase of business operators has created competition among them. For example, the number of operators of management businesses that emphasize musical works out of the classes of works, etc., they handle has risen to thirteen (as of 5 May 2010).

3.2 LEGAL FRAMEWORKS RELATED TO COLLECTIVE MANAGEMENT

Although the following may not fall under the category of collective management in a strict sense of the term, I will give a brief explanation about legal frameworks related to collective management.

3.2.1 Collection of Secondary Use Fees

Pursuant to the provisions of the Copyright Act, any broadcasting organization or wire-broadcasting organization (hereinafter, broadcasting organization, etc.) that broadcasts or wire-broadcasts using a commercial phonogram must pay a secondary use fee to performers whose performance is recorded on the commercial phonogram and the producer of the commercial phonogram.[40]

If there is an association consisting of a considerable number of domestic professional performers and that is designated by the Commissioner of the Agency for Cultural Affairs, performers' rights to receive secondary use fees may be exercised exclusively through the said association.[41] The amount of secondary use fees is determined through negotiations between the designated association and

---

37. See Management Business Act, Art. 19.
38. See Management Business Act, Art. 20.
39. See Management Business Act, Art. 21.
40. See Copyright Act, Arts 95(1) and 97(1).
41. See Copyright Act, Art. 95(3).

broadcasting organizations, etc.[42] The designated association is subject to the supervision of the Commissioner.

With regard to phonogram producers' rights to receive secondary use fees as well, if there is an association consisting of a considerable number of professional producers of commercial phonograms and designated by the Commissioner, the right may be exercised exclusively through the association.[43] With regard to other roles of and regulations for the designated association for producers of phonograms, the provisions for performers apply *mutatis mutandis.*[44]

3.2.2 Collection of Remuneration for Rental

Pursuant to the provisions of the Copyright Act, every person engaged in the business of rental of commercial phonograms to the public must pay remuneration for such rental to performers and producers of phonograms.[45]

Similar to the right to receive secondary use fees for commercial phonograms, the right to receive such remuneration for rental may be exercised exclusively through an association designated by the Commissioner of the Agency for Cultural Affairs.[46] With regard to other legal frameworks, the provisions for secondary use fees apply *mutatis mutandis.*

3.2.3 Designated Associations

Shadan-hôjin Nihon Geinô Jitsuen-ka Dantai Kyôgi-kai (Japan Council of Performers' Organizations, hereinafter Geidankyo, its abbreviation in Japanese) has been designated as the sole designated association for performers' rights to receive secondary use fees and remuneration for rental respectively.

Ippan Shadan-hôjin Nihon Rekôdo Kyôkai (Recording Industry Association of Japan, hereinafter RIAJ) has been designated as the sole designated association for phonogram producers' rights to receive secondary use fees and remuneration for rental respectively.

3.2.4 Collection of Compensation for Private Digital Sound Recordings

Pursuant to the provisions of the Copyright Act, every copyright holder and holder of a neighbouring right is entitled to compensation for digital sound recordings that are made for private use purposes with such devices and media as specified by Cabinet Order.[47]

---

42. See Copyright Act, Art. 95(10).
43. See Copyright Act, Art. 97(3).
44. See Copyright Act, Art. 97(4).
45. See Copyright Act, Art. 95–3(3).
46. See Copyright Act, Art. 95–3(4).
47. See Copyright Act, Art. 30(2).

If there is an association established for those entitled to compensation for private digital sound recordings and designated by the Commissioner of the Agency for Cultural Affairs, the right to receive compensation for private digital sound recordings may be exercised exclusively through the association.[48] *Shadan-hôjin Shiteki Rokuon Hoshô-kin Kanri Kyôkai* (Society for The Administration of Remuneration for Audio Home Recording (sarah)) is the only one designated association with regard to compensation for private digital sound recordings.

Currently, compensation for private digital sound recordings is paid to sarah by manufacturers of such devices or media as designated by the above Cabinet Order by collecting such compensation as a premium on the selling prices of such devices or media.

3.2.5 Collection of Compensation for Private Digital Visual Recordings

Similarly, pursuant to the provisions of the Copyright Act, every copyright holder and holder of a neighbouring right is also entitled to compensation for digital visual recordings that are made for private use purposes with such devices and media as specified by Cabinet Order.[49]

The provisions for compensation for private digital sound recordings apply *mutatis mutandis* to compensation for private digital visual recordings. *Shadan-hôjin Shiteki Rokuga Hoshô-kin Kanri Kyôkai* (Society for Administration of Remuneration for Video Home Recording (SARVH)) is the only association designated by the Commissioner of the Agency for Cultural Affairs with regard to compensation for private digital visual recordings.

4 IMPORTANT REGULATIONS ON COLLECTIVE MANAGEMENT ORGANIZATIONS

Compared to the era of the Intermediary Business Act, regulations on collective management organizations have been greatly relaxed under the Management Business Act. It has become easier to make a new entry into the copyright management business and the determining and changing of tariffs has become freer.

However, this does not mean that there are no regulations on collective management organizations. In the following sections, I will focus on important regulations on collective management organizations imposed by the Management Business Act.

---

48. See Copyright Act, Art. 104-2.
49. See Copyright Act, Art. 30(2).

4.1 REGULATIONS ON TARIFFS

Regulations on tariffs have been relaxed as the preparation or change of tariffs, which required the approval of the Commissioner of the Agency for Cultural Affairs under the Intermediary Business Act, requires only notification to the Commissioner under the Management Business Act. However, operators of management businesses have by no means been given a free hand to set or change tariffs. The Management Business Act regulates the setting or changing of a tariff as follows:

(1) Every operator of management business must determine its tariff, notify the tariff to the Commissioner, and make an outline thereof public and may not charge royalties higher than those prescribed in the notified tariff.[50] Furthermore, any operator of management business must endeavour to hear the opinions of users when changing its notified tariff and notify to the Commissioner any changes thereof.[51] (This is a system to secure the transparency of royalties and protect the interests of users.)

(2) A tariff becomes effective thirty days after notification to the Commissioner (the period during which the enforcement of the tariff is prohibited).[52] The Commissioner may extend the period up to three months after the receipt of notification if the Commissioner deems the tariff will prevent the smooth use of works, etc.[53] (This is a system to secure preparation time for users and time to examine the necessity of an order for business operation improvement.)

(3) Certain operators of management businesses that have a significant impact on standards for royalties are designated by the Commissioner as designated operators of management businesses and governed by the consultation and ruling system with regard to the setting or change of their tariffs.

4.2 SYSTEM OF DESIGNATED OPERATORS OF MANAGEMENT BUSINESSES

The system of designated operators of management businesses can be described as being the centrepiece of the regulations provided in the Management Business Act.

4.2.1 Background to Introduction

The Subcommittee Report (see section 3.2.1), which proposed the review of the Intermediary Business Act, expected that the registration system would stimulate competition among copyright management organizations by new entries into the

---

50. See Management Business Act, Arts 13(1), 13(4) and 15.
51. See Management Business Act, Arts 13(1) and 13(2).
52. See Management Business Act, Art. 14(1).
53. See Management Business Act, Art. 14(2).

copyright management business and make royalties reasonable. On the other hand, the Report suggested 'the relationship between copyright management organizations and users in the case of the authorization of the exploitation of works is different from the relationship between buyers and sellers in the case of general products',[54] pointing out the following three differences:

(1) 'The collective exercise of a copyright, which is a right to authorize, generally tends to prioritize the position of copyright management organizations over that of users.'

(2) The situation of copyright management organizations becomes more advantageous 'because works are highly taste-oriented but not very substitutable, and because all the rights comprising the copyright (or a part of such rights) regarding the same work will in effect not be managed by more than one management organization in cases of the discretionary entrustment of copyrights'.

(3) 'Because royalties have no concept of cost, there are no objective criteria for setting royalties, unlike general products, where a reasonable profit can be added to their cost. Therefore, there is a risk that copyright management organizations may set royalties arbitrarily.'

Acknowledging these differences, the Subcommittee Report pointed out 'it is essential to establish a legal system that allows copyright management organizations and user associations to set royalties through negotiations, to develop a mechanism for protecting users against steep rise in royalties and for the setting of fair royalties'.

The system that has been established based on this suggestion is the system of designated operators of management businesses.

4.2.2 Outline of System

If an operator of management business meets both the requirements (1) and (2) below in an 'exploitation category' (referring to a category by the type and exploitation manner of works, etc.) under its tariff, the Commissioner of the Agency for Cultural Affairs may designate such operator of management business as *Shitei Chosakuken-tô Kanri Jigyô-sha* (literally, the designated operator of management business of copyrights, etc., hereinafter, the 'designated operator of management business') in the exploitation category.[55]

(1) The sum of royalties collected by the operator of management business in any exploitation category under its tariff accounts for a significant share of the sum of royalties collected by all operators of management businesses in the exploitation category.

---

54. There is no official English translation of the Subcommittee Report, so the English translation cited in this paper was arranged by me for the purpose of reference.
55. See Management Business Act, Art. 23(1).

(2) The operator of management business falls under (a) or (b):
   (a) The sum of royalties collected by all operators of management businesses in the exploitation category accounts for a significant share of the sum of royalties collected in the exploitation category.[56]
   (b) The tariff of the operator of management business is widely used as standards for royalties in the exploitation category, and it is deemed particularly necessary to designate the operator of management business for the smooth use of works, etc., in the exploitation category.

The designated operator of management business in an exploitation category must attend consultations on its tariff for the exploitation category if requested by the representative of users in such exploitation category.[57] If an agreement is reached, the designated operator of management business must change said tariff based on the outcome of such consultation.[58]

The representative of users means an individual or organization that is deemed to represent the interests of users in the exploitation category in which the designated operator of management business is designated. When determining whether an individual or organization represents the interests of users, it is necessary to consider (1) the ratio of all direct or indirect members of the organization to the total number of users, (2) the ratio of the sum of royalties paid by the individual or the direct or indirect members of the organization to the sum of royalties paid by all users and (3) other conditions.[59]

If the Commissioner receives a notice from the representative of users that the representative has made a request for consultations to a designated operator of management business, the Commissioner may extend the period during which the enforcement of the tariff is prohibited by up to six months after the receipt of the notification of the tariff.[60] The Commissioner may also order the commencement of consultations if the designated operator of management business refuses to hold consultations and, if no agreement is reached by consultations, may order the resumption of consultations at the request of the representative of users.[61,62]

---

56. The sum includes not only royalties collected by operators of management businesses, but also those collected by other persons (such as copyright holders).
57. See Management Business Act, Art. 23(2). The representative of users must endeavor to hear the opinions of other users (excluding direct or indirect members of the representative) when negotiating with the designated operator of management business on the tariff (see the Management Business Act, Art. 23(3)).
58. See Management Business Act, Art. 23(5).
59. See Management Business Act, Art. 23(2).
60. See Management Business Act, Art. 14(2).
61. See Management Business Act, Art. 23(4).
62. A designated operator of management business, in principle, decides whether an organization or an individual is the representative of users. However, the Commissioner of the Agency for Cultural Affairs has to make that decision if the Commissioner decides whether to extend the period during which the enforcement of the tariff is prohibited or if the Commissioner decides whether to order the commencement or resumption of consultations for designated operators of management businesses. The decision criteria are prescribed in Art. 21 of the Ordinance for Enforcement of the Act on Management Business of Copyright and Neighbouring Rights.

If no agreement is reached during consultations initiated by an order for the commencement or resumption of consultations, the designated operator of management business or the representative of users may apply for a ruling by the Commissioner.[63] If the Commissioner gives a ruling that the tariff should be changed, the designated operator of management business must change its tariff in accordance with the ruling.[64]

The system of designated operators of management businesses can be described as a system to maintain the balance between the freedom of copyright management business activities and the protection of users by narrowing the scope of regulations to fields that significantly affect users.

4.2.3 Number of Designated Operators of Management Businesses

As of 10 May 2009, seven organizations have been designated by the Commissioner of the Agency for Cultural Affairs as designated operators of management businesses. For the details of each organization, see section 5 'Major Operators of Management Businesses'.

4.3 RESCISSION OF REGISTRATION OF OPERATORS OF MANAGEMENT BUSINESSES

Because restrictions on entry into the copyright management business have been relaxed under the Management Business Act, it is necessary to exclude problematic business operators by using procedures strictly.

Two organizations have had their registration rescinded so far on the grounds that they failed to give notification of their tariffs and general conditions of their management commission contracts and did not conduct actual business operations.

5 MAJOR OPERATORS OF MANAGEMENT BUSINESSES

In this section, I will introduce designated operators of management businesses as major operators of management businesses in Japan.

5.1 JAPANESE SOCIETY FOR RIGHTS OF AUTHORS, COMPOSERS AND PUBLISHERS

JASRAC manages the copyrights of lyricists, composers and music publishers. About 15,000 right holders (4,300 lyricists, 3,200 composers, 5,000 song writers

---

63. See Management Business Act, Art. 24(1).
64. See Management Business Act, Art. 24(6).

and 2,500 music publishers) entrust their copyrights to this organization.[65] JASRAC collected JPY 113 billion in total in fiscal 2008.

JASRAC is the designated operator of management business for many exploitation categories of musical works under its tariff.[66]

5.2   WRITERS GUILD OF JAPAN

The Writers Guild of Japan manages the rights of public transmission, screen presentation, reproduction, distribution, publication, performance, etc., on behalf of playwrights. About 1,500 playwrights contract with this organization.[67] According to the Agency for Cultural Affairs, it collected about JPY 2.6 billion in total in fiscal 2004.[68]

The Writers Guild of Japan is the designated operator of management business for several exploitation categories under its tariff, such as the broadcasting and reproduction as commercial videograms and other media of scripts for television and radio programmes.[69]

5.3   JAPAN WRITERS GUILD

The Japan Writers Guild manages the rights of public transmission, reproduction, rental, screen presentation, etc., on behalf of playwrights. About 540 playwrights contract with this organization.[70] According to the Agency for Cultural Affairs, the Japan Writers Guild collected about JPY 575 million in fiscal 2004.[71]

The Japan Writers Guild is the designated operator of management business for one exploitation category under its tariff; namely the broadcasting of theatrical films by broadcasting organizations that have obtained rights of broadcasting.[72]

5.4   JAPAN REPROGRAPHIC RIGHTS CENTER

Shadan-hôjin Nihon Fukusha-ken Sentâ (Japan Reprographic Rights Center) is an operator of management business with respect to the reproduction and other

---

65. See <www.jasrac.or.jp/profile/outline/member.html> (last visited: 5 May 2010).
66. See <www.bunka.go.jp/1tyosaku/pdf/sitei_kanri_jasrac.pdf> (last visited: 5 May 2010).
67. See <www.writersguild.or.jp/wgj/rights.html> (last visited: 5 May 2010).
68. See the final report of *Chosakuken Bunka-kai Keiyaku Ryûtsû Syô-iinkai* (literally, the Contract and Distribution Subcommittee, Subdivision on Copyright, Council for Cultural Affairs.), at 195, <www.bunka.go.jp/chosakuken/singikai/pdf/singi_houkokusho_1801.pdf> (last visited: 5 May 2010).
69. See <www.bunka.go.jp/file_l/1000012479_kyakuhon.pdf> (last visited: 5 May 2010).
70. See <www.j-writersguild.org/s6_0.html> (last visited: 5 May 2010).
71. See the final report of *Chosakuken Bunka-kai Keiyaku Ryûtsû Syô-iinkai* (literally, the Contract and Distribution Subcommittee, Subdivision on Copyright, Council for Cultural Affairs.), at 195, <www.bunka.go.jp/chosakuken/singikai/pdf/singi_houkokusho_1801.pdf> (last visited: 5 May 2010).
72. See <www.bunka.go.jp/file_l/1000012480_sinario.pdf> (last visited: 5 May 2010).

exploitation of publications. It collected about JPY 183 million in fiscal 2008.[73]

The Japan Reprographic Rights Center is the designated operator of management business for one exploitation category under its tariff; namely, the not-for-distribution reproduction of publications.[74]

5.5   RECORDING INDUSTRY ASSOCIATION OF JAPAN

RIAJ manages the neighbouring rights of phonogram producers in connection with the reproduction of phonograms for broadcasting, the act to make transmittable programmes recording phonograms and other exploitation of phonograms. It collected about JPY 1.5 billion in royalties in fiscal 2008.[75] RIAJ is the designated operator of management business for one exploitation category under its tariff; namely, reproduction for broadcasting by NHK, general terrestrial broadcasting organizations and *Hôsô Daigaku Gakuen* (The Open University of Japan).[76]

RAIJ is also designated by the Commissioner of the Agency for Cultural Affairs as (1) the sole association collecting secondary use fees for commercial phonograms and (2) the sole association collecting remuneration for rental of commercial phonograms on behalf of phonogram producers, severally. In fiscal 2008, RIAJ collected about JPY 4.2 billion in secondary use fees and about JPY 3.7 billion in remuneration for rental.[77]

5.6   JAPAN COUNCIL OF PERFORMERS' ORGANIZATIONS

Geidankyo founded an internal independent organization, *Jitsuen-ka Chosaku Rinsetsu-ken Sentâ* (Center for Performers' Rights Administration, (CPRA)),[78] which manages the neighbouring rights of performers in connection with (1) the recording for broadcasting of performances recorded on commercial phonograms, (2) the act to make transmittable performances recorded on commercial phonograms used for broadcast programmes, (3) the secondary use of broadcast programmes (sale, reproduction into videograms and making transmittable), and other categories of exploitation.[79] In fiscal 2006, CPRA collected about JPY 1.3 billion in royalties for the recording for broadcasting.[80] Geidankyo is the designated operator of management business for one exploitation category under its tariff;

---

73. See <www.jrrc.or.jp/document/pdf/jigyouhoukokusyo.pdf> (last visited: 5 May 2010).
74. See <www.bunka.go.jp/file_l/1000012481_hukusha.pdf> (last visited: 5 May 2010).
75. See <www.riaj.or.jp/about/pdf/h20_balance_sheet.pdf> (last visited: 5 May 2010).
76. See <www.bunka.go.jp/file_l/1000012482_record.pdf> (last visited: 5 May 2010).
77. See <www.riaj.or.jp/about/pdf/h20_balance_sheet.pdf> (last visited: 5 May 2010).
78. See <www.cpra.jp/what/message/index.shtml> (last visited: 5 May 2010).
79. See <www.cpra.jp/what/activities/index.shtml> (last visited: 5 May 2010).
80. See <www.fmp.or.jp/aboutfmp/cpra_fmp_distribute.html> (last visited: 5 May 2010).

namely, recording for broadcasting by NHK, general terrestrial broadcasting organizations and the Open University of Japan.[81]

CPRA is also in charge of collecting and distributing secondary use fees and remuneration for rental for commercial phonograms because Geidankyo has been designated by the Commissioner of the Agency for Cultural Affairs as (1) the sole association collecting secondary use fees for commercial phonograms and (2) the sole association collecting remuneration for rental of commercial phonograms on behalf of performers, severally. CPRA collected about JPY 3.6 billion in secondary use fees and about JPY 1.7 billion in remuneration for rental in fiscal 2006.[82]

5.7　　Rental Rights Administration Center for Publications

Ippan Shadan-hôjin Shuppanbutsu Taiyo-ken Kanri Sentâ (Rental Rights Administration Center for publications (RRAC)) manages the rights of rental of publications.[83] The total amount which the RRAC distributed to right holders in fiscal 2009 reached JPY 990 million.[84]

The RRAC is the designated operator of management business for two exploitation categories under its tariff.[85] One category is for when royalties for rental are paid for each publication rented and the other category is for when royalties are paid depending on the number of times publications are rented.

6　　ISSUES RELATING TO COLLECTIVE MANAGEMENT

As a conclusion to this Chapter, I will use this section to look into issues relating to collective management in Japan. First, the arguments over the review of the Management Business Act are introduced. Next, topics related to competition law and movement toward a form of 'one-stop shop' are mentioned as recent themes in collective management. Finally, the weaknesses of collective management and the potential of the 'contract approach' are explored.

6.1　　Review of the Management Business Act

In 2004, *Bunka Shingi-kai Chosakuken Bunka-kai Keiyaku Ryûtsû Syô-iinkai* (literally, the Contract and Distribution Subcommittee, Subdivision on Copyright, Council for Cultural Affairs) deliberated the necessity for a review of the Management Business Act in accordance with Article 7 of the supplementary

---

81. See <www.bunka.go.jp/file_l/1000012483_geinou.pdf> (last visited: 5 May 2010).
82. See <www.fmp.or.jp/aboutfmp/cpra_fmp_distribute.html> (last visited: 5 May 2010).
83. See <www.taiyoken.jp/> (last visited: 5 May 2010).
84. See <www.taiyoken.jp/kenri.html> (last visited: 5 May 2010).
85. See <www.bunka.go.jp/file_l/1000012484_shiteikanri.pdf> (last visited: 5 May 2010).

provisions of that act. The Subcommittee solicited public comments twice during its deliberation process to seek opinions from various concerned parties and released its final report in 2005.[86]

This report assessed the enforcement of the Management Business Act as having created competition among operators of management businesses and consequently reducing management fees and improving services. On the other hand, the report pointed out that on the user side there were opinions to the effect that there were those dissatisfied with the complicated procedures for application as a result of the existence of more than one operator of management business in a field of works, etc. Other users demanded tighter regulations, including regulations on untrustworthy newcomers.[87]

However, the report concluded 'there are no issues to deal with caused by the immediate revision of the Act' on the grounds that on the user side, most complaints, etc., were attributable to the fact that the new system under the Management Business Act had not yet become established. At the same time, the report requested that the Agency for Cultural Affairs should strictly operate the Management Business Act based on opinions from the user side and pointed out the future necessity of considering whether to review the Act.

6.2   ISSUES ABOUT COMPETITION

Some may be afraid that competition among operators of management businesses has not been as active as desired by the Management Business Act. Take music, for example. The enforcement of the Act increased the number of operators of management businesses that deal with musical works to eleven, thanks to newcomers to the market. In monetary terms, however, the market share of newcomers is small while JASRAC still boasts an overwhelming market share. This naturally raises the doubt as to whether there is sound competition in the music copyright business. Needless to say, it would be premature to conclude that this situation is a legal problem because JASRAC's large share is attributable to its long-term efforts.

In February 2009, the Japan Fair Trade Commission (JFTC) concluded that the cause of the small market share of new entrants in the field of broadcasting of musical works was the blanket contract system between JASRAC and broadcast organizations.[88]

Under the blanket contract system, broadcasting organizations are obligated to pay JASRAC a certain percentage of their revenue to be licensed to use music compositions and lyrics managed by JASRAC. Therefore, broadcasting organizations have to pay extra to use music compositions and lyrics managed by any other

---

86. See the final report of the Subcomitee, at 177–213, <www.bunka.go.jp/chosakuken/singikai/pdf/singi_houkokusho_1801.pdf> (last visited: 5 May 2010).
87. Some requested the establishment of a new system that obligates non-designated operators of management business to hear the opinions of the representative of users when changing tariffs.
88. See <www.jftc.go.jp/pressrelease/09.february/090227.pdf> (last visited: 5 May 2010).

operators of management businesses. The JFTC pointed out that this system kept broadcasting organizations from using music compositions and lyrics not managed by JASRAC and had actually restricted new operators entering the music copyright business.

The JFTC issued a cease and desist order to JASRAC, demanding a review of the blanket contract system. However, JASRAC requested a hearing as an objection to the order.[89] No conclusion has been reached as of the time of writing, so the progress of this matter will attract attention.[90]

6.3   'ONE-STOP SHOPPING'

I have already mentioned the complaints that procedures for license application became complicated as under the Management Business Act more than one operator of management business may conduct business in the same field of works (see section 6.1). The movement toward a form of 'one-stop shopping', as shown in the following subsections, can be appreciated as an attempt to resolve such complaints.

6.3.1   Portal Site for Right Holders' Databases

In January 2009, *Chosakuken Mondai wo kangaeru Sôsaku-sha Dantai Kyôgi-kai* (literally, the Council of Creators' Organizations for Copyright Issues) launched a portal site for the searching for authors and copyright holders.[91] This portal site is an entrance to the databases of right holders provided by the member organizations of the Council. This can be said to be an attempt to reduce the time and labour needed to search for authors and copyright holders.

6.3.2   Copyright Data Clearinghouse

In March 2009, music distributors and operators of management businesses related to musical works took the lead in founding a general incorporated association named *Ippan Shadan-hôjin Chosakuken Jôhô Shûchû Shori Kikô* (Copyright Data Clearinghouse (CDC)).[92]

Hitherto, each music distributor has been identifying which operator of management business manages the musical works that it wants to use by making inquires to each operator of management business and in other ways, while reporting the records of exploitation to each operator. On the other hand, each operator of management business has also been answering inquiries from music distributors, checking reports from them and doing other tasks on its own account.

---

89. JASRAC argues that the system does not 'keep users from using' music managed by non-JASRAC entities, contrary to the opinion of the JFTC, and that the system is a popular system adopted by a variety of foreign countries.

90. See <www.jftc.go.jp/pressrelease/09.may/09052703.pdf> (last visited: 5 May 2010).

91. See <www.sousakusya.jp/> (last visited: 5 May 2010).

92. See <www.cdc.or.jp/info/index.htm#1> (last visited: 5 May 2010).

However, as the music distribution business rapidly expands, the workload for these tasks has sharply increased, which has been a heavy burden on both operators of management businesses and music distributors.

The CDC provides a system called 'Fluzo', which functions as a copyright information hub to help report the usage of musical works. It makes the centralization of these tasks possible for the purpose of reducing the burden on both operators of management businesses and music distributors. The CDC began operation of the Fluzo system in April 2010.

6.3.3   Secondary Use of Broadcast Programmes

The potential demand for the secondary use of television programmes, such as DVDs and online distribution, is large because television programmes are one of the most popular forms of content in Japan. However, it is not realistic to obtain permission from each performer appearing in a television programme because there are many such performers. This time-consuming process has come to be regarded as a challenge inherent in the secondary use of television programmes.

Geidankyo, as mentioned in section 5.6, started licensing activities for the secondary use of broadcast programmes in 2006.[93] Yet, under the existing circumstances, as there are many right holders who conduct licensing activities on their own, instead of entrusting their rights to Geidankyo,[94] it is said that collective management has not displayed a sufficient effect.

Thus, Geidankyo and other associations of right holders who do not entrust their rights to Geidankyo are considering the establishment of a new organization to integrate the channels of applications for licenses.[95] The integration of application channels will make it much easier for broadcasters and others to search and contact right holders. This will become the subject of attention as an attempt to promote the secondary use of television programmes.[96]

6.4   WEAKNESSES OF AND A SYSTEM COMPLEMENTARY TO COLLECTIVE MANAGEMENT

6.4.1   Merits of Collective Management

The collective management of copyrights, etc., was 'invented' as a system to be beneficial to both right holders and users.[97] Thanks to collective management,

---

93. The actual activities are conducted by the CPRA.
94. See <www.cpra.jp/web/img/pdf/panpfh.pdf> (last visited: 30 May 2009).
95. See <www.soumu.go.jp/main_content/000021824.pdf> (last visited: 30 May 2009). The provisional name of the new organization is *Ippan Shadan-hôjin Eizô Kontentsu Kenri Syori Kikô* (literally, Video Content Copyright Clearinghouse).
96. Although, according to the press release, the new organization was scheduled to start its operations in April 2010, no additional information about it was available at the time of writing.
97. See, generally, Sakka, *supra* n. 1, at 760.

right holders can reduce considerably the time and expenses necessary for licensing users and detecting infringements. On the other hand, collective management saves users a lot of labour when searching for right holders. In addition, in many cases, users can use the standard license conditions set by collective management organizations without the need to negotiate on license conditions when they apply for licenses.

If consideration is given to these merits, it should be no surprise that as new exploitation forms of works spread, there are growing calls for the enhancement of collective management to cope with such exploitation forms (see section 6.3.3).

6.4.2 Weaknesses of Collective Management

Unfortunately, collective management is not a magic wand. It also has some weaknesses.

First, collective management is unlikely to reflect the intent of individual right holders because, in order to increase the efficiency that is one of the merits of collective management, a collective management organization usually applies standardized terms and conditions to all works, etc., under its management. In addition, under the Management Business Act, operators of management businesses cannot refuse licensing unless they have justifiable grounds. Although I would not go so far as to say that collective management turns copyrights, etc., into rights only regarding the receipt of royalties or compensation, collective management has a tendency to restrict the ability of right holders to control the exploitation of their works, etc.

Second, it is difficult to meet the demand for the exploitation of works, etc., accompanied by modification within the framework of collective management. The advancement of digital and network technologies has facilitated the modification of works, etc.; thus there is great demand for the exploitation of works, etc., accompanied by modification. However, users need to individually obtain the permission of authors or performers for such exploitation because collective management is not consonant to the moral rights of authors or performers.

Third, it is hard for collective management to cope with the situation in which the whole population can become creators and then broadcasters. The spread of digital and network technologies has made it possible for individuals to distribute their works throughout the world. However, it is difficult for such works to be the subject of collective management if the efficiency of such management is considered. Therefore, it is highly likely that they will be placed outside the collective management framework.[98]

Of course, the merits of collective management more than offset its weaknesses. There is no doubt that, despite its weaknesses, collective management should be further enhanced. Keeping this in mind, we next consider a license system complementary to collective management.

---

98. See, for example, Kaoru Okamoto, *Daredemo Wakaru Chosakuken* (literally, *Easy-to-Understand Copyright*) (Tokyo: Zen-nihon Shakai Kyoiku Rengo-kai, 2005), at 324.

6.4.3   Contract Approach

If we enable right holders and users to individually and directly conclude contracts using digital and network technologies, such contracts can be complementary to collective management.[99] (This is a process based on contracts, so it is termed 'contract approach' in the following discussion.)

In contrast to collective management, the contract approach can reflect the intent of right holders and deal with the exploitation of works, etc., that may infringe the moral rights of authors or performers and require their permission. Furthermore, because digital and network technologies reduce to an extent the labour and cost necessary for concluding contracts individually and directly, the contract approach can provide an efficient licensing system for works, etc., not covered by collective management.

There will be three requirements for the contract approach to effectively function. The first requirement is to develop a marketplace of works, etc.[100] There, right holders can offer licenses for their own works, etc., and users can obtain such licenses. The second requirement is for works, etc., to become 'products' suitable for transactions in the marketplace.[101] In this era of digital networks, works, etc., are vulnerable to unauthorized access and illegal reproduction. This means that works, etc., must be protected by encryption technologies and other methods to protect them against illegal use in order that they may become 'products' suitable for market transactions.[102] The third requirement is that license conditions must be 'embedded' in works, etc., because market products have a price tag.[103]

6.4.4   Copymart

'Copymart', the law model proposed by Professor Zentaro Kitagawa, is a typical example of the contract approach.[104] To facilitate understanding of the contract approach, I will give an outline of Copymart.

As shown in Figure 12.1, Copymart consists of two databases – the copyright market and copy market.[105] Right holders register their works, etc., with the copy

---

99. See Zentaro Kitagawa, 'Copymart – For activation of Copyrights as a Private Right', in *Festschrift für Andreas Heldrich: zum 70. Geburstag* (Munich: Back, 2005), at 242 (hereinafter referred to as 'Kitagawa [2005]').

100. See Okamoto, *supra* n. 98, at 324.

101. See Zentaro Kitagawa, 'Copymart as Legal Infrastructure of Information Society', in *Copymart: The Product and its Prospects – Proceedings of the Berlin Symposium (September 5–6, 2002)*, ed. Z. Kitagawa (Kyoto: International Institute for Advanced Studies, 2003), at 59–60 and Kitagawa [2005], *supra* n. 99, at 243.

102. See Zentaro Kitagawa, *Copymart*, (Tokyo: Yuhikaku, 2003), at 88–89.

103. See Kitagawa [2005], *supra* n. 99, at 243.

104. The word 'Copymart' was first used in Zentaro Kitagawa, 'Copymart: A new Concept – An Application of Digital Technology to the Collective management of Copyright', in *WIPO Worldwide Symposium on the Impact of Digital technology on Copyright and Neighboring Rights* (Geneva: WIPO, 1993), at 139–147.

105. See Kitagawa [2005], *supra* n. 99, at 244–245. See also <www.copymart.jp/cmi/about_e_f.html> (last visited: 5 May 2010).

Figure 12.1. Copymart Institute <www.copymart.jp/cmi/about_e_f.html>
(last visited: 5 May 2010).

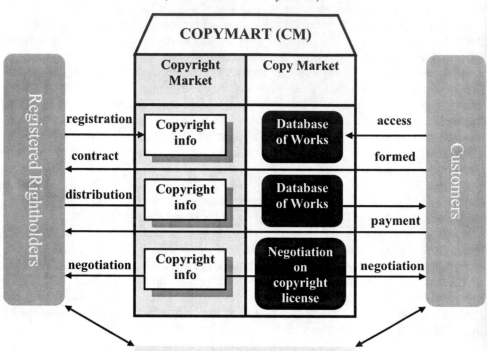

market and the license conditions and other information of the works, etc., with the copyright market. Users can obtain the license conditions and other information of works, etc., that they want to use by searching the copyright market (users can also negotiate on license conditions via Copymart). If a right holder and a user reach agreement, both parties will conclude a contract, under which the user can obtain the works, etc., from Copymart. The organizer of Copymart (Copymart Holder) operates the marketplaces but has no involvement in, nor the intention to become a party to, contracts between right holders and users.

6.4.5   Mutual Complementing

Collective management and the contract approach have different areas of strength. Collective management is suitable for processing a large volume of works, etc. By bundling right holders together, collective management can also provide a human and financial infrastructure that strongly promotes both activities to expose illegal use and educational activities for rights protection. On the other hand, the contract approach has more than a few advantages for works, etc., created by amateurs;

works, etc., the demand for which is very niche; and works, etc., that their right holders want to manage as they wish because of their strong personal feelings about the works, etc.

That is to say, if we mainly take the collective management and take the contract approach to complement it, we can cope with various future environments for the use of works, etc.

If the mutual complementing of collective management and the contract approach develops further an environment through which it is easy to obtain a license for works, it will contribute to a decrease in the illegal use of works, etc. To address such illegal use, needless to say, it is important to expose illegal use and promote educational activities for copyright, etc. In daily life, however, people are sensible enough to properly purchase products, instead of stealing them. This should be true for works, etc. To support people's sensible behaviours, it should be important to enhance licensing environments.

Chapter 13

Collective Management in Asia

*Ang Kwee-Tiang**

| 1 | INTRODUCTION |

Asia is huge, both geographically and demographically. It contains some 3.3 billion of the world's population and is a diverse mixture of ethnic, cultural, social, economic and political interests and conditions. Several factors have greatly influenced the development of copyright and collective management in Asia. The first factor is historical, more specifically, colonization. British colonization brought its system of copyright to countries such as Brunei, Hong Kong, India, Myanmar, Malaysia, Pakistan, Singapore and Sri Lanka; the Dutch introduced its copyright system to Indonesia; French influence is perceptible in Vietnam; Portuguese law is found in Macau; and the American copyright system exerts itself in the Philippines. These colonial influences exist to this day and are not restricted to the copyright system alone but permeate many aspects of the legal and administrative life in this region.

The second factor is political ideology. The manner in which copyright systems developed in Asia also could be clearly delineated between those countries that embraced capitalism vis-à-vis those countries that adopted socialism or communism. Broadly speaking, those countries that embraced communism had a prolonged period in the twentieth century in which there was little emphasis given to

* Director, Asia Pacific Affairs, CISAC.

Daniel Gervais (ed.), *Collective Management of Copyright and Related Rights*, pp. 409–464.
© 2010 Kluwer Law International BV, The Netherlands.

copyright protection, and it was only in the last decade that a fresh impetus for protection emerged in these countries.

A third and no less important factor influencing the regional copyright scene is the level of economic development. Of the 3.3 billion people in Asia, 89.7% (2.96 billion) have average annual incomes below United States Dollar (USD) 900, with approximately half of these, or 1.44 billion people, having average annual incomes below USD 500.[1] At the other end of the scale, only 4.7% of the Asian population have average annual incomes over USD 20,000. These figures are important in the context because there is a correlation between a country's economic development and the level of copyright protection, as well as the viability of collective management organizations (CMOs). Broadly speaking it is more difficult to enforce copyright protection in a country with a low level of economic development.

The fourth factor is the Agreement on Trade-Related Aspects of Intellectual Property (TRIPS). It would be no exaggeration to generalize that the legislative activities in the field of copyright that took place in the region, particularly in the last decade, may be attributed almost singularly to TRIPS.

Macro factors aside, there are also features that are unique to the Asian creative industries.

1.1 INDUSTRY INFRASTRUCTURE

Many Asian composers deal directly with record companies. Hence, if a composer wanted to have a song recorded and distributed, he or she went directly to a record company and was normally paid a lump sum for the work. With the absence of a publishing infra-structure, many copyright rights are sold to recording companies and the full benefits of collective management are thus unlikely to be enjoyed by the creators. Because of this practice, it has often proven problematic for new CMOs to persuade recording companies to agree to the distribution of 50% of the public performance royalties back to the composers. This has been adversely affecting the proper growth of CMOs in the region. In many instances, local creators, being used to the existing system of selling their rights to the recording companies, or working as employed staff of such companies, find it difficult to break from the system to entrust new rights to a CMO. The foregoing difficulty is compounded by the fact that it normally takes quite a number of years before any meaningful distribution of royalties may be made by a CMO. This also exacerbates the reluctance of many Asian right holders to invest or participate in the formation of a CMO and inhibits the development of collective management in the region.

---

1. Dollar amounts are in USD. The latest statistics compiled by the Asian Development Bank for 2003 showed that 1.85 billion or 57% of Asians still live on less than USD 2 per day. The number of people living in extreme poverty – less than USD 1 per day – was estimated at 621 million, or 19.3% of the population. Approximately 93% of those in the latter category lived in India (327 million), South Asian countries apart from India (77 million) and China (173 million).

In several Asian countries, the first task in the creation of a CMO was in fact to convince copyright holders of the benefits of collective management and to persuade them that they have an economic right worth protecting.

1.2   LATE ARRIVAL OF COLLECTIVE MANAGEMENT
        OF COPYRIGHT TO ASIA

Generally speaking, the concept of collective management of copyright was relatively late in coming to Asia. The earliest collective for musical works created in the region was the Japanese Society for Rights of Authors, Composers and Publishers (JASRAC),[2] established in Japan in 1939,[3] administering the rights in musical works. By contrast, in America or Western Europe, some CMOs date back to the mid-1800s Moreover, it has to be pointed out that the early establishment of some of the Asian CMOs was in some instances only on paper. For example, the CMOs in South Korea and the Philippines, although legally established in 1964 and 1965, were not fully operational until 1987 and 1992, respectively.

The recent growth of new and rejuvenated CMOs in Asia has been quite encouraging, as gross incomes from CMOs in the field of music have increased by a thousand-fold in the past two decades from USD 11.6 million in 1990 to an estimated USD 139 million in 2009.

2   THE COLLECTIVE MANAGEMENT OF RIGHTS IN ASIA

2.1   THE ASEAN COUNTRIES

2.1.1   Singapore

The current Singapore Copyright Act,[4] first enacted in 1987, is largely based on the 1968 Australian Act, which in turn was based on the 1956 UK Act. Singapore is a signatory to the Berne Convention, the World Intellectual Property Organization (WIPO) Copyright Treaty (WCT) and WIPO Performances and Phonograms Treaty (WPPT).

---

2. See the Chapter on Japan.
3. Outside Japan and the field of musical works, the first collecting society for sound recordings is Phonographic Performance Limited, an organization administering the public performance rights in sound recordings in India established in 1936.
4. *Copyright Act Revised Edition No. 2 of 1988*, Government Gazette, 20 Feb. 1987, No. 3. The Singapore Government did not accede to any of the international copyright conventions when this Act was passed. Instead, it legislated to provide bilateral protection to copyright works from the UK (which originally excluded Hong Kong but was subsequently amended to include), and the US. Singapore acceded to the Berne Convention only on 21 Dec. 1998, more than a decade after enacting its copyright law. Prior to 1987, the 1911 UK *Copyright Act* applied in Singapore.

2.1.1.1 The Collective Management of Rights in Musical Works in Singapore

In Singapore, the CMO in the field of musical works is called the Composers and Authors Society of Singapore Limited (COMPASS). It collectively administers the public performance right and, to a limited extent, reproduction rights as well.[5] COMPASS was legally formed in 1987 through the joint efforts of the Performing Right Society (UK) and the International Confederation of Societies of Authors and Composers (CISAC) but became operational only in 1991. Because Singapore was a British colony until 1963,[6] the Performing Rights Society (PRS) had operated a licensing agency in Singapore since 1935.[7] For a period of time, the PRS agent was a Singaporean law firm. Collections were not insubstantial[8]; some Singapore Dollar (SGD) 150,000 was collected in 1979. A Singapore branch of the PRS was established around 1982. By 1988, gross income collected by the PRS Agency had reached nearly SGD 1 million.

COMPASS did not have an easy birth. In fact, as far back as May 1980, a feasibility study had proposed the creation of the Composers Association of Singapore Ltd. However, because of the weak copyright situation at the time[9] as well as the perceived lack of support by the Singapore government, the project was shelved. Although COMPASS was eventually incorporated in 1987, it nevertheless remained dormant until 1989. Two events connived to bring about this delay. First, there were issues raised by major music publishers and recording companies[10] who, *inter alia*, indicated that they would join COMPASS only if they were appointed to the Board of Directors and the provisions concerning the management of mechanical rights by COMPASS (contained in the Articles) were deleted. Second, the negotiations for the payment of royalties by the broadcasting station were problematic. The 1987 Copyright Act had abolished the exemption provided to the then government-owned Singapore Broadcasting Corporation (SBC) from payment

---

5. The decision to commence on the collective management of this right was taken in September 1995.
6. The agency also issued a limited number of licenses to users in Malaysia (such as the one issued to Rediffusion, a cable broadcasting company operating both in Malaysia and Singapore at that time, and Malaysian Airline System, the national airline of Malaysia) and Brunei. It also had some Malaysian composers as members.
7. Singapore obtained self-government in 1959, became a state of Malaysia in 1963, and an independent republic in 1965.
8. Particularly given the fact that the then existing law was the UK 1911 Copyright Act, that Singapore was not signatory to any of the international copyright conventions and that the sole government broadcaster, Radio Television Singapore, which used to pay some SGD 25,000 (approximately EUR 12,500 as of November 2005) in royalties, became exempt from payment of royalties when Parliament enacted the Copyright (Gramophone Record and Government Broadcasting) Act in 1969. This exemption was continued by statutory provision contained in the law that created SBC a statutory body in 1980.
9. The applicable copyright law then was the 1911 UK Copyright Act.
10. At that time, the business of music publishing in Singapore was essentially subsumed into the operations of sound recording companies.

of broadcast royalties. Thus, in September 1987, the PRS Singapore Agency started negotiations with SBC to license it for the use of copyright works in its programming. SBC insisted on paying what PRS felt was an unreasonably low sum of royalties[11] and the matter culminated in a referral to the Copyright Tribunal.[12] As a result of these negotiations and the subsequent litigation, PRS did not transfer the international repertory of works that was entrusted to it for administration in Singapore to COMPASS until the decision of the Tribunal in June 1991.

Although the Tribunal decided that it was unable to accept SBC's scheme as a reasonable method for placing a value on the broadcast rights of all works in the PRS repertory, and it accepted the percentage principle as the proper method of arriving at a license fee, the actual tariff itself was not quite what right holders would have liked. The Tribunal increased the number of bands in the PRS license scheme from three to four and lowered the percentage payable as shown in Table 13.1.

Table 13.1 Percentage Payable under PRS License Scheme

Percentage of Music Used in Programming	*Television (%)*	*Radio (%)*
Up to 25% of music	0.1	0.3
Between 26% and 50% of music	0.2	0.6
Between 51% and 75% of music	0.3	0.9
Above 76% of music	0.4	1.2

Because of this decision, broadcast incomes at COMPASS represent a comparatively low percentage of its overall revenues. In 1992, for example, it represented only 13%, although this has since increased to approximately 27% at the end of 2008 as a result of the increase in the percentage of music used by the broadcasting stations.[13] Compare this against the broadcast incomes of the Music Copyright Society of Chinese Taipei (MUST) in Taiwan, which accounted for 39.3% of its gross revenues in 2008, and that of the Composers and Authors Society of Hong Kong Ltd (CASH), which represented 48.8% in 2008.[14]

---

11. It initially proposed a maximum sum, which was less than SGD 12,000 per annum as blanket license fee for usage of all local and Anglo-American musical works in all SBC radio and television productions for a period of two years. SBC's final offer before referring the matter to the Tribunal was SGD 66,000. PRS counter-offered with a sliding percentage scheme from 0.33% to 1.33% for television and 0.67% to 2.67% for radio, depending on extent of music used.
12. This was the first ever reference to the Copyright Tribunal that was formed under the 1987 Act. An interesting incident occurred at that time. Because of a lapse, no registry of the Tribunal was officially published in the gazette so that when the parties wanted to make the reference, they could not do so. SBC filed the reference under s. 163(2) on 24 Jan. 1990 against PRS. COMPASS applied for and was joined as an interested party to the Tribunal proceeding.
13. Of course, there are more radio and television broadcasting stations both in Taiwan and in Hong Kong.
14. The percentages of broadcast incomes have fallen in recent years, in line with similar developments around the world as a result of the impact of online advertising.

With the conclusion of the litigation, the transfer of operations from PRS to COMPASS was completed. It embraced more than just the international repertory. All existing PRS staff, licenses and furniture and fixtures were subrogated, and Singaporean creators who were PRS members were also asked to transfer their membership to COMPASS, made retroactive to 1 January 1990.

COMPASS is a public company limited by guarantee. Its Board comprises twelve directors, of which ten are elected from among members,[15] being six writer-members[16] and four publisher members,[17] one non-member independent director and the Chief Executive Officer.

On admission to COMPASS membership, each member is obligated to assign the performing right in his works to the Society, which includes an assignment of rights 'which now belongs to or shall hereafter be acquired by or be or become vested in the assignor'.[18]

Since its eventful beginnings, COMPASS has embarked on a path of sustained growth. Between 1991 and 2008, its gross revenues grew by just over 920% from SGD 1.4 million to SGD 14.3 million, respectively, whereas expenses fell from 34% to 14.6% over the same period.

One key measure of any successful CMO is the efficiency and accuracy of its distributions of royalties. In its initial years, COMPASS had entered into a technical services agreement with CASH[19] to carry out the distributions of royalties due to foreign right holders.[20] By 1993, COMPASS had completed the computerization of its operations and embarked on its own distributions of royalties due to both local and foreign right holders. Today, COMPASS, in collaboration with the musical works societies in Vietnam, Thailand, India, Indonesia and the Philippines jointly utilizes a common database known as the MIS @ Asia as the documentation and distribution system to perform these processes.

2.1.1.2 Collective Management of Rights in Sound Recordings in Singapore

Singapore copyright law does not accord any public performance, broadcast or cable transmission rights[21] in sound recordings. Thus, the CMO administering the

---

15. The members who are elected as directors must be citizens of Singapore.
16. Which number shall include at least two special elected directors, one representing writers of Malay or Indian music and the other representing serious or classical music; see Art. 39(a)(1)(aa).
17. Of which there shall be at least one local publisher, which is defined in Art. 1(a) (xiv) as a publisher who is a permanent resident or citizen of Singapore and who is ordinarily resident in Singapore, in the case of an individual or in the case of a corporation, wherever incorporated, a publisher in which Singapore citizens or permanent residents who are ordinarily resident in Singapore or Singapore corporations are interested or deemed to be interested by virtue of s. 7 of the Companies Act, in the aggregate, to the whole of the issued share capital of such corporation.
18. Deed of Assignment of COMPASS, Clause 2.
19. The Composers and Authors Society of Hong Kong Limited.
20. It carried out its first distribution to local members in 1992.
21. However, recent amendments (s. 82(1)(d)) have introduced an exclusive right to 'make available' to the public a sound recording by means of, or as a part of, a digital audio transmission.

rights in sound recordings, RIPS[22] relies on the rights in music videos (treated as cinematographic films)[23] to support its licensing activities.[24]

The setup of RIPS is quite distinct from that of COMPASS. It is a private shareholding company, wholly owned by the Recording Industry Association of Singapore (RIAS),[25] an association registered under the Registrar of Societies. All six directors of RIAS are also directors of RIPS, with the chief executive office of RIPS completing the RIPS Board of Directors. Elected directors hold office for two-year terms. Recording companies must first become a member of RIAS before RIPS can administer the public performance right in music videos. Thereafter, the recording company enters into a non-exclusive contractual agreement with RIPS to empower the latter to exercise the rights with respect to the public performance of karaoke and/or music videos and reproduction of the aforementioned on karaoke-on-demand computers. Given its rather restricted rights, the annual collections of RIPS, which have grown threefold in the last decade from about three quarters of a million Singapore dollars in 1995 to over SGD 3.1 million in 2004, are noteworthy.

Before an annual distribution is made, deductions for the operating expenses of RIPS and RIAS, which would include, among other things, the costs of anti-piracy operations, are factored in. Additionally, a stipend is paid to the International Federation for the Phonographic Industry (IFPI)[26] in London and its regional headquarters in Hong Kong. Distribution is decided by the Board of Directors, who take into account factors such as record sales, airplay and cue-sheets provided by the television stations.

2.1.1.3 Collective Management of Reprographic Rights in Singapore

Under section 52,[27] educational institutions in Singapore have a compulsory license to make copies of works under certain conditions. Specifically, section 52(11) provides that an educational institution shall pay to the copyright owner an equitable remuneration for the making of copies as is agreed upon between the owner and the institution or, in default of agreement, as determined by the

---

Section 82(3) specifically provides that the term 'make available' does not include the causing of a sound recording to be heard, otherwise than by means of or as part of a digital audio transmission.

22. RIPS stands for the Recording Industry Performance Singapore Private Limited.
23. Section 83 provides *inter alia* that copyright in relation to a cinematograph film is the exclusive right to ... (b) cause the film ... to be seen in public; (c) communicate the film to the public.
24. Before 1 Jul. 1998, this function was administered by the SPVA, the Singapore Phonogram and Videogram Association, now known as the Recording Industry Association of Singapore (RIAS).
25. There are two main categories of RIAS membership, namely associate members, with no voting rights, and full members, which are in turn divided into three categories based on annual subscription fees that then determines the number of votes that each full paying member has in RIAS.
26. See <www.ifpi.org> (last visited: 10 May 2010).
27. Singapore Copyright Act, Ch. 63, Act 2 of 1987, Revised Edition 1988.

Copyright Tribunal on the application of either party. Despite the fact that this provision was introduced in 1987, the sole CMO in the field of reprographic rights in Singapore, the Copyright Licensing and Administration Society of Singapore Limited (CLASS) was established only in 1999[28] and commenced operations in 2000 with one employee. It was started with funding from the Federation of Reproduction Rights Organizations (IFRRO)[29] and local book publishers. Despite the provisions of the compulsory license requiring the educational institutions in Singapore to pay equitable remuneration, negotiations with the main higher educational institutions took another two years and no royalty payments were made by any Singaporean educational institution to CLASS until 2002. Indeed, it was INSEAD[30] that made the first payment of royalties to CLASS. This delay in royalty payment necessitated another round of fundraising by CLASS.

Like COMPASS, CLASS is a public company limited by guarantee.[31] Membership in CLASS is open to all persons who have appointed it their agent[32] for the reproduction right in some or all of their works.[33] There are two classes of members, namely, author and publisher members. Every member is entitled to one vote.[34]

There are not fewer than three and not more than ten Directors of CLASS,[35] each elected to a two-year term.[36] The Board is composed of three author directors and publisher directors and three independent directors appointed by the elected members of the Board. Quorum is three, with at least one director from each category present.

There was no licensing income earned until the first license agreement with INSEAD, was secured in 2002. Total revenues for that year were SGD 169,000 against expenses of more than SGD 175,000. By 2004, CLASS has secured license agreements with all government-funded and independent schools, junior colleges, universities and polytechnics. Total revenues are expected to surpass SGD 1.4 million in 2009 with expenses at less than 20%. The first ever distribution of royalties by CLASS was carried out in 2005; since then, some SGD 2.8 million have been distributed.

On the legislative front, the Singapore Copyright Act was amended in 2009 to enlarge the powers of the Copyright Tribunal. The Singapore authorities have also very recently proposed a code of conduct to govern the operations of collective

---

28. Incorporated on 25 Sep. 1999. However, discussions to create a Singapore RRO could be traced back to 1995. IFRRO, having entered into an arrangement with the CISAC Asia Pacific Regional Office, developed a two-year business plan, which, *inter alia,* required matching funds to be provided by local book publishers and IFRRO.
29. See <www.ifrro.org> (last visited: 10 May 2010).
30. See <www.insead.edu/singapore_campus/getting/index.cfm> (last visited: 10 May 2010).
31. Each member's guarantee is SGD 1.
32. This arrangement differs from that of COMPASS where members assign their copyright to the organization.
33. Articles of Association of CLASS, Art. 4(b).
34. *Ibid.,* Art. 26.
35. *Ibid.,* Art. 33.
36. *Ibid.,* Art. 35.

management societies in the country. At the time of writing, public feedback is being sought on the draft code.

2.1.2 Malaysia

Like Singapore, Malaysia was a British colony and the 1911 UK Copyright Act applied until independence.[37] Despite gaining independence, the 1956 UK Copyright Act was adopted as the copyright law of Malaysia, and it was only in 1969 that Malaysia enacted its own copyright legislation, which was then replaced by the current Act, passed in 1987.[38]

The Malaysian Copyright Act was further amended on 15 August 2000 to bring the legislation in line with its TRIPS obligations by the introduction of performers' rights. Also, an equitable remuneration right to the performer for the public performance or broadcast or communication to the public was introduced.

2.1.2.1 Collective Management of Musical Works in Malaysia

Efforts to form a CMO for musical works stretched back to 1986 when CISAC commenced discussions with interested parties in Malaysia against the backdrop of the impending 1987 Copyright Act. In the initial stages, the constitution of CASH was used as the basis for forming the Malaysian organization.[39] There were, however, certain substantive modifications, in particular, the role played by PRS in CASH[40] was agreed to be substituted by CISAC with the further modification that the CISAC representatives would not have voting rights, unlike the PRS representatives on the CASH Board.

Despite the early and promising start, the unity soon disintegrated such that by early 1988, the music publishers decided to form their own organization called Malaysian Performing Rights Services Berhad (MPRS) and the writers founded the Malaysian Authors, Composers and Publishers Berhad (MASRAC).[41] Given the unhealthy circumstances, CISAC was requested to step in to attempt to bring the groups together. Meetings were held throughout 1988 in this regard, and it was agreed that a totally new legal vehicle would be incorporated. However, MASRAC representatives quickly developed second thoughts and backed out of the venture. Subsequently, as a result of certain representations that were made to the Malaysian

---

37. Malaysia gained independence on 31 Aug. 1957. The UK Copyright Act 1911 (1911 Ch. 46 1_and_2_Geo_5) applied until then.
38. Malaysian Copyright Act 1987 No. 332, *Gazette of Malaysia*, 21 May 1987.
39. The original name for the organization was CIPTA, a Malay acronym for the Composers, Authors and Publishers Association of Malaysia.
40. See the Section on Hong Kong *infra*.
41. MASRAC was incorporated in October 1987.

government, a meeting was held between CISAC and the Secretary-General[42] of the Ministry of Trade and Industry to explain the situation to the government and obtain their blessings for continuation of the formative work without the MASRAC representatives. Given this, efforts at forming a new CMO under the umbrage of CISAC continued. Late in 1988, CISAC offered to organize an interest free[43] loan of Ringgit, Malaysia Dollar (RYM) 100,000[44] if the local music publishers would match it dollar-for-dollar. With the agreement on financing cobbled together, Music Authors' Copyright Protection (MACP)[45] was officially incorporated as a public company limited by guarantee on 7 September 1989. Both of the first two MACP employees, the General Manager and the Licensing Manager, attended CISAC-funded training at CASH soon after commencement of their employment.

Perhaps as compensation for its rather difficult establishment, MACP's growth in its initial years under its dynamic general manager could be described as truly inspiring. By the end of its first year of operations, its royalty collections[46] had already exceeded its expenditures.[47] It was particularly inspiring as the state television and radio broadcasting stations, RTM did not pay royalties until December 1994. Negotiations with Radio & Television Corporation of Malaysia (RTM) had taken longer than expected.[48] However, when it did, it also honoured its word and paid royalties back to 1989.[49] The retrospective payments made by the Malaysian government-owned broadcast station is to be greatly respected. In the case of many other users, the tactic adopted has been to prolong negotiations and delay payments, and then as a final condition for taking out a license, to insist on forgiveness of royalties for past periods.[50]

As could be imagined, the licensing activities of MACP in their initial months attracted protests from users. Numerous queries and complaints were made to the government regarding its authenticity and authority, particularly because

---

42. The Secretary-General, Dato' Ahmad Sarji, was subsequently appointed as Secretary to the Malaysian Cabinet.
43. An interest rate of 5% per annum for three years was subsequently applied because one of the publishers was prohibited from providing interest-free loans. In lieu of interest, CISAC requested MACP to set aside the equivalent of the interest amount, that is, MYR 15,000 (approximately EUR 3,500 as of November 2005) to establish a music fund within thirty days of the repayment date of the loan.
44. Approximately EUR 22,000 as of November 2005.
45. Even the name of the new society caused some problems; the Registrar of Companies rejected the original name of MAPAC, and the second option of PROMA (Performing Rights Organization of Malaysia) was also rejected. Finally, the name Music Authors' Copyright Protection (MACP) Berhad was approved.
46. Royalty income as of December 1990 was RM 527,000 or approximately EUR 120,000 as of November 2005. MACP issued its first license contract on 15 Apr. 1990, before the Berne Convention came into effect, for a sum of RM 3,251.50 (approx. EUR 750).
47. Expenses were RYM 316,200 or approximately EUR 72,000 as of November 2005.
48. RTM entered into a license agreement with MACP on 8 Dec. 1994.
49. It paid RYM 3.35 million or approximately EUR 760,000 (as of November 2005) as royalties covering the period from 1989 to 1993.
50. As the CMOs are new and struggling to cover costs, they are oftentimes compelled to accept such arrangements.

MASRAC also continued its activities. This thorny issue was finally laid to rest when the Malaysian Trade and Industry Minister attended a copyright symposium in early 1990 organized jointly by MACP and CISAC and took the occasion to officially announce that Malaysia was acceding to the Berne Convention[51] that year. The importance of this seemingly innocuous event cannot be overstated. By attending the MACP/CISAC symposium, and choosing the event to make the official Berne accession announcement, the government issued a very powerful public statement with regard to the legitimacy of the fledgling CMO. Users grudgingly began to accept the valid claims of MACP, and its licensing activities were facilitated greatly.[52]

Up until 2000, MACP only administered the public performance rights in musical works. In 2000, it embarked on a limited administration of the reproduction rights in musical works.[53] To date, mechanical royalties represent a miniscule portion of its total revenues, accounting for only 0.11% of its 2004 gross revenues of MYR 19.2 million.[54]

MACP's growth has been exemplary. As a result of this success, it was able to repay its loans from CISAC and music publishers promptly. Its success is also reflected in its membership growth from the original 16 founder members to over 2,500 members as of 2008. MACP can be justifiably proud of the fact that its expenses, which consume only 9.3% of revenues, are the lowest in the region and in fact among the lowest in the world.

The criterion to qualify as associate writer member or an associate publisher member of MACP is one and five commercially exploited[55] works, respectively. Associate members automatically become full members when they receive a distribution of royalties based on actual monitored usage of works, and full members get downgraded to associate status when they fail to receive such royalties for several years. The key difference between the two classes of membership is the ability of full members to vote and to hold office. Upon election to membership, a member is obligated to assign the public performance rights in his or her works to MACP.

The current MACP Board consists of ten directors, with equal numbers of writer and publisher directors elected by writers and publishers, respectively. Only full members are entitled to stand for election as directors, who hold office for two years.

---

51. Malaysia deposited its instrument of accession with WIPO on 28 Jun. 1990, and the Convention entered into force on 1 Oct. 1990.
52. This could be one of the key reasons why MACP was able to break even financially within its first year of operations.
53. Music publishers continued to administer the mechanical rights directly with recording companies. MACP administered only the reproduction rights of those foreign works entrusted to it by sister societies and which are not sub-published by a Malaysian publisher.
54. Approximately EUR 4.3 million as of November 2005.
55. 'Commercially exploited' is defined to mean a work that has been commercially recorded, published or broadcasted, or performed in public.

To date, MACP is the only society in which a three-party agreement, involving the society, music publishers and sound recording companies, has been concluded and implemented in relation to the licensing of digital usages.

2.1.2.2 The Collective Management of the Rights in Sound Recordings

Sound recordings are listed as one category of works eligible for copyright protection[56] in the Malaysian Copyright Act, together with literary, musical and artistic works. Section 13(1) then expressly provides that sound recordings shall have the identical exclusive rights that are accorded to literary, musical and artistic works.

Public Performance Malaysia Sendiran Berhad[57] (PPM) represents Malaysian and international recording companies in the collective management of the public performance rights in sound recordings in Malaysia. It was established in 1988 and is a private shareholding company whose two issued shares are held by an accounting firm as trustee for the Recording Industry Association of Malaysia (RIM).[58] Like RIPS in Singapore, PPM is a wholly owned subsidiary of RIM, and a sound recording company in Malaysia must first become a RIM member before entering into an agency contract with PPM for the collective management of their rights. The Board of PPM is a mirror of the board of RIM.

PPM distributes its royalties based on usage returns whenever such data are available, such as in broadcasts. In terms of royalties from general public performances such as pubs, bars and restaurants, 50% of the royalties are distributed based on market share of sound recordings, with the balance being distributed based on available usage returns. As a result of the full copyright status of sound recordings in Malaysia, PPM's annual gross revenue[59] is nearly on par with MACP's collections.

2.1.2.3 Performers and Artistes Rights (M) Sendiran Berhad (PRISM)

As mentioned earlier, the amendments made in 2000 to the Malaysian Copyright Act also introduced performers' rights. Additionally, section 16B now provides that 'where a sound recording is . . . publicly performed or used directly for broadcast or other communication to the public, an equitable remuneration for the performance shall be payable to the performer by the user of the sound recording'. Following the introduction of these rights, some Malaysian performers organized the formation of a performers' rights collective called 'Karyawan'.

---

56. Malaysian Copyright Act, *supra* n. 36, s. 7(1)e).
57. Formerly known as Phonographic Performance (Malaysia) Sendiran Berhad.
58. RIM stands for the Recording Industry Association of Malaysia.
59. In 2004, its gross revenue was RYM 17.1 million or approximately EUR 3.9 million as of November 2005.

At about the same time, a separate performers' organization called PRISM, which had the support of the recording companies, was formed. Eventually, PRISM prevailed as the main CMO representing performers' rights in Malaysia. PRISM is a private limited company. The current Board of Directors consists of eight members, of whom three are in their capacity as artists and the other five represent different performers' organizations in Malaysia. PRISM entered into a Memorandum of Understanding on 17 February 2003 with PPM whereby the latter would carry out the licensing of their rights. In 2004, the first distribution of royalties was made by PRISM involving some MYR 200,000 collected on its behalf by PPM.

2.1.2.4 The Collective Management of the Right in Literary Works in Malaysia

There is no operational reprographic rights organization in Malaysia at present. The reason for this is somewhat difficult to fathom because the market potential exists for such an organization to function profitably. Discussions to either restart the organization or create a new one have taken place recently, however.

2.1.3 Thailand

Thailand has the distinction of being the earliest of the ASEAN countries to introduce its own copyright legislation.[60] On 17 July 1931, Thailand acceded to the Berne Convention, among one of the first independent Asian countries to do so at that time.[61] The latest Thai Copyright Act[62] became effective in 1995. Unlike many of the other Asian countries, though, the Thai copyright law has a very wide definition of the term 'communication to the public', subsuming the public performance, broadcast and cable transmission rights into this term.[63] Moreover, the Thai law also accords full copyright protection to sound recordings,[64] much like Malaysia. Another unique feature of the Thai copyright protection system is the

---

60. In 1894, the National Library issued a pronouncement prohibiting any person from publishing any part of the Vajirayarnvises books without prior permission. In 1902 and 1914, the Copyright Acts B.E. 2445 and 2457 were enacted; both protected only the copyright in literary works. In line with Thailand's Berne accession, a new copyright law, the Act for the Protection of Literary and Artistic Works B.E. 2474, encompassing international concepts of copyright protection was enacted on 16 Jun. 1931. Protection for audiovisual works, sound recordings and video broadcast works was given only under Copyright Act B.E. 2521 (1978).
61. However, it is not signatory to the Rome Convention for the Protection of Performers, Producers of Phonograms and Broadcasting Organizations, Convention for the Protection of Producers of Phonograms Against Unauthorized Duplication of Their Phonograms, the WCT or the WPPT.
62. Copyright Act B.E.2537, *Government Gazette,* 21 Dec. 1994, Vol. 111, Part. 59a.
63. Section 4 defines 'Communication to the public' to mean making a work available to the public by means of performing, lecturing, preaching, playing music, causing the perception by sound or image, constructing, distributing or by any other means.
64. Section 6 states that 'copyright works ... means works of authorship in the categories of literary, dramatic, artistic, musical ... sound recording ...'. Section 15 then goes on to accord a full bundle of exclusive rights to copyright works.

establishment of the Central Intellectual Property and International Trade (IPIT) Court in December 1997. The IPIT Court has jurisdiction over civil and criminal cases involving IP matters and is staffed by both career and associate judges.

2.1.3.1 Collective Management of Rights in Musical Works in Thailand

As early as 1978, several studies[65] were made in relation to the copyright situation, and the feasibility of establishing an authors' society in Thailand. In 1982, the CISAC Administrative Council gave its approval for a project to be formulated and implemented under the supervision of the CISAC Asian Committee. The studies indicated that the environment was somewhat premature for the launch of a CMO; hence, a decision was taken by CISAC with a group of Thai creators to first establish a Copyright Information Office[66] whose main role would be to conduct public education programmes so that the concepts of copyright protection and collective management were properly disseminated to pave the way for the establishment and operation of a collective. Eventually, the first CMO in the field of musical works, Music Copyright (Thailand) Limited (MCT)[67] was established on 14 June 1994 with funding[68] provided entirely by CISAC.

The Thai music market is predominantly local and dominated by two particularly large domestic recording companies.[69] Against this backdrop,[70] one could have thought that these two companies would be invited to join MCT as members early on. However, two factors probably played crucial roles in keeping them out of MCT. The first was MCT's insistence that the recording companies agree to distribute 50% of public performance royalties to composers and authors. Historically, Thai creators routinely assigned their entire copyright rights to sound recording producers or were otherwise employed[71] by these companies, with the result that the entire set of copyrights in this body of musical works vested in the

---

65. Some of these initial studies were carried out by MCOS on behalf of CISAC, and one was carried out by Professor Alan Latman, New York University Law Center on behalf of UNESCO. Professor Latman's study was on the formation of a national copyright information office, which was taken up by CISAC.
66. The TCIO started operations around December 1986 under the auspices of the Thai Composers Association and was funded by CISAC.
67. His Majesty, the King of Thailand was for a period of time, the royal patron of MCT. This was a rather special privilege as he was seldom known to lend his name to private shareholding companies.
68. Aside from various grants, interest-free loans totaling almost 7 million Bahts (approximately EUR 146,000 as of November 2005) were provided by CISAC to MCT.
69. Grammy Records and RS Records, both of which are estimated to have market share totaling 60% to 70% of Thai music.
70. Coupled with the history of lump sum buy-outs of the rights in musical works.
71. Section 9 states that 'copyright in a work creator by author in the course of employment shall vest in the authors unless otherwise agreed in writing, provided that the employer shall be entitled to communicate such work to the public in accordance with the purpose of the employment'.

sound recording companies. The other hurdle was the requirement by MCT that copyright be assigned to it.

Without the participation of these two large Thai music companies,[72] and with limited representation of slightly more than hundred composers, MCT's early development was hampered and the rapid growth of the CMOs that was experienced in Malaysia, Singapore and Indonesia could not be replicated here.

2.1.3.2 The Collective Management of Rights in Musical Works in Thailand

One unique feature distinguishes MCT from other music CMOs established in Asia. Based on their lawyers' advice at the time of incorporation to the effect that Thai corporate law did not allow an association to carry out the intended functions of a CMO, MCT was incorporated as a private company. Owing to this legal structure, a provision was then built into its Statutes to ensure that only the following persons may hold MCT shares namely: (1) any individual author or composer of musical works with at least one published work, (2) any natural or juristic person owning the copyrights in ten or more published musical works, (3) any successors-in-title to copyrights and (4) any other person approved by the Board of Directors for the specific purpose of holding MCT's shares that have not been issued. Strong restrictions on the transfer of shares and the issuance of dividends also exist.

The MCT Board of Directors consists of up to eleven Directors comprising three authors, three composers and three music publishers and two other directors nominated by the Thai Composers Association. The corporate articles also provide for the appointment of a general manager who must not be a member of the Board or a shareholder.

MCT, together with the Filipino Society of Composers, Authors, and Publishers (FILSCAP), probably had the most difficulty in breaking even financially. It took four years after its formation before gross annual incomes exceeded expenses. However, if cumulative losses were taken into consideration, MCT only managed to generate more income than accumulated expenses by the end of 2000. In fact, it took MCT a full fourteen months before it was finally able to issue its first three licenses to two karaokes and one restaurant for a total of B 108,000. At the end of 1995, sixteen months after its inception, its gross revenue was just slightly more than Baht (THB) 600,000.[73]

The pioneering work carried out by MCT in establishing the collective management of rights in Thailand led to a new challenge. A number of Thai recording companies decided to enter the fray by establishing profit-making companies, initially to collect royalties from karaoke establishments utilizing

---

72. One of the companies did join MCT for a couple of years but withdrew its membership and subsequently started a profit-making company to carry out the licensing of its public performance rights.
73. This was approximately equivalent to EUR 12,500 as of November 2005.

their music.[74] Because of its profit-making nature, the tariffs applied by them were comparatively high. This led to at least one protest organized by karaoke operators. The Thai government did react and issued regulations[75] specifying the conditions[76] under which CMOs could collect public performance royalties for the exercise of such rights.

As a consequence of the situation, MCT and Phonorights, the sound recording collecting society established by IFPI, decided to come together in a joint venture[77] in 2003 to offer licenses covering both the public performance rights in musical works and sound recordings to users in Thailand for primarily international repertory, plus the Thai works that are represented through MCT.

A Board of Directors oversees the functions of the joint venture composed of two directors appointed by each organization. There is no Chairman of the Board, and all decisions pertaining to the joint venture are made by way of consensus. Both MCT and Phonorights agreed to make available its own licensing staff to undertake the licensing work of the joint venture. All licenses of each organization then in existence were transferred to the joint venture through the expiry of time, and the joint venture Board determines the new licensing rates and licenses. The joint venture has worked well for both organizations as incomes have increased despite the difficulties caused by the dozen or so private companies attempting to license the exercise of the public performance rights in Thailand. Before the formation of the Joint Venture, MCT's gross revenue in 2002 was 6.5 million Bahts.[78] In 2008, its collections have grown five-fold to 32 million Bahts.[79]

2.1.3.3 The Collective Management of Rights in Sound Recordings

Phonorights (Thailand) Limited started its activities in 1997. It is private shareholding company whose shares are held largely by the Thai Entertainment Content Association (TECA)[80] and the representatives of the local recording companies that are its members. The Board of Directors comprises six directors. Although strongly encouraged, a recording company need not become a member of TECA to entrust the public performance rights in sound recordings to it for collective

---

74. These companies now license or attempt to license all categories of establishments publicly performing music.
75. The Minister of Commerce, in his capacity as Chairman of the Central Price Fixing Commission issued a notification under the Price of Goods and Services Act B.E. 2542 in 2003.
76. Such as having a paid up capital of one million Bahts, maintaining a register of members, providing the Department of Intellectual Property with a list of the licensing personnel, etc.
77. The joint venture is called JV 1-Stop and was for an initial period of one year. Because of the success of the joint venture, its operations have been extended beyond this trial period.
78. Approximately EUR 13,500 as of November 2005.
79. Similarly, the gross revenue of Phonorights increased from THB 15.5 million in 2002 to THB 19 million in 2004 (or from approximately EUR 325,000 to EUR 400,000 as of November 2005).
80. The shares are held by its general manager. TECA is largely owned by the subsidiaries of the international recording companies.

management. Presently, all royalties collected by Phonorights, after deduction of its expenses, are given to TECA for anti-piracy operations and are not distributed.

Because of the negative side effects of having multiple CMOs collecting royalties for the public performance rights, the Thai government has been working on numerous drafts of laws to govern the collective management of rights in Thailand. Its representatives have visited countries as diverse as Hungary, the United Kingdom and Japan to better understand the situation and work on the draft is ongoing at the time of writing; more developments are expected.

2.1.4 The Philippines

Copyright law in the Philippines can be traced back to 1879 when Spanish law was enforced in all its colonies. Then, US copyright law applied after the country was handed by Spain to the United States in 1898. In 1924, the first Filipino law on copyright was enacted. This was in turn repealed by Presidential Decree 49 of 1972 during the martial law years until replaced by the Intellectual Property Code of the Philippines (Republic Act No. 8293) of 6 June 1997.[81] The Philippines is signatory to the Berne Convention and became a signatory to the WCT and the WPPT in October 2002. Despite the long history of copyright legislation, the first CMO was created only forty years ago.

2.1.4.1 Collective Management of Rights in Musical Works in the Philippines

The sole CMO for the rights in musical works is the Filipino Society of Composers, Authors and Publishers, Incorporated (FILSCAP). FILSCAP, incorporated as a non-stock and non-profit corporation on 13 May 1965, is one of the earliest CMOs in the field of musical works in Asia. However, despite its early start, political developments[82] intervened to put a long hiatus to its development. CISAC attempted to resuscitate the collective in the mid-1980s, after people's power toppled Marcos. Unfortunately, in 1989, economic conditions under the new democratic government were not particularly ideal, with daily blackouts severely disrupting work of all kinds. In 1989, CISAC[83] terminated all financial assistance to FILSCAP as certain conditions were not met. In 1992, at the invitation of the Chairman of FILSCAP, CISAC returned and implemented a comprehensive rehabilitation plan.

When CISAC started on the rehabilitation effort, FILSCAP had a total of six public performance licensees. Annual income that year was about Philippines Peso

---

81. This new law came into effect on 1 Jan. 1998.
82. Martial law was declared in 1972 by President Ferdinand Marcos and, among other companies, all broadcasting companies were nationalized. ASCAP, assisting FILSCAP, had just managed to negotiate an agreement for some of the broadcasters to pay royalties.
83. See <www.cisac.org> (last visited: 11 May 2010).

(PDP) 600,000[84] while expenses were PDP 50,000 higher. CISAC funded the salary[85] of the new general manager who was recruited with its assistance. By February 1995, the total number of licenses had grown to 98 and FILSCAP had turned the corner. In fact, a modest sum of about PDP 1 million from the 1994 collections[86] was available for distribution.

As could be imagined, given the many years during which FILSCAP existed but was unable to license the users in the Philippines, its revival and renewed attempts at licensing were simply ignored.[87] Given this backdrop, it was apparent that FILSCAP had to begin litigation against selected users in order to put teeth to its revival. The first legal case was brought against Nikko Hotel in 1993.[88] As a direct consequence of this legal action and its settlement in 1994, FILSCAP was able to enter into an agreement with the Hotel and Restaurant Association of the Philippines (HRAP), which required the HRAP to exhort to all of its members throughout the Philippines to secure public performance licenses from FILSCAP. The importance and significance of this result cannot be underestimated. First, it endowed FILSCAP with desperately needed legitimacy with a key section of the music using market. Second, it smoothed the path of negotiations between the society and this category of users. Third, it soon provided sufficient income for FILSCAP to cover its costs and to concentrate on other important market segments, such as broadcasting.

It would not be complete to recount the history of FILSCAP's development to date without mention of its efforts to license the broadcasters in the country. Negotiations with the broadcasters' organization *Kapisanan Ng Mga Brodkaster Ng Pilipinas* (KBP) started soon after the CISAC rehabilitation plan of FILSCAP was put in place,. The KBP suggested that negotiations be conducted first for the payment of royalties by FM radio stations. Thus, a Memorandum of Understanding for the payment of royalties by FM stations was signed in December 1995. This was followed by a Memorandum of Understanding for the payment of royalties by AM stations.[89] Negotiations with the KBP for the payment of royalties by their television station members then started in earnest. However, it eventually became apparent that the KBP was not in a position to move the negotiations forward. FILSCAP broke off negotiations with the association in 2001 and entered into

---

84. Approximately EUR 10,000 as of November 2005.
85. Training was also arranged and funded by CISAC at COMPASS and CASH, followed by visits to ASCAP and BMI, and a further sum of money was prepared to fund intended litigation against the broadcasters.
86. Gross collections in 1994 exceeded PDP 3 million or approximately EUR 47,000 as of November 2005.
87. Indeed, there was much debate within CISAC on whether to fund the rehabilitation of FILSCAP because there was a strong view that a new society should be started as a result of FILSCAP's long but unsuccessful history.
88. Nikko Hotel was a previous licensee that had stopped payment of royalties given the ineffectuality of FILSCAP before the rehabilitation effort.
89. It should be highlighted that despite the MOUs, many FM and AM radio stations have still not obtained any license from FILSCAP to date. This shows the weakness of industry-based negotiations and agreements in which there is no punitive measure provided for failure to follow.

discussions with the two main television stations, ABS-CBN and GMA7, directly. FILSCAP rejected an offer of PDP 1.3 million[90] as annual license fees for the use of its worldwide repertory of music and decided to commence litigation, asking for damages as well as preliminary and temporary injunctions in relation to four works used in two prime-time drama series. Against the backdrop of litigation, negotiations were restarted, and a contract with ABS-CBN was signed in November 2004; royalties were paid retroactive to 1996, albeit at a much reduced rate. The agreement extended to 2009 and marked the first time in history that ABS-CBN has paid royalties for the broadcast of musical works in their programming.[91] However, the honour of being the first Filipino television station to pay such royalties in the Philippines goes to its rival station, GMA7,[92] which entered into a license agreement with FILSCAP on 1 July 2004. It also paid royalties retrospective to 1996.[93] The licensing of the Filipino television stations probably qualifies as one of the longest negotiating sagas in Asia.

With the successful licensing of the broadcasters, albeit at comparatively low rates, FILSCAP's income for 2008 amounted to PDP 60 million,[94] a substantial increase from the PDP 600,000 in 1992.

FILSCAP has three categories of members – regular, associate and successors. Regular members are those with published works and are accorded full voting rights.[95] Those without published works may join as associate members with no voting rights. In an interesting departure from other societies, successor members have a right to vote,[96] but cannot become directors. Upon election to membership, a member has to execute an assignment of the public performance right to FILSCAP.

FILSCAP is the only CMO within the ASEAN region to levy an entrance[97] and annual membership fee.[98] This provision was introduced in 1993 when the society was in dire need of money, and the introduction of such fees was seen as one of the ways to raise some operational funds. The FILSCAP Board of Directors is composed of fifteen members; nine writers (authors or composers) and at least

---

90. Equivalent to approximately EUR 20,500. FILSCAP had in response dropped its earlier tariff of 0.3% of gross advertising revenues less commissions, to PDP 4 million per annum.
91. The basic license fee is PDP 3 million (approximately EUR 48,000 as of November 2005) per annum.
92. An administrative action before the Intellectual Property Office was filed by FILSCAP against GMA7 for payment of royalties. FILSCAP chose this path with GMA7 in order to determine the speediest method of resolving licensing deadlocks.
93. At more than 68% against the agreed annual lump sum fees to be paid from 2003 to 2005.
94. This figure included back royalties as well as royalties for 2006. It is the approximate equivalent of EUR 900,000 as of November 2005.
95. Each member has one vote, either in person or by proxy.
96. This is similar to ASCAP provisions. See the chapter on the United States for more information on ASCAP.
97. Entrance fee is PDP 100 for individuals, PDP 500 for sole proprietorships and PDP 1,000 for corporations.
98. Annual membership fee is PDP 50 for individuals, PDP 200 for sole proprietorships and PDP 500 for corporations or approximately EUR 1, 3 and 8 (as of November 2005).

three publishers who are elected by regular and successor members every other year.

The use of Anglo-American musical works is prevalent in the Philippines, although this has lessened to some degree in recent years. Thus, if distributions to sub-publishers of international works are excluded, a fairly substantial share of FILSCAP royalties is distributed to foreign right holders. Section 5 of FILSCAP's Corporate Articles specifically provide, *inter alia*, that royalties collected will be apportioned in accordance with international distribution practices, provided that in no case shall any publisher be entitled to more than 50% of such royalties.

2.1.4.2   Collective Management of Other Rights in the Philippines

Filipino copyright law maintains a distinction between copyright works[99] and objects of related rights.[100] In relation to the communication to the public right for sound recordings, a single remuneration right[101] to both producers of sound recordings and performers based on Article 12 of the Rome Convention is provided. The sound recording companies in the Philippines, while operating together as the Philippine Association of the Record Industry, Inc. (PARI), have not yet started to license the public performance rights in their products, concentrating their efforts in the fight against piracy.

Although Filipino performers created their own CMO called Performers' Rights Society of the Philippines (PRSP) in 2002, it is not operational and without any licensing activity as yet. PRSP is a non-stock, non-profit corporation registered under the Securities Exchange Commission of the Philippines; it has no fulltime employees. The Executive Director of OPM[102] helps out when needed, and OPM is currently also hosting the PRSP office. It has 100 members, with the majority coming from the music industry. To date, the society has been able to put up a database of performing works with funds granted by the National Commission for Culture and the Arts.[103] Although the well-known performers have been able to provide such data, many supporting musicians and actors have been unable to do so.

With regard to literary works, a reprographic rights organization called the Philippine Reprographic Rights Organization Incorporation (PRRO) was registered in 2001. According to its Articles of Incorporation, its primary purpose

---

99. The categories of protected copyright works are set out in s. 172.
100. The rights accorded to sound recordings are set out in Ch. XIII.
101. Section 209 states that 'If a sound recording published for commercial purposes ... is used directly for broadcasting or for other communication to the public, or is publicly performed with the intention of making and enhancing profit, a single equitable remuneration for the performer or performers, and the producer of the sound recording shall be paid by the user to both the performers and the producer, who, in the absence of any agreement shall share equally.'
102. OPM stands for Organisasyon Ng Pilipinong Mang-aawit or the Organization of Filipino Musicians.
103. Which comes directly under the office of the President of the Philippines.

is to 'control the widespread unauthorized copying of works' and for the purpose of centrally managing the exchange of permission to reproduce works and payment of royalties'. The Articles of the PRRO provide for three categories of members: founding members, regular members and associate members. The organization is to be governed by a Board comprising thirteen members who shall hold office for two years.[104] Despite being formed in 2001, and still in existence legally, the PRRO has not begun operations. In the meantime, a new reprographic rights organization (RRO) has been created. The Filipinas Copyright Licensing Society, Inc. (FILCOLS) was organized on 8 January 2008 and has started on its licensing attempts. It has a board comprising five author and four publisher representatives.[105]

One of the latest CMOs to be established in this region is the Filipino Visual Arts and Design Rights Organization (FILVADRO), established in January 2010. The Philippines is one of only three Asian countries with a resale royalty right. Hence, the first agenda item for FILVADRO is to push for the enactment of enabling regulations so that the resale right may be implemented. FILVADRO will be looking to FILSCAP for funding and administrative support in its initial years because it will be facing a daunting challenge to enforce its rights.

2.1.5 Indonesia

The colonial Dutch government introduced the first copyright legislation into Indonesia in 1912. Although Indonesia became an independent republic in 1945, the 1912 legislation continued in force until it was replaced in 1982. Indonesia's current copyright law[106] was enacted on 29 July 2002 and came into force exactly one year later. The Indonesian copyright law is unique in Asia in that it simply encapsulates all the exclusive rights of an author into 'the exclusive rights to publish or reproduce'.[107] Indonesia is of course the first Asian country to accede to the WCT[108] when it also acceded to the Berne Union.[109] On 15 November 2004, it also ratified the WPPT.[110]

---

104. There are special provisions for the first four years after incorporation. See Art. V, s. 1.
105. There are two local publishers, one foreign publisher representative and one representative from the Book Development Association of the Philippines.
106. Law No. 19 of July 29, 2002 on Copyright, *State Gazette of the Republic of Indonesia*, 2002, No. 85.
107. Article 2(1). The term 'publication' is defined in Art. 1 to mean 'the reading, broadcasting, exhibition, sale, distribution of dissemination of a work, by utilizing whatever means including the Internet, or by any manner so that such work is capable of being read, heard or seen by any other person'. Thus, the public performance or communication to the public right is included in this term.
108. It ratified the treaty on 5 Jun. 1997, on the same day that it ratified the Berne Convention. The treaty came into force in Indonesia on 6 Mar. 2002, when the WCT itself came into force with the requisite number of accessions.
109. The Berne Convention became applicable on 5 Sep. 1997.
110. Which came into force on 15 Feb. 2005.

2.1.5.1   The Collective Management of Rights in Musical Works in Indonesia

The sole collective in Indonesia, the Yayasan Karya Cipta Indonesia (KCI) was established as a private foundation by twelve persons and one organizational founder, Persatuan Artis Pencipta Penata Music Rekaman Indonesia (PAPPRI), in 1990.[111] At that time, the foundation structure was considered the best choice for the CMO because foundations were generally better regarded, compared to any other kind of legal vehicle. In this regard, KCI differs from all other CMOs in Asia[112] because composers, authors and music publishers are strictly speaking not members.

The Dutch music collective BUMA/STEMRA[113] and CISAC were intimately involved in KCI's creation. Both organizations extended substantial financial assistance toward its start up. In fact, KCI was the first Asian recipient of financial assistance from the then newly created CISAC Solidarity Fund.[114] In 1990, a sum of USD 20,000 was provided by CISAC to KCI, and in 1991, another sum of USD 90,000[115] was extended. In addition, BUMA/STEMRA extended a further interest-free loan of USD 20,000,[116] aside from funding the training of KCI staff and Indonesian government officials. CISAC member societies also contributed further by agreeing to forgo the distribution of a diminishing share[117] of royalties due to their respective members to defray the high costs[118] associated with its establishment.

Like almost all of the new CMOs created around this time, KCI commenced only with the administration of public performance rights. In 1992, it entered into an agreement with STEMRA to commence the administration of the reproduction rights in musical works in relation to foreign works reproduced in Indonesia.[119]

---

111. Under a new law governing foundations, KCI was re-registered in 2004 with eight individual founders; under this new law, PAPPRI could not continue as a founder-member.
112. A recent similar organization would be the Vietnam Center for Protection of Music Copyright (VCPMC) in Vietnam.
113. See <www.bumastemra.nl.> (last visited: 11 May 2010).
114. CISAC members contribute a small part of their collections toward the Solidarity Fund, which is used to finance the creation of new societies, where they do not exist, or to fund the growth and development of developing authors' societies around the world.
115. This sum was provided by way of a three-year interest-free loan.
116. It subsequently donated USD 10,000 back to KCI to fund the establishment of a mechanical rights division.
117. Societies agreed that KCI could retain 100%, 60%, 30% of royalties due to the use of international repertory from its first, second and third years of collections. From the fourth year on, all royalties due to foreign societies were to be distributed based on usage returns. Indonesia did not accede to the Berne Convention until 1997, so only American works were protected in Indonesia in KCI's early years. The amount of royalties involved was not insignificant. In 1991, the retained royalties totaled USD 66,605 (approximately EUR 57,000 as of November 2005).
118. It was expressly agreed that these retained royalties were not to be distributed to local members.
119. STEMRA entered into agreements with two CD replication plants in Batam and Jakarta for the reproduction of foreign works by them and KCI was involved in administered parts of the agreements with technical support by STEMRA.

KCI secured its first licensing agreement with the government broadcaster, TVRI on 25 May 1991. Together with Garuda Airlines, these royalties proved instrumental in its early financial success.[120] Both licensees were government-owned establishments, and KCI's experience in this regard best sums up the pivotal role that governments can play in the early success of CMOs – by respecting the copyright laws enacted by them and paying royalties for the use of works. Sadly, this is not always the case in the region.

In 1991, the Japanese music collective JASRAC[121] sent, at its own costs, a documentation and distribution expert to assist KCI in setting up such a department. Such assistance reduces the startup expenses of new CMOs and spreads out the costs among a number of more developed collectives. It also avoids mistakes experienced by other CMOs and shortens the learning curve. On 30 March 1992, KCI made its first distribution of royalties to its members. A total of Rupiah (IDR) 136 million[122] were distributed to 257 Indonesian composers. From 1994, KCI started to distribute royalties to foreign right holders as well, averaging about 15% of its distributable royalties annually.

In recent years, KCI has been buffeted by management issues that have dented its early successes. It is undergoing a slow re-structuring process that would hopefully put it on the path toward continued growth.

2.1.6 Brunei

Right holders in Brunei are accorded protection under the Constitution of Brunei Darussalam Emergency (Copyright) Order 1999, which came into force on 1 May 2000. This law is based essentially on the UK's 1988 Copyright Act. Before the enactment of this law, the 1911 UK Copyright Act had force in the country. To date, Brunei has not yet acceded to the Berne Convention. However, its World Trade Organization (WTO) membership obliges it to grant protection compatible with the TRIPS Agreement.

At the time of writing, local composers are working with CISAC to establish a CMO named Bruneian Authors and Composers Association (BeAT) Berhad with the assistance of the Attorney-General's Chambers.[123] Given its small population size, BeAT will undertake membership and licensing activities, and the back room operations of documentation and distribution will be contracted out to another society. It is also likely that this office would eventually administer all of the different categories of rights. It is anticipated that BeAT will become operational in 2010.

---

120. Royalties from these two users represented 88.5% of KCI's total revenues in 1991.
121. See Chapter 12 on Japan.
122. Approximately EUR 11,500 as of November 2005.
123. Due to historical links, PRS (UK) issues a couple of licenses to certain users in Brunei.

2.1.7 Vietnam

Copyright is a relatively new concept in Vietnam, and many industry practices are still based on traditional arrangements, usually on agreements between users and right holders, rather than on copyright law. The copyright legislation of present-day Vietnam was first enacted in 1986.[124] In 1994, the Standing Committee to the National Assembly adopted the ordinance on copyright protection. In 1995, the National Assembly approved the civil code of Vietnam with an entire chapter[125] on copyright.[126] It acceded to the Berne Convention on 26 October 2004. At the same time, it has bilateral copyright agreements with the United States of America, the European Union and Switzerland.

2.1.7.1 Collective Management of Rights in Musical Works in Vietnam

The history of collective management in Vietnam started with the Vietnam Musicians' Association (VMA), a non-governmental organization created in 1957 to serve as a liaison centre for all musicians throughout Vietnam. Two committees govern the VMA, namely the Central Committee, consisting of nine members, and the Secretariat, consisting of five members comprising one secretary-general, three vice secretary-generals and one ordinary committee member elected from the Central Committee.[127] The Secretariat performs the day-to-day functions of the VMA and meets twice per year with the Central Committee. The members of the Central Committee[128] are elected by its membership[129] once every five years. The VMA receives annual financial assistance from the government; these monies are spent largely on promoting new works and creativity. The VMA established the Vietnam Centre for Protection of Music Copyright (VCPMC)[130] to perform the functions of a CMO on 19 April 2002.[131]

The VCPMC is a non-profit and non-governmental organization that operates[132] under the management of the VMA. It administers both the public

---

124. Decree Number 142/HDBT. A new copyright law was passed by the Vietnamese Parliament on 19 Nov. 2005 as part of a new IP Code.
125. Chapter 1, Part 6.
126. This came into force on 1 Jul. 1996. There also exist a number of other decrees and circulars largely on issues of implementation and enforcement. A new draft copyright law is being circulated for discussions in line with its desire to join the WTO.
127. Apart from the Secretary General and the permanent Vice Secretary General, the members of the Secretariat do not work fulltime. It has approximately 20 employees.
128. And hence also the Secretariat.
129. It currently has about 900 members of which approximately 50% are composers and the balance consists of music teachers, critics and performers.
130. The VCPMC is a legal entity that is separate from the VMA.
131. It was officially launched on 22 May 2002.
132. In accordance with Art. 3 of the Charter of VCPMC, its 'operational objectives' *inter alia* include (1) the exploitation and protection of musical copyright, and (2) the support of state management agencies in the development and implementation of copyright policies. Art. 5 of

performance and reproduction rights in musical works. It is not a membership-based CMO; instead, management of the rights is based on copyright authorization contracts.[133] The VCPMC does not obtain a transfer or assignment of rights from right holders. Instead, the fiduciary contract authorizes the VCPMC to collectively administer these rights for an initial period of five years, which will automatically renew unless terminated. According to the contract, the VCPMC undertakes to make bi-annual distributions.[134] It is not a membership organization, so there are no provisions for members to vote. Hence, the main control mechanism over VCPMC comes from electing the VMA representatives.

The organizational structure of the VCPMC consists of a Management Council (MC), a Board of Directors, a Board of Inspectors and a Board of Consultants, which advises the Management Council and the Board of Directors. The fifteen members of the MC, appointed by the Secretariat of the VMA, meet every six months to review VCPMC's operations and the activities of the Board of Directors. The Board of Directors is nominated by the MC and appointed by the Secretariat of the VMA. The Directors are responsible for the day-to-day management of VCPMC, including the recruitment, appointment, suspension and/or dismissal of staff. The Board of Inspectors, appointed by the MC, inspects the implementation of the VCPMC's Charter, performs general inspection of assets and finance of VCPMC and inspects the activity of the Board of Directors.

The growth of VCPMC since its inception has been spectacular. From the Vietnamese Dongs (VND) 165 million collected in its first year of operations, it grossed some VND 23.2 billion in 2009. VCPMC distributes royalties to its local members four times per year, and international royalties are distributed once a year.

An organization representing authors of literary works, the Vietnam Literary Copyright Center (VLCC), has existed since August 2004 and is attempting to license for the usage of such works.

2.1.8 Cambodia

The ASEAN jigsaw became complete when Cambodia became its tenth Member States in 1999. Cambodia enacted a new copyright law, which came into force on 5 March 2003. It is not yet a signatory to the Berne Convention.

Article 56 of the copyright legislation provides that an author or a related right holder can establish CMOs to protect and manage their economic rights.

VCPMC's Charter sets out its duties as to cooperate with relevant agencies to disseminate knowledge on copyright laws; to inform VCPMC's activities to copyright holders, to exercise rights authorized by right holders in the field of music including to issue licenses and collect royalties; to annually distribute proceeds gained from works exploitation; etc., and to cooperate with foreign copyright protection organizations to make full use of their support and to protect mutual legitimate rights.

133. Chapter III of Charter of VCPMC. Over 400 composers have entered into fiduciary contracts with the VCPMC, which represents approximately 50% of currently performed works.
134. Note that this differs from the Charter of VCPMC, which provides for an annual distribution.

The establishment of such CMOs requires the recognition of the Ministry of Culture and Fine Arts.[135] Article 49 states:

> If a phonogram has been produced for commercial purposes, or a reproduction of such phonogram is used directly for broadcasting or other communication to the public, or is publicly performed, *a single equitable remuneration, for the performers and the producer of the phonogram, shall be paid by the user to the organization governing this collective right.*

The law also makes the reproduction and communication to the public of copyright works without authority an offence.[136]

Cambodia is the second least developed country (LDC) to join the WTO[137] through the full process of negotiation since the WTO was established in 1995. It underwent a difficult and demanding negotiating process and is the eighth ASEAN member of the WTO, leaving Vietnam and Laos still in the process of accession.

There is presently no CMO in Cambodia because the market is considered as not yet commercially viable.

2.1.9 Myanmar

The existing copyright legislation in Myanmar is still the 1911 United Kingdom Copyright Act, which came into force in 1914, a remnant of colonization. Although Myanmar is a member of the WTO, it is classified as an LDC and work is ongoing to introduce new copyright legislation. There is at present no CMO in Myanmar.

2.2 THE EAST ASIAN COUNTRIES

2.2.1 China

The year 1990 witnessed a momentous copyright event when China enacted new copyright legislation, the first in its recent history.[138] Another historic occurrence took place when it acceded to the Berne Convention in 1992.

Key amendments were made in 2001. Under Article 43 of the previous Chinese copyright law, a radio or television station that broadcasts a published

---

135. The establishment of a CMO for broadcasting requires the recognition of the Ministry of Information.
136. Article 64. Such infringements are punishable by one to three months' imprisonment and/or a fine of 1–5 million Cambodian Riels (or from approximately EUR 200–1,000 as of November 2005). Where several offences are committed, the punishment is multiplied by the number of offences.
137. It became the 148th WTO member on 13 Oct. 2004.
138. Copyright Law (Adopted at the 15th Session of the Standing Committee of the Seventh National People's Congress on 7 Sep. 1990, and Amended According to the Decision on the Revision of the Copyright Law of the People's Republic of China, Adopted at the 24th Session of the Standing Committee of the Ninth National People's Congress on 27 Oct. 2001).

sound recording for non-commercial purposes did not need to obtain permission from or pay remuneration to the right holders. Almost all broadcasters in China saw themselves as public broadcasters and invoke the indemnity under Article 43, and thus they neither obtained permission for their use of copyright works nor paid any royalties. Under the amendments, broadcasters are given a statutory license to utilize published works[139] and sound recordings[140] in their broadcasts but are required to pay remuneration for such uses. The concluding sentence of Article 43 provides that 'specific measures in this regard shall be formulated by the State Council'. It took the State Council, which is the equivalent of the Chinese Cabinet, a full eight years before it finally published the 'State Council Order 566' on the 'Measures for the Payment of Royalties by Radio and Television Stations for the Broadcast of Recorded Works' with effect from 1 January 2010.[141]

In summary, the Order empowers the broadcasters to negotiate an annual remuneration with the relevant CMO.[142] However, if the parties are unable to arrive at a mutually agreeable arrangement, they may base their payment on one of the two following methods. The parties may opt for royalties to be paid on a percentage of the broadcaster's annual total advertising income or for the royalties payable to be calculated based on a per-minute rate. If the parties are still unable to arrive at an agreement based on one of the foregoing basis of payment, the Order provides that the percentage basis shall prevail.[143]

By all accounts, the Order appears to be a very well-thought-out measure, befitting the length of time that it took to come into being. Additional measures taking into account the lower level of economic growth in the Central and Western Chinese regions were crafted; 50% and 90% reductions[144] of the prescribed rate are provided, respectively.[145]

Chinese broadcasters have yet to pay any royalties for the use of copyright works and/or sound recordings in their broadcasts despite the introduction of the Order. At the time of writing, the parties are still in negotiation.

There are three provisions on the collective management contained in the Chinese Copyright Law. Article 8 provides that copyright and related right holders may authorize a CMO to exercise their rights. It further provides that upon authorization, a CMO may, *inter alia*, participate as a party in legal proceedings in its own name for the copyright or related right holder. This provision was required because users have sought to challenge the *locus standi* of a CMO to bring legal actions on behalf of right holders. The article also expressly requires CMOs to be non-profit entities. Aside from those provisions, the law provides that regulations

---

139. *Ibid.*, Art. 42.
140. *Ibid.*, Art. 43.
141. Signed by the Chinese Prime Minister Wen Jia Bao on 10 Nov. 2009.
142. Article 4, Order of State Council, People's Republic of China, Number 566.
143. *Ibid.*, Art. 8.
144. There are additional detailed provisions.
145. *Ibid.*, Art. 10.

concerning their establishment, rights and obligations, collection and distribution of fees are to be separately formulated by the State Council.

2.2.1.1 Regulations Governing the Collective Management of Rights

The first CMO established in China started in 1992. With experience, it became increasingly obvious that some regulatory measures had to be introduced to facilitate the functioning of CMOs. The government eventually enacted and brought into effect on 1 March 2005 the Regulations on Copyright Collective Administration. The Regulations prohibit any organization or person from carrying out copyright collective management unless the collective is established in accordance with its provisions.[146] In addition, however, Article 7(2) of the Regulations states that there can only be one CMO in each 'field of rights'. The Regulations also contain detailed provisions on how a CMO is to be constituted and managed. The Regulations further empower[147] the National Copyright Administration of China (NCAC) to supervise CMOs by checking their accounts, annual budgets and finance reports and by sending a representative as an observer to attend the general membership and Board meetings. A peculiar provision, perhaps reflecting the situation in China, makes a government official liable for administrative or criminal sanctions if he is negligent in his duty or abuses his power.[148]

It is also expressly provided that the general membership, meeting at least once a year, is the institution of power of the CMO.[149] A Board of Directors, comprising no fewer than nine directors, is also elected for a four-year term.[150] A CMO is proscribed from refusing to administer the rights of a copyright holder who meets its qualifying criteria.[151] Conversely, and dealing a situation that is quite problematic throughout Asia,[152] a copyright holder is not allowed to exercise or authorize any others to exercise the rights that have been entrusted to a CMO for administration.[153] Finally, Article 29 of the Regulations provides that all licensing fees collected shall, after deduction for administration fees to maintain its regular activities, be completely distributed among owners and may not be diverted for any other purpose. Distribution records must be maintained for a minimum period of ten years.

---

146. *Ibid.*, Art. 6.
147. *Ibid.*, Art. 37.
148. *Ibid.*, Art. 45.
149. *Ibid.*, Art. 17.
150. *Ibid.*, Art. 18.
151. *Ibid.*, Art. 19. This provision is of course also targeted as ensuring that a collective management organization does not abuse its monopoly position. See also Art. 23(3).
152. This problem of self exercise of rights and/or multiple assignments of the rights that have already been entrusted to a CMO has been experienced in Thailand, Taiwan, Philippines, for examples.
153. Copyright Law, *supra* n. 144, Art. 20.

Coming as they did more than a decade after its Copyright Law was enacted and its first CMO established, the Regulations provide a perspective on the problems that had developed and required governmental intervention. Countries in the region would do well to ponder the Chinese experience.

2.2.1.2 The Collective Management of the Rights in Musical Works in China

The Music Copyright Society of China (MCSC) was created on 15 September 1992 as a non-profit social organization to administer the public performance and reproduction rights in musical works. The qualifying criterion for membership is one published or performed work at the provincial level or above. Every member has, *inter alia*, the right to be elected as a director of the CMO.[154] Its Articles also provide for representatives from the state copyright administration to be on the Board. In fact, a recent Director General of MCSC was the former Director-General of the copyright division of the NCAC, while the former deputy director general of the NCAC remains the vice chairman of the organization. This link between the CMO and the national copyright office was probably a blessing[155] to MCSC, particularly in its formative years, as the close relationship would have given it some legitimacy in the eyes of the public as well as the Chinese government.

A couple of observations may be made about MCSC's development since its inception. Firstly, unlike most Southeast Asian CMOs, a sizable component of its current revenues flow from reproduction income. For example, 54% and 37%[156] of its 2001 and 2002 gross incomes respectively may be attributed to 'mechanical' collections. There is a restricted license[157] for the reproduction of published musical works under Chinese law.[158] Second, its real growth only started in 2001[159] when its gross revenues have increased annually by more than 50% each year.[160] Prior to that, its growth could at best be described as anaemic. In 2004, MCSC's net revenues were over Chinese Yuan Renminbi (RMB) 39 million.[161]

It is noteworthy that MCSC made its first distribution of royalties to local members in June of 1993, within four months of its formation. However, any

---

154. General membership meetings are held once every four years, the longest period among the Asian societies.
155. There is a contrary view that this has in fact hobbled its natural development as the decision-making process tended to be conservative and pro-government, and users which are part of the Chinese government machinery tended to pay only lip service to their copyright obligations.
156. It was 43% and 33% in 2003 and 2004, respectively.
157. The approved statutory rate is 3.5% of wholesale price, which is lower than the 5.4% of published price to dealer applicable under an industry agreement throughout much of Asia.
158. Copyright Law, *supra* n. 134, Art. 39.
159. In 2000, its gross revenue was RMB 4.9 million. This nearly doubled to RMB 9.7 million in 2001.
160. In fact, its gross income doubled in 2001 over 2000 and doubled again the following year.
161. Approximately EUR 4.2 million as of November 2005.

conclusion drawn from this impressive fact is likely to be misleading. As mentioned, MCSC's collections in fact remained relatively flat for quite a number of years after its inception and it made its first distribution to overseas societies in 2002, with a sum of RMB 2.02 million.[162] This sum represents royalties due to foreign right holders, which had been accumulated over the years and not distributed because the amounts involved were considered too small. Another noteworthy fact is that there are occasional net surpluses of royalties flowing into China versus the distribution by it of royalties to foreign societies. For instance, in 2004, it distributed RMB 3.6 million overseas while receiving RMB 4.78 million in return.[163] MCSC also has the distinction of making quarterly distributions[164] to its members compared to the more usual one or two annual distributions of CMOs in the region. The distributions are for different categories of uses, namely mechanical royalties, Internet royalties, performance royalties and overseas royalties.

It is obvious that development in the collective management of rights in China has not kept pace with the country's economic growth. In 2008, MCSC's total revenues were only approximately RMB 37 million. Although the publication of the broadcast tariff and eventual payment of royalties by the Chinese broadcasters would go some distance to improve MCSC's revenues, the comparatively low broadcast tariff could at the same time stymie the proper development of MCSC for some time to come.

2.2.1.3 Administration of Sound Recordings in China

No general public performance or communication to the public right applies to sound recordings in China. There is a right of 'making *[a sound recording]* available to the public through information networks and to receive remuneration therefrom'.[165] Although there is no definition provided to explain what this right covers in relation to sound recordings, a similar term for copyright works is defined based on the 1996 WIPO Treaties as 'the right to make a work available to the public by wire or by wireless means so that people may have access to the work from a place and at a time individually chosen by them'.[166] Given the limited rights accorded by the Chinese law, recording companies adopted a strategy that has been successfully implemented in numerous Asian countries – they rely on the public performance

---

162. Approximately EUR 215,000 as of November 2005.
163. Approximately EUR 380,000 and EUR 505,000, respectively, as of November 2005. In 2003, it experienced a small deficit, having distributed RMB 2.94 million overseas while receiving RMB 2.54 million (approximately EUR 270,000). In 2002, it experienced a net inflow of royalties. In 2008, MCSC received approximately RMB 4 million as overseas income while distributing some RMB 10 million.
164. So does the Korea Music Copyright Association (KOMCA) in relation to certain categories of rights administered.
165. Copyright Law, *supra* n. 134, Art. 41, which goes on to state that 'anyone who ... makes *[a sound recording]* available to the public through information networks shall, in addition, obtain permission from, and pay remuneration to both the copyright owner and the performer'.
166. *Ibid.*, Art. 10(12).

rights in music videos[167] to collect public performance license fees from establishments that use such works. This is done through the China Audio Visual Copyright Association (CAVCA). CAVCA's main pre-occupation is in the licensing of karaokes for which the National Copyright Administration of China has issued a notice for the daily charge of RMB 12 per karaoke room. As a result of substantial resistance toward the payment of this royalty rate, CAVCA has had to file numerous law suits against karaoke operators in different provinces. Royalties collected are thus to be shared between the recording companies and MCSC for the public performance rights in musical works. Because of the manner with which the rights in audiovisual products have been licensed, there currently exist certain issues relating to the sharing of the royalties collected. It had taken a long time for CAVCA to obtain all of the necessary operating licenses, and it was finally authorized only in June 2008.

2.2.1.4 Collective Management of Rights in Literary Works in China

The China Written Works Copyright Society (CWWCS) was established on 24 October 2008 to collectively manage the rights of authors and publishers in literary works in China by 12 publishing institutions[168] and more than 500 authors. Although formed, CWWCS has not commenced on the collective management of rights in the traditional sense as such. It has, however, taken on negotiations with Google over the scanning of thousands of Chinese works

2.2.2 Chinese Taipei

The latest amendments to the Taiwanese Copyright Act[169] were promulgated on 13 May 2009. This amendment makes Taiwan one of two Asian countries to have a law requiring Internet service providers to terminate the connection of a user who has received three prior infringement notifications.[170] Earlier, major amendments had been passed by the Legislative Yuan on 6 June 2003 which, *inter alia*, introduced an exclusive right of 'public transmission',[171] created a Copyright

---

167. Which would be categorized as 'cinematographic films'.
168. The twelve institutions include the Chinese Writers' Association, the Development Research Centre of the State Council, the China Federation of Literary and Art Circles, the All-China Journalists Association, the Chinese Academy of Sciences, Chinese Academy of Engineering, Chinese Academy of Social Sciences and China Association of Science and Technology.
169. Copyright Act, Presidential Order No. (87) Hua-Zong-(1)-Yi-Zih 87000126405. Because of its unique relationship with China, Taiwan is not a signatory to the Berne or any other international copyright or neighbouring rights conventions. Its WTO membership thus provides a crucial link to the international intellectual property community.
170. Article 90 quinquies.
171. *Ibid.*, Art. 3.10, which defines it as 'making available or communicating to the public the contents of a work through sounds or images by wire or wireless network, or other means of communication, including enabling the public to receive the content of such work by any of the above means at a time or place individually chosen by them'.

Examination and Mediation Committee[172] charged with handling copyright matters under the Ministry of Economic Affairs – which mediates disputes between CMOs and users concerning compensation for use[173] – and granted a remuneration right in sound recordings used in public performances.[174] Other provisions in the copyright law that warrant mention include, first, a compulsory license[175] for the reproduction of musical works that have been commercially released for more than six months,[176] a prohibition on the sale of copies of sound recordings made under such licenses outside of Taiwan[177]and Article 81, which provides that 'economic rights holders may, with the approval of the specialized agency in charge of copyright matters, establish copyright intermediary organizations for the purpose of exercising rights or for collecting and distributing compensation for use'. Pursuant to this article, the Copyright Intermediary Organization Act was passed.

The history of how a specific law governing CMOs in Taiwan came about bears some recounting. Before 1989, Taiwanese law permitted the formation of only one organization in each industry. The Copyright Holders' Association of the Republic of China (CHA), which was formed in 1972, was the sole CMO entitled to carry out collective management of rights. CHA was a multi-rights CMO, with a membership that included composers, book authors, visual artists and even inventors. Toward the late 1980s, it commenced work in the field of collective management of the rights in musical works. Because it was not able at that time to secure the rights from foreign CMOs in its early years, it laboriously identified the works that have been broadcast by the television stations and obtained loans from commercial lenders to finance the distribution of royalties to local and foreign[178] right holders based on the identified works. With the receipts for these payments, it then negotiated with the stations for payment. In 1989, legal changes removed the restraint that there should only be one CMO in each industry and the number of collectives proliferated.[179] A point was reached when there were a dozen or so CMOs, mainly in the field of musical works. Some were established in name only and conducted little licensing. This multiplicity of CMOs caused confusion among right holders and users for many years and not surprisingly, also stunted the proper

---

172. *Ibid.*, Art. 82.
173. *Ibid.*
174. *Ibid.*, Art. 26(3). Before to this, there was no public performance right in sound recordings.
175. *Ibid.*, Art. 69.
176. *Ibid.*, Art. 12 of the Regulations governing application for approval of compulsory license of musical works fixes the rate at 5.4% of whole sale price of the sound recording with a minimum fee of TWD $20,000 (which may be waived under appropriate circumstances).
177. *Ibid.*, Art. 70.
178. These royalties, distributed through CASH in Hong Kong, were not insubstantial. Between 1990 and 1995, CHA remitted some USD 4.1 million to foreign right holders while USD 1.8 million was distributed to local members. From 1995, CHA carried out its own distributions. At that time, only works from Hong Kong, the United Kingdom and the United States were protected in Taiwan.
179. By 1990, there were already four CMOs claiming to administer the rights in musical works.

development of a strong and efficient CMO in Taiwan. In November 1997, the Copyright Intermediary Organization Act (CIOA) was enacted to regulate the establishment and operations of collectives.

2.2.2.1 The Copyright Intermediary Organization Act

At the very outset, the CIOA makes it illegal for any person, not registered in accordance with the Act, to carry out any collective management activity.[180] In applying to operate a CMO, an applicant is required to submit its proposed license tariffs to the competent authority for approval.[181] Article 10 prohibits a person from joining two or more intermediary organizations managing the same category of works at the same time. The law goes on to state that if a person joins two or more organizations simultaneously, he shall be deemed to have joined none of them, and if he joins at different times, the first in time prevails. The law further expressly states that 'a member shall not grant or cause a third party to grant any license (within the scope of management by the society) on his or her behalf'. This highlights the perennial difficulty of multiple assignments and dealings over the same set of rights, resulting in conflicting claims among users as well as tripping up distributions. A CMO is not permitted to refuse to administer the rights of a non-member if requested to do so.[182] The CIOA imposes on CMOs the need for its distributions to be approved by the Board of Supervisors of the CMO.[183] Another special clause is Article 35, which mandates that a CMO shall allocate 10% of its management fees annually for social, educational and cultural purposes.

The enactment of the CIOA resulted in the formation of a new authors' society for musical works in Taiwan called the Music Copyright Intermediary Society of Chinese Taipei (MUST) in 1999 as CHA could no longer continue in its current form.[184] Despite the enactment of a new law to govern the collective management of rights, there is still more than one CMO in Taiwan in each field of rights. Thus, for example, there are three major collectives in relation to the public performance right in musical works and two in relation to the public performing rights in sound recordings.

---

180. Copyright Intermediary Organization Act, promulgated by the President on 5 Nov. 1997, Art. 9. See also Art. 41 for sanctions which include fines and/or imprisonment.
181. *Ibid.*, Art. 4.
182. *Ibid.*, Art. 28.
183. This has led to at least one known case in which the supervisors had refused to sign off and the Board of Directors was compelled to proceed with the distribution with subsequent ratification of its general membership. Under Art. 38 of the law, *ibid.*, the relevant government supervisory authority may also call for documents and/or carry out inspections of the business of a CMO.
184. CHA still exists, and it has made numerous unsuccessful applications to be registered as a CMO.

2.2.2.2　　　　Music Copyright Intermediary Society of Chinese Taipei

MUST was formed[185] through the efforts of Taiwanese creators, music publishers and CISAC[186] under the CIOA. Any composer or author who owns at least five musical works and any publisher who represents at least twenty-five musical works that have been commercially recorded, published or publicly performed or broadcast is eligible to apply for membership of MUST. When MUST was first created, there was only one category of membership, although divided into individual and group membership, and all members have equal rights. However, this was subsequently amended and a new category of associate membership was introduced for those who did not meet the requirements in an attempt to attract more members in competition with other societies in Taiwan.

The MUST Board of Directors has thirteen members consisting of not fewer than two and not more than seven individual members and not fewer than one and not more than six group members. A segregated voting system for directors is in use – individual members can only vote for individual directorships and likewise for publishers. The term of office is limited to two years, with a requirement that at least three writers and publishers each must be replaced. In accordance with the requirements of Taiwanese law, there is also constituted a Board of Supervisors comprising not more than three individual and two group supervisors. This practice of having supervisors[187] appears more prevalent in the societies from the East Asian territories, and we see them provided for in the constitutions of societies in China, Japan and South Korea. In the ASEAN countries, apart from Vietnam, there are no such oversight provisions. In essence, the key responsibility of the Board of Supervisors is to oversee the performance and execution of duties by the Board of Directors. Two specific functions of the Supervisory Board are the auditing of the distribution statements and the business and financial condition of the society.

Another noteworthy feature of MUST's Articles is a provision that its expenses shall not exceed 25% of annual royalty collections in its first year of operations and that this shall be adjusted annually downward to be less than 20% from the fifth year of operations on.[188] Although the intention behind this provision is to be commended, it did lead to difficult financial constraints in the initial years of MUST's existence. As was to be expected with all startup operations, expenses in the early years greatly exceeded this limit. In fact, MUST had to seek the approval of its general membership when the time came for it to repay the startup loans to music publishers, sister societies and CISAC because the repayments would have pushed its expenses beyond the expense limit allowed by its constitution.

---

185. Its application was formally approved by the government in May 1999.
186. CISAC and the music publishers jointly put together an TWD 8.3 million loan to fund the start up of MUST.
187. They are termed as 'Councilors' in KOMCA and JASRAC.
188. Corporate Art. 82.

Given that MUST was formed with the assistance of CISAC, it is to be expected that foreign societies will enter into reciprocal agreements with it, and it alone will then administer foreign rights in Taiwan. Domestically, its main group of members comprises Mandarin language composers, writers and music publishers, as well as a strong core of local dialect creators and right holders. Until 2004, MUST administered only the public performance rights. Since then, it carries on an extremely limited administration of reproduction rights in musical works, that is, in relation to the reproduction of Japanese works.

The fact that CHA had been licensing some of the key users in Taiwan for several years coupled with the fact that a couple of key staff members of MUST left CHA to join MUST, the new society was able to achieve a relatively decent gross income of almost TWD 25 million[189] in its first year of operation. This jumped substantially to almost TWD 75 million the following year, remained flat for the next two years and surpassed TWD 150 million[190] in 2008. One final observation about MUST; like MCSC, its foreign income represents a fairly decent portion of its total revenues; 13.9% of its gross revenues in 2001 and 20.5% in 2004.

2.2.2.3 Music Copyright Association of Taiwan (MCAT)

The history of MCAT[191] could be traced back to about 1993 and to efforts to unify the many different groups attempting to carry out the collective management of copyrights at that time. Although amalgamation efforts proved unsuccessful, it spawned MCAT. Following a second unsuccessful attempt at unification in 1997 and the enactment of the CIOA soon after, MCAT became the first CMO to be officially registered under the new law in January 1999. It would be fairly accurate to say that the repertory represented by MCAT comprises largely a section of the local '*ming nan*' dialect composers and music companies. Despite its lesser repertory, it is nevertheless able to collect revenues in the region of that achieved by MUST.

As mentioned, there are three CMOs in the field of musical works, and the third organization in existence in Taiwan is called the Taiwan Music Copyright Intermediary Society (TMCS). TMCS is an extremely small setup that represents probably no more than 5% of musical works being used in the market.

The existence of multiple CMOs in the same field in such a small territory obviously affects the proper development of collective management. Thus, despite the importance of the Taiwanese music market in the region, the total amount of royalties collected in 2007 by all societies, including those representing the sound recording companies, reached only TWD 266 million.

---

189. Approximately EUR 640,000 as of November 2005.
190. This figure includes some back royalties. It is the approximate equivalent of EUR 3 million as of November 2005.
191. Its original name could be loosely translated as the Joint Association of Rightsholders of Musical Works. The name MCAT was officially adopted on 27 Dec. 2003.

2.2.2.4 Collective Management of the Rights in Sound Recordings

Although a sound recording is classified as one category of protected works[192] under the Taiwanese copyright law, the rights accorded to it are spelt out separately. Article 26[193] grants a right to remuneration in sound recordings when they are publicly performed. If a performer is involved, the remuneration is shared between them.[194] The society that administers rights in sound recordings is the Association of Recording Copyright Owners of R.O.C. (RCO). It was founded in September 1989 to collectively manage the broadcast rights in sound recordings and is now also authorized to collect royalties under Article 26. The members of ARCO comprise some thirty sound recording companies in Taiwan. It is governed by a Board of fifteen directors and five supervisors elected for two-year terms.[195] Unlike MUST, each member has one vote.[196] Because of its more restricted rights, its collections are only a fraction of that collected by MUST and MCAT.

2.2.2.5 Collective Management of Rights in Literary Works

There is a limited compulsory license found in the Taiwanese copyright law. Article 47 of the Law provides that 'within a reasonable scope, and for the purpose of editing textbooks used for teaching ... the works of another person that have been publicly released may be reproduced, adapted or compiled'.[197] Additionally, all schools may publicly broadcast works within a reasonable scope and for the purposes of education.[198] Users are required to notify the right holders and pay compensation, as set by the competent authorities,[199] for the use.

An application made by a group of writers to establish a CMO named Chinese Oral & Literary Copyright Intermediary Association (COLCIA) in the field of literary works was presented to the competent authorities in 2002 but approved only on 8 August 2006. To date, although COLCIA has signed agreements with a small number of photocopy shops, they have not been implemented and no royalties have been collected. Since its formation, COLCIA has been funded largely through the resources and resourcefulness of its key founder with a small grant from IFRRO as well.

---

192. *Copyright Act, supra* n. 157, Art. 5.8.
193. *Ibid.*, Art. 26(3).
194. *Ibid.*, Art. 26(4).
195. Constitution of ARCO, Arts 19 and 25.
196. *Ibid.*, Art. 13.
197. The next paragraph of the same article extends the compulsory license to include supplementary aids that are ancillary to the textbooks.
198. Copyright Act, *supra* n. 157, Art. 47.
199. *Ibid.*

2.2.3   Hong Kong

The governing copyright law in Hong Kong was enacted on 27 June 1997,[200] just days before the handover of the territory back to China. It is a well-crafted legislation and contained interesting innovations. Through China, Hong Kong continues to be a part of the Berne Convention. Among the innovations are certain provisions governing CMOs.[201] A collective copyright licensing body[202] may be registered with the Registrar of Copyright Licensing Bodies. The basic requirement for registration is that the licensing body must be willing to make publicly available information concerning its royalty rates for different uses. The validity of the registration depends on compliance by the registered licensing body in charging royalties that do not exceed the published rates.[203]

Every licensing scheme[204] implies that the licensing body undertakes to indemnify licensees against any liability incurred by reason of having infringed copyright in a work in circumstances within the apparent scope of the license.[205] Where an indemnity is implied, the amount of damages that a court may award in favour of the copyright owner who is not a member of the scheme for copyright infringement must not exceed the amount the copyright owner would have received if he was a member of the licensing body,[206] provided that the award will not result in a conflict with a normal exploitation of the work or unreasonably prejudice the legitimate interests of the copyright owner.[207] Any proposed[208] or existing[209] copyright licensing schemes may be referred to the Copyright Tribunal[210] for a determination. In determining the reasonableness of a licensing scheme, the Copyright Tribunal will take into account the public interest and some additional specific matters,[211] the overriding consideration being to ensure that the exercise of its power will not result in a conflict with the normal exploitation of the

---

200. Copyright Ordinance, *Gazette*, 27 Jun. 1997, L.N. 92 of 1997. Before this, the governing law in Hong Kong was the 1956 United Kingdom Copyright Act.
201. Described as 'collective copyright licensing body' in the legislation.
202. Copyright Ordinance, *supra* n. 198, Art. 145(4), which defines such a body as one whose main object is to grant copyright licenses covering works of more than one author.
203. Copyright Ordinance, *ibid.*, Arts. 149(2) and 150.
204. A licensing scheme means anything in the nature of a scheme, whether described as a scheme or tariff or by any other name: Section 145(4), so far as they relate to copying a work, renting of a computer program or a sound recording, performing the work in public, broadcasting the work or including it in a cable programme service, issuing or making available of the work to the public, making adaptation of the work and any other act restricted by copyright in the work: s. 154.
205. Copyright Ordinance, *supra* n. 198, Art. 168.
206. *Ibid.*, Art. 168(6).
207. *Ibid.*, Art. 168(7).
208. *Ibid.*, Art. 162.
209. *Ibid.*, Arts 156 and 163.
210. *Ibid.*, Art. 169 provides that the Tribunal shall consist of one Chairman and one Deputy Chairman, each of whom must be qualified for appointment as a District Judge, and seven other ordinary members.
211. *Ibid.*, Art. 167(1).

work or unreasonably prejudice the legitimate interests of the copyright owner.[212] Moreover, the Copyright Tribunal may, on the application of a person wishing to make a copy of a fixation of a performance, give consent in a case where the identity or whereabouts of the person entitled to the right of reproduction cannot be ascertained by reasonable enquiry.[213] Where a reference has been made regarding a proposed or expiring copyright license, the Copyright Tribunal may award interim copyright royalty payment by the licensee to the licensing body[214] and may order the licensing body not to apply for an interlocutory injunction against the licensee.[215]

2.2.3.1 Collective Management of Rights in Musical Works

Much like in Singapore, PRS (United Kingdom) had set up a licensing agency in Hong Kong in 1946, which continued its activities till 1977, when the Composers and Authors Society of Hong Kong (CASH) was established to assume its functions. Given its historical roots, CASH, like PRS, is a public company limited by guarantee. As a result of the transfer of operations, which included existing licenses, from the PRS Agency to CASH, the society was in the enviable position of being able to immediately register a surplus of revenues[216] against expenses in its initial fifteen months of operations.[217]

In its early years, CASH administered only the public performance rights in musical works. In 1981, a decision was taken to start[218] a new division for the collection of mechanical royalties. The administration of reproduction rights by CASH has always been of limited scope as the music publishers, in the main, dealt directly with the recording companies.[219] In 1989, CASH also started issuing a very limited number of grand right licenses.

CASH has three main classes of members – associate, full and successor. Any person upon becoming a member ordinarily becomes an associate member. Associate and successor members have no voting rights and cannot be elected to office. When voting is by way of a poll, each full member is entitled to one basic vote and one additional vote for every Hong Kong Dollar (HKD) 5,000 of royalties received by such full member during the preceding financial year. There is an important

---

212. *Ibid.*, Art. 167(3).
213. *Ibid.*, Art. 213.
214. *Ibid.*, Art. 164(1).
215. *Ibid.*, Art. 164(2).
216. Gross revenues were HKD 5,479,682.98 against expenses of HKD 480,495.43 plus a further sum of HKD 921,479.86 as management fees paid to PRS.
217. From September 1977 to December 1978.
218. Actual operation of this division started in 1982, and the first distribution of mechanical royalties was made in August 1983.
219. In 1996, CASH reached an agreement with the Music Publishers Association to represent the latter in licensing broadcasters in Hong Kong on reproduction rights when they produced television programmes for broadcasting purposes. Hitherto, this right had never been exercised in the territory.

proviso to this weighted voting clause, however. No full member is entitled to exercise more than 10% of all the votes cast by all full members.[220] However, if the poll concerns the election of directors, the 10% limit applies to the total number of writer or publisher votes. The rationale behind such a provision is simple enough to understand – a desire to ensure that no one member shall dominate the key decision-making processes of the CMO. This is particularly so in relation to the major music publishers as each of their aggregated royalties received from a society is often much larger than that paid to any one individual author or composer.

The CASH Board of Directors, termed the 'Council' in its Articles of Association, comprises up to twelve members, namely four Writer Directors elected by Writer Members; four Publisher Directors elected by Publisher Members and up to four Directors appointed by the CASH Council 'from persons who, either are members or, not being members, are prominent individuals in the musical or literary field or alternatively in a position to contribute to the development of the society'.[221] Directors serve a term of office of three years and may be re-elected or re-appointed. The quorum for the conduct of Board meetings is similarly set at three.[222] For historical reasons, the CASH Board had four directors who were appointed by PRS from its inception until 1996. The first Chairman of CASH, who served as such from 1977 till 2001,[223] was appointed by PRS. In 1996, the constitution of CASH was amended and the power of appointment accorded to PRS was abolished and entrusted to the elected CASH directors instead.

In its first five years, distributions of royalties collected by CASH were carried out by PRS. The net distributable incomes for the first year were in fact allocated 30:70 to domestic and international repertory, respectively, based on agreement between CASH and PRS. This percentage split was used pending the collation of statistics to determine the actual usage patterns. Since then, the upward trend in favour of local members has been maintained, with local members receiving 67.66% of distributed royalties in 2003. The experience of CASH in this connection could well serve as an excellent indication of how a good copyright system and a CMO can work to encourage and nurture local creativity.

This approach of assisting young start-up collectives is invaluable in the development of such organizations in Asia. In recent years, CASH has also moved to replicate its DIVA computer system[224] in MUST as well as MCSC. It is quite an achievement that CASH eventually went on to assist CHA,[225] MCSC, COMPASS and MACP to carry out international distributions on their behalf in the formative years of these societies.

---

220. Articles of Association of CASH, Art. 27c.
221. Article 35aiii of the Articles of Association of CASH.
222. Articles of Association of CASH, Art. 51.
223. With the change in the Articles of Association, Mr Malcolm Bennett became a CASH-appointed director after 1996. He retired on 16 Jan. 2001 when the current chairman Professor Chan Wing Wah was appointed.
224. The development of DIVA was started in April 2002 and launched in August 2003.
225. From 1990 to 1995.

In terms of collections, CASH is ranked fourth among societies collectively managing the rights in musical works in the Asia Pacific region, behind JASRAC, APRA and KOMCA. Its revenues grew from HKD 5.5 million in 1978 to reach HKD 155 million in 2008.[226] As an indication of its achievements, in 1990 the society was co-opted[227] onto the CISAC Administrative Council, the highest decision-making body of CISAC. CASH also participated in the formation of the CISAC Asian Regional Office, which was located within CASH from 1982 to 1989 and conducted training for many of the new general and departmental managers and staff of new CMOs in the region.[228]

2.2.3.2   Collective Management of the Rights in Sound Recordings in Hong Kong

Established in 1984 by IFPI, Phonographic Performance (South East Asia) Limited administers the public performance and broadcast rights in sound recordings, music videos and karaoke videos in Hong Kong. It was subsequently transferred to the IFPI (Hong Kong Group)[229] as its subsidiary company in 1998. This arrangement has since splintered into two organizations. Phonographic Performance (South East Asia) Ltd (PPSEAL) now represents largely the local sound recording companies, whereas the majors – EMI, Sony, Universal and Warner created a new collective in October 2008 called the Hong Kong Recording Industry Alliance Limited (HKRIA). Naturally, this has led to market confusion.

2.2.3.3   Collective Management of the Rights in Literary Works in Hong Kong

The Hong Kong Reprographic Rights Licensing Society (HKRRLS), established in 1995, is an agency operating under the umbrella of IFRRO. Apart from representing local authors and publishers, it represents authors and publishers under the IFFRO[230] umbrella. Its authority to collectively administer the rights of its members is acquired by way of an agency arrangement rather that the assignment approach adopted by CASH. Its licensing activities started only in 2000, and its annual gross collections in 2008 reached HKD 7.4 million. Like CLASS in Singapore, HKRRLS has achieved fairly decent growth in recent years.

Apart from HKRRLS, members of the Newspaper Society of Hong Kong founded the Hong Kong Copyright Licensing Association (HKCLA) in October

---

226. Approximately EUR 605,000 and EUR 13 million, respectively, as of November 2005.
227. In 1992, CASH was elected onto the CISAC Administrative Council. It is the only Asian society, apart from JASRAC, to have been elected so in the history of CISAC.
228. So much so that some jokingly called it the CASH University.
229. The IFPI (HK Group) is a national group of IFPI that represents over fifty recording companies in Hong Kong, which includes all the major local recording companies.
230. See <www.ifrro.org> (last visited: 11 May 2010).

2001 offering a one-stop collective licensing scheme[231] for photocopying of newspapers. HKCLA does not administer its rights directly but has appointed the Hong Kong Copyright Licensing Services Limited (HKCLS) as its exclusive service company to assist it in the delivery of a series of licensing services to individuals and the vast corporate sector.

2.2.4 Macau

The boom in the Macau gaming industry has resulted in the formation of a new CMO in Macau that is called the Macau Association of Composers, Authors and Publishers Association (MACA). Started in January 2009, MACA's first license was issued to the Macau Cultural Institute for certain concerts of the 23rd Macau International Music Festival. This license has symbolic importances as it signifies the ready acceptance of the Macau government to respect copyright in the conduct of its affairs. Naturally, among MACA's key licensing targets would be the casinos that are offering a plethora of entertainment activities, many of which copyright works are integral. Because of the limited size of Macau, it is possible that MACA's activities will eventually extend to include non-musical works. The establishment of MACA is being funded by interest-free loans extended to it by a number of CISAC societies.

An interesting facet of MACA is that many of the established local composers and writers are already members of CASH in Hong Kong. Moreover, again as a result of its size, MACA is likely to focus on only membership and licensing activities in the foreseeable future, contracting its backroom functions of documentation and distribution to CASH because it would not be cost effective for MACA to establish a fully fledged support system.

2.2.5 South Korea

The current Korean copyright law was promulgated on 31 December 1986 and came into force on 1 July 1987.[232] It was subsequently amended on numerous occasions, including major amendments in 2000 and 2003. South Korea acceded to the Berne Convention only on 21 August 1996.[233] It was till then a signatory only to the Universal Copyright Convention.[234] It is still not a signatory to the Rome

---

231. HKCLA has been authorized by twelve Hong Kong newspapers to issue photocopy licenses for internal references, instructional purposes (only applicable to kindergartens, primary and secondary schools under prescribed conditions), inclusion in course packs and news monitoring purposes.

232. Copyright Act, Act No. 3916, 31 Dec. 1986.

233. Thus, up until the time South Korea joined the Berne Convention, not all repertories received copyright protection. For example, US works created before October 1987 were then not protected under the Universal Commercial Code (UCC).

234. The UCC came into force in South Korea on 1 Oct. 1987.

Convention, although it did ratify the 1971 Geneva Phonograms Convention.[235] It acceded to the WCT in 2004[236] and to the WPPT in 2009.[237]

The South Korean Copyright Act contains limitations that affect the collective management of rights. Article 23 provides for a compulsory license for educational institutions at the level of high schools or lower to reproduce 'to the extent deemed necessary' a work that has already been published in textbooks.[238] Article 23(3) further provides that compensation shall be paid to copyright holders according to criteria prescribed by the relevant Ministry. Article 26 provides that it is permissible to publicly perform or broadcast a published work for non-profit purposes and without charging fees to an audience, spectators or third persons, provided that the performers concerned are not paid any remuneration for their performances.[239] The Act also contains provisions concerning the collective management of copyright and neighbouring rights in a chapter entitled 'Copyright Management Services'. The relevant legal provisions divide such services into two categories – namely 'copyright trust services' and 'copyright agency (or brokerage) services'. A copyright trust service[240] is the equivalent to the majority of CMOs, that is, it is about the exercise of copyright or neighbouring rights by the right holders themselves organized into a society. The term 'copyright agency or brokerage service'[241] is self-explanatory; there is no transfer of rights. This distinction has important repercussions.

A CMO[242] must receive government approval for its operations,[243] whereas copyright management agencies have only to report their activities to the Ministry for Culture and Tourism.[244] There are over 200 such management agencies in Korea. Because of much stricter requirements for engaging in copyright trust services, there are currently only eight CMOs in South Korea. Moreover, the

---

235. Which came into force on 1 Oct. 1987.
236. 24 Jun. 2004. See <www.wipo.int> (last visited: 11 May 2010).
237. 18 Mar. 2009. See <www.wipo.int> (last visited: 11 May 2010).
238. There is also provision that certain education institutions may publicly perform, broadcast or reproduce a published work to the extent necessary for the purpose of education and no payment or compensation is obligated.
239. Copyright Act, *supra* n. 216, Art. 26.
240. *Ibid.*, Arts 2–18, which was newly provided as part of amendments introduced on 12 Jan. 2000, defines 'copyright trust services' to mean 'a line of business in which one holds in trust and continuously manages author's property rights, publication rights, neighbouring rights or exploitation rights on behalf of the holders of the aforementioned rights'.
241. *Ibid.*, Arts 2–19, also introduced on 12 Jan. 2000, defines 'copyright agency or brokerage services' to mean a line of business in which one acts as an agent (excluding a general agent concerning exploitation) or a broker on behalf of the owner of author's property rights, public rights or neighbouring rights with regard to the exploitation of works or of performance, phonograms or broadcasting, which are the subject matters of neighbouring rights.
242. Termed as an organization offering 'copyright trust services' in the Korean Copyright Act.
243. Copyright Act, *supra* n. 226, Art. 78(1) stipulates that 'any person who intends to engage in copyright trust services shall obtain a permit from the Minister of Culture and Tourism'.
244. Amendments to the Korean Copyright Act carried out in 1994 changed the need for such services to obtain operating licenses from the relevant ministry to a reporting system.

practice by the Korean government is to allow just one copyright trust service organization for each field of exploitation or right.[245] The government's control over collecting societies and copyright agencies extends to requiring reports on their activities and suspension of their activities if they carry on their business in breach of the provisions of the Copyright Act. Government approval might be withdrawn in extreme cases.[246]

2.2.5.1 The Collective Management of Rights in Musical Works in South Korea

Established on 8 March 1964, KOMCA ranks as one of the earliest CMOs of musical works created in Asia, second only to JASRAC in Japan. At present, it also ranks as one of the largest CMOs in Asia both in terms of membership, with over 5,000[247] members in 2004, and in terms of royalty collections. It administers both the public performance and reproduction rights in musical works. In the administration of the public performance rights, KOMCA has a monopoly. As for mechanical rights administration, the major music publishers account directly among themselves in relation to the reproduction of 'international works' only. Hence, if an independent recording company in Korea reproduces an international work, KOMCA does the royalty collection. Moreover, KOMCA collects reproduction royalties on all local works, unless they are published by one of the local or major publishers, in which case, the major publishers will account directly among themselves and KOMCA will collect royalties from the local recording companies for both the local and major publishers.

Authors, composers, arrangers and music publishers or any other copyright owner may apply to become a KOMCA member. Article 7 of KOMCA's Statutes divides its membership into ordinary and associate members.[248] All members join as associate members in the first instance. For a long time, promotion to ordinary membership is decided by the Board of Directors, who used a rather convoluted calculation which results in only a small minority of its members being full members. Its qualification rules to become a full member was finally amended on 24 March 2009 such that any writer or music publisher who has been an associate member for three years could now qualify to become a full member. The foregoing aside, publishers have to meet some additional criteria. Thus, publishers could now qualify to become full members of KOMCA unlike the situation in the past. Article 12 of KOMCA's Statutes states that once a member becomes an ordinary member, he or she will not be demoted or removed unless he or she commits a

---

245. There is no express legal restriction on the number of trust organizations per category of rights.
246. Copyright Act, *supra* n. 226, Art. 80.
247. There were 5,073 members as at 31 Jan. 2004, of which 586 were full members, and 4,487 were associate members, including seventy-five music publisher members.
248. Ordinary Members' are described as 'those who have engaged in substantial musical creation out of associate members and been approved by the Board of Directors under separately stipulated provisions' and 'Associate Members' are defined as 'those who have entrusted the management of musical works to the Society or taken over the Copyright Trust Contract'.

serious offence against the society. Only ordinary members can attend and vote at the annual general meeting and are eligible for election to the board of directors.

KOMCA's Board of Directors comprises twenty-one members of which there are four music composers, two national classical music composers, two nursery music composers and ten popular music composers. The President nominates three other directors. Only full or ordinary members are entitled to stand for election or be appointed to become directors.[249]

Although KOMCA was formally organized in 1964, it could be said to have truly commenced operations only under the new copyright law of 1987. Thus, in 1988, it recorded gross revenues of some Korean Wons (KRW) 679 million.[250] Throughout the last decade of the millennium, its growth was not spectacular, particularly when set against the backdrop of the country's impressive economic progress. At the turn of the millennium, its gross revenue was KRW 27 billion. However, between 2000 and 2008, it almost trebled its gross income to reach KRW 78.2 billion[251] in 2008. KOMCA's licensing[252] operations are divided into two departments, namely the Licensing Department and the Regional Office Administration Department. The former is further subdivided into four sections covering mechanical licensing, transmission rights licensing, mechanical (piracy) licensing and broadcast licensing. The Regional Office Administration Department oversees the general licensing activities throughout South Korea.

Until January 1990, KOMCA did not enter into any reciprocal representation agreement with any foreign society. A representative of the Ministry of Culture and Information had visited ASCAP and BMI in October 1989, on KOMCA's behalf, to propose the payment of USD 10,000[253] for the use of US works from 1987 to 1989 to clear the way for bilateral agreements to be entered into between KOMCA and foreign societies. Bilateral agreements were entered into by KOMCA with the two main US performing rights CMOs, ASCAP and BMI[254] in mid-1990, followed by an agreement with Hong Kong's CASH (including PRS repertory).[255] In early 1994, the German music CMO GEMA, representing twenty-nine other CMOs, entered into a reciprocal agreement on mechanical rights administration. By April 2001, KOMCA had entered into agreements with thirty-two collectives in thirty countries for performance rights and thirty-two CMOs covering thirty-four countries for reproduction rights.

---

249. The term of office is three years.
250. Approximately EUR 570,000 as of November 2005.
251. Approximately EUR 46 million as of November 2005.
252. KOMCA's license tariffs must be approved by the government. Note also that the relevant Korean authorities must also approve any changes to the articles of association of KOMCA, as well as its distribution rules.
253. This arrangement was accepted.
254. See Ch. 11 on the United States.
255. August 1990.

2.2.5.2   Collective Management of Other Rights in South Korea

The Korean Society of Authors (KOSA) was founded on 19 May 1984 and was the first CMO established in South Korea for the protection of copyright in literary and scientific works.[256] In 2004, it had some 1606 individual members and fifty-seven organizational members. Its Board consists of seventeen members, with two auditors. The secretariat consists of four regular employees and multiple part-time staff members. In 2003, it collected the equivalent of USD 1,569,749 and distributed some USD 906,129 to members.

2.2.5.3   Korea Reprographic and Transmission Rights Association (KRTRA)

The KRTRA started with six member organizations[257] on 1 July 2000. Compared with the growth of the RROs in Hong Kong or Singapore, KRTRA has lagged behind with collections of about KRW 340 million achieved in 2007.

2.2.5.4   Korean Television and Radio Writers Association (KTRWA)

KTRWA was established in December 1957 and has 1,663 individual members in 2003 with collections of about KRW 4.4 billion.

2.2.5.5   Korea Scenario Writers Association

Although this association was established in 1954, it was given permission to operate as a CMO only on 21 September 2000. It has 327 members, of which 150 are regular members, 107 are associate members and 70 are special members.

2.2.5.6   Federation of Korea Art Performers Association (PAK)

Started on 4 June 1988, PAK currently has thirteen member-organizations.

2.2.5.7   Korean Association of Phonogram Producers (KAPP)

The KAPP was started on 5 September 2001 and currently has more than 400 members.

---

256. Under its license with the Ministry for Culture and Tourism, KOSA is authorized to operate in the fields of literary works of literature and sciences, dramatic works, cinematographic works, artistic works and photographic works.
257. Five authors' association and one publisher association – Korean Society of Authors, Korean Publishers Association, Korea Music Copyright Association, Korea TV & Radio Writers Association, Korean Association of Academic Societies.

2.2.5.8 Korean Broadcasting Performers Association

This organization was started in 2001, has 2,200 members and collected about KRW 30 million in 2003.

South Korea is now one of two Asian countries with a 'three-strikes' law that requires Internet service providers to terminate the accounts of users who have thrice infringed copyright laws.

2.2.6 North Korea

It may come as a surprise to some that North Korea acceded to the Berne Convention, which took effect on 28 April 2003. It is not surprising, however, that there is no other information with regard to copyright and collective management of rights in North Korea.

2.2.7 Mongolia

Mongolia is a large country geographically, but a relatively small one population-wise, with only 2.5 million people with a per capita gross national income (GNI) of USD 430 or less than EUR 400 in 2002.[258] About 500,000 people live in the capital, Ulan Bator, and the rest of the population is still largely nomadic.

Copyright protection[259] has existed in Mongolia as part of the civil law since 1963 under the socialist regime. These changed under a new 1992 Mongolian Constitution and with the enactment of a new copyright law in 1993.[260] Mongolia is both a signatory to the Berne Convention[261] and a member of the WTO. It also acceded to the WCT and WPPT on 25 October 2002.

2.2.7.1 The Collective Management of Rights in Musical Works in Mongolia

The first CMO in Mongolia, the Mongolian Society for the Rights of Authors and Composers (MOSRAC), which was established in 2000 with a financial loan provided by the Japanese CMO JASRAC, shut its doors as a result of a proliferation of for-profit licensing agencies. The situation remains confused, and there are ongoing attempts to regulate it.

Mongolia is one of the rare Asian countries[262] that provides for a *droit de suite* (resale right) in its law. Article 12.2 provides for a 5% resale royalty when an

---

258. World Development Indicators Database, April 2004, The World Bank Group.
259. Authors had only a remuneration right, and the State and Government agencies could exploit without the authorization of and payment to the author.
260. Law of Mongolia on Copyright, [publication info]. Amended most recently in 1999 to bring Mongolia's copyright law into compliance with the country's TRIPS obligations.
261. 12 Mar. 1998. See <www.wipo.int> (last visited: 11 May 2010).
262. Only two other Asian countries have *droit de suite*, namely, India and the Philippines.

original copy of a work of fine art or applied art is sold through an auctioneer or agent. However, there is as yet no collective management of this right.

2.3   THE SAARC[263] COUNTRIES

All South Asian countries except Bhutan are WTO members. In this part of Asia, the majority of copyright legislations are essentially based on UK law with south Asian characteristics superimposed onto it.

2.3.1   Bangladesh

Bangladesh acceded to the Berne Convention on 4 May 1999 and amended its 1962 Copyright Ordinance in 2000 to comply with its international obligations. It is classified as a least developed country and its population of 136 million has a per capita GNI of USD 380. There is presently no collective management of rights in Bangladesh.

2.3.2   Bhutan

With the teeming masses in Asia, it is sometimes forgotten that there are also extremely small countries in the region. Bhutan, while landlocked between the two Asian giants, India and China, has a population of only 800,000 people. The first copyright legislation of Bhutan was enacted in July 2001,[264] and it acceded to the Berne Convention on 25 November 2004. The Act contains some provisions, which has reference to or possible impact on the collective management of rights. Sections 12(1)(b)(ii) and 13(a)(iii) provide for the making of copies of works for teaching in educational purposes and by libraries and archives without the authorization of the author provided that, *inter alia*, 'there is no collective license available (i.e., offered by a CMO in a way that the educational institution is aware or should be aware of the availability of the license) under which such reproduction can be made'. Hence, if a CMO exists, these fair dealing exemptions would no longer be valid and the foregoing categories of users would be required to obtain a reproduction license from the CMO. Section 34 empowers the Minister for Trade and Industry 'to regulate by order questions whose regulation may be necessary for the implementation of the Act, including the setting up of one or more organizations to administer rights on behalf of the owners of such rights and determining the conditions under which such organizations shall work'. Section 25 provides that a single equitable remuneration shall be paid to the performer or performers and the

---

263. Bangladesh, Bhutan, India, Maldives, Nepal, Pakistan and Sri Lanka have organized themselves into a regional grouping called the South Asian Association for Regional Cooperation (SAARC) in 1985 and there is a working group on intellectual property rights.
264. Before this, there was no copyright protection in Bhutan. Indeed, until six years ago, the reception of television signals by ordinary Bhutanese was prohibited.

producer of the sound recording if a sound recording, published for commercial purposes, or a reproduction of such sound recording is used directly for broadcasting or for other communication to the public, or is publicly performed.

There is presently no CMO in Bhutan. Given the limited market size,[265] the plan is to create some form of collective management of rights within the Intellectual Property Office.

2.3.3   India

Copyright law in India is governed by the Copyright Act of 1957,[266] last amended in late 1999. It became a Berne signatory on 1 April 1928. Chapter VII of the Indian Copyright Act, entitled 'Copyright Societies',[267] contains various provisions on collective management. Section 33 generally proscribes any person from carrying out the work of a collective except in accordance with registration granted under the Chapter. The proviso to section 33(3) states that 'the central government shall not ordinarily register more than one copyright society to do business in respect of the same class of works'.[268] Section 36 requires every copyright society to submit to the registrar of copyrights such returns as may be prescribed. With regard to distribution, apart from requiring the society to obtain the approval of members for its distribution procedures, and for non-distribution-related utilization of royalties,[269] the Act specifies that as far as possible it should be in proportion to the actual use of their works.[270] There is also a legal provision that a CMO shall not discriminate in regard to the terms of license or the distribution of fees collected between rights in Indian and other works. If the government is of the opinion, based on a complaint by the registrar of copyrights, or a copyright holder, that it is in the interests of members of a CMO to do so, it may, after conducting any inquiry into the complaint, suspend[271] or cancel[272] the registration of the society.

A compulsory license exists under section 52 of the Indian Copyright Act in relation to the making of sound recordings. The unique feature is that this

---

265. The Bhutanese economy, one of the world's smallest, is based on agriculture and forestry, which provide the main livelihood for 90% of the population and account for about 40% of gross domestic product.
266. The Indian Copyright Act, 1957, *Official Gazette*, No. 14 of 1957, adopted many of the principles and provisions of the 1956 UK Copyright Act.
267. *Ibid.*, Art. 2 defines a 'copyright society' as a society registered under subs. (3) of s. 33. There is also an entire Ch. V contained in the Copyright Rules on copyright societies.
268. *Ibid.*
269. *Ibid.*, Art. 35(1).
270. *Ibid.*, Art. 35(2).
271. Suspension may be for up to a period of one year, and the government shall appoint an administrator to discharge the functions of the society.
272. Cancellation of registration could be carried out on the following grounds, namely, the society is being managed in a manner detrimental to the interests of the holders of rights concerned or if the copyright society persistently fails to manage its affairs properly or if it persistently fails to properly maintain its accounts and get them audited or it utilizes its funds for purposes other than the copyright business.

compulsory license applies not only to sound recordings made of musical works, but also to sound recordings made of any literary or dramatic work.

The Indian cabinet approved proposals at the end of 2009 to amend the Indian copyright law in its first major revision in a decade. The proposed amendments are the outcome of India's desire to comply with the Internet treaties as well as to legislate measures to regulate certain practices in the Indian music industry. According to the government press release, the proposed amendments are, *inter alia*, to 'give independent rights to authors of literary and musical works in films, which were hitherto denied and wrongfully exploited by the producers and music companies'. The amendment is intended to ensure 'that the authors of the works, particularly songs included in the cinematograph film or sound recordings, receive royalty for the commercial exploitation of such work'. Additionally, the amendments will 'introduce a system of statutory licensing to ensure that the public has access to musical works over the radio and television networks'.

2.3.3.1 Collective Management of Rights in Musical Works

British colonial rule of India began in the east of the country in the mid-eighteenth century and did not end until 15 August 1947, with not only the independence of India but also the creation of the new state of Pakistan.[273] Naturally, therefore, before the formation of the Indian Performing Rights Society (IPRS), performing rights in non-Indian music was administered by PRS (UK) for its own members and affiliated societies. It did this through an agent in Calcutta, Natsin (India) Private Limited (Natsin). The collections made by this agent were for the use of foreign repertory by All India Radio only. The IPRS was formed in 1969. It began licensing in June 1970,[274] when it attempted to license cinema theatres in the country. The Eastern India Motion Picture Association resisted this attempt firstly before the Copyright Board, which ruled in favour of IPRS, and then in the High Court of Calcutta,[275] which overruled the decision of the Copyright Board. IPRS appealed to the Supreme Court,[276] which affirmed the decision of the high court.

---

273. East and West Pakistan. East Pakistan subsequently became an independent country, Bangladesh.
274. In accordance with the provisions of s. 33 of the Copyright Act, IPRS published its licensing tariffs on 27 Sep. and 29 Nov. 1969 in the 'Statesman' and the '*Gazette of India*', respectively. A number of persons including various associations of film producers who claim to be owners of films, including the sound tracks thereof filed objections in accordance with s. 34 of the Copyright Act.
275. The High Court held that unless there is a contract to the contrary, a composer who writes a lyric or music for the first time for valuable consideration for a cinematograph film does not acquire any copyright in respect to either the film or its sound track, which he or she is capable of assigning, and that the owner of the film becomes the first holder of the copyright in the composition.
276. *Indian Performing Rights Society v. Eastern India Motion Picture Association*, Civil Appeal Number 967 of 1975.

On 1 April 1972, IPRS entered into an agency agreement with PRS for the licensing of the international music repertory in India. However, it had to be conducted through the services of Natsin. This was followed in the next year with a reciprocal agency agreement with Mechanical Copyright Protection Society Ltd., London (MCPS) for the administration of the reproduction rights in musical works. In 1975, the Society entered into a reciprocal agreement with PRS, whereby the latter was vested with the right to administer Indian works outside India. However, the licensing of both Indian and non-Indian music continued to be carried out by Natsin as licensing agent. This state of affairs led a renowned South Indian composer, M. B. Srinivasan to campaign for IPRS members to assume full management of the Society. A case was filed in the Bombay High Court against Natsin, and eventually IPRS was able to terminate its agency contract with Natsin in December 1977 and assumed full operations of the organization. In the immediate aftermath, the agent filed various civil suits against the Society and its staff, severely crimping the activities of IPRS for some time. To make matters worse, the decision of the Supreme Court in the *Eastern India Motion Picture Association* case that same year was interpreted as preventing IPRS from licensing the performing rights in Indian music. In 1992, upon a review of operations, it was realized that the judgment had the effect of only restricting IPRS from the licensing of musical works when used simultaneously with the film but did not restrict IPRS from the licensing of film music used separately from films. As a result of the misunderstanding, IPRS hitherto only collected license fees for the use of Western music and distributed these collections to its members.

Until 1992, IPRS had a reciprocal arrangement with PRS (UK) by which each party was collecting royalties in its own territory on behalf of the other but retained the sums so collected for distribution among its own members.[277] This was renegotiated in 1992[278] for the royalties collected to be remitted to each other.[279] In 1993, IPRS received its first overseas distribution from PRS (UK) in the amount of Indian Rupees (INR) 3,845,110.[280] In the same year, IPRS admitted publisher members for the first time. In 1994, IPRS received mechanical royalties for the first time of INR 418,350[281] from MCPS and also issued its first ever mechanical license for the utilization of Indian music in India.[282]

Despite its early formation, the annual revenue of IPRS remained dismally low for a long time. In 1992, it was only INR 1.9 million[283] whereas expenses were 1.2 million. With the change in arrangements between IPRS and PRS, the

---

277. IPRS made its first distribution of Indian Rupees (INR) 900 to five members in its first distribution in 1973.
278. CISAC provided a grant of USD 9,000 to purchase computers for its distribution system.
279. All foreign repertory continued to be channelled to IPRS through its reciprocal contract with PRS (UK). With effect from 1 Jan. 1996, IPRS started to enter into direct reciprocal contracts with other societies.
280. Approximately EUR 72,000 as of November 2005.
281. Approximately EUR 8,000 as of November 2005.
282. Before this, IPRS had sporadically issued licenses in India for the use of international music. In 2004, it took the unusual decision of terminating its administration of mechanical rights.
283. Approximately EUR 36,000 as of November 2005.

remittances of foreign royalties substantially increased its incomes. For several years thereafter, foreign royalties constituted a sizable proportion of its total income. In 2004, for example, foreign income comprised 37.9% of its total incomes. Thus, looking at domestic royalty collections in 2004 (INR 58 million[284]), it may be concluded that given its history and size, IPRS has not been able to achieve its market potential in terms of collections. This situation has dramatically changed in the past few years. For the year ended 31 March 2008, IPRS turned in domestic revenues of R214.2 million, which comprised 85% of its gross revenues. Despite the substantial rise in revenues in recent years, the total royalties collected by IPRS indicate that the society still has some way to go before achieving its market potential.

IPRS ranks among the earliest CMOs established in Asia. It is a company limited by guarantee[285] and does not have a share capital. According to its Memorandum of Association,[286] the society is authorized to collectively administer the public performance, broadcast, cable transmission and reproduction rights in musical works. Membership in IPRS is open to any composer, author, writer or owner, as well as any successor in title, and based on the latest IPRS constitution, which was substantially amended in 2008, there are two classes of membership – owner members and members. A member is defined as 'those . . . who have created their respective works . . . but are not copyright owners and not owner members'. The composition of the Board of Directors also underwent major alteration to provide for six members who represent music publishers, two composers and lyricists each and twelve directors nominated by the board. Such a composition effectively places IPRS in the control of music publishers, which in the case of India, are essentially the music recording companies. Apart from the nominee directors, only 'owner members' qualify to be directors. This term 'owner' is defined in the constitution as 'any person owning wholly or partially the copyrights in the literary, musical works, dramatic works or cinematograph film'. Moreover, to qualify to stand for election as a Board member, a writer and publisher must have 300 and 2,000 published works, respectively.

2.3.3.2 Collective Management of Rights in Sound Recordings

The Indian Phonographic Industry (IPI), precursor of the Indian Music Industry, started in 1936 as a non-profit association of producers of sound recordings. In 1994, the association changed its name to The Indian Music Industry (IMI). It is a non-commercial, non-profit organization affiliated to the International Federation of Phonographic Industry (IFPI). IMI members had formed a collecting society in 1941 to administer rights in sound recordings called Phonographic Performance Ltd. (PPL), which is registered with the Registrar of Copyrights.

---

284. Approximately EUR 1.1 million as of November 2005.
285. Liability is limited to INR 100 per member.
286. Article IIIA1.

PPL administers broadcasting/telecasting and public performance rights on behalf of over 120 music companies which are its members.

2.3.3.3 Collective Management of Rights in Literary Works

Members of the Federation of Indian Publishers registered an organization named Indian Reprographic Rights Organization in 2000 to collectively manage the rights in literary works. Unfortunately, to date, there is little or no licensing or distributing of royalties to speak of.

2.3.3.4 *Droit de Suite*

Section 53A of the Indian Copyright Act establishes a *droit de suite* in the case of resale of an original work of painting, sculpture or drawing or of the original manuscript of a literary or dramatic or musical work exceeding INR 10,000.[287] The Copyright Board, who may fix different shares for different classes of works, shall fix the share in the resale price. No CMO presently exists to administer this right in India. There are discussions ongoing regarding the formation of an Indian visual arts society.

2.3.4 Nepal

The latest Copyright Act of Nepal was enacted in April 2002.[288] Further to the enactment, copyright rules were passed in August 2004. The Berne Convention came into force on 11 January 2006 in Nepal, which was admitted as a WTO member, together with Cambodia, in 2003 and is categorized as an LDC. The Copyright Rules expressly regulate the formation of CMOs. Section 39 provides that generally one CMO shall be formed for each category of right holders with a minimum of fifty members in each organization. The Registrar is empowered under section 30(2)(a) to monitor and control the CMO. Section 39(2) requires a CMO to be registered with the Registrar. Further, section 39(5) expressly permits a collective to sue and be sued in its own name.

2.3.4.1 Collective Management of Copyrights

The Copyright Protection Society of Nepal (CPSN) was established in March 1997 as an autonomous corporate body. One of the key objectives of CPSN is to collect and distribute royalties to right holders for use of copyright works. Since its inception, CPSN has spent a great deal of time lobbying for amendments to the copyright law. As a result of the inadequacy in the previous copyright law, CPSN had not commenced on its management activities. After the enactment of the

---

287. Approximately EUR 190 as of November 2005.
288. It received royal assent on 15 Aug. 2002.

2000 copyright law, CPSN worked on the establishment of a music CMO; the outcome was Music Royalty Collection Society Nepal (MRCSN).

MRCSN was established in June, 2007, with the objective of collecting royalty for public performance of music in the first phase and mechanical royalty later. It has more than 165 music composers and song writers as members at present, with a rapidly growing membership. Its Executive Committee has eleven members, of which five are elected from among music composers and five from among lyricists. The Chairman is elected directly. Its day-to-day work is supervised by the Chairman of the Executive Committee, who works on voluntary basis. He is assisted by two paid staff members. At present, MRCSN is supported by a small annual grant of USD 4,000 provided by the Government of Nepal. Despite operating in less than ideal conditions, MRCSN has been able to extract a promise by Nepal Radio to pay 1% of its advertising revenues as royalties. It has also started on the collection and distribution of ring tone royalties. MRCSN is now working to very quickly establish proper documentation and distribution systems to ensure that royalties collected may be distributed speedily and equitably to the rightful owners.

2.3.5   Pakistan

The governing law in Pakistan is the *Copyright Ordinance*.[289] Pakistan is a signatory to the Berne Convention.[290] Historically, the PRS (UK), like in India, also had an agent in Pakistan till the mid-1990s. This arrangement was terminated, and to date no collective, in the field of musical works or any other field, has been formed. There is a chapter devoted to performing rights societies to be found in the Ordinance that, *inter alia*, requires every performing rights society to publish and file with the Registrar statements of all fees, charges and royalties it proposes to collect for the grant of licenses for the performance in public of works in respect to which it has authority to grant such licenses. If any such society fails to act in accordance with the aforementioned provisions, no action or other proceedings to enforce any remedy, civil or criminal, for infringement of the performing rights in that work shall be commenced except with the consent of the Registrar. Objections to the published fees may be lodged with the Registrar's office, and a Copyright Board is then empowered to inquire into such objections. No CMO has yet been established in Pakistan, although there has been some recent interest expressed by various parties.

2.3.6   Sri Lanka

The current Sri Lankan copyright legislation is embodied in its Intellectual Property Act[291] of 2003. Sri Lanka has been a Berne Union member since 20 July 1959.

---

289. Copyright Ordinance No. XXXIV of 1962, *The Gazette of Pakistan*, Extra, 2 Jun. 1962 (as amended by Copyright (Amendment) Ordinance, 2000 dated 29 Sep. 2000).
290. Which entered into force on 5 Jul. 1948.
291. Intellectual Property Act of 2003, No. 36 of 2003.

There are numerous provisions contained in the latest law that affects the collective management of rights. Section 2(1)(b) creates the position of a Director-General of Intellectual Property, who 'shall take all necessary steps to promote and encourage the establishment and proper functioning of organizations or societies to protect and administer copyright and related rights'. Section 25(1)(a) provides that no person shall commence or carry on the business of a CMO unless authorized under the Act. It is also provided that the Director-General shall not ordinarily register more than one such society to do business in respect to the same class of rights. Every CMO submits to the Director-General such returns as may be prescribed. The Director-General may, if he is satisfied that the CMO is being managed in a manner detrimental to the interests of the owners of rights concerned, cancel or suspend the registration of the society and the permission to commence or carry on business. Where the Director-General suspends the registration of a society, he appoints an administrator to carry out the functions of the CMO. Every collective is subject to the control of the right holders. All fees distributed among right holders are, as far as may be, distributed in proportion to the actual use of their works. An equitable remuneration right in sound recordings is provided.[292] This provision is substantially identical to Article 12 of the Rome Convention with one key difference – the Sri Lankan provision extends the remuneration right to include any public performance of a sound recording. It is further implied that the producer collects the royalties from the users and pays half to the performer in the absence of agreement to the contrary.[293]

2.3.6.1   Collective Management of Rights in Musical Works in Sri Lanka

There now legally exist three collecting societies in Sri Lanka.

2.3.6.2   Sri Lanka Performing Rights Society (SLPRS)

Before enactment of the new law, there existed a CMO called the Sri Lanka Performing Rights Society (SLPRS), which was incorporated as a company limited by guarantee under the Sri Lankan Companies Act in September 1981. When the new Intellectual Property Act was passed in 2003, SLPRS was, for a period of time, unable to collect any royalties because the regulations governing collecting societies were not enacted and it could not register to operate under the new law. It was able to register only in 2006. Thereafter, licensing became more difficult as three societies in the field of musical works were registered under the new law. Since then, SLPRS has only been able to collect an annual average of about USD 900 from about twenty-five licenses with one fulltime employee[294] – the field officer who

---

292. *Ibid.*, Art. 19.
293. *Ibid.*, Art. 19(2).
294. He has been a fulltime employee for 25 years and is about 45 years of age.

collects the royalties. It operates out of a 100-square feet office,[295] which it uses rent-free. Since its inception, SLPRS has made only three small distributions. Thus, despite a history spanning almost three decades, SLPRS has had little result to show for it. This dismal record has eroded the trust and confidence of its members in the society and also acts as a deterrent to the new and upcoming composers and lyric writers joining it. The outcome of this is the creation of other societies such as the Outstanding Song Creators' Association (OSCA) and the Creative Value Protection Society (CVPS) as 'competing' societies.

2.3.6.3   Creative Value Protection Society (CVPS)

CVPS was officially incorporated as a limited[296] company under the Sri Lankan Companies Act on 20 May 2005. The fifteen promoters in the formation of CVPS include musicians, a professor, an attorney-at-law, a photographer, film directors, writers, a dancing instructress, an artist and a government officer.

Since its incorporation, CVPS has not issued any public performance or mechanical right licenses and does not have any full- or part-time employee.

2.3.6.4   Outstanding Song Creators Association (OSCA)

OSCA was officially incorporated as a limited company under the Companies Act on 10 April 2002, with a primary welfare intention of its members; members receive free medical care and insurance coverage, and meeting facilities are provided by the current Chairman at the hospital where he is also the chairman. Because of its welfare-oriented origins, some members of OSCA are also members of SLPRS. However, OSCA has also been registered as a CMO, although its constitution is not specifically designed to perform this function. Moreover, its current membership cuts across all creative genres.

The existing multiple-society situation in Sri Lanka is on its face contrary to the provisions of the copyright law that states that there shall ordinarily be only one society permitted in each field of rights. Of course, it could be argued that the situation is less than ordinary, hence, three societies. However, this simply complicates the matter further. Having said the foregoing, we should view this matter in perspective. Sri Lanka has just emerged from a bruising civil war, the aftermath of which is still working its way through the country's political, social, legal and economic spheres. The collective management of copyright, unfortunately, is not likely to rank high in the priority list.

---

295. The office is owned by a leading book publisher who is currently a member of the Board of SLPRS and a member of the advisory committee of the National Intellectual Property Office Sri Lanka (NIPOS).
296. The liability of each member is limited to INR 100.

3   CONCLUDING REMARKS

It would be appropriate to conclude with some remarks on the impact of digital usages on the activities of CMOs in the Asian region. Broadly speaking, Asian CMOs have had little success in effectively licensing digital usages throughout most of the region, with perhaps four exceptions – Japan, South Korea, Hong Kong and, increasingly, Malaysia.

TRIPS has been the dominant driving force in the legislative changes that have taken place in the Asia Pacific region, particularly in the last decade. Increasingly, however, collective management is accepted as an efficient way of administering certain rights. A trend toward legislative intervention in the field of collective management has also been observed in recent years. At the time of writing, Indonesia is considering the enactment of regulations while a proposed code of conduct has surfaced in Singapore for public feedback. However, the collective management of rights remains totally undeveloped in quite a large number of Asian territories. The CMOs that do exist continue to struggle to collect royalties that should rightfully be paid to them. In the former category, there are countries such as Pakistan, Bangladesh, Bhutan, Sri Lanka, Myanmar, Laos, Cambodia and Brunei. In the latter category, there are examples in Thailand, the Philippines, China, Mongolia and India, where CMOs have existed for quite some time with less than optimal results. The collective management of other rights, such as the 'mechanical right' in musical works, the reprographic rights in literary works, the visual arts, etc., are largely embryonic and face daunting challenges in their development.

We have seen lively developments in Asia in the last decade and a half. However, the economic benefits are still not being fully realized by the right holders. Governments in the region can take the lead in encouraging the development of CMOs by ensuring, *inter alia*, that they pay reasonable amounts of royalties when their departments and government-linked organizations utilize copyright materials. Another crucial area would be the reform of the judicial systems in some of the Asian countries. Without this latter reform, the continued development in the field of collective management would be quite seriously hampered. We can certainly look forward to another exciting decade in the field of copyright development in the Asia Pacific region at the start of the new millennium.

Chapter 14
Collective Management of Copyright in Latin America

Karina Correa Pereira*

1 INTRODUCTION

The countries discussed in this chapter are Argentina, Brazil, Chile, Costa Rica, Mexico, Peru, Uruguay and Venezuela. This group was selected to represent different regions of Latin America, each with different social realities as well as various political and cultural environments. The three largest countries – Argentina, Brazil and Mexico – are considered first because those are the most important markets in the region, not only for demographic reasons but also arguably because of the cultural relevance of these three nations' heritage, both locally and internationally. Peru and Venezuela are members of the Andean Community. Chile is a regional leader and an example of economic growth after the fall of its military regime. Uruguay might be a small player in the regional scene, but it is the current headquarters of LATINAUTOR, a regional cooperation project centralizing Ibero-American Collective Management Organizations (CMOs). Finally, Costa Rica was considered in order to include a representative of Central America.

All countries considered are signatory to major international treaties concerning intellectual property,[1] have enacted 'modern' laws protecting copyright and, in some

---

* LLM, University of Ottawa. JD equivalent Universidade Presbiteriana Mackenzie. Admitted to the Brazilian Bar Association – São Paulo Chapter.
1. See s. 3 of this chapter.

Daniel Gervais (ed.), *Collective Management of Copyright and Related Rights*, pp. 465–495.
© 2010 Kluwer Law International BV, The Netherlands.

cases, have established guidelines for the collective management of copyright. However, the enforcement of national laws is often jeopardized by weak legal institutions and the lack of copyright's awareness by their populations. This lack of awareness, combined with the lower purchasing power of most Latin American countries, may lead to increasing piracy of copyright products. It is a market in which CMOs can conduct a variety of preventive actions and start litigation procedures.

The purpose of this chapter is to analyse the activities and gain a better understanding of CMOs throughout Latin America based on (1) organizational and transparency levels achieved by CMOs in each given country and its relation to governmental control and (2) effectiveness of the activities of CMOs, especially in relation to collecting licensing fees and distributing funds to its members. Those two different criteria are closely related because the latter depends on the former. Furthermore, these two criteria aid in determining whether a governmentally controlled system can be more effective for CMOs than a strictly private one.

2 CMOs THROUGHOUT LATIN AMERICA

This section presents active CMOs in Latin America as well as associations of right holders that have an important role in the fight against piracy and the spread of awareness among the local populations. It is important to adequately describe the current situation before commencing further analysis.

2.1 BRAZIL

The first Brazilian CMO, *Sociedade Brasileira de Autores Teatrais* (Brazilian Society of Theatre Authors (SBAT)) was established in 1917.[2] SBAT is still active and is one of the most dynamic CMOs in the country. Originally, it managed only theatrical works, but it now collects and distributes amounts related to the commercialization of all kinds of literary works. The widening of its scope caused a change to its initial name to *Sociedade Brasileira de Autores;* however, the acronym SBAT is still used.

After the creation of this first CMO, many others followed:

- 1942 – *União Brasileira de Compositores* (Brazilian Union of Composers (UBC));[3]
- 1946 – *Sociedade Brasileira de Autores Compositores e Editores* (Brazilian Society of Authors, Composers and Publishers (SBACEM));[4]
- 1956 – *Sociedade Arrecadadora de Direitos de Execuções Musicais no Brasil* (Society of Music Performing Rights of Brazil (SADEMBRA));

---

2. See <www.sbat.com.br> (last visited: 8 Dec. 2009).
3. See <www.ubc.org.br> (last visited: 8 Dec. 2009).
4. See <www.sbacem.org.br> (last visited: 8 Dec. 2009).

- 1960 – *Sociedade Independente de Compositores e Autores Musicais* (Independent Society of Composers and Music Authors (SICAM));[5]
- 1962 – *Sociedade Brasileira de Administração e Proteção de Direitos Intelectuais* (Brazilian Society of Management and Protection of Intellectual Property Rights (SOCINPRO)).[6]

The large number of associations made it difficult for authors and users of artistic works to collect and distribute money.[7] The principal reason for a large number of associations is the fact that authors freely got together to establish as many associations as they wanted, which was easily done at the time because governmental approval was not a prerequisite and no formal or legal requirements prevented a CMO from opening its doors.

In an attempt to organize the collection and distribution of amounts related to musical works, in 1973 the government intervened and enacted Federal Law No. 5988/73 providing for the establishment of a central office for collection and distribution of amounts related to musical performances. Known as the *Escritório Central de Arrecadação e Distribuição* (National Collection and Distribution Office (ECAD)),[8] its primary function is to collect and distribute money from musical performances.

The same law that created ECAD also created a governmental authority called *Conselho Nacional de Direito Autoral* (National Copyright Council (CNA)).[9] All collective management associations were obliged to send a copy of their accounts and other relevant information to the CNA,[10] which was also responsible for enacting the statutes of ECAD. The existence of a governmental authority with control over the activity of CMOs demonstrates the involvement of the Brazilian government. This is perhaps a reflection of Brazilian politics at the time, with the military government restricting cultural manifestations it considered dangerous, at the government's sole discretion. In the 1970s, CNA and the military police had authority over Brazilian cultural events; no musical concert or event could take place without the authorization of the military police. Much has changed since the 1970s – CNA no longer exists, and collective management in Brazil has been completely privatized. ECAD remains as a centralizing agent. It now acts on behalf of CMOs, which, in turn, act on behalf of authors. ECAD represents many foreign CMOs in Brazil.

The associations that are part of ECAD can be 'effective' associations or 'administered' associations. Effective associations are part of ECAD's general council, and help set prices, enact collection and distribution rules, etc.

---

5. See <www.sicam.org.br> (last visited: 8 Dec. 2009).
6. See <www.socinpro.org.br> (last visited: 8 Dec. 2009).
7. According to the organizational criteria, in countries where the government exercises control over the CMO activity there is a smaller number of organizations and less chance of confusion by authors.
8. See <www.ecad.org.br> (last visited: 8 Dec. 2009).
9. CNA acted as the auditing agent for CMOs.
10. There was no explanation as to what this relevant information was. It could be anything, at the government's discretion.

Administered associations do not participate in the administration of ECAD. Associations in both categories, as of today, are discussed in the following section.

2.1.1 Effective Associations

The following list identifies the effective associations:

- *Associação Brasileira de Música*[11] (Brazilian Music Association (ABRA-MUS)) was founded in 1982 and as of 2004 had 5,000 authors, publishers, singers, musicians and arrangers as members.
- *Associação de Músicos, Arranjadores e Regentes*[12] (Association of Musicians, Arrangers and Producers (AMAR)) was created in 1980. It is a Brazilian society that gathers authors, composers, performers, musicians, publishers and independent phonogram producers. AMAR is the outcome of a movement called SOMBRÁS (Brazilian sound), created in the 1970s to claim the enactment of specific legislation on copyright, non-existent in Brazil at the time, as well as the restructuring of the CMOs. This CMO is also known as AMAR-SOMBRÁS, *Associação de Músicos Arranjadores e Regentes-Sociedade Musical Brasileira.* It fought for copyright in the 1970s and denounced the control of copyright by the phonographic industry.
- *Sociedade Brasileira de Autores, Compositores e Escritores de Música* (Brazilian Society of Music Authors, Composers and Writers (SBACEM)) is one of the oldest associations. It has more than 5,000 members, including some of the most renowned Brazilian composers.
- *Sociedade Independente de Compositores e Autores Musicais* (Independent Society of Music Authors and Composers (SICAM)) is another association that helped establish ECAD. It claims to have more than 38,000 members. This association has taken an initiative to divulge its members' works on the Internet by offering downloadable music and licensing of works. Its intention is to spread Brazilian music worldwide.
- *Sociedade Brasileira de Administração e Proteção de Direitos Intelectuais* (Brazilian Society for the Protection and Management of Intellectual Rights (SOCINPRO)) has 13,000 members and aims to protect the rights of authors, musicians, composers, singers, publishers and producers. SOCIN-PRO is part of the National Council of Culture Incentive, an action of the Ministry of Culture that offers musical instruments and help of any sort to authors.
- *União Brasileira de Compositores* (Brazilian Union of Composers (UBC)). In 1938, although musical composers had their own 'department' at SBAT, they felt they needed an association of their own to protect their interests. Consequently, *Associação Brasileira de Compositores e Autores* (ABCA)

---

11. See <www.abramus.org.br> (last visited: 8 Dec. 2009).
12. See <www.amar.art.br> (last visited: 8 Dec. 2009).

was created. However, not all composers joined ABCA; some remained at SBAT. In an attempt to unify the efforts conducted in the musical domain by both associations – SBAT and ABCA – musical composers decided to start a third association, namely UBC, in 1942.

2.1.2 Administered Associations[13]

The following list details the administered associations:

- *Associação Brasileira de Autores, Compositores, Intérpretes e Músicos* (Brazilian Association of Music Authors, Composers and Performers (ABRAC));
- *Associação Nacional de Autores, Compositores e Intérpretes de Musica* (National Association of Authors, Composers and Performers of Music (ANACIM));
- *Associação de Intérpretes e Músicos* (Association of Performers and Musicians (ASSIM)).[14]
- *Sociedade Administradora de Direitos de Execução Musical do Brasil* (Society for the Management of Music Performing Rights of Brazil (SADEMBRA)).

ECAD's collections and distribution have increased steadily from 2000 as Table 14.1 demonstrates.[15]

Table 14.1   ECAD's Collections

Year	Total amount collected (in BRL)	Total amount distributed (in BRL)
2000	112,000,000	84,000,000
2001	157,000,000	103,000,000
2002	177,000,000	121,000,000
2003	209,000,000	156,000,000
2004	227,261,841	187,794,398
2005	254,747,161	212,867,782

13. When this chapter was first written, in 2005, ECAD had two more administered associations: *Associação de Titulares de Direitos Autorais* (Association of Copyright Holders (ATIDA)) and *Associação de Compositores e Intérpretes Musicais do Brasil* (Association of Music Composers and Performers of Brazil (ACIMBRA)). ATIDA was expelled from ECAD in 2006 under accusations of corruption. Its members have been transferred to ACIMBRA, which was later also accused of corruption. Neither association could be contacted. See <www.administradores. com.br/artigos/dapica_estaria_daniel_dantas_por_tras_do_ecad/26080/> (last visited: 14 Dec. 2009).
14. See <www.assimassociacao.com> (last visited: 15 Dec. 2009).
15. As of 9 Nov. 2005, 10 Dec. 2009, 1 Brazilian Real (BRL) is equivalent to Euro (EUR) 0.38, United States Dollar (USD) 0.44 56. BRL 112 million is the approximate equivalent of EUR 43 million, and BRL 227 million is the equivalent of EUR 87 million.

Table 14.1   (cont'd)

Year	Total amount collected (in BRL)	Total amount distributed (in BRL)
2006	268,368,828	205,939,540
2007	302,206,444	250,490,071
2008	332,298,825	271,485,547

BRL: Brazilian Real.

The percentage of foreign works in ECAD's distributions over the same period varied from a low of 9.88% in 2001 to a high of 27% in 2008, perhaps caused by the better availability of foreign works documentation.

2.1.3   Other Associations

Besides the associations directly linked to ECAD, Brazil has other associations that are active in the defence of copyright.

– *Associação Brasileira de Direitos Reprográficos* (Brazilian Association for Reprographic Rights (ABDR)).[16] Established in 1992, ABDR started collecting reprographic reproduction fees in 1998. Its main objective is the collection of copyright fees for photocopies. It also endeavors to develop an awareness and information about the damages caused by the unauthorized reproduction of books. ABDR, also defends authors and publishers against the violation of their rights in the court. In 2004, it declared 77 publishers and 357 authors as members and that it had issued 186 licenses to universities, libraries and copy shops.

– *Associação Defensora de Direitos Autorais* (Association for the Defence of Authors' Rights (ADDAF)).[17] This association was created in 1958 by former members of UBC. The aim of ADDAF is to protect mechanical rights, differently from ECAD and its associations that protect the live execution of works. ADDAF is the only association in Brazil that protects only the rights of reproduction. ADDAF is a member of LATINAUTOR.

– *Associação Brasileira de Direitos de Autores Visuais* (Brazilian Association for the Rights of Visual Authors (AUTVIS)).[18] AUTVIS is the first CMO dedicated exclusively to authors of visual works. It was created in November 2002 by a group of photographers, plastic artists and designers.

---

16. See <www.abdr.org.br> (last visited: 10 Dec. 2009).
17. See <www.addaf.org.br> (last visited: 10 Dec. 2009).
18. See <www.autvis.org.br> (last visited: 10 Dec. 2009).

2.2   ARGENTINA

In comparison with Brazil, the Argentinean legal system allows for higher governmental control of the activities of CMOs. This may explain why there are fewer CMOs in Argentina (the particularities of the Argentinean legal system will be addressed in the next section of this chapter). CMOs currently operating in Argentina are:

- *Sociedad Argentina de Autores y Compositores de Musica* (Argentinean Society of Authors and Composers of Music (SADAIC)) is the main CMO in Argentina.[19] SADAIC has been representing authors and composers of all kinds of music since 1936.
- *Sociedad General de Autores de la Argentina* (General Society of Authors of Argentina (ARGENTORES)).[20] ARGENTORES was officially recognized as a CMO 1973, through Law No. 20.115. This law authorized ARGENTORES to collect copyright remuneration regarding literary works, drama pieces, musical dramas, cinema and television. An agreement between ARGENTORES and *Sociedad Argentina de Escritores* (SADE) allows ARGENTORES to collect remuneration for works of SADE's members. ARGENTORES is an ordinary member of the International Confederation of Societies of Authors and Composers (CISAC) and works with the Motion Picture Association Latin America office and the Writers Guild of America.
- *Sociedad Argentina de Musicos* (Argentinean Society of Musicians (SADEM)) plays a role that may seem similar to a labour union.[21] It promotes the works of its members and collects remuneration for such works, and it also contracts labour agreements with radio stations and television channels representing its members. It acts together with the musicians' labour union *Sindicato Argentino de Musicos*, the popular school of music *Escola Popular de Musica* (EPM), *Federacion Internacional de Musicos* (FIM), *Confederacion General del Trabajo* (CGT), with *Confederacion Sindical de Trabajadores de los Medios de Comunicacion Social* (COSIT-MECOS), *Secretariado Internacional de Sindicatos de Artes, Medios de Comunicacion y Espectaculos* (ISETU) and *Federacion Panamericana de Sindicatos de Artes, Medios de Comunicacion y Espetaculos* (PANARTES).
- *Centro de Administracion de Derechos Reprograficos* (Centre for the Management of Reprographic Rights (CADRA)). CADRA's members are authors and publishers.[22] Founded in 2002, the main objectives of this CMO are the licensing of published works, collection and distributions of funds

---

19.   See <www.sadaic.org.ar> (last visited: 10 Dec. 2009).
20.   See <www.argentores.org.ar> (last visited: 10 Dec. 2009).
21.   See <www.sadem.org.ar> (last visited: 10 Dec. 2009).
22.   See <www.cadra.org.ar> (last visited: 10 Dec. 2009).

and the legal representation of its members. In 2004 it collected Argentine Peso (ARS) 175,980 or approximately EUR 50,000.

2.3   MEXICO

CMOs operating in Mexico face a situation similar to that in Argentina, namely, strong government oversight and little competition. The existing CMOs in Mexico are:

- *Sociedad General de Escritores de México* (General Society of Writers of Mexico (SOGEM)).[23] Even though SOGEM was officially established on 23 August 1976, its activities date back to 1902 under the name *Sociedad Autoral*. In 1976, all prior existing writers' societies got together to form SOGEM. The organization aims to foment the intellectual production of its members with the purpose of improving national culture. It is composed of poets; narrators; playwrights; cinema; video and television writers; periodical publication writers; social, technical and scientific researchers; and all others who produce written materials. SOGEM is an ordinary member of CISAC. SOGEM also works as the registrar for works in the following domains: television, cinema, radio, theatre and literature in general. SOGEM was also involved in the fight against retaining income tax from copyright. Traditionally exempt from this tax, authors saw a change in legislation in 2002 make their business less profitable. However, SOGEM was able to obtain an exemption for works charged at up to twenty minimum wages in Mexico, which mainly benefits writers in the beginning of their careers. In 2002, SOGEM's collection revenues totaled more than MXN 34 million,[24] including PDP 21.45 million from television broadcasts, over PDP 9.2 million from theatres and PDP 3,175 million from cinemas.[25]
- *Sociedad de Autores y Compositores de Música* (Society of Authors and Composers of Music (SACM)) originated in 1945 as the first assembly of musical authors and composers in Mexico and claims to be the only society authorized to collect music royalties in Mexico.[26]
- *Sociedad Mexicana de Coreografos* (Mexican Society of Choreographers (SOMEC)). This society received its authorization to operate from INDAUTOR in 1998.

---

23. See <www.sogem.org.mx> (last visited: 10 Dec. 2009).
24. As of 14 Dec. 2009, 1 MXN is equivalent to: EUR 0.0530, USD 0.0775. PDP 34 million is the approximate equivalent of EUR 1.8 million.
25. See <www.sogem.org.mx/html/pag34.pdf> (last visited: 25 Oct. 2005).
26. See <www.sacm.org.mx> (last visited: 10 Dec. 2009).

- *Sociedad Mexicana de Autores de las Artes Plasticas* (Mexican Society of Authors of Plastic Arts (SOMAAP)).[27] This society received its authorization to operate from INDAUTOR in 1998.
- *Associacion Nacional de Interpretes* (National Association of Interpreters) received authorization to conduct business in 2004.[28]
- *Sociedad Mexicana de Directores Realizadores de Obras Audiovisuales* (Mexican Society of Directors of Audiovisual Works (DIRECTORES)) was authorized to act as a CMO in 1998 and protects the rights of movie directors and writers.[29]
- *Union Ibero Americana de Humoristas Gráficos.*[30] The idea of an association of cartoonists began in Cuba during an international meeting in 1997. The association was formed in 1999 and received its governmental approval in 2002. It is important to note that this CMO has been international from the beginning of its activities, because it originated from the common vision of cartoonists from different parts of Latin America.
- *Centro Mexicano de Protección y Fomento a los Derechos de Autor* (Mexican Centre for the Protection and Development of Copyright (CEMPRO)) was created in 1998.[31] It administers reproduction rights on behalf of Mexican publishers and authors. With its international agreements, it claims to administer rights to 95% of the Mexican repertory. In the reprographic area, it licenses mostly educational users. Its 2004 collections amounted to PDP 961,633 or approximately EUR 76,000.
- EJECUTANTES, also known as 'EJE' (Association of Music Performers) received its authorization to act as a CMO in 1999. It represents the copyright of musical performers.[32]
- *Sociedad Mexicana de Autores de Obras Fotográficas* (Mexican Society of Authors of Photographic Works (SMAOF)) received its authorization to act as a CMO in 2000.
- *Sociedad Mexicana de Productores de Fonogramas, Videogramas y Multimedia* (Mexican Society of Producers of Phonograms, Videograms and Multimedia (SOMEXFON)) was authorized to act as a CMO in 2001.
- *Sociedad Mexicana de Ejecutantes de Musica* (Mexican Society of Music Performers (SOMEM)) was authorized to act as a CMO in 2002 and represents the copyrights of music performers.[33]
- *Sociedad de Autores de Obras Visuales Imagen del Tercer Milenio* (Society of Authors of Visual Works – Images of the Third Millennium)

---

27. See <www.somaap.com> (last visited: 10 Dec. 2009).
28. See <www.andi.org.mx> (last visited: 10 Dec. 2009).
29. See <www.cinedirectores.com> (last visited: 10 Dec. 2009).
30. See <www.editorialcarton.com.mx> (last visited: 10 Dec. 2009).
31. See <www.cempro.com.mx> (last visited: 10 Dec. 2009).
32. The decision authorizing EJE EJECUTANTES to operate is available online: <www.sep.gob.mx/wb2/sep/sep_Resolucion_del_14_de_junio_de_1999> (last visited: 25 Oct. 2005).
33. The decision authorizing SOMEM to operate is available online: <www.sep.gob.mx/wb2/sep/sep_Resolucion_del_25_de_noviembre_de_2002> (last visited: 25 Oct. 2005).

was authorized to act as a CMO in 2002 and it represents authors of visual works.[34]

2.4 PERU

Peru is a smaller market compared to those presented above. The government adopts the policy of approving the operation only of CMOs that represent a significant number of artists in their domain. The ones currently approved and operating are as follows:

- *Associacion Peruana de Autores y Compositores* (Peruvian Association of Authors and Composers (APDAYC)).[35] Founded on 20 February 1952, it was the first CMO in Peru, and its foundation documents included the signatures of almost all active musicians in Peru at that time. Today, it claims to represent more than 4,000 authors who are either originally from Peru or who are residents of Peru, in addition to the international authors it represents through CISAC.[36]
- *Associacion Peruana de Artistas Visuales* (Peruvian Association of Visual Artists (APSAV)).[37] This CMO first began its activities in 1996 under the business name *Agencia Peruana de Sociedades de Autores Visuales*, with the support of *Visual Entidad de Gestion de Artistas Plasticos* (VEGAP), a Spanish agency that aimed to divulge copyright among visual artists. At that time, visual artists were not aware that they had the same kind of copyright as writers and musicians. So, in the early stage of its activities, APSAV had an informational role among visual artists. The change from agency to collective only happened in 1999, when APSAV complied with the legal requirements and obtained its authorization to operate as a CMO. APSAV became a provisional member of CISAC in July 2005.

2.5 VENEZUELA

There are three CMOs legally authorized to operate in Venezuela, as follows:

- *Sociedad de Autores y Compositores de Venezuela* (Society of Authors and Composers of Venezuela (SACVEN)).[38] This society started its activities in

---

34. The decision authorizing this CMO to operate is available online: <www.sep.gob.mx/wb2/sep/sep_Resolucion_del_17_de_diciembre_de_2002> (last visited: 25 Oct. 2005).
35. See <www.apdayc.org.pe> (last visited: 10 Dec. 2009).
36. CISAC was founded in 1926 in France and initially had 18 members. The main goal of CISAC was to coordinate the work of member societies, to improve national and international copyright law and to foster the diffusion of creative works. In 2004, CISAC was formed by 210 CMOs from 109 different countries. <www.cisac.org> (last visited: 10 Dec. 2009).
37. See <www.apsav.org.pe> (last visited: 10 Dec. 2009).
38. See <www.sacven.org> (last visited: 14 Dec. 2009).

1955 and represents authors of musical, dramatic and musical-dramatic works. SACVEN has been an important player on the Venezuelan cultural scene from the beginning of its activities. The activities of the forty authors that initially formed SACVEN ended up reviewing the copyright law of 1928. SACVEN became a member of CISAC in 1964.

Current Venezuelan copyright legislation[39] requires CMOs to obtain a license to operate. SACVEN received its license on 15 October 1996, but was forced to restructure itself to ensure compliance with the new regulations. Following the requirements under the National Copyright Law, SACVEN tariffs are published in two newspapers and become effective thirty days after publication. If a user of SACVEN's services or a broadcasting organization finds tariffs to be abusive, it can require an arbitral procedure before SAPI (Servicio Autónomo de la Propiedad Intelectual) for a ten-day period following publication.

Assuming its position as a leader in the copyright domain, SACVEN is currently proposing new amendments to the Copyright Law, according to the new Constitution of 2000. Some issues that are considered by the new Constitution and are not included in the Copyright legislation are traditional knowledge and folklore.

– AUTORARTE. This CMO has been authorized by the *Directorio Nacional del Derecho de Autor* (National Directorate of Copyright (DNDA)[40] to operate since 1999. It represents authors of visual works and is a member of CISAC. Unlike SACVEN, AUTORARTE started its activities only shortly before governmental licensing, with its first meetings in 1998. Despite the fact that it started activities recently, it already represents many foreign CMOs. AUTORARTE and SACVEN have agreed to do their collections together for a period of five years.

– *Associacion Venezuelana de Interpretes y Productores Fonograficos* (Venezuelan Association of Performers and Phonogram Producers (AVINPRO)).[41] This CMO has been authorized by DNDA to operate, but records of its activities are not easily obtained.

2.6   URUGUAY

– LATINAUTOR,[42] a Latin American authors' rights organization based in Uruguay and a member of CISAC, is a regional cooperation project between Latin American musical and dramatic CMOs, which encompasses

---

39. Official Journal No. 4.638 (1 Oct. 1993), as amended and with applicable regulations, including the regulation implementing Decision No. 351 and the Cartagena Agreement. See (in Spanish) <www.analitica.com/bitblioteca/home/derechos_del_autor.asp> (last visited: 15 Dec. 2009).
40. DNDA – Directorio Nacional del Derecho de Autor (National Directorate of Copyright).
41. See <www.avinpro.com> (last visited: 10 Dec. 2009).
42. See <www.cisac.org> (last visited: 26 Oct. 2005).

most of those in Latin America, as well as in Spain and Portugal. It promotes the integration of the musical repertoires across Latin America and ensures its correct identification and protection. LATINAUTOR also assists well-structured CMOs and helps small CMOs to establish themselves in local or regional markets with the intent of ensuring that authors, copyright owners, broadcasting organizations, professional users and society in general are confident in Latin American CMOs. LATINAUTOR has been appointed as an International Standard Musical Works Code (ISWC) agency.

- *Asociación General de Autores del Uruguay* (General Association of Authors of Uruguay (AGADU)) is the main CMO in Uruguay.[43] It collects contributions for its members and also for CUD and SUDEI.
- *Camara Uruguaya del Disco* (Uruguayan Book Chamber (CUD)).[44] This association represents phonogram producers, but the collection and distribution of amounts perceived by its members is actually effectuated by AGADU.
- *Sociedad Uruguaya de Artistas y Interpretes* (Uruguayan Society of Performing Artists (SUDEI)) started its activities in 1951 and was the first one to be legally recognized by the government. It has more than 3,000 members and represents literary and musical authors. The collection and distribution of amounts perceived by its members is also effectuated by AGADU.
- *Asociación Uruguaya para la Tutela Organizada de los Derechos Reprográficos* (Uruguayan Association for the Protection of Reprographic Rights (AUTOR)). This Montevideo-based reprographic rights organization (RRO) was incorporated in 2005. In its first report to the International Federation of Reprographic Rights Organizations (IFRRO),[45] it claims to have sixty-seven members.

2.7   CHILE

The Chilean situation is marked by the presence of a very strong CMO, *Sociedad Chilena del Derecho de Autor* (Chilean Society of Authors (SCD)), and smaller CMOs that rely on the operational expertise of SCD.

SCD received its authorization from the Ministry of Education in 1992.[46] It represents authors of musical works, with or without text, synchronized or not with audiovisual, theatrical or choreographic works. SCD represents approximately 2,000 authors and thirty-five foreign CMOs.

SCD provides financial aid to its members. Grants through the programme called *Fondo de Fomento a la Produccion Musical* are of up to 50% of the total project cost and cannot exceed the total amount distributed to the author by SCD in

---

43. See <www.agadu.org> (last visited: 10 Dec. 2009).
44. See <www.cudisco.org> (last visited: 10 Dec. 2009).
45. See <www.ifrro.org> (last visited: 10 Dec. 2009).
46. See <www.scd.cl> or <www.autor.cl> (last visited: 10 Dec. 2009).

the year before the author requests the grant. There are also grants that can be received by SCD's members in the case of medical or social difficulties. Furthermore, there are emergency funds available and a 'guaranteed minimum right' for authors over 60 years old. This is a guarantee that elderly authors will receive at least a minimum fixed amount even if the collection of amounts for the exploitation of their works does not achieve that minimum amount.

- *Sociedad de Autores Nacionales de Teatro, Cine y Audiovisuales*[47] (Society of National Authors of Theatre, Cinema and Audiovisual Works (ATN)) is a member of CISAC. The creation of this society was motivated by the challenges imposed by new technologies on the distribution of copyright works. ATN began its operations in December 1995 with the help and assistance of SCD. To cover the costs of its operations, ATN charges from 5% to 10% of the total amounts collected. Unlike other CMOs in other countries, the author is the one who establishes the price for the license of his or her work. There are minimum standards to be followed, but the author is the one who puts a final price on the commercialization of his or her work.
- CREAIMAGEN (*Image Creations*) represents authors of fixed images, such as photographers, painters, plastic artists and drawers.[48] Like ATN, It was founded in 1997 with the administrative help and support of SCD. CREAIMAGEN protects the copyright of its members, manages the use of the copyright of its members, detects and avoids non-authorized use and establishes reciprocity agreements with other CMOs around the world. CREAIMAGEN is also a member of CISAC.
- *Corporacion de Actores de Chile* (Chilean Authors Corporation (CHILEACTORES)).[49] This society, which represents actors, was founded in 1996 with the support of SCD. CHILEACTORES protects the copyright of its members, licenses works and collects and distributes funds.
- *Sociedad Chilena de Interpretes* (Chilean Society of Performers (SCI)) was founded in 1998 based on the support received from SCD.[50] SCI is a member of *Federacion Ibero Latinoamericana de Artistas, Interpretes y Ejecutantes* (FILAIE)). SCI represents the copyright of Chilean nationals abroad and the copyright of foreign authors in Chile. It studies national legislation aiming its improvement and promotes cultural and artistic activities.
- *Sociedad de Derechos Literarios* (Society of Literary Rights (SADEL)).[51] This RRO was incorporated in 2003. It declared 100 authors and 20 publishers as members in 2004 but had not begun collecting license fees.

---

47. See <www.atn.cl> (last visited: 10 Dec. 2009).
48. See <www.creaimagen.cl> (last visited: 10 Dec. 2009).
49. See <www.chileactores.cl> (last visited: 10 Dec. 2009).
50. See <www.musicos.cl> (last visited: 10 Dec. 2009).
51. See <www.sadel.cl> (last visited: 15 Dec. 2009).

2.8   Costa Rica

With fewer than 5,000,000 inhabitants, Costa Rica has only one active CMO:

- *Associacion de los Compositores y Autores Musicales de Costa Rica* (Association of Composers and Music Authors of Costa Rica (ACAM)).[52] This non-profit association started its activities in 1990. ACAM has more than 500 members and is a member of CISAC. As the local agent of LATINAUTOR, ACAM manages copyright licensing in all countries of Central America. It represents around 25 million musical works. In 1993, ACAM gave birth to *Compositores y Autores Musicales de Costa Rica, Sociedad Anonima* (SACAM), responding to questions that arose from the Costa Rican government with regard to the carrying out of the collection of amounts by an association and not by a commercial company. This fact proves that, even though the law mentions that a CMO might have a non-profit nature, the government understands that the collective management of copyright is a commercial business.

3   LEGAL FRAMEWORK AND ITS APPLICATION

All countries included in this analysis are contracting parties to the Berne Convention for the Protection of Literary and Artistic Works (Berne Convention), the Rome Convention for the Protection of Performers, Producers of Phonograms and Broadcasting Organizations (Rome Convention) and the Convention for the Protection of Producers of Phonograms Against Unauthorized Duplication of Their Phonograms (Geneva Convention).[53] However, as of 15 December 2009, Brazil has not signed and Venezuela has not ratified both the WIPO Copyright Treaty ('WCT') and the WIPO Performances and Phonograms Treaty (WPPT).[54]

Terms of copyright protection varies among the analysed countries, as demonstrated in Table 14.2.

---

52. See <www.acamcostarica.com> (last visited: 10 Dec. 2009).
53. Full references to these Treaties are provided at the beginning of the book. More information on the contracting parties to these Treaties can be found at the following websites: <www.wipo.int/treaties/en/documents/pdf/e-berne.pdf>, <www.wipo.int/treaties/en/documents/pdf/k-rome.pdf> and <www.wipo.int/treaties/en/documents/pdf/o-phongr.pdf> (last visited: 26 Oct. 2005).
54. More information on the contracting parties to these Treaties can be found at the following websites: <www.wipo.int/treaties/en/documents/pdf/s-wct.pdf> and <www.wipo.int/treaties/en/documents/pdf/s-wppt.pdf> (last visited: 26 Oct. 2005).

Table 14.2   Copyright Protection Terms

Country	Term of Protection[55]
Brazil	Seventy years.
Argentina	Seventy years. Copyright over photographic works are protected for twenty years from the first publication of the photograph. Copyright over cinematographic works are protected for fifty years from the death of the last collaborator (director, producer or composer)
Mexico	Seventy-five years. Protection for the work of performers is of fifty years from (i) the first fixing of the performance in a phonogram; (ii) the first performance of works not recorded on phonograms; (iii) the first transmission by radio, television or other medium
Peru	Seventy years
Venezuela	Sixty years
Uruguay	Fifty years
Chile	Fifty years[56]
Costa Rica	Seventy years

3.1   BRAZIL

As discussed in section 1 of this chapter, the Brazilian market contains many active CMOs, some of them in the same artistic domain. Live musical performances have their collections and distributions centralized at ECAD, according to Federal Law No. 5988/73. Besides the creation of ECAD, Brazilian legislation does not restrict or regulate collective management societies. The activity is strictly private. With regard to copyright itself, Brazilian legislation is very simple and does not establish guidelines for contracts as is the practice of many other countries in the region. The Brazilian legislator rather leaves contractual provisions to be determined by the parties and does not differentiate the negotiation of copyright from the negotiation of other assets.

3.2   ARGENTINA

In comparison with Brazil, Argentinean CMOs receive stronger guidance from the government. Some of the existing CMOs have had their existence confirmed by the

---

55. The term of protection includes the life of the author plus the term indicated in this table. The indicated term starts from 1 January after the death of the author.
56. Chile has a peculiar exception to the term of protection. According to Art. 10 of Law No. 17.336 (1970) on Intellectual Property, *Diario Oficial*, 2 Oct. 1970, No. 27.761, in the event that upon expiration of the fifty-year term of protection, the author's widow is still alive,

government through the enactment of a federal law. However, this is not a legal requirement.

Some categories of domestic copyright works need to be registered in order to be fully protected. Law No. 11.723/33 determines which works must be registered with the *Registro Nacional de Propiedad Intelectual* (National Intellectual Property Register). This is the case for translated works,[57] periodical publications[58] and transfers and assignments of literary, scientific or musical works.[59] With regard to translated works, no copyright is granted on the translated version before registration with the designated authorities. As to transfers and assignments of works, failure to present such works for registration may invalidate the transaction. Failure to present published works for registration suspends copyright protection and obliges the editor to pay a penalty in the amount of ten times the amount of the work not presented for registration. Independently of the kind of work, registration is compulsory if the work has been created with subsidies from the Argentinean government.

Although registration is not always compulsory, the majority of Argentinean artists tend to present their works for registration to safeguard their economic rights. Government regulations requiring certain works to be published and simply not mentioning other kinds of works make it difficult for artists to believe that their rights are protected without registration. Considering that registration is an efficient proof in an eventual dispute over copyright,[60] one could argue that Argentinean artists would rather register all their works.

3.2.1 The National Intellectual Property Register

The National Intellectual Property Register is a group of collective management organizations and artistic associations, which, under the supervision of the Ministry of Justice, have the duty of registering copyright works, according to governmental directives.

Books and other publications, art work pieces, multimedia works, videos, films and agreements are presented for registration before the *Camara Argentina del Libro* (Argentinean Book Chamber (CAL) a publishers' association).[61] Web pages and works published under legal representation (including theatre plays, television, radio and exhibited shows) may be registered at the DNDA,[62] which is a service (not a CMO) provided by the Ministry of Justice.

---

the author's daughters are single or widowed or any of the author's sons-in-law are not capable of work, the fifty-year term of protection will be extended until the death of the last survivor.

57. Law No. 11.723 – Legal Intellectual Property Regime, *Boletín Oficial*, 30 Sep. 1933 and 11 Nov. 1998, Art. 23.
58. *Ibid.*, Art. 30.
59. *Ibid.*, Art. 53.
60. See <www.jus.gov.ar> (last visited: 15 Dec. 2009).
61. See <www.editores.org.ar> (last visited: 15 Dec. 2009).
62. See <www.jus.gov.ar> (last visited: 15 Dec. 2009).

CAMARA ARGENTINA DEL LIBRO[63] started its activities in 1938, under the name *La Associacion Camara Argentina del Libro*. The validation of its activities happened in 1941 through a federal decree. The original association later merged with *Sociedad Argentina de Editores and Camara Argentina de Editores de Libros* and became CAL.

The main activities of CAL are the fight against piracy, the management of International Standard Book Numbers (ISBNs) and the determination of bar codes for all books across the nation. Furthermore, CAL assists its members in negotiating large book sales (CAL's members are mainly editors, publishers and bookstores), especially when sales are for the government. CAL's activities consist of informing its members on the types of books needed by different authorities of the Argentinean government, such as the Ministry of Education, Provincial Ministries and the *Comisión Nacional Protectora de Bibliotecas Populares* (National Protection Commission of Public Libraries (CONABIP)).

Software programs can be registered at *Camara de Empresas de Tecnología de la Información de Argentina* (Chamber of Information Technology Enterprises of Argentina (CESSI)).[64] CESSI is not a CMO, but rather a business association that aims to develop the technology information sector in Argentina. CESSI lobbies the government for new measures to increase software production in Argentina and stimulate competition of Argentinean information technology products in the international market. CESSI is the result of the merger between the former *Camara de Empresas de Software* (CES: *Chamber of Software Companies* and *Camara Empresaria de Servicios de Computación* (Chamber of Commerce of Computing Services (CAESCO)).

Musical works are received for registration by SADAIC, which, as mentioned earlier, is the most important CMO in Argentina.

Periodical publications have to be presented for registration before the *Asso-ciacion Argentina de Revistas* (Argentinean Magazines Association).[65] This association was established in 1948, and its members publish 85% of Argentina's magazines.

Phonograms can be presented either at *Camara Argentina de Productores de Fonogramas* (Argentinean Chamber of Phonogram Producers (CAPIF)), *Associa-cion para la Proteccion de los Derechos Intelectuales sobre Fonogramas y Video-gramas Musicales* (Association for the Protection of Intellectual property Rights on Music Videograms and Phonograms (APDIF))[66] or the *Fondo Nacional de las Artes* (National Arts Fund (FNA)).[67] The FNA was created in 1958 with the purpose of financing cultural activities.

---

63. See <www.editores.org.ar> (last visited: 15 Dec. 2009).
64. See <www.cessi.org.ar> (last visited: 15 Dec. 2009).
65. See <www.editores-revistas.com.ar> (last visited: 15 Dec. 2009).
66. As mentioned earlier in this paper, CAPIF and APDIF act jointly. APDIF has its focus on anti-piracy actions. More information is available online: <www.capif.org.ar/Default.asp?CodOp=MDLM&CO=1> (last visited: 15 Dec. 2009.
67. See <www.fnartes.gov.ar> (last visited: 15 Dec. 2009).

3.3   MEXICO

Mexican copyright law[68] has many provisions on copyright contracts. These provisions aim to protect authors during copyright negotiations and might be useful for authors who are at the beginning of their career. However, limitations on how copyright can be negotiated may end up restricting the freedom of authors to negotiate their works. It has been argued that because of unequal bargaining power, this may be required to safeguard the interests of authors.

According to the Mexican copyright law, any transfer of economic rights has to provide remuneration for the author. Remuneration can be either a percentage of the amounts recuperated from the exploitation of the work or a fixed amount.[69] This provision also indicates that licenses free of charge are not allowed in certain circumstances. Thus, if an author decides to license a given work for free, he or she may be breaking the law.

Legal guidelines also apply to license terms and conditions. If there is no express provision in the license agreement, the term is deemed to be five years. Licenses for more than fifteen years are allowed only in exceptional cases. Again, this measure restricts the freedom of authors, because it determines for the length of time their work can be exploited. Although this measure might be helpful for unknown authors who have little bargaining power, well-known authors might have trouble renewing their contracts for a period longer than fifteen years. It is important to stress that this limitation does not apply to literary works.[70]

Acts, agreements and contracts transferring economic rights shall be entered in the Public Copyright Register in order to be binding on third parties.[71]

The law also establishes practical measures for the launch of a work, such as who handles costs of publication, distribution, promotion, advertising and publicity; who determines the price that should be set on copies of the work for sale; the obligations of both author (or owner of economic rights) and publisher; information that the printer must display on works he or she prints; and the time limit for a work to be placed on sale after being made available to the publisher; etc. It also determines reasons for terminating a publishing contract.[72] One of them is the inability of the publisher to provide the necessary number of copies of a work to the public.[73] If a work goes out of print or if the publisher does not distribute the work on agreed conditions, the publishing contract may be terminated.

Another strong provision limits the parties' ability to define how to cope with *force majeure* situations. The effects of an audiovisual production contract[74] lapses

---

68. Federal Law on Copyright of 5 Dec. 1996, *Diario Oficial de la Federación*, 24 Dec. 1996, 39.
69. *Ibid.*, Art. 31.
70. *Ibid.*, Art. 43.
71. *Ibid.*, Art. 32.
72. *Ibid.*, Art. 56.
73. Which in some jurisdictions is linked to the notion of 'publication' and/or reversions of right.
74. According to s. 68 of the Federal Copyright Law, *supra* n. 66, an audiovisual production contract is a contract where the authors or owners of economic rights grant the exclusive ownership of the economic rights of reproduction, distribution, communication, to the public and subtitling of the work to the producer.

if the work does not start on the scheduled date or if there is a force majeure event.[75] In this situation, rather than permitting the parties to decide what to do once there is a delay on a scheduled event, the law simply terminates the agreement. The parties can always opt to redefine the negotiated terms.

Advertising and commercial announcements have time limitations under the law. They can be broadcast for a six-month period after the first communication. After said period, every new communication is subject to additional payments per six-month period. Three years following the first communication, any new use of the work requires permission from the authors and owners of neighbouring rights on the work. This is another provision that could be easily established by the parties exercising their free will, instead of being determined by Federal law. Furthermore, this provision is not needed to protect authors, because advertising agencies have enough bargaining power to negotiate the terms of their deals.

An interesting provision of the law concerns economic rights on works made under an individual employment contract. In this case, the Mexican copyright law determines that in the absence of agreement to the contrary, the economic rights shall be shared equally between the employer and the employee. In the absence of an employment contract, the economic rights shall accrue to the employee.[76]

Mexican copyright law also permits the possibility of publishing or translating a work, without the author's consent, if and when the work is considered to be in the public interest.[77] Works in the public interest are those considered necessary for the advancement of science, national culture or education. Such a publication or translation will be made against payment of compensatory remuneration. Notwithstanding the fact that the definition of public interest under the law is very broad,[78] the 'government' interest is not always synonymous with the 'public' interest. The language of Article 147 allows the Mexican government to publish *any* work.

The collective management of copyright has a specific section under Mexican copyright law. Section 192 defines a collective society as:

> a legal entity without gainful intent that is set up under this Law with a view to protecting both national and foreign authors and owners of neighbouring rights, and also collecting and delivering to those persons the sums payable to them by virtue of their copyright or neighbouring rights.[79]

The societies 'shall be set up with a view to the provision of mutual assistance for their members, and shall base their action on principles of collaboration, equality

---

75. *Ibid.*, Art. 70.
76. *Ibid.*, Art. 84.
77. *Ibid.*, Art. 147.
78. *Ibid.*, Art. 147 posits a work of public interest as one that is 'necessary for the advancement of science, national culture and education'.
79. *Ibid.* Translation from the original in Spanish available online: <www.wipo.int/clea/docs_new/en/mx/mx003en.html> (last visited: 27 Oct. 2005).

and equity, in addition to which they shall operate on the principles laid down by this Law, which make them into public-interest bodies'.[80]

CMOs can operate only upon prior authorization of the *Instituto Nacional del Derecho de Autor* (National Copyright Institute (INDAUTOR)).[81] Such authorization shall be published at the *Official Gazette of the Federation*. Authorization may be revoked by the Institute in the following situations: (1) failure to comply with the obligations placed on CMOs by the Law or (2) if a dispute arises among its members that leaves it without a director or without management, with the result that the purpose and objective of the society is affected, to the detriment of the rights of its members. In the circumstances mentioned, prior notice shall be given to the Institute, which shall set a period not exceeding three months for the situation reported to be remedied or rectified.[82]

This provision demonstrates governmental control over those societies. However, individuals may freely choose which society to join or whether to negotiate their rights personally. In the latter case, societies cannot intervene in the collection of royalties. Members of a society who have chosen the society to collect royalties on their behalf can stop the society from collecting royalties by revoking the mandate.[83]

The law also foresees the presence of an agent acting on the author's behalf. The agent has to be a natural person and also needs prior authorization from the Institute to collect royalties for the author.[84] Power of attorneys granted to agents can be neither replaced nor delegated. Powers of attorney granted to collectives shall confer powers for litigation and collection.[85]

All instruments, agreements and contracts between CMOs and authors, owners of economic rights or owners of neighbouring rights, as well as those between CMOs and users of the works, shall be in written format.[86] The following documents are entered in the Public Copyright Register once a CMO has been licensed to operate – articles of association and statutes, together with their rules of collection and distribution; the contracts concluded with users and the representation contracts that they have with counterpart societies; and the instruments and documents by which members of their governing and supervisory bodies, directors and agents are appointed, all within thirty days following approval, conclusion, election or appointment, as the case may be. These provisions relate to the principles of 'publicity' and transparency.[87] The Law also requires some provisions to be included in the societies' statutes, such as how to avoid over-representation of members and the voting system for the exclusion of its members, which shall

---

80. *Ibid.*, Art. 192.
81. *Ibid.*, Art. 193.
82. *Ibid.*, Art. 194.
83. *Ibid.*, Art. 195.
84. *Ibid.*, Art. 196.
85. *Ibid.*, Art. 197.
86. *Ibid.*, Art. 201.
87. *Ibid.*, Art. 203.

invariably be one vote per member, and consent shall require 75% of the votes of those present at the Assembly.[88]

The right of publicity appears again in section 207, which determines that the Institute can require a collective society to provide information of any kind and shall order inspections and audits in the society upon request of at least 10% of the membership.

3.3.1　　　The National Intellectual Property Register

INDAUTOR is the authority responsible for registration of works, as well as of agreements concerning the licensing of copyright and acts related to CMOs. It is part of the *Secretaría de Educacion Publica* and depends on the *Secretaría de Educación Superior e Investigación Científica* (Secretariat for Higher Education and Scientific Research).

INDAUTOR's largest activity is the maintenance of the Public Registry Directory, which contains information on all registered, copyright works. Another task performed by INDAUTOR is the maintenance of the Reserved Rights Directory, which contains registered titles, names, distinctive physical and psychological characteristics or original characteristics applied to periodical publications and typical real-life human or fictional or symbolic characters, persons or groups devoted to artistic activities and promotional advertising.

Even though there is an extensive section on collective management organizations in the Mexican copyright law, information obtained from the Legal Directory of INDAUTOR indicates that authorization to start its activities is the only control exercised by the government over these organizations. Once the organization receives its governmental approval, through INDAUTOR, it is free to operate and be administered as their representatives' wish. Given the amount of legislative particularities imposed on Mexican CMOs, however, governmental presence is stronger in Mexico than in both Brazil and Argentina.

3.4　　　PERU AND VENEZUELA

Peru and Venezuela are members of the Andean Community, which is also formed by Colombia, Bolivia and Ecuador. The Andean Community is a subregional organization endowed with international legal status. The Andean Integration System (AIS) is composed of bodies and organizations that aim to intensify Andean subregional integration, to promote its external projection and to reinforce the actions connected with the process.[89] Decisions taken by the AIS are binding on member countries. National laws do not require reception procedures to be fully effective. Furthermore, the Andean Court of Justice has repeatedly emphasized that Andean Community Law prevails over national provisions.

88.　*Ibid.*, Art. 205.
89.　See <www.comunidadandina.org/ingles/who.htm> (last visited: 28 Oct. 2005).

Decision No. 351 of the Cartagena Agreement establishes that the term of protection for copyright cannot be shorter than the life of the author plus fifty years.[90] Section 28 of the Decision provides for protection of databases under copyright, as long as the selection and arrangement of their contents constitute an intellectual creation. The Decision has a chapter on collective societies, which provides that 'societies for the collective administration of copyright and neighbouring rights shall be subject to inspection and supervision by the State, and shall be required to obtain the appropriate operating license from the competent national office'.[91] Affiliation to societies is voluntary. National laws can set additional requirements for the grant of license to CMOs, but the Decision establishes that the corporate object of the CMO has to be the administration of copyright or neighbouring rights; the members of the society must have the right to participate in the decisions of the society; the equitable distribution of the amounts collected should be distributed according to the use of the work; except where expressly authorized by a General Assembly, the remuneration collected is not to be used for purposes other than the covering of the actual cost of administering the rights concerned – the balance of remuneration after deduction of such costs should thus be distributed to right holders; and, finally, it prohibits CMOs from admitting members of other CMOs of the same type, whether national or foreign, that have not first expressly renounced membership in the other CMO.

Section 50 of the Decision provides that, for the action of CMOs to be enforceable against third parties:

> collective administration societies shall be obliged to register with the competent national office, in terms specified by the domestic legislation of the Member Countries, the names and titles of the members of their governing bodies, and also the instruments evidencing the mandates that they exercise on behalf of foreign associations or organizations.

The licensing, inspecting and supervising of CMOs is realized by National Copyright and Neighbouring Rights Offices. CMOs already existing at the time of entry into force of Decision No. 351 would have three months from the date of entry into force to comply with the provisions of the Decision.

3.4.1 Peru

Legislative Decree No. 822 is the Peruvian copyright law.[92] It defines collective societies as legally constituted, non-profit-making associations under civil law

---

90. Decision No. 351 of 17 Dec. 1993 of the Commission of the Cartagena Agreement on the Common Provisions on Copyright and Neighboring Rights, *Gaceta Oficial del acuerdo de Cartagena*, 21 Dec. 1993, No. 145 [Cartagena Agreement], <www.wipo.int/clea/docs_new/pdf/en/pe/pe002en.pdf> (last visited: 27 Oct. 2005).
91. *Ibid.*, Art. 43.
92. Copyright Law – Legislative Decree No. 822 of 23 Apr. 1996, *Diario Oficial El Peruano*, 24 Apr. 1996, 139, 104 [Legislative Decree No. 822], <www.wipo.int/clea/docs_new/pdf/en/pe/pe003en.pdf> (last visited: 15 Dec. 2009).

devoted to the management of copyright or neighbouring rights of economic character on behalf and in the interest of a number of authors or owners of such rights. Such associations must obtain from the Copyright Office of the *Instituto Nacional de Defensa de la Competencia y de la Protección de la Propiedad Intelectua* (National Institute for the Defense of Competition and Intellectual Property (INDECOPI)) an operating license provided for in the Law.

3.4.1.1 The National Intellectual Property Register

The national intellectual property register (managed by INDECOPI)[93] is responsible for authorizing and inspecting CMOs. CMOs in Peru are legally prohibited from exercising any religious or political activities, as well as activities not related to their essential purpose. Licenses to start activities are granted upon presentation of the CMOs' statutes to INDECOPI. The decision granting authorization or refusing the license to operate is published in the supplement of legal provisions of the Official Gazette, *El Peruano*.

CMOs can only operate after governmental authorization. To grant such authorizations, INDECOPI uses the following criteria: (1) the number of owners who have undertaken to entrust the management of their rights to the candidate society; (2) the size of the repertoire that it proposes to manage and the actual use of that repertoire by the most significant users in the course of the preceding year; (3) the number and importance of the potential users; (4) the suitability of the statutes and of the human, technical, financial and material resources available for the achievement of its objectives; and (5) the potential effectiveness of the management of the repertoire that it proposes to manage in other countries, in the form of prospective reciprocal representation contracts with societies of the same nature that operate abroad.[94]

These requirements show that even though operation is allowed only after authorization is granted, the CMO has to be sufficiently organized – including having some potential affiliates together with the complete list of the works the CMO will manage – in order for authorization to be granted. These requirements also prove the control exercised by the government over the activities of CMOs in Peru. In this case, governmental control seems to be effective, because it forces CMOs to be organized and maintain clear records of their portfolio. An example is section 153, which determines obligations to be fulfilled by the management of CMOs.[95]

---

93. See <www.indecopi.gob.pe> (last visited: 15 Dec. 2009).
94. Legislative Decree No. 822, *supra* n. 90, Art. 150.
95. Obligations listed under this section concern the daily administration of a CMO, such as the obligation to enter into agreements to negotiate the rights administered by the CMO; the obligation to collect amounts resulting from the exploitation of works; the obligation to distribute amounts not later than one year after collection; the maximum of 30% from the total of collections of a CMO to be spent with administrative costs; etc.

Besides those requirements, Peru's copyright law also enlists a series of provisions that have to be included in all CMOs statutes, including the classes of owners of rights included in the scope of its operations; the general rules of the contract of association, which is different from the individual membership contract; conditions concerning acquisition and termination of membership; the principles to which the distribution of amounts collected are subject; and provisions that ensure that the management of the CMOs repertoire is free of all interference from users – preventing any preferential use of works, performances or productions under management.

After the grant of authorization to operate, CMOs have to register all of their initial corporate documents – and changes thereto – with INDECOPI. CMOs are also legally obliged to accept membership of any author whose work is under its domain.[96]

The Copyright Office is entitled to impose sanctions on CMOs for infringement of their own statutes or regulations or the relevant legislation, or those that are involved in acts affecting the interests of those that they represent, without prejudice to any criminal sanctions or civil actions that may be appropriate.[97]

INDECOPI provides arbitration services in disputes concerning intellectual property and competition. These services might also be used in the event that a union or association representing users considers that the tariff determined by a CMO is abusive.

3.4.2　　　Venezuela

The Venezuelan Constitution was enacted on 24 March 2000.[98] Sections 98 and 124 of the Constitution protect intellectual property rights. The Venezuelan copyright law was enacted on 14 August 1993. It establishes a term of protection of copyright of sixty years after the death of the author. According to the Law – and following the provisions of the Cartagena Agreement previously explained – the collective administration of copyright is under the supervision of the National Directorate of Copyright. CMOs can start operations only after receiving a license from the State. However, Venezuelan Copyright Law provides some basic guidelines to the operation of CMOs.

Like Mexico and Peru, Venezuela has special sections in its copyright law concerning copyright agreements – a section on performance contracts, a section on publishing contracts and a section on the assignment of press articles. Even though among the three countries Venezuela has the fewest legal requirements, the number of provisions determining how copyright negotiations should be conducted demonstrates higher governmental presence in the area.

---

96. Legislative Decree No. 822, *supra* n. 90, Art. 153.
97. Legislative Decree No. 822, *supra* n. 90, Art. 165.
98. Published in the extraordinary *Official Gazette* No. 5453.

Besides the provisions in the Venezuelan copyright law, there are also specific statutes dealing with books,[99] national cinematography,[100] piracy[101] and statutory deposit.[102] The main purpose of these specific bills is to promote actions aiming to enhance the cultural activity in the country and to protect the cultural heritage.

3.4.2.1   The National Intellectual Property Register

Servicio Autonomo de la Propiedad Intelectual is the Venezuelan Intellectual Property Register is (SAPI).[103] This authority is under the direction of the Ministry of Production and Commerce; it began operation in 1998 when the services of both copyright and industrial property were united.

DNDA is the Copyright division. DNDA not only registers copyright works but also licenses and supervises the activities of CMOs. Another activity exercised by DNDA is arbitration. Arbitration is conducted upon request of one of the parties and might be among copyright holders, CMOs and their members, CMOs and copyright holders or CMOs and users of copyright works.

3.5   URUGUAY

Uruguayan CMOs need to be approved by the Executive Power in order to legally operate. Approval is granted after the opinion of the *Consejo de Derechos de Autor* (Copyright Council).[104]

The copyright law establishes a set of obligations that need to be fulfilled by CMOs,[105] such as the need to distribute amounts collected in time periods not superior to one year and to periodically present its accounted expenses to the *Consejo de Derechos de Autor*. Differently than in other countries analysed in this chapter, those obligations are more general and mainly concerned with the transparency of a CMO's administration. However, as in other Latin American countries, the government retains the right to supervise and inspect CMOs.[106]

---

99. Law on Books of 18 Apr. 1997, *Gaceta Oficial de la República de Venezuela*, 21 Apr. 1997, No. 36.189. Regulation to the Law on Books, *Gaceta Oficial de la República de Venezuela*, 18 Dec. 1998, No. 5.285.
100. National Cinematography Law of 15 Aug. 1993, *Gaceta Oficial de la República de Venezuela*, 8 Sep. 1993, No. 4.626. Regulation to the National Cinematography Law, *Gaceta Oficial de la República de Venezuela*, 2 Feb. 1994, No. 4.689.
101. Institutional Agreement Against Piracy (4 Jun. 1996).
102. Statutory Deposit Law of 10 Aug. 1993, *Gaceta Oficial de la República de Venezuela*, 3 Sep. 1993, No. 4.623. Regulation to the Statutory Deposit Law of 23 Jul. 1997, *Gaceta Oficial de la República de Venezuela*, 13 Aug. 1997, No. 5.163.
103. See <www.sapi.gov.ve> (last visited: 10 Dec. 2009).
104. Law on Copyright No. 9.739 of 17 Dec. 1937, as amended on 10 Jan. 2003, s. 58.
105. *Ibid.*
106. *Ibid.*

3.6   CHILE

Section 21 of Chilean copyright law[107] guarantees the freedom of authors to negotiate their works. The authorization granted by authors to CMOs does not restrict authors' right to directly negotiate their work. As already mentioned, it has been argued that this freedom may not be beneficial for less famous authors when dealing with larger publishers or other users.

The chapter on CMOs was introduced by Law No. 19.166,[108] which updated the copyright law. According to this chapter, CMOs must be private entities. Their sole social purpose must be the activities of management, protection and collection of monies related to the intellectual property rights of their members. Social funds remaining after the distribution of amounts to their members can be used for the promotion of activities or services to their members.

Besides the legal requirements addressed to all private entities, CMOs have to include in their statutes the specification of the intellectual rights they manage; the voting regime; rules for the distribution of amounts collected, as well as the percentage reserved for administrative costs, which cannot exceed 30% of the total collected; and the destination of the CMO's assets in case of liquidation, as well as the rights of members in such a case.[109]

Authorization to start operations is granted by the Ministry of Education[110] by the publication in the *National Official Gazette* and presentation of the statutes to the Ministry, together with proof that the CMO represents at least 20% of national authors in the field of the CMO or of foreign authors with permanent residence in Chile. Another requirement is that the data presented to the Ministry of Education indicates that the CMO has the necessary conditions to safely and duly manage the works of its members and members.

The *Registro de la Propiedad Intelectual* is under supervision of the *Dirección de Bibliotecas, Archivos y Museos* (Directorate for Libraries, Archives and Museums (DIBAM)).[111] DIBAM is a governmental authority that promotes knowledge and creation and contributes to national development.

3.7   COSTA RICA

Unlike in Chile, the Costa Rican copyright law[112] does not dedicate a specific chapter to CMOs. It mentions CMOs only in section 132, which provides that the mere association to a CMO is enough for the CMO to consider itself the

---

107. Law No. 17.336 (1970) on Intellectual Property, *Diario Oficial*, 2 Oct. 1970, No. 27.761.
108. *Ibid.*, as last amended on 17 Sep. 1992.
109. *Ibid.*, Art. 93.
110. See <www.mineduc.cl> (last visited: 10 Dec. 2009).
111. See <www.dibam.cl> (last visited: 10 Dec. 2009).
112. Law No. 6683 on Copyright and Neighbouring Rights (as last amended by law No. 8039 of 10 Oct. 2000), *La Gaceta*, 27 Oct. 2000, <www.wipo.int/clea/docs_new/pdf/en/cr/cr001en. pdf> (last visited: 28 Oct. 2005).

representative of a right holder. There is no need for a specific mandate to represent artists. Furthermore, section 132 also provides that CMOs can be associations or commercial societies, allowing CMOs to earn profits. This is the first country from all of the countries covered in this research that allows the CMO activity to be a commercial business.

The *Registro Nacional de Derechos de Autor y Conexos*[113] (Register of Copyright and Related Rights) is attached to the Public Registry of Property and is the authority responsible for registering copyright works.

4　　　　　CHALLENGES FACED BY CMOs IN LATIN AMERICA

Even though the group of countries analysed have myriad detailed legal frameworks to regulate CMO activity, there are some general patterns when it comes to the challenges they face. Piracy, lack of awareness of the duty to properly remunerate authors and new digital technologies are the most commonly cited difficulties faced by CMOs in Latin America.

4.1　　　　PIRACY

The piracy of copyrighted materials is sometimes mentioned as a means to finance organized crime activities, including drug trafficking. Besides this fact, the economic situation of countries in the region and the relatively low purchasing power of the populations of many Latin American countries may contribute to the sale of low-quality, pirated products on a large scale. According to one source, pirate CDs and DVDs represent 70% of the Brazilian market.[114] The fight against piracy is thus one of the most demanding activities conducted by CMOs and associations of right holders throughout Latin America.

4.2　　　　LACK OF AWARENESS

The lack of awareness of the obligation to properly remunerate authors and other right holders can also be seen in the Judiciary. To tackle this problem, CMOs organize seminars and educative campaigns to make government officials understand that commercial use of copyright works deserve to be properly remunerated.[115] This is not always easy, and the effect of the misperception that copyright works should be free even when used in a commercially significant way

---

113.　See <www.registronacional.go.cr> (last visited: 10 Dec. 2009).
114.　Information obtained from an interview with Mr Chico Ribeiro, Supervisor of Artists at ABRAMUS (Brazil) on 7 Jul. 2005.
115.　Information obtained from an interview with Dr Maria Huerta, Legal Director of SADAIC (Argentina) on 5 Jul. 2005.

is reflected in the average amounts collected by CMOs in Latin America. According to information received from the Artists Supervisor of ABRAMUS (Brazil),[116] if all outstanding amounts were to be paid, collection values would double. In other words, only half of the due amount is actually collected in Brazil.

Radio channels and television stations are on the top of the debtors' list, and this makes the problem even harder to solve. For example, because radio channels and television stations are governmental concessions in Brazil – many of the concessions have been granted to Brazilian politicians who profit from the visibility they gain through communication media – getting those stations to pay copyright fees is politically difficult. To put it differently, besides making use of the high visibility they acquire and the controlling power they have over content, politicians many times view themselves as above justice and do not believe they will be judicially compelled to pay amounts they decide not to pay. These facts discourage many CMOs from initiating judicial actions against politicians.[117] The same problem is faced by ADDAF (Brazil) for its mechanical works. Many of those works are used in advertising pieces without prior authorization or clearance of rights.[118]

SADAIC (Argentina) believes that those who refuse to pay often do not discuss the amounts involved but rather the underlying copyright itself.[119] This problem becomes even larger when one considers copyrights that are not related to musical works. This is the problem faced by SOCEM (the Mexican Society of Choreographers). This CMO suffers from the non-acceptance of its right to charge contributions for the works of its members.[120] Besides SOCEM, the only society that also collects and distributes amounts related to the performance of choreographers in Latin America is ARGENTORES (Argentina).[121] Visual artists have similar problems, and one of the activities exercised by visual arts' CMOs is public education about copyrights on visual works. This problem was also specifically mentioned by APSAV (Peru). APSAV even had to deal with a collective refusal to pay copyright from all local newspapers in 2002.[122]

Recourse to the judicial system is often avoided in Latin America because the system is slow and procedures are costly. In some cases, not only time and money are at issue but also the fact that the Judiciary power might be corrupt. There is thus no guarantee that justice will be achieved through litigation. Leaving corruption, time and money aside, if one launches a judiciary process, one will have to face the reality that many courts are not well equipped to deal with copyright issues. There

---

116. See *supra* n. 110.
117. See *supra* n. 110.
118. Information obtained from the legal department of ADDAF in an interview on 4 Jul. 2005.
119. See *supra* n. 111.
120. The protection of choreographies is linked to the protection of traditional knowledge, including sacred dances and dances derived from traditional sources. See Daniel Gervais, 'Spiritual but Not Intellectual? The Protection of Sacred Intangible Traditional Knowledge', *Cardozo Journal of Inernational & Comparative Law* 11 (2003): 467.
121. Information obtained from Ms. Patricia Aulestia at SOCEM in an interview on 8 Jul. 2005.
122. Information obtained from Ms. Villa Illacencio in an interview on 7 Jul. 2005.

are no specialized courts for the subject, and many judges do not 'believe in' copyright. This situation was mentioned, for example, in the case of Argentina.[123]

In an attempt to solve this problem, some national copyright registrars offer specialized arbitration services to their members. This is the case in Peru and Venezuela, two countries with very similar governmental control provisions – not surprisingly because they are both part of the Andean Community. Despite the fact that arbitral tribunals have been created in both countries under the supervision of the national copyright registrars, tribunal decisions are not publicly available for consultation. This publication might help enhance the modernization of those two countries' copyright systems.

Courts in Uruguay have confirmed not only the legitimacy of CMOs and their right to act on behalf of their members but also that collective management is a more efficient way to negotiate the use of copyright material.

4.3   ORGANIZATIONAL PROBLEMS

In Argentina, Decree No. 1671/74 required CAPIF, AADI (*Associación Argentina de Intérpretes* (Argentine Association of Interpreters)), SADEM and ADIVA to change their statutes, based on a previous agreement executed by these collectives with the purpose of avoiding the double collection of amounts for the same uses. Although the Decree and the agreement among the collectives is more than twenty years old, lawsuits dealing with the legality of such agreements are still being pursued and the legality of the Decree is still being analysed by the courts.[124]

AADI and CAPIF are at the top of the list of recent decisions concerning the collective management of copyright in Argentina. The large majority of claims regard the legitimacy of AADI and CAPIF in the representation of authors. Opponents of the CMOs' activity allege that their legal representation is unconstitutional and that the regulation validating the AADI-CAPIF agreement was not enacted by the Legislative power, but by the Executive. However, although some hotels and night clubs admit that the agreement among the four collectives has been properly established and is not unconstitutional, those who do not contest the constitutionality of AADI-CAPIF's activity, maintain that the entities have legitimacy only to collect and distribute money in the representation of authors, not to initiate lawsuits to collect outstanding amounts.

In Costa Rica, some suits claim that ACAM is not entitled to collect contributions on behalf of its members.[125] Others pledge that ACAM does not determine for which works it is collecting contributions and invoices commercial establishments the amount it judges fair (Docket No. 04-006203-0007-CO of 25 June 2004). Some lawsuits have tried to question the legitimacy of ACAM and SACAM, but

---

123. See *supra* n. 111.
124. See <www.scba.gov.ar/> (last visited: 28 Oct. 2005).
125. Sentence No. 11593, Lawsuit No. 04-008357-0007-CO of 10 Oct. 2004.

thus far without success (Sentence No. 273; Docket No. 00-000093-0011-CI of 12 July 2000).[126]

4.4 NEW TECHNOLOGIES

New technologies are another very important and demanding challenge, not only in Latin America, but everywhere in the world. There is no specific legislation dealing with music on the Internet. Therefore, some say that music can be downloaded from the Internet without compensation to the copyrights' owner. Most CMOs are essentially powerless because there is no specific legal provision allowing or prohibiting the free transit of music files on the Internet. SADAIC and ABRAMUS listed new technologies as one of their biggest challenges today.[127]

Besides the three points mentioned previously, a particular difficulty faced by Mexico and Peru is the level of formalism required by the law to deal with copyright licensing. The legal requirements contained in the Mexican Law (e.g., to have a mandate recognized by a notary) not only slows down the process of joining a CMO, but may also keep authors who do not have many works to license away from CMOs. SOGEM (Mexico) mentioned excessive formalism as one of the reasons that makes their activity harder and creates problems for authors, especially those beginning their careers that might not have the necessary means to afford notary services. APSAV (Peru) mentions the periodical audits conducted to comply with legal requirements as a costly and unnecessary measure. Considering that APSAV is administered by authors themselves there should be no need for the government to approve its accountancy because authors themselves will benefit from sound accountancy procedures.

5 CONCLUSION

Brazil and Argentina are examples of successful, privately run CMOs. CMOs in those two countries – together with Mexico – are the oldest and strongest in the region. They are well established, and their activities are generally well understood and supported. Lawsuits that reach superior courts in those countries have mostly confirmed the importance of the role of CMOs. Collection and distribution numbers in both countries – as well as in Mexico – are available for consultation by the public, and approximately 80% of the total collected is actually distributed.[128] Brazilian and Argentinean CMOs do not require governmental assistance in the execution of their activities. Authors themselves have started CMOs and managed to organize the activity in a manner that fulfils their needs. This is also beneficial for users who obviously prefer to rely on efficient institutions to obtain licenses.

---

126. See <www.poder-judicial.go.cr/> (last visited: 29 Oct. 2005).
127. See *supra* nn. 110 and 111.
128. Reference to ECAD's data.

Considering the group of the three biggest and richest countries in the region, Mexico's CMOs are under a higher level of government supervision compared to CMOs in Brazil and Argentina. This is despite the fact that Mexico is considered a regional leader and adopts a free market approach, reflected, *inter alia*, in its North American Free Trade Agreement (NAFTA) membership. Mexico maintains that the regulations are an attempt to prove to Mexico's North American partners the seriousness and transparency of its copyright institutions.

The global position of Latin American countries as members of the developing world may justify governmental assistance in the setting up of new collective management organizations in some countries. Looking back at our research, Peru and Venezuela are the two countries with a higher degree of governmental presence in the activities of local CMOs. They also have the lowest per capita gross-domestic product (GDP)[129] among the group of countries under review. In spite of governmental aid for their startup phase, CMOs in those two countries (in Peru mainly) complain about the lack of awareness by, and the lack of a legal structure for effective support from, the government, not only in the establishment of CMOs but also in the day-to-day operations, especially when disputes with users arise. Local CMOs cannot always rely on the Government or on the Judiciary to help.

In Uruguay and Chile, the government has the right to audit and supervise the activities of CMOs. Local CMOs consider State control as a formal process and not as an invasion of their rights to freely develop their activities. Those countries possess stable economies and politics, and this reflects not only on their legal institutions but also on their understanding of the importance of copyright.

In Costa Rica, the situation is *sui generis* compared to the group of countries under review, because it views CMOs as commercial businesses and allows CMOs to operate for profit, something that is prohibited in many Latin American countries.

From our research, for those countries where institutions and the economy are not stable, governmental guidance is not only helpful but often also a necessary ingredient of successful collective management. However, this guidance is only a small step in the consolidation of the activity in those countries. Once CMOs start their activities they need to be supported by the government – mainly through recognition of their activities by the Judiciary. Ideally, CMOs should receive governmental aid until they acquire the necessary expertise to conduct their activities independently and until users and others better understand copyright. When this stage is reached, CMOs should be run privately and independently, that is, managed and administered by the right holders themselves. This is the scenario in place in Argentina and Brazil.

---

129. Peru's per capita GDP: USD 5,600, Venezuela's: USD 5,800. See <www.cia.gov> (last visited: 29 Oct. 2005).